Because It's There

Because It's There

A Celebration of Mountaineering from 200 B.C. to Today

Edited and Translated by Alan Weber

TAYLOR TRADE PUBLISHING
Lanham • New York • Oxford

First Taylor Trade Publishing edition 2003

This paperback edition of *Because It's There* is an original publication. It is published by arrangement with the editor.

Published by Taylor Trade Publishing
A Member of the Rowman & Littlefield Publishing Group
4501 Forbes Boulevard, Suite 200
Lanham, Maryland 20706

Distributed by National Book Network

Library of Congress Cataloging-in-Publication Data

Because it's there : a celebration of mountaineering from 200 B.C. to
 today / edited by Alan Weber.
  p. cm.
 Includes bibliographical references.
 ISBN 0-87833-303-7 (pbk. : alk. paper)
 1. Mountaineering. I. Weber, Alan, 1963–

GV200 .B42 2003
796.52'2—dc21

                                                              2002152198

∞ ™ The paper used in this publication meets the minimum requirements of American National Standard for Information Sciences—Permanence of Paper for Printed Library Materials, ANSI/NISO Z.39.48-1992.
Manufactured in the United States of America.

Contents

CONTENTS

CONTENTS

Acknowledgments

This book would not have been possible without the support of a research fellowship arranged by Pat Wasyliw, Susan Tarrow, and Jonas Pontusson of the Institute for European Studies at Cornell University for 1999–2000. I would also like to thank Charles Burroughs and CEMERS of the State University of New York at Binghamton for their continuing support. The Kroch Rare Book Room, Cornell University Libraries, and SUNY Interlibrary Loan were instrumental in obtaining rare materials.

Chronology

3300 B.C.	The **Ice Man** becomes lost in the Oetzal region of the Alps and perishes.
200 B.C.	**Hannibal** crosses the Alps with elephants to attack Rome.
1336 A.D.	**Petrarch** climbs Ventoux with his brother.
1545	**Conrad Gesner** writes on mountains in his book on milk production.
1574	**Josias Simler** writes his history of the Alps.
1684	**Thomas Burnet** writes *On the Sacred Theory of the Earth*, an important early scientific work on mountains.
1732	**Albrecht von Haller** publishes a widely read series of poems on the Alps.
1744	Englishman **William Windham** travels over alpine glaciers and publishes his account of his journey.
1786	**Dr. Michel-Gabriel Paccard** and **Jacques Balmat** climb Mont Blanc.
1802	**Alexander von Humboldt** climbs to 5,500 meters on Chimborazo in Ecuador and accurately describes altitude sickness.
1808	**Maria Paradis** is the first woman to ascend Mont Blanc.
1820	**Zachariah Wilson** and **Rifleman Verplank** climb Pikes Peak in Colorado.
1829	**Killar Khasirov** climbs Mount Elbrus in the Caucasus, the highest mountain in Europe.
1843	**John Ruskin** writes the first volume of *Modern Painters*, a work on painting containing two seminal chapters on mountains.
1846	**Henry David Thoreau** climbs Ktaadn in Maine and writes about his experience in *The Maine Woods*.
1852	**Albert Smith** stages the variety show "The Ascent of Mt. Blanc," popularizing climbing in Britain.
1854	**Alfred Wills** ascends the Wetterhorn in the Alps, and later writes *Wanderings among the High Alps*.
1861	**John Tyndall** makes the first ascent of the Weisshorn.
1865	**Edward Whymper's** spectacular accident on the Matterhorn occurs.
	A. W. Moore climbs the Brenva face of Mont Blanc.
1870	**Hazard Stevens** and **Philemon Van Trump** climb Mount Ranier.
1876	**William Cecil Slingsby** climbs Store Skagastolstind in Norway.
1880	**Whymper** climbs Chimborazo.

1881	**B. Venetz** and **A. F. Mummery** reach the top of the Grépon by setting new rock climbing standards on the Mummery Crack.
1889	**Hans Meyer** and **Ludwig Purtscheller** climb Kilimanjaro.
1895	**A. F. Mummery** and two Ghurkas disappear on Nanga Parbat in the Himalayas.
1896	**Norman Collie** climbs Sgurr Coire an Lochain on the Island of Skye, the last unclimbed British mountain.
1897	The guide **Mattias Zurbriggen** of **Edward Fitzgerald's** expedition scales Aconcagua.
1902	American Alpine Club founded with assistance from **Annie Peck**.
1906	Founding of Japanese Alpine Club by **Walter Weston** and **Usui Kojima**. **Duke of Abruzzi** climbs most of the peaks in the Ruwenzori range in Uganda.
1908	**Annie Peck** climbs Huascarán in Peru, setting the women's world altitude record.
1909	**Owen Glynne Jones** writes *Rock Climbing in the English Lake District*, containing one of the first systems to describe the difficulty of a particular climb. **The Duke of Abruzzi** attempts K2.
1911	**Karl Blodig** of Bregenz completes his climbs of all 4,000 meter peaks in the Alps. **Josef Knubel**, **G. W. Young** and others climb the east face of the Grépon, which had defeated Mummery.
1913	**Walter Harper** of **Hudson Stuck's** expedition makes it to the top of Mt. McKinley in Alaska.
1922	First major British attempt on Everest led by **C. G. Bruce**. **Bruce** and **George Finch** reach a record 27,300 feet.
1924	Another British Everest attempt with first use of oxygen equipment; **George Leigh Mallory** and **Sandy Irvine** disappear after possibly reaching summit.
1931	**Frank Smythe** and **Eric Shipton** summit of Kamet.
1933	**Frank Smythe** reaches 28,000 feet on Everest. Mallory's or Irvine's ice axe found.
1938	The Eigerwand, which has claimed numerous lives, is first climbed by **Fritz Kasparek**, **Heini Harrer**, **Anderl Heckmair**, and **Ludwig Vorg**.
1944	British Mountaineering Council formed.
1950	A strong team of **Louis Lachenal**, **Lionel Terray**, and **Gaston Rébuffat**, led by **Maurice Herzog**, climb K2, the first 8,000-meter peak ever climbed.

1953	**Sir Edmund Hillary** and **Tenzing Norgay** reach the summit of Everest.
1975	Unsuccessful U.S. attempt on K2 led by the **Whittakers**.
1978	**Peter Habeler** and **Reinhold Messner** climb Everest without supplemental oxygen.
1980	**Reinhold Messner** climbs Everest solo.
	Martine Rolland becomes the first official woman guide in the Alps.
1991	"Otzi" the **Ice Man**, a neolithic wanderer of the Alps, discovered by hikers.
1996	A group of guides and climbers die in Everest disaster. **Jon Krakauer** describes the experience in his book *Into Thin Air*.
1999	Body of **George Leigh Mallory** discovered by **Conrad Anker** expedition.

Introduction

Pestered by an eager journalist who insisted on knowing why he climbed mountains, George Leigh Mallory once allegedly quipped "Because it's there." Mallory and the mountaineers in the room knew that men and women do not flippantly risk their lives and fortunes for mere recreation, but what could one answer, after all, to someone so terribly oblivious to the obsession that propels climbers to a possible death or loss of extremities? Thus far Mallory's response has sufficed to this question.

A relatively new phenomenon, mountain climbing and mountain appreciation only began in earnest in the 1830s and 1840s in Europe and America. For the greater part of history, mountains were either worshiped silently as the homes of gods, stoically accepted as facts of life, or else ignored entirely. From a practical standpoint, ranges such as the Alps, Caucasus, and the Himalayas rendered travel impossible and hindered trade as well, although in times of wars and conflict, many a tribe welcomed their sheltered caves and defensible positions. It is no accident that the remnants of conquered peoples have more often than not been mountain people by necessity, the Welsh and Basque being cases in point. Until modern times, mountains were places where no sane person would be, unless driven there by circumstance. Hence, when Hannibal crossed the Alps during the Second Punic War against Rome, he was defying conventional wisdom so thoroughly that even the Roman historians Livy and Polybius had no choice but to grudgingly admire the Carthaginian's audacity. That he dared to bring elephants with him and cut his own rock steps when the stones blocked his way likewise raised him to mythic proportions in the Roman public mind.

Mountains, like the sky and the sea, have always provided us with a rough means of dividing our surroundings, and have consequently played a central role in the human psyche for millennia. Mountains simply cannot be missed, and their brooding presence permeates the lives of those who live in their shadow. The blessed gods of the Greeks, of course, chose forbidding Olympus for their playground, as far away from the mundane cares of workaday humanity as possible. Olympus remains a place of stark beauty and visual purity, where the air is rarified and light, and the landscape stripped to its essentials, almost distilled into the Platonic idea itself. In Old French, the word *Olympe* is synonymous with sky, the region where mountains scratch the dome of heaven.

It was probably Petrarch in the Western world, however, who first truly recognized the spiritual dimensions of mountains after the passing of the influence of the pagan religions, when standing on Ventoux in 1336, he opened his copy of Augustine's *Confessions* and read "Men travel to admire the high mountains, and to view the great seas . . . and yet they forget themselves." Shame and exhilaration fought for dominion in his mind at that moment. He had briefly mounted towards God, but could a man sustain himself at that height, or would he be forced by the something-bigger-than-he to descend down further where his flesh would corrupt, where he could breathe and eat normally again (and that a kind of death) only to be called upon to mount again?

The scattered documents on mountains which survive from the Middle Ages and Renaissance after Petrarch's watershed ascent indicate that the poet did not start a craze, or inspire others to sacrifice life or limb for spiritual or recreational ends. Josias Simler and Conrad Gesner in the sixteenth century, however, did attempt to describe these alien landscapes, and to capture their beauty and strangeness in elegant Latin prose, but they were natural philosophers interested in all of creation (particularly the world's unknown corners), not the harbingers of a new sport.

The first serious and sustained attempts at reaching the summits of mountains were inspired by scientific curiosity, and perhaps a variant of the pioneering and expeditionary spirit of science has always propelled mountaineering—the natural philosopher asks, "what will the valleys look like from on high, what kinds of rocks and plants are there, how far can we ascend until the air is gone," but inwardly, the scientist asks like the ordinary explorer, "Am I worthy and am I strong?" When Horace Bénédict de Saussure in the eighteenth century ascended Mount Blanc on the path blazed for him by Balmat and Paccard, he recorded the temperature, humidity, and barometric pressure, but secretly he sought a measure of his own human strength against a nature infinitely more powerful than his books and instruments.

Edward Whymper almost ruined the sport of mountaineering in its infancy when three prominent Englishmen and their guide tumbled to their deaths on the Matterhorn in 1865. Queen Victoria and her public promptly denounced mountain climbing as the most shocking display of reckless folly, a pastime for madmen. Although he persevered in his stunning series of first ascents around the globe, Whymper's subsequent career was permanently cast into shadow, and he could never shake the suspicion that he, or his guide Peter Taugwalder, had deliberately employed a faulty rope which snapped when the lead man fell, sparing Whymper and the guides, but dooming their four companions to a 4,000-foot free fall.

After the accident, the public was as perplexed as Mallory's journalist in understanding the why of mountaineering, an endeavor, as most mountaineers will admit, in which every step represents a simple dividing line between what you are and what you might become. It is perhaps this simplicity, mirrored by the uncomplicatedness of the mountain landscape, which has drawn thousands to scramble upon the sloping hills, to gaze in stupefaction at the unearthly patterns of the frozen couloir or the supernatural perpendicularity of the aiguille. In this respect, climbing approaches pure experience at its limits, existence stripped to the essentials: epiphanies explode in the consciousness when the mind is focused solely on safely ascending and descending rock and snow, when one realizes that all humanity really needs to survive is food, drink, sleep, and a good pair of dry boots. Mortgages, nothing. Sickness, nothing. Overpopulation, nothing. The clang and grate of modern living, all foolishness and nothing.

In fact, a climber's greatest performances—when a superhumanly difficult wall has been scaled with ease and an impassible overhang surmounted—occur during these intense periods of focus. For this reason, a great number of mountaineering accidents occur when climbers, either from hubris or fatigue, believing themselves safe and over the rough spots, turn their minds briefly from their tasks: "It was stupid, really. I had just come off a hellishly steep wall, one I thought I would never get off alive, and brought myself up to a ledge big enough to park a lorry on. Gathering up the rope, I tripped on my own boot and tumbled ten feet down onto a lower ledge. Thank God for the ledge! Stupid, really."

The twentieth century has been riddled with fatal mountaineering accidents. As the easier climbs of the Alps fell in succession in the nineteenth century, climbing techniques became standardized and refined and a brash younger generation was emboldened to seek harder and more dangerous routes. Fortunately the safety of the sport has improved dramatically since the days of hemp ropes and hobnailed boots. Since the end of the First World War, a growing number of amateurs have safely ventured unto the hills. Once only the sport of wealthy Victorian gentlemen who could finance the siege-style expeditions of porters, cooks, and well-supplied base camps, a certain democratization of climbing occurred from the 1920s to the present day, in which anyone with a few hundred dollars worth of equipment, a wiry frame, and the willingness to sacrifice all of their free hours on the rock could aspire to a world-class climbing reputation.

When the summit of Mount Everest, the highest point on earth, finally fell in 1953 to a lanky New Zealander, Sir Edmund Hillary, and his Sherpa companion, Tenzing Norgay, mountaineers wondered what was left for them to do. Mountaineering has always thrived on records and record-breaking, and there has been no diminution of new and astounding feats following the unheard of achievements of climbers of the 1950s and 1960s equipped with oxygen, lightweight gear, and over a century of hard-won accumulated knowledge of the mountain environment. The first ascent of Everest without oxygen, the first woman on K2, the longest bivouac over 28,000 feet . . . new records are invented and broken. As long as they are there, mountains will always provide an opportunity for climbers to test their perseverance, creativity, audacity, and foolhardiness.

The following essays, poems, and firsthand accounts may not adequately answer the question of why men and women climb mountains, and why they admire and fear them and have been so obsessed with standing on their summits, but the selections do describe how mountains are climbed, and how the climbers have felt climbing them, and how mountains have permanently affected those who have fallen under their sometimes fatal spell.

ALAN WEBER
Ithaca, New York
March 2002

Titus Livius

"Hannibal Crosses the Alps"

Titus Livius (59 B.C.E.–17 C.E.) was a Roman historian whose influential volumes on the rise of the Roman Empire contain the most complete account of Hannibal's crossing of the Alps during the Second Punic War between Rome and Carthage from 218–202 B.C.E. Harassed by hostile mountain tribes who stoned him from the heights, Carthaginian General Hannibal lost thousands of men, horses, and elephants in the narrow mountain passages. His troops were eventually forced to cut steps through the mountainside by heating the rocks with bonfires and pouring vinegar onto the hot stones. Hannibal's invasion through these natural defensive bulwarks was as much a psychological tactic as a strictly military maneuver: the Romans had come to believe that the impregnable Alps would always protect them from northern European invasions. Hannibal's move further underscored the vulnerability of the rising Roman Empire from overseas enemies. Rome fought a bitter and expensive war against the Africans until Hannibal finally succumbed to Scipio Africanus at Zama in 202 B.C.E. Hannibal's exploits were a popular theme in European schoolbooks up until modern times, and have provided us with such figures of speech as "Hannibal at the door." A parallel account written by the Greek historian Polybius also survives.

Whilst the elephants were conveyed over, Hannibal, in the mean time, had sent five hundred Numidian horsemen towards the camp of the Romans, to observe where and how numerous their forces were, and what they were designing. The three hundred Roman horsemen sent, as was before said, from the mouth of the Rhone, meet this band of cavalry; and a more furious engagement than could be expected from the number of the combatants takes place. For, besides many wounds, the loss on both sides was also nearly equal: and the flight and dismay of the Numidians gave victory to the Romans, now exceedingly fatigued. There fell of the conquerors 160, not all Romans, but partly Gauls: of the vanquished more than two hundred. This commencement, and at the same time omen of the war, as it portended to the Romans a prosperous issue of the whole, so did it also the success of a doubtful and by no means bloodless contest. When, after the action had thus occurred, his own men returned to each general, Scipio could adopt no fixed plan of proceeding, except that he should form his measures from the plans and undertakings of the enemy: and Hannibal, uncertain whether he should pursue the march he had commenced into Italy, or fight with the Roman army which had first presented itself, the arrival of ambassadors from the Boii, and of a petty prince called Magalus,

---

Titus Livius, *The History of Rome*, trans. D. Spillan and Cyrus Edmonds (London: Henry G. Bohn, 1849).

diverted from an immediate engagement; who, declaring that they would be the guides of his journey and the companions of his dangers, gave it as their opinion, that Italy ought to be attacked with the entire force of the war, his strength having been no where previously impaired. The troops indeed feared the enemy, the remembrance of the former war not being yet obliterated; but much more did they dread the immense journey and the Alps, a thing formidable by report, particularly to the inexperienced.

Hannibal, therefore, when his own resolution was fixed to proceed in his course and advance on Italy, having summoned an assembly, works upon the minds of the soldiers in various ways, by reproof and exhortation. He said, that "he wondered what sudden fear had seized breasts ever before undismayed: that through so many years they had made their campaigns with conquest; nor had departed from Spain before all the nations and countries which two opposite seas embrace, were subjected to the Carthaginians. That then, indignant that the Romans demanded those, whosoever had besieged Saguntum, to be delivered up to them, as on account of a crime, they had passed the Iberus to blot out the name of the Romans, and to emancipate the world. That then the way seemed long to no one, though they were pursuing it from the setting to the rising of the sun. That now, when they saw by far the greater part of their journey accomplished, the passes of the Pyrenees surmounted, amid the most ferocious nations, the Rhone, that mighty river, crossed, in spite of the opposition of so many thousand Gauls, the fury of the river itself having been overcome, when they had the Alps in sight, the other side of which was Italy, should they halt through weariness at the very gates of the enemy, imagining the Alps to be—what else than lofty mountains? That supposing them to be higher than the summits of the Pyrenees, assuredly no part of the earth reached the sky, nor was insurmountable by mankind. The Alps in fact were inhabited and cultivated;—produced and supported living beings. Were they passable by a few men and impassable to armies? That those very ambassadors whom they saw before them had not crossed the Alps borne aloft through the air on wings; neither were their ancestors indeed natives of the soil, but settling in Italy from foreign countries, had often as emigrants safely crossed these very Alps in immense bodies, with their wives and children. To the armed soldier, carrying nothing with him but the instruments of war, what in reality was impervious or insurmountable? That Saguntum might be taken, what dangers, what toils were for eight months undergone! Now, when their aim was Rome, the capital of the world, could any thing appear so dangerous or difficult as to delay their undertaking? That the Gauls had formerly gained possession of that very country which the Carthaginian despairs of being able to approach. That they must, therefore, either yield in spirit and valour to that nation which they had so often during those times overcome; or look forward, as the end of their journey, to the plain which spreads between the Tiber and the walls of Rome."

He orders them, roused by these exhortations, to refresh themselves and prepare for the journey. Next day, proceeding upward along the bank of the Rhone, he makes for the inland part of Gaul: not because it was the more direct route to the Alps, but believing that the farther he retired from the sea, the Romans would be less in his way; with whom, before he arrived in Italy, he had no intention of engaging. After four days' march he came to the Island: there the streams of the Arar and the Rhone, flowing down from different branches of the Alps, after embracing a pretty large tract of country, flow into one. The name of the Island is given to the plains that lie between them. The Allobroges dwell near, a nation even in those days inferior to none in Gaul in power and fame. They were at that time at variance. Two brothers were contending for the sovereignty. The elder, named Brancus, who had before been king, was driven out by his younger brother and a party of the younger men, who, inferior in right, had more of power. When the decision of this quarrel was most opportunely referred to Hannibal, being appointed arbitrator of the kingdom, he restored the sovereignty to the elder, because such had been the opinion of the senate and the chief men. In return for this service, he was assisted with a supply of provisions, and plenty of all necessaries, particularly clothing, which the Alps, notorious for extreme cold, rendered necessary to be prepared. After composing the dissensions of the Allobroges, when he now was proceeding to the Alps, he directed his course thither, not by the straight road, but turned to the left into the country of the Tricastini, thence by the extreme boundary of the territory of the Vocontii he proceeded to the Tricorii; his way not being any where obstructed till he came to the river Druentia. This stream, also arising amid the Alps, is by far the most difficult to pass of all the rivers in Gaul; for though it rolls down an immense body of water, yet it does not admit of ships; because, being restrained by no banks, and flowing in several and not always the same channels, and continually forming new shallows and new whirlpools (on which account the passage is also uncertain to a person on foot), and rolling down besides gravelly stones, it affords no firm or safe passage to those who enter it; and having been at that time swollen by showers, it created great disorder among the soldiers as they crossed, when, in addition to other difficulties, they were of themselves confused by their own hurry and uncertain shouts.

Publius Cornelius the consul, about three days after Hannibal moved from the bank of the Rhone, had come to the camp of the enemy, with his army drawn up in square, intending to make no delay in fighting: but when he saw the fortifications deserted, and that he could not easily come up with them so far in advance before him, he returned to the sea and his fleet, in order more easily and safely to encounter Hannibal when descending from the Alps. But that Spain, the province which he had obtained by lot, might not be destitute of Roman auxiliaries, he sent his brother Cneius Scipio with the principal part of his forces against Hasdrubal, not only to defend the old allies and conciliate new, but also to drive Hasdrubal out of Spain. He himself, with a very small force, returned to Genoa, intending to defend Italy with the army which was around the Po. From the Druentia, by a road that lay principally through plains, Hannibal arrived at the Alps without molestation from the Gauls that inhabit those regions. Then, though the scene had been previously anticipated

3

from report (by which uncertainties are wont to be exaggerated), yet the height of the mountains when viewed so near, and the snows almost mingling with the sky, the shapeless huts situated on the cliffs, the cattle and beasts of burden, withered by the cold, the men unshorn and wildly dressed, all things, animate and inanimate, stiffened with frost, and other objects more terrible to be seen than described, renewed their alarm. To them, marching up the first acclivities, the mountaineers appeared occupying the heights over head; who, if they had occupied the more concealed valleys, might, by rushing out suddenly to the attack, have occasioned great fight and havoc. Hannibal orders them to halt, and having sent forward Gauls to view the ground, when he found there was no passage that way, he pitches his camp in the widest valley he could find, among places all rugged and precipitous. Then, having learned from the same Gauls, when they had mixed in conversation with the mountaineers, from whom they differed little in language and manners, that the pass was only beset during the day, and that at night each withdrew to his own dwelling, he advanced at the dawn to the heights, as if designing openly and by day to force his way through the defile. The day then being passed in feigning a different attempt from that which was in preparation, when they had fortified the camp in the same place where they had halted, as soon as he perceived that the mountaineers had descended from the heights, and that the guards were withdrawn, having lighted for show a greater number of fires than was proportioned to the number that remained, and having left the baggage in the camp, with the cavalry and the principal part of the infantry, he himself with a part of light-armed, consisting of all the most courageous of his troops, rapidly cleared the defile, and took post on those very heights which the enemy had occupied.

At dawn of light the next day the camp broke up, and the rest of the army began to move forward. The mountaineers, on a signal being given, were now assembling from their forts to their usual station, when they suddenly behold part of the enemy over-hanging them from above, in possession of their former position, and the others passing along the road. Both these objects, presented at the same time to the eye and the mind, made them stand motionless for a little while; but when they afterwards saw the confusion in the pass, and that the marching body was thrown into disorder by the tumult which itself created, principally from the horses being terrified, thinking that whatever terror they added would suffice for the destruction of the enemy, they scramble along the dangerous rocks, as being accustomed alike to pathless and circuitous ways. Then indeed the Carthaginians were opposed at once by the enemy and by the difficulties of the ground; and each striving to escape first from the danger, there was more fighting among themselves than with their opponents. The horses in particular created danger in the lines, which, being terrified by the discordant clamours which the groves and reechoing valleys augmented, fell into confusion; and if by chance struck or wounded, they were so dismayed that they occasioned a great loss both of men and baggage of every description: and as the pass on both sides was broken and precipitous, this tumult threw many down to an im-

4

mense depth, some even of the armed men; but the beasts of burden, with their loads, were rolled down like the fall of some vast fabric. Though these disasters were shocking to view, Hannibal however kept his place for a little, and kept his men together, lest he might augment the tumult and disorder; but afterwards, when he saw the line broken, and that there was danger that he should bring over his army, preserved to no purpose if deprived of their baggage, he hastened down from the higher ground; and though he had routed the enemy by the first onset alone, he at the same time increased the disorder in his own army: but that tumult was composed in a moment, after the roads were cleared by the flight of the mountaineers; and presently the whole army was conducted through, not only without being disturbed, but almost in silence. He then took a fortified place, which was the capital of that district, and the little villages that lay around it, and fed his army for three days with the corn and cattle he had taken; and during these three days, as the soldiers were neither obstructed by the mountaineers, who had been daunted by the first engagement, nor yet much by the ground, he made considerable way.

He then came to another state, abounding, for a mountainous country, with inhabitants; where he was nearly overcome, not by open war, but by his own arts of treachery and ambuscade. Some old men, governors of forts, came as deputies to the Carthaginian, professing, "that having been warned by the useful example of the calamities of others, they wished rather to experience the friendship than the hostilities of the Carthaginians: they would, therefore, obediently execute his commands, and begged that he would accept of a supply of provisions, guides of his march, and hostages for the sincerity of their promises." Hannibal, when he had answered them in a friendly manner, thinking that they should neither be rashly trusted nor yet rejected, lest if repulsed they might openly become enemies, having received the hostages whom they proffered, and made use of the provisions which they of their own accord brought down to the road, follows their guides, by no means as among a people with whom he was at peace, but with his line of march in close order. The elephants and cavalry formed the van of the marching body; he himself, examining every thing around, and intent on every circumstance, followed with the choicest of the infantry. When they came into a narrower pass, lying on one side beneath an overhanging eminence, the barbarians, rising at once on all sides from their ambush, assail them in front and rear, both at close quarters and from a distance, and roll down huge stones on the army. The most numerous body of men pressed on the rear; against whom the infantry, facing about and directing their attack, made it very obvious, that had not the rear of the army been well supported, a great loss must have been sustained in that pass. Even as it was they came to the extremity of danger, and almost to destruction: for while Hannibal hesitates to lead down his division into the defile, because, though he himself was a protection to the cavalry, he had not in the same way left any aid to the infantry in the rear; the mountaineers, charging obliquely, and on having broken through the middle of the army, took possession of the road; and one night was spent by Hannibal without his cavalry and baggage.

5

Next day, the barbarians running in to the attack between (the two divisions) less vigorously, the forces were re-united, and the defile passed, not without loss, but yet with a greater destruction of beasts of burden than of men. From that time the mountaineers fell upon them in smaller parties, more like an attack of robbers than war, sometimes the van, sometimes on the rear, according as the ground afforded them advantage, or stragglers advancing or loitering gave them an opportunity. Though the elephants were driven through steep and narrow roads with great loss of time, yet wherever they went they rendered the army safe from the enemy, because men unacquainted with such animals were afraid of approaching too nearly. On the ninth day they came to a summit of the Alps, chiefly through places trackless; and after many mistakes of their way, which were caused either by the treachery of the guides, or, when they were not trusted, by entering valleys at random, on their own conjectures of the route. For two days they remained encamped on the summit; and rest was given to the soldiers, exhausted with toil and fighting: and several beasts of burden, which had fallen down among the rocks, by following the track of the army arrived at the camp. A fall of snow, it being now the season of the setting of the constellation of the Pleiades, caused great fear to the soldiers, already worn out with weariness of so many hardships. On the standards being moved forward at daybreak, when the army proceeded slowly over all places entirely blocked up with snow, and languor and despair strongly appeared in the countenances of all, Hannibal, having advanced before the standards, and ordered the soldiers to halt on a certain eminence, whence there was a prospect far and wide, points out to them Italy and the plains of the Po, extending themselves beneath the Alpine mountains; and said "that they were now surmounting not only the ramparts of Italy, but also of the city of Rome; that the rest of the journey would be smooth and down-hill; that after one, or, at most, a second battle, they would have the citadel and capital of Italy in their power and possession." The army then began to advance, the enemy now making no attempts beyond petty thefts, as opportunity offered. But the journey proved much more difficult than it had been in the ascent, as the declivity of the Alps being generally shorter on the side of Italy is consequently steeper; for nearly all the road was precipitous, narrow, and slippery, so that neither those who made the least stumble could prevent themselves from falling, nor, when fallen, remain in the same place, but rolled, both men and beasts of burden, one upon another.

They then came to a rock much more narrow, and formed of such perpendicular ledges, that a light-armed soldier, carefully making the attempt, and clinging with his hands to the bushes and roots around, could with difficulty lower himself down. The ground, even before very steep by nature, had been broken by a recent falling away of the earth into a precipice of nearly a thousand feet in depth. Here when the cavalry had halted, as if at the end of their journey, it is announced to Hannibal, wondering what obstructed the march, that the rock was impassable. Having them gone himself to view the place, it seemed clear to him that he must lead his army round it, by however great a circuit, through the pathless and untrodden regions around. But

6

this route also proved impracticable; for while the new snow of a moderate depth remained on the old, which had not been removed, their footsteps were planted with ease as they walked upon the new snow, which was soft and not too deep; but when it was dissolved by the trampling of so many men and beasts of burden, they then walked on the bare ice below, and through the dirty fluid formed by the melting snow. Here there was a wretched struggle, both on account of the slippery ice not affording any hold to the step, and giving way beneath the foot more readily by reason of the slope; and whether they assisted themselves in rising by their hands or their knees, their supports themselves giving way, they would tumble again; nor were there any stumps or roots near, by pressing against which, one might with hand or foot support himself; so that they only floundered on the smooth ice and amid the melted snow. The beasts of burden sometimes also cut into this lower ice by merely treading upon it, at others they broke it completely through, by the violence with which they struck in their hoofs in their struggling, so that most of them, as if taken in a trap, stuck in the hardened and deeply frozen ice.

At length, after the men and beasts of burden had been fatigued to no purpose, the camp was pitched on the summit, the ground being cleared for that purpose with great difficulty, so much snow was there to be dug out and carried away. The soldiers being then set to make a way down the cliff, by which alone a passage could be effected, and it being necessary that they should cut through the rocks, having felled and lopped a number of large trees which grew around, they make a huge pile of timber; and as soon as a strong wind fit for exciting the flames arose, they set fire to it, and, pouring vinegar on the heated stones, they render them soft and crumbling. They then open a way with iron instruments through the rock thus heated by the fire, and soften its declivities by gentle windings, so that not only the beasts of burden, but also the elephants could be led down it. Four days were spent about this rock, the beasts nearly perishing through hunger: for the summits of the mountains are for the most part bare, and if there is any pasture the snows bury it. The lower parts contain valleys, and some sunny hills, and rivulets flowing beside woods, and scenes more worthy of the abode of man. There the beasts of burden were sent out to pasture, and rest given for three days to the men, fatigued with forming the passage: they then descended into the plains, the country and the dispositions of the inhabitants being now less rugged.

In this manner chiefly they came to Italy in the fifth month (as some authors relate) after leaving New Carthage, having crossed the Alps in fifteen days. What number of forces Hannibal had when he had passed into Italy is by no means agreed upon by authors. Those who state them at the highest, make mention of a hundred thousand foot and twenty thousand horse; those who state them at the lowest, of twenty thousand foot and six thousand horse. Lucius Cincius Alimentus, who relates that he was made prisoner by Hannibal, would influence me most as a authority, did he not confound the number by adding the Gauls and Ligurians. Including these (who, it is more probable, flocked to him afterwards, and so some authors assert), he says, that

7

eighty thousand foot and ten thousand horse were brought into Italy; and that he had heard from Hannibal himself, that after crossing the Rhone he had lost thirty-six thousand men, and an immense number of horses, and other beasts of burden, among the Taurini, the next nation to the Gauls, as he descended into Italy. As this circumstance is agreed on by all, I am the more surprised that it should be doubtful by what road he crossed the Alps; and that it should commonly be believed that he passed over the Pennine mountain, and that thence[1] the name was given to that ridge of the Alps. Cœlius says, that he passed over the top of Mount Cremo; both which passes would have brought him, not to the Taurini, but through the Salassian mountaineers to the Libuan Gauls. Neither is it probable that these roads into Gaul were then open, especially since those which lead to the Pennine mountain would have been blocked up by nations half German; nor by Hercules (if this argument has weight with any one) do the Veragri, the inhabitants of this ridge, know of the name being given to these mountains from the passage of the Carthaginians, but from the divinity, whom the mountaineers style Penninus, worshipped on the highest summit.

—C. 200 B.C.E.

Note

1. From Pænus, Cathaginian.

8

Francesco Petrarcha
"Petrarch Climbs Mont Ventoux"

Inspired by Hannibal's crossing of the Alps and Philip of Macedon's ascent of Mount Hemus in Thessaly, Italian poet Francesco Petrarcha (1304–1374) climbed Mons Ventosus (the "Windy Mount") in southern France on April 26, 1336, with his younger brother. He then wrote this letter to his former confessor Father Dionighi, interpreting his overfondness of the pleasing vistas he found on the mountain as a spiritual blindness to the care of the soul. Petrarch's brother does not hesitate to take the difficult, steep, and thorny route directly to the summit, while Petrarch flounders and loses the path several times by sticking to the seemingly "easier" slopes. Upon reaching the summit, he opened his copy of The Confessions of St. Augustine, *and the first words his eyes fell upon were "Men travel to admire the high mountains, and to view the great seas . . . and yet they abandon themselves." A complex spiritual allegory of sin and redemption, Petrarch's letter represents one of Western literature's most enduring moral homilies.*

TO FATHER DIONIGHI DA BORGO SAN SEPOLCRO [APRIL 26, 1336]

Today I climbed the highest mountain in this region, which is not without reason called the "Windy Mount," led solely by the desire to experience the great height of the summit. I had intended to take this journey for many years; as you know, these parts have been my home since my childhood, on account of the destiny which governs the fates of men. This mountain, which is visible from afar and from all sides, was always before my eyes. An irresistible desire seized me to make the journey which I rehearsed every day in my mind, especially a few days ago when I was re-reading Titus Livius's *Roman History*, and I by chance fell upon the passage in which Philip, the King of Macedonia (the one who made war against the Romans), climbed Mount Hemus. It is said that he saw two seas—the Adriatic and Euxine—from the summit of that Thessalian mountain. Philip believed this, but is it true or false? I cannot confirm this, because Mount Hemus is far from our region and the disagreement of the ancient authorities makes the case doubtful. Without citing all of them, Pomponius Mela the cosmographer, for example, states without the least hesitation that the account is exact, while Titus Livius believes that it is a legend. As for myself, I would not have left the question in doubt any longer if the climbing of Hemus were as easy as Ventoux. But, to drop that matter and to take up the story at hand, I thought that a young person might attempt a feat that an old king was not criticized for undertaking.

Francesco Petrarcha, "Petrarch Climbs Mont Ventoux, 1336." Translation by Alan Weber, based on the text of Francis Gribble, *The Early Mountaineers* (London: T. Fisher Unwin, 1899).

I thought about a travelling companion, and surprisingly, I could scarcely find a single one of my friends who appeared suitable on all points, so rare is it to find even among the most cherished companions that perfect balance of feelings and temperament. This one was too phlegmatic, that one too lively; one was too slow, the other too quick; one was too sad, the other too gay; finally, that one was too crazy, and another one wiser than I wanted. I was scared by the silence of the one, and the chatter of the other, the heaviness and stoutness of one, and the thinness and debility of another. In another, the cold indifference discouraged me, in the same way as the ardent officiousness of another. Such annoyances are tolerable at home, because charity mends all such affronts, and friendship refuses no burden, but on a journey, these same faults are difficult to accept.

———

Thus did my fastidious spirit, seized with an honest desire, weigh the dispositions of each of my friends without straining my friendships and I condemned in silence everything that might have been a hindrance to the planned climb. In the end, I turned to my family and I revealed my plan to my only brother, who is younger than me and whom you know well. He could not imagine a more agreeable proposition and he expressed the desire to go not only as a brother, but as a friend.

On the appointed day, we left the house and by the evening had arrived at Malaucène, a village situated at the foot of the mountain on the north side. We rested there for one day. Today, finally, each accompanied by a servant, we ascended the mountain, but not without great difficulty. The mountain consists of a mass of rocky earth, abrupt and almost inaccessible. But the poet has said well "persistent labor conquers all." The length of the day, the sweetness of the air, the vigor of our spirits, the strength and agility of our bodies and other such advantages all favored our enterprise. There was no other obstacle except the nature of the place.

On the mountain ridges, we met an ancient shepherd, who tried to discourage us from our climb with a great many words. Fifty years previously, he said, the same youthful ardor had driven him to mount the final summit, and he had gained nothing from it but regret and fatigue, as well as torn clothes and scratches from the rocks and thorny bushes. Never before or after had he heard that anyone in the country had risked a similar ascent. But he shouted himself hoarse in vain, because in the face of opposition, young people—deaf to the counsel of elders—feel an increase in their desires. As soon as he saw the futility of his efforts, the old man accompanied us a little while among the rocks and pointed out with his finger a craggy path, while redoubling his advice which he reiterated to our backs as our group moved away. Since we had left with him all of the clothes and baggage which loaded us down (only keeping the equipment that was strictly necessary for the climb), we climbed with a brisk step.

But as it often happens, fatigue greeted our great efforts, and not far from where we left the shepherd, we stopped on a rock. Then we started again, but more slowly; I especially walked on the mountain path at a more moderate pace. My brother, taking a shortcut directly across the ridges, climbed towards the heights. But I, being less robust than he, turned along the slopes and when he called to me and showed me a more direct route, I told him that I was trying to find easier access from another side and that I didn't mind a longer route where I could march on a more even plane.

―――――

But it was an excuse to hide my weakness and the others already occupied the ridges while I was still wandering in the hollows, without finding an easier way up. On the contrary, the road lengthened, and I increased my futile labors. Completely disgusted, however, I soon regretted my tardiness in winding sinuously up the mountain and right away I decided to win the heights. My brother was waiting for me. He had renewed his forces with a long rest, and when I finally reached him I felt exhausted and weak. For a while we walked side by side. But scarcely had we left the ridge, and forgetting my previous words, I threw myself again into a downward descent: and as I traversed the hollows and while I was looking for the easy way along the longer route, I again fell into great difficulties. Thus I deferred the fatigue of the ascent, but the human spirit does not know how to overcome the laws of nature and it is impossible for a body to rise by travelling downwards.

In sum, not without making my brother laugh and me angry, these misadventures repeated themselves three or more times within several hours. After being deceived several times about the way, I sat down in a hollow. There, my thoughts moved rapidly from material to spiritual things and I addressed myself in terms similar to this: "Don't forget that the same trials that you (among many others) endured today, will also be met on the road to blessedness. But this is not easy to discern, because the movements of the body are visible to the eyes, while those of the soul are invisible and hidden. Yes, the life that we call happy is situated at an elevated height: narrow is the route that leads there, so it is said. Many escarpments arise there also, and one must advance from virtue to virtue by glorious degrees. At the summit is the supreme end, the termination of the voyage we have undertaken. Everyone desires to arrive there, but as Ovid says: 'To want counts little; to triumph, you must ardently desire.' And you, unless you are mistaken as in many cases, undoubtedly not only want, but also yearn with passion. What is it that holds you back then? Nothing more, certainly, than the road of gross and earthly pleasures which at first seems easier and more level. But after much wandering, you will be forced to climb to the heights of blessedness, under the weight of the pains you have avoided, or else fall cowardly into the pit of your sins. And (I tremble to think), if the dark shadows of death find you in that spot, you will live in an eternal night with ceaseless torments."

You will never know how these thoughts brought strength to my soul and body for what I needed to complete on the mountain. God wished that my soul would make its beautiful voyage for which I sigh night and day, since my feet, after having finally surmounted the difficulties, would achieve today the earthly route. And I wonder if what can be understood by the agile and immortal soul without movement

11

and in the wink of an eye is not easier than that which a mortal and perishable body can do over a period of time under the heavy weight of its members.

One height rises above all the others: the mountain people call it Filiolus ("Little Son"); why, I don't know, unless by antiphrasis, I imagine, since this peak truly appears to be the father of all the neighboring mountains. A small flat area can be found on the summit. There we stopped for a rest.

———

And since you have listened to the reflections which assailed my spirit during the climb, my father, please listen to the rest, and I pray you lend me an hour of your time to read about what I did on that day. Suddenly, vividly aware of the strangeness of the breeze which was blowing and because of the extent of the view, I remained immobile as if in a stupor. I looked around and the clouds floated around my feet. And already I was less unbelieving about the myths of Athos and Olympus when I realized that what I have read or heard could be verified on a mountain of lesser renown. From there my view was led towards Italy where my heart inclines. Bristling and snowy, the Alps themselves where formerly the fierce enemy of the name of Rome opened a passage by breaking the rocks with vinegar (if one believes the story), appeared right next to me, despite the great distance. I confess that I sighed for that Italian air, more sensible to my soul than to my eyes and I was seized with an inexpressible longing to see both my friend and country again. This longing, however, was accompanied by severe self-reproach for the weakness of my unmanly feeling in thinking of the two—yet I might be excused for these feelings with ample support from other authorities.

Then a new thought arose in my mind and I passed from place to time. I told myself that on this day ten years had elapsed since I finished my youthful studies and left Bologna; and, O immortal God, O immutable Wisdom, how many important changes in my conduct has that interval witnessed! But the course of my life is not yet finished, so let us leave that, for I have not yet arrived at a safe harbor from which to view in safety my stormy past. Perhaps there will come a time when I will review all my actions in order, and take as my text the words of St. Augustine: "I wish to recollect my past uncleanness, and the carnal corruptions of my soul not because I love them, but because I love Thee, O my God." Indeed I still confront turmoils on my uncertain and arduous route. That which I loved, I no longer love. No, I am telling a lie—I do love it, but with more moderation. But I have lied again: I love, but with more caution, and more sadness. Now I have come to the truth. Yes, I love, but I love that which I would not like to love, that which I desire to hate. I love, however, but in spite of myself, unwillingly, and in tears and affliction—and I feel in myself this little celebrated bit of verse:

I will hate if I can;
If not, I will love, but in spite of myself.

Three years had not passed when that perverse and guilty feeling which entirely possessed me and reigned alone and unopposed in the palace of my heart, began to feel the resistance of a rebellious feeling. For a long time in my mind, the two men in me have fought a bitter and still undecided battle for pre-eminence. Thus did my thoughts turn to the previous ten years of my life. Then, led by my cares, my mind suddenly jumped to the future, and I asked myself "if you are lucky enough to prolong this ephemeral life for ten more years, and during this time to approach virtue as much as you have during the last two years due to the struggle between your old and new dispositions, pushing aside your original obstinacy, couldn't you, although without certainty, but hoping nevertheless, confront death at the age of forty, and give up that final part of life which declines into old age? These and similar thoughts agitated my mind, my father. I was encouraged by my progress, my imperfections made me cry, and I pitied the common inconstancy of human deeds. I forgot the place where I was and why I had come. This continued until, leaving these preoccupations to a more suitable occasion, I looked around and saw what I had come to see—it was time to return, as the descending sun and the passing shadow of the mountain warned me. I roused myself, so to speak, and turned to look towards the west. The frontier of France, and the Pyrenees of Spain were not to be seen (though nothing that I know of intervened, except the impotence of mortal sight). But I could very clearly see the mountains about Lyons on the right and on the left the bay of Marseilles, and the waves which beat against Aigue-Mortes, which are distant some days journey. The Rhône itself flowed beneath our eyes. But while I was admiring these sights—at times abandoning myself to earthly joy, at other times letting my soul (by the example of my body) rise towards the heights—it occurred to me to look into the book of Augustine's *Confessions* which I owe to your kindness, and which I keep in memory of the author and the giver. I generally carry it about with me, as it is a volume of small dimensions that fits in the palm, though of infinite sweetness. I opened it at a venture, meaning to read whatever might present itself—for what could I have found that was not pious and devout? The volume fell open by chance at the tenth book.

My brother was standing attentively waiting to hear some words of St. Augustine from my mouth. I take God and my brother as witnesses, these are the words I found. The first passage that my eyes fell upon were: "men go to admire the mountains and the immense waves of the ocean and the vast courses of rivers and the circuit of the sea and the revolutions of the stars, and they abandon themselves."

I admit that I was stunned. I asked my brother, eager to hear more, not to disturb me, and I closed the book. I was irritated with myself for admiring earthly things, when I should have learned long since from the pagan philosophers that nothing is as admirable as the soul, and in comparison with the soul, nothing is as great.

―――

Then, satiated with the sight of the mountain, I turned my sight inwards and from that moment onwards no one heard me speak a word, until we arrived at the bottom.

13

The words of Augustine, which had transported me, were enough to occupy me for the rest of the journey and I can't believe that I had discovered the passage randomly. On the contrary, I was persuaded that everything that I had read in the passage had been addressed specifically to me and to none other. I recall that the same thought occurred to Augustine, when, as he himself reports, he was reading the Epistles, and he fell on these lines: "Let us conduct ourselves becomingly as in the day, not in reveling and drunkenness, not in debauchery and licentiousness, not in quarrelling and jealousy. But put on the Lord Jesus Christ, and make no provision for the flesh, to gratify its desires" [Paul, *Ad Rom*, 13.13–14].

The same thing happened to Anthony, when he was listening to the Gospel where it is written, "if you would be perfect, go, sell what you possess, and give to the poor, and you will have treasure in heaven; and come, follow me" [Matthew 19.21]. And, as if these lines had been read only for him, according to his biographer Athanasius, he went and submitted himself wholly to the omnipotence of our Lord. And just as Anthony, having heard these words, asked nothing more, and just as Augustine, having read those words, enquired no further, I stopped my reading at the passage which I mentioned earlier. I reflected in silence on the poverty of wisdom in men who, neglecting the most noble part of their being, fritter away themselves on trifles, and dissipate themselves in vain spectacles, and go looking outside for what they can find within themselves.

I also marvelled at the nobility of our soul, when it doesn't turn away by willing degradation from its first holy origin, or turn to shame the gifts that God creates for its glory. How often on the return journey—don't doubt it—did I look behind me at the peak of the mountain. It hardly seemed higher than a cubit in comparison with the height of human thought, when it doesn't fall into earthly mud and filth.

With each step, another reflexion also arose in my spirit: "If you didn't hesitate to suffer so much sweat and pain to drag your body a little closer to heaven, as little as that might be, what cross, what prison, what rack of torture could frighten your soul when it approaches God and crushes the proud summit and mortal destiny beneath its feet?" And this other thought: "How few there are who are not turned away from this path by the fear of hardship and their passionate attachment to desire." How happy is that man, if one exists any where. The poet, in my opinion, was thinking of this man when he wrote:

Happy is he who knows the first causes of things
And who casts beneath his feet
All superstitious fear and immovable destiny
And the noise of insatiable Acheron.

With great ardor we should strive to trample beneath our feet not the earthly heights, but the passions which arouse human impulses in us. Insensible to the stones of the pathway and carrying a turbulent heart, I returned at nightfall to the rustic inn from

14

whence I had departed at daybreak. The moon, which was shining brightly that night, blessed our journey. While the servants were preparing dinner, I retired to an out of the way room to write to you in haste without stopping. I was afraid that if I procrastinated, a change of place might change my feelings and my desire to write to you would cool.

So you see, my dear father, how I have not attempted to conceal anything from you, because I offer you not only my entire life, but each one of my thoughts. And by the grace of God, pray that those thoughts so vagabond and inconstant, will one day come together, and after having been vainly tossed in every direction, they might turn to a singular pursuit of the good, the true, the certain, and the immovable.

Vale. VI Kal Maias. Malaucène.
—1336

Conrad Gesner

"On the Admiration of Mountains"

The sixteenth-century letter of Conrad Gesner (1516–1565) to his friend Jacob Vogel origi-
nally served as a preface to a treatise on milk, Libellus de lacte et operibus lactariis *(Little*
Book on Milk and Milk Production, 1545). The letter is remarkable for its favorable view
of mountains, generally regarded with fear and superstition throughout Europe during the
Middle Ages and Renaissance. Mountains were more often viewed as barriers to travel and
the home of devils and apparitions, rather than as places of beauty, recreation, and spiritual
reflection. Born in Zürich, Switzerland, Gesner was one of the most learned men of his age in
languages, science, and medicine. He published a Greek-Latin dictionary in 1537 and prac-
ticed medicine, eventually securing an appointment as city physician for Zürich in 1554. He
was noted for his Historiae animalium *(History of Animals, 1551–1557), which was*
translated into many languages. He relied on direct observations of animal behavior when pos-
sible rather than on the authority of ancient authors.

LETTER TO JACOB VOGEL ON THE ADMIRATION OF MOUNTAINS, BY CONRAD GESNER, PHYSICIAN.
TO THE DISTINGUISHED M. JACQUES VOGEL, THE PHYSICIAN CONRAD GESNER GREETS YOU:

I have decided, my learned Vogel, that from now on, as long as God will allow, I will
ascend several mountains each year, or at least one, in the season when all of the
plants are in full bloom, to examine them and procure myself some noble exercise, as
well as the renewing of my spirits. Is it not a great pleasure? What a delight for the
justly moved soul, to admire the spectacle presented by the enormity of these mountains, and to lift one's head into the bosom of the clouds. Although I cannot explain
why, my spirit is struck by these astonishing heights and I am carried away in contemplation of the Divine Architect. Nothing surprises those with heavy spirits; they
crouch in their lodgings, instead of going out to witness the theater of the world, retired in their corner like dormice during the winter. They don't realize that man was
placed on earth in order to deduce from these marvels the existence of a superior being, of the Sovereign God himself. Such is their apathy, that like pigs, they look incessantly towards the ground, without ever contemplating the heavens with raised
heads, without ever raising their eyes towards the stars. Thus do they grovel and roll

---

Conrad Gesner, "Epistola ad Jacobum Avienum de montium admiratione, authore Conrado Gesnero
medico," *Libellus de lacte et operibus lactariis* [Zürich: Chr. Froschauer, 1541] in W. A. B. Coolidge, *Josias Sim-*
ler et Les Origines de l'Alpinisme jusqu'en 1600 (Grenoble: Imprimerie Allier Frères, 1904), i–xvii. Translated
by Alan Weber.

in their own dirt, occupied by greed and servile occupations. Those who are animated by wisdom, however, will continue to observe with the eyes of the body and the eyes of the soul the spectacles of this earthly paradise. And not least among these marvels are the elevated and abrupt summits of the mountains, the inaccessible escarpments—the enormity of their sides raised towards heaven—the difficult rocks and the thick forests.

———

Why, I ask you, —and here I cite the text of our learned friend Grynaeus,—"does such a great mass of rocks, a very considerable weight, since the soft ground yields readily, not sink under the earth by its own heaviness according to natural law?" All the more astonishing since nowhere is the ground so soft and swampy than at the base of mountains. So well are the mountains supported that one might suppose that their bases are extraordinarily deep, or that they are dispersed, like tree roots, over a large area. And why are the rocks suspended, as if by design, in such a menacing position? What force has conjured them into this centuries-old and precarious state? And, to what ends are such summits elevated? Here is the answer: a continuous stream of water, which will soon gush out violently, forms itself in the receptacles of the mountains, while the enclosed air in the interior cavities sends the water back up, under pressure at low temperatures, drop by drop without interruption; these drops promptly reunite and quickly form into springs, which we see in great abundance feeding lakes, ponds, and rivers. This is the process which throws up these great masses of rock, due to the astonishing natural miracle which occurs secretly in the interior. Other less precipitous heights are rich in little hillocks exposed to the heat of the sun in plains used for various purposes, and these small hills protect, like a wall, against some dangerous corner of the world; often these hills divert the course of rivers toward neighboring plains and dam them up. Also, mountains commonly supply iron ore and raw materials not only for agriculture and building, such as wood, stone, and iron, but also materials for the managing of business affairs, such as silver and gold." Thus says Grynaeus in his commentary on Aristotle's *De mundo*. Having already expressed my profound respect for his judgement and style, and above all because of my intention to enter into philosophical considerations, I wanted to cite his work directly rather than treat the subject myself with less facility; and if I use my own words to entertain you briefly about mountains, I seek your pardon.

Thus I declare anyone an enemy of nature who doesn't regard the high mountains as a dignified subject of contemplation. Certainly the highest summits seem to be exempt from ordinary weather conditions and escape storms, as if they were part of another world. On the heights, the action of the all-powerful sun and the air and the winds is not the same as in the vallies. The snows there are eternal, and that extremely soft matter which melts in the fingers cares little for the burning of the sun or fire; and far from disappearing with time, it congeals into very hard ice and indissoluble crystals. Letters inscribed in the ash on the summit of Mount Olympus remain there for one year. Who could catalogue precisely the species of animals and the feeding grounds of the savage animals which one meets in the mountains? Besides, everything that nature normally produces helter-skelter and with parsimony, she displays and gives forth in the mountains in complete abundance, like a mound stretching all its riches and joys before our eyes.

Also, all of the elements and diversity of nature can be found in the mountains. One can contemplate there the monstrous burden of the earth, as if nature were parading her forces and wanted to prove her power in raising such a great weight, which presses downwards, always sinking with an enormous force. Often lakes are found on the summits, as if by some trick nature took pleasure in lifting and elevating water from the deep wells which the caverns hold. In the mountains, one can look around and see air expanding in every direction, engorged with subtle vapors exhaled by the mountain waters. Sometimes the vapors, imprisoned within vast cavities, provoke earthquakes, which occur constantly in some spots. One can even find fire in the interior, whose subterranean action fashions metals like a forge. In addition, thermal springs which are good for the health, bear witness to that internal fire, most notably in many places in Switzerland. Also there are erupting flames, as on Etna, Vesuvius, and on a mountain near Grenoble. In other parts also, but without betraying its presence, fire remains hidden in the entrails of the mountain. But why, across the long stretch of the centuries, have mountains not sunk down into the earth? Why have they not been destroyed either by the storms which strike them without end, or by the rains which fall in torrents? Evidently this is due to fire, both the creator and preserver of the mountains, as the philosopher Philo has observed: the igneous matter enclosed in the earth, being naturally driven higher, follows its proper direction, and when it finds an issue, however narrow it may be, the fire raises along with itself a voluminous mass of earth (such is the case of the craters of Etna).

At the same time that the earth shakes, the fire travels along the shortest route. Then, constrained to yield to the thrust of the trembling fire, the earth rises to a considerable height and then contracts in time to terminate in a pointed peak, at the limits of the elemental fire. It is inevitable at this moment that the lightest and the heaviest elements, which oppose each other, enter into a struggle, since each one of them, by the effect of its proper tendency, is drawn towards its true place and drawn in an opposite direction by the violence of the other element. Thus the element of fire which arises from the earth is constrained to lower itself under the weight of the terrestrial element; the terrestrial element, on the other hand, forced to descend by the laws of its equilibrium, but suspended by the fire which naturally rises up in the air (in the end vanquished by the heavy and elevating force which propels it) rises in the place of fire and maintains itself there. This is why the Stoics call fire the "habitus" of the mountains, that is to say the bond that holds

18

the mountains together with universal tension, stretching out from the center, where fire originates, out to the extremities.

———

Also, when the power of all the elements and of all of nature manifests itself on mountains in such an intense manner, it is not surprising that the ancients admired a certain divinity in the mountains, and consequently, imagined a crowd of mountain deities, like Fauns, Satyrs, and Pan, which they represented with goat's feet, calling these gods demi-rams, ram-footed, and ram-legged, because of the roughness of the rocky mountains and because these animals roamed in the mountain pastures. They also feared them because the contemplation of such high and wooded areas causes a surge of fear in our souls beyond the terrors which attend our normal activities. Pan in particular, the mountain dweller, is the symbol of the universe from which the elements of mountains arise, exercising their powerful energy there. This is also why Pan is crowned with pine boughs: the pine stands for the mountains, the forest and for magnificence. Bucalion is said to be his son, the one who first taught man how to graze cattle. All of the imagined and honored nymphs were found in the various corners of the mountains: the Oreades, the Alseides, Helionomes, Hydriades, Crenides, Epipotamades, Limnades, Naiades, Limoniades, Epimelides, Dryades, Hamadryades. Diane the Huntress loved the mountains; the muses ran laughing among the summits of Parnassus from the Helicon to the summits of Aonie and Pieria. These are certainly myths, but myths which have a grain of truth to them.

But, however (to return to my point of departure), the reason that the passing years do no damage to the mountains absolutely escapes those who (in the same way that they misunderstand the mode of mountain formation) don't hesitate to say that in essence the mountains and trees are identical in every way. In the same way that trees, following the law of the seasons, lose and regain their leaves in turn, so certain parts of the mountains are torn asunder, and other parts in turn are rebuilt. The growth of mountains, however, only appears after a long time, because trees, endowed with a more rapid development, grow without delay, while the life of a mountain progresses more slowly. And this is why new parts of mountains are scarcely perceived by our senses except after the passage of time. Let us leave these people, however, and their philosophical systems.

But why do we see mountains pitted with such great caverns, almost like meeting halls, which cannot have been constructed, it seems, without a great effort? Is it from the torrential waters which violently open a route by dragging earth and stones along with them? Is it that since its origin, the earth, unequally ravaged by the action of fire, has accidently preserved cavities in its empty sides? Or is it that the fire in rising later on has destroyed a great part of whatever stood in its way? Or finally, is it that the parts of mountains struck by the earthquakes (which ravage them often), break into half-open crevasses?

19

———

Furthermore, it is a great wonder that the bases of the mountains are so crumbling and light, compared to the summits which are almost exclusively rocky. Without doubt the flowing waters produce that softness of the base, which is only moderately subjected to the influences of the sun and wind. The summit, on the other hand, exposed to the sun and winds, is dried out and all the moisture flows out of it, leaving it arid. The watery and least dense parts disappear and the hard, compact and essentially earthy element remains and subsequently becomes petrified under the influence of cold or burning heat, produced by the interior fire (fire is always the most intense in compact and hard bodies). Although very inactive in the lower regions and surrounding areas, this fire is very powerful at the summit because of its pyramidal structure. Why then do we see snow persisting on the mountain tops, while it melts on the sides and base of the mountain? It is because the lower atmospheric layer heats up from the reverberation of the solar rays and melts the snows, while the reflection of these rays, which doubles the strength of each ray, is not felt at the summit. But why are the snows not melted by that natural fire which operates above all at the summit? It is because the action of the fire stops just below the summit (if not it would spurt out like in volcanoes), and that the earth and thick rocks form a sort of cover that the cone of fire cannot penetrate through to the summit; in addition, near its culminating point, the cone is thin and blunted, crushed as it is by the particularly heavy and massive rock. Thus the flame stops at the underside of the summit; as for the snows, the cold air and the moist and icy vapors feed them and maintain them.

But why are mountains so well forested? It is because the mountains are so rich in nutritive elements: spring waters, frequent rains, and abundant snows (these are particularly helpful, because melting little by little, they penetrate into the soil, such that a great volume of water is not suddenly lost in a single downpour). For that same reason, the temperature of the earth rises to that of the imprisoned heat which surrounds it, because the exterior crushing force and the pressure of the cold increases the heat of the interior (a phenomenon well known from wells in which the temperature is higher during the winter). This heat drawn by the roots distributes itself through the entire plant. We should add that mountain plants are nearly sterile, or at least do not show the luxuriant fecundity of cultivated plants, a fecundity which contributes in large part to shortening their lives. Neither are they attacked by disease, according to Theophrastus. Where does this abundance of water which nourishes the mountain plants come from? It comes from the great quantity of vapors produced by the internal fire, which, formed in the cavities of caverns, are condensed by the cold at the moment when they issue from the earth. The same thing happens to our own bodies, which heated by exercise, allow our emanations to escape, which soon change into drops of sweat by the lightest cooling of the atmosphere; the same happens in the retorts invented by the chemists to distill liquids vaporized by the heat of fire.

For many other reasons, the viewing of mountains delights me immensely; and as the mountains of our country are very high and richer in the variety of plants than other countries, a great desire seized me to visit them, spurred by your friendship. However, in order not to address a dear friend with empty hands, I have decided to fulfill your request and compile everything I have found in the ancient authors concerning milk and the industries connected with it. The subject does not seem devoid of interest for the inhabitants of your region, of which many are milk producers and who make various food products from milk, such as, among others, the famous smooth cheese seasoned with aromatic herbs, which is in vogue among the foreigners who habitually buy it. Now I have attempted a number of things out of order, and you must pardon me, remembering that ordinarily, one reads without boredom that which offers variety.

Vale, Zurich, June 1541.

Josias Simler

from *Vallesiae et alpinum descriptio*

Josias Simler (1530–1576) was born near Zürich. He studied theology and classical languages at the University of Basle. He became world famous for compiling a short version of Conrad Gesner's Bibliotheca universalis *(1555), a list of the known Latin, Hebrew, and Greek authors throughout history. Simler wrote several works on the geography and history of the Alps and Switzerland, including* Vallesiae et alpinum descriptio *(1574),* Commentarius de Alpibus *(1574), and* De Helvetiorum Republicâ *(1576). Simler's "De itinerum Alpinorum difficultatibus et periculis, et quomodo haec superari possint" ("On the Difficulties and Dangers of Alpine Journeys, and the Manner in Which They Are Overcome"), translated below, represents the first Alpine climbing guide, outlining the equipment and techniques required for mountain travel. The work contains the first description of the use of metal crampons. Interestingly, many of the techniques and equipment used in modern alpine climbing—alpenstocks, snowshoes, crampons, glissading, roping together over crevasses—were in common use in the sixteenth century. Simler's work also describes early attempts at snow plowing the alpine passes with oxen to keep them open in the winter. In addition, Simler describes an effective remedy for frostbite: gradually heating the frozen member in successfully warmer water baths. Although he wrote extensively on the Alps, he was never able to explore them personally for any length of time, perhaps due in part to constitutional gout.*

I have just described the passes which are frequently used in the Alps; now I will describe the difficulties and dangers which await travelers who traverse them, and the manner in which they successfully conquer their difficulties. These difficulties and dangers arise either from the narrowness of the footpaths, or the precipices, or the ice, or the snow, or in the end the cold, wind, and suffering. First of all, the passages of the high mountains are almost everywhere naturally difficult and narrow; sometimes they have been cut from the rock with great labor, but still they are so narrow as to be impractical for beasts of burden and in certain spots, their width does not exceed 2 feet. Often when the path is lost, a beam is thrown across two rocks as a bridge, or else stays are fixed on the smooth rock walls. Suspended pathways can be constructed using long poles (longerines), turf, and bundles of sticks. Often, even though the rocks do not make the road narrow, the paths do not allow any passage through the deep snows where a man-made route would normally provide a safe way. The soft and deep snows

Josias Simler, *Vallesiae et alpinum descriptio* (1574; Reprint, Lugduni Batavorum: Elzeviriana, 1633). Translated by Alan Weber from the second Latin edition in the Kroch Memorial Library and the text established by W. A. B. Coolidge.

do not allow a traveler to get through. Many times in these places, the sight of the vallies extending below the feet of the travelers inspires such fear, that from dizzying terror, they allow themselves to be lead by the hand by local guides who are used to these heights. Sometimes they even ride their horses, which can successfully traverse these difficult and narrow spots. Also, and even though there is no col in the Alps which is truly impassable, the narrowness of the pathways prevents armies from crossing because of the difficulty of transporting the baggage and artillery. And as often happens in the mountains where the mountain passages are easier, long gorges are found on the route, and the locals take care that travelers come to no harm. Above all, the local people ensure that these gorges don't endanger the shepherds who lead herds of large cattle or horses along their sides; each year, actually, a great number of cows and horses are herded over the transalpine regions from Switzerland and Germany into Italy. And since there is the danger that disbanded and frightened herds might run off the cliffs and die, the travelers in the Alps and above all those who herd cattle or lead beasts of burden, fix the hours for beginning a journey before meeting at the culminating point of a col which is sometimes found on a plateau. But if it sometimes happens that two groups meet anyway, there are rules which determine which of the two groups can stay on the path, and which must yield the right of way. The difficulty of the pathways is increased by the precipices and the escarpments, especially when ice covers the passages. Thus the travelers, shepherds, and hunters who habitually haunt the high mountains have learned to return safely by various means. To assure their step on the slippery surface of the ice, they often solidly attach iron soles on their shoes, similar to horseshoes, equipped with three sharp points. Similarly, others arm themselves with pointed irons, using straps to attach spurs to the bottom of their shoes. And there are other ways that travelers prevent themselves from slipping. In certain places, they used batons with an iron point, which are customarily used to ascend and descend the yielding slopes. These batons are called alpenstocks and are most often used by shepherds. Sometimes the shepherds and hunters, finding themselves on the steep and practically perpendicular slopes, where, moreover, there is no path, cut tree branches (generally pines), sit down and slide down as if they were on a horse. But when they have heavily loaded carts that they must get down from a rough spot, they sometimes slide them down with great ropes, worked by capstans and tackle. This process was known to the Romans, as Ammianus Marcellinus bears witness, whom we have already cited above in the text in our descriptions of the Cottian Alps. Lambert of Hersfeld reports similarly, in his story of the great troubles that the emperor Henri IV suffered when he crossed the Alps in mid-winter: "the Empress and the Ladies of her entourage were placed on cow skins, and the guides dragged them along. The horses were likewise lowered by the aid of machines or else led, after having their legs hobbled. Many died on the journey, or perished later, exhausted." Steep sides are present in great numbers on the same mountain; because if from a distance the apparent continuity of the mountain makes one believe from a distance that the ridge, where the path crosses, descends once, one arrives at the summit of the col, and then one finds after that crest another slope to climb. This is a

23

disagreeable discovery for those people who are not used to these regions. These people in effect convince themselves that the mountains are not so high or steep, because, viewing them from a distance, they judge them to be less elevated then they actually are; but once at grips with reality, they realize that they are deceived in their point of view and they regret the increase in their labors. Silius observed this phenomenon and described in elegant Latin verses the state of mind of those who climbed in the Alps: "The more they have risen and made an effort to climb and traverse the mountain, the more their pain increases. Exhausted, they discover and see another escarpment peeking out, and at that point they find that they cannot have the satisfaction of measuring the dangers over which they have triumphed and from which they have escaped with so much pain, since other spectacles arise which strike them with terror. They see nothing before them, as far as they can see, but a field of white snow." Thus it is on the high seas, after the seafarer has lost sight of his beloved land and when the sails hang useless on the mast, he gazes out on the immense watery flatness and rests his eyes, which are exhausted from sounding the abyss, on the heavens. The ice in the Alps not only makes the paths dangerous because it is slippery, but it creates even greater difficulties. In certain places, huge rocks loom over the path and terrified travelers who are unused to them imagine that these rocks will rain destruction down on them; but these rocks are seldom dangerous and more often danger arises from the ice, which sometimes breaks off from the high summits and falls to the paths below them, covering and obstructing them, which is a great danger to those who are passing beneath them at the time. Strabo mentions these dangers in the following words: "blocks of ice, perilously situated on the heights, fall down, entirely covering the pathways and rushing down to the vallies below. Often, in fact, the new ice covers the old, especially when snow falls before the sun has entirely melted the icy crust which covers the soil." In addition, this old ice, upon which one is often forced to walk, is pitted with deep crevasses 3 or 4 feet wide, and often even larger, into which every fall would undoubtedly be fatal. It often happens that these crevasses are hidden under freshly fallen or blown snow. Therefore travelers who cross the Alps hire locals who know the region to guide them; these guides gird themselves with a rope to which they also attach several of those who are following them. Those who proceed first sound the way with a long baton and search the crevasses in the snow attentively, and if from carelessness a guide falls in one, the others tied to the rope catch him and draw him out. When there is no snow to hide these abysses, there is less danger, but then it is necessary to jump over them, because in the Alps there are absolutely no bridges, except sometimes rarely. Those who lead beasts of burden in this region carry beams with them with which they make culverts for their passage. The snows in the Alps, moreover, are so deep in many spots that if a man or beast gets bogged down, they perish there with certainty, and the danger is the same as if they had plunged into water. This is why Claudian says: "many a warrior remains bogged down in the high and deep snows. Often carts along with the beasts hauling them become submerged and mired in the abyss, shivering with whiteness." To warn travelers that they should be on their guard, the locals often plant long poles,

24

called "stili lignei" by Ammianus Marcellinus, which travelers must follow. But most of the time they neglect to do this, to force the travelers who don't know the route to hire their services. And in order to assure the passability of the route, the neighboring residents are compelled by the local magistrates to maintain the path, and this duty causes them great fatigue and danger. Consequently almost every day the men of the neighboring villages on each side of the slope explore the path towards the col, and if they see any danger they warn the travellers and repair the path. In many places, as soon as the first snow has fallen, the villagers draw cattle across the snow along the path who break the snow not only with their hooves but also with their legs and chest. These cattle also drag after them a long pole for flattening the path. These animals, it is believed, recognize the path better than horses and are more adept than them at flattening and re-establishing it. If this method is not sufficient for opening the path, numerous workers are hired who, armed with spades, shovels or other tools, remove the snow and re-open the route. The merchants also, when some bad weather arrives, have the route cleared by laborers, hired at great cost, in order to transport their merchandise. In addition, those who wish to traverse the deep snows where there is no trail use the following method to avoid being swallowed by the snow: they take small thin planks, or circles of wood like those which are used to join barrels together, and interlace them in every direction in the form of a trellis, with a one-foot diameter cord, and they attach them to their shoes. By this method, they enlarge the imprint of the step, and they avoid being swallowed by the snow and don't flounder around. We read a similar thing in Xenophon: the Greeks, crossing the mountains of Armenia on a road full of snow, were instructed by the inhabitants to place small sacs on the feet of the horses and beasts of burden, who without them sank down into the snow up to their stomachs with their naked feet.

The greatest danger in the Alps consists of the falling of accumulated snow, what we call Löuwinen, and among the Rhaetians "Labinae," a word derived, no doubt, from "labor" (I slide), from which also comes the German word, from the corruption of "labinae." The slightest thing shakes these snowy masses; the passage of a bird or other animal, or even a strong wind, or the cry of someone passing can shake the snow on the high part of a treeless and steeply inclined mountain; in the case of a cry, the air, agitated by the simple percussion of the voice (in other words, an echo), puts the snow into movement. The result of such motions, even very light ones, is that the snow forms first into a ball. Then after turning upon itself numerous times, this ball becomes irregularly enlarged. The uneven and massive form of the ball hinders it from rolling further, and it slides downward with a greater violence, growing larger with each step. Acquiring a considerable power, and enveloping in its fall rocks, trees, clusters of plants and animals, men, houses and everything it encounters in its path, the ball carries them all right down to the foot of the mountain. These projecting snowy masses often cover several acres, and strike the mountain with such force that

25

even the earth appears to waver, and from a distance one would believe, if nothing had been seen, to be hearing thunder. Avalanches of this kind, however, fall neither in every season, nor in every place, but only on the steep slopes from which the ground has been deforested. More often avalanches occur when the heat of spring causes the snows to melt and soften, or when in autumn and in winter great masses of new snow fall suddenly on the old snow which is icy and solid, and which the cold has hardened under clear skies. There are two types of avalanches: one made exclusively from fresh and soft snow, which gathers together and slips down; and the other which also drags old snow and carries with it a thick covering of earth. This last type is both more re-markable and does greater harm than the first kind. Several years ago, in the valley of Rheinwald in Rhaetia, near the source of the Rhine, an enormous avalanche fell from the mountain and crushed and enveloped in its fall a forest and gigantic pines. Sixty men and more of a Swiss group who were crossing the Alps were crushed under the mass. Sometimes, however, men buried in a mass of snow survive, thanks to the as-sistance of the locals, and are brought to light, or, so to speak, recalled from another world. This almost always happens when the snow mass is composed only of fresh snow, and swallows someone close to the valley which arrests his fall: because if the unfortunate victim thus buried can move his hands under the snow and manages to create a little space in front of his face, he can possibly breathe and perhaps stay alive there for two or even three days. Moreover, when masses of this kind of snow begin to fall, the mountain people ask themselves immediately if any travelers had set out that day, and calculating the elapsed time, they can guess where they were buried by the snow. In these cases, the most experienced among the rescuers digs right away and attempts to discover if anyone is buried there whom they can carry to safety and save his life. All these masses of snow, after having fallen, stop and pile up on the plains and in the vallies. And there they often bar the passage of rivers into which they fall, and if the locals don't open up a new outlet, the stopped up and accumulated wa-ters sometimes end up rupturing the new dyke, oftentimes to the peril of the inhabi-tants nearby. In the places where there is a fear of avalanches at the foot of the slopes, one finds neither house, chalet, nor cattle stable, because the inhabitants normally build and live in a place next to a slope rising between them and the avalanches, thus placing a barrier between themselves and the avalanche. In the canton of Uri, at the foot of Saint-Gothard, stretches a vast and magnificent forest of pines; one might call it a barrier of nature against avalanches, because in no other corner of the mountain can trees or forests be found. It is planted in the form of a triangle, of such a sort that, although the snows customarily strike the trees, there is no danger that the trees are thrown down, because the angle which the snow turns from the slope breaks the falling mass and prevents it from spreading out, making it always larger and thicker. Sometimes, because of the narrowness of the vallies, the paths pass under locations where there is avalanche danger because there is no other alternative. But to escape this peril, those forced to make a journey in avalanche conditions ordinarily leave in the morning, when the danger is least, and in the fastest possible way without saying a word, they cross these dangerous areas. The mountain inhabitants, who know these regions well and who can guess the imminence of the peril by observing certain signs, warn the travelers of the precautions they should take. Finally, when a great mass of snow has fallen on the path, it scarcely melts for a long time and one must pass over it, like a new little mountain or some hill which has all of a sudden arisen in the road. Silius describes these avalanches in which great amounts of snow tumble from the heights: "there where the path was intercepted by the sparkling slope of the hill which the cold had severely hardened, [Hannibal] struck the resisting ice with iron: the detached snow drew the men into a gulf, and crumbling away with rapidity, the high mountains covered the living squadrons." The author represents in perfectly worded terms Hannibal crossing the icy and steep slopes, covered with a great quantity of snow, but soft and melting, in which the soldiers who ventured forth were swallowed, as if drawn into a gulf; then he describes the snow falling from the heights and carrying away entire squadrons. Only on the elevated mountains and on steep slopes and above all when the snow softens and begins to melt, the accumulated snows fall in avalanches. Also perhaps there is an allusion in the verses of Claudian about this phenomenon, although he is speaking of ice, not snow: "Often, the ice beginning to slide, the mountain carries a sudden ruin downwards, under the warm fires of the stars, the foundations of the frozen mass precariously poised on an angled ground."

Among the other plagues of the Alps, the rigorous cold is notable, and most injurious to those who cross the mountains when the north wind begins to blow. Also, the members of the body are burnt by the penetrating cold; on some it is the ears and the nostrils, on others the hands or feet, and the feet swell and die; finally, many lose their sight if they are forced to walk along snow fields often. There are many ways to protect against these dangers, such as placing either a dark vizor in front of the eyes or what are called "lunettes." As for other parts of the body, they are preserved from the cold by means of skins and thick clothes; finally, paper or parchment perfectly protects the chest from cold winds. When the feet are swollen and the night arriving, after removing the shoes, the feet are plunged into ice water into which is poured little by little warm water, because this method, it is believed, restores sensibility. But the greatest protection against the penetrating cold is to keep walking, because it sometimes happens that during the ascent, the body is heated by exercise and the cold cannot be felt, but if one sits down in the snow to rest, drowsiness creeps in, and without the least pain while one is sleeping, one freezes and dies. About this Claudian says in his verses describing the Rhaetian Alps: "Many a warrior, as if he had looked on Medusa, is frozen by the cold." Why is movement a unique protection against fatal cold? Xenophon describes this fact in elegant terms, and I cite him here: "when I found a man frozen and sunk down, who by sluggishness, seemed ready to give himself over to his enemies, I struck him and ordered him to get up and walk around, because I felt that sitting down in a penetrating cold would only increase the sluggishness and slowness of his body. If by accident I stopped (as often happened when helping those who were charged with gathering the baggage), I felt the cold freeze my legs. Thus instructed by my own danger, as soon as I

27

saw a man giving in to his torpor and almost frozen by the cold, I roused him, knowing well that movement and manly exercise of the body warms the limbs and aids respiration. Repose and slowness in marching causes the blood, on the other hand, coagulated by the cold, to congeal and consequently the fingers and the feet freeze, which, as you know, is a frequent occurrence." Similarly our Swiss peasants, instructed not by Xenophon but by their own long experience, protect themselves against the cold.

All these dangers, finally, are augmented by various torments, because violent and deadly storms arise not only on the seas, but also in the highest mountains. The winds in the Alps are always cold and active; sometimes, however, they blow more strongly than normal and are unleashed with excessive violence. It is impossible to travel if it snows, rains, or hails; because not only are these things disagreeable, but they also prevent the voyager from seeing and using the road. The same thing happens if the wind blows the old snow into drifts. Just as in Africa the sands driven by the Simoun sometimes suffocate the caravans, so in the Alps, the snows driven by the wind cause great risks to travelers. It is not prudent, above all, to pass through a narrow and rough passageway; one must fear being thrown from a precipice by the wind. Also, when bad weather arrives suddenly, one is often forced to stop for two or three days on the summit of a col, until the weather is passed and the passes are reopened and re-established by the inhabitants in the neighboring vallies. Happily hospices abound on almost every col frequented by merchants, but they are only as good as the regions permit them to be, and to the extent that beasts of burden can resupply them with provisions. Nor was Silius ignorant of the dangers in the mountains and he describes them thus in these verses: "The terrible wind Corus, after amassing the snow into a deadly whirlwind, sometimes sprays it with his wings into the face of the traveller, or breathing in rage, seizes the arms which crush even the brave warrior, and turning them in a circle, carries them into a cloud twirling in the opposite direction." It is not without reason that here Silius calls the strongest wind "Corus," named Argestis by the Greeks. This wind is one of the coldest; it carries hail, and it seems to be the same one as the Circius (or Mistral) of Provence, of which Pliny says "there is no equal to its violence since it is able to tear off roof tops." Cato also, speaking of the inhabitants of the Spanish mountains, says thus: "When one speaks, this wind fills the mouth; it can knock over a man in arms or a chariot with its load." There is one example of the violence of this wind in Xenophon. This author writes, on the subject of Cleombrotus in book V of the *Hellenics*: "As he parted, an excessively strong wind arose; certain among them saw it as a warning, and in fact, the army suffered greatly, because as they descended Creusis by a slope looming over the sea, a great number of pack animals were thrown from the precipices. The soldiers tried to turn their weapons against the wind, but they were blown away in the same manner as the animals. Many others, incapable of carrying their weapons any further, were forced to abandon them on the summit after weighting them down with rocks."

—1574

28

Andrew Marvell

"Upon the Hill and Grove at Bill-Borow"

Restoration poet Andrew Marvell (1621–1671) addressed this hymn to the pleasant sloping hills at Bill Barrow owned by his patron-friend Lord Thomas Fairfax (d. 1671). Fairfax served with distinction as a general for the parliamentary forces during the English Civil War. Marvell himself was sympathetic to the Commonwealth and he wrote several laudatory odes to its leader Oliver Cromwell. Marvell assisted John Milton as Latin secretary to the Commonwealth and later he may have been instrumental in saving Milton's life when Charles II was restored to the English throne. In this poem, Marvell contrasts the gentle, humble landscape of Lord Fairfax's estate to the more unjust and more abrupt mountains "That do with your hook-shoulder'd height / The Earth deform and heaven fright." His best-known poem is the widely anthologized "To His Coy Mistress."

"UPON THE HILL AND GROVE AT BILL-BOROW"

To the Lord Fairfax
See how the archèd Earth does heare
Rise in a perfect hemisphere!
The stiffest compass could not strike
A line more circular and like;
Nor softest pensel draw a brow   5
So equal as this hill does bow;
It seems as for a model laid,
And that the World by it was made.
Here learn, ye mountains more unjust,
Which to abrupter greatness thrust;   10
That do, with your hook-shoulder'd height,
The Earth deform, and heaven fright;
For whose excrescence, ill design'd,
Nature must a new center find;
Learn here those humble steps to tread,   15
Which to securer glory lead.
See what a soft access, and wide,

Andrew Marvell, *Complete Poems of Andrew Marvell*, The Fuller Worthies' Library (printed for private circulation, 1872).

Lyes open to its grassy side;
Nor with the rugged path deterrs
The feet of breathless travellers;   20
See then how courteous it ascends,
And all the way it rises, bends;
Nor for it self the height does gain,
But only strives to raise the plain;
Yet thus it all the field commands,   25
And in unenvy'd greatness stands,
Discerning further than the cliff
Of heaven-daring Teneriff.
How glad the weary seamen haste,
When they salute it from the mast!   30
By night, the northern star their way
Directs, and this no less by day.
Upon its crest, this mountain grave,
A plume of agèd trees does wave;
No hostile hand durst ere invade,   35
With impious steel, the sacred shade;
For something alwaies did appear
Of the GREAT MASTER'S terrour there,
And men could hear his armour still,
Rattling through all the Grove and Hill.   40
Fear of the MASTER, and respect
Of the great Nymph, did it protect;
VERA, the nymph, that him inspir'd,
To whom he often here retir'd,
And on these okes engrav'd her name;—   45
Such wounds alone these woods became:
But ere he well the barks could part,
'Twas writ already in their heart;
For they ('tis credible) have sense,
As we, of love and reverence,   50
And underneath the coarser rind
The Genius of the house do bind.
Hence they successes seem to know,
And in their lord's advancement grow;
But in no memory were seen,   55
As under this, so straight and green;
Yet now no further strive to shoot,
Contented, if they fix their root;
Nor to the winds' uncertain gust

Their prudent heads too far intrust;   60
Onely sometimes a flutt'ring breez
Discourses with the breathing trees;
Which in their modest whispers name
Those acts that swell'd the cheeks of Fame.
'Much other groves,' say they, 'than these,   65
And other hills, him once did please;
Through groves of pikes he thunder'd then,
And mountains rais'd of dying men;
For all the civic garlands due
To him, our branches are but few;   70
Nor are our trunks enough to bear
The trophees of one fertile year.'
'Tis true, ye trees, nor ever spoke
More certain oracles in oak;
But peace, if you his favour prize!   75
That courage its own praises flies:
Therefore to your obscurer seats,
From his own brightness he retreats;
Nor he the hills, without the groves,
Nor height, but with retirement, loves.   80

—1681

Thomas Burnet

from *Telluris sacra theoria* (On the Sacred Theory of the Earth)

Thomas Burnet (1635–1715) was born in Croft, Durham, England, of Scottish ancestry. He was educated at Cambridge University. Burnet's influential Latin work on geology, Telluris sacra theoria *was so popular that King James II requested an English translation of it in 1684. Burnet attempted to reconcile divine scripture with his scientific theory of the creation of mountains. Burnet, following ancient sources, proposed that the earth at the time of the Garden of Eden was smooth and symmetrical—a "mundane egg"—but as a result of the sin of Adam and the Fall of Man, the present disordered and mountainous state of the earth's crust had resulted. A believer in proportion, harmony, and symmetry, Burnet frequently describes mountains in negative and unflattering terms—the words "ruine," "broken heaps," "confusion," and "rubbish" appear throughout his work, since mountains reflected for him an imperfect, sin-defiled world.*

CHAPTER XI

Concerning the Mountains of the Earth, their greatness and irregular Form, their Situation, Causes, and Origin.

We have been in the hollows of the Earth, and the chambers of the Deep, amongst the damps and steams of those lower Regions; let us now go air our selves on the tops of the Mountains, where we shall have a more free and large Horizon, and quite another face of things will present it self to our observation.

The greatest objects of Nature are, methinks, the most pleasing to behold; and next to the great Concave of the Heavens, and those boundless Regions where the Stars inhabit, there is nothing that I look upon with more pleasure than the wide Sea and the Mountains of the Earth. There is something august and stately in the Air of these things that inspires the mind with great thoughts and passions; We do naturally upon such occasions think of God and his greatness, and whatsoever hath but the shadow and appearance of INFINITE, as all things have that are too big for our comprehension, they fill and over-bear the mind with their Excess, and cast it into a pleasing kind of stupor and admiration.

And yet these Mountains we are speaking of, to confess the truth, are nothing but great ruines; but such as show a certain magnificence in Nature; as from old Temples and broken Amphitheaters of the *Romans* we collect the greatness of that people. But the grandeur of a Nation is less sensible to those that never see the remains and monuments

Thomas Burnet, *Telluris sacra theoria (On the Sacred Theory of the Earth)* (London: R. Norton for Walter Kettilby, 1684).

they have left, and those who never see the mountainous parts of the Earth, scarce ever reflect upon the causes of them, or what power in Nature could be sufficient to produce them. The truth is, the generality of people have not sense and curiosity enough to raise a question concerning these things, or concerning the Original of them. You may tell them that Mountains grow out of the Earth like Fuzz-balls, or that there are Monsters under ground that throw up Mountains as Moles do Mole-hills; they will scarce raise one objection against your doctrine; or if you would appear more Learned, tell them that the Earth is a great Animal, and these are Wens that grow upon its body. This would pass current for Philosophy; so much is the World drown'd in stupidity and sensual pleasures, and so little inquisitive into the works of God and Nature.

There is nothing doth more awaken our thoughts or excite our minds to enquire into the causes of such things, than the actual view of them; as I have had experience my self when it was my fortune to cross the *Alps* and *Appennine* Mountains, for the sight of those wild, vast and indigested heaps of Stones and Earth, did so deeply strike my fancy, that I was not easie till I could give my self some tolerable account how that confusion came in Nature. 'Tis true, the height of Mountains compar'd with the Diameter of the Earth is not considerable, but the extent of them and the ground they stand upon, bears a considerable proportion to the surface of the Earth; and if from *Europe* we may take our measures for the rest, I easily believe, that the Mountains do at least take up the tenth part of the dry land. The Geographers are not very careful to describe or note in their Charts, the multitude or situation of Mountains; They mark the bounds of Countries, the site of Cities and Towns, and the course of Rivers, because these are things of chief use to civil affairs and commerce, and that they design to serve, and not Philosophy or Natural History. But *Cluverius* in his description of *Ancient Germany, Switzerland* and *Italy*, hath given Maps of those Countries more approaching to the natural face of them, and we have drawn (at the end of this Chapter) such a Map of either Hemisphere, without marking Countries or Towns, or any such artificial things; distinguishing only Land and Sea, Islands and Continents, Mountains and not Mountains; and 'tis very useful to imagine the Earth in this manner, and to look often upon such bare draughts as shew us Nature in an undress; for then we are best able to judge what her true shapes and proportions are.

'Tis certain that we naturally imagine the surface of the Earth much more regular than it is; for unless we be in some Mountainous parts there seldom occur any great inequalities within so much compass of ground as we can at once reach with our Eye; and to conceive the rest we multiply the same *Idea,* and extend it to those parts of the Earth that we do not see; and so fancy the whole Globe much more smooth and uniform than it is. But suppose a man was carri'd asleep out of a Plain Country, amongst the *Alps,* and left there upon the top of one of the highest Mountains, when he wak'd and look'd about him; he would think himself in an enchanted Country, or carri'd into another World; Every thing would appear to him so different to what he had ever seen or imagin'd before. To see on every hand of him a multitude of vast bodies thrown together in confusion, as those Mountains are; Rocks standing naked round

33

about him; and the hollow Valleys gaping under him; and at his feet, it may be, an heap of frozen Snow in the midst of Summer. He would hear the thunder come from below, and see the black Clouds hanging beneath him: It would not be easie to him to perswade himself that he was still upon the same Earth; but if he did, he would be convinc'd at least that there are some Regions of it strangely rude, and ruine-like, and very different from what he had ever thought of before. But the inhabitants of these wild places are even with us; for those that live amongst the *Alps* and the great Mountains, think that all the rest of the Earth is like their Country, all broken into Mountains and Valleys and Precipices; They never see other, and most people think of nothing but what they have seen at one time or another.

These *Alps* we are speaking of are the greatest range of Mountains in *Europe*; and 'tis prodigious to see and to consider of what extent these heaps of Stones and Rubbish are; one way they overspread *Savoy* and *Dauphiné*, and reach through *France* to the *Pyrenean* Mountains, and so to the Ocean. The other way they run along the skirts of *Germany*, through *Stiria*, *Pannonia*, and *Dalmatia*, as far as *Thrace* and the Black Sea. Then backwards they cover *Switzerland* and the parts adjacent; and that branch of them which we call the *Appennines*, strikes through *Italy*, and is, as it were, the backbone of that Country. This must needs be a large space of ground which they stand upon; Yet 'tis not this part of *Europe* only that is laden with Mountains, the Northern part is as rough and rude in the face of the Country as in the manners of the people; *Bohemia*, *Silesia*, *Denmark*, *Norway*, *Sweedland*, *Lapland*, and *Iseland*, and all the coasts of the *Baltick Sea*, are full of Clifts, and Rocks, and Crags of Mountains: Besides the *Riphean* Mountains in Muscovy, which the Inhabitants there use to call the *Stone-girdle*, and believe that it girds the Earth round about.

Nor are the other parts of our Continent more free from Mountains than *Europe*, nor other parts of the Earth than our Continent: They are in the New World as well as the Old; and if they could discover two or three New worlds or Continents more, they would still find them there. Neither is there any Original Island upon the Earth, but is either all a Rock, or hath Rocks and Mountains in it. And all the dry Land, and every Continent, is but a kind of Mountain, though that Mountain hath a multitude of lesser, and Valleys, and Plains, and Lakes, and Marshes, and all variety of grounds.

In *America* the *Andes*, or a ridge of Mountains so call'd, are reported to be higher than any we have, reaching above a thousand Leagues in length, and twenty in breadth, where they are the narrowest. In *Africk* the Mountain *Atlas*, that for its height was said to bear the heavens on its back, runs all along from the Western Sea to the borders of *Ægypt*, parallel with the *Mediterranean*. There also are the Mountains of the *Moon*, and many more whereof we have but an imperfect account, as neither indeed of that Country in the remote and inner parts of it. *Asia* is better known, and the Mountains thereof better describ'd: *Taurus*, which is the principal, was adjug'd by the ancient Geographers the greatest in the World. It divides *Asia* into two parts, which have their denomination from it: And there is an *Anti-Taurus* the greater and the less, which accordingly divide *Armenia* into greater and less. Then the *Cruciform* Mountains of *Imaus*, the famous *Caucasus*, the long Chains of *Tartary* and *China*, and the Rocky and Mountainous *Arabia*. If one could at once have a prospect of all these together, one would be easily satisfied, that the Globe of the Earth is a more rude and indigested Body than 'tis commonly imagin'd; If one could see all the Kingdoms of the Earth at one view, how they lie in broken heaps; The Sea hath overwhelm'd one half of them, and what remains are but the taller parts of a ruine. Look upon those great ranges of Mountains in *Europe* or in *Asia*, whereof we have given a short survey, in what confusion do they lie? They have neither form nor beauty, nor shape nor order, no more than the Clouds in the Air. Then how barren, how desolate, how naked are they? how they stand neglected by Nature? neither the Rains can soften them, nor the Dews from heaven make them fruitful.

I have given this short account of the Mountains of the Earth to help to remove that prejudice we are apt to have, or that conceit that the present Earth *is regularly form'd*. And to this purpose I do not doubt but that it would be of very good use to have *natural* Maps of the Earth, as we noted before, as well as *civil*; and done with the same care and judgment. Our common Maps I call *Civil*; which note the distinction of Countries and of Cities, and represent the Artificial Earth as inhabited and cultivated: But natural Maps leave out all that, and represent the Earth as it would be if there was not an Inhabitant upon it, nor ever had been; the Skeleton of the Earth, as I may so say, with the site of all its parts. Methinks also every Prince should have such a Draught of his Country and Dominions, to see how the ground lies in the several parts of them, which highest, which lowest; what respect they have to one another, and to the Sea; how the Rivers flow, and why; how the Mountains lie, how Heaths, and how the Marches. Such a Map or Survey would be useful both in time of War and Peace, and many good observations might be made by it, not only as to Natural History and Philosophy, but also in order to the perfect improvement of a Country. But to return to our Mountains.

As this Survey of the multitude and greatness of them may help to rectifie our mistakes about the form of the Earth, so before we proceed to examine their causes, it will be good to observe farther, that these Mountains are plac'd in no order one with another, that can either respect use or beauty; And if you consider them singly, they do not consist of any proportion of parts that is referable to any design, or that hath the least footsteps of Art or Counsel. There is nothing in Nature more shapeless and ill-figur'd than an old Rock or a Mountain, and all that variety that is among them is but the various modes of irregularity; so as you cannot make a better character of them in short, than to say they are of all forms and figures except regular. Then if you could go within these Mountains, for they are generally hollow, you would find all things there more rude, if possible, than without: And lastly, if you look upon an heap of them together, or a Mountainous Country, they are the greatest examples of confusion that we know in Nature; no Tempest or Earthquake puts things into more disorder. 'Tis true, they cannot look so ill now as they did at first; a ruine that is fresh looks much worse than afterwards, when the Earth grows discolour'd and

35

skin'd over. But I fancy if we had seen the Mountains when they were new-born and raw, when the Earth was fresh broken, and the waters of the Deluge newly retir'd, the fractions and confusions of them would have appear'd very gastly and frightful.

After this general Survey of the Mountains of the Earth and their properties, let us now reflect upon the causes of them. There is a double pleasure in Philosophy, first that of Admiration, whilst we contemplate things that are great and wonderful, and do not yet understand their Causes; for though admiration proceed from ignorance, yet there is a certain charm and sweetness in that passion. Then the second pleasure is greater and more intellectual, which is that of distinct knowledge and comprehension, when we come to have the Key that unlocks those secrets, and see the methods wherein those things come to pass that we admir'd before; The reasons why the World is so or so, and from what causes Nature or any part of Nature came into such a state; and this we are now to enquire after as to the mountains of the Earth, what their original was, how and when the Earth came into this strange frame and structure? In the beginning of our World, when the Earth rise from a Chaos, 'twas impossible it should come immediately into this mountainous form; because a mass that is fluid, as a Chaos is, cannot lie in any other figure than what is regular; for the constant laws of Nature do certainly bring all Liquors into that form: And a Chaos is not call'd so from any confusion or brokenness in the form of it, but from a confusion and mixture of all sorts of ingredients in the composition of it. So we have already produc'd, in the precedent Chapters, a double argument that the Earth was not originally in this form, both because it rise from a Chaos, which could not of it self, or by any immediate concretion settle into a form of this nature, as hath been shown in the Fourth and Fifth Chapters; as also because if it had been originally made thus, it could never have undergone a Deluge, as hath been prov'd in the Second and Third Chapters. If this be than a secondary and succedaneous form, the great question is from what causes it arises.

Some have thought that Mountains and all other irregularities in the Earth have rise from Earthquakes, and such like causes; others have thought that they came from the universal Deluge; yet not from any dissolution of the Earth that was then, but only from the great agitation of the waters, which broke the ground into this rude and unequal form. Both these causes seem to me very incompetent and insufficient. Earthquakes seldom make Mountains, they often take them away, and sink them down into the Caverns that lie under them; Besides, Earthquakes are not in all Countries and Climates as Mountains are; for, as we have observ'd more than one, there is neither Island that is original, nor Continent any where in the Earth, in what latitude soever, but hath Mountains and Rocks in it. And lastly, what probability is there, or how is it credible that those vast tracts of Land which we see fill'd with Mountains both in *Europe, Asia* and *Africa*, were rais'd by Earthquakes, or any eruptions from below. In what Age of the world was this done, and why not continued? As for the Deluge, I doubt not but Mountains were made in the time of the general Deluge, that great change and transformation of the Earth happen'd then, but not from such causes as are pretended, that is, the bare rowling and agitation of the waters; For if the Earth was smooth and plain before the Flood, as they seem to suppose as well as we do, the waters could have little or no power over a smooth surface to tear it any way in pieces, no more than they do a meadow or low ground when they lie upon it; for that which makes Torrents and Land-floods violent, is their fall from the Mountains and high Lands, which our Earth is now full of, but if the Rain fell upon even and level ground, it would only sadden and compress it; there is no possibility how it should raise Mountains in it. And if we could imagine an universal Deluge as the Earth is now constituted, it would rather throw down the Hills and Mountains than raise new ones; or by beating down their tops and loose parts, help to fill the Valleys, and bring the Earth nearer to evenness and plainness.

Seeing then there are no hopes of explaining the Origin of Mountains, either from particular Earthquakes, or from the general Deluge, according to the common notion and Explication of it; these not being causes answerable to such vast effects; Let us try our *Hypothesis* again; which hath made us a Channel large enough for the Sea, and room for all subterraneous Cavities, and I think will find us materials enough to raise all the Mountains of the Earth. We suppose the great Arch or circumference of the first Earth to have fallen into the Abyss at the Deluge, and seeing that was larger than the surface it fell upon, 'tis absolutely certain, that it could not all fall flat, or lie under the water: Now as all those parts that stood above the water made dry Land, or the present habitable Earth, so such parts of the dry Land as stood higher than the rest made Hills and Mountains; And this is the first and general account of them, and of all the inequalities of the Earth. But to consider these things a little more particularly; There is a double cause and necessity of Mountains, first this now mention'd, because the exteriour Orb of the Earth was greater than the interiour which it fell upon, and therefore it could not all fall flat; and secondly, because this exteriour Orb did not fall so flat and large as it might, or did not cover all the bottom of the Abyss, as it was very capable to do; but as we shewed before in explaining the Chanel of the Ocean, it left a gaping in the middle, or an *Abyss-chanel*, as I should call it; and the broader this Abyss-chanel was, the more Mountains there would be upon the dry Land; for there would be more Earth, or more of the falling Orb left, and less room to place it in, and therefore it must stand more in heaps.

In what parts of the Earth these heaps would lie, and in what particular manner, it cannot be expected that we should tell; but all that we have hitherto observ'd concerning Mountains, how strange soever and otherwise unaccountable, may easily be explain'd, and deduc'd from this original; we shall not wonder at their greatness and vastness, seeing they are the ruines of a broken World; and they would take up more or less of the dry Land, according as the Ocean took up more or less space of our Globe: Then as to their figure and form, whether External or Internal, 'tis just such as answers our expectation, and no more than what the *Hypothesis* leads us to; For you would easily believe that these heaps would be irregular in all manner of ways, whether consider'd apart, or in their situation to one another. And they would lie

37

commonly in Clusters and in Ridges, for those are two of the most general postures of the parts of a ruine, when they fall inwards. Lastly, we cannot wonder that Mountain should be generally hollow; For great bodies falling together in confusion, or bearing and leaning against one another must needs make a great many hollownesses in them, and by their unequal Applications empty spaces will be intercepted. We see also from the same reason, why mountainous Countries are subject to Earthquakes; and why Mountains often sink and fall down into the Caverns that lie under them; their joynts and props being decay'd and worn, they become unable to bear their weight. And all these properties you see hang upon one and the same string, and are just consequences from our supposition concerning the dissolution of the first Earth. And there is no surer mark of a good *Hypothesis*, than when it doth not only hit luckily in one or two particulars, but answers all that it is to be appli'd to, and is adequate to Nature in her whole extent.

But how fully or easily soever these things may answer Nature, you will say, it may be, that all this is but an *Hypothesis*; that is, a kind of fiction or supposition that things were so and so at first, and by the coherence and agreement of the Effects with such a supposition, you would argue and prove that they were really so. This I confess is true, this is the method, and if we would know any thing in Nature further than our senses go, we can know it no otherwise than by an *Hypothesis*. When things are either too little for our senses, or too remote and inaccessible, we have no way to know the inward Nature, and the causes of their sensible properties, but by reasoning upon an *Hypothesis*. If you would know, for example, of what parts Water, or any other Liquor consists, they are too little to be discern'd by the Eye, you must therefore take a supposition concerning their invisible figure and form, and if that agrees and gives the reason of all their sensible qualities, you understand the nature of Water. In like manner, if you would know the nature of a Comet, or of what matter the Sun consists, which are things inaccessible to us, you can do this no otherwise than by an *Hypothesis*; and if that *Hypothesis* be easie and intelligible, and answers all the *Phœnomena* of those two bodies, you have done as much as a *Philosopher* or as *Humane reason* can do. And this is what we have attempted concerning the Earth and concerning the Deluge; We have laid down an *Hypothesis* that is easie and perspicuous, consisting of a few things, and those very intelligible, and from this we have given an account how the Old World was destroy'd by a Deluge of water, and how the Earth came into this present form; so distinguish'd and interrupted with Sea and Land, Mountains and Valleys, and so broken in the surface and inward parts of it.

But to speak the Truth, this Theory is something more than a bare *Hypothesis*; because we are assur'd that the general ground that we go upon is true, namely, that the Earth rise at first from a Chaos; for besides Reason and Antiquity, Scripture it self doth assure us of that; and that one point being granted, we have deduc'd from it all the rest by a direct chain of consequences, which I think cannot be broken easily in any part or link of it. Besides, the great hinge of this Theory upon which all the rest turns, is the distinction we make of the Ante-diluvian Earth and Heavens from the

Post-diluvian, as to their form and constitution. And it will never be beaten out of my head, but that S. *Peter* hath made the same distinction sixteen hundred years since, and to the very same purpose; so that we have sure footing here again, and the Theory riseth above the character of a bare *Hypothesis*. And whereas an *Hypothesis* that is clear and proportion'd to Nature in every respect, is accounted morally certain, we must in equity give more than a moral certitude to the Theory. But I mean this only as to the general parts of it; for as to particularities, I look upon them only as problematical, and accordingly I affirm nothing therein but with a power or revocation, and a liberty to change my opinion when I shall be better inform'd. Neither do I know any Author that hath treated a matter new, remote, and consisting of a multitude of particulars, who would not have had occasion, if he had liv'd to have seen his *Hypothesis* fully examin'd, to have chang'd his mind and manner of explaining things, in many material instances.

To conclude both this Chapter and this Section, we have here added a Map or Draught of the Earth, according to the Natural face of it, as it would appear from the Moon, if we were a little nearer to her; or as it was at first after the Deluge, before Cities were built, distinctions of Countries made, or any alterations by humane industry. 'Tis chiefly to expose more to view the Mountains of the Earth, and the proportions of Sea and Land, to shew it as it lies in it self, and as a Naturalist ought to conceive and consider it. 'Tis true, there are far more Mountains upon the Earth than what are here represented, for more could not conveniently be plac'd in this narrow Scheme; But the best and most effectual way of representing the body of the Earth as it is by Nature, would be, not in plain Tables, but by a *rough Globe*, expressing all the considerable inequalities that are upon the Earth. The smooth Globes that we use, do but nourish in us the conceit of the Earths regularity, and though they may be convenient enough for Geographical purposes, they are not so proper for Natural Science; nothing would be more useful in this respect than a rough Globe of the largest dimensions, wherein the Chanel of the Sea should be really hollow, as it is in Nature, with all its unequal depths according to the best soundings, and the shores exprest both according to matter and form, little Rocks standing where there are Rocks, and Sands and Beaches in the places where they are found; And all the Islands planted in the Sea-chanel in a due form, and in their solid dimensions. Then upon the Land should stand all the ranges of Mountains, in the same order or disorder that Nature hath set them there: And the in-land Seas, and great Lakes, or rather the beds they lie in, should be duly represented; as also the vast desarts of Sand as they lie upon the Earth. And this being done with care and due Art, would be a true Epitome or true model of our Earth. Where we should see, besides other instructions, what a rude Lump our World is which we are so apt to dote upon.

—1684

39

J. J. Scheuchzer

from *The Swiss Mountain Roamer*

J. J. Scheuchzer (1672–1733) was a Zürich physician who personally explored the Alps and compiled a history of mountain stories and anecdotes, which "he had upon good account." His collection The Swiss Mountain Roamer *includes a number of eyewitness accounts of dragon sightings along with his famous engravings of the fearsome Dragons of the Alps. These fantastic pictures were frequently reprinted in subsequent books on the Alps. These mountains were at the time the source of great superstition, fear, and apprehension among the local inhabitants. Isolated and under the effects of altitude, and fully expecting frightful beasts, gnomes, and trolls, the imaginations of mountain travelers undoubtedly turned bats, snakes, and large birds into terrifying, mythical beasts. Scheuchzer believed firmly in the existence of dragons in the Alps, and collected eyewitness accounts of these animals. The dragons described by reputable witnesses, often under oath, came in a wide variety of shapes and sizes: the only common feature seems to be that they breathed fire.*

On Mount Frumsanus, in the Barony of Altensaxus, two varieties of dragons or large serpents are met with—the one with feet, and the other without feet. They are thus described by Wagner, in his *Natural History of Helvetia*, pp. 247 and 251: "John Tinner, of the Commune of Frumsen, in the Barony of Altensaxus, an honorable man, whose word can be trusted, and who, at the present time, is still living, solemnly deposed to me that, twelve years since, at the end of month of April, he repaired to the neighboring mountain, the Frumsenberg, and that there, in the place commonly known as the Hanwelen, encountered a terrible serpent, black and grey in color, which first coiled itself up and then raised itself upright. Its length, he said, was at least seven feet; its girth was about that of an apple tree; it had a head like the head of a cat, but no feet whatsoever. He said that he struck and slew it with the assistance of his brother Thomas. He added that before the serpent was killed, the inhabitants of the vicinity complained that the milk was drawn from the udders of their cows, and that they could never discover the author of the mischief, but that, after the serpent was killed the mischief ceased."

———

J. J. Scheuchzer, *The Swiss Mountain Roamer* (Lugduni Batavorum: Peter Vander, 1723). Selection based on the text of Francis Gribble, *The Early Mountaineers* (London: T. Fisher Unwin, 1899).

. . . John Bueler, of the Parish of Sennwald, member of the Ecclesiastical Assembly, went to the Frumsenberg, in the summer season, eleven years ago, and in a place called Erlawäld, beside the stream called the Kalenbach, saw an enormous black beast, emerging, in a state of the greatest amazement, from a thicket, and standing upon its four legs, which were of no excessive length. Its girth was about the thickness of an apple tree, and it carried a crest, half a foot long, on its head. Its entire length, however, he could not observe, because its hinder parts lay hidden in the thicket among the briars.

Christopher Schorer wrote:

. . . In the year 1649, I was contemplating the beauty of the heavens by night, when lo! and behold, I saw a bright and shining dragon issue from a large cave in the mountain commonly called Pilatus, and fly about, swiftly flapping its wings. It was very large with a long tail. Its neck extended and its head terminated in the serrated jaw of a serpent. While it was flying, it threw out sparks, just as the red hot horseshoe does when hammered by the blacksmith. My first impression was that I saw a meteor, but after careful observation, I recognized that it was a dragon, from the nature of its movements and the structure of its various limbs.

—1723

Albrecht von Haller

"Die Alpen"

Albrecht Haller (1708–1777) was born in Bern, Switzerland, and trained as a physician at Leiden. Haller's series of poems on his beloved Alps (1732) were immensely popular in Europe. Haller is better known, however, as a natural philosopher and medical scientist who published substantial contributions on Swiss flora and the theory of physiological irritability, though he still enjoys a considerable reputation as a poet. His Historia stirpium indigenarium helvetiae inchoata *(1768) or* An Unfinished History of the Indigenous Plants of Switzerland *was a notable eighteenth-century work on Swiss flora. Haller's medical research laid the foundations of modern neurology and the understanding of muscle contraction. The poems translated below reveal his Rousseau-inspired championing of native primitivism against the corruptions of urban life, a cherished theme since the Odes of the Roman poet Horace. Although there are many similarities between Jean-Jacques Rousseau's and Haller's philosophy in their mutual love of nature, mountains, and the simple outdoor life, Haller was not a supporter or follower of Rousseau.*

"DIE ALPEN"

Sobald der rauhe Nord der Lüfte Reich verlieret
Und ein belebter Saft in alle Wesen dringt,
Wann sich der Erde Schoss mit neuem Schmucke zieret,
Den ihr ein holder West auf lauen Flügeln bringt,
Sobald flieht auch das Volk aus den verhassten Gründen,
Woraus noch kaum der Schnee mit trüben Strömen fliesst,
Und eilt den Alpen zu, das erste Gras zu finden,
Wo kaum noch durch das Eis der Kräuter Spitze spriesst;
Das Vieh verlässt den Stall und grüsst den Berg mit Freuden,
Den Frühling und Natur zu seinem Nutzen kleiden.

[Translation:]

As soon as the raw north wind loses its power
And a life-giving sap flows throughout all beings
When the lap of the earth is adorned with new jewels
And a dear West wind floats on soothing wings

Albrecht von Haller, "Die Alpen" in *Versuch Schweizerischer Gedichte* (Berne, 1732). Translated by Alan Weber from *Albrecht von Hallers Gedichte*, ed. Ludwig Hirzel (Frauenfeld: J. Huber, 1882).

Then the people flee their hated dwellings
Where the snow still melts in muddy streams
And rush to the Alps to find the first grass,
Although the plants have scarcely sprouted through the ice.
The cattle leave their barns, and greet the mountain with joy
Which Spring and Nature have clothed for their use.

Ein angenehm Gemisch von Bergen, Fels und Seen
Fällt nach und nach erbleicht, doch deutlich, ins Gesicht,
Die blaue Ferne schliesst ein Kranz beglänzter Höhen,
Worauf ein schwarzer Wald die letzten Strahlen bricht;
Bald zeigt ein nah Gebürg die sanft erhobnen Hügel,
Wovon ein laut Geblök im Tale widerhallt;
Bald scheint ein breiter See ein Meilen-langer Spiegel,
Auf dessen glatter Flut ein zitternd Feuer wallt;
Bald aber öffnet sich ein Strich von grünen Tälern,
Die, hin und her gekrümmt, sich im Entfernen schmälern.

[Translation:]

A pleasant variety of mountains, rocks and lakes
Comes palely, yet clearly, little by little into sight
The blue distance encloses a wreath of gleaming peaks
On which the last rays break upon a dark forest;
Now a nearby mount displays its gently elevated slopes
Where a loud bleating echoes in the valley
Now a bright lake shines like a mile-long mirror;
Upon its smooth surface a quaking fire undulates
Now a length of green valleys opens up
Which bend here and there, and disappear into the distance.

—1732

William Windham

from *An Account of the Glaciers or Ice Alps in Savoy, in Two Letters*

The English gentleman William Windham (1768–1833) toured Geneva and Chamonix in 1741 with his traveling companion Richard Pococke. Their desire to explore the local glaciers and mountains was viewed by the local inhabitants as another instance of English eccentricity. Departing from Chamonix with local guides, they explored Montenvers and the Mer de Glace ("Sea of Ice"). Thus, Windham and Pococke were the originators of the English "guided climbing" in the Alps, which in the nineteenth century would develop into an institutionalized sport with clubs, regulations, journals, and guidebooks. Windham published an account of his mountain travels in 1744 in the form of a letter to Peter Martel, along with Martel's reply.

[I]

A LETTER *from an* English *Gentleman to Mr.* Arlaud, *a celebrated Painter at* Geneva, *giving an Account of a Journey to the* Glacieres, *or* Ice Alps *in Savoy, written in the Year 1741. Translated from the* French.

Sir,
According to your Desire I send you an Account of our Journey to the *Glacieres*. I shall give it you in the plainest Manner, although the Beauty and Variety of the Situations and Prospects that we observed in this unfrequented Part of the World, would well deserve to be described by one, who, like you, join to so great a Skill in Painting so lively and poetical an Imagination; but these not being my Talents, I will, as I said before, confine myself to the giving you a faithful Relation of the Incidents of our Journey, and acquainting you with the Observations we made. I shall add a few Hints, which may be useful to such as shall hereafter have the same Curiosity that we had, and who may perhaps have Advantages and Conveniences which we had not to make more accurate Observations. It is really Pity that so great a Curiosity, and which lies so near you, should be so little known; for through *Scheuchzer*, in his *Iter Alpinum*, describes the *Glacieres* that are in the Canton of *Berne*, yet they seem to me by his description to be very different from those in *Savoy*.

William Windham, *An Account of the Glaciers or Ice Alps in Savoy, in Two Letters* (London: Peter Martel, 1744).

I had long had a great Desire to make this Excursion, but the Difficulty of getting Company had made me defer it: Luckily in the Month of *June* last Dr. *Pococke*[1] arrived at *Geneva* from his Voyages into the *Levant* and *Egypt*, which Countries he had visited with great Exactness. I mentioned to him this Curiosity, and my Desire to see it, and he who was far from fearing Hardships, expressing a like Inclination, we immediately agreed to go there; when some others of our Friends found a Party was made, they likewise came into it, and I was commissioned to provide what was necessary for our setting out.

As we were assured on all hands, that we should fearcely find any of the Necessaries of Life in those Parts, we took with us Sumpter Horses, loaded with Provisions, and a Tent, which was of some use to us, though the terrible Description People had given us of the Country was much exaggerated. I had provided several Mathematical Instruments to take Heights, and make Observations with, hoping that Mr. *Williamson*, an able Mathematician, Governor to Lord *Hadinton*, would have been of the Party; but he declining it, on account of the Fatigue which he fear'd he should not be able to support, I chose not to take the Trouble of carrying them, there being no Person in the Company so capable as he of making a proper use of them.

We set out from *Geneva* the 19th of *June*, N. S. we were Eight in company,[2] besides five Servants, all of us well arm'd, and our Baggage-Horses attending us, so that we had very much the Air of a Caravan. The first Day we went no farther than *Bonneville*, a Town about four Leagues distant from *Geneva*, according to the way of reckoning there; these four Leagues took us more than six Hours riding. This Place is situated at the Foot of the *Maule*, and close by the River *Arve*; 'tis surrounded with beautiful Meadows and high Mountains, covered with Trees, which form all together a very delightful Situation. There is a very good Stone-Bridge near the Town, but it had suffered in the late Innundation of the *Arve*, which had carried away part of it. Our Inn was a tolerable one for *Savoy* as to every thing but Beds.

The next Day being the 20th, we set out very early in the Morning, and passed the *Arve*; our Road lay between that River and the Mountains, all along which we were entertained with an agreeable Variety of fine Landskips. They reckon two Leagues from *Bonneville* to *Cluse*, but we were three Hours and an half in going it.

Cluse is situated in a narrow Pass between the Mountains, which almost meet in this Place [leaving only room for the *Arve*, which is thus hemm'd in for above a League together.] Before you come to *Cluse* there is a kind of Hermitage, upon a Rock on the Right Hand, where we climb'd up in order to enjoy the Prospect, which is *delicious*; after that we passed the *Arve* over a fine Stone Bridge, of one very large Arch, and continued our Journey for about an Hour and an half through a narrow Road, along the *Arve*, between Rocks of a prodigious Height, which look'd as if they had been split on purpose to give the River a Passage. Not to mention the Beauty of the Views all along, we were extremely entertained by continual Echoes, and the prodigious rattling, caused by cracking a Whip, or firing a Pistol, which we repeated several Times. We saw Cascades on every Side, which fell from the Top of high Rocks

45

into the *Arve*. There is one among the rest of singular Beauty, it is called the *Nan d' Arpena*, 'tis a great Torrent, which falls from a very high Rock; all the Company agreed it must be higher than *Saleve*.[3] As for my Part, I will not pretend to decide about it, I however may venture to say, that the Cascade of *Terni* does not fall from near so great a Height; but then the Quantity of Water, when we saw it, was much less than at this last mentioned Place; tho' the People of the Country assured us, that at certain times the Water is much more abundant than it was then.

After about three Hours riding from *Cluse*, we came to Saint *Martin*'s Bridge, right against *Salanches*, which is on the other Side of the *Arve*. We did not care to go out of our Way into the Town; but chose rather to encamp in a fine Meadow near the Bridge, in order to refresh ourselves. From thence we set out again on our Journey, and after four Hours riding through very bad Ways, being obliged to cross some dangerous Torrents, we arrived at a little Village called *Servoz*. Our Horses suffered here very much, being tied to Pickets all Night in the open Air for want of Stabling; besides, there was neither Oats, nor any other Forrage, but Grass fresh cut; as for ourselves, as we had brought all Necessaries along with us, we were well enough off, except as to Beds, and that want was supplied by clean Straw in a Barn.

From thence we set forward at break of Day, and passed the *Arve* once more over a very bad wooden Bridge, and after having clim'd over a steep Mountain, where we had no small Difficulty with our Horses, their Shoes coming off continually, and they often running the risque of tumbling into the *Arve*, which run at the Bottom of the rock, we came into a pleasant Valley, where we pass'd the *Arve* a fourth time over a Stone Bridge, and then first had a View of the *Glacieres*. We continued our Journey on to *Chamouny*, which is a Village upon the North-side of the *Arve*, in a Valley, where there is a Priory belonging to the Chapter of *Salanches*; here we encamp'd, and while our Dinner was preparing, we inquired of the People of the Place about the *Glacieres*. They shewed us at first the Ends of them which reach into the Valley, and were to be seen from the Village; these appear'd only like white Rocks, or rather like immense Icicles, made by Water running down the Mountain. This did not satisfy our Curiosity, and we thought we were come too far to be contented with so small a Matter; we therefore strictly inquired of the Peasants whether we could not by going up the Mountain discover something more worth our Notice. They told us we might, but the greatest Part of them represented the Thing as very difficult and laborious; they told us no-body ever went there but those whose Business it was to search for Crystal, or to shoot *Bouquetins*[4] and *Chamois*, and that all the Travellers, who had been to the *Glacieres* hitherto, had been satisfied with what we had already seen.

The Prior of the Place was a good old Man, who shewed us many Civilities, and endeavoured also to dissuade us; there were others who represented the Thing as mighty easy; but we perceived plainly, that they expected, that after we had bargain'd with them to be our Guides, we should soon tire, and that they should earn their Money with little Trouble. However our Curiosity got the better of these Discouragements, and relying on our Strength and Resolution, we determined to attempt climbing the Mountain. We took with us several Peasants, some to be our Guides, and others to carry Wine and Provisions. These People were so much persuaded that we should never be able to go through with our Talk, that they took with them Candles and Instruments to strike Fire, in case we should be overcome with Fatigue, and be obliged to spend the Night on the Mountain. In order to prevent those among us who were the most in wind, from fatiguing the rest, by pushing on too fast, we made the following Rules: That no one should go out of his Rank; That he who led the way should go a slow and even pace; That who ever found himself fatigued; or out of Breath, might call for a Halt; And lastly, that when ever we found a Spring we should drink some of our Wine, mixed with Water, and fill up the Bottles, we had emptied, with Water, to serve us at other Halts where we should find none. These Precautions were so useful to us, that, perhaps, had we not observed them, the Peasants would not have been deceived in their Conjectures.

We set out about Noon, the 22d of *June*, and crossed the *Arve* over a wooden Bridge. Most Maps place the *Glacieres* on the same Side with *Chamoigny*, but this is a Mistake. We were quickly at the Foot of the Mountain, and began to ascend by a very steep Path through a Wood of Firs and Larche Trees. We made many Halts to refresh ourselves, and take breath, but we kept on at a good Rate. After we had passed the Wood, we came to a kind of Meadow, full of large Stones, and Pieces of rocks, that were broke off, and fallen down from the Mountain; the Ascent was so steep that we were obliged sometimes to cling to them with our Hands, and make use of Sticks, with sharp Irons at the End, to support ourselves. Our Road lay slant Ways, and we had several Places to cross where the *Avalanches*[5] of Snow were fallen, and had made terrible Havock; there was nothing to be seen but Trees torn up by the Roots, and large Stones, which seemed to lie without any Support; every step we set, the Ground gave way, the Snow which was mixed with it made us slip, and had it not been for our Staffs, and our Hands, we must many times have gone down the Precipice. We had an uninterrupted View quite to the Bottom of the Mountain, and the Steepness of the Descent, join'd to the Height where we were, made a View terrible enough to make most People's Heads turn. In short, after climbing with great Labour for four Hours and three Quarters, we got to the Top of the Mountain; from whence we had the Pleasure of beholding Objects of an extraordinary Nature. We were on the Top of a Mountain, which, as well as we could judge, was at least twice as high as Mount *Saleve*, from thence we had a full View of the *Glacieres*. I own to you that I am extremely at a Loss how to give a right Idea of it; as I know no one thing which I have ever seen that has the least Resemblance to it.

The Description which Travellers give of the Seas of *Greenland* seems to come the nearest to it. You must imagine your Lake put in Agitation by a strong Wind, and frozen all at once, perhaps even that would not produce that same Appearance.

The *Glacieres* consist of three large Valleys, that form a kind of Y, the Tail reaches into the *Val d' Aoste*, and the two Horns into the Valley of *Chamoigny*, the Place where we ascended was between them, from whence we saw plainly the Valley, which forms one of these Horns.

I had unluckily left at *Chamoigny* a pocket Compass, which I had carried with me, so that I could not well tell the Bearings as to its Situation; but I believe it to be pretty nearly from North to South. These Valleys, although at the Top of a high Mountain, are surrounded with other Mountains; the Tops of which being naked and craggy Rocks, shoot up immensely high; something resembling old *Gothic* Buildings or Ruines, nothing grows upon them, they are all the Year round covered with Snow; and our Guides assured us, that neither the *Chamois*, nor any Birds, ever went so high as the Top of them.

Those who search after Crystal, go in the Month of *August* to the Foot of these Rocks, and strike against them with Pick-axes; if they hear them resound as if they were hollow, they work there, and opening the Rock, they find Caverns full of Crystalisations. We should have been very glad to have gone there, but the Season was not enough advanced, the Snow not being yet sufficiently melted. As far as our Eye-sight could reach, we saw nothing but this Valley; the Height of the Rocks, which surrounded it, made it impossible for the Eye to judge exactly how wide it was; but I imagine it must be near three Quarters of a League. Our Curiosity did not stop here, we were resolved to go down upon the Ice; we had about four hundred Yards to go down, the Descent was excessively steep, and all of a dry crumbling Earth, mixt with Gravel, and little loose Stones, which afforded us no firm footing; so that we went down partly falling, and partly sliding on our Hands and Knees. At length we got upon the Ice, where our Difficulty ceased, for that was extremely rough, and afforded us good footing; we found in it an infinite Number of Cracks,[6] some we could step over, others were several Feet wide. These Cracks were so deep, that we could not even see to the Bottom; those who go in search of Crystal are often lost in them, but their Bodies are generally found again after some Days, perfectly well preserved. All our Guides assured us, that these Cracks change continually, and that the whole *Glaciere* has a kind of Motion. In going up the Mountain we often heard something like a Clap of Thunder, which, as we were informed by our Guides, was caused by fresh Cracks then making; but as there were none made while we were upon the Ice, we could not determine whether it was that, or *Avalanches* of Snows, or perhaps Rocks falling; though since Travellers observe, that in *Greenland* the Ice cracks with a Noise that resembles Thunder, it might very well be what our Guides told us. As in all Countries of Ignorance people are extremely superstitious, they told us many strange Stories of Witches, &c. Who came to play their Pranks upon the *Glacieres*, and dance to the Sound of Instruments. We should have been surprised if we had not been entertained in these Parts, with some such idle Legends. The *Bouquetins* go in Herds often to the Number of fifteen or sixteen upon the Ice, we saw none of them, there were some *Chainois* which we shot at, but at too great a Distance to do any Execution.

There is Water continually issuing out of the *Glacieres*, which the People look on as so very wholesome, that they say it may be drank of in any Quantities without Danger, even when one is hot with Exercise.

The Sun shone very hot, and the Reverberation of the Ice, and circumjacent Rocks, caused a great deal of thaw'd Water to lie in all the Cavities of the Ice; but I fancy it freezes there constantly as soon as Night comes on.

48

Our Guides assured us, that, in the time of their Fathers, the *Glaciere* was but small, and that there was even a Passage thro' these Valleys, by which they could go into the *Val d' Aoste* in six Hours: But that the *Glaciere* was so much increased, that the passage was then quite stopped up, and that it went on increasing every Year.

We found on the Edge of the *Glaciere* several Pieces of Ice, which we took at first for Rocks, being as big as a House; these were pieces quite separate from the *Glaciere*. It is difficult to conceive how they came to be formed there.

Having remained about half an Hour upon the *Glaciere*, and having drank there in Ceremony Admiral *Vernon*'s Health, and Success to the *British* Arms, we climb'd to the Summit, from whence we came, with incredible Difficulty, the Earth giving way at every step we set. From thence, after having rested ourselves a few Minutes, we began to descend, and arrived at *Chamouny* just about Sun-set, to the great Astonishment of all the People of the Place, and even of our Guides, who owned to us they thought we should not have gone through with our Undertaking.

Our Curiosity being fully satisfied, we left *Chamouny* the next Day, and lying at *Salanches*, we got the 23d to *Bonneville*. The Nearness of this Place to the *Maule* raised in us an Inclination to go up it. We set about this Task the next Day early in the Morning; we fancied that after the *Glacieres* every Mountain would be easy to us, however it took us more than five Hours hard labour in getting up; the Ascent being extremely steep; though, after two thirds of the Way, there is a fine green Turf quite up to the Top, which ends in a Point, the Mountain being like a Sugar-Loaf on one Side, and quite perpendicular on that Part which lies farthest from *Geneva*. From this Point there is a most delightful View, on one Side, upon the Lake, *Geneva*, and the adjacent Parts; on the other, upon high Mountains cover'd with Snow, which rise around, in form of an Amphitheatre, and make a most Picturesque Prospect. After having stay'd some time here, we returned back, and went on to *Annecy*, where we lay, from whence the next Day we got to *Geneva*.

Those who are desirous to undertake this Journey, ought not to set out till towards the Middle of *August*; they would at that time find not so much Snow on the Mountain. They might go to the Crystal Mines, and divert themselves with shooting of *Bouquetins*; the Oats would then be cut, and their Horses would not suffer so much. Although we met with nothing which had the Appearance of Danger, nevertheless I would recommend going well armed; 'tis an easy Precaution, and on certain Occasions very useful, one is never the worse for it, and oftentimes it helps a Man out of a Scrape. Barometers to measure the Height of the Mountains, portable Thermometers, and a Quadrant to take Heights with, would be useful, if there were a Mathematician in Company. A Tent would not be necessary, unless for those who had a Mind to examine every thing with the greatest Exactness, and make Observations; in this Case one might pitch it upon the Mountain, and pass the Night in it, if it were necessary, for it did not seem very cold there.

With these Precautions one might go through the other Parts of these Valleys, which form the Y, and one might find out whether the Cracks change daily as we were told; one might also Measure those excessive high Rocks which are on the Side of the *Glaciere*, and make many other curious Observations, according to the Taste and Genius of the Travellers; who, if they were inclined to Botany, might find an ample Field of Amusement.

One who understood Drawing might find wherewithal to imploy himself, either on the Road, or in the Place itself; in short, a Man of Genius might do many things which we have not done. All the Merit we can pretend to is having opened the way to others who may have Curiosity of the same Kind.

It would be right to take Victuals ready dress'd, and Salt Meat, Bread and Wine, for there are some Places where one can get no Provisions, and the little there is to be had in other Places, is very bad. We bought a Sheep, which we killed, and dressed upon the spot.

It is necessary to carry Halter to tie the Horses, cut Shoes, Nails, Hammer, &c. for they lose their Shoes continually in those stoney Roads.

With such Precautions all kinds of Journeys become easy and agreeable, even in the most desart Countries, and one is then more in a Condition to observe with Care and Accuracy, whatever occurs worth Notice.

This is the Substance, Sir, of what I can recollect of our Journey. My having so long defer'd giving you this Account is owing to the Incapacity I found in myself to say any thing worth being pretenede to a Person of so good a Taste as yourself. However, upon the whole, 'tis your good Taste which ought to encourage me: Your Lively and penetrating Imagination, which unites in one, both the Poet and Painter, will at once lay hold and perfect what I have but flightly sketched. I am, with the greatest Esteem,

SIR,
Your most Obedient Humble Servant.

—1744

Notes

1. The same who has lately published so accurate and ingenious an Account of his Travels.

2. Viz. Lord *Hadinton*, the Honourable Mr. *Bailhe* his Brother, and Mess. *Chetwynd*, *Aldworth*, *Pococke*, *Price*, *Windham* and *Stillingfleet*.

3. *Saleve* is a Mountain, about three Miles from *Geneva*, whose perpendicular Height is about 1150 *French* Feet.

4. The *Bouquetins* are Animals much larger, and less Shaggy than a Goat. They live in the highest Mountains, and come down very rarely, for which reason the Trouble and Danger of Hunting them is very great; they are very courageous, making use of their great Horns for Defence, when attack'd; they are very cunning, and by the Wind smell the Hunter a vast way off; when chased, they leap an incredible Distance, and being pursued closely will throw themselves down high Precipices, and by falling upon their Horns break their Fall so as not to hurt themselves. The Edges of their Hoofs, or Claws, are so sharp and hard, that the Impression of

50

them may be seen on Stones. Their Blood is esteemed as a sovereign Remedy in Pleuritick Disorders, which is reckoned to be owing to the Herbs they feed on in these Mountains, particularly an Herb called, in the Language of the Country, *Genepi*. Chamois is a Kind of Goat, only stronger. They keep on the high Mountains of the *Alps*; they are very fond of licking certain Rocks, of a kind of soft crumbling Stone, which is Salt, and in those Places the Hunters go to look for them, and surprise them, which is however very difficult, for they always have some of the Herd standing on high Rocks as Centries, and when they perceive any Danger they give the Alarm by a Noise they make, upon which the rest betake themselves to the Precipices, where it is impossible to follow them. Sometimes this kind of Sport becomes dangerous, not only by reason of the craggy Rocks one must climb up to, but because it often happens that the Hunter persues the *Chamois* into some narrow Pass, where there is but just Foot hold for one Person, having on one side a steep Rock above him, and beneath a frightful Precipice; the *Chamois* then having no way to escape is obliged to turn upon the Hunter, and endeavours either to jump over him, or else squeeze between him and the Rock, in which case be pushes the Man down the Precipice; so that all he has to do is either to lay down, or else, by struggling, make good his Place, and thrust the Beast down the Rock. It is with their Horns that the little Reed-canes Ladies carry are generally tipt, and of their Skins is made the true Shammy Leather.

5. *Avalanche.* To explain the meaning of this Word, I believe it will not be unentertaining to the Reader to cite some Passages from the *Delices da la Suisse*, which contain some curious Particulars relating to those mountainous Parts of the World.

"Besides these Ice Mountains, the Snows are extremely dangerous to Travellers. There often fall from these high Mountains immense Balls of Snow, which are called *in German Lawinen*, in *Italian Lavine*, in *French Avalanches*, which by the Impetuosity of their Fall make a Noise like a Clap of Thunder; so great those that are at a Distance imagine it to be really so, as I remember it happened to myself some Years since, having heard one that fell in the *Vallais*, though I was above twenty Leagues distant from it. Sometimes it is caused by the new fallen Snow, which being driven by the Violence of the Wind, forms vast Snowballs, which gather by rolling, and overwhelm every thing they meet, both Men and Beasts. As it is very difficult to avoid them, because they are extremely sudden, so, being very light, a Man may remain under them longer without being suffocated; but there are others which are occasioned by the Thaws in the Spring, which are much more dangerous, great Masses of old snow, melting underneath, fall off at once, making a terrible Noise, but still more Ravage, not only destroying Men and Cattle, but even Trees and Houses. *Claudian,* who lived in the fourth and fifth Centuries, informs us, that such Accidents were known in his Time, *Vide* 4t *Consul. Honorii:*

multos hausere profundae
Vasta mole nives; cumque ipsis saepe juvencis
Naufraga candenti merguntur plaustra barathro,
Interdum subitam, Glacie labente, ruinam
Mors dedit.

A Trifle will produce these terrible Accidents in the *Alps*, the Flight of a Bird, the Leaping of a *Chamois*, the firing of a Pistol, a Shout, speaking loud, the Bells of the Mules and Pack-Horses, or even a gentle Rain are sufficient to loosen this Snow, and bring it down to the Destruction of Passengers, so little hold has it on these steep Places. For this Reason they always take great Care to caution Travellers in Places where there is danger of this Sort, to travel early, and in great Silence, and to get through as fast as possible, as one would out of a House on Fire: And the *Voiturins* fill with Hay or Straw the Bells of their Beasts, in some Places, as in the *Val d' Aversa*; in the *Grisons* they put the Bells only a Foot above the Ground, that their Sound should not extend so far as to cause Danger, and in several Places they do not use them at all for that Reason. In the Lower *Engadine*, between the Villages of *Lavin* and *Guardia*, there are all along the Road several Caves made in the rocks for Travellers to retire into when they see any of these Mountains of Snow falling; but if they are so unfortunate as not to be able to reach such a Place, the only way is to get as close to some Rock as possible, and cling to it, so as not to be carried away, and to endeavour to keep their Head free, to be able to breath till Assistance comes; for in all these Places there are People paid by the Magistrates to look after the Ways, and keep them always open; and as soon as there is fallen any Quantity of Snow, they go and mend the Ways, smooth the Snows with large Pieces of Wood, drawn by Oxen, and shovel it away, and at the same time examine all dangerous Places to see if there is no poor Traveller buried under the Snow. The Histories of *Switzerland* are full of the terrible Ravages made in several Places, at different times, by these *Avalanches* in 1499. When the Emperor Maximilian made War upon the *Grisons*, a Body of 2000 Men of his Troups having been ordered to pass a high Mountain to go into the *Engadine*, an *Avalanche* falling suddenly upon them, buried 400 Soldiers, which at first caused great Confusion and Terror in the rest, which was soon turned into Laughter, when they saw all the 400 Men safe and sound out of their snowy Tomb, not one being lost: But the Year following a Body of *Switzers*, going into *Italy* for the Service of the *French*, was surprized on the Mount of St. *Bernard*, by a horrible *Avalanche* which destroyed a hundred of them. And in our Memory, in the Year 1695, on the 21st of *February*, at Ten o'Clock at Night, a violent Wind brought down a most terrible *Avalanche* of above 100 Yards in width upon a Village in the *Vall Madia*, which destroyed eleven Houses, with as many Barns and Stables, so entirely, that there scarce remained one Stone upon another, and very much damaged nineteen other Houses that remained. The Violence of the Wind blew open the Windows of some Houses, and filled them with Snow; thirty-four Persons perished in this Storm, some were taken alive, almost miraculously from under the Snow, amongst others a Mother and two Children. It happens very often that Travellers who are caught in the Snows are happily preserved and saved from Death. When any one is found seemingly dead, without Sense or Motion, the first Remedy is to plunge him in cold Water. To some it will appear both barbarous and ridiculous to dip a Man, who is frozen, and almost dead with Cold, into cold Water; but let them know that it would be certain Death to any one to give him heat suddenly when he is frozen. They begin therefore with dipping him into cold Water, upon which his whole Body is covered with a Crust of Ice; afterward he is put into luke-warm Water, then proceeding by Degrees, they get him into a Bed well warmed, and finish his Cure by Cordials and Fomentations. And this Rule holds good also with regard to Fruits, when the frost has caught them; one must never carry them at once into a warm Place, but the way is to dip them into cold Water, and then into warm Water, by which means they become pretty good again. I will not leave this Subject without observing a thing, which is truly a physical Paradox, which is, that the Water that runs from the *Gletschers*, or Ice Mountains, that I have mentioned before, is the best and wholsomest that one can drink. A Traveller that passes those Mountains can drink no other Water if he is heated, without Danger of catching a fatal Distemper; but he may without Danger drink this Ice Water, whether fasting, or after eating, and it has a kind of balsamick Virtue to restore and fortify after any Fatigue; this is a known Fact, and proved by constant Experience. The Inhabitants of the *Alps* know no other Remedy in Diarrhoea's, Dysenteries, and Fevers, than this Water of the *Gletschers*, and a celebrated Physician has recommended it for the Tooth-Ach. A Man who passes thro' these Parts ought carefully to avoid two Things, *viz.* drinking common Water, and sleeping near a Fountain, or in the Snow, since they commonly prove fatal."

6. "In some Places there are found Mountains of Ice, which not only never melt, but always increase by the falling of fresh Snow, so that by little and little they extend themselves, and cover the Country all about them. The *Germans* call them *Gletscher*, we call them commonly *Glacieres*. These Ice Mountains are mostly of an immense Height, and sometimes they split from Top to Bottom, which they do with so horrible a Noise, that one would think the whole Mountain was breaking in Pieces; these Clefts differ as to the Width and Depth; there are some two, three, or four Feet wide, and three or four hundred Yards deep, and if a Man falls in he is almost inevitably lost, being either killed by the cold, or drowned in the melted Snow: However, in many Places, one is obliged to pass over these Mountains, there being no other Way, and when there is any Snow new fallen it is very dangerous, for the Ice covers these terrible Clefts, so that the Travellers are taken as birds in a Snare, and fall in and perish. To avoid these Misfortunes Travellers take Guides, who with long Poles found the way to see there is no Cleft, and when they find one they must jump over, or else they pass over a Board, which they carry for that Purpose. The Difficulty augments when there is Snow new fallen, for then one sees no track of the way at all, and one must observe certain Poles set up to shew the way, which the *Grifons* call *Stazas*, but in many Places the Inhabitants set up none, that the Travellers may be obliged to pay them well for being their Guides. On these Occasions it is necessary to have iron Cramps to ones Shoes, not to slip, and withal take great Care where one sets one's Feet, and on this Occasion I hope the Reader will not blame me for inserting a wonderful Adventure which happened some Years ago to a Hunter of *Glaris*, name *Gasper Stöeri*. This Man being in pursuit of Chamois, with two other Hunters on Mount *Limmeren*, and thinking he was walking on the Snow very safely, fell into a deep Cleft of the Ice: His Companions, who lost sight of him, were in great Uneasiness, and expected no otherwise than that he must be killed, either by the Fall, or by the Cold of the Ice. Nevertheless that they might not reproach themselves with letting him perish, without endeavouring to help him, they ran to the nearest Cottage, which was full a League off, to look for a Rope, or something else to assist him; but finding nothing there but an old Blanket, they cut it into long Slips, and went to the Hole where their Companion was. While they were going and coming, poor *Stöeri* was almost dead with Cold, being up to his Middle in ic'd Water. The Depth of which was so great under him, that he could not see to the Bottom, and by extending his Arms and Legs, he held himself fast against the Sides of the Cleft of Ice, so that he was shut up there, as it were, in a close, cold, and deep Dungeon. You may imagine in what a Situation he was, he expected nothing but Death, and was recommending his Soul to God, when his Companions arrived, who let down the Slips they had cut, to pull him out; he had Strength enough to tie them about his Body, and by this Mean was drawn up to the Top of the Pit; but as he was just upon the Point of being delivered, unhappily the Slip which held him up broke, and he fell again into the iced Water, and was in greater Danger than before. He carried down with him a piece of the Slip which broke, and the Remainder was not long enough to reach him, and as an additional Misfortune, in this second Fall he broke his Arm. However his Companions did not lose Courage, they divided the Slip again, and joining the Pieces end to end, lower'd them down to him, he with great Difficulty, with his broken Arm, tied it round his Body, while with the other he held to the Sides of his Dungeon and with this weak Instrument, by a Miracle of Providence, was drawn out of this terrible Pit, and though he had at first fainted away, God gave him Strength to come to himself, and to bear the Fatigue of being carried to a House where he entirely recovered." *Vid. Delices de la Suisse, Tem.* 1. *Pag* 22 *& seq.*

53

Jacques Balmat, as told to Alexandre Dumas

from *The First Ascent of the Great White Mountain [Mont Blanc]*

Internationally known scientist Horace-Bénédict de Saussure inspired the later glaciological investigations of Louis Agassiz, James Forbes, and John Tyndall, who all took a serious scientific interest in the origin and movement of glacial ice and the physics, morphology, and chemistry of frozen water. Saussure offered a financial reward to anyone who would climb Mont Blanc. The challenge was taken up by Jacques Balmat (1762–1834), a local rock-crystal hunter, and Dr. Michel-Gabriel Paccard, who made a daring ascent on August 8, 1786, in the midst of bitter cold and high winds. They returned from their fourteen-hour ordeal as snow-blinded and frostbitten local heroes. Although Paccard seems to have been the key member of the duo, Balmat claimed the contrary and their roles in the climb were the subject of a bitter dispute between the two men for years afterward. Balmat later led Saussure on a successful ascent in 1787. The account below was recounted to Alexandre Dumas (1802–1870) in 1832 by the aging Balmat and translated by Edward Whymper, one of the most controversial climbers of the nineteenth century.

CHAPTER III.

THE FIRST ASCENT OF THE GREAT WHITE MOUNTAIN.

JACQUES BALMAT DISCOVERS THE *ANCIEN PASSAGE* AND NEARLY REACHES THE SUMMIT— DR. PACCARD AND BALMAT MAKE THE FIRST ASCENT—DE SAUSSURE GIVES INSTRUCTIONS TO LEVEL THE WAY—RECRIMINATIONS—WHO IS THIS DR. PACCARD?

Along with the three who it has been mentioned ascended from the valley of Chamonix, there was a fourth, who attached himself to the others almost against their will—a young man named Jacques Balmat. Just before they started, he is said to have passed a couple of days in searching for a route upon his own account, and he was returning, with his clothes sticking to him half frozen, when he met the others ascending. They were unwilling that he should accompany them. *They* wanted the reward, and so did *he*. But he went with them, and when the others turned back, he lin-

Jacques Balmat as told to Alexandre Dumas, "The First Ascent of the Great White Mountain [Mont Blanc]." Translated by Edward Whymper, *A Guide to Chamonix and the Range of Mont Blanc* (London: John Murray, 1896).

gered behind to look about, and they went on, it is said, and deserted him intentionally. "Balmat is lively," said the others ironically, "and will catch us up." "I found myself alone," said he, "and was divided between a wish to rejoin them, and an ambition to attempt the ascent alone. I was piqued at being left behind, and something told me that, this time, I should succeed." He decided on the latter course; descended on to a great snowy plain that is about 2600 feet below the summit (the Grand Plateau), and remounted by the exceedingly steep snow,[1] digging out footsteps with the point of his bâton, until high enough to see all the rest of the way clear to the top. "It wasn't either easy or amusing, I can tell you, to be hung up so to speak on one leg, with an abyss underneath, and obliged to fashion this sort of staircase. But at last I got to the Rocher Rouge.[2] Oh! I am there, I said. There was nothing further to hinder one—no more steps to make." Night was approaching, there were clouds about, and he did not try to go to the top—less from fear of losing himself than from the conviction that he would not be seen, and that no one would believe he had been there. He came down again the same way, but on arriving at the Grand Plateau was nearly blind. "The snow had so affected my eyes that I couldn't see anything. I sat down, closed my eyes, and put my head between my hands. At the end of half an hour sight came back, but night had come. I hadn't taken two hundred steps when I felt with my bâton that the snow was giving way under my feet. I was on the edge of the great crevasse which we had crossed in the morning by a snow-bridge. I sought for it and couldn't find it. Something had to be done. I put my knapsack on the snow, tied my handkerchief round my face, and prepared to pass the night as well as I could. From the place where I was I saw the lights of Chamonix,[3] where my comrades were sitting cozily round the fire, or, it may be, were in their beds. Perhaps none of them gave a thought of me; or, if he did, it would be only to say, when stirring up the embers or drawing the counterpane over the ears, 'Just now that fool of a Jacques is beating his feet to keep them warm.'" Next morning he returned alone to his village. "All was right at home. My wife gave me something to eat, though I was more sleepy than hungry. She wanted me to go to bed in my room, but I was afraid of being tormented by the flies; so, shutting myself up in the barn, I laid down upon the hay, and slept twenty-four hours without waking."

Balmat, at this time, was twenty-four years old, and though so young had already made two attempts to ascend Mont Blanc. Once he had passed a night on the top of the Montagne de la Côte, and on the next day reached the Grand Plateau, *alone*. He had now done a more notable thing, but still did not awake to find himself famous; for no one, not even his wife, knew the information he had gained. If he divulged it, he could not hope to profit. Hence, "upon return to Chamonix, at first he kept his discovery a secret. But as he understood that Dr. Paccard was thinking of making some attempts on the mountain he communicated his secret to him, and offered to act as his guide" to the summit. So says De Saussure in Vol. IV of his *Voyages*. Paccard, the Village Doctor, was known to Chamoniards as a mountaineering amateur, and in 1786 was about thirty-four years of age. Though he might be little service as a companion, he could be useful as a witness. Paccard agreed to go. Then three weeks of bad weather intervened; but at last, on August 8, 1786, it seemed fine enough to start. "All our little matters having been arranged," said Balmat,[4] "and good-bye said to our wives, we set out about five in the afternoon, one taking the right and the other the left bank of the River Arve, in order that no one should guess what we were about, and we rejoined each other at the village of La Côte." They camped at the top of the Montagne de la Côte (the long buttress extending from the valley towards the summit), about 5500 feet above Chamonix. So far there was no difficulty. "I slept like a top," said Balmat, "until about half-past one," and then awoke the doctor. "The sun arose cloudless, bright and shining, promising us a grand day."

The top of the Montagne de la Côte abuts on the glaciers which extend continuously to the summit of Mont Blanc. The Glacier de Taconnaz descends on its right and the Glacier des Bossons on its left, and at the place where they separate the ice is extremely fissured and difficult to traverse. Balmat made no fuss about this. "In a quarter of an hour," said he, "we took to the Glacier de Taconnaz. The first steps of the doctor were rather unsteady, but seeing how I managed he gained confidence. We soon left the Grands Mulets behind us.[5] I pointed out the place where I had passed my first night. He made a significant grimace; and held his tongue for ten minutes, then said all at one, 'Do you think, Balmat, that we shall get to the top to-day?' I promised nothing. For two hours more we continued to ascend in the same way. After the (Grand) Plateau, the wind rose, and grew higher and higher. At last, on arriving where the rocks which we called the Petit Mulet[6] peep out, a violent gust carried away the doctor's hat. I saw it scuttling away, while he looked after it with outstretched arms. 'Oh! Doctor,' I said, 'you will have to go into mourning; you'll see it no more. It's off to Piedmont. Good-bye!'

"I had hardly shut my mouth when there came such a squall as made us lie flat on our stomachs, and for ten minutes we couldn't get up again. The doctor was discouraged. As for me, just then I was thinking only about the shop-keeper who ought to be looking out for us,[7] and I stood up at the first opportunity, but the doctor would only follow on all fours. In this fashion we came to a place where the village could be seen; I got out my glass, and twelve thousand feet below in the valley made out our gossip, and a crowd of others looking at us through telescopes. Considerations of self-respect influenced the doctor to get on his legs, and the moment he was up they recognised us, he in his big frock-coat and I in my regular dress. Down below they waved their hats, and I replied with mine.

"Paccard had used up his strength in getting on his legs, and neither the encouragement we received nor that which I gave him made him continue upwards. After I had exhausted all my eloquence and saw that I was only losing time, I told him to keep in movement and as warm as possible. He listened without hearing, and answered 'Yes, yes,' to get rid of me. He was suffering from the cold, and I myself was benumbed. I went off by myself, saying that I would come back to look for him. 'Yes, yes,' he replied. I recommended him again not to keep still; but I had not gone thirty steps, when, on looking round, I saw that, instead of running about and beating his feet to keep them alive, he was sitting with his back to the wind.

"From this time the way did not present any particular difficulty, but, as I got higher, the air became less and less fit to breathe. Every ten steps I was obliged to stop. It seemed as if I had an empty chest and no lungs, and the cold laid hold of me more and more. I went on, with face lowered, but presently, not knowing where I was, raised my head and saw that at last I was on the summit of Mont Blanc. Looking around, trembling lest I was mistaken, and should see some fresh aiguille or new point which I should not have strength to scale, the joints of my legs only seemed to hold together by the help of my trousers. But no! no! I was at the end of my journey. I was where no one had ever been before. Then I turned towards Chamonix, waving my hat at the end of my bâton, and saw through my glass that they answered me. When this exciting moment was over, I thought of my poor doctor; and, descending to him as quickly as possible, called him by name—quite frightened not to hear him answer. At the end of a quarter of an hour I saw him from afar, round as a ball, not moving, notwithstanding the shouts which he certainly must have heard. I found him doubled up with his head between his knees, like a cat making itself into a muff. I slapped him on the shoulder, and he mechanically raised his head. I told him that I had reached the summit of Mont Blanc, but that appeared to interest him very little, for he only answered by inquiring where he could lie down and go to sleep. I told him that he had come on purpose to go to the top of the mountain, and that he must go there. I shook him, took him by the shoulders, and made him go a few steps; but he appeared stupefied, and as if it were all the same whether he went one way or another, either up or down. However, the exercise I compelled him to take restored his circulation somewhat, and he asked if I hadn't by chance another pair of gloves in my pocket like those which were on my hands. They were of hareskin and had been made expressly for the occasion, without divisions between the fingers. In a similar situation, I would have refused *both* to my brother, but I gave him *one*. Soon after six we were on the summit of Mont Blanc.

"Seven o'clock came; there were only two hours and a half more of daylight; it was time to be off. I caught Paccard again under the arm, waved my hat as a last signal to those below, and we began to go down. There was no track to direct us except the little holes which had been made with the points of our iron-shod bâtons. Paccard was no better than a child, without will or energy, whom I guided over the good bits and carried over the bad ones. Night began to close in when we crossed the big crevasse, and caught us below the Grand Plateau. Paccard stopped every moment, declaring that he could go no farther, and I was obliged to compel him to go forward, not by persuasion but by force. At eleven o'clock we got out of the ice-world, and set foot on *terra firma*."

They had now got back to the top of the Montagne de la Côte. Balmat remarked here that the doctor made no use of his hands, and found that he had lost sensation in them. "I drew off his gloves; his hands were white, and as if dead." One of Balmat's own hands was in a similar state.

"I told him that there were three frost-bitten hands between the two of us, but he only wanted to lie down and go to sleep, though he told me to rub my hand with snow. The remedy wasn't far off. I commenced on him, and finished on myself. Presently the blood came back, and with it warmth, but with the most exquisite pain . . . I rolled up my doll in the rug, put him under shelter of a rock, we ate a bit, drank a drop, pressed one against the other as close as we could, and went to sleep."

Next morning the doctor was snow-blind, and was led down holding on to a strap of his guide's knapsack; and Balmat said that he himself was unrecognisable. "I had red eyes, a black face, and blue ears." Four days afterwards he left for Geneva to announce his success.

But before Balmat and Paccard came back, a special messenger was already on his way to Geneva, sent by a sharp innkeeper, who hoped to secure the patronage of De Saussure. The reply which came from the Professor is an interesting document. It commenced thus:

"I am very much obliged to you, my dear Jean-Pierre, for sending an express to inform me of the happy result of Dr. Paccard's expedition. I was so delighted at the news that I gave two new crowns to the messenger. . . .

"Now, I am going to tell you something that you must keep a profound secret, and this is that I myself wish to try the same route; not that I flatter myself I shall get to the top, for I have neither the youth nor the agility of Monsieur the Doctor; but I may get, anyhow, to a considerable elevation, and make there some observations and experiments which will be very important to me. Now, as it appears that it is very troublesome to get across the glacier which is above the Montagne de la Côte, I wish you to send at once five or six men to level the way, so far as such a thing is possible. You will give them good wages. . . . You can put at their head this Jacques Balmat, who made the journey with Monsieur Paccard, and give him higher pay."

And then, after various other directions, comes this curious passage. "But, in all this, I expressly forbid you to mention my name: say that all this has been ordered by an Italian nobleman, who does not wish to be known. I have the strongest reasons for wanting not to be talked about, and that no one shall know I have got this idea in my head." What these reasons were we do not know. He came to Chamonix a week after writing the letter,[8] but bad weather set in, and another *year* passed before De Saussure stood on the summit of Mont Blanc. On August 1, 1787, he set out with seventeen men led by Jacques Balmat, and passed the first night on the top of the Montagne de la Côte, the next under tent near the edge of the Grand Plateau, and upon August 3, at 11 A.M., "I enjoyed," he said, "the pleasure of the accomplishment of the project which I had planned twenty-seven years before, namely, upon my first journey to Chamonix in 1760—a project which I had often abandoned and taken up again, which was a constant matter of care and anxiety to my family."

In the book by M. de Saussure a plate of Mont Blanc is given, with his track marked thereon; and, although this plate inaccurately represents the mountain, one can tell from it where he went, and the route that was first of all discovered by Balmat, which was subsequently followed by Balmat and Paccard. The opinion of De Saussure (printed nine years after his ascent) was that this route was "very certainly the only one by which the summit could be gained." In this he was mistaken—the mountain has, since then, been ascended from half-a-dozen different directions. But the route taken on the first ascent is the most direct of all, and, in some respects, is the most natural one.[9]

An episode relating to Jacques Balmat remains to be mentioned, which appears to have been overlooked or ignored by writers on Mont Blanc. In the number of the *Journal de Lausanne* for February 24, 1787, an anonymous article appeared questioning the accuracy of the account of the ascent which was generally received. It claimed that Paccard had discovered the route which was followed; it stated that he had 'selected' Jacques Balmat to accompany him, and had done so merely because the other guides were away and he was the only one unoccupied; and that he was selected not as a *guide* but as a *workman*. "He was guided," said this anonymous communication, "and encouraged by M. Paccard. Paccard pressed him to go on when he wanted to turn back. Balmat was useful to him, doubtless, but not in attaining the summit . . . Balmat did *not* get there the first—M. Paccard has certificates which prove this"—and he "was not unrewarded, for the Doctor gave him money."

M. Bourrit took up his pen in defence of the Chamonix guide, and sent a letter to the *Journal de Lausanne*, which appeared in its numbers for March 10 and 17, 1787. He contradicted point-blank some of the above statements, and challenged the production of the certificates. "If M. Paccard rewarded Balmat," said Bourrit, "It must have been *after* the publication of my letter; for I know that he offered him a crown, and that Balmat refused it." This caused the publication in the *Journal de Lausanne* for May 12, 1787, of two declarations (purporting to be signed by Balmat), which were prefaced by the following editorial remarks. "Our impartiality led us to insert, in our 13th, 15th, and 16th numbers, the complaints of Dr. Paccard[10] and M. Bourrit. . . . We admit to-day the following certificates, which we do not feel able to refuse to insert. But we will say now, to those interested in this dispute, that the scheme of our paper will not allow us to occupy the attention of our readers any longer on such matters, which, perhaps, are not generally interesting." Then follow the declarations.

"I the undersigned Jacques, son of J. T. Balmat, of Pelerins, Commune of Chamonix, declare to all those it may concern, that I offered my services to Doctor M. Paccard, having learned that he wished to make a new attempt on Mont Blanc, in continuation of those which he had already made, and knowing that his own guide was away.

"As he proposed to go by the side of the Montagne de la Côte, which we thought was an impracticable route, I had doubts as to the success of the enterprise; but he told me that he had examined this direction, for the space of three years, with his telescope.

"I declare that except for the steady manner in which he proceeded we should never have succeeded; that he continually encouraged me; that he shared my labour, and sometimes himself carried a portion of the things he had given me to carry; that when I wanted to come down, as I had promised, to be of assistance to my wife and a child who was ill (this latter died on the 8th of August), he regarded my representations as excuses.

"He would not follow the route which we had taken on our last attempt, but kept straight on to the middle of the plain which is above the Glacier des Bossons. He himself traced for me his new route, by going before me, up a steep slope, which is at the foot of the great Mont Blanc. As he had always said that we should sleep out on the mountain, he made me look for a camping-place, as soon as we got to the top of this slope, whilst he ascended to examine the rocks. Not finding any, he determined to ascend the same evening to the summit, the object we were in pursuit of. He called to me, and I followed. At the same moment, I saw something dark pass above me—it was his hat, which the wind carried away with such velocity that we saw it no more.

"The Doctor continued to ascend numbly. We came to a little rock, behind which I sheltered myself from the wind, whilst he examined it, and made collections. We were near the top of the mountain. I bore away to the left to avoid a snow slope, which Mons. Paccard courageously scaled to get straight to the summit of Mont Blanc. The detour I made delayed me somewhat, and I was obliged to run, to be nearly as soon as he was on the aforesaid spot.

"He made experiments there, and observations, which he wrote down. He left a mark there, and we then came down at once, quickly, following our track, and looking for it in turn. We arrived on the top of the Montagne de la Côte, where Mons. Paccard slept, on the side exposed to the glacier.

"He fed me, he paid me, and handed over money which had been given to him to transmit. In witness of which I sign this at the Bourg of Chamonix, this 18th of October, 1786, in presence of the undersigned witnesses."
JACQUES BALMAT.
"Counter-signed by Joseph Pot and Joseph Marie Crussa, the requisite witnesses, called expressly."

———

SECOND TESTIMONY OF THE AFORESAID J. BALMAT.

"I, the undersigned, certify having received of Dr. Paccard a new crown on the part of the Baron de Gersdorf, on August 10, 1786, at the same time as my wage.
JACQUES BALMAT.
"Chamonix, 25th of March, 1787."

It must be taken for granted that Balmat actually signed these documents, but the question arises, did he know what he was signing? Their obvious aim is the glorification of Paccard. From first to last it is Paccard who said this or did that. The merit of having pointed out and led the way, and the honour of first reaching the summit, are declared to be his. It is Paccard who helps and encourages Balmat, not Balmat who assists the doctor. If one believes Balmat, the village doctor cut a sorry figure on

60

Mont Blanc. If one credits Paccard, the part taken by Balmat was quite subordinate. Though these curious documents may have answered their purpose at the time of publication, posterity has not estimated Paccard so highly as he might have wished. A monument has been raised in Chamonix to Balmat, and another to De Saussure. Whilst their names are remembered with gratitude, that of the village doctor is well-nigh forgotten; and, if one were to make inquiries about him, it is more than likely that the answer would be, "Who is this Doctor Paccard?"[11]

—1786

Notes

1. This is now termed the *"ancien passage"* (*i.e.*, the old way).

2. The Rocher Rouge is the great cliff. Its situation in relation to the summit will be understood by reference to a large engraving of Mont Blanc from the Brevent.

3. It is to be remarked, however, that Chamonix cannot be seen from the Grand Plateau.

4. The account that follows of the ascent with Paccard is principally taken from the relation of it which was given by Balmat to Alexandre Dumas in 1832, forty-six years after the event.

5. The Grands Mulets is the name given to the first little group of Aiguilles which appear through the ice, above the Montagne de la Côte.

6. Balmat disposes of the greater part of the ascent in half-a-dozen lines. The Petits Mulets (as the rocks to which he refers are now termed) are a small patch only 350 feet below the summit, 600 feet above the top of the Rochers Rouges, and about 5300 feet above the Grands Mulets.

7. Before leaving Chamonix, they had told a *marchande de sirop* to look out for them, near the top of the mountain, at a certain time.

8. The original letter *from* De Saussure was recently, and I suppose is still, in existence. It was given by Mons. Edward Tairraz to the late Mr. Albert Smith. The letter *to* De Saussure, advising him that Mont Blanc had been ascended, was written by Jean Pierre Tairraz, who kept a little inn.

9. The first route has been improved upon, and to some extent has been superseded. The usual course is to proceed from Chamonix (3445 feet) to the Pierre Pointue (6723). So far there is a mule path. From the Pierre Pointue to the spot called Pierre l'Echelle (7910), at the edge of the right bank of the Glacier des Bossons, there is a rough path. The Glacier des Bossons is then crossed to the rocks called the Grands Mulets (10,113), and there the original route is taken up, and followed so far as the Grand Plateau (about 12,900). Balmat's route is then departed from, and there are two ways, which are used about equally—one by the ridge of the Bosses, and the other by what is termed "the Corridor"—a steep bank of glacier leading from a break in the Mont Maudit ridge down to the Grand Plateau. Those who ascend by the latter way take up Balmat's route again upon reaching the top of the Rochers Rouges.

10. Hence it appears that the anonymous article was written by Dr. Paccard.

11. Dr. Paccard continued to live at Chamonix for many years, and is referred to in several of the accounts of early ascents of Mont Blanc. At the conclusion of the famous interview between Alexandre Dumas and Balmat in 1832 the former enquired:

"'Et le docteur Paccard, est-il resté aveugle?'

'Ah! oui, aveugle! Il est mort il y a onze mois, à l'âge de soixante-dix-neuf ans, et il lisait encore sans ses lunettes. Seulement il avait les yeux diablement rouges.'

'Des suites de son ascension?'

'Oh! que non!'

'Et de quoi alors?'

'Le bonhomme levait un peu le coude.'"

Percy Bysshe Shelley

"Mont Blanc: Lines Written in the Vale of Chamouni"

A graduate of Eton College, Percy Bysshe Shelley (1792–1822) was later expelled from Oxford University, along with Thomas Hogg, for writing The Necessity of Atheism. *This disgrace, along with Shelley's elopement with Harriet Westbrook, alienated him further from his wealthy family. After leaving England, Shelley traveled throughout Europe and became involved in radical politics, while writing a steady stream of plays, poems, and pamphlets. In 1814, Shelley eloped with Mary Godwin, the author of* Frankenstein, *and Harriet drowned herself in 1816. Shelley's enduring poem on "Mont Blanc" represents the greatest tribute to the Arve Ravine and western Europe's highest mountain. Shelley wrote "Mont Blanc" during a summer excursion with Lord Byron in Geneva. The poem was published in a collaborative volume of Shelley's and Mary Shelley's writings entitled* History of a Six Weeks Tour. *An example of the awakening of the aesthetic sublime in romantic poetics, Shelley's lines inspired a school of mountain poetry and literature. Shelley drowned in a shipwreck near Livorno, Tuscany, in 1822.*

I.

The everlasting universe of things
Flows through the mind, and rolls its rapid waves,
Now dark—now glittering—now reflecting gloom—
Now lending splendour, where from secret springs
The source of human thought its tribute brings
Of waters,—with a sound but half its own,
Such as a feeble brook will oft assume
In the wild woods, among the mountains lone,
Where waterfalls around it leap for ever,
Where woods and winds contend, and a vast river
Over its rocks ceaselessly bursts and raves.

II.

Thus thou, Ravine of Arve—dark, deep Ravine—
Thou many-coloured, many-voiced vale,

Percy Bysshe Shelley, "Mont Blanc: Lines Written in the Valley of Chamouni," in Mary Shelley, *History of a Six Weeks Tour* (London: T. Hookham, 1817).

Over whose pines, and crags, and caverns sail
Fast cloud shadows and sunbeams: awful scene,
Where Power in likeness of the Arve comes down
From the ice gulphs that gird his secret throne,
Bursting through these dark mountains like the flame
Of lightning thro' the tempest;—thou dost lie,
Thy giant brood of pines around thee clinging,
Children of elder time, in whose devotion
The chainless winds still come and ever came
To drink their odours, and their mighty swinging
To hear—an old and solemn harmony;
Thine earthly rainbows stretched across the sweep
Of the ethereal waterfall, whose veil
Robes some unsculptured image; the strange sleep
Which when the voices of the desart fail
Wraps all in its own deep eternity;—
Thy caverns echoing to the Arve's commotion,
A loud, lone sound no other sound can tame;
Thou art pervaded with that ceaseless motion,
Thou art the path of that unresting sound—
Dizzy Ravine! and when I gaze on thee
I seem as in a trance sublime and strange
To muse on my own separate phantasy,
My own, my human mind, which passively
Now renders and receives fast influencings,
Holding an unremitting interchange,
With the clear universe of things around;
One legion of wild thoughts, whose wandering wings
Now float above thy darkness, and now rest
Where that or thou art no unbidden guest,
In the still cave of the witch Poesy,
Seeking among the shadows that pass by
Ghosts of all things that are, some shade of thee,
Some phantom, some faint image; till the breast
From which they fled recalls them, thou art there!

III.

Some say that gleams of a remoter world
Visit the soul in sleep,—that death is slumber,
And that its shapes the busy thoughts outnumber
Of those who wake and live.—I look on high;

Has some unknown omnipotence unfurled
The veil of life and death? or do I lie
In dream, and does the mightier world of sleep
Spread far around and inaccessibly
Its circles? For the very spirit fails,
Driven like a homeless cloud from steep to steep
That vanishes among the viewless gales!
Far, far above, piercing the infinite sky,
Mount Blanc appears,—still, snowy, and serene—
Its subject mountains their unearthly forms
Pile around it, ice and rock; broad vales between
Of frozen floods, unfathomable deeps,
Blue as the overhanging heaven, that spread
And wind among the accumulated steeps;
A desart peopled by the storms alone,
Save when the eagle brings some hunter's bone,
And the wolf tracts her there—how hideously
Its shapes are heaped around! rude, bare, and high,
Ghastly, and scarred, and riven.—Is this the scene
Where the old Earthquake-dæmon taught her young
Ruin? Were these their toys? Or did a sea
Of fire, envelope once this silent snow?
None can reply—all seems eternal now.
The wilderness has a mysterious tongue
Which teaches awful doubt, or faith so mild,
So solemn, so serene, that man may be
But for such faith with nature reconciled;
Thou hast a voice, great Mountain, to repeal
Large codes of fraud and woe; not understood
By all, but which the wise, and great, and good
Interpret, or make felt, or deeply feel.

IV.

The fields, the lakes, the forests, and the streams,
Ocean, and all the living things that dwell
Within the dædal earth; lightning, and rain,
Earthquake, and fiery flood, and hurricane,
The torpor of the year when feeble dreams
Visit the hidden buds, or dreamless sleep
Holds every future leaf and flower;—the bound
With which from that detested trance they leap;

The works and ways of man, their death and birth,
And that of him and all that his may be;
All things that move and breathe with toil and sound
Are born and die; revolve, subside and swell.
Power dwells apart in its tranquillity
Remote, serene, and inaccessible:
And *this*, the naked countenance of earth,
On which I gaze, even these primæval mountains
Teach the adverting mind. The glaciers creep
Like snakes that watch their prey, from their far fountains
Slow rolling on; there, many a precipice,
Frost and the Sun in scorn of mortal power
Have piled: dome, pyramid, and pinnacle,
A city of depth, distinct with many a tower
And wall impregnable of beaming ice.
Yet not a city, but a flood of ruin
Is there, that form the boundaries of the sky
Rolls its perpetual stream; vast pines are strewing
Its destined path, or in the mangled soil
Branchless and shattered stand; the rocks, drawn down
From yon remotest waste, have overthrown
The limits of the dead and living world,
Never to be reclaimed. The dwelling-place
Of insects, beasts, and birds, becomes its spoil;
Their food and their retreat for ever gone,
So much of life and joy is lost. The race
Of man, flies far in dread; his work and dwelling
Vanish, like smoke before the tempest's stream,
And their place is not known. Below, vast caves
Shine in the rushing torrent's restless gleam,
Which from those secret chasms in tumult welling
Meet in the vale, and one majestic River,
The breath and blood of distant lands, for ever
Rolls its loud waters to the ocean waves,
Breathes its swift vapours to the circling air.

V.

Mont Blanc yet gleams on high:—the power is there,
The still and solemn power of many sights,
And many sounds, and much of life and death.
In the calm darkness of the moonless nights,

In the lone glare of day, the snows descend
Upon that Mountain; none beholds them there,
Nor when the flakes burn in the sinking sun,
Or the star-beams dart through them:—Winds contend
Silently there, and heap the snow with breath
Rapid and strong, but silently! Its home
The voiceless lightning in these solitudes
Keeps innocently, and like vapour broods
Over the snow. The secret strength of things
Which governs thought, and to the infinite dome
Of heaven is as a law, inhabits thee!
And what were thou, and earth, and stars, and sea,
If to the human mind's imaginings
Silence and solitude were vacancy?

—June 23, 1816

Lord Byron (George Gordon)

"Lachin y Gair" and "When I Roved a Young Highlander"

Although born in London in 1788, Lord Byron (1788–1824) moved to Aberdeen, Scotland, with his mother in 1790 to escape his profligate father Captain John Byron, Jr. Byron fell into unexpected wealth after his father died on the continent and he inherited his Great Uncle William's estate and title at age ten, becoming the sixth Lord Byron. Byron attended Cambridge University and took up his hereditary seat in the House of Lords in 1809. After a world tour of Spain, Turkey, and Greece, he published part of one of his most successful poems, Childe Harold's Pilgrimage *in 1812. Byron's best-known poem is* Don Juan, *a satiric look at English society. In the midst of rumors of improprieties with his half sister Augusta Leigh, he left England for Geneva, Switzerland. The Bernese Alps formed the backdrop for Byron's romantic drama* Manfred. *By 1823 he had become heavily involved in the Greek movement for independence from Turkey. He died at Missolonghi in 1824 while helping to prepare Greek soldiers for the war. Although he never returned to England after 1816, Byron frequently recalled his beloved Scottish highlands in such poems as "Lachin y Gair" and "When I Roved a Young Highlander."*

"LACHIN Y GAIR"

Away, ye gay landscapes, ye gardens of roses!
In you let the minions of luxury rove;
Restore me the rocks where the snow-flake reposes,
Though still they are sacred to freedom and love.
Yet, Caledonia, beloved are thy mountains,
Round their white summits though elements war;
Though cataracts foam 'stead of smooth-flowing fountains,
I sigh for the valley of dark Loch na Garr.

Ah! There my young footsteps in infancy wander'd;
My cap was the bonnet, my cloak was the plaid;
On chieftains long perish'd my memory ponder'd,
As daily I strode through the pine-cover'd glade:

Lord Byron (George Gordon), "Lachin y Gair" and "When I Roved a Young Highlander," *Byron's Complete Poetical Works* (Cambridge: Riverside Press, 1905).

I sought not my home til the day's dying glory
Gave place to the rays of the bright polar star;
For fancy was cheer'd by traditional story,
Disclosed by the natives of dark Loch na Garr.

'Shades of the dead! have I not heard your voices
Rise on the night-rolling breath of the gale?'
Surely the soul of the hero rejoices,
And rides on the wind, o'er his own Highland vale.
Round Loch na Garr while the stormy mist gathers,
Winter presides in his cold icy car:
Clouds there encircle the forms of my fathers;
They dwell in the tempests of dark Loch na Garr.

'Ill-starr'd, though brave, did no visions foreboding
Tell you that fate had forsaken your cause?'
Ah! were you destined to die at Culloden,
Victory crown'd not your fall with applause:
Still were you happy in death's earthy slumber,
You rest with your clan in the caves of Braemar;
The pibroch resounds, to the piper's loud number,
Your deeds on the echoes of dark Loch na Garr.

Years have roll'd on, Loch na Garr, since I left you,
Years must elapse ere I tread you again:
Nature of verdure and flow'rs has bereft you,
Yet still are you dearer than Albion's plain.
England! thy beauties are tame and domestic
To one who has roved on the mountains afar:
Oh for the crags that are wild and majestic!
The steep frowning glories of dark Loch na Garr!

"WHEN I ROVED A YOUNG HIGHLANDER"

When I roved a young Highlander o'er the dark heath,
And climb'd thy steep summit, oh Morven of snow!
To gaze on the torrent that thunder'd beneath,
Or the mist of the tempest that gather'd below,
Untutor'd by science, a stranger to fear,
And rude as the rocks where my infancy grew,
No feeling, save one, to my bosom was dear;
Need I say, my sweet Mary,[1] 't was centered in you?

Yet it could not be love, for I knew not the name,—
What passion can dwell in the heart of a child?
But still I perceive an emotion the same
As I felt, when a boy, on the crag-cover'd wild:
One image alone on my bosom impress'd,
I loved my bleak regions, nor panted for new;
And few were my wants, for my wishes were bless'd;
And pure were my thoughts, for my soul was with you.
I arose with the dawn; with my dog as my guide,
From mountain to mountain I bounded along;
I breasted the billows of Dee's rushing tide,
And heard at a distance the Highlander's song:
At eve, on my heath-cover'd couch of repose,
No dreams, save of Mary, were spread to my view;
And warm to the skies my devotions arose,
For the first of my prayers was a blessing on you.

I left my bleak home, and my visions are gone;
The mountains are vanish'd, my youth is no more;
As the last of my race, I must wither alone,
And delight but in days I have witness'd before:
Ah! splendour has raised, but embitter'd, my lot;
More dear were the scenes which my infancy knew:
Though my hopes may have fail'd, yet they are not forgot;
Though cold is my heart, still it lingers with you.

When I see some dark hill point its crest to the sky,
I think of the rocks that o'ershadow Colbleen;
When I see the soft blue of a love-speaking eye,
I think of those eyes that endear'd the rude scene;
When, haply, some light-waving locks I behold,
That faintly resemble my Mary's in hue,
I think on the long flowing ringlets of gold,
The locks that were sacred to beauty, and you.

Yet the day may arrive when the mountains once more
Shall rise to my sight in their mantles of snow;
But while these soar above me, unchanged as before,
Will Mary be there to receive me?—ah, no!
Adieu, then, ye hills where my childhood was bred!
Thou sweet flowing Dee, to thy waters adieu!
No home in the forest shall shelter my head,—
Ah, Mary! What home could be mine but with you?

—c. 1820

Note

1. The "Mary" of this poem is not Mrs. Chaworth Musters, nor is it his distant cousin Mary Duff, but the daughter of James Robertson, of the farmhouse of Ballatrich on Deeside.

Matthew Arnold

"Stanzas in Memory of the Author of Obermann"

Matthew Arnold (1822–1888) was an influential Victorian literary critic, poet, and educational reformer. He published several volumes of poetry, but spent most of his career as a school inspector in the British Isles. He also served from 1857 to 1867 as a professor of poetry at Oxford University, where he had obtained his degree. Arnold composed a substantial number of critical essays, including his still widely read Culture and Anarchy, *in which he divided British society into social groups he called Philistines, Barbarians, and the Populace. Arnold made several trips (both for business and pleasure) to the Swiss Alps, though a childhood weakness in his legs prevented him from becoming a serious climber. He was, of course, influenced by the recent popularity of the new sport of mountain climbing as well as by romantic mountain literature such as Byron's* Manfred *and Shelley's poems on Mont Blanc. Arnold's poem is dedicated to Etienne Pivert de Senancour, the author of* Obermann, *the story of an Alpine philosopher who retreats to the mountains for Stoic meditation and spiritual redemption. Arnold's poem revisits many of the themes of Senancour's work. Several years later, Arnold wrote a companion poem on the same topic entitled "Obermann Once More."*

"STANZAS IN MEMORY OF THE AUTHOR OF *OBERMANN*"

November, 1849.

In front the awful Alpine track
Crawls up its rocky stair;
The autumn storm-winds drive the rack,
Close o'er it, in the air.

Behind are the abandon'd baths
Mute in their meadows lone;
The leaves are on the valley paths,
The mists are on the Rhone—

The white mists rolling like a sea!
I hear the torrents roar.

Matthew Arnold, "Stanzas in Memory of the Author of *Obermann*" (1849), *Poems*, vol. 2 (London: Macmillan and Co., 1877).

—Yes, Obermann, all speaks of thee;
I feel thee near once more!

I turn thy leaves! I feel their breath
Once more upon me roll;
That air of languor, cold, and death,
Which brooded o'er thy soul.

Fly hence, poor wretch, whoe'er thou art,
Condemn'd to cast about,
All shipwreck in thy own wear heart,
For comfort from without!

A fever in these pages burns
Beneath the calm they feign;
A wounded human spirit turns,
Here, on its bed of pain.

Yes, though the virgin mountain-air
Fresh through these pages blows;
Though to these leaves the glaciers spare
The soul of their white snows;

Though here a mountain-murmur swells
Of many a dark-bough'd pine;
Though, as you read, you hear the bells
Of the high-pasturing kine—

Yet, through the hum of torrent lone,
And brooding mountain-bee,
There sobs I know not what ground-tone
Of human agony.

Is it for this, because the sound
Is fraught too deep with pain,
That, Obermann! the world around
So little loves thy strain?

Some secrets may the poet tell,
For the world loves new ways;
To tell too deep ones is not well—
It knows now what he says.

BECAUSE IT'S THERE

Yet, of the spirits who have reign'd
In this our troubled day,
I know but two, who have attain'd,
Save thee, to see their way.

By England's lakes, in grey old age,
His quiet home one keeps;
And one, the strong much-toiling sage,
In German Weimar sleeps.

But Wordsworth's eyes avert their ken
From half of human fate;
And Goethe's course few sons of men
May think to emulate.

For he pursued a lonely road,
His eyes on Nature's plan;
Neither made man too much a God,
Nor God too much a man.

Strong was he, with a spirit free
From mists, and sane, and clear;
Clearer, how much! than ours—yet we
Have a worse course to steer.

For though his manhood bore the blast
Of a tremendous time,
Yet in a tranquil world was pass'd
His tenderer youthful prime.

But we, brought forth and rear'd in hours
Of change, alarm, surprise—
What shelter to grow ripe is ours?
What leisure to grow wise?

Like children bathing on the shore,
Buried a wave beneath,
The second wave succeeds, before
We have had time to breathe.

Too fast we live, too much are tried,
Too harass'd, to attain

Wordsworth's sweet calm, or Goethe's wide
And luminous view to gain.

And then we turn, thou sadder sage,
To thee! we feel thy spell!
—The hopeless tangle of our age,
Thou too hast scann'd it well!

Immoveable thou sittest, still
As death, composed to bear!
Thy head is clear, thy feeling chill,
And icy thy despair.

Yes, as the son of Thetis said,
One hears thee saying now:
Greater by far than thou are deud;
Strive not! die also thou!

Ah! two desires toss about
The poet's feverish blood;
One drives him to the world without,
And one to solitude.

The glow, he cries, *the trill of life,*
Where, where do these abound?—
Not in the world, not in the strife
Of men, shall they be found.

He who hath watch'd, not shared, the strife,
Knows how the day hath gone.
He only lives with the world's life,
Who hath renounced his own.

To thee we come, then! Clouds are roll'd
Where thou, O seer! art set;
Thy realm of thought is drear and cold—
The world is colder yet!

And thou hast pleasures, too, to share
With those who come to thee—

BECAUSE IT'S THERE

Balms floating on thy mountain-air,
And healing sights to see.

How often, where the slopes are green
On Jaman, hast thou sate
By some high chalet-door, and seen
The summer-day grow late;

And darkness steal o'er the wet grass
With the pale crocus starr'd,
And reach that glimmering sheet of glass
Beneath the piny sward,

Lake Leman's waters, far below!
And watch'd the rosy light
Fade from the distant peaks of snow;
And on the air of night

Heard accents of the eternal tongue
Through the pine branches play—
Listen'd, and felt thyself grow young!
Listen'd, and wept—Away!

Away the dreams that but deceive!
And thou, sad guide, adieu!
I go, fate drives me; but I leave
Half of my life with you.

We, in some unknown Power's employ,
Move on a rigorous line;
Can neither, when we will, enjoy,
Nor, when we will, resign.

I in the world must live;—but thou,
Thou melancholy shade!
Wilt not, if thou can'st see me now,
Condemn me, nor upbraid.

For thou art gone away from earth,
And place with those dost claim,

The Children of the Second Birth,
Whom the world could not tame;

And with that small, transfigured band,
Whom many a different way
Conducted to their common land,
Thou learn'st to think as they.

Christian and pagan, king and slave,
Soldier and anchorite,
Distinctions we esteem so grave,
Are nothing in their sight.

They do not ask, who pined unseen,
Who was on action hurl'd,
Whose one bond is, that all have been
Unspotted by the world.

There without anger thou wilt see
Him who obeys thy spell
No more, so he but rest, like thee,
Unsoil'd;—and so, farewell!

Farewell!—Whether thou now liest near
That much-loved inland sea,
The ripples of whose blue waves cheer
Vevey and Meillerie;

And in that gracious region bland,
Where with clear-rustling wave
The scented pines of Switzerland
Stand dark round thy green grave,

Between the dusty vineyard-walls
Issuing on that green place
The early peasant still recalls
The pensive stranger's face,

And stoops to clear thy moss-grown date
Ere he plods on again;—

BECAUSE IT'S THERE

Or whether, by maligner fate,
Among the swarms of men,

Where between granite terraces
The blue Seine rolls her wave,
The Capital of Pleasure sees
Thy hardly-heard-of grave;—

Farewell! Under the sky we part,
In this stern Alpine dell.
O unstrung will! O broken heart!
A last, a last farewell!

—1849

Alfred Wills

from *Wanderings among the High Alps*

Alfred Wills (1828–1912) was an English judge and also the first to reach the top of the Wetterhorn from Grindelwald. Wills's party was constantly shadowed by another uninvited group. Wills was incensed that the rival party was trying to beat them to the top. The groups entered within speaking distance on the mountain and almost came to blows, but the mysterious expedition (consisting of several chamois hunters and the Alpine guides Christian Almer and Ulrich Kaufmann) agreed to let Wills capture the honors. When Wills arrived near the top, he was shocked to find another flag within ten feet of the summit—the earlier party apparently having been defeated by a difficult cornice. Wills's party surmounted the difficulty and was the first men to set foot on the top. A dangerous descent of the mountain followed, with an unplanned glissade down the icy slopes.

ASCENT OF THE WETTERHORN

Thou wert to me,
That minute, with thy brow in Heaven,
As sure a sign of Deity
As e'er to mortal man was given.
Nor ever, were I destined yet
To live my life twice o'er again,
Can I the deep-felt awe forget—
The ecstasy that filled me then! MOORE.

J'avoue, que si l'on m'avait demandé mon opinion sur la possibilité d'escalader le Wetterhorn de ce côté, j'aurais vraisemblablement déclaré la chose impossible.—DESOR.

———

I admit that if one had asked for my opinion on scaling the Wetterhorn from this side, I truly would have declared it to be impossible.

———

Alfred Wills, *Wanderings among the High Alps* (London: Richard Bentley, 1856).

RESOLUTION TO ASCEND THE WETTERHORN—"SAMPSON"—LAUENER—START FROM GRINDELWALD—DESCRIPTION OF THE WETTERHORN—BOHREN—THE ENGE—THE FLAG— SALUTE FROM BELOW—SUNSET—NIGHT ENCAMPMENT—UNCOMFORTABLE QUARTERS— SOLEMN SCENE—EARLY MORNING—ROCK DIFFICULTIES—THE UPPER PLATEAU—PIRATES— THE LAST ROCKS—HAZARDOUS ASCENT—OVERHANGING CORNICE—STARTLING ARRIVAL AT THE SUMMIT—NARROW EDGE—MAGNIFICENT PANORAMA—SEEN FROM GINDELWALD— PLANTING THE FLAG AND THE FIR-TREE—FAILURE OF PREVIOUS ATTEMPTS—AWFUL DE- SCENT—"TO THE HEALTH OF THE WETTERHORN"—A RACE ON THE ROCKS AND A ROLL ON THE ICE—TROUBLESOME FLOCK OF SHEEP—FEU DE JOIE—SAFE ARRIVAL—BLACK FACES— EXCITEMENT AT GRINDELWALD—REMARKS.

———

Towards the end of my tour in 1854, I was anxious to make some more considerable glacier expedition than I had been able to effect during the course of that journey. We were staying at Interlaken; and, as I gazed upon the graceful form of the Jungfrau, which rose opposite the window at which I sat, an irrepressible longing came over me to win that lofty and difficult summit, and look down upon the boundless prospect that must stretch on every side. I had crossed many a lofty Col, and wound my way among many a labyrinth of profound and yawning crevasses. I had slept on the moraine of a glacier, and on the rugged mountain side; but I had never yet scaled any of those snowy peaks which rise in tempting grandeur above the crests of Cols and the summits of the loftiest passes. The ascent of the Jungfrau would be an achievement that would worthily crown autumn's campaign. Took Balmat into my counsels; and he was de- lighted at the prospect. He could hardly conceal his satisfaction, though we agreed to say not a word about the matter, until all was in train; and, in the course of the evening, he came to me in great exultation. He had fallen in with a Chamouni friend, who had just terminated an engagement, and was about to return home. He was one of the best mountaineers that could be found, Balmat said; of great strength, endurance, courage and prudence, and well acquainted with the glaciers, and would be of the greatest serv- ice in any difficult expedition. He was going to stay a day or two at Interlaken, for the chance of further employment, and Balmat would take care not to lose sight of him. I went out and had a chat with him, and found him a man of great size and strength, with an air of modest self-reliance which promised well. His name was Auguste Si- mond; but it was not long before we altered it to Sampson, on account of his powerful frame. Balmat said he had seen him hold out a man at the end of his arm.

The next day, we made an excursion to Lauterbrunnen, to take counsel of Ulrich Lauener,[1] the most renowned guide of the Oberland, an elder brother of Christian who, two years before, had been my guide over the Tschingel pass. Unfortunately, he was gone to Grindelwald; and when we came back from a visit to the upper end of the valley, near the Schmadribach fall (an expedition perfectly practicable for ladies, and of no common interest), he was still absent. We, therefore, left word for him to come the next day to Interlaken, and seek us at the Hôtel de la Jungfrau. Accordingly, the following afternoon, on returning from the Giesbach Falls, we saw a tall, straight, active, knowing-looking fellow, with a cock's feather stuck jauntily in his high-crowned hat, whom I recognized at once as possessing the true Lauener cut, perched on the railings in front of the hotel, lazily dangling his long legs in the air. He was soon closeted with us, and questioned as to the possibility of ascending the Jungfrau. It could be done, he said, but would take six days, as we must go, by way of the Grimsel, to the back of the chain and ascend from the chalets of Merglen. This was an expenditure of time I was not prepared for; and I asked if we could not mount from the side of the Grimsel. He said it was possible in the height of summer, but not now; it was too late in the season. I asked if it could not be compassed, by taking proper measures. He replied by an expressive shake of the head, and a "Nein, nein, Herr; man muss zwei Nächte am Gletscher schlafen; und die Nächte sind zu länge; es macht sehr kalt am Eis." (No, no, Sir; you must sleep two nights on the glacier, and the nights are too long; it is very cold on the ice.) I knew something of what a night on the glacier meant, and could quite believe that, with the scanty stock of appliances we should be able to carry, and without the possibility of making a fire, the cold would probably be intolerable, and was reluctantly obliged to abandon the idea of reaching the summit of the Jungfrau, that year. I then asked him if we could attempt the Finster Aarhorn or the Schreckhorn; but he made the same objection. The autumn was too far advanced to sleep on a glacier, which we must do in either case. The Wetterhorn next occurred to me; and I asked him if that were practicable. He answered with a ready "Ja, ja, Herr," adding that no one had yet succeeded in the ascent;[2] but he thought it was possible, and at all events worth the trial.

The resolution was quickly taken; and we appointed to meet Lauener the next day, towards noon, at Grindelwald, whither he was to proceed, early in the day, to make all necessary preparations. The party was to consist of myself, with Lauener, Balmat and Simond for guides; and I gave Lauener authority to engage a porter, should he find it necessary so to do, to help in conveying to our sleeping-place whatever might be required. My wife was to stay with her brother, for that night, at Grindelwald, where we hoped to rejoin them the next evening. Sampson was now spoken to, and retained; and, with a caution to the men to drop no hint of our project at Interlaken, for fear we should ignominiously fail, we parted till the morrow.

Next morning (16th September, 1854), we started from Interlaken about eight, and proceeded by voiture to Grindelwald, which we found already full of the bustle of preparation. Many idlers were lounging about the doors of the inn, waiting our arrival; and the guides' room was full of people smoking, chattering, and crowding about Lauener, who was packing a great basket with ropes, crampons, and other necessaries for an excursion of this sort. He called me aside, and begged permission to retain another guide, one Peter Bohren, of Grindelwald, who he said had been three times this season to the plateau out of which the peaks of the Wetterhörner spring, and would, therefore, prove a valuable auxiliary. I was somewhat annoyed at having this additional expense put upon me, but did not like to oppose the wishes of the leading guide in such

81

a matter, and assented; so that I had four guides, besides which, we were obliged to hire a porter, as there was much to carry, making our party six in all. I ordered dinner for ourselves; and while it was getting ready, went again to look at the preparations. I was a little staggered at their magnitude, and at the serious air of the men, who were far more grave and quiet than is usual on such occasions; and I heard so much on every side of the difficulties and dangers we were to encounter, that I almost began to fear we were bent on a rash enterprize. However, I resolved we would run no foolish risks, and if we found the difficulties too great for us prudently to face, we would abandon the undertaking; but I was seriously afraid that, when I was gone, the people would alarm my wife with exaggerated accounts of the horrors of our track.

The Chamouni men, who do these things in a more quiet and business-like manner than their fellows of the Oberland, were quite disgusted with the noise and confusion. Balmat said they made his head ache; and Sampson applied himself assiduously to encourage my wife, assuring her with a seriousness and solemnity which made us all laugh, that he would answer for my safety with his own, and that, if we did not run into danger, danger would not come to us. Altogether, I was glad when the hour of departure arrived. The landlord wrung Balmat's hand, as we pushed our way through the crowd of loiterers, and issued from the inn. "Try," said he, "to return all of you alive; but—" he broke off, and shook his head gravely. Lauener and Bohren had pressed me to allow them to take a "Flagge" with them, to plant on the summit. I thought this seemed rather like a tempting of Nemesis, but yielded to their importunities; and they now told me it was not ready, and asked to wait for it. I inquired where it was being made, and was told, to my surprise, at the blacksmith's. It seemed an odd place to go to for a flag; but I supposed the blacksmith was some mechanic of a versatile genius, who would be applied to for everything out of the common way, and asked no more questions, but told them to stay behind for the flag, and overtake the rest of us; and then, bidding adieu to my wife and her brother, I set off at once, with Balmat and Sampson, very glad to escape the honours and inconveniences of distinction.

The Wetterhorn consists, speaking very generally, of a huge mass of rock, perpendicular on every side, except where it joins the chain which runs back towards the Grimsel and the main chain of the Bernese Oberland, of both of which it is a kind of outwork. Its precipices are tremendous; I know scarcely any to compare with them; they rise from the valley of Grindelwald in one abrupt and shaggy wall for thousands and thousands of feet; and are crowned by a vast plateau of snow, out of which spring three peaks—the Rosenhorn, nearest the Grimsel, the Mittelhorn and the Wetterhorn proper, which last overhangs the Great Scheideck pass, from Grindelwald to Meyringen, and on that side is, literally, one sheer precipice from the bottom nearly to the summit, which soars proudly aloft, in a sharp, snow-clad peak, that seems to defy approach. Whether this or the Mittelhorn be the higher, is a point as to which some doubts have been entertained. There is not much difference; but we all thought that what slight difference exists is in favour of the sharper and bolder summit of the Wetterhorn proper. It is of little consequence; but, from its position and the uninterrupted nature of the view on the northern side, there cannot be a doubt that the Wetterhorn commands a finer view. There can be as little doubt that it is far more difficult of approach. This was the peak we determined to assail.

The North-western and South-western faces of the mountain are nearly at right angles to one another; and beside the south-western precipices, the upper glacier of Grindelwald streams down to the valley, guarded on one side by the Wetterhorn, on the other by the scarcely less awful crags of the Mettenberg, a spur of the Shreckhorn. This glacier communicates with, and in fact descends from, the snowy plateau of the Wetterhorn. It pours round the interior extremity of the wall of rock described as forming one of its barriers, and which runs back from the valley of Grindelwald, till it loses itself in the general mass. The plateau of snow, seen from below, appears directly to overhang this flanking defence of the glacier; but, in reality, a broad and deep valley lies between them, the upper end of which is filled partly by a glacier descending from beneath the actual peak of the Wetterhorn, partly by a range of precipices, two or three thousand feet high which, though apparently inaccessible, afford the only means of attaining the plateau. These precipices and the adjoining glacier arc completely hidden from the spectator in the valley by the intervening ridge, which rises immediately above the glacier. In the hollow just described, we were to pass the night, and this spot, accordingly, formed the goal of our first day's journey. It was about five hours' walk from Grindelwald.

It was half past one when we left the door of the hotel; the sun was hot, and we walked slowly across the beautiful meadows which clothe the northern slopes of the valley of Grindelwald, and give to it that character of mingled loveliness and grandeur, for which it is so eminently distinguished, and in which, so far as I know, the valley of Fée is its only superior. Balmat and I chatted pleasantly on the many scenes of glory we had witnessed together in various parts of Switzerland and Sardinia; now and then, we cast an upward glance at the great peak before us, and wondered whether we should find more difficulty in scaling the Wetterhorn, than in descending the icy arête of the Findelen, whether we should be as well rewarded for our toil as we had been on that eventful day, and whether Lauener would prove as excellent a guide as our good friend of Saas. The moments flew quickly by, and in less than an hour we were overtaken by Bohren, who told us Lauener was still behind; but would soon be on our track.

A few minutes afterwards, we halted for a moment at a chalet near the foot of the glacier, where Bohren's father lived, with a number of his almost numberless progeny, all of whom came forth, and with much interest bid their brother and ourselves, God speed. Bohren took it all very philosophically, borrowed a better pipe than his own, and a larger stock of tobacco, and set off again, smoking like a chimney-pot. Passing the end of the glacier, we made, first of all, for the great wall of rock which forms the side of the Scheideck pass, and after scrambling some distance up its face, by inequalities of the surface scarcely perceptible from below, gained a narrow goat-walk (known as the Enge), which hugs the brink of terrible precipices, often but an inch or two from the path, and is itself surmounted by others equally formidable, the base of which we could sometimes almost touch with one hand, while a pebble dropped from the other would fall hundreds of feet before it touched the earth. The path, however, when you are on it, does not look so bad as this description might seem to imply; little tufts of grass and brushwood grow freely on the edge of the precipice, and conceal from the eye its depth and its perpendicularity. This wild track leads, with little ascent, for about half an hour, back, in a direction towards Grindelwald, till it arrives at the corner of the mountain, which is almost as square as if it were the work of the mason; it there takes a turn, and continues along the other face of the mountain, at right angles to its former course. At the angle, there was a little platform of sloping turf, just large enough for us all to lay ourselves down in the sunshine, while waiting for Lauener.

The view down the valley and towards the snowy heights beyond, with the cataract of ice beneath our feet, was abundantly striking; but my eye could not help wandering to the glittering spire of Grindelwald, as my imagination strove in vain to paint the scenes I should have gazed upon, before I was welcomed back again by those I had left behind me. While we lay on the grass, a magnificent avalanche came crashing down the precipices of the Shreckhorn, just across the glacier, and added to the great bank of dead white dust beneath, which told us that we looked upon a track which the avalanches were much wont to take. We had not long to wait; a loud, clear, ringing shout of greeting, and a cheery laugh announced the presence of Lauener; and it did not require two glances to show why he had sought the blacksmith for the "Flagge." Strapped on his back was a sheet of iron, three feet long and two feet wide, with two rings strongly welded to one of the shorter edges, and he stood leaning upon a bar of the same metal, ten or twelve feet long, and as thick as a man's thumb. He pointed, first to the "Flagge," and then with an exulting look on high, and set up a shout of triumph which made the rocks ring again. Bohren took up the note, and presently a chorus of wild shouts came faintly borne on the air from the valley below. It was Bohren's affectionate relatives, answering from the chalet at the foot of the glacier.

Balmat and Sampson were men of less boisterous spirit; and were far from delighted with either the "drapeau," or the shouting. Sampson went so far as to call the unwieldy iron machine, which cannot have weighed less than twenty or thirty pounds, a "bêtise" (which may be freely rendered "a confounded piece of nonsense"), and Balmat thought it would be time to shout when we were here again, the next evening, on our way down.

I could not help admiring Lauener's figure, as he stood there, straight as an arrow, more than six feet high, spare, muscular and active, health and vigour glowing in his open and manly countenance, his clear blue eyes sparkling with vivacity and good temper, a slight dash of rough and careless swagger in his attitude and manner, which suited well with the wild scenery around, and made him look like the genius of the place.

The path now directly overhangs the Upper Grindelwald glacier; for some distance you descend, in order to avoid a torrent which leaps down the precipices above, and which there is not room to pass, except near the edge of the glacier. After crossing this stream, you ascend by a bank of moraine, and afterwards, in a slanting direction, along the face of the cliff. The rock is marked in Desor's map as gneiss, but the footing is so bad, that I took it for limestone, which is the very worst of all rocks to walk over. It is slippery and deceptive, to a degree not readily understood by those who are not familiar with it. "Oh! le mauvais calcaire!" was an exclamation frequent enough on our lips, when compelled to walk in difficult places upon this treacherous stone. In many spots, steps had been hewn in the smooth slopes or slabs of gneiss, without which it would have been very difficult and dangerous to traverse them. As it was, we slipped uncomfortably often, and were very glad to reach a small shoulder of the mountain, round which the glacier comes pouring from the left, and which is covered with a rich carpet of luxuriant herbage, affording excellent pasturage to the numerous flocks which are driven hither, and into the valley behind, to fatten during the summer months. From this shoulder, we had a few minutes of very steep descent, and then passed beneath a ridge of rocks which support, like a terrace, the valley we were seeking. Several clear streams pour in beautiful showers, over the ledge thus formed. Above the head of one, a delicate rainbow played fitfully—a glory placed there by the Eternal hand. Further on, the ridge gave way to a bank of earth and boulder-stones, up which we climbed, and entered upon a turf slope, dotted with rocks rolled down from above, and occupying the bed of a broad valley. This valley was closed at the head by a glacier streaming from the base of the peak we aspired to climb, and by a wall of crags as hopeless, to all appearance, as the precipice of the Ghemmi. On our right was a range of lofty rocks, capped by the great plateau of ice, and on our left the ridge up whose opposite side we had fought our way, and behind which the glow of sunset had already flushed the western sky.

Half an hour's ascent over the herbage and among the boulders brought us to a stone under which we were to pass the night. It was a splendid wild scene—no distant prospect, but we were in the very heart of the crags and the ice—surrounded by some of the grandest glaciers, and precipices in the Alps. I climbed alone a neighbouring height; the glacier, by whose side we had ascended, lay white and cold at its base; but the tints of the evening sky over the mountains which border the valley of Lauterbrunnen were wonderfully rich, while every peak and glacier around was bathed in a flood of purple:

"O'er the vale
Light falls like a thick veil of golden motes,
And flings a glow, like a whole shower of roses,
Over the face of the vast precipice.[3]
No sight beside, no motion and no sound—
Silence, the desert, and that solemn height.

* * *

Heaven's eve, the failing sun,
Will soon be closed, and Darkness shall keep watch
Over her slumbering sister, Solitude."

85

I cast one look towards that majestic summit upon which I hoped, before tomorrow's sunset, to have stood, and returned to more practical cares and occupations, stimulated by a pleasing excitement, and filled with all that mingled wonder, delight and awe, which takes possession of the soul, when evening falls amidst the solemn silence of these Alpine fastnesses, and which no man can, or would, repress.

> Night opes the noblest scenes, and sheds an awe,
> Which gives these venerable scenes full weight,
> And due reception in the intender'd heart,

I found our sleeping-den to consist of a low, arched cave, formed by two or three rocks, one of which, somewhat hollow on the under side, had fallen curiously upon the others, so as to make a kind of vaulted roof. Two sides were supplied by the boulders on which it rested, and in the course of time, the earth had so accumulated about them, that all round their bases they were hermetically sealed, and the ground without was two or three feet higher than the floor of the cavern. Mould had also gathered about their points of contact, so that the holes and crannies were filled up, and the shelter was complete. Only one narrow entrance was left, and the care of the hunters had blocked this up with stones, which we removed. There was barely room for one to enter at a time, and we were obliged to creep backwards through the aperture. Within, the hunters, whose calling had led them to sleep in this natural chamber, had strewn the floor of earth with a thick covering of short mountain hay, which gave an unexpected look of warmth and comfort to the place. It was small enough for half a dozen men to sleep in; it was difficult to see how we should all pack; but at all events, we must try. Our first care—that is Balmat's and mine—was to inspect the blankets before it was quite dark; for we did not think it likely that mine host of Grindelwald, would have lent us his best and cleanest; and it turned out to be as well that we had done so. We were not left quite "all alone by ourselves," we found, when we came to lie down. Certain reminiscences of chalet life were obtruded upon us, as it was; but we should have been much worse off, if we had not made "la chasse" to begin with.

The men had brought up with them a stock of wood—for was none to be grubbed up here, as at the Tacul; and abundance of fresh water was supplied by a brawling glacier stream, which leaped and bounded over a rocky bed, by the side of our queer little hut. A fire was lighted outside, and some good black coffee made. The supper was not so luxurious as at the Tacul. We felt the want of that refinement of good cheer, which the company of a lady gives a fair excuse for indulging in. There was no boiled cream, or cold chicken, this time. A mug of coffee without milk, a hunch of cold veal, and a log of sour bread, carved with one's pocket knife, formed the evening repast. But it was a cheerful meal, and a hearty one, for all that; and the great, bright stars looked down upon us with a merry

86

twinkle in their roguish eyes, as if they too enjoyed the fun. There was no moon, and the vast, white glaciers gleamed faintly through the night, like the battlements of phantom-castles.

At length, the supper was over; the coffee pot and cups were rinsed clean in the noisy stream; the fire was carefully trodden out, that none of our scanty stock of fuel might be wasted; a light was struck; and one by one we entered the cavern, and laid ourselves down in our places. They gave me what they meant to be the place of honour—at the opposite extremity of the cavern, away from the entrance; but is was where the floor was highest, and the roof was lowest (and it was nowhere high enough for a man to stand upright). When we were all arranged, the candle was put out, and we were left in the thick darkness. Suddenly, the three Swiss struck up a hymn in German. They sang well; there was a good tenor and a rich, manly bass. The effect, in that strange place, in "darkness visible," couched as we were beneath the shadows of the eternal mountains, was inexpressibly solemn; when the song of praise was sung, no one spoke, and presently the deep breathing all around announced that most of them were sunk in sleep.

I must say, I was desperately uncomfortable; they had built up again the aperture by which we entered, and what with the smell of the hay, and the presence of so many persons, the air soon became insufferably hot and close; a great fellow (Lauener, I think) had laid his head on my feet, and when I moved further back to get rid of him, he followed, even in his sleep, and insisted upon using me for a pillow. I moved back half-a-dozen times, but invariably with the same result, and at length I was in the corner; I could retreat no further, the roof was cold and clammy, not six inches from my face, and the air stifling. Had I been near the entrance, I should have made my escape; but I could only do that, by walking over the prostrate bodies of four or five other men, in their first deep and sweet sleep, after a good day's work, and with we knew not what before them on the morrow. I waxed restless and feverish, and all chance of sleep deserted me. The cold veal seemed to rise up in judgment upon me; and I thought of "Pierre L'Echelle," and his potato supper. I passed a miserable night. I could not, however, fail to be struck with the solemnity of the place and time; all night long, I lay in palpable darkness, beneath a hollow rock, and on a bed of stones, with a foaming glacier torrent brawling past my head, not six feet from me, save for the noise of which, all nature was still and silent as the grave.

This profound tranquillity, however, was broken by frequent and startling interruptions;

> All in a moment, crash on crash,
> From precipice to precipice,
> An avalanche's ruins dash
> Down to the nethermost abyss,
> Invisible! The ear alone

Pursues the uproar, till it dies;
Echo to echo, groan to groan,
From deep to deep replies.

Silence again the darkness seals,
Darkness that may be felt.

It was eight o'clock, when we entered the cave: I lay uneasily for many hours, but at length I could endure it no longer; I spoke to Balmat, who was near me, and found he too was very uncomfortable, and we agreed to make our escape. We got across the sleepers, somehow, knocked out the stones, and emerged. Oh! How grateful was that cool fresh air! How refreshing that draught at the mountain torrent! The stars were shining as I never saw them before in my life, like so many balls of fire in the black concave; the glaciers were sparkling in the soft light of the waning moon, now in her fourth quarter. It was just two o'clock, but not cold, and a bracing air blew briskly, yet pleasantly, from the North-west. I had been up before the sun, many a morning, on many a mountain height, and had seen, I thought, almost every phase of Alpine night-scenery; but so beautiful a nocturnal view as this I never yet had beheld; it spoke well for the promise of the day. Presently, some of the men came out, a fire was kindled, and tea and coffee made. I stripped, and had a bathe in the dashing torrent; it was icy-cold, but did me more good than the weary night in the hole. Balmat and I were urgent with Lauener to start as early as possible, for we all expected a long day, and we wished to reach the snow while it was yet crisp; but he refused to start before half-past four, saying that in an hour we should reach the glacier, and that the moon was not bright enough to light us across it. It was still dark when, at the hour appointed we set off, and for some time we groped our way by the help of a lantern. During the first hour and a half, we mounted amongst a mass of débris, and amidst great boulders of rock, which lie below, or form part of, the terminal moraine of the glacier. It was disagreeable walking in the dark, and we were frequently stumbling and falling. Long before we reached the glacier, day had began to dawn, and a cold, clear grey was stealing over the sky.

"Lo! On the eastern summit, clad in grey,
Morn, like a horseman girt for travel, comes;
And from his tower of mist
Night's watchman hurries down."

I could not help thinking, despite Lauener's precautions, that we might perfectly well have traversed the glacier before daybreak, as there was but one crevasse of any magnitude, which we crossed without much difficulty. We were nearly an hour upon the ice, on leaving which we approached the abrupt wall of rock I have spoken of before, as affording the only means of access to the upper plateau. It turned out to be not

88

absolutely precipitous, but full of small ledges and steep slopes covered with loose stones and schisty débris, which gave way at every step. The substratum appeared to be a schistaceous gneiss, very friable and much disintegrated by the weather; so that every particle had to be tried, before it was safe to trust hand or foot to it. It was extremely steep; very often the ledges which gave us foot-hold were but an inch or two wide, and throughout, it was a marvel to me that rocks which, from a short distance off, looked such absolute precipices could be climbed at all. At length, we came to a very singular formation. Standing out from a nearly perpendicular wall of rock were a series of thin parallel wedges of rock, planted, with the thin edge upwards, at right angles to the body of the mountain, and separated from one another by deep intervening clefts and hollows. Each of these was two or three hundred feet in height, seventy or eighty in width at the base, but narrowing off to the thickness of a few inches, and presenting, at the top, a rough and jagged ridge, forty or fifty feet long, by which we must pass, to reach the plateau which lay just beyond. We first climbed to the top of one of these wedges, and then had to make our way along its crest.

It was nervous work; a good head, a stout heart, a steady hand and foot were needed. Lauener went first, carrying a rope, which was stretched by the side of the ridge, so as to form a protection to the next passer. Bohren went next; then came my own turn. It was certainly the worst piece of scrambling I ever did. The rock was much shattered by exposure to the frost and snow, and there was hardly a single immoveable piece, along the whole length. Every bit had to be tried before it was trusted to, and many were the fragments (some, as large as a shoulder of mutton, and something of that shape) which came out, when put to the test, and went crashing down till out of sight, making an avalanche of other stones as they fell. I passed my right arm over the top of the ridge, and thus secured myself, having the rock between that arm and my body, on one side, and the rope stretched below me, on the other. Every one had to pass much in the same way, and it was a long quarter of an hour before we were all safely landed on the snow beyond.

A few minutes later, we came to the brink of a precipice on the Grindelwald side, and here, for the first time to-day, we had a view of that rich and verdant valley, which looked lovelier than ever, by contrast with the desolation which surrounded us. We could not only distinguish the village, but, as we thought, the inn, which, with the telescope, we made out easily enough. It was from the brink of a dizzy height that we looked down; stones that we kicked over were out of sight in a moment, and were heard, at distant intervals, striking against the precipice as they fell, till the sound gradually died away in the silence of distance. A small quantity of black débris jutted out of the snow, upon which we sat down, at nine o'clock, to take our morning meal. I had been ill with indigestion, all the way up, but thanks to the fresh air of the mountains was at length recovering, and felt quite ready for a meal; but, to my mortification, I found all the meat they had brought tainted with garlic—the object of my peculiar detestation. I could not eat a mouthful, and a crust of bread, from time to time, with a cup of mingled wine and snow, was all my food throughout this laborious day.

At this spot, we left everything we had brought with us, except a flask of brandy and our alpenstocks. The sticks the Oberland men carried were admirably suited for their work. They were stout pieces of undressed wood, with the bark and knots still upon them, about four feet long, shod with a strong iron point at one end, and fixed at the other into a heavy iron head, about four inches long each way; one arm being a sharp spike, with which to hew out the ice, where needed, the other, wrought into a flat blade, with a broad point, something like a glazier's knife. This part of the instrument was extremely useful in climbing rocks. It ran into clefts and fissures too high to be accessible, or too small to admit the hand, and, once well planted, formed a secure and certain support. This kind of alpenstock is hardly ever seen at Chamouni. Our ice hatchet on the Col du Géant and the Col Imseng was perfectly different, though better adapted to the mere ice-work we had then to perform; and its great utility called forth repeated expressions of admiration from the Chamouni men, to whom it was new. The Swiss men put on their crampons and offered some to us; but we (that is, Balmat, Sampson and myself) preferred the double-headed points I have mentioned before, of which we had brought a stock from Chamouni, and which we screwed into our boots. Crampons are hardly safe things to wear, unless you are accustomed to them, and I found Balmat, who knew perfectly well how to use them, uniformly reject them. We now fastened ourselves all together with ropes, and commenced the last ascent. It lay near the edge of a long and steep arête, which connects the Mittelhorn with the Wetterhorn; at the place where we gained the plateau, the ridge was nearly level, but almost immediately began to rise sharply towards the peak. We were now at the back of the mountain, as seen from the valley of Grindelwald, which was, of course, completely hidden from the view. When we had stopped to take something to eat, we were at an extremity of the ridge which runs up to the actual summit, and, as it were, peeped round a corner. We were not to see the valley again, till we stood upon the summit.

The ascent was rapid, and commenced in deep snow; but it was not long before the covering of snow became thinner, and the slope more rapid, and every minute a step or two had to be cut. In this way, we zig-zagged onwards for nearly an hour, in the course of which we made, perhaps, a thousand feet of ascent, having the satisfaction, every time we could look round, to see a wider expanse of prospect risen into view. About ten o'clock, we reached the last rocks; which were a set of black, sloping, calcareous crags, whose inclination was hardly less than that of the glacier, left bare by the melting of the snow; they were much disintegrated by the weather, and the rough and shaly débris on their surface was, for the most part, soaked with the water that trickled from the snows above. Here we sat down and unharnessed ourselves. It was neither too hot nor too cold. A gentle breeze tempered the heat of the sun, which shone gloriously upon a sparkling sea of ice-clad peaks, contrasting finely with the deep blue of the cloudless heaven.

While we had been making our short halt at the edge of the plateau, we had been surprised to behold two other figures, creeping along the dangerous ridge of rocks we

90

had just passed. They were at some little distance from us, but we saw that they were dressed in the guise of peasants, and when we first perceived them, Lauener (who was a great hunter himself) shouted excitedly, "Gems-jägers!" but a moment's reflection convinced us that no chamois-hunter would seek his game in this direction; and immediately afterwards, we observed the one carried on his back a young fir tree, branches, leaves and all. We had turned aside a little to take our refreshment, and while we were so occupied, they passed us, and on our setting forth again, we saw them on the snow slopes, a good way ahead, making all the haste they could, and evidently determined to be the first at the summit. After all our trouble, expense and preparations, this excited the vehement indignation of my Chamouni guides—they declared that, at Chamouni, any one who should thus dog the heels of explorers and attempt to rob them of their well-earned honours would be scouted; nor were they at all satisfied with the much milder view which the Oberlanders took of the affair. The pacific Balmat was exceedingly wroth, and muttered something about "coups de poigns," and they at length roused our Swiss companions to an energetic expostulation. A great shouting now took place between the two parties, the result of which was, that the piratical adventurers promised to wait for us on the rocks above, whither we arrived very soon after them. They turned out to be two chamois-hunters, who had heard of our intended ascent, and resolved to be even with us, and plant their tree side by side with our "Flagge." They had started very early in the morning, had crept up the precipices above the upper glacier of Grindelwald, before it was light, had seen us soon after daybreak, followed on our trail, and hunted us down. Balmat's anger was soon appeased, when he found they owned the reasonableness of his desire that they should not steal from us the distinction of being *the first* to scale that awful peak, and instead of administering the fisticuffs he had talked about, he declared they were "bons enfants" after all, and presented them with a cake of chocolate; thus the pipe of peace was smoked, and tranquillity reigned between the rival forces.

Once established on the rocks, and released from the ropes, we began to consider our next operations. A glance upwards, showed that no easy task awaited us. In front rose a steep curtain of glacier, surmounted, about five or six hundred feet above us, by an overhanging cornice of ice and frozen snow, edged with a fantastic fringe of pendants and enormous icicles. This formidable obstacle bounded our view, and stretched from end to end of the ridge. What lay beyond it, we could only conjecture; but we all thought that it must be crowned by a swelling dome, which would constitute the actual summit. We foresaw great difficulty in forcing this imposing barrier; but after a short consultation, the plan of attack was agreed upon, and immediately carried into execution. Lauener and Sampson were sent forward to conduct our approaches which consisted of a series of short zig-zags, ascending directly from where we were resting to the foot of the cornice. The steep surface of the glacier was covered with snow; but it soon became evident that it was not deep enough to afford any material assistance. It was loose and uncompacted, and lay to the thickness of two or three inches only; so that every step had to be hewn, out of the solid ice. Lauener went first, and cut a hole just sufficient to afford him a foot-hold while he cut another. Sampson followed, and doubled the size of the step, so as to make a safe and firm resting-place. The line they took ascended, as I have said, directly above the rocks on which we were reclining, to the base of the overhanging fringe. Hence, the blocks of ice, as they were hewn out, rolled down upon us, and shooting past, fell over the brink of the arête by which we had been ascending, and were precipitated into a fathomless abyss beneath. We had to be on the *qui vive* to avoid these rapid missiles, which came accompanied by a very avalanche of dry and powdery snow. One, which I did not see in time, struck me a violent blow on the back of the head, which made me keep a better look out for its successors. I suggested, that they should mount by longer zig-zags, which would have the double advantage of sending the débris on one side, and of not filling up the footsteps already cut with the drifts of snow. Balmat's answer, delivered in a low, quiet tone, was conclusive. "Mais où tomberaient-ils, monsieur, si, par un malheur, ils glissaient? A présent, il y aurait la chance que nous pourrions les aider; mais si on glissait à côté—violà, monsieur!" pointing to a block of ice which passed, a little on one side, and bounded into the frightful gulf.

For nearly an hour, the men laboured intently at their difficult task, in which it was impossible to give them help; but, at length, they neared the cornice, and it was thought advisable that we should begin to follow them. Balmat went first, then I, then Bohren, and the two chamois hunters, who now made common cause with us, brought up the rear. We were all tied together. We had to clear out all the foot-holes afresh, as they were filled with snow. A few paces after starting, when we were clear of the rocks, I ascertained the angle of the slope, by planting my alpenstock upright, and measuring the distance from a given point in it to the slope, in two directions, vertically and horizontally. I found the two measurements exactly equal; so that the inclination of the glacier was 45°; but at every step it became steeper; and when, at length, we reached the others, and stood, on below another, close to the base of the cornice, the angle of inclination was between 60° and 70°! I could not help being struck with the marvellous beauty of the barrier which lay, still to be overcome, between us and the attainment of our hopes. The cornice curled over towards us, like the crest of a wave, breaking at irregular intervals along the line into pendants and inverted pinnacles of ice, many of which hung down to the full length of a tall man's height. They cast a ragged shadow on the wall of ice behind, which was hard and glassy, not flecked with a spot of snow, and blue as the "brave o'erhanging" of the cloudless firmament. They seemed the battlements of an enchanted fortress, framed to defy the curiosity of man, and to laugh to scorn his audacious efforts.

A brief parley ensued. Lauener had chosen his course well, and had worked up to the most accessible point along the whole line, where a break in the series of icicles allowed him to approach close to the icy parapet, and where the projecting crest was narrowest and weakest. It was resolved to cut boldly into the ice, and endeavour to hew deep enough to get a sloping passage on to the dome beyond. He stood close, not facing the parapet, but turned half round, and struck out as far away from himself as he could. A few strokes of his powerful arm brought down the projecting crest, which, after rolling a few feet, fell headlong over the brink of the arête, and was out of sight in an instant. We all looked on in breathless anxiety; for it depended upon the success of this assault, whether that impregnable fortress was to be ours, or whether we were to return, slowly and sadly, foiled by its calm and massive strength.

Suddenly, a startling cry of surprise and triumph rang through the air. A great block of ice bounded from the top of the parapet, and before it had well lighted on the glacier, Lauener exclaimed, "Ich schaue den blauen himmel!" (I see blue sky!) A thrill of astonishment and delight ran through our frames. Our enterprise had succeeded! We were almost upon the actual summit. That wave above us, frozen, as it seemed, in the act of falling over, into a strange and motionless magnificence, was the very peak itself! Lauener's blows flew with redoubled energy. In a few minutes, a practicable breach was made, through which he disappeared; and in a moment more, the sound of his axe was heard behind the battlement under whose cover we stood. In his excitement, he had forgotten us, and very soon the whole mass would have come crashing upon our head. A loud shout of warning from Sampson, who now occupied the gap, was echoed by five other eager voices, and he turned his energies in a safer direction. It was not long before Lauener and Sampson together had widened the opening; and then, at length, we crept slowly on. As I took the last step, Balmat disappeared from my sight; my left shoulder grazed against the angle of the icy embrasure, while, on the right, the glacier fell abruptly away beneath me, towards an unknown and awful abyss; a hand from an invisible person grasped mine; I stepped across, and had passed the ridge of the Wetterhorn!

The instant before, I have been face to face with a blank wall of ice. One step, and the eye took in a boundless expanse of crag and glacier, peak and precipice, mountain and valley, lake and plain. The whole world seemed to lie at my feet. The next moment, I was almost appalled by the awfulness of our position. The side he had come up was steep; but it was a gentle slope, compared with that which now fell away from where I stood. A few yards of glittering ice at our feet, and then, nothing between us and the green slopes of Grindelwald, nine thousand feet beneath. I am not ashamed to own that I experienced, as this sublime and wonderful prospect burst upon my view, a profound and almost irrepressible emotion—an emotion which, if I may judge by the low ejaculations of surprise, followed by a long pause of breathless silence, as each in turn stepped into the opening, was felt by others as well as myself. Balmat told me repeatedly, afterwards, that it was the most awful and startling moment he had known in the course of his long mountain experience. We felt as in the more immediate presence of Him who had reared this tremendous pinnacle, and beneath the "majestical roof" of whose deep blue Heaven we stood, poised, as it seemed, half way between the earth and sky.

In a few minutes, Lauener and Sampson had cut away a length of about ten feet of the overhanging cornice, and we hastened, for the sake of security, to place ourselves astride on the ridge that was exposed. It was a saddle, or more properly, a kind of knife-edge, of ice; I never sat on so narrow-backed a horse. We worked ourselves along this ridge, seated ourselves in a long row upon it, and untied the ropes. After a few minutes, when we had become more accustomed to the situation, I ventured to stand upright on that narrow edge—not four inches wide—and then, at length, I became fully aware of the extent and magnificence of the panorama. To the East and South lay a boundless sea of mighty peaks, stretching from the great Ortler Spitz, and his giant companions of the Tyrol, in the solemn distance, past the fine group of the Monte Leone, the many summits of Monte Rosa, and the sharp peak of the Weisshorn, towards the Western extremity of the Pennine chain. Mount Blanc was hidden behind the mountains of the Oberland, whose stupendous masses looked but a stone's throw from us. Between us and the far off snows of the Ortler Spitz, lay group behind group of the mountains of the Grisons and of Uri, green at the base, dark and craggy above, and capped by broken patches of glacier and snow, intersected by numerous deep and narrow valleys, at the foot of which tortuous mountain torrents and glacier streams glittered like silver threads.

The long range stretching back from the Wetterhorn towards the Grimsel seemed, from this point of view, to join on with the clustered peaks which lay beyond the valley of the Rhône. In this direction, we gazed upon an icy sea, in which scarcely one islet of rock was perceptible. The summit nearest to us was the Mittelhorn, seen edgeways, rising majestically, in a kind of half-dome, from the plateau, and connected with us by the arête along whose precipitous brink we had won our hard fought way. Immediately beneath this arête lay a fearful abyss, terminating in the upper basin of the glacier of Rosenlaui, broken and rifted into a chaos of crevasses, almost as formidable as those of the Col du Géant. It was all dazzling white, and there was a little to remind us of those exquisite deep blue vaults of transparent ice, for which of the lower end of the glacier is so justly celebrated.

The immediate group of the Oberland presented a scene of indescribable grandeur and sublimity. The Shreckhorn was the nearest of these mountains, a massive pyramid of gneiss, chequered with patches of snow and glacier, which clung to the ledges and lay amongst the recesses of its precipitous sides. Between this[4] and the Eiger was seen the magnificent amphitheatre of glacier and precipice—one of the finest in the Alps—which bounds, on the South-east, the plateau of the Lower Grindelwald glacier, marked by the sharp peaks of the Viescher Hörner; and then came the wedge-like form of the Eiger, rising in a thin slice a thousand feet above the height on which we stood. This mountain, too steep to allow more than a thin and broken coating of snow to rest upon its northern side, presents, from this point of view, a peculiarly majestic and imposing appearance. It appears to raise itself directly from the valley South of the Wengern Alp, and to shoot upward, almost in one unbroken and uniform plane, from the base to the summit. From this distance, it seemed as if anything let slip from the top would slide many thousands of feet, before it met with any obstacle to divert it, in the least, from its original direction.

The other mountains of the Bernese chain were nearly in a line with us and the Eiger, but we saw the graceful summit of the Jungfrau under a new and interesting aspect. The Silberhörner, instead of appearing, as they generally do, close to the face of the Jungfrau, and almost on the same line, stand boldly out as separate peaks, divided from the summit by a broad and deep valley of crag and ice.

Turning towards the North, we were greeted by a scene of pleasing contrast to this majestic, but desolate, spectacle. Far as the eye could reach or the mind could grasp, lay a vast expanse of verdure-covered mountains and fertile plains. A soft, rich green was the pervading colour of the landscape, and peace and plenty the prevailing ideas which it suggested. The heights above the valley of Lauterbrunnen, capped here and there with snow, lay next to the mighty barrier of ice and crag, which seemed to cry "Here shalt thou cease," to the wave of life and fertility which was borne upward towards it from the great plain of Switzerland, on the gradually increasing heights which border the Emmenthal, the valley of Lauterbrunnen and the Kanderthal. Conspicuous in the North-west, were the well-known and characteristic forms of the Niesen and the Stockhorn; then came the plain of Switzerland, bounded by the distant Jura,[5] the Lake of Thun, peacefully nestled beneath a chain of mountain ramparts, the fir-clad group about the Brünig, the Lakes of Lungern, Sarnen, Lucerne, Zug and Zürich, forming a chain of dark blue islands in that mighty ocean of green. The Righi was with some difficulty distinguished, amidst a multitude of summits of nearly equal altitude; to the East of which, the mountains rise again, and snow-capped peaks, in distant Schwyz and Glarus, mark the approach, in this direction, to the vast domains where frost and ice hold sway. I was very much struck with the nearer prospect eastward, where it was curious to look down into valley after valley, and follow them as on a map. We were so high that we could trace, in this manner, the course of pass after pass in several directions, from the foot of their ascent to the crest or col to which they led; many of them wound through valleys, both sides of which we could see from top to bottom. I never, from any other point, got so good an idea of the grouping of mountains, and of the manner in which the passes lie amongst them.

After all, however, the most interesting and striking part of the view lay nearer to us. It was impossible long to turn the eye from the fearful slope at the top of which we stood. For twenty or thirty yards below us, the glacier curved away steeper and steeper, until its rounded form limited our view, and prevented our seeing what shape it took, beneath. Nothing else broke the terrific void, and the next objects on which the eye rested were the green pastures of the Scheideck, nearly two miles of absolute depth below us. This was the prospect that had startled us so much, when we mounted the breach Lauener had effected, and made our hearts beat quicker with a solemn and strange emotion. The imagination shrank from contemplating the abyss, and picturing to itself the fearful precipices which must be beneath, to raise us to that dizzy height.

Further down the valley lay the peaceful Grindelwald, and I thought I could even distinguish the inn. We did not venture to use our telescopes, as we did not wish to run any chance of weakening the steadiness of the eye, on which we had still much to depend. I thought that, most probably, my wife and brother-in-law would be

95

watching from below, and I took off my hat and waved it many times round my head; the action, however, was not perceived; but they had recognized us, as we appeared on the summit, as was proved by their being able to tell us correctly in what order we arrived. The chamois hunters puzzled them dreadfully, and were a mystery to them, till we could explain the phenomenon; but the rest of us were easily distinguished. Sampson was the tallest and broadest, Bohren the shortest of the party, Balmat had a blouse, and I a pair of white flannel trousers.

The chamois hunters and Bohren, while I was standing up, began an unearthly series of yells, which broke discordantly upon the solemnity and silence of the scene; but the prudent Balmat instantly checked them, and I was glad of it, for the ringing shouts produced a strange and unpleasant effect upon the nerves, which must not now be disturbed unnecessarily. "Il ne faut jamais s'écrier dans les hautes sommités," was Balmat's comment; "on ne sait jamais ce qui peut arriver." Lauener did not need the caution; brave as a lion, active as a chamois, the best hunter and the best guide, in the Oberland, he could hardly conceal a strong emotion. Balmat assured me—and neither did he, nor do I, mention it as any disparagement to his manliness—he saw him, and felt him, tremble like a child, when he helped him through the gap. No wonder: his elder brother, Johann, who was reputed a more bold and adventurous mountaineer than even Ulrich, had perished, but a few months before, while hunting his favourite game, by slipping over the edge of a less dangerous precipice.

While I was standing on the ridge, where there was not room to place my two feet side by side, the guides were busy driving the long iron bar of the "Flagge" into the solid ice. I took my turn at it for a minute; it was planted five or six feet deep in the glacier, and seemed firm enough to defy the tempest, even at this aerial height; the broad sheet of iron was fitted in its place, resting on a rim in the staff, on which it played freely; and, finally, was secured with a nut, screwed on to the top. It was then turned towards Grindelwald, whence, as well as from all the country round, it long remained a conspicuous object. It was planted a few paces nearer to Grindelwald than the opening where the cornice was cut away, so as to have the white wall of snow behind for a background, by which means it was rendered far more easy to be seen. Side by side with it, the chamois hunters planted their green tree which had a strange appearance, as if it were growing vigorously out of a soil of ice. While standing up, I dropped a glove; it rolled for a few yards down the bank of glacier on the Grindelwald side, and there rested against a crust of snow. Despite my earnest requests, and even commands, to the contrary, Bohren insisted upon cutting his way down, and regaining it; a piece of folly and rashness of which I was an unwilling spectator.

When I sat down again, Balmat pointed out to me what I had not observed before—a flag just like ours, planted deep in the ice, a few feet below, on the side we had ascended, and near the end of the ridge. We knew that the ascent had been attempted that year by a gentleman whose flag still floated over the more attainable peak of the Mittelhorn; but no better comment could be devised on the reality and greatness of the difficulty we had overcome in passing the cornice. These explorers had actually arrived within ten feet of the summit; but had been arrested by that frowning barrier of overhanging ice. They had attempted to get round the eastern end of the ridge; but had been foiled by the excessive steepness of the arête in which it terminated, had planted their flag where we found it, and had returned without any idea of their proximity to the summit. This Balmat learned subsequently, happening to meet the gentleman—a very intrepid and hardy mountaineer—in another part of Switzerland. They had supposed, as we had from below, that the actual summit would be found to consist of a dome. I had spoken, the day before, to a man who professed to have been one of his guides; but I am inclined to think he was telling a lie, as I did not find one of the kind of difficulties which he described as the most formidable—namely, those presented by deep and dangerous crevasses—and he said little or nothing about the passage of the rocks and the last ascent, which were the real difficulties of the day. Balmat made me crawl along the edge of the ice, and shake the "drapeau" of our predecessors, in assertion of our own supremacy. In doing so, I caught a glimpse of the arête below, ending in the glacier of Schwarzwald, which made me shudder.

We spent about twenty minutes on the summit; we arrived at twenty minutes past eleven, and remained till twenty minutes to twelve; long enough to impress indelibly upon the memory the immense and varied panorama we had beheld.[6] It was now necessary to descend the slope by which we had mounted. Just as we were about to start, Sampson said, "Maintenant, à la garde de Dieu!" an observation for which Balmat took him severely to task. Balmat was right. No sound should have been uttered which could tend to shake the nerves, or aid the imagination in magnifying the danger of the descent. I proposed that we should tie ourselves together again; but they all dissented, thinking, as they told me afterwards, that an accident to any one would, in that case, have involved the destruction of the whole party. Going down proved, as might be expected, a worse task than ascending; the difficulty and danger stared us in the face; it was a trial for the stoutest nerves, to look down the steep curtain of glacier, on which a single slip might (perhaps must) have entailed fatal consequences. Balmat and Simond both urged me to descend with my face to the ice, so that I might not see what lay before me; but I felt confident of my own presence of mind, and preferred to look my work boldly in the face.

The descent was conducted with extreme caution. Before we took a step, we planted our alpenstocks firmly in the glacier, and laid hold of them close to the snow, or cut holes with them, into which we could put a couple of fingers, and so get a grasp of the ice. When we were about fifty yards on the way down, someone remembered that we had forgotten to drink the health of the Wetterhorn. The first impulse was unanimous, to return; but second thoughts told us that would be an unjustifiable imprudence, and rectified the omission, then and there, as we stood on the ice, each tossing off, bareheaded, a draught of brandy and snow to "the health of the Wetterhorn." Then we continued our descent with the same care and deliberation, and in about half an hour reached the rocks on which we had lain so long, while

Lauener and Sampson were toiling at the steps. We looked back from this place, with no small pride and satisfaction; for now the worst part of our day's work was over. Presently, we were able to descend much more rapidly, and by about a quarter to one we were at the spot where we had left our provender. Here we sat down for a hearty meal, though I was still limited to bread. We shared our stock with the two hunters, who had brought little with them, and were very glad of some wine and meat, though flavoured with garlic. They had by this time completely established their character as "bons enfants," and we were all the best friends possible. We drank again more solemnly and deliberately to "the health of the Wetterhorn," in a rousing bumper of iced red wine, and, this time, Balmat raised no objection to as loud a shout as human lungs could utter. Lauener astounded us all by the strength and clearness of his manly voice.

We stayed here but half an hour, and then crossed again, with extreme care, the dangerous ridge of rocks, which was the last serious difficulty we had to encounter. Once at the base of the wedge to which it belonged, we found the abundance of small loose stones which had impeded us so much in the morning, when climbing up the steep slopes of rock on which they lay, afford us the greatest facilities for descending. We jumped upon a bank of them, and stones and man all slid down, a dozen feet at a time, till stopped by some ledge, which we always took care to look out for, before taking a leap. In this way, we came down at a tremendous pace. Till now, we had been in doubt as to whether we should be able to reach Grindelwald that evening. My wife had been told to prepare herself for our being absent a second night; for all agreed, that if five o'clock should pass while we were still above our sleeping-place, it would be madness to think of descending the slippery rocks of gneiss, and the narrow goat-track of the Enge, in a waning light. It was not till they saw how I could manage the descent over the rocks beneath the plateau, that the Oberland men would pronounce an opinion as to the hour at which we should arrive; had I been nervous or slow, they said, we must have taken hours to pass this part, and might not have arrived at the cavern till nearly dusk. When they saw me lead the way, and run Lauener a race down here, they shouted for joy, and exclaimed that we should be at Grindelwald by eight.

We reached the glacier, at a point higher than where we had quitted it in the morning. It was a grand place for a glissade. There was but one crevasse of any consequence, some distance below, and I marked a wide bridge of snow and ice in the middle, which made it perfectly safe in that direction. Accordingly, I made for a point in the glacier above this bridge, having gained which, I took a little run, planted my alpenstock behind me, and went sliding down at railroad pace. Lauener was behind, and never having been out with me before, was not assured that I knew what I was about, and how to direct my course towards the point where the crevasse was safe. Accordingly, he set off after me with a shout of "Halte! halte!" and overtaking me, seized me by the arm to stop me. The consequence was, we both rolled over together, and had the greatest difficulty in stopping ourselves. My hand, grasping my alpenstock, got ground between his heavy body and the hard, granulated snow; the skin was taken off all the knuckles; but fortunately we succeeded in checking our descent, with no worse result. The crevasse was soon passed, we slid and ran down the glacier as hard as we could go, and what had taken us an hour to ascend in the morning, was descended in a few minutes. The steep bit of turf, strewn with boulders, which lay below the glacier, we found to be now soaked with the drainings of the snow above, and very slippery. Most of us had a tumble as we passed rapidly down towards our hut, but a slip mattered little now; and we actually reached the sleeping-place at ten minutes to three. Here we picked up our porter, who had stayed for the sake of company on the way back. Our early return, after so successful an enterprize, put us in the highest possible spirits; and a bottle of champagne which I had brought up, and reserved to be drunk only in honour of success, added to our festivity. We stayed but half an hour, and then, building up again the entrance of the cavern, to keep it dry and clean for future wanderers, we collected our traps, and set forth once more, lighter by the iron standard, and by many pounds of bread, cheese, meat, wine and coffee, than when we had arrived thither, some twenty hours before.

So bare and exposed a rock as the upper part of the Wetterhorn consists of, is not likely to support much vegetable life. I looked everywhere for specimens of its flora; but above the first glacier, I found only one plant—a beautiful specimen of *campanula cenisia*, whose delicate flowers made beautiful spots of bright blue against the dark and gloomy crags around. Between the glacier and the sleeping-place, the gentians flourished abundantly, though they were not fine. There appeared, however, to be three species only, *acaulis*, *verna* and *nivalis*.

When we came to the bad place, over the slabs of treacherous rock, we were terribly annoyed by a large flock of sheep, which would follow us and roll down stones upon us, in a very dangerous fashion. These animals rarely see any human being, unless it be the shepherd who comes at intervals to tend them, or to give them salt; and whenever a man comes near them, they cluster round him, and besiege him with their importunate caresses. They can pass securely, where the foot of man would slip; and they climbed above our track, disturbing the stones, both great and small, which lay on the rock, wanting but the smallest impetus to set them rolling. They are, thus often very dangerous companions. We pelted them with fragments of rock, but in vain; we were compelled to charge them five or six times, and drive them far away at the point of the alpenstock. Even then, they clustered together, the moment our backs were turned, and followed us again, though at a more respectful distance. The last time, in pursuing them somewhat farther than usual, I came upon a touching sight. A couple of very young lambs had been deserted by their dam. One had just ceased to breath, and was still warm. The other was bleating piteously, but in a very exhausted state. Bohren and Balmat both declared there was no chance of the dam's returning. It had left one to die, and the other would soon share the same fate; and Bohren mercifully put it out of its misery, and saved it from starving to death.

We now descended the "mauvais pas," slowly and cautiously, but relieved from the undesirable companionship of the sheep, and presently came in sight of the chalet where old Bohren and his family lived. They were not on the look-out, as they did not expect us for several hours; but some one happened to catch sight of us, and they fired a salute of two guns to announce our safe approach. My wife and her brother were at that moment on the upper glacier, exploring some of its beautiful deep blue caverns and crevasses. She had had a little chat with the old man as she went to the glacier, and he had pointed to the two cannons, ready loaded, with which he meant to greet us; but she could scarcely believe her ears, and thought it was a mistake, till there was a great bawling from the chalet, and they shouted that they had seen us. She hurried to old Bohren's; and presently afterwards, we again came in sight, and rested for a moment on the little platform of turf near the Enge. We were welcomed by the yells of the whole assembled family of Bohrens, not unworthily responded to by our Bohren and Lauener, who bawled themselves black in the face. We could distinguish the chalet easily enough, but hardly the figures. They were not, as we were, cut out sharply against a face of rock. Balmat, however, put my glass to his eye, and exclaimed: "Violà Madame, qui agite son mouchoir"; and I fancied I saw a faint gleam of flickering white. Then, he exclaimed again: "Elle se cache derrière la grange; on va tirer encore"; and, as he said it, we saw a puff of white smoke, and, after a considerable interval, a faint report reached our ears. We put ourselves in motion again, and rapidly traversed the Enge, and by a quarter past five arrived at the turf beneath. We stopped for one moment, to quaff our last draught of wine—a welcome refreshment after our energetic descent—and then set off at a run, and raced down the grassy slopes, leaping over several fences. I was a-head; and Lauener and I took a hedge, at the same instant, which divided the meadow from the path towards the Scheideck, when suddenly, and very much to our mutual astonishment, we found ourselves within ten paces of my wife and her brother, who were strolling out to meet us. They could scarcely conceive, nor could we easily realize, that we had come from the summit in less than six hours, including an hour of rest.

They told me my face was quite livid and purple. I knew it must be very much sunburnt, for all the day long we had none of us dared to wear a veil, as we needed to make full use of our eyes, almost from the first moment we entered upon the upper plateau until we quitted it; and, indeed, I felt that my face was scorched and sore, but I had not expected the other effect. It was due, in part, probably to the congestion of the vessels of the skin, which always takes place, more or less, at great elevations—and which is familiar to us in the case of persons who ascend to the summit of Mont Blanc—and partly to the rapid descent, which, as I have elsewhere noticed, is apt to produce temporary deafness from the same cause. The superficial vessels of the drum of the ear, in common with all the finer vessels of the head, get swollen and a little congested, and hearing is impaired. I have known persons whose noses always bled, if they made a long and hurried descent. It was the case on several occasions with my friend H., who had been frequently mentioned as my companion in 1852, and who is one of the best walkers and strongest men I know.

My wife and her brother turned back with us, and retraced their steps to old Bohren's, where we were received with vociferous greetings; and another salute of two guns was fired in honour of our arrival. We offered to drop our Bohren here; but he preferred to go on to Grindelwald, a good hour further, for the sake of figuring in a sort of triumphal procession, which I soon found they were arranging for our entrance into the village. My wife mounted her mule; and we returned slowly by the road. The men cut across the fields, and must have gained nearly half an hour upon us, but we found them all waiting at a corner of the road, not far from Grindelwald, where they fell into rank, and made the most of our forces. The chamois hunters had left us, when we stopped half an hour at the sleeping-place, to gather up our baggage, else they, no doubt, would have been pressed into the service. Lauener had made us all decorate our hats with bunches of a brilliant red berry we found on the Enge, so that we wore quite a holiday look. It was a quarter past five, when we had met my wife; and we marched into Grindelwald, and were received by the whole assembled village, at half-past six, a full hour and half before the most sanguine had ventured to expect, when we were on the rocks beneath the plateau.

It was curious and amusing to learn the interest our expedition had excited. Telescopes were seen, for some days to come, fixed against the principal windows of both inns, and when any of us walked about the village, we were pointed at, as people who had done something extraordinary. My wife told me that, for two hours at mid-day, after our success was known, the whole village had turned out and occupied itself in gazing intently at the peak, where, of course, nothing could by any possibility be seen, except two little black specks against the snow, invisible to all but the very keenest eyes, unaided by a glass. The landlord took the earliest opportunity of telegraphing the news to Berne, where the great telescope of the observatory was brought to bear, and from a distance of forty miles they were able to discern our standard and the fir-tree, though what the latter object meant was for some days a puzzle.

Balmat told me that among the guides and people of that kind, the affair had created an extraordinary sensation, and that he found himself quite a man of note. I had not been surprized to see that both he and Sampson had created in Lauener a strong feeling of respect for their manly and mountaineer-like qualities, and the feeling was mutual. Balmat always called Lauener "le capitaine," and a very hearty feeling of regard evidently existed between them. The next evening, as we were returning from the Wengern Alp, a peasant entered into an animated conversation with our mule-driver, in the course of which I heard myself styled by the countryman "Der Wetterhörner Herr." It was unquestionably a very difficult enterprize, and Balmat and Sampson, who had each been many times to the summit of Mont Blanc declared repeatedly (and I overheard them saying the same in their conversations with one another), that the ascent of Mont Blanc was a "bagatelle," in comparison, as far as difficulty was concerned, though, of course, its superior elevation makes the fatigue much greater. Mont Blanc is 15,732 feet, and the Wetterhorn about 12,500 feet above the level of the sea, so that Mont Blanc is the loftier of the two by nearly the height of Snowdon. The last three thousand feet make a prodigious difference in the fatigue. But there are no difficulties, on the side of Mont Blanc, like those of the Wetterhorn. There are no such bad passages of rock, the Mur de la Côte is far less steep than the last slope of the Wetterhorn, and is much sooner passed, and, finally, there is no such obstacle as the overhanging cornice, which as we saw, had baffled other explorers, within a dozen feet of the summit. Balmat, who visited me in London, the following winter, told me that when he arrived at Chamouni, whither the fame of his exploit had preceded him, he was instantly sent for to the chief guide's office, where he had to tell the story over and over again, to fresh troops of eager listeners; and his journey from Interlaken to Chamouni, along which route he was well known, was like a triumphal progress. At Martigny, he was surrounded, as he was crossing the square, by a host of guides and acquaintances, who beset him with questions innumerable, which he had to answer before he was allowed to proceed to his inn.

The expedition, though full of difficulties, did not appear to me to be dangerous, with really good guides, and abundant precaution. Of course, no one ought to undertake such an enterprize, who was not tolerably familiar with Alpine climbing, or who had not had practice and experience enough to know whether he could safely trust his head and his nerves, in such scenes and situations as I have attempted to describe. The first half hour of the descent would be terrible indeed, to a person who lost, in any degree, his self-possession or self-reliance. Indeed, it would be a task full of danger, if such were the case with any one of the party; and the whole descent would be immensely prolonged. Bohren told me he had accompanied a French gentleman to the plateau, who was very nervous in the descent, and that he had thought they would never reach the bottom of the rocks. The expense is necessarily considerable; the guides ask fifty francs apiece for the "course," and it is not at all too much. The porter receives ten or fifteen francs, as he carries a heavy load, up a difficult and laborious path, and is out two, or perhaps three, days. Three guides are absolutely necessary for the expedition, which is a very laborious one for them, upon whom the labour of cutting the steps devolves. All these men have to be fed, for the greatest part of two days; and the bill for eatables is not a small one. The landlord at Grindelwald charged me sixty francs for the provisions, exclusive of wine; an atrocious attempt at imposition, which I am happy to say failed entirely. But still, they must form a considerable item of expenditure; men cannot climb the mountains and eat moderately. The expedition cost me, in the whole, nearly £10. I think it might be done for between £6 and £7; but the fourth guide I was obliged to take made the cost between £2 and £3 more than it need have been. The "Flagge" cost some eight or ten francs; but, in the end, even Balmat and Sampson approved the investment. I never saw such a race of unbelievers as the people at Grindelwald. Our flag was planted at the eastern extremity of a ridge of some length, and of nearly equal height all along. Consequently, from Grindelwald, the western extremity, being nearer, looked a trifle higher, and it was with some difficulty that we could persuade them that the point at which our standard was planted was as high as the rest of the ridge. I am quite sure, if we had not left a very substantial proof of our presence, they never would have believed that we had reached the summit at all.

I found the fatigue not at all more than a good night's rest would dispel. I walked, the next day, to the summit of the Wengern Alp, and back, and spent twelve hours, the day after, in an excursion to the Eismeer, the upper part or plateau of the lower glacier of Grindelwald—one of the sublimest scenes the Alps afford—which I explored thoroughly, while my wife rested on the rocks at its side. The third day after, we ascended the Faulhorn, and I experienced what Balmat said he had almost always suffered from, three or four days after a great "course"—a raging and insatiable thirst; but this was the only uncomfortable effect left by the greatest and grandest expedition of my life. I am inclined to think that in ordinary years, the difficulty and the fatigue would be less than we found them; but the year 1854 was remarkable, in Switzerland, for the unusually small quantity of snow on the high mountains; and the same cause that rendered Mont Blanc so easy of access, that no less than five or six times the usual number of ascents were made, immensely increased the difficulty of climbing the last slope of the Wetterhorn.

—1856

Notes

1. Johann, mentioned in the last chapter—the eldest of the three brothers—was dead. He had fallen over a precipice, in his eager chase of the chamois, and had perished.

2. This was not strictly correct; Desor, in his "Séjours et Excursions dans les glaciers et dans les hautes régions des Alpes," mentions an ascent by two of his guides and it is stated in "Murray's Hand-Book" that it was ascended in 1845 by a Scotch gentleman, named Speer. It is certain, however, that no one at Grindelwald appeared to have heard of any ascent of the peak of the Wetterhorn proper, previous to mine. There are two other peaks—the Rosenhorn and the Mittelhorn, both of which are classed with the peak I ascended under the generic name of "Wetterhörner," and have several times been attained; in fact, they present no extraordinary difficulty, especially from the side of the glacier of Gauli. One of these summits may have been that referred to in "Murray." I should not have thought it likely that the fact would have been altogether forgotten, if the actual Wetterhorn *had* been reached before our attempt. One of my guides was a Grindelwald, and another a Lauterbrunnen man, the former being one of a very numerous family, most of whom were mountaineers and hunters, and neither of them had heard of any previous successful ascent. They both spent the morning of the day on which we started, at Grindelwald, where our preparations excited a vast deal of attention, but certainly did not hear such a fact mentioned by any of the Grindelwald people, though several cases of failure were related; and I am therefore inclined to think it probable the ascent spoken of in "Murray" must have been to one of the other summits. We were certainly regarded, at Grindelwald and in the neighbourhood, as the first adventurers who had succeeded.

3. I hope the Rev. Mr. White, should he ever chance to see these pages, will pardon the liberty I have taken, in altering two or three words in his very beautiful lines, to make them suit the context better than the original would have done. The alteration has been made, I can assure

him, in no spirit of disrespect to the author of some of the most touching and poetical dramas that the modern stage has produced.

4. I have no recollection of seeing the Finster Aarhorn, and I find no note of it. It lies immediately behind the Shreckhorn, and probably was hidden by that massive mountain.

5. Varying in distance from fifty to a hundred miles.

6. Part of the details of the foregoing picture are necessarily told from memory. It is possible, therefore, that as to some of the less important features in the view, an error may here and there occur. I am satisfied, however, of the general fidelity of my account, and have a strong belief that it is correct, even in the detail.

John Ruskin

"Mountain Glory"

English artist and critic John Ruskin (1819–1900) began drawing and sketching from an early age. His father, a successful London wine merchant, took the Ruskin family on trips to the Alps when John was young. While at Oxford, Ruskin was advised to travel to a warmer climate to relieve a possible case of tuberculosis. On his travels he again passed through Switzerland. He published volume one of Modern Painters, *his best-known work on art and aesthetics, in 1843. In 1845 Ruskin explored little-known mountains and towns in northern Italy. His 1848 unconsummated marriage to Euphemia Gray was a great source of anxiety for Ruskin and the marriage was annulled in 1854. In his later years, he lived in Switzerland, near Geneva. In the section entitled "Mountain Gloom," Ruskin focuses on the poverty, dirtiness, and lack of culture of Alpine peasants as a prelude to his celebratory "Mountain Glory" chapter, in which he praises* all *aspects of the mountain climate, scenery, and way of life.*

I have dwelt, in the foregoing chapter, on the sadness of the hills with the greater insistance that I feared my own excessive love for them might lead me into too favorable interpretation of their influences over the human heart; or, at least, that the reader might accuse me of fond prejudice, in the conclusions to which, finally, I desire to lead him concerning them. For, to myself, mountains are the beginning and the end of all natural scenery; in them, and in the forms of inferior landscape that lead to them, my affections are wholly bound up; and though I can look with happy admiration at the lowland flowers, and woods, and open skies, the happiness is tranquil and cold, like that of examining detached flowers in a conservatory, or reading a pleasant book; and if the scenery be resolutely level, insisting upon the declaration of its own flatness in all the detail of it, as in Holland, or Lincolnshire, or Central Lombardy, it appears to me like a prison, and I cannot long endure it. But the slightest rise and fall in the road,—a mossy bank at the side of a crag of chalk, with brambles at its brow, overhanging it,—a ripple over three or four stones in the stream by the bridge,—above all, a wild bit of ferny ground under a fir or two, looking as if, possibly, one might see a hill if one got to the other side of the trees, will instantly give me intense delight, because the shadow, or the hope, of the hills is in them.

And thus, although there are few districts of Northern Europe, however apparently dull or tame, in which I cannot find pleasure, though the whole of Northern France (except Champagne), dull as it seems to most travellers, is to me a perpetual Paradise; and putting Lincolnshire, Leicestershire, and one or two such other perfectly

John Ruskin, "Mountain Glory," *Modern Painters*, vol. 4 (London: Macmillan, 1860).

flat districts aside, there is not an English county which I should not find entertainment in exploring the cross-roads of, foot by foot; yet all my best enjoyment would be owing to the imagination of the hills, coloring, with their faraway memories, every lowland stone and herb. The pleasant French coteau, green in the sunshine, delights me, either by what real mountain character it has in itself (for in extent and succession of promontory the flanks of the French valleys have quite the sublimity of true mountain distances), or by its broken ground and rugged steps among the vines, and rise of the leafage above, against the blue sky, as it might rise at Vevay or Como. There is not a wave of the Seine but is associated in my mind with the first rise of the sandstones and forest pines of Fontainebleau; and with the hope of the Alps, as one leaves Paris with the horses' heads to the south-west, the morning sun flashing on the bright waves at Charenton. If there be *no* hope or association of this kind, and if I cannot deceive myself into fancying that perhaps at the next rise of the road there may be seen the film of a blue hill in the gleam of sky at the horizon, the landscape, however beautiful, produces in me even a kind of sickness and pain; and the whole view from Richmond Hill or Windsor Terrace,—nay, the gardens of Alcinous, with their perpetual summer,—or of the Hesperides (if they were flat, and not close to Atlas), golden apples and all,—I would give away in an instant, for one mossy granite stone a foot abroad, and two leaves of lady-fern.[1]

I know that this is in great part idiosyncrasy; and that I must not trust to my own feelings, in this respect, as representative of the modern landscape instinct; yet I know it is not idiosyncrasy, in so far as there may be proved to be indeed an increase of the absolute beauty of all scenery in exact proportion to its mountainous character, providing that character be *healthily* mountainous. I do not mean to take the Col de Bon Homme as representative of hills, any more than I would take Romney Marsh as representative of plains; but putting Leicestershire or Staffordshire fairly beside Westmoreland, and Lombardy or Champagne fairly beside the Pays de Vaud or the Canton Berne, I find the increase in the calculable sum of elements of beauty to be steadily in proportion to the increase of mountainous character; and that the best image which the world can give of Paradise is in the slope of the meadows, orchards, and cornfields on the sides of a great Alp, with its purple rocks and eternal snows above; this excellence not being in any wise a matter referable to feeling, or individual preferences, but demonstrable by calm enumeration of the number of lovely colors on the rocks, the varied grouping of the trees, and quantity of noble incidents in stream, crag, or cloud, presented to the eye at any given moment.

For consider, first, the difference produced in the whole tone of landscape color by the introductions of purple, violet, and deep ultramarine blue, which we owe to mountains. In an ordinary lowland landscape we have the blue of the sky; the green of grass, which I will suppose (and this is an unnecessary concession to the lowlands) entirely fresh and bright; the green of trees; and certain elements of purple, far more rich and beautiful than we generally should think, in their bark and shadows (bare hedges and thickets, or tops of trees, in subdued afternoon sunshine, are nearly perfect purple, and of an exquisite tone), as well as in ploughed fields, and dark ground in general. But among mountains, in *addition* to all this, large unbroken spaces of pure violet and purple are introduced in their distances; and even near, by films of cloud passing over the darkness of ravines or forests, blues are produced of the most subtle tenderness; these azures and purples[2] passing into rose-color of otherwise wholly unattainable delicacy among the upper summits, the blue of the sky being at the same time purer and deeper than in the plains. Nay, in some sense, a person who has never seen the rose-color of the rays of dawn crossing a blue mountain twelve or fifteen miles away, can hardly be said to know what *tenderness* in color means at all; *bright* tenderness he may, indeed, see in the sky or in a flower, but this grave tenderness of the far-away hill-purples he cannot conceive.

Together with this great source of preeminence in *mass* of color, we have to estimate the influence of the finished inlaying and enamel-work of the color-jewellery on every stone; and that of the continual variety in species of flower; most of the mountain flowers being, besides, separately lovelier than the lowland ones. The wood hyacinth and wild rose are, indeed, the only *supreme* flowers that the lowlands can generally show; and the wild rose is also a mountaineer, and more fragrant in the hills while the wood hyacinth, or grape hyacinth, at its best cannot match even the dark bell-gentian, leaving the light-blue star-gentian in its uncontested queenliness, and the Alpine rose and Highland heather wholly without similitude. The violet, lily of the valley, crocus, and wood anemone are, I suppose, claimable partly by the plains as well as the hills; but the large orange lily and narcissus I have never seen but on hill pastures, and the exquisite oxalis is preeminently a mountaineer.[3]

To this supremacy in mosses and flowers we have next to add an inestimable gain in the continual presence and power of water. Neither in its clearness, its color, its fantasy of motion, its calmness of space, depth, and reflection, or its wrath, can water be conceived by a lowlander, out of sight of sea. A sea wave is far grander than any torrent—but of the sea and its influences we are not now speaking; and the sea itself, though it *can* be clear, is never calm, among our shores, in the sense that a mountain lake can be calm. The sea seems only to pause; the mountain lake to sleep, and to dream. Out of sight of the ocean, a lowlander cannot be considered ever to have seen water at all. The mantling of the pools in the rock shadows, with the golden flakes of light sinking down through them like falling leaves, the ringing of the thin currents among the shallows, the flash and the cloud of the cascade, the earthquake and foam-fire of the cataract, the long lines of alternate mirror and mist that lull the imagery of the hills reversed in the blue of morning,—all these things belong to those hills as their undivided inheritance.

To this supremacy in wave and stream is joined a no less manifest preeminence in the character of trees. It is possible among plains, in the species of trees which properly belong to them, the poplars of Amiens, for instance, to obtain a serene simplicity of grace, which, as I said, is a better help to the study of gracefulness as such, than any of the wilder groupings of the hills; so also, there are certain conditions of symmetrical luxuriance developed in the park and avenue, rarely rivalled in their way among mountains; and yet the mountain superiority in foliage is, on the whole, nearly as complete as it is in water; for exactly as there are some expressions in the broad reaches of a navigable lowland river, such as the Loire or Thames, not, in their way, to be matched among the rock rivers, and yet for all that a lowlander cannot be said to have truly seen the element of water at all; so even in his richest parks and avenues he cannot be said to have truly seen trees. For the resources of trees are not developed until they have difficulty to contend with; neither their tenderness of brotherly love and harmony, till they are forced to choose their ways of various life where there is contracted room for them, talking to each other with their restrained branches. The various action of trees rooting themselves in inhospitable rocks, stooping to look into ravines, hiding from the search of glacier winds, reaching forth to the rays of rare sunshine, crowding down together to drink at sweetest streams, climbing hand in hand among the difficult slopes, opening in sudden dances round the mossy knolls, gathering into companies at rest among the fragrant fields, gliding in grave procession over the heavenward ridges,—nothing of this can be conceived among the unvexed and unvaried felicities of the lowland forest: while to all these direct sources of greater beauty are added, first the power of redundance,—the mere quantity of foliage in the folds and on the promontories of a single Alp being greater than that of an entire lowland landscape (unless a view from some cathedral tower); and to this charm of redundance, that of clearer *visibility*,—tree after tree being constantly shown in successive height, one behind another, instead of the mere tops and flanks of masses, as in the plains; and the forms of multitudes of them continually defined against the clear sky, near and above, or against white clouds entangled among their branches, instead of being confused in dimness of distance.

Finally, to this supremacy in foliage we have to add the still less questionable supremacy in clouds. There is no effect of sky possible in the lowlands which may not in equal perfection be seen among the hills; but there are effects by tens of thousands, for ever invisible and inconceivable to the inhabitant of the plains, manifested among the hills in the course of one day. The mere power of familiarity with the clouds, of walking with them and above them, alters and renders clear our whole conception of the baseless architecture of the sky; and for the beauty of it, there is more in a single wreath of early cloud, pacing its way up an avenue of pines, or pausing among the points of their fringes, than in all the white heaps that fill the arched sky of the plains from one horizon to the other. And of the nobler cloud manifestations,—the breaking of their troublous seas against the crags, their black spray sparkling with lightning; or the going forth of the morning along their pavements of moving marble, level-laid between dome and dome of snow;—of these things there can be as little imagination or understanding in an inhabitant of the plains as of the scenery of another planet than his own.

And, observe, all these superiorities are matters plainly measurable and calculable, not in any wise to be referred to estimate of *sensation*. Of the grandeur or expression of the hills I have not spoken; how far they are great, or strong, or terrible, I do not for the moment consider, because vastness, and strength, and terror, are not to all minds subjects of desired contemplation. It may make no difference to some men whether a natural object be large or small, whether it be strong or feeble. But loveliness of color, perfectness of form, endlessness of change, wonderfulness of structure, are precious to all undiseased human minds; and the superiority of the mountains in all these things to the lowland is, I repeat, as measurable as the richness of a painted window matched with a white one, or the wealth of a museum compared with that of a simply furnished chamber. They seem to have been built for the human race, as at once their schools and cathedrals; full of treasures of illuminated manuscript for the scholar, kindly in simple lessons to the worker, quiet in pale cloisters for the thinker, glorious in holiness for the worshipper. And of these great cathedrals of the earth, with their gates of rock, pavements of cloud, choirs of stream and stone, alters of snow, and vaults of purple traversed by the continual stars,—of these, as we have seen, it was written, nor long ago, by one of the best of the poor human race for whom they were built, wondering in himself for whom their Creator *could* have made them, and thinking to have entirely discerned the Divine intent in them—"They are inhabited by the Beasts."

Was it then indeed thus with us, and so lately? Had mankind offered no worship in their mountain churches? Was all that granite sculpture and floral painting done by the angels in vain?

Not so. It will need no prolonged thought to convince us that in the hills the purposes of their Maker have indeed been accomplished in such measure as, through the sin or folly of men, He ever permits them to be accomplished. It may not seem, from the general language held concerning them, or from any directly traceable results, that mountains have had serious influence on human intellect; but it will not, I think, be difficult to show that their occult influence has been both constant and essential to the progress of the race.

Consider, first, whether we can justly refuse to attribute to their mountain scenery some share in giving the Greeks and Italians their intellectual lead among the nations of Europe.

There is not a single spot of land in either of these countries from which mountains are not discernible; almost always they form the principal feature of the scenery. The mountain outlines seen from Sparta, Corinth, Athens, Rome, Florence, Pisa, Verona, are of consummate beauty; and whatever dislike or contempt may be traceable in the mind of the Greeks for mountains ruggedness, their placing the shrine of Apollo under the cliffs of Delphi, and his throne upon Parnassus, was a testimony to all succeeding time that they themselves attributed the best part of their intellectual inspiration to the power of the hills. Nor would it be difficult to show that every great writer of either of those nations, however little definite regard he might manifest for the landscape of his country, had been mentally formed and disciplined by it, so that even such enjoyment as Homer's of the ploughed ground and poplar groves owes its intensity and delicacy to the excitement of the imagination produced, without his own consciousness, by other and grander features of the scenery to which he had been accustomed from a child; and differs in every respect from the tranquil, vegetative, and prosaic affection with which the same ploughed land and poplars would be regarded by a native of the Netherlands.

The vague expression which I have just used—"intellectual lead," may be expanded into four great heads; lead in Religion, Art and Literature, War, and Social Economy.

It will be right to examine our subject eventually under these four heads; but I shall limit myself, for the present, to some consideration of the first two, for a reason presently to be stated.

1ST. INFLUENCE OF MOUNTAINS ON RELIGIOUS TEMPERAMENT.

I. We have before had occasion to note the peculiar awe with which mountains were regarded in the Middle Ages, as bearing continual witness against the frivolity or luxury of the world. Though the sense of this influence of theirs is perhaps more clearly expressed by the medieval Christians than by any other sect of religionists, the influence itself has been constant in all time. Mountains have always possessed the power, first, of exciting religious enthusiasm; secondly, of purifying religious faith. These two operations are partly contrary to one another: for the faith of enthusiasm is apt to be *im*pure, and the mountains, by exciting morbid conditions of the imagination, have caused in great part the legendary and romantic forms of belief; on the other hand, by fostering simplicity of life and dignity of morals, they have purified by action what they falsified by imagination. But, even in their first and most dangerous influence, it is not the mountains that are to blame, but the human heart. While we mourn over the fictitious shape given to the religious visions of the anchorite, we may envy the sincerity and the depth of the emotion from which they spring: in the deep feeling, we have to acknowledge the solemn influences of the hills; but for the erring modes or forms of thought, it is human wilfulness, sin, and false teaching, that are answerable. We are not to deny the nobleness of the imagination because its direction is illegitimate, nor the pathos of the legend because its circumstances are groundless; the ardor and abstraction of the spiritual life are to be honored in themselves, though the one may be misguided and the other deceived; and the deserts of Osma, Assisi, and Monte Viso are still to be thanked for the zeal they gave, or guarded, whether we find it in St. Francis and St. Dominic, or in those whom God's hand hid from them in the clefts of the rocks.

And, in fact, much of the apparently harmful influence of hills on the religion of the world is nothing else than their general gift of exciting the poetical and inventive faculties, in peculiarly solemn tones of mind. Their terror leads into devotional cast of thought; their beauty and wildness prompt the invention at the same time; and where the mind is not gifted with stern reasoning powers, or protected by purity of teaching, it is sure to mingle the invention with its creed, and the vision with its prayer. Strictly speaking, we ought to consider the superstitions of the hills, universally, as a form of poetry; regretting only that men have not yet learned how to distinguish poetry from well-founded faith.

110

And if we do this, and enable ourselves thus to review, without carping or sneering, the shapes of solemn imagination which have arisen among the inhabitants of Europe, we shall find, on the one hand, the mountains of Greece and Italy forming all the loveliest dreams, first of the Pagan, then of the Christian mythology; on the other, those of Scandinavia to be the first sources of whatever mental (as well as military) power was brought by the Normans into Southern Europe. Normandy itself is to all intents and purposes a hill country; composed, over large extents, of granite and basalt, often rugged and covered with heather on the summits, and traversed by beautiful and singular dells, at once soft and secluded, fruitful and wild. We have thus one branch of the Northern religious imagination rising among the Scandinavian fiords, tempered in France by various encounters with elements of Arabian, Italian, Provençal, or other Southern poetry, and then reacting upon Southern England; while other forms of the same rude religions' imagination, resting like clouds upon the mountains of Scotland and Wales, met and mingled with the Norman Christianity, retaining even to the latest times some dark color of superstition, but giving all its poetical and military pathos to Scottish poetry, and a peculiar sternness and wildness of tone to the Reformed faith, in its manifestations among the Scottish hills.

It is on less disputable ground that I may claim the reader's gratitude to the mountains, as having been the centres not only of imaginative energy, but of purity both in doctrine and practice. The enthusiasm of the persecuted Covenanter, and his variously modified claims to miraculous protection or prophetic inspiration, hold exactly the same relation to the smooth proprieties of lowland Protestantism, that the demon-combats, fastings, visions, and miracles of the mountain monk or anchorite hold to the wealth and worldliness of the Vatican. It might indeed happen, whether at Canterbury, Rheims, or Rome, that a good bishop should occasionally grasp the crozier; and a vast amount of prudent, educated, and admirable piety is to be found among the ranks of the lowland clergy. But still the large aspect of the matter is always, among Protestants, that formalism, respectability, orthodoxy, caution, and propriety, live by the slow stream that encircles the lowland abbey or cathedral; and that enthusiasm, poverty, vital faith, and audacity of conduct, characterize the pastor dwelling by the torrent side. In like manner, taking the large aspects of Romanism, we see that its worst corruptions, its cunning, its worldliness, and its permission of crime, are traceable for the most part to lowland prelacy; but its self-denials, its obediences, humilities, sincere claims to miraculous power, and faithful discharges of pastoral duty, are traceable chiefly to its anchorites and mountain clergy.

It is true that the "Lady Poverty" of St. Francis may share the influence of the hills in the formation of character; and that, since the clergy who have little interest at court or conclave are those who in general will be driven to undertake the hill services, we must often attribute to enforced simplicity of life, or natural bitterness of feeling, some of the tones of thought which we might otherwise have ascribed to the influence of mountain scenery. Such causes, however, affect the lowland as much as the highland religious character in all districts far from cities; but they do not produce the same effects.

The curate or hermit of the field and fen, however simple his life, or painful his lodging, does not often attain the spirit of the hill pastor or recluse: we may find in him a decent virtue or a contented ignorance, rarely the prophetic vision or the martyr's passion. Among the fair arable lands of England and Belgium extends an orthodox Protestantism or Catholicism; prosperous, creditable, and drowsy; but it is among the purple moors of the highland border, the ravines of Mont Genèvre, and the crags of the Tyrol, that we shall find the simplest Evangelical faith, and the purest Romanist practice.

Of course the inquiry into this branch of the hill influence is partly complicated with that into its operation on domestic habits and personal character, of which hereafter: but there is one curious witness borne to the general truth of the foregone conclusions, by an apparently slight, yet very significant circumstance in art. We have seen, in the preceding volume, how difficult it was sometimes to distinguish between honest painters, who truly chose to paint sacred subjects because they loved them, and the affected painters, who took sacred subjects for their own pride's sake, or for merely artistical delight. Amongst other means of arriving at a conclusion in this matter, there is one helpful test which may be applied to their various works, almost as easily and certainly as a foot-rule could be used to measure their size; and which remains an available test down to the date of the rise of the Claudesque landscape schools. Nearly all the genuine religious painters use *steep mountain distances*. All the merely artistical ones, or those of intermediate temper, in proportion as they lose the religious element, use flat or simply architectural distances. Of course the law is liable to many exceptions, chiefly dependent on the place of birth and early associations of painter; but its force is, I think, strongly shown in this;—that, though the Flemish painters never showed any disposition to paint, *for its own sake*, other scenery than of their own land (compare vol. III, Chap. XIII. § 20), the sincerely religious ones continually used Alpine distances, bright with snow. In like manner Giotto, Perugino, Angelico, the young Raphael, and John Bellini, always, if, with any fitness to their subject, they can introduce them, use craggy or blue mountain distances, and this with definite expression of love towards them; Leonardo, conventionally, as feeling they were necessary for his sacred subjects, while yet his science and idealism had destroyed his mountain sincerity; Michael Angelo, wholly an artist, and Raphael in later years, show no love of mountains whatever, while the relative depths of feeling in Tintoret, Titian, and Veronese, are precisely measurable by their affection to mountains. Tintoret, though born in Venice, yet, because capable of the greatest reaches of feeling, is the first of the old painters who ever drew mountain detail rightly:[4] Titian, though born in Cadore, and recurring to it constantly, yet being more worldly-minded, uses his hills somewhat more conventionally, though, still in his most deeply felt pictures, such as the St. Jerome in the Brera, giving to the rocks and forests a consummate nobleness; and Veronese, in his gay grasp of the outside aspects of the world, contentedly includes his philosophy within proticos and pillars, or at the best overshadows it with a few sprays of laurel.

The test fails, however, utterly, when applied to the later or transitional landscape schools, mountains being there introduced in mere wanton savageness by Salvator, or vague conventionalism by Claude, Berghem, and hundreds more. This need not, however, in the least invalidate our general conclusions: we surely know already that it is possible to misuse the best gifts, and pervert the purest feelings; nor need we doubt the real purpose, or, on honest hearts, the real effect, of mountains, because various institutions have been founded among them by the banditti of Calabria, as well as by St. Bruno.

I cannot leave this part of my subject without recording a slight incident which happened to myself, singularly illustrative of the religious character of the Alpine peasant when under favorable circumstances of teaching. I was coming down one evening from the Rochers de Naye, above Montreux, having been at work among the limestone rocks, where I could get no water, and both weary and thirsty. Coming to a spring at a turn of the path, conducted, as usual, by the herdsman into a hollowed pine-trunk I stooped to it and drank deeply: as I raised my head, drawing breath heavily, some one behind me said, "Celui qui boira de cette eau-ci, aura encore soif." I turned, not understanding for the moment what was meant; and saw one of the hill-peasants, probably returning to his châlet from the market place at Vevay or Villeneuve. As I looked at him with an uncomprehending expression, he went on with the verse:—"Mais celui qui boira de l'eau que je lui donnerai, n'aura jamais soif."

I doubt if this would have been thought of, or said, by even the most intelligent lowland peasant. The thought might have occurred to him, but the frankness of address, and expectation of being at once understood without a word of preparative explanation, as if the language of the Bible were familiar to all men, mark, I think, the mountaineer.

2ND. INFLUENCE OF MOUNTAINS ON ARTISTICAL POWER.

We were next to examine the influence of hills on the artistical power of the human race. Which power, so far as it depends on the imagination, must evidently be fostered by the same influences which give vitality to religious vision. But, so far as artistical productiveness and skill are concerned, it is evident that the mountaineer is at a radical and insurmountable disadvantage. The strength of his character depends upon the absence of luxury; but it is eminently by luxury that art is supported. We are not, therefore, to deny the mountain influence, because we do not find finished frescoes on the timbers of châlets, or delicate bas-reliefs on the bastion which protects the mountain church from the avalanche; but to consider how far the tone of mind shown by the artists laboring in the lowland is dependent for its intensity on the distant influences of the hills, whether during the childhood of those born among them, or under the casual contemplation of men advanced in life.

Glancing broadly over the strength of the mediaeval—that is to say, of the peculiar and energetic—art of Europe, so as to discern, through the clear flowing of its waves over France, Italy, and England, the places in the pool where the fountain-heads are, and where the sand dances, I should first point to Normandy and Tuscany. From the cathedral of Pisa, and the sculpture of the Pisans, the course is straight to Giotto, Angelico, and Raphael—to Oreagna and Michael Angelo;—the Venetian school, in many respects mightier, being, never the subsequent and derivative. From the cathedrals of Caen and Coutances the course is straight to the gothic of Chartres and Notre-Dame of Paris, and thence forward to all French and English noble art, whether ecclesiastical or domestic. Now the mountain scenery about Pisa is precisely the most beautiful that surrounds any great Italian city, owing to the wonderful outlines of the peaks of Carrara. Milan and Verona have indeed fine ranges in sight, but rising farther in the distance, and therefore not so directly affecting the popular mind The Norman imagination, as already noticed, is Scandinavian in origin, and fostered by the lovely granite scenery of Normandy itself. But there is, nevertheless, this great difference between French art and Italian, that the French paused strangely at a certain point, as the Norman hills are truncated at the summits, while the Italian rose steadily to a vertex, as the Carrara hills to their crests. Let us observe this a little more in detail.

The sculpture of the Pisans was taken up and carried into various perfection by the Lucchese, Pistojans, Sienese, and Florentines. All these are inhabitants of truly mountain cities, Florence being as completely among the hills as Inspruck is, only the hills have softer outlines. Those around Pistoja and Lucca are in a high degree majestic. Giotto was born and bred among these hills. Angelico lived upon their slope. The mountain towns of Perugia and Urbino furnish the only important branches of correlative art; for Leonardo, however individually great, originated no new school; he only carried the *executive* delicacy of landscape detail so far beyond other painters as to necessitate my naming the fifteenth-century manner of landscape after him, though he did not invent it; and although the school of Milan is distinguished by several peculiarities, and definitely enough separable from the other schools of Italy, all its peculiarities are mannerisms, not inventions.

Correggio, indeed, created a new school, though he himself is almost its only master. I have given in the preceding volume the mountain outline seen from Parma. But the only entirely great group of painters after the Tuscans are the Venetians, and they are headed by Titian and Tintoret, on whom we have noticed the influence of hills already; and although we cannot trace it in Paul Veronese, I will not quit the mountain claim upon him; for I believe all that gay and gladdening strength of his was fed by the breezes of the hills of Garda, and brightened by the swift glancing of the waves of the Adige.[5]

Observe, however, before going farther, of all the painters we have named, the one who obtains most executive perfection is Leonardo, who on the whole lived at the greatest distance from the hills. The two who have most feeling are Giotto and Angelico, both hill-bred. And generally, I believe, we shall find that the hill country gives its inventive depths of feeling to art, as in the work of Oreagna, Perugino, and Angelico, and the plain country executive neatness. The executive precision is joined with feeling in Leonardo, who saw the Alps in the distance; it is totally unaccompanied by feeling in the pure Dutch schools, or schools of the dead flats.

I do not know if any writer on art, or on the development of national mind, has given his attention to what seems to me one of the most singular phenomena in the

114

history of Europe,—the pause of the English and French in pictorial art after the fourteenth century. From the days of Henry III, to those of Elizabeth, and of Louis IX, to those of Louis XIV, the general intellect of the two nations was steadily on the increase. But their art intellect was as steadily retrograde. The only artwork that France and England have done nobly is that which is centralized by the Cathedral of Lincoln, and the Sainte Chapelle. We had at that time (*we*—French and English—but the French first) the incontestable lead among European nations; no thirteenth-century work in Italy is comparable for majesty of conception, or wealth of imaginative detail, to the cathedrals of Chartres, Rheims, Rouen, Amiens, Lincoln, Peterborough, Wells, or Lichfield. But every hour of the fourteenth century saw French and English art in precipitate decline, Italian in steady ascent; and by the time that painting and sculpture had developed themselves in an approximated perfection, in the work of Ghirlandajo and Mino of Fésole, we had in France and England no workman, in any art, deserving a workman's name; nothing but skilful masons, with more or less love of the picturesque, and redundance of undisciplined imagination, flaming itself away in wild and rich traceries, and crowded bosses of grotesque figure sculpture, and expiring at last in barbarous imitation of the perfected skill and erring choice of Renaissance Italy. Painting could not decline, for it had not reached any eminence; the exquisite arts of illumination and glass design had led to no effective results in other materials; they themselves, incapable of any higher perfection than they had reached in the thirteenth century, perished in the vain endeavor to emulate pictorial excellence, bad *drawing* being substituted, in books, for lovely *writing*, and opaque precision, in glass, for transparent power; nor in any single department of exertion did artists arise of such calibre or class as any of the great Italians; and yet all the while, in literature, *we* were gradually and steadily advancing in power up to the time of Shakespeare; the Italians, on the contrary, not advancing after the time of Dante.

Of course I have no space here to pursue a question such as this; but I may state my belief that *one* of the conditions involved in it was the mountain influence of Italian scenery, inducing a disposition to such indolent or enthusiastic reverie, as could only express itself in the visions of art; while the comparatively flat scenery and severer climate of England and France, fostering less enthusiasm, and urging to more exertion, brought about a practical and rational temperament, progressive in policy, science, and literature, but wholly retrograde in art; that is to say (for great art my be properly so defined), in the Art of *Dreaming*.

3RD. INFLUENCE OF MOUNTAINS ON LITERARY POWER.

§ 25. III. In admitting this, we seem to involve the supposition that mountain influence is either unfavorable or inessential to literary power; but for this also the mountain influence is still necessary, only in a subordinate degree. It is true, indeed, that the Avon is no mountain torrent, and that the hills round the vale of the Stratford are not sublime; true, moreover, that the cantons Berne or Uri have never yet, so far as I know, produced a great poet; but neither, on the other hand, has Antwerp or Amsterdam.

115

And, I believe, the natural scenery which will be found, on the whole, productive of most literary intellect is that mingled of hill and plain, as all available light is of flame and darkness; the flame being the active element, and the darkness the tempering one.

In noting such evidence as bears upon this subject, the reader must always remember that the mountains are at an unfair disadvantage, in being much *out of the way* of the masses of men employed in intellectual pursuits. The position of a city is dictated by military necessity or commercial convenience; it rises, flourishes, and absorbs into its activity whatever leading intellect is in the surrounding population. The persons who are able and desirous to give their children education naturally resort to it; the best schools, the best society, and the strongest motives assist and excite those born within its walls; and youth after youth rises to distinction out of its streets, while among the blue mountains, twenty miles away, the goatherds live and die in unregarded lowliness. And yet this is no proof that the mountains have little effect upon the mind, or that the streets have a helpful one. The men who are formed by the schools, and polished by the society of the capital, may yet in many ways have their powers shortened by the absence of natural scenery; and the mountaineer, neglected, ignorant, and unambitious, may have been taught things by the clouds and streams which he could not have learned in a college, or a coterie.

And in reasoning about the effect of mountains we are therefore under a difficulty like that which would occur to us if we had to determine the good or bad effect of light on the human constitution, in some place where all corporal exercise was necessarily in partial darkness, and only idle people lived in the light. The exercise might give an advantage to the occupants of the gloom, but we should neither be justified in therefore denying the preciousness of light in general, nor the necessity to the workers of the few rays they possessed; and thus I suppose the hills around Stratford, and such glimpses as Shakespeare had of sandstone and pines in Warwickshire, or of chalk cliffs in Kent, to have been essential to the development of his genius. This supposition can only be proved false by the rising of a Shakespeare at Rotterdam or Bergen-op-Zoom, which I think not probable; whereas, on the other hand, it is confirmed by myriads of collateral evidences. The matter could only be *tested* by placing for half a century the British universities at Keswick and Beddgelert, and making Grenoble the capital of France; but if, throughout the history of Britain and France, we contrast the general invention and pathetic power, in ballads or legends, of the inhabitants of the Scottish border with those manifested in Suffolk or Essex; and similarly the inventive power of Normandy, Provence, and the Bearnois with that of Champagne or Picardy, we shall obtain some convincing evidence respecting the operation of hills on the masses of mankind, and be disposed to admit, with less hesitation, that the apparent inconsistencies in the effect of scenery on greater minds proceed in each case from specialities of education, accident, and original temper, which it would be impossible to follow out in detail. Sometimes only, when the original resemblance in character of intellect is very marked in two individuals, and they are submitted to definitely contrary circumstances of education, an approximation to evidence may be obtained. Thus Bacon and Pascal appear to be men

116

naturally very similar in their temper and power of mind. One, born in York House, Stand, of courtly parents, educated in court atmosphere, and replying, almost as soon as he could speak, to the queen asking how old he was—"Two years younger than Your Majesty's happy reign!"—has the world's meanness and cunning engrafted into his intellect, and remains smooth, serene, unenthusiastic, and in some degree base, even with all his sincere devotion and universal wisdom; bearing, to the end of life, the likeness of a marble palace in the street of a great city, fairly furnished within, and bright in wall and battlement, yet noisome in places about the foundations. The other, born at Clermont, in Auvergne, under the shadow of the Puy de Dôme, though taken to Paris at eight years old, retains for ever the impress of his birthplace; pursuing natural philosophy with the same zeal as Bacon, he returns to his own mountains to put himself under their tutelage, and by their help first discovers the great relations of the earth and the air: struck at last with mortal disease; gloomy, enthusiastic, and superstitious, with a conscience burning like lava, and inflexible like iron, the clouds gather about the majesty of him, fold after fold; and, with his spirit buried in ashes, and rent by earthquake, yet fruitful of true thought and faithful affection, he stands like that mound of desolate scoria that crowns the hill ranges of his native land, with its sable summit far in heaven, and its foundations green with the ordered garden and the trellised vine.

When, however, our inquiry thus branches into the successive analysis of individual characters, it is time for us to leave it; noting only one or two points respecting Shakespere, whom, I doubt not, the reader was surprised to find left out of all our comparisons in the preceding volume. He seems to have been sent essentially to take universal and equal grasp of the *human* nature; and to have been removed, therefore, from all influences which could in the least warp or bias his thoughts. It was necessary that he should lean *no* way; that he should contemplate, with absolute equality of judgment, the life of the court, cloister, and tavern, and be able to sympathize so completely with all creatures as to deprive himself, together with his personal identity, even of his conscience, as he casts himself into their hearts. He must be able to enter into the soul of Falstaff or Shylock with no more sense of contempt or horror than Falstaff or Shylock themselves feel for or in themselves; otherwise his own conscience and indignation would make him unjust to them; he would turn aside from something, miss some good, or overlook some essential palliation. He must be utterly without anger, utterly without purpose; for if a man has any serious purpose in life, that which runs counter to it, or is foreign to it, will be looked at frowningly or carelessly by him. Shakespere was forbidden of Heaven to have any *plans*. To *do* any good or *get* any good, in the common sense of good, was not to be within his permitted range of work. Not, for him, the founding of institutions, the preaching of doctrines, or the repression of abuses. Neither he, nor the sun, did on any morning that they rose together, receive charge from their Maker concerning such things. They were both of them to shine on the evil and good; both to behold unoffendedly all that was upon the earth, to burn unappalled upon the spears of kings, and undisdaining, upon the reeds of the river.

Therefore, so far as nature had influence over the early training of this man, it was essential to his perfectness that the nature should be quiet. No mountain passions were to be allowed in him. Inflict upon him but one pang of the monastic conscience; cast upon him but one cloud of the mountain gloom; and his serenity had been gone forever—his equity—his infinity. You would have made another Dante of him; and all that he would have ever uttered about poor, soiled, and frail humanity would have been the quarrel between Sinon and Adam of Breseia,—speedily retired from, as not worthy a man's hearing, nay, not to be heard without heavy fault. All your Falstaffs, Slenders, Quicklys, Sir Tobys, Lances, Touchstones, and Quinces would have been lost in that. Shakespere would be allowed no mountains; nay not even any supreme natural beauty. He had to be left with his kingcups and clover;—pansies—the passing clouds—the Avon's flow—and the undulating hills and woods of Warwick; nay, he was not to love even these in any exceeding measure, lest it might make him in the least overrate their power upon the strong, full-fledged minds of men. He makes the quarrelling fairies concerned about them; poor lost Ophelia find some comfort in them; fearful, fair, wise-hearted Perdita trust the speaking of her good will and good hostess-ship to them; and one of the brothers of Imogen confide his sorrow to them,—rebuked instantly by his brother for "wench-like words";[6] but any thought of them in his mighty men I do not find: it is not usually in the nature of such men; and if he had loved the flowers the *least* better himself, he would assuredly have been offended at this, and given a botanical turn of mind to Caesar, or Othello.

And it is even among the most curious proofs of the necessity to all high imagination that it should paint straight from the life, that he has *not* given such a turn of mind to some of his great men;—Henry the Fifth, for instance. Doubtless some of my readers having been accustomed to hear it repeated thoughtlessly from mouth to mouth that Shakespere conceived the spirit of all ages, were as much offended as surprised at my saying that he only painted human nature as he saw it in his own time. They will find, if they look into his work closely, as much antiquarianism as they do geography, and no more. The commonly received notions about the things that had been, Shakespere took as he found them animating them with pure human nature, of any time and all time; but inquiries into the minor detail of temporary feeling, he despised as utterly as he did maps; and wheresoever the temporary feeling was in anywise contrary to that of his own day, he errs frankly, and paints from his own time. For instance in this matter of love of flowers; we have traced already, far enough for our general purposes, the mediaeval interest in them, whether to be enjoyed in the fields, or to be used for types of ornamentation in dress. If Shakespere had cared to enter into the spirit even of the early fifteenth century, he would assuredly have marked this affection in some of his knights, and indicated, even then, in heroic tempers, the peculiar respect for loveliness of *dress* which we find constantly in Dante. But he could not do this; he had not seen it in real life. In his time dress had become an affectation and absurdity. Only fools, or wise men in their weak moments, showed much concern about it; and the facts of human nature which appeared to him general in the matter were the soldier's disdain, and the coxcomb's care of it. Hence Shakespere's good soldier is almost always in plain or battered armor; even the speech of Vernon in Henry the Fourth, which, as far as I remember, is the only one that bears fully upon the beauty of armor, leans more upon the spirit and hearts of men— "bated, like eagles having lately bathed"; and has an under-current of slight contempt running though the following line, "Glittering in golden coats, *like images*"; while the beauty of the young Harry is essentially the beauty of fiery and perfect youth, answering as much to the Greek, or Roman, or Elizabethan knight as to the mediaeval one; whereas the definite interest in armor and dress is opposed by Shakespere in the French (meaning to depreciate them), to the English rude soldierliness:

> "*Con.* Tut, I have the best armor of the world. Would it were day!
> *Orl.* You have an excellent armor, but let my horse have his due."

And again:

> "My lord constable, the armor that I saw in your tent to-night, are those stars, or suns, upon it?"

while Henry, half proud of his poorness of array, speaks of armorial splendor scornfully; the main idea being still of its being a gilded show and vanity—

> "Our gayness and our *gilt* are all besmirched."

This is essentially Elizabethan. The quarterings on a knight's shield, or the inlaying of his armor, would never have been thought of by him as mere "gayness or gilt" in earlier days.[7] In like manner, throughout every scale of rank or feeling, from that of the French knights down to Falstaff's "I looked he should have sent me two-and-twenty yards of satin, as I am true knight, and he sends me security!" care for dress is always considered by Shakespere as contemptible; and Mrs. Quickly distinguishes herself from a true fairy by her solicitude to scour the *chairs of order*—and "each fair instalment, coat, and several crest"; and the association in her mind of the flowers in the fairy rings with the

> "Sapphire, pearl, and rich embroidery,
> Buckled below fair knighthood's bending knee";

While the true fairies, in field simplicity, are only anxious to "sweep the dust behind the door"; and

119

"With this field dew consecrate,
Every several chamber bless
Through this palace with sweet peace."

Note the expression "Field dew consecrate." Shakespere loved courts and camps; but he felt that sacredness and peace were in the dew of the Fields only.

There is another respect in which he was wholly incapable of entering into the spirit of the Middle Ages. He had no great art of any kind around him in his own country, and was, consequently, just as powerless to conceive the general influence of former art, as a man of the most inferior calibre. Therefore it was, that I did not care to quote his authority respecting the power of imitation, in the second chapter of the preceding volume. If it had been needful to add his testimony to that of Dante (given in § 5), I might have quoted multitudes of passages wholly concurring with that, of which the "fair Portia's counterfeit," with the following lines, and the implied ideal of sculpture in the Winter's Tale, are wholly unanswerable instances. But Shakespere's evidence in matters of art is as narrow as the range of Elizabethan art in England, and resolves itself wholly into admiration of two things,—mockery of life (as in this instance of Hermione as a statue), or absolute splendor, as in the close of Romeo and Juliet, where the notion of *gold* as the chief source of dignity of aspect, coming down to Shakespere from the times of the Field of the Cloth of Gold, and, as I said before, strictly Elizabethan, would interfere seriously with the pathos of the whole passage, but for the sense of sacrifice implied in it:

"As *rich* shall Romeo by his lady lie,
Poor sacrifices of our enmity."

And observe, I am not giving these examples as proof of any smallness in Shakespere, but of his greatness; that is to say, of his contentment, like every other great man who ever breathed, to paint nothing but *what he saw*; and therefore giving perpetual evidence that his sight was of the sixteenth, and not of the thirteenth century, beneath all the broad and eternal humanity of his imagination. How far in these modern days, emptied of splendor, it may be necessary for great men having certain sympathies for those earlier ages, to act in this differently from all their predecessors; and how far they may succeed in the resuscitation of the past by habitually dwelling in all their thoughts among vanished generations, are questions, of all practical and present ones concerning art, the most difficult to decide; for already in poetry several of our truest men have set themselves to this task, and have indeed put more vitality into the shadows of the dead than most others can give the presences of the living. Thus Longfellow, in the Golden Legend, has entered more closely into the temper of the Monk, for good and for evil, than ever yet theological writer or historian, though they may have given their life's labor to the analysis: and, again, Robert Browning is

120

unerring in every sentence he writes of the Middle Ages; always vital, right, and profound; so that in the matter of art, with which we have been specially concerned, there is hardly a principle connected with the mediaeval temper, that he has not struck upon in those seemingly careless and too rugged rhymes of his. There is a curious instance, by the way, in a short poem referring to this very subject of tomb and image sculpture, and illustrating just one of those phases of local human character which, though belonging to Shakespere's own age, he never noticed, because it was specially Italian and un-English; connected also closely with the influence of mountains on the heart, and therefore with our immediate inquiries. I mean the kind of admiration with which a southern artist regarded the *stone* he worked in; and the pride which populace or priest took in the possession of precious mountain substance, worked into the pavements of their cathedrals, and the shafts of their tombs.

Observe, Shakespere, in the midst of architecture and tombs of wood, or freestone, or brass, naturally thinks of *gold* as the best enriching and ennobling substance for them;—in the midst also of the fever of the Renaissance he writes, as every one else did, in praise of precisely the most vicious master of that school—Giulio Romano; but the modern poet, living much in Italy, and quite of the Renaissance influence, is able fully to enter into the Italian feeling, and to see the evil of the Renaissance tendency, not because he is greater than Shakespere, but because he is in another element, and has *seen* other things. I miss fragments here and there not needed for my purpose in the passage quoted, without putting asterisks, for I weaken the poem enough by the omissions, without spoiling it also by breaks.

"The Bishop orders his Tomb in St. Praxed's Church.

"As here I lie
In this state chamber, dying by degrees,
Hours, and long hours, in the dead night, I ask,
Do I live—am I dead? Peace, peace, seems all:
St. Praxed's ever was the church for peace.
And so, about this tomb of mine. I fought
With tooth and nail to save my niche, ye know;
Old Gandolf[8] cozened me, despite my care.
Shrewd was that snatch from out the corner south
He graced his carrion with.
Yet still my niche is not so cramped but thence
One sees the pulpit o' the epistle side,
And somewhat of the choir, those silent seats;
And up into the aery dome where live
The angels, and a sunbeam's sure to lurk.
And I shall fill my slab of basalt there,
And 'neath my tabernacle take my rest,

With those nine columns round me, two and two,
The odd one at my feet, where Anselm[9] stands;
Peach-blossom marble all.
Swift as a weaver's shuttle fleet our years:
Man goeth to the grave, and where is he?
Did I say basalt for my slab, sons? Black—
'Twas ever antique-black[10] I meant! How else
Shall ye contrast my frieze to come beneath?
The bas-relief in bronze ye promised me,
Those Pans and Nymphs ye wot of, and perchance
Some tripod, thyrsus, with a vase or so,
The Saviour at his sermon on the mount,
St. Praxed in a glory, and one Pan,
And Moses with the tables . . . but I know
Ye mark me not! What do they whisper thee,
Child of my bowels, Anselm? Ah, ye hope
To revel down my villas while I gasp,
Bricked o'er with beggar's mouldy travertine,
Which Gandolf from his tomb-top chuckles at!
Nay, boys, ye love me—all of jasper, then!
There's plenty jasper somewhere in the world—
And have I not St. Praxed's ear to pray
Horses for ye, and brown Greek manuscripts.
That's if ye carve my epitaph aright,
Choice Latin, picked phrase, Tully's every word,
No gaudy ware like Gandolf's second line—
Tully, my masters? Ulpian serves *his* need."

I know no other piece of modern English, prose or poetry, in which there is so much told, as in these lines, of the Renaissance spirit,—its worldliness, inconsistency, pride, hypocrisy, ignorance of itself, love of art, of luxury, and of good Latin. It is nearly all that I said of the central Renaissance in thirty pages of the "Stones of Venice" put into as many lines, Browning's being also the antecedent work. The worst of it is that this kind of concentrated writing needs so much *solution* before the reader can fairly get the good of it, that people's patience fails them, and they give the thing up as insoluble; though, truly, it ought to be to the current of common thought like Saladin's talisman, dipped in clear water, not soluble altogether, but making the element medicinal.

It is interesting, by the way, with respect to this love of stones in the Italian mind, to consider the difference necessitated in the English temper merely by the general domestic use of wood instead of marble. In that old Shakesperian England, men must have rendered grateful homage to their oak forests, in the sense of all that they owed to their goodly timbers in the wainscot and furniture of the rooms they loved best, when the blue of the frosty midnight was contrasted, in the dark diamonds of the lattice, with the glowing brown of the warm, fire-lighted, crimson-tapestried walls. Not less would an Italian look with a grateful regard on the hill summits, to which he owed, in the scorching of his summer noonday, escape into the marble corridor or crypt palpitating only with cold and smooth variegation of the unfevered mountain veins. In some sort, as, both in our stubbornness and our comfort, we not unfitly describe ourselves typically as Hearts of Oak, the Italians might in their strange and variegated mingling of passion, like purple color, with a cruel sternness, like white rock, truly describe themselves as Hearts of Stone.

Into this feeling about marble in domestic use, Shakespere, having seen it even in northern luxury, could partly enter, and marks it in several passages of his Italian plays. But if the reader still doubts his limitation to his own experience in all subjects of imagination, let him consider how the removal from mountain influence in his youth, so necessary for the perfection of his lower human sympathy, prevented him from ever rendering with any force the feelings of the mountain anchorite, or indicating in any of his monks the deep spirit of monasticism. Worldly cardinals or nuncios he can fathom to the uttermost; but where, in all his thoughts, do we find St. Francis, or Abbot Samson! The "Friar" of Shakespere's plays is almost the only stage conventionalism which he admitted; generally nothing more than a weak old man who lives in a cell, and has a rope about his waist.

While, finally, in such slight allusions as he makes to mountain scenery itself, it is very curious to observe the accurate limitation of his sympathies to such things as he had known in his youth; and his entire preference of human interest, and of courtly and kingly dignities to the nobleness of the hills. This is most marked in Cymbeline, where the term "mountaineer" is, as with Dante, always one of reproach; and the noble birth of Arviragus and Guiderius is shown by their holding their mountain cave as

"A cell of ignorance; travelling abed.
A prison for a debtor";

and themselves, educated among hills, as in all things contemptible:

"We are beastly; subtle as the fox, for prey;
Like warlike as the wolf, for what we eat:
Our valor is to chase what flies; our cage
We make our choir, as doth the prisoned bird."

A few phrases occur here and there which might justify the supposition that he had seen high mountains, but never implying awe or admiration. Thus Demetrius:

"These things seem *small* and *indistinguishable*,
Like far off mountains, turned into clouds."

123

"Taurus snow," and the "frosty Caucasus," are used merely as types of purity or cold; and though the avalanche is once spoken of as an image of power, it is with instantly following depreciation:

"Rush on his host, as doth the melted snow
Upon the vallies, whose low vassal seat
The Alps doth spit and void his rheum upon."

There was only one thing belonging to hills that Shakespere seemed to feel as noble—the pine tree, and that was because he had seen it in Warwickshire, clumps of pine occasionally rising on little sandstone mounds, as at the place of execution of Piers Gaveston, above the lowland woods. He touches on this tree fondly again and again.

"As rough,
Their royal blood enchafed as the rud'st wind,
That by his top doth take the mountain pine,
And make him stoop to the vale
The strong-based promontory
Have I made shake, and by the spurs plucked up
The pine and cedar."

Where note his observance of the peculiar horizontal roots of the pine, spurred as it is by them like the claw of a bird, and partly propped, as the aiguilles by those rock promontories at their base which I have always called their spurs, this observance of the pine's strength and animal-like grasp being the chief reason for his choosing it, above all other trees, for Ariel's prison. Again:

"You may as well forbid the mountain pines
To wag their high tops, and to make no noise
When they are fretted with the gusts of heaven"

And yet again:

"But when, from under this terrestrial ball,
He fires the proud tops of the eastern pines."

We may judge, by the impression which this single feature of hill scenery seems to have made on Shakespere's mind, because he had seen it in his youth, how his whole temper would have been changed if he had lived in a more sublime country, and how essential it was to his power of contemplation of mankind that he should be

124

removed from the sterner influences of nature. For the rest, so far as Shakespere's work has imperfections of any kind,—the trivialness of many of his adopted plots, for instance, and the comparative rarity with which he admits the ideal of an enthusiastic virtue arising out of principle; virtue being with him for the most part founded simply on the affections joined with inherent purity in his women or on mere manly pride and honor in his men;[11]—in a word, whatever difference, involving inferiority, there exists between him and Dante, in his conceptions of the relation between this world and the next, we may partly trace as we did the difference between Bacon and Pascal, to the less noble character of the scenes around him in his youth; and admit that, though it was necessary for his special work that he should be put, as it were, on a level with his race, on those plains of Stratford, we should see in this a proof, instead of a negation, of the mountain power over human intellect. For breadth and perfectness of condescending sight, the Shakesperian mind stands alone; but in *ascending* sight it is limited. The breadth of grasp is innate; the stoop and slightness of it was given by the circumstances of scene; and the difference between those careless masques of heathen gods, or unbelieved though mightily conceived visions of fairy, witch, or risen spirit, and the earnest faith of Dante's vision of Paradise, is the true measure of the difference in influence between the willowy banks of Avon, and the purple hills of Arno.

Our third inquiry, into the influence of mountains on domestic and military character, was, we said, to be deferred; for this reason, that it is too much involved with the consideration of the influence of simple rural life in unmountainous districts, to be entered upon with advantage until we have examined the general beauty of vegetation, whether lowland or mountainous. I hope to pursue this inquiry, therefore, at the close of the next volume, only desiring, in the meantime, to bring one or two points connected with it under the consideration of our English travellers.

For, it will be remembered, we first entered on this subject in order to obtain some data as to the possibility of a Practical Ideal in Swiss life, correspondent, in some measure, to the poetical ideal of the same, which so largely entertains the European public. Of which possibility, I do not think, after what we have even already seen of the true effect of mountains on the human mind, there is any reason to doubt, even if that ideal had not been presented to us already in some measure, in the older life of the Swiss republics. But of its possibility, *under present circumstances*, there is, I grieve to say, the deepest reason to doubt; and that the more, because the question is not whether the mountaineer can be raised into a happier life by the help of the active nations of the plains; but whether he can yet be protected from the infection of the folly and vanity of those nations. I urged, in the preceding chapter, some consideration of what might be accomplished, if we chose to devote to the help what we now devote to the mockery of the Swiss. But I would that the enlightened population of Paris and London were content with doing nothing;—that they were satisfied with expenditure upon their idle pleasures, in their idle way; and would leave the Swiss to their own mountain gloom of unadvancing independence. I believe that every frac now spent by travellers among the Alps tends more or less to the undermining of whatever special greatness there is in the Swiss character; and the persons I met in Switzerland, whose position and modes of life rendered them best able to give me true information respecting the present state of their country, among many causes of national deterioration, spoke with chief fear of the influx of English wealth, gradually connecting all industry with the wants and ways of strangers, and inviting all idleness to depend upon their casual help; thus gradually resolving the ancient consistency and pastoral simplicity of the mountain life into the two irregular trades of innkeeper[12] and mendicant.

I could say much on this subject if I had any hope of doing good by saying anything. But I have none. The influx of foreigners into Switzerland must necessarily be greater every year, and the greater it is, the larger, in the crowd, will be the majority of persons whose objects in travelling will be, first, to get as fast as possible from place to place, and, secondly, at every place where they arrive, to obtain the kind of accommodation and amusement to which they are accustomed in Paris, London, Brighton, or Baden. Railroads are already projected round the head of the Lake of Geneva, and through the town of Fribourg; the head of the Lake of Geneva being precisely and accurately the one spot of Europe whose character, and influence on human mind, are special; and unreplaceable if destroyed, no other spot resembling, or being in any wise comparable to it, in its peculiar way: while the town of Fribourg is in like manner the only mediaeval mountain town of importance left to us; Inspruck and such others being wholly modern, while Fribourg yet retains much of the aspect it had in the fourteenth and fifteenth centuries. The valley of Chamouni, another spot also unique in its way, is rapidly being turned into a kind of Cremorne Gardens; and I can see, within the perspective of but few years, the town of Lucerne consisting of a row of symmetrical hotels round the foot of the lake, its old bridges destroyed, an iron one built over the Reuss, and an acacia promenade carried along the lake-shore, with a German band playing under a Chinese temple at the end of it, and the enlightened travellers, representative of European civilization, performing before the Alps, in each afternoon summer sunlight, in their modern manner, the Dance of Death.

All this is inevitable; and it has its good as well as its evil side. I can imagine the zealous modernist replying to me that when all this is happily accomplished, my melancholy peasants of the valley of Trient will be turned into thriving shopkeepers, the desolate streets of Sion into glittering thoroughfares, and the marshes of the Valais into prosperous market-gardens. I hope so; and indeed am striving every day to conceive more accurately, and regulate all my efforts by the expectation of, the state of society, not now, I suppose, much more then twenty years in advance of us, when Europe, having satisfactorily effaced all memorials of the past, and reduced itself to the likeness of America, or of any other new country (only with less room for exertion), shall begin to consider what is next to be done, and to what newness of arts and interests may best be devoted the wealth of its marts, and the strength of its multitudes. Which anticipations and estimates, however, I have never been able, as yet,

126

to carry out with any clearness, being always arrested by the confused notion of a necessity for solitude, disdain of buying and selling, and other elements of that old mediaeval and mountain gloom, as in some way connected with the efforts of nearly all men who have either seen far into the destiny, or been much helpful to the souls, of their race. And the grounds of this feeling, whether right or wrong, I hope to analyze more fully in the next volume; only noting, finally, in this, one or two points for the consideration of those among us with whom it may sometimes become a question, whether they will help forward, or not, the turning of a sweet mountain valley into an abyss of factory-stench and toil, or the carrying of a line of traffic through some green place of shepherd solitude.

For, if there be any truth in the impression which I have always felt, and just now endeavored to enforce, that the mountains of the earth are its natural cathedrals, or natural altars, overlaid with gold, and bright with broidered work of flowers, and with their clouds resting on them as the smoke of a continual sacrifice, it may surely be a question with some of us, whether the tables of the moneychanger, however fit and commendable they may be as furniture in other places, are precisely the thing which it is the whole duty of man to get well set up in the mountain temple.

And perhaps it may help to the better determination of this question, if we endeavor, for a few patient moments, to bear with that weakness of our forefathers in feeling an *awe* for the hills; and, divesting ourselves, as far as may be, of our modern experimental or exploring activity, and habit of regarding mountains chiefly as places for gymnastic exercise, try to understand the temper, not indeed altogether exemplary, but yet having certain truths and dignities in it, to which we owe the founding of the Benedictine and Carthusian cloisters in the thin Alpine air. And this monkish temper we may, I suppose, best understand by considering the aspect under which mountains are represented in the Monk's book. I found that in my late lectures, at Edinburgh, I gave great offence by supposing, or implying, that scriptural expressions could have any force as bearing upon modern practical question; so that I do not now, nor shall I any more, allude to such expressions as in any wise necessarily bearing on the worldly business of the practical Protestant, but only as necessary to be glanced at in order to understand the temper of those old monks, who had the awkward habit of understanding the Bible literally; and to get any little good which momentary sympathy with the hearts of a large and earnest class of men may surely bring to us.

The monkish view of mountains, then, already alluded to,[13] was derived wholly from that Latin Vulgate of theirs; and, speaking as a monk, it may perhaps be permitted me to mark the significance of the earliest mention of mountains in the Mosaic books; at least, of those in which some Divine appointment or command is stated respecting them. They are first brought before us as refuges for God's people from the two judgments of water and fire. The ark *rests* upon the "mountains of Ararat"; and man, having passed through that great baptism unto death, kneels upon the earth first where it is nearest heaven, and mingles with the mountain clouds the smoke of his sacrifice of thanksgiving. Again: from the midst of the first judgment by fire, the command

127

of the Deity to His servant is, "Escape to the mountain"; and the morbid fear of the hills, which fills any human mind after long stay in places of luxury and sin, is strangely marked in Lot's complaining reply: "I cannot escape to the mountain, lest some evil take me." The third mention, in way or ordinance, is a far more solemn one: "Abraham lifted up his eyes, and saw the place afar off." "The Place," the Mountain of Myrrh, or of bitterness, chosen to fulfil to all the seed of Abraham, far off and near, the inner meaning of promise regarded in that vow: "I will lift up mine eyes unto the hills, from whence cometh mine help."

AND THE FOURTH IS THE DELIVERY OF THE LAW ON SINAI.

§ 46. It seemed, then, to the monks, that the mountains were appointed by their Maker to be to man, refuges from Judgment, signs of Redemption, and altars of Sanctification and obedience; and they saw them afterwards connected, in the manner the most touching and gracious, with the death, after his task had been accomplished, of the first anointed Priest; the death, in like manner, of the first inspired Lawgiver; and, lastly, with the assumption of his office by the Eternal Priest, Lawgiver, and Saviour.

Observe the connection of these three events. Although the *time* of the deaths of Aaron and Moses was hastened by God's displeasure, we have not, it seems to me, the slightest warrant for concluding that the *manner* of their deaths was intended to be grievous or dishonorable to them. Far from this: it cannot, I think, be doubted that in the denial of the permission to enter the Promised Land, the whole punishment of their sin was included; and that as far as regarded the manner of their deaths, it must have been appointed for them by their Master in all tenderness and love; and with full purpose of ennobling the close of their service upon the earth. It might have seemed to *us* more honorable that both should have been permitted to die beneath the shadow of the Tabernacle, the congregation of Israel watching by their side; and all whom the loved gathered together to receive the last message from the lips of the meek lawgiver, and the last blessing from the prayer of the anointed priest. But it was not thus they were permitted to die. Try to realize that going forth of Aaron from the midst of the congregation. He who had so often done sacrifice for their sin, going forth now to offer up his own spirit. He who had stood, among them, between the dead and the living, and had seen the eyes of all that great multitude turned to him, that by his intercession their breath might yet be drawn a moment more, going forth now to meet the Angel of Death face to face, and deliver himself into his hand. Try if you cannot walk, in thought, with those two brothers, and the son, as they passed the outmost tents of Israel, and turned, while yet the dew lay round about the camp, towards the slopes of Mount Hor; talking together for the last time, as step by step, they felt the steeper rising of the rocks, and hour after hour, beneath the ascending sun, the horizon grew broader as they climbed, and all the folded hills of Idumea, one by one subdued, showed amidst their hollows in the haze of noon, the windings of that long desert journey, now at last to close. But who shall enter into the thoughts of the High Priest, as his eye followed those paths of ancient pilgrimage; and, through the silence of the arid and endless hills, stretching even to the dim peak of Sinai, the whole history of those forty years was unfolded before him, and the mystery of his own ministries revealed to him; and that other Holy of Holies, of which the mountain peaks were the altars, and the mountain clouds the veil, the firmament of his Father's dwelling, opened to him still more brightly and infinitely as he drew nearer his death; until at last, on the shadeless summit,—from him on whom sin was to be laid no more—from him, on whose heart the names of sinful nations were to press their graven fire no longer,—the brother and the son took breast-plate and ephod, and left him to his rest.

There is indeed a secretness in this calm faith and deep restraint of sorrow, into which it is difficult for us to enter; but the death of Moses himself is more easily to be conceived, and had in it circumstances still more touching, as far as regards the influence of the external scene. For forty years Moses had not been alone. The care and burden of all the people, the weight of their woe, and guilt, and death, had been upon him continually. The multitude had been laid upon him as if he had conceived them; their tears had been his meat, night and day, until he had felt as if God had withdrawn His favor from him, and he had prayed that he might be slain, and not see his wretchedness.[14] And now, at last, the command came, "Get thee up into this mountain." The weary hands that had been so long stayed up against the enemies of Israel, might lean again upon the shepherd's staff, and fold themselves for the shepherd's prayer—for the shepherd's slumber. Not strange to his feet, though forty years unknown, the roughness of the bare mountain-path, as he climbed from ledge to ledge of Abarim; not strange to his aged eyes the scattered clusters of the mountain herbage, and the broken shadows of the cliffs, indented far across the silence of uninhabited ravines; scenes such as those among which, with none, as now, beside him but God. He had led his flocks so often; and which he had left, how painfully! taking upon him the appointed power, to make of the fenced city a wilderness, and to fill the desert with songs of deliverance. It was not to embitter the last hours of his life that God restored to him, for a day, the beloved solitudes he had lost; and breathed the peace of the perpetual hills around him, and cast the world in which he had labored and sinned far beneath his feet, in that mist of dying blue;—all sin, all wandering, soon to be forgotten for ever; the Dead Sea—a type of God's anger understood by him, of all men, most clearly, who had seen the earth open her mouth, and the sea his depth, to overwhelm the companies of those who contended with his Master—laid waveless beneath him; and beyond it, the fair hills of Judah, and the soft plains and banks of Jordan, purple in the evening light as with the blood of redemption, and fading in their distant fulness into mysteries of promise and of love. There, with his unabated strength, his undimmed glance, lying down upon the utmost rocks, with angels waiting near to contend for the spoils of his spirit, he put off his earthly armor. We do deep reverence to his companion prophet, for whom the chariot of fire came down from heaven; but was his death less noble, whom his Lord Himself buried in the vales of Moab, keeping, in the secrets of the eternal counsels, the knowledge of a sepulchre, from which he was to be called, in the fulness of time, to talk with that Lord, upon Hermon, of the death that He should accomplish at Jerusalem!

And lastly, let us turn our thoughts for a few moments to the cause of the resurrection of these two prophets. We are all of us too much in the habit of passing it by, as a thing mystical and inconceivable, taking place in the life of Christ for some purpose not by us to be understood, or, at the best, merely as a manifestation of His divinity by brightness of heavenly light, and the ministering of the spirits of the dead, intended to strengthen the faith of His three chosen apostles. And in this, as in many other events recorded by the Evangelists, we lose half the meaning and evade the practical power upon ourselves, by never accepting in its fulness the idea that our Lord was "perfect man," "tempted in all things like as we are." Our preachers are continually trying, in all manner of subtle ways, to explain the union of the Divinity with the Manhood, an explanation which certainly involves first their being able to describe the nature of Deity itself, or, in plain words, to comprehend God. They never can explain, in any one particular, the union of the natures; they only succeed in weakening the faith of their hearers as to the entireness of either. The thing they have to do is precisely the contrary of this—to insist upon the *entireness* of both. We never think of Christ enough as God, never enough as Man; the instinctive habit of our minds being always to miss of the Divinity, and the reasoning and enforced habit to miss of the Humanity. We are afraid to harbor in our own hearts, or to utter in the hearing of others, any thought of our Lord, as hungering, tired, sorrowful, having a human soul, a human will, and affected by events of human life as a finite creature is; and yet one half of the efficiency of His atonement, and the whole of the efficiency of His example, depend on His having been this to the full.

Consider, therefore, the Transfiguration as it relates to the human feelings of our Lord. It was the first definite preparation for His death. He had foretold it to His disciples six days before; then takes with Him the three chosen ones into "an high mountain apart." From an exceedingly high mountain, at the first taking on Him the ministry of life, He had beheld, and rejected the kingdoms of the earth, and their glory: now, on a high mountain, He takes upon Him the ministry of death. Peter and they that were with him, as in Gethsemane, were heavy with sleep. Christ's work had to be done alone.

The tradition is, that the Mount of Transfiguration was the summit of Tabor; but Tabor is neither a high mountain, nor was it in any sense a mountain *"apart"*; being in those years both inhabited and fortified. All the immediately preceding ministries of Christ had been at Cesarea Philippi. There is no mention of travel southward in the six days that intervened between the warning given to His disciples, and the going up into the hill. What other hill could it be than the southward slope of that goodly mountain, Hermon, which is indeed the centre of all the Promised Land, from the entering in of Hamath unto the river of Egypt; the mount of fruitfulness, from which the springs of Jordan descended to the valleys of Israel. Along its mighty forest avenues, until the grass grew fair with the mountain lilies, His feet dashed in the dew of Hermon, He must have gone to pray His first recorded prayer about death; and from the steep of it, before He knelt, could see to the south all the dwelling-place of the people that had sat in darkness, and seen the great light, the land of Zabulon and of Naphtali, Galilee of the nations;—could see, even with His human sight, the gleam of that lake by Capernaum and Chorazin, and many a place loved by Him, and vainly ministered to, whose house was now left unto them desolate; and, chief of all, far in the utmost blue, the hills above Nazareth, sloping down to His old home: hills on which yet the stones lay loose, that had been taken up to cast at Him, when He left them for ever.

"And as he prayed, two men stood by him." Among the many ways in which we miss the help and hold of Scripture, none is more subtle than our habit of supposing that, even as man, Christ was free from the Fear of Death. How could He then have been tempted as we are? since among all the trials of the earth, none spring from the dust more terrible than that Fear. It had to be borne by Him, indeed, in a unity, which we can never comprehend, with the foreknowledge of victory,—as His sorrow for Lazarus, with the consciousness of the power to restore him; but it *had* to be borne, and that in its full earthly terror; and the presence of it is surely marked for us enough by the rising of those two at His side. When, in the desert, He was girding Himself for the work of life, angels of life came and ministered unto Him; now, in the fair world, when He is girding Himself for the work of death, the ministrants come to Him from the grave.

But from the grave conquered. One, from that tomb under Abarim, which His own hand had sealed so long ago; the other from the rest into which he had entered, without seeing corruption. There stood by Him Moses and Elias, and spake of His decease.

Then, when the prayer is ended, the task accepted, first, since the star paused over Him at Bethlehem, the full glory falls upon Him from heaven, and the testimony is borne to his everlasting Sonship and power. "Hear ye him."

If, in their remembrance of these things, and in their endeavor to follow in the footsteps of their Master, religious men of by-gone days, closing themselves in the hill solitudes, forgot sometimes, and sometimes feared, the duties they owed to the active world, we may perhaps pardon them more easily than we ought to pardon ourselves, if we neither seek any influence for good nor submit to it unsought, in scenes to which thus all the men whose writings we receive as inspired, together with their Lord, retired whenever they had any task or trial laid upon them needing more than their usual strength of spirit. Nor, perhaps, should we have unprofitably entered into the mind of the earlier ages, if among our other thoughts, as we watch the chains of the snowy mountains rise on the horizon, we should sometimes admit the memory of the hour in which their Creator, among their solitudes, entered on His travail for the salvation of our race; and indulge the dream, that as the flaming and trembling mountains of the earth seem to be the monuments of the manifesting of His terror on Sinai,—these pure and white hills, near to the heaven, and sources of all good to the earth, are the appointed memorials of that Light of His Mercy, that fell, snow-like, on the Mount of Transfiguration.

—1860

131

Notes

1. In tracing the *whole* of the deep enjoyment to mountain association, I of course accept whatever feelings are connected with the observance of rural life, or with that of architecture. None of these feelings arise out of the landscape, properly so called: the pleasure with which we see a peasant's garden fairly kept, or a ploughman doing his work well, or a group of children playing at a cottage door, being wholly separate from that which we find in the fields or commons around them; and the beauty of architecture, or the associations connected with it, in like manner often ennobling the most tame scenery;—yet not so but that we may always distinguish between the abstract character of the unassisted landscape, and the charm which it derives from the architecture. Much of the majesty of French landscape consists in its grand and grey village churches and turreted farmhouses, not to speak of its cathedrals, castles, and beautifully placed cities.

2. One of the principal reasons for the false supposition that Switzerland is not picturesque, is the error of most sketchers and painters in representing pine forest in middle distance as dark *green*, or grey green, whereas its true color is always purple, at distances of even two or three miles. Let any traveller coming down the Montanvert look for an aperture, three or four inches wide, between the near pine branches, through which, standing eight or ten feet from it, he can see the opposite forests on the Breven or Flegère. Those forests are not above two or two and a half miles from him; but he will find the aperture is filled by a tint of nearly pure azure or purple, not by green.

3. The Savoyard's name for its flower, "Pain du Bon Dieu," is very beautiful; from, I believe, the supposed resemblance of its white and scattered blossom to the fallen manna.

4. See reference to his painting of stones in the last note to § 28 of the chapter on Imagination Penetrative, Vol. II.

5. In saying this I do not, of course, forget the influence of the sea on the Pisans and Venetians; but that is a separate subject, and must be examined in the next volume.

6. "With fairest flowers
   While summer lasts, and I live here, Fidele,
   I'll sweeten thy sad grave. Thou shalt not lack
   The flower that's like thy face—pale primrose, nor
   The azured harebell—like thy veins; no, nor
   The leaf of eglantine, whom not to slander,
   Outsweetened not thy breath. The ruddock would
   With charitable bill bring thee all this;
   Yea, and furred moss besides, when flowers are none,
   To winter-ground thy corse.
   Gui. Prithee, have done,
   And do not play in wench-like words with that
   Which is so serious."

Imogen herself, afterwards in deeper passion, will give weeds—not flowers—and something more:
"And when
With wildwood leaves, and weeds, I have strewed his grave,

132

And on it said a century of prayers,
Such as I can, twice o'er, I'll weep, and sigh,
And, leaving so his service, follow you."

7. If the reader thinks that in Henry the Fifth's time the Elizabethan temper might already have been manifesting itself, let him compare the English herald's speech, act 2, scene 2, of King John; and by way of specimen of Shakespere's historical care, or regard of mediaeval character, the large use of *artillery* in the previous scene.

8. The last bishop.

9. His favorite son; nominally his nephew.

10. "Nero Antico" is more familiar to our ears; but Browning does right in translating it; as afterwards "cipollino" into "onion-stone." Our stupid habit of using foreign words without translation is continually losing us half the force of the foreign language. How many travellers hearing the term "cipollino" recognize the intended sense of a stone splitting into concentric coats, like an onion?

11. I mean that Shakespere almost always implies a total difference in nature between one human being and another; one being from the birth, pure and affectionate, another base and cruel; and he displays each, in its sphere, as having the nature of dove, wolf, or lion, never much implying the government or change of nature by any external principle. There can be no question that in the main he is right in this view of human nature; still, the other form of virtue does exist occasionally, and was never, as far as I recollect, taken much note of by him. And with this stern view of humanity, Shakespere joined a sorrowful view of Fate, closely resembling that of the ancients. He is distinguished from Dante eminently by his always dwelling on last causes instead of first causes. Dante invariably points to the moment of the soul's choice which fixed its fate, to the instant of the day when it read no farther, or determined to give bad advice about Penestrino. But Shakespere always leans on the force of fate, as it urges the final evil; and dwells with infinite bitterness on the power of the wicked, and the infinitude of result dependent seemingly on little things. A fool brings the last piece of news from Verona, and the dearest lives of its noble houses are lost; they might have been saved if the scristan had not stumbled as he walked. Othello mislays his handkerchief, and there remains nothing for him but death. Hamlet gets hold of the wrong foil, and the rest is silence. Edmund's runner is a moment too late at the prison, and the feather will not move at Cordelia's lips. Salisbury a moment too late at the tower, and Arthur lies on the stones dead. Goneril and Iago have on the whole, in this world, Shakespere sees, much of their own way, though they come to a bad end. It is a pin that Death pierces the king's fortress wall with; and Carelessness and Folly sit sceptred and dreadful, side by side with the pin-armed skeleton.

12. Not the old hospitable innkeeper, who honored his guests and was honored by them, than whom I do not know a more useful or worthy character; but the modern innkeeper, proprietor of a building in the shape of a factory, making up three hundred beds; who necessarily regards his guests in the light of Numbers 1, 2, 3–300, and is too often felt or apprehended by them only as a presiding influence of extortion.

13. Vol. III. Chap. xiv. § 10.

14. Numbers, xi. 12, 15.

John Tyndall
"The Weisshorn"

John Tyndall (1820–1893) succeeded Michael Faraday as superintendent of the scientific Royal Institution and conducted research on magne-crystallic phenomena, infrared radiation, and microbial action. In England he supported Louis Pasteur's theories of fermentation and bacteria. Tyndall visited the Alps every summer for a number of years where he continued the pioneering experiments of Saussure and James David Forbes on the structure, movement, and "regelation" of glacial ice. His works on mountaineering and glaciers include The Glaciers of the Alps *(1860),* Hours of Exercise in the Alps *(1871), and* Forms of Water in Clouds, Rivers, Ice and Glaciers *(1872). Tyndall became a key figure in British Golden Age climbing with his numerous technically demanding climbs in the 1860s, including the first ascent of the Weisshorn, described in this passage.*

IX.

THE WEISSHORN.

On Friday, the 16th of August, I rose at 4:30; the eastern heaven was hot with the glow of the rising sun, and against it were drawn the mountain outlines. At 5:30 I bade good-bye to the excellent little auberge of the Bel Alp,[1] and went straight down the mountain to Brieg, took the diligence to Visp, and engaged a porter immediately to Randa. I had sent Bennen thither to inspect the Weisshorn. On my arrival I learned that he had made the necessary reconnaissance, and entertained hopes of our being able to gain the top.

This noble mountain, which is 14,800 feet high, had been tried on various occasions and from different sides by brave and competent climbers, but all efforts had been hitherto unavailing.

Previous to quitting Randa to assail this formidable peak I had two pairs of rugs sewed together so as to form two sacks. These and other coverlets, together with our wine and provisions, were sent on in advance of us. At 1 P.M. on the 18th of August Bennen, Wenger, and myself quitted the hotel, and were soon zigzagging among the pines of the opposite mountain. Wenger had been the guide of my friend Forster, and had showed himself so active and handy on the Strahleck that I commissioned Bennen to engage him. During the previous night I had been very unwell, and as I climbed the slope I suffered from intense thirst. Water seemed powerless to quench the desire for drink. We reached a chalet, and at our request a smart young Senner

John Tyndall, "The Weisshorn," *Hours of Exercise in the Alps* (London: Macmillan, 1861).

caught up a pail, and soon returned with it full of delicious milk. The effect of the milk was astonishing. It seemed to lubricate every atom of my body, and to exhilarate with its fragrance my brain.

Two hours' additional climbing brought us to our bivouac, a ledge of rock which jutted from the mountain-side, and formed an overhanging roof. On removing the stones from beneath the ledge, a space of comparatively dry clay was laid bare. This was to be my bed, and to soften it Wenger considerably stirred it up with his axe. This position was excellent, for lying upon my left side I commanded the whole range of Monte Rosa, from the Mischabel to the Breithorn. We were on the edge of an amphitheatre. Beyond the Schallenbach was the stately Mettelhorn. A row of eminences swept round to the right linked by lofty ridges of cliffs, which embraced the Schallenberg glacier. They formed, however, only a spur of the vaster Weisshorn, the cone of which was not visible from our dormitory. In company with Bennen I afterwards skirted the mountain until the whole colossal pyramid stood facing us. When I first looked at it my hopes sank, but both of us gathered confidence from a more lengthened gaze. The mountain is a pyramid with three faces, the intersections of which form three sharp edges or *arêtes*. The end of the eastern ridge was nearest to us, and on it our attention was principally fixed. We finally decided on the route to be pursued next morning, and with a chastened hope in both our breasts we returned to our shelter.

Water was our first necessity: it seemed everywhere, but there was none to drink. It was locked to solidity in the ice and snow. The sound of it came booming up from the Vispbach, as it broke into foam or rolled its boulders over its waterworn bed; and the swish of many a minor streamlet mingled with the muffled roar of the large one. Bennen set out in search of the precious liquid, and after a long absence returned with a jug and pan full. At our meal, Wenger, who is a man rich in small expedients, turned the section of a cheese towards the flame of our pine fire; it fizzed and blistered and turned viscous, and, the toasted surface being removed, was consumed with relish by us all. The sunset had been unspeakably grand, steeping the zenith in violet, and flooding the base of the heavens with crimson light. Immediately opposite to us rose the Mischabel, with its two peaks, the Grubenhorn and the Täschhorn, each barely under 15,000 feet in height. Next came the Alphubel, with its flattened crown of snow; then the Allaleinhorn and Rympfischhorn; then the Cima di Jazzi; next the mass of Monte Rosa, flooded with light from bottom to top. The face of the Lyskamm turned towards us was for the most part shaded, but here and there its projecting portions jutted forth red hot as the light fell upon them. The "Twins" were most singularly illuminated; across the waist of each of them was drawn a black bar, produced by the shadow of a corner of the Breithorn, while their bases and crowns were exposed to the crimson light. Over the rugged face of the Breithorn itself the light fell as if in splashes, igniting its glaciers and swathing its black crags in a layer of transparent red. The Mettelhorn was cold, so was the entire range governed by the Weisshorn, while the glaciers they embraced lay grey and ghastly in the twilight shade.

The sunlight lingered, while up the arch of the opposite heavens the moon, within one day of being full, seemed hastening to our aid. She finally appeared exactly behind the peak of the Rympfischhorn, the cone of the mountain being projected for a short time as a triangle on the lunar disc. Only for a short time, however; the silver sphere soon cleared the mountain, and bore away through the tinted sky. The motion was quite visible, and resembled that of a vast balloon. As the day approached its end the scene assumed the most sublime aspect. All the lower portions of the mountains were deeply shaded, while the loftiest peaks, ranged upon a semicircle, were fully exposed to the sinking sun. They seemed pyramids of solid fire, while here and there long stretches of crimson light drawn over the higher snow-fields linked the summits together. An intensely illuminated geranium flower seems to swim in its own colour, which apparently surrounds the petals like a layer, and defeats by its lustre any attempt of the eye to seize upon the sharp outline of the leaves. A similar effect was here observed upon the mountains; the glory did not seem to come from them alone, but seemed also effluent from the air around them. As the evening advanced, the eastern heavens low down assumed a deep purple hue, above which, and blending with it by infinitesimal gradations, was a belt of red, and over this again zones of orange and violet. I walked round the corner of the mountain at sunset, and found the western sky glowing with a more transparent crimson than that which overspread the east. The crown of the Weisshorn was imbedded in this magnificent light. After sunset the purple of the cast changed to a deep neutral tint, and against the faded red which spread above it the sun-forsaken mountains laid their cold and ghastly heads. The ruddy colour vanished more and more; the stars strengthened in lustre, until finally the moon and they held undisputed possession of the sky.

My face was turned towards the moon until it became so chilled that I was forced to protect it by a light handkerchief. The power of blinding the eyes is ascribed to the moonbeams, but the real mischief is that produced by radiations from the eyes into clear space, and the inflammation consequent upon the chill. As the cold increased I was fain to squeeze myself more and more underneath the ledge, so as to lessen the space of sky against which my body could radiate. Nothing could be more solemn than the night. Up from the valley came the low thunder of the Vispbach. Over the Dom flashed in succession the stars of Orion, until finally the entire constellation hung aloft. Higher up in heaven was the moon, and her beams as they fell upon the snow-fields and pyramids were sent back in silvery lustre by some, while others remained a dead white. These, as the earth twirled round, came duly in for their share of the glory. The Twins caught it at length and retained it long, shining with a pure spiritual radiance, while the moon continued above the hills.

At twelve o'clock I looked at my watch, and a second time at 2 A.M. The moon was then just touching the crest of the Schallenberg, and we were threatened with the withdrawal of her light. This soon occurred. We rose at 2:15 A.M., consumed our coffee, and had to wait idly for the dawn. A faint illumination at length overspread the sky, and with this promise of the coming day we quitted our bivouac at 3:30 A.M. No cloud was to be seen; as far as the weather was concerned we were sure to have fair play. We rounded the shingly shoulder of the mountain to the edge of a snow-field, but before entering upon it I disburthened myself of my strong shooting jacket, leaving it on the mountain-side. The sunbeams and my own exertion would, I knew, keep me only too warm during the day. We crossed the snow, cut our way through a piece of entangled glacier, reached the Bergschrund, and passed it without a rope. We ascended the frozen snow of the couloir by steps, but soon diverged from it to the rocks at our right, and mounted them to the end of the eastern *arête* of the mountain.

A snow saddle separated us from the higher rocks. With our staff-pikes at one side of the saddle, we pass by steps cut upon the other. We find the rocks hewn into fantastic turrets and obelisks, while the loose chips of this sculpture are strewn confusedly upon the ridge. Amid these we cautiously pick our way, winding round the towers or scaling them amain. The work was heavy from the first, the bending, twisting, reaching, and drawing up calling upon all the muscles of the frame. After two hours of this work we halted, and, looking back, saw two moving objects on the glacier below us. At first we took them to be chamois, but they were men. The leader carried an axe, and his companion a knapsack and an alpenstock. They followed our traces, losing them apparently now and then, and waiting to recover them. Our expedition had put Randa in a state of excitement, and some of its best climbers had urged Bennen to take them with him. This he did not deem necessary, and now here were two of them determined to try the thing on their own account, and perhaps to dispute with us the honour of the enterprise. On this point, however, our uneasiness was small.

Resuming our gymnastics, the rocky staircase led us to the flat summit of a tower, where we found ourselves cut off from a similar tower by a deep gap bitten into the mountain. The rope was here our refuge. Bennen coiled it round his waist; we let him down along the surface of the rock, until he fixed himself on a ledge, where he could lend me a helping hand. I followed him, and Wenger followed me. By a kind of screw motion we twisted ourselves round the opposite tower, and reached the ridge behind it. Work of this kind, however, is not to be performed by the day, and, with a view of sparing our strength, we quitted the ridge and endeavoured to get along the southern slope of the pyramid. The mountain was scarred by long couloirs, filled with clear hard ice. The cutting of steps across these couloirs proved to be so tedious and fatiguing that I urged Bennen to abandon them and try the ridge once more. We regained it and worked along it as before. Here and there upon the northern side the snow was folded over, and we worked slowly upward along the cornice snow. The ridge became gradually narrower, and the precipices on each side more sheer. We reached the end of one of its subdivisions, and found ourselves separated from the next rocks by a gap about twenty yards across. The ridge was here narrowed to a mere wall, which, however, as rock, would present no serious difficulty. But upon the wall of rock was placed a second wall of snow, which dwindled to a pure knife-edge at the top. It was white, of very fine grain, and a little moist. How to pass this snow catenary I knew not, for I did not think a human foot could trust itself upon so frail a support. Bennen's practical sagacity, however, came into play. He tried the snow by squeezing it with his foot, and to my astonishment began to cross it. Even after the pressure of his feet the space he had to stand on did not exceed a hand-breadth. I followed him, exactly as a boy walking along a horizontal pole, with toes turned outwards. Right and left the precipices were appalling. We reached the opposite rock, and an earnest smile rippled over Bennen's countenance as he turned towards me. He knew that he had done a daring thing, though not a presumptuous one. "Had the snow," he said, "been less perfect, I should not have thought of attempting it; but I knew after I had set my foot upon the ridge that we might pass without fear."

It is quite surprising what a number of things the simple observation made by Faraday in 1846 enables us to explain. Bennen's instinctive act is justified by theory. The snow was fine in grain, pure, and moist. When pressed, the attachments of its granules were innumerable, and their perfect cleanness enabled them to freeze together with a maximum energy. It was this freezing which gave the mass its sustaining power.

Two fragments of ordinary table ice brought carefully together freeze and cement themselves at their place of junction; or if two pieces floating in water be brought together, they instantly freeze, and by laying hold of either of them gently you can drag the other after it through the water. Imagine such points of attachment distributed in great numbers through a mass of snow. The substance becomes thereby a semi-solid instead of a mass of powder. My guide, however, unaided by any theory, did a thing from which I should have shrunk, though backed by all the theories in the world.

After this we found the rocks on the ridge so shaken that it required the greatest caution to avoid bringing them down upon us. With all our care, moreover, we sometimes dislodged vast masses, which leaped upon the slope adjacent, loosened others by their shock, these again others, until finally a whole flight of them would escape, setting the mountain in a roar as they whizzed and thundered along its side to the snow-fields 4,000 feet below us. The day was hot, the work hard, and our bodies were drained of their liquids as by a Turkish bath. To make good our loss we halted at intervals where the melted snow formed liquid veins, and quenched our thirst. A bottle of champagne, poured sparingly into our goblets over a little snow, furnished Wenger and myself with many a refreshing draught. Bennen feared his eyes, and would not touch champagne. We, however, did not find halting good; for at every pause the muscles became set, and some minutes were necessary to render them again elastic. But for both mind and body the discipline was grand. There is scarcely a position possible to a human being which, at one time or another during the day, I was not forced to assume. The fingers, wrist, and forearm were my main reliance, and as a mechanical instrument the human hand appeared to me this day to be a miracle of constructive art.

For the most part the summit was hidden from us, but on reaching the successive eminences it came frequently into view. After three hours spent on the *arête*—about five hours, that is, subsequent to starting—we saw the summit over another minor summit, which gave it an illusive proximity. "You have now good hopes," I re-marked, turning to Bennen. "I do not allow myself to entertain the idea of failure," he replied. Well, six hours passed on the ridge, each of which put in its inexorable claim to the due amount of mechanical work; and at the end of this time we found our-selves apparently no nearer to the summit than when Bennen's hopes cropped out in confidence. I looked anxiously at my guide as he fixed his weary eyes upon the dis-tant peak. There was no confidence in his expression; still I do not believe that either of us entertained for a moment the thought of giving in. Wenger complained of his lungs, and Bennen counselled him several times to remain behind; but this the Ober-land man refused to do. At the commencement of a day's work one often feels anx-ious, if not timid; but when the work is very hard we become callous and sometimes stupefied by the incessant knocking about. This was my case at present, and I kept watch lest my indifference should become carelessness. I repeatedly supposed a case where a sudden effort might be required of me, and felt all through that I had a fair residue of strength to fall back upon should such a call be made. This conclusion was sometimes tested by a spurt; flinging myself suddenly from rock to rock, I proved my condition by experiment instead of relying on surmise. An eminence in the ridge which cut off the view of the summit was now the object of our exertions. We reached it; but how hopelessly distant did the summit appear! Bennen laid his face upon his axe for a moment; a kind of sickly despair was in his eye as he turned to me, re-marking, "Lieber Herr, die Spitze ist noch sehr weit oben."

Lest the desire to gratify me should urge him beyond the bounds of prudence, I told my guide that he must not persist upon my account; that I should cheerfully re-turn with him the moment he thought it no longer safe to proceed. He replied that, though weary, he felt quite sure of himself, and asked for some food. He had it, and a gulp of wine, which mightily refreshed him. Looking at the mountain with a firmer eye, he exclaimed, "Herr! wir müssen ihn haben," and his voice, as he spoke, rung like steel within my heart. I thought of Englishmen in battle, of the qualities which had made them famous: it was mainly the quality of not knowing when to yield—of fighting for duty even after they had ceased to be animated by hope. Such thoughts helped to lift me over the rocks. Another eminence now fronted us, behind which, how far we knew not, the summit lay. We scaled this height, and above us, but clearly within reach, a silvery pyramid projected itself against the blue sky. I was assured ten times over by my companions that it was the highest point before I ventured to stake my faith upon the assertion. I feared that it also might take rank with the illusions which had so often beset our ascent, and I shrunk from the consequent moral shock. A huge prism of granite, or granitic gneiss, terminated the arête, and from it a knife-edge of pure white snow ran up to a little point. We passed along the edge, reached that point, and instantly swept with our eyes the whole range of the horizon. We stood upon the crown of the redoubtable Weisshorn.

The long-pent feelings of my two companions found vent in a wild and reiterated cheer. Bennen shook his arms in the air and shouted as a Valaisian, while Wenger

139

raised the shriller yell of the Oberland. We looked downwards along the ridge, and far below, perched on one of its crags, could discern the two Randa men. Again and again the roar of triumph was sent down to them. They had accomplished but a small portion of the ridge, and soon after our success they wended their way homewards. They came, willing enough, no doubt, to publish our failure had we failed; but we found out afterwards that they had been equally strenuous in announcing our success; they had seen us, they affirmed, like three flies upon the summit of the mountain. Both men had to endure a little persecution for the truth's sake, for nobody in Randa would believe that the Weisshorn could be scaled, and least of all by a man who for two days previously had been the object of Philomène the waitress's constant pity, on account of the incompetence of his stomach to accept all that she offered for its acceptance. The energy of conviction with which the men gave their evidence had, however, proved conclusive to the most sceptical, before we arrived.

Bennen wished to leave some outward and visible sign of our success on the summit. He deplored having no suitable flag; but as a substitute for such it was proposed that he should use the handle of one of our axes as a flagstaff, and surmount it by a red pocket-handkerchief. This was done, and for some time subsequently the extempore banner was seen flapping in the wind. To his extreme delight, it was shown to Bennen himself three days afterwards by my friend Mr. Francis Galton, from the Riffelberg hotel.

Every Swiss climber is acquainted with the Weisshorn. I have long regarded it as the noblest of all the Alps, and most other travellers share this opinion. The impression it produces is in some measure due to the comparative isolation with which it juts into the heavens. It is not masked by other mountains, and all around the Alps its final pyramid is in view. Conversely, the Weisshorn commands a vast range of prospect. Neither Bennen nor myself had ever seen anything at all equal to it. The day, moreover, was perfect; not a cloud was to be seen; and the gauzy haze of the distant air, though sufficient to soften the outlines and enhance the colouring of the mountains, was far too thin to obscure them. Over the peaks and through the valleys the sunbeams poured, unimpeded save by the mountains themselves, which sent their shadows in bars of darkness through the illuminated air. I had never before witnessed a scene which affected me like this one. I opened my note-book to make a few observations, but soon relinquished the attempt. There was something incongruous, if not profane, in allowing the scientific faculty to interfere where silent worship seemed the "reasonable service."

We had been ten hours climbing from our bivouac to the summit, and it was now necessary that we should clear the mountain before the close of day. Our muscles were loose and numbed, and, unless extremely urged, declined all energetic tension: the thought of our success, however, ran like a kind of wine through our fibres and helped us down. We once fancied the descent would be rapid, but it was far from being so. As in ascending, Bennen took the lead; he slowly cleared each crag, paused till I joined him, I pausing till Wenger joined me, and thus one or other of us was always in motion. Our leader showed a preference for the snow, while I held on to the rocks, where my hands could assist my feet. Our muscles were sorely tried by the twisting round the splintered turrets of the *arête*, but a long, long stretch of the ridge must be passed before we can venture to swerve from it. We were roused from our stupefaction at times by the roar of the stones which we loosed from the ridge and sent leaping down the mountain. Soon after recrossing the snow catenary already mentioned we quitted the ridge to get obliquely along the slope of the pyramid. The face of it was scarred by couloirs, of which the deeper and narrower ones were filled with ice, while the others acted as highways for the rocks quarried by the weathering above. Steps must be cut in the ice, but the swing of the axe is very different now from what it was in the morning. Bennen's blows descended with the deliberateness of a man whose fire is half-quenched; still they fell with sufficient power, and the needful cavities were formed. We retraced our morning steps over some of the ice-slopes. No word of warning was uttered here as we ascended, but now Bennen's admonitions were frequent and emphatic—"Take care not to slip." I imagined, however, that even if a man slipped he would be able to arrest his descent; but Bennen's response when I stated this opinion was very prompt—"No! it would be utterly impossible. If it were snow you might do it, but it is pure ice, and if you fall you will lose your senses before you can use your axe." I suppose he was right. At length we turned directly downwards, and worked along one of the ridges which lie in the line of steepest fall. We first dropped cautiously from ledge to ledge. At one place Bennen clung for a considerable time to a face of rock, casting out feelers of leg and arm, and desiring me to stand still. I did not understand the difficulty, for the rock, though steep, was by no means vertical. I fastened myself on to it, Bennen being on a ledge below, waiting to receive me. The spot on which he stood was a little rounded protuberance sufficient to afford him footing, but over which the slightest momentum would have carried him. He knew this, and hence his caution. Soon after this we quitted our ridge and dropped into a couloir to the left of it. It was dark, and damp with trickling water. Here we disencumbered ourselves of the rope, and found our speed greatly augmented. In some places the rocks were worn to a powder, along which we shot by glissades. We swerved again to the left, crossed a ridge, and got into another and dryer couloir. The last one was dangerous, as the water exerted a constant slapping action upon the rocks. From our new position we could hear the clatter of stones descending the gulley we had just forsaken. Wenger, who had brought up the rear during the day, is now sent to the front; he has not Bennen's power, but his legs are longer and his descent rapid. He scents out the way, which becomes more and more difficult. He pauses, observes, dodges, but finally comes to a dead stop on the summit of a precipice, which sweeps like a rampart round the mountain. We moved to the left, and after a long *détour* succeeded in rounding the precipice.

Another half-hour brings us to the brow of a second precipice, which is scooped out along its centre so as to cause the brow to overhang. Chagrin was in Bennen's face: he turned his eyes upwards, and I feared mortally that he was about to propose a reascent

141

of the *arête*. It was very questionable whether our muscles could have responded to such a demand. While we stood pondering here, a deep and confused roar attracted our attention. From a point near the summit of the Weisshorn, a rock had been discharged down a dry couloir, raising a cloud of dust at each bump against the mountain. A hundred similar ones were immediately in motion, while the spaces between the larger masses were filled by an innumerable flight of smaller stones. Each of them shook its quantum of dust in the air, until finally the avalanche was enveloped in a cloud. The clatter was stunning, for the collisions were incessant. Black masses of rock emerged here and there from the cloud, and sped through the air like flying fiends. Their motion was not one of translation merely, but they whizzed and vibrated in their flight as if urged by wings. The echoes resounded from side to side, from the Schallenberg to the Weisshorn and back, until finally, after many a deep-sounding thud in the snow, the whole troop came to rest at the bottom of the mountain. This stone avalanche was one of the most extraordinary things I had ever witnessed, and in connection with it I would draw the attention of future climbers of the Weisshorn to the danger which would infallibly beset any attempt to ascend it from this side, except by one of its *arêtes*. At any moment the mountain-side may be raked by a fire as deadly as that of cannon.

After due deliberation we moved along the precipice westward, I fearing that each step forward but plunged us deeper into difficulty. At one place, however, the precipice bevelled off to a steep incline of smooth rock, along which ran a crack, wide enough to admit the fingers, and sloping obliquely down to the lower glacier. Each in succession gripped the rock and shifted his body sideways along the crack until he came near enough to the glacier to reach it by a rough glissade. We passed swiftly along the glacier, sometimes running, and, on steeper slopes, sliding, until we were pulled up for the third time by a precipice which seemed even worse than either of the others. It was quite sheer, and as far as I could see right or left altogether hopeless. To my surprise, both men turned without hesitation to the right. I felt desperately blank, but I could notice no expression of dismay in the countenance of either of my companions. They inspected the moraine matter over which we walked, and at length one of them exclaimed, "Da sind die Spuren," lengthening his strides at the same moment. We looked over the brink at intervals, and at length discovered what appeared to be a mere streak of clay on the face of the precipice. On this streak we found footing. It was by no means easy, but to hard-pushed men it was a deliverance. The streak vanished, and we must get down the rock. This fortunately was rough, so that by pressing the hands against its rounded protuberances, and sticking the boot-nails against its projecting crystals, we let ourselves gradually down. A deep cleft separated the glacier from the precipice; this was crossed, and we were free, being clearly placed beyond the last bastion of the mountain.

In this admirable fashion did my guides behave on this occasion. The day previous to my arrival at Randa they had been up the mountain, and they then observed a solitary chamois moving along the base of this very precipice, and making ineffectual attempts to get up it. At one place the creature succeeded; this spot they fixed in their

142

memories, and when they reached the top of the precipice they sought for the traces of the chamois, found them, and were guided by them to the only place where escape in any reasonable time was possible. Our way was now clear; over the glacier we cheerfully marched, escaping from the ice just as the moon and the eastern sky contributed about equally to the illumination. The moonlight was afterwards intercepted by clouds. In the gloom we were often at a loss, and wandered half-bewildered over the grassy slopes. At length the welcome tinkle of cow-bells was heard in the distance, and guided by them we reached the chalet a little after 9 P.M. The cows had been milked and the milk disposed of, but the men managed to get us a moderate draught. Thus refreshed we continued the descent. I was half famished, for my solid nutriment during the day consisted solely of part of a box of meat lozenges given to me by Mr. Hawkins. Bennen and myself descended the mountain deliberately, and after many windings emerged upon the valley, and reached the hotel a little before 11 P.M. I had a basin of broth, *not* made according to Liebig, and a piece of mutton boiled probably for the fifth time. Fortified by these, and comforted by a warm footbath, I went to bed, where six hours' sound sleep chased away all consciousness of fatigue. I was astonished on the morrow to find the loose atoms of my body knitted so firmly by so brief a rest. Up to my attempt upon the Weisshorn I had felt more or less dilapidated, but here all weakness ended, and during my subsequent stay in Switzerland I was unacquainted with infirmity.

—1861

Note

1. Now a substantial and well-known hotel.—L. C. T.

Henry David Thoreau

"Ktaadn"

When Henry David Thoreau (1817–1862) climbed Mount Ktaadn in 1846, the Maine wilderness was remote, wild, and inhospitable. The journey to and from the foot of Katahdin, passing through mostly uninhabited lands, was an adventure in itself. Thoreau is associated with the American transcendentalist movement and its main figure, Thoreau's friend Ralph Waldo Emerson. Thoreau's book Walden, *recounting his stay in a cabin on Walden Pond near Concord, Massachusetts, remains a classic study of self-reliance, nature, and humankind's place in the universe. Graduating from Harvard University in 1837, Thoreau failed at school teaching (though he briefly established his own school) and eventually returned to his family's pencil-making business. He later devoted his energies to poetry and writing. He popularized the act of "Civil Disobedience" in an essay by that name, spending a night in jail to protest the U.S. endorsement of slavery and aggression against Mexico. The memorable descriptions of the Maine countryside and the climb to Katahdin in Thoreau's work* The Maine Woods *(published after his death) are tellingly counterpoised with quotes from Milton's* Paradise Lost, *weaving a subtle subtextual commentary on the "nature of nature." Comparing himself to Milton's Satan flying through Chaos provides a disturbing undercurrent to Thoreau's experiences in the Maine wilderness, in which he found a beautiful savagery.*

On the 31st of August, 1846, I left Concord in Massachusetts for Bangor and the backwoods of Maine, by way of the railroad and steamboat, intending to accompany a relative of mine engaged in the lumber-trade in Bangor, as far as a dam on the west branch of the Penobscot, in which property he was interested. From this place, which is about one hundred miles by the river above Bangor, thirty miles from the Houlton military road, and five miles beyond the last log-hut, I proposed to make excursions to Mount Ktaadn, the second highest mountain in New England, about thirty miles distant, and to some of the lakes of the Penobscot, either alone or with such company as I might pick up there. It is unusual to find a camp so far in the woods at that season, when lumbering operations have ceased, and I was glad to avail myself of the circumstance of a gang of men being employed there at that time in repairing the injuries caused by the great freshet in the spring. The mountain may be approached more easily and directly on horseback and on foot from the northeast side, by the Aroostook road, and the Wassataquoik River; but in that case you see much less of the wilderness, none of the glorious river and lake scenery, and have no experience of the batteau and the boatman's life. I was fortunate also in the season of the year, for in the summer myriads of black

---

Henry David Thoreau, "Ktaadn," *The Maine Woods* (Boston: Ticknor and Fields, 1864).

flies, mosquitoes, and midges, or, as the Indians call them, "no-see-ems," make travelling in the woods almost impossible; but now their reign was nearly over.

Ktaadn, whose name is an Indian word signifying highest land, was first ascended by white men in 1804. It was visited by Professor J. W. Bailey of West Point in 1836; by Dr. Charles T. Jackson, the State Geologist, in 1837; and by two young men from Boston in 1845. All these have given accounts of their expeditions. Since I was there, two or three other parties have made the excursion, and told their stories. Besides these, very few, even among backwoodsmen and hunters, have ever climbed it, and it will be a long time before the tide of fashionable travel sets that way. The mountainous region of the State of Maine stretches from near the White Mountains, northeasterly 160 miles wide. The wild or unsettled portion is far more extensive. So that some hours only of travel in this direction will carry the curious to the verge of a primitive forest, more interesting, perhaps, on all accounts, than they would reach by going a thousand miles westward.

The next forenoon, Tuesday, September 1st, I started with my companion in a buggy from Bangor for "up river," expecting to be overtaken the next day night at Mattawamkeag Point, some sixty miles off, by two more Bangoreans, who had decided to join us in a trip to the mountain. We had each a knapsack or bag filled with such clothing and articles as were indispensable, and my companion carried his gun.

Within a dozen miles of Bangor we passed through the villages of Stillwater and Oldtown, built at the falls of the Penobscot, which furnish the principal power by which the Maine woods are converted into lumber. The mills are built directly over and across the river. Here is a close jam, a hard rub, at all seasons; and then the once green tree, long since white, I need not say as the driven snow, but as a driven log, becomes lumber merely. Here your inch, your two and your three inch stuff begin to be, and Mr. Sawyer marks off those spaces which decide the destiny of so many prostrate forests. Through this steel riddle, more or less coarse, is the arrowy Maine forest, from Ktaadn and Chesuncook, and the head-waters of the St. John, relentlessly sifted, till it comes out boards, clapboards, laths, and shingles such as the wind can take, still perchance to be slit and slit again, till men get a size that will suit. Think how stood the white-pine tree on the shore of Chesuncook, its branches soughing with the four winds, and every individual needle trembling in the sunlight,—think how it stands with it now,—sold, perchance, to the New England Friction-Match Company! There were in 1837, as I read, 250 saw-mills on the Penobscot and its tributaries above Bangor, the greater part of them in this immediate neighborhood, and they sawed two hundred millions of feet of boards annually. To this is to be added the lumber of the Kennebec, Androscoggin, Saco, Passamaquoddy, and other streams. No wonder that we hear so often of vessels which are becalmed off our coast, being surrounded a week at a time by floating lumber from the Maine woods. The mission of men there seems to be, like so many busy demons, to drive the forest all out of the country, from every solitary beaver-swamp and mountainside, as soon as possible.

At Oldtown we walked into a batteau-manufactory. The making of batteaux is quite a business here for the supply of the Penobscot River. We examined some on the stocks. They are light and shapely vessels, calculated for rapid and rocky streams, and to be carried over long portages on men's shoulders, from twenty to thirty feet long, and only four or four and a half wide, sharp at both ends like a canoe, though broadest forward on the bottom, and reaching seven or eight feet over the water, in order that they may slip over rocks as gently as possible. They are made very slight, only two boards to a side, commonly secured to a few light maple or other hard-wood knees, but inward are of the clearest and widest white-pine stuff, of which there is a great waste on account of their form, for the bottom is left perfectly flat, not only from side to side, but from end to end. Sometimes they become "hogging" even, after long use, and the boatmen then turn them over and straighten them by a weight at each end. They told us that one wore out in two years, or often in a single trip, on the rocks, and sold for from fourteen to sixteen dollars. There was something re-freshing and wildly musical to my ears in the very name of the white man's canoe, reminding me of Charlevoix and Canadian Voyageurs. The batteau is a sort of mon-grel between the canoe and the boat, a fur-trader's boat.

The ferry here took us past the Indian island. As we left the shore, I observed a short, shabby, washer-woman-looking Indian—they commonly have the woe-begone look of the girl that cried for spilt milk—just from "up river"—land on the Oldtown side near a grocery, and, drawing up his canoe, take out a bundle of skins in one hand, and an empty key or half-barrel in the other, and scramble up the bank with them. This picture will do to put before the Indian's history, that is, the history of his extinction. In 1837 there were 362 souls left of this tribe. The island seemed deserted to-day, yet I observed some new houses among the weather-stained ones, as if the tribe still a design upon life; but generally they have a very shabby, forlorn, and cheerless look, being all back side and woodshed, not homesteads, even Indian homesteads, but instead of home or abroad-steads, for their life is *domi aut militiæ*, at home or at war, or now rather *venatus*, that is, a hunting, and most of the latter. The church is the only trim-looking building, but that is not Abenaki, that was Rome's do-ings. Good Canadian it may be, but it is poor Indian. These were once a powerful tribe. Politics are all the rage with them now. I even thought that a row of wigwams, with a dance of powwows, and a prisoner tortured at the stake, would be more re-spectable than this.

We landed in Milford, and rode along on the east side of the Penobscot, having a more or less constant view of the river, and the Indian islands in it, for they retain all the islands as far up as Nickatow, at the mouth of the East Branch. They are generally well-timbered, and are said to be better soil than the neighboring shores. The river seemed shallow and rocky, and interrupted by rapids, rippling and gleaming in the sun. We paused a moment to see a fish-hawk dive for a fish down straight as an ar-row, from a great height, but he missed his prey this time. It was the Houlton road on which we were now travelling, over which some troops were marched once towards

Mars' Hill, though not to Mars' *field*, as it proved. It is the main, almost the only, road in these parts, as straight and well made, and kept in a good repair, as almost any you will find anywhere. Everywhere we saw signs of the great freshet,—this house standing awry, and that where it was not founded, but where it was found, at any rate, the next day; and that other with a water-logged look, as if it were still airing and drying its basement, and logs with everybody's marks upon them, and sometimes the marks of their having served as bridges, strewn along the road. We crossed the Sunkhaze, a summery Indian name, the Olemmon, Passadumkeag, and other streams which make a greater show on the map than they now did on the road. At Passadumkeag we found anything but what the name implies,—earnest politicians, to wit,—white ones, I mean,—on the alert, to know how the election was likely to go; men who talked rapidly, with subdued voice, and a sort of factitious earnestness, you could not help believing, hardly waiting for an introduction, one on each side of your buggy, endeavoring to say much in little, for they see you hold the whip impatiently, but always saying little in much. Caucuses they have had, it seems, and caucuses they are to have again,—victory and defeat. Somebody may be elected, somebody may not. One man, a total stranger, who stood by our carriage in the dusk, actually frightened the horse with his asseverations, growing more solemnly positive as there was less in him to be positive about. So Passadumkeag did not look on the map. At sundown, leaving the river-road awhile for shortness, we went by way of Enfield, where we stopped for the night. This, like most of the localities bearing names on this road, was a place to name, which, in the midst of the unnamed and unincorporated wilderness, was to make a distinction without a difference, it seemed to me. Here, however, I noticed quite an orchard of healthy and well-grown apple-trees, in a bearing state, it being the oldest settler's house in this region, but all natural fruit, and comparatively worthless for want of a grafter. And so it is generally, lower down the river. It would be a good speculation, as well as a favor conferred on the settlers, for a Massachusetts boy to go down there with a trunk full of choice scions, and his grafting apparatus, in the spring.

The next morning we drove along through a high and hilly country, in view of Cold-Stream Pond, a beautiful lake four or five miles long, and came into the Houlton road again, here called the military road, at Lincoln, forty-five miles from Bangor, where there is quite a village for this country,—the principal one above Oldtown. Learning that there were several wigwams here, on one of the Indian islands, we left our horse and wagon, and walked through the forest half a mile to the river, to procure a guide to the mountain. It was not till after considerable search that we discovered their habitations,—small huts, in a retired place, where the scenery was unusually soft and beautiful, and the shore skirted with pleasant meadows and graceful elms. We paddled ourselves across to the island-side in a canoe, which we found on the shore. Near where we landed sat an Indian girl ten or twelve years old, on a rock in the water, in the sun, washing, and humming or moaning a song meanwhile. It was an aboriginal strain. A salmon-spear, made wholly of wood, lay on the shore, such as they might have used before white men came. It had an elastic piece of wood fastened to one side of its point, which slipped over and closed upon the fish, somewhat like the contrivance for holding a bucket at the end of a well-pole. As we walked up to the nearest house, we were met by a sally of a dozen wolfish-looking dogs, which may have been lineal descendants from the ancient Indian dogs, which the first voyageurs describe as "their wolves." I suppose they were. The occupant soon appeared, with a long pole in his hand, with which he beat off the dogs, while he parleyed with us. A stalwart, but dull and greasy-looking fellow, who told us, in his sluggish way, in answer to our questions, as if it were the first serious business he had to do that day, that there *were* Indians going "up river"—he and one other—to-day, before noon. And who was the other? Louis Neptune, who lives in the next house. Well, let us go over and see Louis together. The same doggish reception, and Louis Neptune makes his appearance,—a small, wiry man, with puckered and wrinkled face, yet he seemed the chief man of the two; the same, as I remembered, who had accompanied Jackson to the mountain in '37. The same questions were put to Louis, and the same information obtained, while the other Indian stood by. It appeared that they were going to start by noon, with two canoes, to go up to Chesuncook to hunt moose,—to be gone a month. "Well, Louis, suppose you get to the Point [to the Five Islands, just below Mattawamkeag], to camp, we walk on up the West Branch to-morrow,—four of us,—and wait for you at the dam, or this side. You overtake us to-morrow or next day, and take us into your canoes. We stop for you, you stop for us. We pay you for your trouble." "Ye!" replied Louis, "may be you carry some provision for all,—some pork,—some bread,—and so pay." He said, "Me sure get moose"; and when I asked if he thought Pomola would let us go up, he answered that we must plant one bottle of rum on the top; he had planted good many; and when he looked again, the rum was all gone. He had been up two or three times: he had planted letter,—English, German, French, &c. These men were slightly clad in shirt and pantaloons, like laborers with us in warm weather. They did not invite us into their houses, but met us outside. So we left the Indians, thinking ourselves lucky to have secured such guides and companions. . . .

[Thoreau describes his journey through the Maine wilderness toward Ktaadn] . . . In the next nine miles, which were the extent of our voyage, and which it took us the rest of the day to get over, we rowed across several small lakes, poled up numerous rapids and thoroughfares, and carried over four portages. I will give the names and distances, for the benefit of future tourists. First, after leaving Ambejijis Lake, we had a quarter of a mile of rapids to the portage, or carry of ninety rods around Ambejijis Falls; then a mile and a half through Passamagamet Lake, which is narrow and river-like, to the falls of the same name,—Ambejijis stream coming in on the right; then two miles through Katepskonegan Lake to the portage of ninety rods around Katepskonegan Falls, which name signifies "carrying-place,"—Passamagamet stream coming in on the left; then three miles through Pockwockomus Lake, a slight expansion of the river, to the portage of forty rods around the falls of the same name,—Katepskonegan stream coming in on the left; then three quarters of a mile through Aboljacarmegus Lake, similar to the last, to the portage of forty rods around the falls of the same name;

148

then half a mile of rapid water to the Sowadnehunk dead-water, and the Aboljackna-gesic stream.

This is generally the order of names as you ascend the river: First, the lake, or, if there is no expansion, the dead-water; then the falls; then the stream, emptying into the lake, or river above, all of the same name. First we came to Passamagamet Lake, then to Passamagamet Falls, then to Passamagamet stream emptying in. This order and identity of names, it will be perceived, is quite philosophical, since the dead-water or lake is always at least partially produced by the stream emptying in above; and the first fall below, which is the outlet of that lake, and where that tributary water makes its first plunge, also naturally bears the same name.

At the portage around Ambejijis Falls I observed a pork-barrel on the shore, with a hole eight or nine inches square cut in one side, which was set against an upright rock; but the bears, without turning or upsetting the barrel, had gnawed a hole in the opposite side, which looked exactly like an enormous rat hole, big enough to put their heads in; and at the bottom of the barrel were still left a few mangled and slabbered slices of pork. It is usual for the lumberers to leave such supplies as they cannot conveniently carry along with them at carries or camps, to which the next comers do not scruple to help themselves, they being the property, commonly, not of an individual, but a company, who can afford to deal liberally.

I will describe particularly how we got over some of these portages and rapids, in order that the reader may get an idea of the boatman's life. At Ambejijis Falls, for instance, there was the roughest path imaginable cut through the woods; at first up hill, at an angle of nearly forty-five degrees, over rocks and logs without end. This was the manner of the portage. We first carried over our baggage, and deposited it on the shore at the other end; then returning to the batteau, we dragged it up the hill by the painter, and onward, with frequent pauses, over half the portage. But this was a bungling way, and would soon have worn out the boat. Commonly, three men walk over with a batteau weighing from three to five or six hundred pounds on their heads and shoulders, the tallest standing under the middle of the boat, which is turned over, and one at each end, or else there are two at the bows. More cannot well take hold at once. But this requires some practice, as well as strength, and is in any case extremely laborious, and wearing to the constitution, to follow. We were, on the whole, rather an invalid party, and could render our boatmen but little assistance. Our two men at length took the batteau upon their shoulders, and, while two of us steadied it, to prevent it from rocking and wearing into their shoulders, on which they placed their hats folded, walked bravely over the remaining distance, with two or three pauses. In the same manner they accomplished the other portages. With this crushing weight they must climb and stumble along over fallen trees and slippery rocks of all sizes, where those who walked by the sides were continually brushed off, such was the narrowness of the path. But we were fortunate not to have to cut our path in the first place. Before we launched our boat, we scraped the bottom smooth again, with our knives, where it had rubbed on the rocks, to save friction.

To avoid the difficulties of the portage, our men determined to "warp up" the Passamagamet Falls; so while the rest walked over the portage with the baggage, I remained in the batteau, to assist in warping up. We were soon in the midst of the rapids, which were more swift and tumultuous than any we had poled up, and had turned to the side of the stream for the purpose of warping, when the boatmen, who felt some pride in their skill, and were ambitious to do something more than usual, for my benefit, as I surmised, took one more view of the rapids, or rather the falls; and, in answer to our question, whether we couldn't get up there, the other answered that he guessed he'd try it. So we pushed again into the midst of the stream, and began to struggle with the current. I sat in the middle of the boat to trim it, moving slightly to the right or left as it grazed a rock. With an uncertain and wavering motion we wound and bolted our way up, until the bow was actually raised two feet above the stern at the steepest pitch; and then, when everything depended upon his exertions, the bowman's pole snapped in two; but before he had time to take the spare one, which I reached for him, he had saved himself with the fragment upon a rock; and so we got up by a hair's breadth; and Uncle George exclaimed that that was never done before, and he had not tried it if he had not known whom he got in the bow, nor he in the bow, if he had not known him in the stern. At this place there was a regular portage cut through the woods, and our boatmen had never known a batteau to ascend the falls. As near as I can remember, there was a perpendicular fall here, at the worst place of the whole Penobscot River, two or three feet at least. I could not sufficiently admire the skill and coolness with which they performed this feat, never speaking to each other. The bowman, not looking behind, but knowing exactly what the other is about, works as if he worked alone. Now sounding in vain for a bottom in fifteen feet of water, while the boat falls back several rods, held straight only with the greatest skill and exertion; or, while the sternman obstinately holds his ground, like a turtle, the bowman springs from side to side with wonderful suppleness and dexterity, scanning the rapids and the rocks with a thousand eyes; and now, having got a bite at last, with a lusty shove, which makes his pole bend and quiver, and the whole boat tremble, he gains a few feet upon the river. To add to the danger, the poles are liable at any time to be caught between the rocks, and wrenched out of their hands, leaving them at the mercy of the rapids,—the rocks, as it were, lying in wait, like so many alligators, to catch them in their teeth, and jerk them from your hands, before you have stolen an effectual shove against their palates. The pole is set close to the boat, and the prow is made to overshoot, and just turn the corners of the rocks, in the very teeth of the rapids. Nothing but the length and lightness, and the slight draught of the batteau, enables them to make any headway. The bowman must quickly choose his course; there is no time to deliberate. Frequently the boat is shoved between rocks where both sides touch, and the waters on either hand are a perfect maelstrom.

Half a mile above this, two of us tried our hands at poling up a slight rapid; and we were just surmounting the last difficulty when an unlucky rock confounded our calculations; and while the batteau was sweeping round irrecoverably amid the whirlpool, we were obliged to resign the poles to more skilful hands.

Katepskonegan is one of the shallowest and weediest of the lakes, and looked as if it might abound in pickerel. The falls of the same name, where we stopped to dine, was considerable and quite picturesque. Here Uncle George had seen trout caught by the barrelful; but they would not rise to our bait at this hour. Half-way over this carry, thus far in the Maine wilderness on its way to the Provinces, we noticed a large, flaming, Oak Hall hand-bill, about two feet long, wrapped round the trunk of a pine, from which the bark had been stript, and to which it was fast glued by the pitch. This should be recorded among the advantages of this mode of advertising, that so, possibly, even the bears and wolves, moose, deer, otter, and beaver, not to mention the Indian, may learn where they can fit themselves according to the latest fashion, or, at least, recover some of their own lost garments. We christened this, the Oak Hall carry.

The forenoon was as serene and placid on this wild stream in the woods, as we are apt to imagine that Sunday in summer usually is in Massachusetts. We were occasionally startled by the scream of a bald-eagle, sailing over the stream in front of our batteau; or of the fish-hawks, on whom he levies his contributions. There were, at intervals, small meadows of a few acres on the sides of the stream, waving with uncut grass, which attracted the attention of our boatmen, who regretted that they were not nearer to their clearings, and calculated how many stacks they might cut. Two or three men sometimes spend the summer by themselves, cutting the grass in these meadows, to sell to the loggers in the winter, since it will fetch a higher price on the spot than in any market in the State. On a small isle, covered with this kind of rush, or cut grass, on which we landed, to consult about our further course, we noticed the recent track of a moose, a large, roundish hole, in the soft wet ground, evincing the great size and weight of the animal that made it. They are fond of the water, and visit all these island-meadows, swimming as easily from island to island as they make their way through the thickets on land. Now and then we passed what McCauslin called a poke-logan, an Indian term for what the drivers might have reason to call a poke-logs-in, an inlet that leads nowhere. If you get in, you have got to get out again the same way. These, and the frequent "run-rounds" which come into the river again, would embarrass an inexperienced voyager not a little.

The carry around Pockwockomus Falls was exceedingly rough and rocky, the batteau having to be lifted directly from the water up four or five feet on to a rock, and launched again down a similar bank. The rocks on this portage were covered with the *dents* made by the spikes in the lumberers' boots while staggering over under the weight of their batteaux; and you could see where the surface of some large rocks on which they had rested their batteaux was worn quite smooth with use. As it was, we had carried over but half the usual portage at this place for this stage of the water, and launched our boat in the smooth wave just curving to the fall, prepared to struggle with the most violent rapid we had to encounter. The rest of the party walked over the remainder of the portage, while I remained with the boatmen to assist in warping up. One had to hold the boat while the others got in to prevent it from going over the falls. When we had pushed up the rapids as far as possible, keeping close to the shore, Tom

151

seized the painter and leaped out upon a rock just visible in the water, but he lost his footing, notwithstanding his spiked boots, and was instantly amid the rapids; but recovering himself by good luck, and reaching another rock, he passed the painter to me, who had followed him, and took his place again in the bows. Leaping from rock to rock in the shoal water, close to the shore, and now and then getting a bite with the rope round an upright one, I held the boat while one reset his pole, and then all three forced it upward against any rapid. This was "warping up." When a part of us walked round at such a place, we generally took the precaution to take out the most valuable part of the baggage, for fear of being swamped.

As we poled up a swift rapid for half a mile above Aboljacarmegus Falls, some of the party read their own marks on the huge logs which lay piled up high and dry on the rocks on either hand, the relics probably of a jam which had taken place here in the Great Freshet in the spring. Many of these would have to wait for another great freshet, perchance, if they lasted so long, before they could be got off. It was singular enough to meet with property of theirs which they had never seen, and where they had never been before, thus detained by freshets and rocks when on its way to them. Methinks that must be where all my property lies, cast up on the rocks on some distant and unexplored stream, and waiting for an unheard-of freshet to fetch it down. O make haste, ye gods, with your winds and rains, and start the jam before it rots!

The last half-mile carried us to the Sowadnehunk dead-water, so called from the stream of the same name, signifying "running between mountains," an important tributary which comes in a mile above. Here we decided to camp, about twenty miles from the Dam, at the mouth of Murch Brook and the Aboljacknagesic, mountain streams, broad off from Ktaadn, and about a dozen miles from its summit; having made fifteen miles this day.

We had been told by McCauslin that we should here find trout enough: so, while some prepared the camp, the rest fell to fishing. Seizing the birch-poles which some party of Indians, or white hunters, had left on the shore, and baiting our hooks with pork, and with trout, as soon as they were caught, we cast our lines into the mouth of the Aboljacknagesic, a clear, swift, shallow stream which came in from Ktaadn. Instantly a shoal of white chivin (*Leucisci pulchelli*), silvery roaches, cousin-trout, or what not, large and small, prowling thereabouts, fell upon our bait, and one after another were landed amidst the bushes. Anon their cousins, the true trout, took their turn, and alternately the speckled trout, and the silvery roaches, swallowed the bait as fast as we could throw in; and the finest specimens of both that I have ever seen, the largest one weighing three pounds, were heaved upon the shore, though at first in vain, to wriggle down into the water again, for we stood in the boat; but soon we learned to remedy this evil: for one, who had lost his hook, stood on shore to catch them as they fell in a perfect shower around him,—sometimes, wet and slippery, full in his face and bosom, as his arms were outstretched to receive them. While yet alive, before their tints had faded, they glistened like the fairest flowers, the product of primitive rivers; and he could hardly trust his senses, as he stood over them, that these jewels should have swam away in that Aboljacknagesic water for so long, so many dark ages;—these bright fluviatile flowers, seen of Indians only, made beautiful, the Lord only knows why, to swim there! I could understand better, for this, the truth of mythology, the fables of Proteus, and all those beautiful sea-monsters,—how all history, indeed, put to a terrestrial use, is mere history; but put to a celestial, is mythology always.

But there is the rough voice of Uncle George, who commands at the frying-pan, to send over what you've got, and then you may stay till morning. The pork sizzles, and cries for fish. Luckily, for the foolish race, and this particularly foolish generation of trout, the night shut down at last, not a little deepened by the dark side of Ktaadn, which, like a permanent shadow, reared itself from the eastern bank. Lescarbot, writing in 1609, tells us that the Sieur Champdoré, who, with one of the people of the Sieur de Monts, ascended some fifty leagues up the St. John in 1608, found the fish so plenty, "qu'en mettant la chaudière sur le feu ils en avoient pris suffisamment pour eux dîsner avant que l'eau fust chaude." Their descendants here are no less numerous. So we accompanied Tom into the woods to cut cedar-twigs for our bed. While he went ahead with the axe, and lopt off the smallest twigs of the flat-leaved cedar, the arbor vitæ of the gardens, we gathered them up, and returned with them to the boat, until it was loaded. Our bed was made with as much care and skill as a roof is shingled; beginning at the foot, and laying the twig end of the cedar upward, we advanced to the head, a course at a time, thus successively covering the stub-ends, and producing a soft and level bed. For us six it was about ten feet long by six in breadth. This time we lay under our tent, having pitched it more prudently with reference to the wind and the flame, and the usual huge fire blazed in front. Supper was eaten off a large log, which some freshet had thrown up. This night we had a dish of arbor-vitæ, or cedar-tea, which the lumberer sometimes uses when other herbs fail,—

"A quart of arbor-vitæ,
to make him strong and mighty,"

but I had no wish to repeat the experiment. It had too medicinal a taste for my palate. There was the skeleton of a moose here, whose bones some Indian hunters had picked on this very spot.

In the night I dreamed of trout-fishing; and, when at length I awoke, it seemed a fable that this painted fish swam there so near my couch, and rose to our hooks the last evening, and I doubted if I had not dreamed it all. So I arose before dawn to test its truth, while my companions were still sleeping. There stood Ktaadn with distinct and cloudless outline in the moonlight; and the rippling of the rapids was the only sound to break the stillness. Standing on the shore, I once more cast my line into the stream, and found the dream to be real and the fable true. The speckled trout and silvery roach, like flying-fish, sped swiftly through the moonlight air, describing bright arcs on the dark side of Ktaadn, until moonlight, now fading into daylight, brought satiety to my mind, and the minds of my companions, who had joined me.

153

By six o'clock, having mounted our packs and a good blanketful of trout, ready dressed, and swung up such baggage and provision as we wished to leave behind, upon the tops of saplings, to be out of the reach of bears, we started for the summit of the mountain, distant, as Uncle George said the boatmen called it about four miles, but as I judged, and as it proved, nearer fourteen. He had never been any nearer the mountain than this, and there was not the slightest trace of man to guide us farther in this direction. At first, pushing a few rods up the Aboljacknagesic, or "open-land stream," we fastened our batteau to a tree, and travelled up the north side, through burnt lands, now partially overgrown with young aspens, and other shrubbery; but soon, recrossing this stream, where it was about fifty or sixty feet wide, upon a jam of logs and rocks,—and you could cross it by this means almost anywhere,—we struck at once for the highest peak, over a mile or more of comparatively open land, still very gradually ascending the while. Here it fell to my lot, as the oldest mountain-climber, to take the lead. So, scanning the woody side of the mountain, which lay still at an indefinite distance, stretched out some seven or eight miles in length before us, we determined to steer directly for the base of the highest peak, leaving a large slide, by which, as I have since learned, some of our predecessors ascended, on our left. This course would lead us parallel to a dark seam in the forest, which marked the bed of a torrent, and over a slight spur, which extended southward from the main mountain, from whose bare summit we could get an outlook over the country, and climb directly up the peak, which would then be close at hand. Seen from this point, a bare ridge at the extremity of the open land, Ktaadn, presented a different aspect from any mountain I have seen, there being a greater proportion of naked rock rising abruptly from the forest; and we looked up at this blue barrier as if it were some fragment of a wall which anciently bounded the earth in that direction. Setting the compass for a northeast course, which was the bearing of the southern base of the highest peak, we were soon buried in the woods.

We soon began to meet with traces of bears and moose, and those of rabbits were everything visible. The tracks of moose, more or less recent, to speak literally, covered every square rod on the sides of the mountain; and these animals are probably more numerous there now than ever before, being driven into this wilderness, from all sides, by the settlements. The track of a full-grown moose is like that of a cow, or larger, and of the young, like that of a calf. Sometimes we found ourselves travelling in faint paths, which they had made, like cow-paths in the woods, only far more indistinct, being rather openings, affording imperfect vistas through the dense underwood, than trodden paths; and everywhere the twigs had been browsed by them, clipt as smoothly as if by a knife. The bark of trees was stript up by them to the height of eight or nine feet, in long, narrow strips, an inch wide, still showing the distinct marks of their teeth. We expected nothing less than to meet a herd of them every moment, and our Nimrod held his shooting-iron in readiness; but we did not go out of our way to look for them, and, though numerous, they are so wary that the unskilful hunter might range the forest a long time before he could get sight of one. They are sometimes dangerous to encounter, and will not turn out for the hunter, but furiously rush upon him and trample him to death, unless he is lucky enough to avoid them by dodging round a tree. The largest are nearly as large as a horse, and weigh sometimes one thousand pounds; and it is said that they can step over a five-feet gate in their ordinary walk. They are described as exceedingly awkward-looking animals, with their long legs and short bodies, making a ludicrous figure when in full run, but making great headway nevertheless. It seemed a mystery to us how they could thread these woods, which it required all our suppleness to accomplish,—climbing, stooping, and winding, alternately. They are said to drop their long and branching horns, which usually spread five to six feet, on their backs, and make their way easily by the weight of their bodies. Our boatmen said, but I know not with how much truth, that their horns are apt to be gnawed away by vermin while they sleep. Their flesh, which is more like beef than venison, is common in Bangor market.

We had proceeded on thus seven or eight miles, till about noon, with frequent pauses to refresh the weary ones, crossing a considerable mountain stream, which we conjectured to be Murch Brook, at whose mouth we had camped, all the time in woods, without having once seen the summit, and rising very gradually, when the boatmen, beginning to despair a little, and fearing that we were leaving the mountain on one side of us, for they had not entire faith in the compass, McCauslin climbed a tree, from the top of which he could see the peak, when it appeared that we had not swerved from a right line, the compass down below still ranging with his arm, which pointed to the summit. By the side of a cool mountain rill, amid the woods, where the water began to partake of the purity and transparency of the air, we stopped to cook some of our fishes, which we had brought thus far in order to save our hard bread and pork, in the use of which we had put ourselves on short allowance. We soon had a fire blazing, and stood around it, under the damp and sombre forest of firs and birches, each with a sharpened stick, three or four feet in length, upon which he had spitted his trout, or roach, previously well gashed and salted, our sticks radiating like the spokes of a wheel from one centre, and each crowding his particular fish into the most desirable exposure, not with the truest regard always to his neighbor's rights. Thus we regaled ourselves, drinking meanwhile at the spring, till one man's pack, at least, was considerably lightened, when we again took up our line of march.

At length we reached an elevation sufficiently bare to afford a view of the summit, still distant and blue, almost as if retreating from us. A torrent, which proved to be the same we had crossed, was seen tumbling down in front, literally from out of the clouds. But this glimpse at our whereabouts was soon lost, and we were buried in the woods again. The wood was chiefly yellow birch, spruce, fir, mountain-ash, or round-wood, as the Maine people call it, and moose-wood. It was the worst kind of travelling; sometimes like the densest scrub-oak patches with us. The cornel, or bunch-berries, were very abundant, as well as Solomon's seal and moose-berries. Blueberries were distributed along our whole route; and in one place the bushes were drooping with the weight of the fruit, still as fresh as ever. It was the 7th of September. Such patches afforded a grateful repast, and served to bait the tired party forward. When any lagged behind, the cry of "blueberries" was most effectual to bring them up. Even at this elevation we passed through a moose-yard, formed by a large flat rock, four or five rods square, where they tread down the snow in winter. At length, fearing that if we held the direct course to the summit, we should not find any water near our camping-ground, we gradually swerved to the west, till, at four o'clock, we struck again the torrent which I have mentioned, and here, in view of the summit, the weary party decided to camp that night.

While my companions were seeking a suitable spot for this purpose, I improved the little daylight that was left, in climbing the mountain alone. We were in a deep and narrow ravine, sloping up to the clouds, at an angle of nearly forty-five degrees, and hemmed in by walls of rock, which were at first covered with low trees, then with impenetrable thickets of scraggy birches and spruce-trees, and with moss, but at last bare of all vegetation but lichens, and almost continually draped in clouds. Following up the course of the torrent which occupied this,—and I mean to lay some emphasis on this word *up*,—pulling myself up by the side of perpendicular falls of twenty or thirty feet, by the roots of firs and birches, and then, perhaps, walking a level rod or two in the thin stream, for it took up the whole road, ascending by huge steps, as it were, a giant's stairway, down which a river flowed, I had soon cleared the trees, and paused on the successive shelves, to look back over the country. The torrent was from fifteen to thirty feet wide, without a tributary, and seemingly not diminishing in breadth as I advanced; but still it came rushing and roaring down, with a copious tide, over and amidst masses of bare rock, from the very clouds, as though a waterspout had just burst over the mountain. Leaving this at last, I began to work my way, scarcely less arduous than Satan's anciently through Chaos, up the nearest, though not the highest peak. At first scrambling on all fours over the tops of ancient black spruce-trees (*Abies nigra*), old as the flood, from two to ten or twelve feet in height, their tops flat and spreading and their foliage blue, and nipt with cold, as if for centuries they had ceased growing upward against the bleak sky, the solid cold. I walked some good rods erect upon the tops of these trees, which were overgrown with moss and mountain-cranberries. It seemed that in the course of time they had filled up the intervals between the huge rocks, and the cold wind had uniformly levelled all over. Here the principle of vegetation was hard put to it. There was apparently a belt of this kind running quite round the mountain, though, perhaps, nowhere so remarkable as here. Once, slumping through, I looked down ten feet, into a dark and cavernous region, and saw the stem of a spruce, on whose top I stood, as on a mass of coarse basket-work, fully nine inches in diameter at the ground. These holes were bears' dens, and the bears were even then at home. This was the sort of garden I made my way *over*, for an eighth of a mile, at the risk, it is true, of treading on some of the plants, not seeing any path *through* it,—certainly the most treacherous and porous country I ever travelled.

"Nigh foundered on he fares,
Treading the crude consistence, half on foot,
Half flying."

But nothing could exceed the toughness of the twigs,—not one snapped under my weight, for they had slowly grown. Having slumped, scrambled, rolled, bounced, and walked, by turns, over this scraggy country, I arrived upon a side-hill, or rather side-mountain, where rocks, gray, silent rocks, were the flocks and herds that pastured, chewing a rocky cud at sunset. They looked at me with hard gray eyes, without a bleat or a low. This brought me to the skirt of a cloud, and bounded my walk that night. But I had already seen that Maine country when I turned about, waving flowing, rippling, down below.

When I returned to my companions, they had selected a camping-ground on the torrent's edge, and were resting on the ground; one was on the sick list, rolled in a blanket, on a damp shelf of rock. It was a savage and dreary scenery enough; so wildly rough, that they looked long to find a level and open space for the tent. We could not well camp higher, for want of fuel; and the trees here seemed so evergreen and sappy, that we almost doubted if they would acknowledge the influence of fire; but fire prevailed at last, and blazed here, too, like a good citizen of the world. Even at this height we met with frequent traces of moose, as well as of bears. As here was no cedar, we made our bed of coarser feathered spruce; but at any rate the feathers were plucked from the live tree. It was, perhaps, even a more grand and desolate place for a night's lodging than the summit would have been, being in the neighborhood of those wild trees, and of the torrent. Some more aerial and finer-spirited winds rushed and roared through the ravine all night, from time to time arousing our fire, and dispersing the embers about. It was as if we lay in the very nest of a young whirlwind. At midnight, one of my bedfellows, being startled in his dreams by the sudden blazing up to its top of a fir-tree, whose green boughs were dried by the heat, sprang up, with a cry, from his bed, thinking the world on fire, and drew the whole camp after him.

In the morning, after whetting our appetite on some raw pork, a wafer of hard bread, and a dipper of condensed cloud or waterspout, we all together began to make our way up the falls, which I have described; this time choosing the right hand, or highest peak, which was not the one I had approached before. But soon my companions were lost to my sight behind the mountain ridge in my rear, which still seemed ever retreating before me, and I climbed alone over huge rocks, loosely poised, a mile or more, still edging toward the clouds; for though the day was clear elsewhere, the summit was concealed by mist. The mountain seemed a vast aggregation of loose rocks, as if some time it had rained rocks, and they lay as they fell on the mountain sides, nowhere fairly at rest, but leaning on each other, all rocking-stones, with cavities between, but scarcely any soil or smoother shelf. They were raw materials of a planet dropped from an unseen quarry, which the vast chemistry of nature would anon work up, or work down, into the smiling and verdant plains and valleys of earth. This was an undone extremity of the globe; as in lignite, we see coal in the process of formation.

At length I entered within the skirts of the cloud which seemed forever drifting over the summit, and yet would never be gone, but was generated out of that pure air as fast as it flowed away; and when, a quarter of a mile farther, I reached the summit of the ridge, which those who have seen in clearer weather say is about five miles long, and contains a thousand acres of table-land, I was deep within the hostile ranks of clouds, and all objects were obscured by them. Now the wind would blow me out a yard of clear sunlight, wherein I stood; then a gray, dawning light was all it could accomplish, the cloud-line ever rising and falling with the wind's intensity. Sometimes it seemed as if the summit would be cleared in a few moments, and smile in sunshine: but what was gained on one side was lost on another. It was like sitting in a chimney and waiting for the smoke to blow away. It was, in fact, a cloud-factory,— these were the cloud-works, and the wind turned them off done from the cool, bare rocks. Occasionally, when the windy columns broke in to me, I caught sight of a dark, damp crag to the right or left; the mist driving ceaselessly between it and me. It reminded me of the creations of the old epic and dramatic poets, of Atlas, Vulcan, the Cyclops, and Prometheus. Such was Caucasus and the rock where Prometheus was bound. Æschylus had no doubt visited such scenery as this. It was vast, Titanic, and such as man never inhabits. Some part of the beholder, even some vital part, seems to escape through the loose grating of his ribs as he ascends. He is more lone than you can imagine. There is less of substantial thought and fair understanding in him, than in the plains where men inhabit. His reason is dispersed and shadowy, more thin and subtile, like the air. Vast, Titanic, inhuman Nature has got him at disadvantage, caught him alone, and pilfers him of some of his divine faculty. She does not smile on him as in the plains. She seems to say sternly, why came ye here before time? This ground is not prepared for you. Is it not enough that I smile in the valleys? I have never made this soil for they feet, this air for thy breathing, these rocks for thy neighbors. I cannot pity nor fondle thee here, but forever relentlessly drive thee hence to where I *am* kind. Why seek me where I have not called thee, and then complain because you find me but a stepmother? Shouldst thou freeze or starve, or shudder thy life away, here is no shrine, nor altar, nor any access to my ear.

"Chaos and ancient Night, I come no spy
With purpose to explore or to disturb
The secrets of your realm, but . . .
.   .   .   .   .   as my way
Lies through your spacious empire up to light."

The tops of mountains are among the unfinished parts of the globe, whither it is a slight insult to the gods to climb and pry into their secrets, and try their effect on our humanity. Only daring and insolent men, perchance, go there. Simple races, as savages, do not climb mountains,—their tops are sacred and mysterious tracts never visited by them. Pomola is always angry with those who climb to the summit of Ktaadn. According to Jackson, who, in his capacity of geological surveyor of the State, has accurately measured it,—the altitude of Ktaadn is 5,300 feet, or a little more than one mile above the level of the sea,—and he adds, "It is then evidently the highest point in the State of Maine, and is the most abrupt granite mountain in New England." The peculiarities of that spacious table-land on which I was standing, as well as the remarkable semi-circular precipice or basin on the eastern side, were all concealed by the mist. I had brought my whole pack to the top, not knowing but I should have to make my descent to the river, and possibly to the settled portion of the State alone, and by some other route, and wishing to have a complete outfit with me. But at length, fearing that my companions would be anxious to reach the river before night, and knowing that the clouds might rest on the mountain for days, I was compelled to descend. Occasionally, as I came down, the wind would blow me a vista open, through which I could see the country eastward, boundless forests, and lakes, and streams, gleaming in the sun, some of them emptying into the East Branch. There were also new mountains in sight in that direction. Now and then some small bird of the sparrow family would flit away before me, unable to command its course, like a fragment of the gray rock blown off by the wind.

I found my companions where I had left them, on the side of the peak, gathering the mountain cranberries, which filled every crevice between the rocks, together with blueberries, which had a spicier flavor the higher up they grew, but were not the less agreeable to our palates. When the country is settled, and roads are made, these cranberries will perhaps become an article of commerce. From this elevation, just on the skirts of the clouds, we could overlook the country, west and south, for a hundred miles. There it was, the State of Maine, which we had seen on the map, but not much like that,—immeasurable forest for the sun to shine on, that eastern *stuff* we hear of in Massachusetts. No clearing, no house. It did not look as if a solitary traveller had cut so much as a walking-stick there. Countless lakes,—Moosehead in the southwest, forty miles long by ten wide, like a gleaming silver platter at the end of the table; Chesuncook, eighteen long by three wide, without an island; Millinocket, on the south, with its hundred islands; and a hundred others without a name; and mountains also, whose names, for the most part, are known only to the Indians. The forest looked like a firm grass sward, and the effect of these lakes in its midst has been well compared, by one who has since visited this same spot, to that of a "mirror broken into a thousand fragments, and wildly scattered over the grass, reflecting the full blaze of the sun." It was a large farm for somebody, when cleared. According to the Gazetteer, which was printed before the boundary question was settled, this single Penobscot county, in which we were, was larger than the whole State of Vermont, with its fourteen counties; and this was only a part of the wild lands of Maine. We are concerned now, however, about natural, not political limits. We were about 80 miles, as the bird flies, from Bangor, or 115, as we had rode, and walked, and paddled. We had to console ourselves with the reflection that this view was probably as good as that from the peak, as far as it went; and what were a mountain without its attendant clouds and mists? Like ourselves, neither Bailey nor Jackson had obtained a clear view from the summit.

Setting out on our return to the river, still at an early hour in the day, we decided to follow the course of the torrent, which we supposed to be Murch Brook, as long as it would not lead us too far out of our way. We thus travelled about four miles in the very torrent itself, continually crossing and recrossing it, leaping from rock to rock, and jumping with the stream down falls of seven or eight feet, or sometimes sliding down on our backs in a thin sheet of water. This ravine had been the scene of an extraordinary freshet in the spring, apparently accompanied by a slide from the mountain. It must have been filled with a stream of stones and water, at least twenty feet above the present level of the torrent. For a rod or two, on either side of its channel, the trees were barked and splintered up to their tops, the birches bent over, twisted, and sometimes finely split, like a stable-broom; some, a foot in diameter, snapped off, and whole clumps of trees bent over with the weight of rocks piled on them. In one place we noticed a rock, two or three feet in diameter; lodged nearly twenty feet high in the crotch of a tree. For the whole four miles, we saw but one rill emptying in, and the volume of water did not seem to be increased from the first. We travelled thus very rapidly with a downward impetus, and grew remarkably expert at leaping from rock to rock, for leap we must, and leap we did, whether there was any rock at the right distance or not. It was a pleasant picture when the foremost turned about and looked up the winding ravine, walled in with rocks and the green forest, to see, at intervals of a rod or two, a red-shirted or green-jacketed mountaineer against the white torrent, leaping down the channel with his pack on his back, or pausing upon a convenient rock in the midst of the torrent to mend a rent in his clothes, or unstrap the dipper at his belt to take a draught of the water. At one place we were startled by seeing, on a little sandy shelf by the side of the stream, the fresh print of a man's foot, and for a moment realized how Robinson Crusoe felt in a similar case; but at last we remembered that we had struck this stream on our way up, though we could not have told where, and one had descended into the ravine for a drink. The cool air above, and the continual bathing of our bodies in mountain water, alternate foot, sitz, douche, and plunge baths, made this walk exceedingly refreshing, and we had travelled only a mile or two, after leaving the torrent, before every thread of our clothes was as dry as usual, owing perhaps to a peculiar quality in the atmosphere.

After leaving the torrent, being in doubt about our course, Tom threw down his pack at the foot of the loftiest spruce tree at hand, and shinned up the bare trunk, some twenty feet, and then climbed through the green tower, lost to our sight, until he held the topmost spray in his hand.[1] McCauslin, in his younger days, had marched through the wilderness with a body of troops, under General Somebody, and with one other man did all the scouting and spying service. The General's word was, "Throw down the top of that tree," and there was no tree in the Maine woods so high that it did not lose its top in such a case. I have heard a story of two men being lost once in these woods, nearer to the settlements than this, who climbed the loftiest pine they could find, some six feet in diameter at the ground, from whose top they discovered a solitary clearing and its smoke. When at this height, some two hundred feet from the ground, one of them became dizzy, and fainted in his companion's arms, and the latter had to accomplish the descent with him, alternately fainting and reviving, as best he could. To Tom we cried, Where away does the summit bear? where the burnt lands? The last he could only conjecture; he described, however, a little meadow and pond, lying probably in our course, which we concluded to steer for. On reaching this secluded meadow, we found fresh tracks of moose on the shore of the pond, and the water was still unsettled as if they had fled before us. A little farther, in a dense thicket, we seemed to be still on their trail. It was a small meadow, of a few acres, on the mountain side, concealed by the forest, and perhaps never seen by a white man before, where one would think that the moose might browse and bathe, and rest in peace. Pursuing his course, we soon reached the open land, which went sloping down some miles toward the Penobscot.

Perhaps I most fully realized that this was primeval, untamed, and forever un-tameable *Nature*, or whatever else men call it, while coming down this part of the mountain. We were passing over "Burnt Lands," burnt by lightning, perchance, though they showed no recent marks of fire, hardly so much as a charred stump, but looked rather like a natural pasture for the moose and deer, exceedingly wild and desolate, with occasional strips of timber crossing them, and low poplars springing up, and patches of blueberries here and there. I found myself traversing them familiarly, like some pasture run to waste, or partially reclaimed by man; but when I reflected what man, what brother or sister or kinsman of our race made it and claimed it, I expected the proprietor to rise up and dispute my passage. It is difficult to conceive of a region uninhabited by man. We habitually presume his presence and influence everywhere. And yet we have not seen pure Nature, unless we have seen her thus vast and drear and inhuman, though in the midst of cities. Nature was here something savage and aw-ful, though beautiful. I looked with awe at the ground I trod on, to see what the Pow-ers had made there, the form and fashion and material of their work. This was that Earth of which we have heard, made out of Chaos and Old Night. Here was no man's garden, but the unhandselled globe. It was not lawn, nor pasture, nor mead, nor wood-land, nor lea, nor arable, nor waste-land. It was the fresh and natural surface of the planet Earth, as it was made for ever and ever,—to be the dwelling of man, we say,—so Nature made it, and man may use it if he can. Man was not to be associated with it. It was Matter, vast, terrific,—not his Mother Earth that we have heard of, not for him to tread on, or be buried in,—no, it were being too familiar even to let his bones lie there,—the home, this, of Necessity and Fate. There was there felt the presence of a force not bound to be kind to man. It was a place for heathenism and superstitious rites,—to be inhabited by men nearer of kin to the rocks and to wild animals than we. We walked over it with a certain awe, stopping, from time to time, to pick the blueberries which grew there, and had a smart and spicy taste. Perchance where *our* wild pines stand, and leaves lie on their forest floor, in Concord, there were once reapers, and husbandmen planted grain; but here not even the surface had been scarred by man, but it was a spec-imen of what God saw fit to make this world. What is it to be admitted to a museum, to see a myriad of particular things, compared with being shown some star's surface, some hard matter in its home! I stand in awe of my body, this matter to which I am bound has become so strange to me. I fear not spirits, ghosts, of which I am one,—*that my body might,*—but I fear bodies, I tremble to meet them. What is this Titan that has possession of me? Talk of mysteries!—Think of our life in nature,—daily to be shown matter, to come in contact with it,—rocks, trees, wind on our cheeks! the *solid* earth! the *actual* world! the *common sense! Contact! Contact! Who* are we? *where* are we?

Erelong we recognized some rocks and other features in the landscape which we had purposely impressed on our memories, and, quickening our pace, by two o'clock we reached the batteau.[2] Here we had expected to dine on trout, but in this glaring sunlight they were slow to take the bait, so we were compelled to make the most of the crumbs of our hard bread and our pork, which were both nearly exhausted. Meanwhile we deliberated whether we should go up the river a mile farther, to Gibson's clearing, on the Sowadnehunk, where there was a deserted log-hut, in order to get a half-inch auger, to mend one of our spike-poles with. There were young spruce-trees enough around us, and we had a spare spike, but nothing to make a hole with. But as it was uncertain whether we should find any tools left there, we patched up the broken pole, as well as we could, for the downward voyage, in which there would be but little use for it. Moreover, we were unwilling to lose any time in this expedition, lest the wind should rise before we reached the larger lakes, and detain us; for a moderate wind produces quite a sea on these waters, in which a batteau will not live for a moment; and on one occasion McCauslin had been delayed a week at the head of the North Twin, which is only four miles across. We were nearly out of provisions, and ill prepared in this respect for what might possibly prove a week's journey round by the shore, fording innumerable streams and threading a trackless forest, should any accident happen to our boat.

It was with regret that we turned our backs on Chesuncook, which McCauslin had formerly logged on, and the Allegash lakes. There were still longer rapids and portages above; among the last the Rippogenus Portage, which he described as the most difficult on the river, and three miles long. The whole length of the Penobscot is 275 miles, and we are still nearly one hundred miles from its source. Hodge, the assistant State Geologist, passed up this river in 1837, and by a portage of only one mile and three-quarters crossed over into the Allegash, and so went down that into the St. John, and up the Madawaska to the Grand Portage across to the St. Lawrence. His is the only account that I know, of an expedition through to Canada in this direction. He thus describes his first sight of the latter river, which, to compare small things with great, is like Balboa's first sight of the Pacific from the mountains of the Isthmus of Darien. "When we first came in sight of the St. Lawrence," he says, "from the top of a high hill, the view was most striking, and much more interesting to me from having been shut up in the woods for the two previous months. Directly before us lay the broad river, extending across nine or ten miles, its surface broken by a few islands and reefs, and two ships riding at anchor near the shore. Beyond, extended ranges of uncultivated hills, parallel with the river. The sun was just going down behind them, and gilding the whole scene with its parting rays."

About four o'clock, the same afternoon, we commenced our return voyage, which would require but little if any poling. In shooting rapids the boatmen use large and broad paddles, instead of poles, to guide the boat with. Though we glided so swiftly, and often smoothly, down, where it had cost us no slight effort to get up, our present voyage was attended with far more danger: for if we once fairly struck one of the thousand rocks by which we were surrounded the boat would be swamped in an instant. When a boat is swamped under these circumstances, the boatmen commonly find no difficulty in keeping afloat at first, for the current keeps both them and their cargo up for a long way down the stream; and if they can swim, they have only to work their way gradually to the shore. The greatest danger is of being caught in an eddy behind some larger rock, where the water rushes up stream faster than elsewhere it does down, and being carried round and round under the surface till they are drowned. McCauslin pointed out some rocks which had been the scene of a fatal accident of this kind. Sometimes the body is not thrown out for several hours. He himself had performed such a circuit once, only his legs being visible to his companions; but he was fortunately thrown out in season to recover his breath.[3] In shooting the rapids, the boatman has this problem to solve: to choose a circuitous and safe course amid a thousand sunken rocks, scattered over a quarter or half a mile, at the same time that he is moving steadily on at the rate of fifteen miles an hour. Stop he cannot; the only question is, where will he go? The bow-man chooses the course with all his eyes about him, striking broad off with his paddle, and drawing the boat by main force into her course. The stern-man faithfully follows the bow.

We were soon at the Aboljacarmegus Falls. Anxious to avoid the delay, as well as the labor, of the portage here, our boatmen went forward first to reconnoitre, and concluded to let the batteau down the falls, carrying the baggage only over the portage. Jumping from rock to rock until nearly in the middle of the stream, we were ready to receive the boat and let her down over the first fall, some six or seven feet perpendicular. The boatmen stand upon the edge of a shelf of rock, where the fall is perhaps nine or ten feet perpendicular, in from one to two feet of rapid water, one on each side of the boat, and let it slide gently over, till the bow is run out ten or twelve feet in the air; then, letting it drop squarely, while one holds the painter, the other leaps in, and his companion following, they are whirled down the rapids to a new fall, or to smooth water. In a very few minutes they had accomplished a passage in safety, which would be as foolhardy for the unskilful to attempt as the descent of Niagara itself. It seemed as if it needed only a little familiarity, and a little more skill, to navigate down such falls as Niagara itself with safety. At any rate, I should not despair of such men in the rapids above table-rock, until I saw them actually go over the falls, so cool, so collected, so fertile in resources are they. One might have thought that these were falls, and that falls were not to be waded through with impunity, like a mud-puddle. There was really danger of their losing their sublimity in losing their power to harm us. Familiarity breeds contempt. The boatman pauses, perchance, on some shelf beneath a table-rock under the fall, standing in some cove of back-water two feet deep, and you hear his rough voice come up through the spray, coolly giving directions how to launch the boat this time.

Having carried round Pockwockomus Falls, our oars soon brought us to the Katepskonegan, or Oak Hall carry, where we decided to camp halfway over, leaving our batteau to be carried over in the morning on fresh shoulders. One shoulder of each of the boatmen showed a red spot as large as one's hand, worn by the batteau on this expedition; and this shoulder, as it did all the work, was perceptibly lower than its fellow, from long service. Such toil soon wears out the strongest constitution. The drivers are accustomed to work in the cold water in the spring, rarely ever dry; and if one falls in all over he rarely changes his clothes till night, if then, even. One who takes this precaution is called by a particular nickname, or is turned off. None can lead this life who are not almost amphibious. McCauslin said soberly, what is at any rate a good story to tell, that he had seen where six men were wholly under water at once, at a jam, with their shoulders to handspikes. If the log did not start, then they had to put out their heads to breathe. The driver works as long as he can see, from dark to dark, and at night has not time to eat his supper and dry his clothes fairly, before he is asleep on his cedar bed. We lay that night on the very bed made by such a party, stretching our tent over the poles which were still standing, but reshingling the damp and faded bed with fresh leaves.

In the morning we carried our boat over and launched it, making haste lest the wind should rise. The boatmen ran down Passamagamet, and, soon after, Ambejijis Falls, while we walked round with the baggage. We made a hasty breakfast at the head of Ambejijis Lake, on the remainder of our pork, and were soon rowing across its smooth surface again, under a pleasant sky, the mountain being now clear of clouds, in the northeast. Taking turns at the oars, we shot rapidly across Deep Cove, the foot of Pamadumcook, and the North Twin, at the rate of six miles an hour, the wind not being high enough to disturb us, and reached the Dam at noon. The boatmen went through one of the log sluices in the batteau, where the fall was ten feet at the bottom, and took us in below. Here was the longest rapid in our voyage, and perhaps the running of this was as dangerous and arduous a task as any. Shooting down sometimes at the rate, as we judged, of fifteen miles an hour, if we struck a rock we were split from end to end in an instant. Now, like a bait bobbing for some river monster, amid the eddies, now darting to this side of the stream, now to that, gliding swift and smooth near to our destruction, or striking broad off with the paddle and drawing the boat to right or left with all our might, in order to avoid a rock. I suppose that it was like running the rapids of the Saute de St. Marie, at the outlet of Lake Superior, and our boatmen probably displayed no less dexterity than the Indians there do. We soon ran through this mile, and floated in Quakish Lake.

After such a voyage, the troubled and angry waters, which once had seemed terrible and not to be trifled with, appeared tamed and subdued; they had been bearded and worried in their channels, pricked and whipped into submission with the spike-pole and paddle, gone through and through with impunity, and all their spirit and their danger taken out of them, and the most swollen and impetuous rivers seemed but playthings henceforth. I began, at length, to understand the boatman's familiarity with, and contempt for, the rapids. "Those Fowler boys," said Mrs. McCauslin, "are perfect ducks for the water." They had run down to Lincoln, according to her, thirty or forty miles, in a batteau, in the night, for a doctor, when it was so dark that they could not see a rod before them, and the river was swollen so as to be almost a continuous rapid, so that the doctor *cried*, when they brought him up by daylight, "Why, Tom, how did you see to steer?" "We didn't steer much,—only kept her straight." And yet they met with no accident. It is true, the more difficult rapids are higher up than this.

When we reached the Millinocket opposite to Tom's house, and were waiting for his folks to set us over, for we had left our batteau above the Grand Falls, we discovered two canoes, with two men in each, turning up this stream from Shad Pond, one keeping the opposite side of a small island before us, while the other approached the side where we were standing, examining the banks carefully for muskrats as they came along. The last proved to be Louis Neptune and his companion, now, at last, on their way up to Chesuncook after moose; but they were so disguised that we hardly knew them. At a little distance they might have been taken for Quakers, with their broad-brimmed hats, and overcoats with broad capes, the spoils of Bangor, seeking a settlement in this Sylvania,—or, nearer at hand, for fashionable gentlemen the morning after a spree. Met face to face, these Indians in their native woods looked like the sinister and slouching fellows whom you meet picking up strings and paper in the streets of a city. There is, in fact, a remarkable and unexpected resemblance between the degraded savage and the lowest classes in a great city. The one is no more a child of nature than the other. In the progress of degradation the distinction of races is soon lost. Neptune at first was only anxious to know what we "kill," seeing some partridges in the hands of one of the party, but we had assumed too much anger to permit of a reply. We thought Indians had some honor before. But—"Me been sick. O, me unwell now. You make bargain, then me go." They had in fact been delayed so long by a drunken frolic at the Five Islands, and they had not yet recovered from its effects. They had some young musquash in their canoes, which they dug out of the banks with a hoe, for food, not for their skins, for musquash are their principal food on these expeditions. So they went on up the Millinocket, and we kept down the bank of the Penobscot, after recruiting ourselves with a draught of Tom's beer, leaving Tom at his home.

Thus a man shall lead his life away here on the edge of the wilderness, on Indian Millinocket stream, in a new world, far in the dark of a continent, and have a flute to play at evening here, while his strains echo to the stars, amid the howling of wolves; shall live, as it were, in the primitive age of the world, a primitive man. Yet he shall spend a sunny day, and in this century be my contemporary; perchance shall read some scattered leaves of literature, and sometimes talk with me. Why read history, then, if the ages and the generations are now? He lives three thousand years deep into time, an age not yet described by poets. Can you well go further back in history than this? Ay! Ay!—for there turns up but now into the mouth of Millinocket stream a still more ancient and primitive man, whose history is not brought down even to the former. In a bark vessel sewn with the roots of the spruce, with hornbeam paddles, he dips his way along. He is but dim and misty to me, obscured by the æons that lie between the bark-canoe and the batteau. He builds no house of logs, but a wigwam of skins. He eats no hot bread and sweet cake, but musquash and moose-meat and the fat of bears. He glides up the Millinocket and is lost to my sight, as a more distant and misty cloud is seen flitting by behind a nearer, and is lost in space. So he goes about his destiny, the red face of man.

After having passed the night, and buttered our boots for the last time, at Uncle George's, whose dogs almost devoured him for joy at his return, we kept on down the river the next day, about eight miles on foot, and then took a batteau, with a man to pole it, to Mattawamkeag, ten more. At the middle of that very night, to make a swift conclusion to a long story, we dropped our buggy over the half-finished bridge at Oldtown, where we heard the confused din and clink of a hundred saws, which never rest, and at six o'clock the next morning one of the party was steaming his way to Massachusetts.

——

What is most striking in the Maine wilderness is the continuousness of the forest, with fewer open intervals or glades than you had imagined. Except the few burnt-lands, the narrow intervals on the rivers, the bare tops of the high mountains, and the lakes and streams, the forest is uninterrupted. It is even more grim and wild than you had anticipated, a damp and intricate wilderness, in the spring everywhere wet and miry. The aspect of the country, indeed, is universally stern and savage, excepting the distant views of the forest from hills, and the lake prospects, which are mild and civilizing in a degree. The lakes are something which you are unprepared for; they lie up so high, exposed to the light, and the forest is diminished to a fine fringe on their edges, with here and there a blue mountain, like amethyst jewels set around some jewel of the first water,—so anterior, so superior, to all the changes that are to take place on their shores, even now civil and refined, and fair as they can ever be. These are not the artificial forests of an English king,—a royal preserve merely. Here prevail no forest laws but those of nature. The aborigines have never been dispossessed, nor nature disforested.

It is a country full of evergreen trees, of mossy silver birches and watery maples, the ground dotted with insipid, small, red berries, and strewn with damp and moss-grown rocks,—a country diversified with innumerable lakes and rapid streams, peopled with trout and various species of *leucisci,* with salmon, shad, and pickerel, and other fishes; the forest resounding at rare intervals with the note of the chickadee, the blue-jay, and the woodpecker, the scream of the fish-hawk and the eagle, the laugh of the loon, and the whistle of ducks along the solitary streams; at night, with the hooting of owls and howling of wolves; in summer, swarming with myriads of black flies and mosquitoes, more formidable than wolves to the white man. Such is the home of the moose, the bear, the caribou, the wolf, the beaver, and the Indian. Who shall describe the inexpressible tenderness and immortal life of the grim forest, where Nature, though it be mid-winter, is ever in her spring, where the moss-grown and de-caying trees are not old, but seem to enjoy a perpetual youth; and blissful, innocent Nature, like a serene infant, is too happy to make a noise, except by a few tinkling, lisping birds and trickling rills?

What a place to live, what a place to die and be buried in! There certainly men would live forever, and laugh at death and the grave. There they could have no such thoughts as are associated with the village graveyard,—that make a grave out of one of those moist evergreen hummocks!

Die and be buried who will,
I mean to live here still;
My nature grows ever more young
The primitive pines among.

I am reminded by my journey how exceedingly new this country still is. You have only to travel for a few days into the interior and back parts even of many of the old States, to come to that very America which the Northmen, and Cabot, and Gosnold, and Smith, and Raleigh visited. If Columbus was the first to discover the islands, Americus Vespucius and Cabot, and the Puritans, and we their descendants, have discovered only the shores of America. While the republic has already acquired a history world-wide, America is still unsettled and unexplored. Like the English in New Holland, we live only on the shores of a continent even yet, and hardly know where the rivers come from which float our navy. The very timber and boards and shingles of which our houses are made, grew but yesterday in a wilderness where the Indian still hunts and the moose runs wild. New York has her wilderness within her own borders; and though the sailors of Europe are familiar with the soundings of her Hudson, and Fulton long since invented the steamboat on its waters, an Indian is still necessary to guide her scientific men to its head-waters in the Adirondack country.

Have we even so much as discovered and settled the shores? Let a man travel on foot along the coast, from the Passamaquoddy to the Sabine, or to the Rio Bravo, or to wherever the end is now, if he is swift enough to overtake it, faithfully following the windings of every inlet and of every cape, and stepping to the music of the surf,—with a desolate fishing-town once a week, and a city's port once a month to cheer him, and putting up at the light-houses, when there are any,—and tell me if it looks like a discovered and settled country, and not rather, for the most part, like a desolate island, and No-man's Land.

We have advanced by leaps to the Pacific, and left many a lesser Oregon and California unexplored behind us. Though the railroad and the telegraph have been established on the shores of Maine, the Indian still looks out from her interior mountains over all these to the sea. There stands the city of Bangor, fifty miles up the Penobscot, at the head of navigation for vessels of the largest class, the principal lumber depot on this continent, with a population of twelve thousand, like a star on the edge of night, still hewing at the forests of which it is built, already overflowing with the luxuries and refinement of Europe, and sending its vessels to Spain, to England, and to the West Indies for its groceries,—and yet only a few axe-men have gone "up river," into the howling wilderness which feeds it. The bear and deer are still found within its limits; and the moose, as he swims the Penobscot, is entangled amid its shipping, and taken by foreign sailors in its harbor. Twelve miles in the rear, twelve miles of railroad, are Orono and the Indian Island, the home of the Penobscot tribe, and then commence the batteau and the canoe, and the military road; and sixty miles above, the country is virtually unmapped and unexplored, and there still waves the virgin forest of the New World.

—1864

Notes

1. "The spruce-tree," says Springer in '51, "is generally selected, principally for the superior facilities which its numerous limbs afford the climber. To gain the first limbs of this tree, which are from twenty to forty feet from the ground, a smaller tree is undercut and lodged against it, clambering up which the top of the spruce is reached. In some cases, when a very elevated position is desired, the spruce-tree is lodged against the trunk of some lofty pine, up which we ascend to a height twice that of the surrounding forest."

To indicate the direction of pines, he throws down a branch, and a man at the ground takes the bearing.

2. The bears had not touched things on our possessions. They sometimes tear a batteau to pieces for the sake of the tar with which it is besmeared.

3. I cut this from a newspaper. "On the 11th (instant?) [May, '49], on Rappogenes Falls, Mr. John Delantee, of Orono, Me., was drowned while running logs. He was a citizen of Orono, and was twenty-six years of age. His companions found his body, enclosed it in bark, and buried it in the solemn woods."

Edward Whymper
"The Fatal Accident on the Matterhorn"

The English engraver Edward Whymper (1840–1911) made a series of stunning first ascents in the Alps during the Golden Age of mountaineering, including the first ascent of the Matterhorn in 1865. This expedition ended with the most sensational accident in nineteenth-century mountain climbing: three English climbers and their guide roped together tumbled thousands of feet onto a glacier after one member of the party slipped and the rope snapped. The tragedy almost brought an end to Whymper's climbing career and Queen Victoria seriously considered mounting an enquiry into the safety of the sport. Both the native guides and Whymper became the targets of official inquiries regarding the safety of the rope and the precautions taken by the members of the group. Whymper first wrote a letter on August 8, 1865, to The Times to allay suspicions regarding his conduct, and he later published an expanded account of the accident in his Scrambles amongst the Alps *(1872), reprinted below from the American edition.*

CHAPTER XXI.

THE ASCENT OF THE MATTERHORN.

We started from Zermatt on the 13th of July at half-past five, on a brilliant and perfectly cloudless morning. We were eight in number—Croz, old Peter and his two sons,[1] Lord Francis Douglas, Hadow, Hudson[2] and I. To ensure steady motion, one tourist and one native walked together. The youngest Taugwalder fell to my share, and the lad marched well, proud to be on the expedition and happy to show his powers. The wine-bags also fell to my lot to carry, and throughout the day, after each drink, I replenished them secretly with water, so that at the next halt they were found fuller than before! This was considered a good omen and little short of miraculous.

On the first day we did not intend to ascend to any great height, and we mounted, accordingly, very leisurely, picked up the things which were left in the chapel at the Schwarzsee at 8:20, and proceeded thence along the ridge connecting the Hörnli with the Matterhorn. At half-past eleven we arrived at the base of the actual peak, then quitted the ridge and clambered round some ledges on to the eastern face. We were now fairly upon the mountain, and were astonished to find that places which from the Riffel, or even from the Furggengletscher, looked entirely impracticable, were so easy that we could *run about*.

Edward Whymper, "The Fatal Accident on the Matterhorn," *Scrambles amongst the Alps* (Philadelphia: J. B. Lippincott and Co., 1872).

Before twelve o'clock we had found a good position for the tent, at a height of eleven thousand feet.[3] Croz and young Peter went on to see what was above, in order to save time on the following morning. They cut across the heads of the snow-slopes which descended toward the Furggengletscher, and disappeared round a corner, but shortly afterward we saw them high up on the face, moving quickly. We others made a solid platform for the tent in a well-protected spot, and then watched eagerly for the return of the men. The stones which they upset told that they were very high, and we supposed that the way must be easy. At length, just before 3 P.M., we saw them coming down, evidently much excited. "What are they saying, Peter?" "Gentlemen, they say it is no good." But when they came near we heard a different story: "Nothing but what was good—not a difficulty, not a single difficulty! We could have gone to the summit and returned to-day easily!"

We passed the remaining hours of daylight—some basking in the sunshine, some sketching or collecting—and when the sun went down, giving, as it departed, a glorious promise for the morrow, we returned to the tent to arrange for the night. Hudson made tea, I coffee, and we then retired each one to his blanket-bag, the Taugwalders, Lord Francis Douglas and myself occupying the tent, the others remaining, by preference, outside. Long after dusk the cliffs above echoed with our laughter and with the songs of the guides, for we were happy that night in camp, and feared no evil.

We assembled together outside the tent before dawn on the morning of the 14th, and started directly when it was light enough to move. Young Peter came on with us as a guide, and his brother returned to Zermatt. We followed the route which had been taken on the previous day, and in a few minutes turned the rib which had intercepted the view of the eastern face from our tent platform. The whole of this great slope was now revealed, rising for three thousand feet like a huge natural staircase. Some parts were more and others were less easy, but we were not once brought to a halt by any serious impediment, for when an obstruction was met in front it could always be turned to the right or to the left. For the greater part of the way there was indeed no occasion for the rope, and sometimes Hudson led, sometimes myself. At 6:20 we had attained a height of 12,800 feet, and halted for half an hour: we then continued the ascent without a break until 9:55, when we stopped for fifty minutes at a height of fourteen thousand feet. Twice we struck the north-eastern ridge, and followed it for some little distance—to no advantage, for it was usually more rotten and steep, and always more difficult, than the face. Still, we kept near to it, lest stones perchance might fall.

We had now arrived at the foot of that part which, from the Riffelberg or from Zermatt, seems perpendicular or overhanging, and could no longer continue upon the eastern side. For a little distance we ascended by snow upon the arête—that is, the ridge—descending toward Zermatt, and then by common consent turned over to the right, or to the northern side. Before doing so we made a change in the order of ascent. Croz went first, I followed, Hudson came third: Hadow and old Peter were last. "Now," said Croz as he led off—"now for something altogether different." The work

170

became difficult, and required caution. In some places there was little to hold, and it was desirable that those should be in front who were least likely to slip. The general slope of the mountain at this part was *less* than forty degrees, and snow had accumulated in, and had filled up, the interstices of the rock-face, leaving only occasional fragments projecting here and there. These were at times covered with a thin film of ice, produced from the melting and refreezing of the snow. It was the counterpart, on a small scale, of the upper seven hundred feet of the Pointe des Écrins; only there was this material difference—the face of the Écrins was about, or exceeded, an angle of fifty degrees, and the Matterhorn face was less than forty degrees. It was a place over which any fair mountaineer might pass in safety, and Mr. Hudson ascended this part, and, as far as I know, the entire mountain, without having the slightest assistance rendered to him upon any occasion. Sometimes after I had taken a hand from Croz or received a pull, I turned to offer the same to Hudson, but he invariably declined, saying it was not necessary. Mr. Hadow, however, was not accustomed to this kind of work, and required continual assistance. It is only fair to say that the difficulty which he found at this part arose simply and entirely from want of experience.

This solitary difficult part was of no great extent. We bore away over it at first nearly horizontally, for a distance of about four hundred feet, then ascended directly toward the summit for about sixty feet, and then doubled back to the ridge which descends toward Zermatt. A long stride round a rather awkward corner brought us to snow once more. The last doubt vanished! The Matterhorn was ours! Nothing but two hundred feet of easy snow remained to be surmounted!

You must now carry your thoughts back to the seven Italians who started from Breuil on the 11th of July. Four days had passed since their departure, and we were tormented with anxiety lest they should arrive on the top before us. All the way up we had talked of them, and many false alarms of "men on the summit" had been raised. The higher we rose the more intense became the excitement. What if we should be beaten at the last moment? The slope eased off, at length we could be detached, and Croz and I, dashing away, ran a neck-and-neck race which ended in a dead heat. At 1:40 P.M. the world was at our feet and the Matterhorn was conquered! Hurrah! Not a footstep could be seen.

It was not yet certain that we had not been beaten. The summit of the Matterhorn was formed of a rudely level ridge, about 350 feet long,[4] and the Italians might have been at its farther extremity. I hastened to the southern end, scanning the snow right and left eagerly. Hurrah again! It was untrodden. "Where were the men?" I peered over the cliff, half doubting, half expectant. I saw them immediately, mere dots on the ridge, at an immense distance below. Up went my arms and my hat. "Croz! Croz! come here!" "Where are they, monsieur?" "There—don't you see them down there?" "Ah! The *coquins!* they are low down." "Croz, we must make those fellows hear us." We yelled until we were hoarse. The Italians seemed to regard us—we could not be certain. "Croz, we *must* make them hear us—they *shall* hear us!" I seized a block of rock and hurled it down, and called upon my companion, in the name of friendship,

171

to do the same. We drove our sticks in and prized away the crags, and soon a torrent of stones poured down the cliffs. There was no mistake about it this time. The Italians turned and fled.[5]

Still, I would that the leader of that party could have stood with us at that moment, for our victorious shouts conveyed to him the disappointment of the ambition of a lifetime. He was *the* man, of all those who attempted the ascent of the Matterhorn, who most deserved to be the first upon its summit. He was the first to doubt its inaccessibility, and he was the only man who persisted in believing that its ascent would be accomplished. It was the aim of his life to make the ascent from the side of Italy for the honor of his native valley. For a time he had the game in his hands; he played it as he thought best, but he made a false move, and lost it. Times have changed with Carrel. His supremacy is questioned in the Val Tournanche; new men have arisen, and he is no longer recognized as *the* chasseur above all others; but so long as he remains the man that he is to-day it will not be easy to find his superior.

The others had arrived, so we went back to the northern end of the ridge. Croz now took the tentpole[6] and planted it in the highest snow. "Yes," we said, "there is the flagstaff, but where is the flag?" "Here it is," he answered, pulling off his blouse and fixing it to the stick. It made a poor flag, and there was no wind to float it out, yet it was seen all around. They saw it at Zermatt, at the Riffel, in the Val Tournanche. At Breuil the watchers cried, "Victory is ours!" They raised "bravos" for Carrel and "vivas" for Italy, and hastened to put themselves *en fête*. On the morrow they were undeceived. All was changed: the explorers returned sad—cast down—disheartened—confounded—gloomy. "It is true," said the men. "We saw them ourselves—they hurled stones at us! The old traditions *are* true—there are spirits on the top of the Matterhorn!"[7]

We returned to the southern end of the ridge to build a cairn, and then paid homage to the view.[8] The day was one of those superlatively calm and clear ones which usually precede bad weather. The atmosphere was perfectly still and free from all clouds or vapors. Mountains fifty—nay, a hundred—miles off looked sharp and near. All their details—ridge and crag, snow and glacier—stood out with faultless definition. Pleasant thoughts of happy days in bygone years came up unbidden as we recognized the old, familiar forms. All were revealed—not one of the principal peaks of the Alps was hidden.[9] I see them clearly now—the great inner circles of giants, backed by the ranges, chains and *massifs*. First came the Dent Blanche, hoary and grand; the Gabelhorn and pointed Rothhorn, and then the peerless Weisshorn; the towering Mischabelhörner, flanked by the Allaleinhorn, Strahlhorn and Rimpfischhorn; then Monte Rosa—with its many Spitzes—the Lyskamm and the Breithorn. Behind were the Bernese Oberland, governed by the Finsteraarhorn, the Simplon and St. Gothard groups, the Disgrazia and the Orteler. Toward the south we looked down to Chivasso on the plain of Piedmont, and far beyond. The Viso—one hundred miles away—seemed close upon us; the Maritime Alps—130 miles distant—were free from haze. Then came my first love—the Pelvoux; the Écrins and the Meije; the clusters of the Grainas; and lastly, in the west, gorgeous in the full sunlight, rose the monarch of all—Mont Blanc. Ten thousand feet beneath us were the green fields of Zermatt, dotted with chalets, from which blue smoke rose lazily. Eight thousand feet below, on the other side, were the pastures of Breuil. There were forests black and gloomy, and meadows bright and lively; bounding waterfalls and tranquil lakes; fertile lands and savage wastes; sunny plains and frigid plateaux. There were the most rugged forms and the most graceful outlines—bold, perpendicular cliffs and gentle, undulating slopes; rocky mountains and snowy mountains, sombre and solemn or glittering and white, with walls, turrets, pinnacles, pyramids, domes, cones and spires! There was every combination that the world can give, and every contrast that the heart could desire.

We remained on the summit for one hour—

One crowded hour of glorious life.

It passed away too quickly, and we began to prepare for the descent.

CHAPTER XXII.

DESCENT OF THE MATTERHORN.

Hudson and I again consulted as to the best and safest arrangement of the party. We agreed that it would be best for Croz to go first,[10] and Hadow second; Hudson, who was almost equal to a guide in sureness of foot, wished to be third; Lord F. Douglas was placed next, and old Peter, the strongest of the remainder, after him. I suggested to Hudson that we should attach a rope to the rocks on our arrival at the difficult bit, and hold it as we descended, as an additional protection. He approved the idea, but it was not definitely settled that it should be done. The party was being arranged in the above order whilst I was sketching the summit, and they had finished, and were waiting for me to be tied in line, when someone remembered that our names had not been left in a bottle. They requested me to write them down, and moved off while it was being done.

A few minutes afterward I tied myself to young Peter, ran down after the others, and caught them just as they were commencing the descent of the difficult part. Great care was being taken. Only one man was moving at a time: when he was firmly planted, the next advanced, and so on. They had not, however, attached the additional rope to rocks, and nothing was said about it. The suggestion was not made for my own sake, and I am not sure that it even occurred to me again. For some little distance we two followed the others, detached from them, and should have continued so had not Lord F. Douglas asked me, about 3 P.M., to tie on to old Peter, as he feared, he said, that Taugwalder would not be able to hold his ground if a slip occurred.

———

A few minutes later a sharp-eyed lad ran into the Monte Rosa hotel to Seiler, saying that he had seen an avalanche fall from the summit of the Matterhorn on to the

Matterhorngletscher. The boy was reproved for telling idle stories: he was right, nevertheless, and this was what he saw.

Michel Croz had laid aside his axe, and in order to give Mr. Hadow greater security was absolutely taking hold of his legs and putting his feet, one by one, into their proper positions.[11] As far as I know, no one was actually descending. I cannot speak with certainty, because the two leading men were partially hidden from my sight by an intervening mass of rock, but it is my belief, from the movements of their shoulders, that Croz, having done as I have said, was in the act of turning round to go down a step or two himself: at this moment Mr. Hadow slipped, fell against him and knocked him over. I heard one startled exclamation from Croz, then saw him and Mr. Hadow flying downward: in another moment Hudson was dragged from his steps, and Lord F. Douglas immediately after him.[12] All this was the work of a moment. Immediately we heard Croz's exclamation, old Peter and I planted ourselves as firmly as the rocks would permit:[13] the rope was taut between us, and the jerk came on us both as on one man. We held, but the rope broke midway between Taugwalder and Lord Francis Douglas. For a few seconds we saw our unfortunate companions sliding downward on their backs, and spreading out their hands, endeavoring to save themselves. They passed from our sight uninjured, disappeared one by one, and fell from precipice to precipice on to the Matterhorngletscher below, a distance of nearly four thousand feet in height. From the moment the rope broke it was impossible to help them.

So perished our comrades! For the space of half an hour we remained on the spot without moving a single step. The two men, paralyzed by terror, cried like infants, and trembled in such a manner as to threaten us with the fate of the others. Old Peter rent the air with exclamations of "Chamounix!—oh, what will Chamounix say?" He meant, Who would believe that Croz could fall? The young man did nothing but scream or sob, "We are lost! we are lost!" Fixed between the two, I could move neither up nor down. I begged young Peter to descend, but he dared not. Unless he did, we could not advance. Old Peter became alive to the danger, and swelled the cry, "We are lost! we are lost!" The father's fear was natural—he trembled for his son; the young man's fear was cowardly—he thought of self alone. At last old Peter summoned up courage, and changed his position to a rock to which he could fix the rope: the young man then descended, and we all stood together. Immediately we did so, I asked for the rope which had given way, and found, to my surprise—indeed, to my horror—that it was the weakest of the three ropes. It was not brought, and should not have been employed, for the purpose for which it was used. It was old rope, and, compared with the others, was feeble. It was intended as a reserve, in case we had to leave much rope behind attached to rocks. I saw at once that a serious question was involved, and made them give me the end. It had broken in mid-air, and it did not appear to have sustained previous injury.

For more than two hours afterward I thought almost every moment that the next would be my last, for the Taugwalders, utterly unnerved, were not only incapable of

174

giving assistance, but were in such a state that a slip might have been expected from them at any moment. After a time we were able to do that which should have been done at first, and fixed rope to firm rocks, in addition to being tied together. These ropes were cut from time to time, and were left behind.[14] Even with their assurance the men were afraid to proceed, and several times old Peter turned with ashy face and faltering limbs, and said with terrible emphasis, "*I cannot!*"

About 6 P.M. we arrived at the snow upon the ridge descending toward Zermatt, and all peril was over. We frequently looked, but in vain, for traces of our unfortunate companions: we bent over the ridge and cried to them, but no sound returned. Convinced at last that they were within neither sight nor hearing, we ceased from our useless efforts, and, too cast down for speech, silently gathered up our things and the little effects of those who were lost, preparatory to continuing the descent. When lo! a mighty arch appeared, rising above the Lyskamm high into the sky. Pale, colorless and noiseless, but perfectly sharp and defined, except where it was lost in the clouds, this unearthly apparition seemed like a vision from another world, and almost appalled we watched with amazement the gradual development of two vast crosses, one on either side. If the Taugwalders had not been the first to perceive it, I should have doubted my senses. They thought it had some connection with the accident, and I, after a while, that it might bear some relation to ourselves. But our movements had no effect upon it. The spectral forms remained motionless. It was a fearful and wonderful sight, unique in my experience, and impressive beyond description, coming at such a moment.[15]

I was ready to leave, and waiting for the others. They had recovered their appetites and the use of their tongues. They spoke in patois, which I did not understand. At length the son said in French, "Monsieur." "Yes." "We are poor men; we have lost our Herr; we shall not get paid; we can ill afford this."[16] "Stop!" I said, interrupting him—"that is nonsense: I shall pay you, of course, just as if your Herr were here." They talked together in their patois for a short time, and then the son spoke again: "We don't wish you to pay us. We wish you to write in the hotel-book at Zermatt and to your journals that we have not been paid." "What nonsense are you talking? I don't understand you. What do you mean?" He proceeded: "Why, next year there will be many travelers at Zermatt, and we shall get more *voyageurs*."

Who would answer such a proposition? I made them no reply in words,[17] but they knew very well the indignation that I felt. They filled the cup of bitterness to overflowing, and I tore down the cliff madly and recklessly, in a way that caused them, more than once, to inquire if I wished to kill them. Night fell, and for an hour the descent was continued in the darkness. At half-past nine a resting-place was found, and upon a wretched slab, barely large enough to hold the three, we passed six miserable hours. At daybreak the descent was resumed, and from the Hörnli ridge we ran down to the chalets of Buhl and on to Zermatt. Seiler met me at his door, and followed in silence to my room: "What is the matter?" "The Taugwalders and I have returned." He did not need more, and burst into tears, but lost no time in useless lamentations, and set to work to the village. Ere long a score of men had started to ascend the Hohlicht heights, above Kalbermatt and Z'Mutt, which commanded the plateau of the Matterhorngletscher. They returned after six hours, and reported that they had seen the bodies lying motionless on the snow. This was on Saturday, and they proposed that we should leave on Sunday evening, so as to arrive upon the plateau at daybreak on Monday. Unwilling to lose the slightest chance, the Rev. J. M'Cormick and I resolved to start on Sunday morning. The Zermatt men, threatened with excommunication by their priests if they failed to attend early mass, were unable to accompany us. To several of them, at least, this was a severe trial, and Peter Perrn declared with tears that nothing else would have prevented him from joining in the search for his old comrades. Englishmen came to our aid. The Rev. J. Robertson and Mr. J. Phillpotts offered themselves and their guide, Franz Andermatten: another Englishman lent us Joseph Marie and Alexandre Lochmatter. Frédéric Payot and Jean Tairraz of Chamounix also volunteered.

We started at 2 A.M. on Sunday, the 16th, and followed the route that we had taken on the previous Thursday as far as the Hörnli. From thence we went down to the right of the ridge, and mounted through the *séracs* of the Matterhorngletscher. By 8:30 we had got to the plateau at the top of the glacier, and within sight of the corner in which we knew my companions must be. As we saw one weather-beaten man after another raise the telescope, turn deadly pale and pass it on without a word to the next, we knew that all hope was gone. We approached. They had fallen below as they had fallen above—Croz a little in advance, Hadow near him, and Hudson some distance behind, but of Lord F. Douglas we could see nothing.[18] We left them where they fell, buried in snow at the base of the grandest cliff of the most majestic mountain of the Alps.

All those who had fallen had been tied with the Manila, or with the second and equally strong rope, and consequently there had been only one link—that between old Peter and Lord F. Douglas—where the weaker rope had been used. This had a very ugly look for Taugwalder, for it was not possible to suppose that the others would have sanctioned the employment of a rope so greatly inferior in strength when there were more than 250 feet of the better qualities still of our use.[19] For the sake of the old guide (who bore a good reputation), and upon all other accounts, it was desirable that this matter should be cleared up; and after my examination before the court of inquiry which was instituted by the government was over, I handed in a number of questions which were framed so as to afford old Peter an opportunity of exculpating himself from the grave suspicions which at once fell upon him. The questions, I was told, were put and answered, but the answers, although promised, have never reached me.[20]

Meanwhile, the administration sent strict injunctions to recover the bodies, and upon the 19th of July twenty-one men of Zermatt accomplished that sad and dangerous task. Of the body of Lord Francis Douglas they too saw nothing: it is probably still arrested on the rocks above.[21] The remains of Hudson and Hadow were interred upon the north side of the Zermatt church, in the presence of a reverent crowd of sympathizing friends. The body of Michel Croz lies upon the other side, under a simpler tomb, whose inscription bears honorable testimony to his rectitude, to his courage and to his devotion.[22]

So the traditional inaccessibility of the Matterhorn was vanquished, and was replaced by legends of a more real character. Others will essay to scale its proud cliffs, but to none will it be the mountain that it was to its early explorers. Others may tread its summit-snows, but none will ever know the feelings of those who first gazed upon its marvelous panorama, and none, I trust, will ever be compelled to tell of joy turned into grief, and of laughter into mourning. It proved to be a stubborn foe; it resisted long and gave many a hard blow; it was defeated at last with an ease that none could have anticipated, but, like a relentless enemy conquered but not crushed, it took terrible vengeance. The time may come when the Matterhorn shall have passed away, and nothing save a heap of shapeless fragments will mark the spot where the great mountain stood, for, atom by atom, inch by inch, and yard by yard, it yields to forces which nothing can withstand. That time is far distant, and ages hence generations unborn will gaze upon its awful precipices and wonder at its unique form. However exalted may be their ideas and however exaggerated their expectations, none will come to return disappointed!

The play is over, and the curtain is about to fall. Before we part, a word upon the graver teachings of the mountains. See yonder height! 'Tis far away—unbidden comes the word "Impossible!" "Not so," says the mountaineer. "The way is long, I know: it's difficult—it may be dangerous. It's possible, I'm sure: I'll seek the way, take counsel of my brother mountaineers, and find how they have gained similar heights and learned to avoid the dangers." He starts (all slumbering down below): the path is slippery—maybe laborious too. Caution and perseverance gain the day—the height is reached! and those beneath cry, "Incredible! 'tis superhuman!"

We who go mountain-scrambling have constantly set before us the superiority of fixed purpose or perseverance to brute force. We know that each height, each step, must be gained by patient, laborious toil, and that wishing cannot take the place of working: we know the benefits of mutual aid—that many a difficulty must be encountered, and many an obstacle must be grappled with or turned; but we know that where there's a will there's a way; and we come back to our daily occupations better fitted to fight the battle of life and to overcome the impediments which obstruct our paths, strengthened and cheered by the recollection of the past labors and by the memories of victories gained in other fields.

I have not made myself an advocate or an apologist for mountaineering, nor do I now intend to usurp the functions of a moralist, but my task would have been ill performed if it had been concluded without one reference to the more serious lessons of the mountaineer. We glory in the physical regeneration which is the product of our exertions; we exult over the grandeur of the scenes that are brought before our eyes, the splendors of sunrise and sunset, and the beauties of hill, dale, lake, wood and waterfall; but we value more highly the development of manliness, and the evolution, under combat with difficulties, of those noble qualities of human nature—courage, patience, endurance and fortitude.

Some hold these virtues in less estimation, and assign base and contemptible motives to those who indulge in our innocent sport.

Be thou chaste as ice, as pure as snow, thou shalt not escape calumny.

Others, again, who are not detractors, find mountaineering, as a sport, to be wholly unintelligible. It is not greatly to be wondered at—we are not all constituted alike. Mountaineering is a pursuit essentially adapted to the young or vigorous, and not to the old or feeble. To the latter toil may be no pleasure, and it is often said by such persons, "This man is making a toil of pleasure." Toil he must who goes mountaineering, but out of the toil comes strength (not merely muscular energy—more than that, an awakening of all the faculties), and from the strength arises pleasure. Then, again, it is often asked, in tones which seem to imply that the answer must at least be doubtful, "But does it repay you?" Well, we cannot estimate our enjoyment as you measure your wine or weigh your lead: it is real, nevertheless. If I could blot out every reminiscence or erase every memory, still I should say that my scrambles amongst the Alps have repaid me, for they have given me two of the best things a man can possess—health and friends.

The recollections of past pleasures cannot be effaced. Even now as I write they crowd up before me. First comes an endless series of pictures, magnificent in form, effect and color. I see the great peaks with clouded tops, seeming to mount up for ever and ever; I hear the music of the distant herds, the peasant's yodel and the solemn church-bells; and I scent the fragrant breath of the pines: and after these have passed away another train of thoughts succeeds—of those who have been upright, brave and true; of kind hearts and bold deeds; and of courtesies received at stranger hands, trifles in themselves, but expressive of that good-will toward men which is the essence of charity.

Still, the last sad memory hovers round, and sometimes drifts across like floating mist, cutting off sunshine and chilling the remembrance of happier times. There have been joys too great to be described in words, and there have been griefs upon which I have not dared to dwell; and with these in mind I say, Climb if you will, but remember that courage and strength are naught without prudence, and that a momentary negligence may destroy the happiness of a lifetime. Do nothing in haste, look well to each step, and from the beginning think what may be the end.

APPENDIX.

A. SUBSEQUENT ASCENTS OF THE MATTERHORN.

Mr. Craufurd Grove was the first traveler who ascended the Matterhorn after the accident. This was in August, 1867. He took with him as guides three mountaineers

178

of the Val Tournanche—J.-A. Carrel, J. Bich and S. Meynet, Carrel being the leader. The natives of Val Tournanche were, of course, greatly delighted that his ascent was made upon their side. Some of them however, were by no means well pleased that J.-A. Carrel was so much regarded. They feared, perhaps, that he acquire the monopoly of the mountain. Just a month after Mr. Grove's ascent, six Val Tournanchians set out to see whether they could not learn the route, and so come in for a share of the good things which were expected to arrive. They were three Maquignazes, Caesar Carrel (my old guide), J.-B. Carrel, and a daughter of the last named! They left Breuil at 5 A.M. on September 12, and at 3 P.M. arrived at the hut, where they passed the night. At 7 A.M. the next day they started again (leaving J.-B. Carrel behind), and proceeded along the "shoulder" to the final peak; passed the cleft which had stopped Bennen, and clambered up the comparatively easy rocks on the other side until they arrived at the base of the last precipice, down which we had hurled stones on July 14, 1865. They (young woman and all) were then about 350 feet from the summit! Then, instead of turning to the left, as Carrel and Mr. Grove had done, Joseph and J.-Pierre Maquignaz paid attention to the cliff in front of them, and managed to find a means of passing up, by clefts, ledges and gullies, to the summit. This was a shorter (and it appears to be an easier) route than that taken by Carrel and Grove, and it has been followed by all those who have since then ascended the mountain from the side of Breuil. Subsequently, a rope was fixed over the most difficult portions of the final climb.

In the mean time they had not been idle upon the other side. A hut was constructed upon the eastern face at a height of 12,526 feet above the sea, near to the crest of the ridge which descends toward Zermatt (north-east ridge). This was done at the expense of Monsieur Seiler and of the Swiss Alpine Club. Mons. Seiler placed the execution of the work under the direction of the Knubels, of the village of St. Nicholas, in the Zermatt valley; and Peter Knubel, along with Joseph Marie Lochmatter of the same village, had the honor of making the second ascent of the mountain upon the northern side with Mr. Elliott. This took place on July 24 and 25, 1868. Since then numerous ascents have been made, and of these the only one which calls for mention is that by Signor Giordano, on September 3-5, 1868.

—1865

Notes

1. The two young Taugwalders were taken as porters by desire of their father, and carried provisions amply sufficient for three days, in case the ascent should prove more troublesome than we anticipated.

2. I remember speaking about pedestrianism to a well-known mountaineer some years ago, and venturing to remark that a man who averaged thirty miles a day might be considered a good walker. "A fair walker," he said—"a *fair* walker." "What, then, would you consider *good* walking?" "Well," he replied, "I will tell you. Some time back a friend and I agreed to go to

Switzerland, but a short time afterward he wrote to say he ought to let me know that a young and delicate lad was going with him who would not be equal to great things—in fact, he would not be able to do more than fifty miles a day!" "What became of the young and delicate lad?" "He lives." "And who was our extraordinary friend?" "Charles Hudson." I have every reason to believe that the gentlemen referred to *were* equal to walking more than fifty miles a day, but they were exceptional, not *good* pedestrians.

Charles Hudson, vicar of Skillington in Lincolnshire, was considered by the mountaineering fraternity to be the best amateur of his time. He was the organizer and leader of the party of Englishmen who ascended Mont Blanc by the Aiguille du Goûter, and descended by the Grands Mulets route, without guides, in 1855. His long practice made him surefooted, and in that respect he was not greatly inferior to a born mountaineer. I remember him as a well made man of middle height and age, neither stout nor thin, with face pleasant though grave, and with quiet, unassuming manners. Although an athletic man, he would have been overlooked in a crowd; and although he had done the greatest mountaineering feats which have been done, he was the last man to speak of his own doings. His friend, Mr. Hadow, was a young man of nineteen, who had the looks and manners of a greater age. He was a rapid walker, but 1865 was his first season in the Alps. Lord Francis Douglas was about the same age as Mr. Hadow. He had had the advantage of several seasons in the Alps. He was nimble as a deer, and was becoming an expert mountaineer. Just before our meeting he had ascended the Ober Gabelhorn (with old Peter and Joseph Viennin), and this gave me a high opinion of his powers, for I had examined that mountain all round a few weeks before, and had declined its ascent on account of its apparent difficulty.

My personal acquaintance with Mr. Hudson was very slight; still, I should have been content to have placed myself under his orders if he had chosen to claim the position to which he was entitled. Those who knew him will not be surprised to learn that, so far from doing this, he lost no opportunity in consulting the wishes and opinions of those around him. We deliberated together whenever there was occasion, and our authority was recognized by the others. Whatever responsibility there was devolved upon us. I recollect with satisfaction that there was no difference of opinion between us as to what should be done, and that the most perfect harmony existed between all of us so long as we were together.

3. Thus far the guides did not once go to the front. Hudson or I led, and when any cutting was required we did it ourselves. This was done to spare the guides, and to show them that we were thoroughly in earnest. The spot at which we camped was just four hours' walking from Zermatt.

4. The highest points are toward the two ends. In 1865 the northern end was slightly higher than the southern one. In bygone years Carrel and I often suggested to each other that we might one day arrive upon the top, and find ourselves cut off from the very highest point by a notch in the summit-ridge which is seen from the Théodule and from Breuil. This notch is very conspicuous from below, but when one is actually upon the summit it is hardly noticed, and it can be passed without the least difficulty.

5. I have learned since from J.-A. Carrel that they heard our first cries. They were then upon the south-west ridge, close to the "Cravate," and *1250 feet* below us, or, as the crow flies, at a distance of about one-third of a mile.

6. At our departure the men were confident that the ascent would be made, and took one of the poles out of the tent. I protested that it was tempting Providence: they took the pole, nevertheless.

180

7. Signor Giordano was naturally disappointed at the result, and wished the men to start again. *They all refused to do so, with the exception of Jean-Antoine.* Upon the 16th of July he set out again with three others, and upon the 17th gained the summit by passing (at first) up the south-west ridge, and (afterward) by turning over to the Z'Mutt, or north-western side. On the 18th he returned to Breuil.

Whilst we were upon the southern end of the summit-ridge we paid some attention to the portion of the mountain which intervened between ourselves and the Italian guides. It seemed as if there would not be the least chance for them if they should attempt to storm the final peak directly from the end of the "shoulder." In that direction cliffs fell sheer down from the summit, and we were unable to see beyond a certain distance. There remained the route about which Carrel and I had often talked—namely, to ascend directly at first from the end of the "shoulder," and afterward to swerve to the left (that is, to the Z'Mutt side), and to complete the ascent from the north-west. When we were upon the summit we laughed at this idea. The part of the mountain that I have described was not easy, although its inclination was moderate. If that slope were made only ten degrees sharper its difficulty would be enormously increased. To double its inclination would be to make it impracticable. The slope at the southern end of the summit-ridge, falling toward the north-west, was *much* steeper than that over which we passed, and we ridiculed the idea that any person should attempt to ascend in that direction when the northern route was so easy. Nevertheless, the summit was reached by that route by the undaunted Carrel. From knowing the final slope over which he passed, and from the account of Mr. F. C. Grove—who is the only traveler by whom it has been traversed—I do not hesitate to term the ascent of Carrel and Bich in 1865 the most desperate piece of mountain-scrambling upon record. In 1869 I asked Carrel if he had ever done anything more difficult. His reply was, "Man cannot do anything much more difficult than that."

8. The summit-ridge was much shattered, although not so extensively as the south-west and north-east ridges. The highest rock in 1865 was a block of mica-schist, and the fragment I broke off it not only possesses in a remarkable degree the *character* of the peak, but mimics in an astonishing manner the details of its form.

9. It is most unusual to see the southern half of the panorama unclouded. A hundred ascents may be made before this will be the case again.

10. If the members of the party had been more equally efficient, Croz would have been placed *last*.

11. Not at all an unusual proceeding, even between born mountaineers. I wish to convey the impression that Croz was using all pains, rather than to indicate extreme inability on the part of Mr. Hadow.

12. At the moment of the accident, Croz, Hadow and Hudson were all close together. Between Hudson and Lord F. Douglas the rope was all but taut, and the same between all the others who were *above*. Croz was standing by the side of a rock which afforded good hold, and if he had been aware or had suspected that anything was about to occur, he might and would have gripped it, and would have prevented any mischief. He was taken totally by surprise. Mr. Hadow slipped off his feet on to his back, his feet struck Croz in the small of the back and knocked him right over, head first. Croz's axe was out of his reach, and without it he managed to get his head uppermost before he disappeared from our sight. If it had been in his hand I have no doubt that he would have stopped himself and Mr. Hadow.

Mr. Hadow, at the moment of the slip, was not occupying a bad position. He could have moved either up or down, and could touch with his hand the rock of which I have spoken.

Hudson was not so well placed, but he had liberty of motion. The rope was not taut from him to Hadow, and the two men fell ten or twelve feet before the jerk came upon him. Lord F. Douglas was not favorably placed, and could move neither up nor down. Old Peter was firmly planted, and stood just beneath a large rock which he hugged with both arms. I enter into these details to make it more apparent that the position occupied by the party at the moment of the accident was not by any means excessively trying. We were compelled to pass over the exact spot where the slip occurred, and we found—even with shaken nerves—that *it* was not a difficult place to pass. I have described the *slope generally* as difficult, and it is so undoubtedly to most persons, but it must be distinctly understood that Mr. Hadow slipped at an easy part.

13. Or, more correctly, we held on as tightly as possible. There was no time to change our position.

14. These ends, I believe, are still attached to the rocks, and mark our line of ascent and descent.

15. I paid very little attention to this remarkable phenomenon, and was glad when it disappeared, as it distracted our attention. Under ordinary circumstances I should have felt vexed afterward at not having observed with greater precision an occurrence so rare and so wonderful. I can add very little about it to that which is said above. The sun was directly at our backs— that is to say, the fog-bow was opposite to the sun. The time was 6:30 P.M. The forms were at once tender and sharp, neutral in tone, were developed gradually, and disappeared suddenly. The mists were light (that is, not dense), and were dissipated in the course of the evening.

It has been suggested that the crosses are incorrectly figured in the Illustration, and that they were probably formed by the intersection of other circles or ellipses, as shown in the annexed diagram. I think this suggestion is very likely correct, but I have preferred to follow my original memorandum.

In Parry's *Narrative of an Attempt to Reach the North Pole*, 1828, there is, at pp. 99, 100, an account of the occurrence of a phenomenon analogous to the above-mentioned one: "At half-past 5 P.M. we witnessed a very beautiful natural phenomenon. A broad white fog-bow first appeared opposite to the sun, as was very commonly the case," etc. I follow Parry in using the term fog-bow.

16. They had been traveling with, and had been engaged by, Lord F. Douglas, and so considered him their employer, and responsible to them.

17. Nor did I speak to them afterward, unless it was absolutely necessary, so long as we were together.

18. A pair of gloves, a belt and boot that had belonged to him were found. This, somehow, became publicly known, and gave rise to wild notions, which would not have been entertained had it been also known that the boots of *all* those who had fallen *were off*, and were lying upon the snow near the bodies.

19. I was one hundred feet or more from the others whilst they were being tied up, and am unable to throw any light on the matter. Croz and old Peter no doubt tied up the others.

20. This is not the only occasion upon which M. Clemenz (who presided over the inquiry) has failed to give up answers that he has promised. It is greatly to be regretted that he does not feel that the suppression of the truth is equally against the interests of travelers and of the guides. If the men are untrustworthy, the public should be warned of the fact, but if they are blameless, why allow them to remain under unmerited suspicion?

Old Peter Taugwalder is a man who is laboring under an unjust accusation. Notwithstanding repeated denials, even his comrades and neighbors at Zermatt persist in asserting or insinuating that he *cut* the rope which led from him to Lord F. Douglas. In regard to this infamous charge, I say that he *could* not do so at the moment of the slip, and that the end of the rope in my possession shows that he did not do so beforehand. There remains, however, the suspicious fact that the rope which broke was the thinnest and weakest one that we had. It is suspicious, because it is unlikely that any of the four men in front would have selected an old and weak rope when there was abundance of new and much stronger rope to spare: and on the other hand, because if Taugwalder thought that an accident was likely to happen, it was to his interest to have the weaker rope where it was placed.

I should rejoice to learn that his answers to the questions which were put to him were satisfactory. Not only was his act at the critical moment wonderful as a feat of strength, but it was admirable in its performance at the right time. I am told that he is now nearly incapable of work—not absolutely mad, but with intellect gone and almost crazy; which is not to be wondered at, whether we regard him as a man who contemplated a scoundrelly meanness, or as an injured man suffering under an unjust accusation.

In respect to young Peter, it is not possible to speak in the same manner. The odious idea that he propounded (which I believe emanated from *him*) he has endeavored to trade upon, in spite of the fact that his father was paid (for both) in the presence of witnesses. Whatever may be his abilities as a guide, he is not one to whom I would ever trust my life or afford any countenance.

21. This or a subsequent party discovered a sleeve. No other traces have been found.

22. At the instance of Mr. Alfred Wills, a subscription-list was opened for the benefit of the sisters of Michel Croz, who had been partly dependent upon his earnings. In a short time more than 280 pounds were raised. This was considered sufficient, and the list closed. The proceeds were invested in French Rentes (by Mr. William Mathews), at the recommendation of M. Dupui, at that time maire of Chamounix.

Leslie Stephen
"Sunset on Mont Blanc"

Widely acknowledged as one of the finest pieces of Alpine writing, Sir Leslie Stephen's (1832–1904) "Sunset on Mont Blanc" examines the effect of mountains on the human spirit. The Playground of Europe, *which contains this essay, appeared in 1871, the same year as Edward Whymper's* Scrambles amongst the Alps, *and helped to reestablish climbing as a respectable sport after Whymper's Matterhorn disaster six years earlier. Many newspaper editorials complained about the sport of climbing after the sensational deaths of four climbers on the Matterhorn in 1865, but Stephen's work argued for the beauty, serenity, and spiritual strength that could be derived from climbing. He also wrote* The History of English Thought in the Eighteenth Century *(1876) and edited* Cornhill *magazine. The father of Virginia Woolf and a noted philosopher who edited the* Dictionary of National Biography, *Stephen, along with John Tyndall, helped to popularize mountaineering in Victorian times and he acted as climbing's spokesman and defender. As a climber, Stephen forged new routes up Mont Blanc and the Dolomites.*

CHAPTER XI

SUNSET ON MONT BLANC

I profess myself to be a loyal adherent of the ancient Monarch of Mountains, and, as such, I hold as a primary article of faith the doctrine that no Alpine summit is, as a whole, comparable in sublimity and beauty to Mont Blanc. With all his faults and weaknesses, and in spite of a crowd of upstart rivals, he still deserves to reign in solitary supremacy. Such an opinion seems to some mountaineers as great an anachronism as the creed of a French Legitimist. The coarse flattery of guide-books has done much to surround him with vulgarising associations; even the homage of poets and painters has deprived his charms of their early freshness, and climbers have ceased to regard his conquest as a glorious, or, indeed, as anything but a most commonplace exploit. And yet Mont Blanc has merits which no unintelligent worship can obscure, and which bind with growing fascination the unprejudiced lover of scenery. Tried by a low, but not quite a meaningless standard, the old monarch can still extort respect. He can show a longer list of killed and wounded than any other mountain in the Alps, or almost than all other mountains put together. In his milder moods he may be approached with tolerable safety even by the inexperienced; but in angry moments,

---

Leslie Stephen, "Sunset on Mont Blanc," *The Playground of Europe* (London: Longmans, Green, and Co., 1871).

when he puts on his robe of clouds and mutters with his voice of thunder, no mountain is so terrible. Even the light snow-wreaths that eddy gracefully across his brow in fine weather sometimes testify to an icy storm that pierces the flesh and freezes the very marrow of the bones. But we should hardly estimate the majesty of men or mountains by the length of their butcher's bill. Mont Blanc has other and less questionable claims on our respect. He is the most solitary of all mountains, rising, Saul-like, a head and shoulders above the crowd of attendant peaks, and yet within that single mass there is greater prodigality of the sublimest scenery than in whole mountain districts of inferior elevation. The sternest and most massive of cliffs, the wildest spires of distorted rock, bounding torrents of shattered ice, snowfields polished and even as a sea-shell, are combined into a whole of infinite variety and yet of artistic unity. One might wander for days, were such wandering made possible by other conditions, amongst his crowning snows, and every day would present new combinations of unsuspected grandeur.

Why, indeed, some critics will ask, should we love a ruler of such questionable attributes? Scientifically speaking, the so-called monarch is but so many tons of black granite determining a certain quantity of aqueous precipitation. And if for literary purposes it be permissible to personify a monstrous rock, the worship of such a Moloch has in it something unnatural. In the mouth of the poet who first invested him with royal honours, the language was at least in keeping. Byron's misanthropy, real or affected, might identify love of nature with hatred of mankind: and a savage, shapeless and lifeless idol was a fitting centre for his enthusiasm. But we have ceased to believe in the Childe Harolds and the Manfreds. Become a hermit—denounce your species, and shrink from their contact, and you may consistently love the peaks where human life exists on sufferance, and whose message to the valleys is conveyed in wasting torrents or crushing avalanches. Men of saner mind who repudiate this anti-social creed should love the fertile valleys and grass-clad ranges better than these symbols of the sternest desolation. All the enthusiasm for the wilder scenery, when it is not simple affectation, is the product of a temporary phase of sentiment, of which the justification has now ceased to exist. To all which the Zealot may perhaps reply most judiciously, Be it as you please. Prefer, if you see fit, a Leicestershire meadow or even a Lincolnshire fen to the cliff and glacier, and exalt the view from the Crystal Palace above the widest of Alpine panoramas. Natural scenery, like a great work of art, scorns to be tied down to any cut-and-dried moral. To each spectator it suggests a different train of thought and emotion, varying as widely as the idiosyncrasy of the mind affected. If Mont Blanc produces in you nothing but a sense of hopeless savagery, well and good; confess it honestly to yourself and to the world, and do not help to swell the chorus of insincere ecstasy. But neither should you quarrel with those in whom the same sight produces emotions of a very different kind. That man is the happiest and wisest who can draw delight from the most varied objects: from the quiet bandbox scenery of cultivated England, or from the boundless prairies of the West; from the Thames or the Amazon, Malvern or Mont Blanc, the Virginia

Water or the Atlantic Ocean. If the reaction which made men escape with sudden ecstasy from trim gardens to round mountain sides was somewhat excessive, yet there was in it a core of sound feeling. Does not science teach us more and more emphatically that nothing which is natural can be alien to us who are part of nature? Where does Mont Blanc end, and where do I begin? That is the question which no metaphysician has hitherto succeeded in answering. But at least the connection is close and intimate. He is a part of the great machinery in which my physical frame is inextricably involved, and not the less interesting because a part which I am unable to subdue to my purposes. The whole universe, from the stars and the planets to the mountains and the insects which creep about their roots, is but a network of forces eternally acting and reacting upon each other. The mind of man is a musical instrument upon which all external objects are beating out infinitely complex harmonies and discords. Too often, indeed, it becomes a mere barrel-organ, mechanically repeating the tunes which have once been impressed upon it. But in proportion as it is more vigorous or delicate, it should retain its sensibility to all the impulses which may be conveyed to it from the most distant sources. And certainly a healthy organisation should not be deaf to those more solemn and melancholy voices which speak through the wildest aspects of nature. "Our sweetest songs," as Shelley says in his best mood, "are those which tell of saddest thought." No poetry or art is of the highest order in which there is not blended some strain of melancholy, even to sternness. Shakespeare would not be Shakespeare if it were not for that profound sense of the transitory in all human affairs which appears in the finest sonnets and in his deepest dramatic utterances. When he tells us of the unsubstantial fabric of the great globe itself, or the glorious morning which "flatters the mountain tops with sovereign eye," only to be hidden by the "basest clouds," or, anticipating modern geologists, observes

The hungry ocean gain
Advantage on the kingdom of the shore,

he is merely putting into words the thoughts obscurely present to the mind of every watcher of the eternal mountains which have outlasted so many generations, and are yet, like all other things, hastening to decay. The mountains represent the indomitable force of nature to which we are forced to adapt ourselves; they speak to man of his littleness and his ephemeral existence; they rouse us from the placid content in which we may be lapped when contemplating the fat fields which we have conquered and the rivers which we have forced to run according to our notions of convenience. And, therefore, they should suggest not sheer misanthropy, as they did to Byron, or an outburst of revolutionary passion, as they did to his teacher Rousseau, but that sense of awestruck humility which befits such petty creatures as ourselves.

It is true, indeed, that Mont Blanc sometimes is too savage for poetry. He can speak in downright tragic earnestness; and any one who has been caught in a storm on some of his higher icefields, who has trembled at the deadly swoop of the gale, or at the ominous sound which heralds an avalanche, or at the remorseless settling down of the blinding snow, will agree that at times he passes the limits of the terrible which comes fairly within the range of art. There are times, however, at which one may expect to find precisely the right blending of the sweet and the stern. And in particular, there are those exquisite moments when the sunset is breathing over his calm snowfields its "ardours of rest and love." Watched from beneath, the Alpine glow, as everybody knows, is of exquisite beauty; but unfortunately the spectacle has become a little too popular. The very sunset seems to smell of "Baedeker's Guide." The flesh is weak; and the most sympathetic of human beings is apt to feel a slight sense of revulsion when the French guests at a *table-d'hôte* are exclaiming in chorus, "Magnifique, superbe!" and the Germans chiming in with "Wunderschön!" and the British tourist patting the old mountain on the back, and the American protesting that he has shinier sunsets at home. Not being of a specially sympathetic nature, I had frequently wondered how that glorious spectacle would look from the solitary top of the monarch himself. This summer I was fortunate enough, owing to the judicious arrangements of one of his most famous courtiers—my old friend and comrade M. Gabriel Loppé—to be able to give an answer founded on personal experience. The result was to me so interesting that I shall venture—rash as the attempt may be—to give some account of a phenomenon of extraordinary beauty which has hitherto been witnessed by not more than some half-dozen human beings.

It was in the early morning of August 6, 1873, that I left Chamonix for the purpose. The sun rose on one of those fresh dewy dawns unknown except in the mountains, when the bouyant air seems as it were to penetrate every pore in one's body. I could almost say with Sir Galahad—

This mortal armour that I wear,
This weight and size, this heart and eyes,
Are touch'd and turn'd to finest air.

The heavy, sodden framework of flesh and blood which I languidly dragged along London streets has undergone a strange transformation, and it is with scarcely a conscious effort that I breast the monstrous hill which towers above me. The pinewoods give out their aromatic scent, and the little glades are deep in ferns, wild-flowers and strawberries. Even here, the latent terrors of the mountains are kept in mind by the huge boulders which, at some distant day, have crashed like cannon-balls through the forest. But the great mountain is not now indulging in one of his ponderous games at bowls, and the soft carpeting of tender vegetation suggests rather luxurious indolence, and, maybe, recalls lazy picnics rather than any more strenuous memories. Before long, however, we emerged from the forest, and soon the bells of a jolly little company of goats bade us farewell on the limits of the civilised world, as we stepped upon the still frozen glacier

187

and found ourselves fairly in the presence. We were alone with the mighty dome, daz-zling our eyes in the brilliant sunshine, and guarded by its sleeping avalanches. Luckily there was no temptation to commit the abomination of walking "against time" or racing any rival caravan of climbers. The whole day was before us, for it would have been un-desirable to reach the chilly summit too early; and we could afford the unusual luxury of lounging up Mont Blanc. We took, I hope, full advantage of our opportunities. We could peer into the blue depths of crevasses, so beautiful that one might long for such a grave, were it not for the awkward prospect of having one's bones put under a glass case by the next generation of scientific travellers. We could record in our memories the strange forms of the shattered séracs, those grotesque ice-masses which seem to suggest that the monarch himself has a certain clumsy sense of humour. We lingered longest on the summit of the Dôme du Goûté, itself a most majestic mountain were it not overawed by its gigantic neighbour. There, on the few ledges of rock which are left exposed in sum-mer, the thunder has left its scars. The lightning's strokes have covered numbers of stones with little glass-like heads, showing that this must be one of its favourite haunts. But on this glorious summer day the lightnings were at rest; and we could peacefully count over the vast wilderness of peaks which already stretched far and wide beneath our feet. The lower mountain ranges appeared to be drawn up in parallel ranks like the sea waves heaved in calm weather by a monotonous ground-swell. Each ridge was blended into a uniform hue by the intervening atmosphere, sharply defined along the summit line, and yet only distinguished from its predecessor and successor by a delicate gradation of tone. Such a view produces the powerful but shadowy impression which one expects from an opium dream. The vast perspective drags itself out to an horizon so distant as to blend imperceptibly with the lower sky. It has a vague suggestion of rhyth-mical motion, strangely combined with eternal calm. Drop a pebble into a perfectly still sheet of water; imagine that each ripple is supplanted by a loftly mountain range, of which all detail is lost in purple haze, and that the furthest undulations melt into the mysterious infinite. One gazes with a sense of soothing melancholy as one listens to plaintive modulations of some air of linked "sweetness long drawn out." Far away among the hills we could see long reaches of the peaceful Lake of Geneva, just gleaming through the varying purple; but at our backs the icy crest of the great mountain still rose proudly above us, to remind us that our task was not yet finished. Fortunately for us, scarcely a cloud was to be seen under the enormous concave of the dark blue heavens; a few light streamers of cirrus were moving gently over our heads in those remote abysses from which they never condescend even to the loftiest of Alpine summits. Faint and evanescent as they might be, they possibly had an ominous meaning for the future, but the present was our own; the little puffs of wind that whispered round some lofty ledges were keen enough in quality to remind us of possible frost-bites, but they had scarcely force enough to extinguish a lucifer match.

Carefully calculating our time, we advanced along the "dromedary's hump" and stepped upon the culminating ridge of the mountain about an hour before sunset. We had time to collect ourselves, to awake our powers of observation, and to prepare for the grand spectacle, for which preparations were already being made. There had been rehearsals enough in all conscience to secure a perfect performance. For millions of ages the lamps had been lighted and the transparencies had been shown with no human eye to observe or hand to applaud. Twice, I believe only twice, before, an audience had taken its place in this lofty gallery; but on one of those occasions, at least, the observers had been too unwell to do justice to the spectacle. The other party, of which the chief member was a French man of science, Dr. Martens, had been obliged to retreat hastily before the lights were extinguished; but their fragmentary account had excited our curiosity, and we had the pleasure of verifying the most striking phenomenon which they described. And now we waited eagerly for the performance to commence; the cold was sufficient to freeze the wine in our bottles, but in still air the cold is but little felt, and by walking briskly up and down and adopting the gymnastic exercise in which the London cabman delights in cold weather, we were able to keep up a sufficient degree of circulation. I say "we," but I am libelling the most enthusiastic member of the party. Loppé sat resolutely on the snow, at the risk, as we might have thought, of following the example of Lot's wife. Superior, as it appeared, to all the frailties which beset the human frame suddenly plunged into a temperature I know not how many degrees below freezing-point, he worked with ever increasing fury in a desperate attempt to fix upon canvas some of the magic beauties of the scene. Glancing from earth to heaven and from north to south, sketching with breathless rapidity the appearance of the eastern ranges, and then wheeling round like a weathercock to make hasty notes of the western clouds, breaking out at times into uncontrollable exclamations of delight, or reproving his thoughtless companions when their opaque bodies eclipsed a whole quarter of the heavens, he enjoyed, I should fancy, an hour of as keen delight as not often occurs to an enthusiastic lover of the sublime in nature. We laughed, envied and admired, and he escaped frost-bites. I wish that I could substitute his canvas—though, to say the truth, I fear it would exhibit a slight confusion of the points of the compass—for my words; but, as that is impossible, I must endeavour briefly to indicate the most impressive features of the scenery. My readers must kindly set their imaginations to work in aid of feeble language; for even the most eloquent language is but a poor substitute for a painter's brush, and a painter's brush lags far behind these grandest aspects of nature. The easiest way of obtaining the impression is to follow in my steps; for in watching a sunset from Mont Blanc one feels that one is passing one of those rare moments of life at which all the surrounding scenery is instantaneously and indelibly photographed on the mental retina by a process which no second-hand operation can even dimly transfer to others. To explain its nature requires a word or two of preface.

The ordinary view from Mont Blanc is not specially picturesque—and for a sufficient reason. The architect has concentrated his whole energies in producing a single impression. Everything has been so arranged as to intensify the sense of vast height and an illimitable horizon. In a good old guide-book I have read, on the authority (I think) of Pliny, that the highest mountain in the world is 300,000 feet above the sea; and one is apt to fancy, on ascending Mont Blanc, that the guess is not so far out. The effect is perfectly unique in the Alps; but it is produced at a certain sacrifice. All dangerous rivals have been removed to such a distance as to become apparently insignificant. No grand mass can be admitted into the foreground; for the sense of vast size is gradually forced upon you by the infinite multiplicity of detail. Mont Blanc must be like an Asiatic despot, alone and supreme, with all inferior peaks reverently couched at his feet. If a man, previously as ignorant of geography as a boy who has just left a public school, could be transported for a moment to the summit, his impression would be that the Alps resembled a village of a hundred hovels grouped round a stupendous cathedral. Fully to appreciate this effect requires a certain familiarity with Alpine scenery, for otherwise the effect produced is a dwarfing of the inferior mountains into pettiness instead of an exaltation of Mont Blanc into almost portentous magnificence. Grouped around you at unequal distances lie innumerable white patches, looking like the tented encampments of scattered army corps. Hold up a glove at arm's length, and it will cover the whole of such a group. On the boundless plain beneath (I say "plain," for the greatest mountain system of Europe appears to have subsided into a rather uneven plain), it is a mere spot, a trifling dent upon the huge shield on whose central boss you are placed. But you know, though at first you can hardly realise the knowledge, that that insignificant discoloration represents a whole mountain district. One spot, for example, represents the clustered peaks of the Bernese Oberland; a block, as big as a pebble, is the soaring Jungfrau, the terrible mother of avalanches; a barely distinguishable wrinkle is the reserve of those snowy wastes of the Blümlis Alp, which seem to be suspended above the terrace of Berne, thirty miles away; and that little whitish streak represents the greatest ice-stream of the alps, the huge Aletsch glacier, whose monstrous proportions have been impressed upon you by hours of laborious plodding. One patch contains the main sources from which the Rhine descends to the German Ocean, two or three more overlook the Italian plains and encircle the basin of the Po; from a more distant group flows the Danube, and from your feet the snows melt to supply the Rhone. You feel that you are in some sense looking down upon Europe from Rotterdam to Venice and from Varna to Marseilles. The vividness of the impression depends entirely upon the degree to which you can realise the immense size of all these immeasurable details. Now, in the morning, the usual time for an ascent, the details are necessarily vague, because the noblest part of the view lies between the sun and the spectator. But in the evening light each ridge, and peak, and glacier stands out with startling distinctness, and each, therefore, is laden with its weight of old association. There, for example, was the grim Matterhorn: its angular dimensions were of infinitesimal minuteness; it would puzzle a mathematician to say how small a space its image would occupy on his retina; but, within that small space, its form was defined with exquisite accuracy; and we could recognise the precise configuration of the wild labyrinth of rocky ridges up which the earlier adventurers forced their way from the Italian side. And thus we not only knew, but felt that at our feet was lying a vast slice of the map of Europe. The

190

effect was to exaggerate the apparent height, till the view had about it something portentous and unnatural: it seemed to be such a view as could be granted not even to mountaineers of earthy mould, but rather to some genie from the "Arabian Nights," flying high above a world tinted with the magical colouring of old romance.

Thus distinctly drawn, though upon so minute a scale, every rock and slope preserved its true value, and the impression of stupendous height became almost oppressive as it was forced upon the imagination that a whole world of mountains, each of them a mighty mass in itself, lay couched far beneath our feet, reaching across the whole diameter of the vast panorama. And now, whilst occupied in drinking in that strange sensation, and allowing our minds to recover their equilibrium from the first staggering shock of astonishment, began the strange spectacle of which we were the sole witnesses. One long delicate cloud, suspended in mid-air just below the sun, was gradually adorning itself with prismatic colouring. Round the limitless horizon ran a faint fog-bank, unfortunately not quite thick enough to produce that depth of colouring which sometimes makes an Alpine sun-set inexpressibly gorgeous. The weather— it was the only complaint we had to make—erred on the side of fineness. But the colouring was brilliant enough to prevent any thoughts of serious disappointment. The long series of western ranges melted into a uniform hue as the dun declined in their rear. Amidst their folds the Lake of Geneva became suddenly lighted up in a faint yellow gleam. To the east a blue gauze seemed to cover valley by valley as they sank into night and the intervening ridges rose with increasing distinctness, or rather it seemed that some fluid of exquisite delicacy of colour and substance was flooding all the lower country beneath the great mountains. Peak by peak the high snowfields caught the rosy glow and shone like signal-fires across the dim breadths of delicate twilight. Like Xerxes, we looked over the countless host sinking into rest, but with the rather different reflection, that a hundred years hence they would probably be doing much the same thing, whilst we should long have ceased to take any interest in the performance. And suddenly began a more startling phenomenon. A vast cone, with its apex pointing away from us, seemed to be suddenly cut out from the world beneath; night was within its borders and the twilight still all round; the blue mists were quenched where it fell, and for the instant we could scarcely tell what was the origin of this strange appearance. Some unexpected change seemed to have taken place in the programme; as though a great fold in the curtain had suddenly given way, and dropped on to part of the scenery. Of course a moment's reflection explained the meaning of this uncanny intruder; it was the giant shadow of Mont Blanc, testifying to his supremacy over all meaner eminences. It is difficult to say how sharply marked was the outline, and how startling was the contrast between this pyramid of darkness and the faintly-lighted spaces beyond its influence; a huge inky blot seemed to have suddenly fallen upon the landscape. As we gazed we could see it move. It swallowed up ridge by ridge, and its sharp point crept steadily from one landmark to another down the broad Valley of Aosta. We were standing, in fact, on the point of the gnomon of a gigantic sundial, the face of which was formed by thousands of square miles of mountain and valley. So clear was the outline that, if figures had been scrawled upon glaciers and ridges, we could have told the time to a second; indeed, we were half-inclined to look for our own shadows at a distance so great that whole villages would be represented by a scarcely distinguishable speck of colouring. The huge shadow, looking ever more strange and magical, struck the distant Becca di Nona, and then climbed into the dark region where the broader shadow of the world was rising into the eastern sky. By some singular effect of perspective, rays of darkness seemed to be converging from above our heads to a point immediately above the apex of the shadowy cone. For a time it seemed that there was a kind of anti-sun in the east, pouring out not light, but deep shadow as it rose. The apex soon reached the horizon, and then to our surprise began climbing the distant sky. Would it never stop, and was Mont Blanc capable of overshadowing not only the earth but the sky? For a minute or two I fancied, in a bewildered way, that this unearthly object would fairly rise from the ground and climb upwards to the zenith. But rapidly the lights went out upon the great army of mountains; the snow all round took the livid hue which immediately succeeds an Alpine sunset, and almost at a blow the shadow of Mont Blanc was swallowed up in the general shade of night. The display had ceased suddenly at its culminating point, and it was highly expedient for the spectators to retire. We had no time to lose if we would get off the summit before the grip of the frost should harden the snows into an ice-crust; and in a minute we were running and sliding downwards at our best pace towards the familiar Corridor. Yet as we went the sombre magnificence of the scenery seemed for a time to increase. We were between the day and the night. The western heavens were of the most brilliant blue with spaces of transparent green, whilst a few scattered cloudlets glowed as if with internal fire. To the east the night rushed up furiously, and it was difficult to imagine that the dark purple sky was really cloudless and not blackened by the rising of some portentous storm. That it was, in fact, cloudless, appeared from the unbroken disc of the full moon, which, if I may venture to say so, had a kind of silly expression, as though it were a bad imitation of the sun, totally unable to keep the darkness in order.

With how sad steps, O moon, thou climb'st the sky,
How silently and with how wan a face!

as Sidney exclaims. And truly, set in that strange gloom the moon looked wan and miserable enough; the lingering sunlight showed by contrast that she was but a feeble source of illumination; and, but for her half-comic look of helplessness, we might have sympathised with the astronomers who tell us that she is nothing but a vast perambulating tombstone, proclaiming to all mankind in the words of the familiar epitaph, "As I am now, you soon shall be!" To speak after the fashion of early mythologies, one might fancy that some supernatural cuttlefish was shedding his ink through the heavens to distract her, and that the poor moon had but a bad chance of escaping his clutches. Hurrying downwards with occasional glances at the sky, we had soon reached

192

the Grand Plateau, whence our further retreat was secure, and from that wildest of mountain fastnesses we saw the last striking spectacle of the evening. In some sense it was perhaps the most impressive of all. As all Alpine travellers know, the Grand Plateau is a level space of evil omen, embraced by a vast semicircle of icy slopes. The avalanches which occasionally descend across it, and which have caused more than one catastrophe, give it a bad reputation; and at night the icy jaws of the great mountain seem to be enclosing you in a fatal embrace. At this moment there was something half grotesque in its sternness. Light and shade were contrasted in a manner so bold as to be almost bizarre. One half of the cirque was of a pallid white against the night, which was rushing up still blacker and thicker, except that a few daring stars shone out like fiery sparks against a pitchy canopy; the other half, reflecting the black night, was re-lieved against the last gleams of daylight; in front a vivid band of blood-red light burnt along the horizon, beneath which seemed to lie an abyss of mysterious darkness. It was the last struggle between night and day, and the night seemed to assume a more ghastly ferocity as the day sank, pale and cold, before its antagonist. The Grand Plateau, in-deed, is a fit scene for such contrasts; for there in mid-day you may feel the reflection of the blinding snows like the blast of a furnace, where a few hours before you were re-alising the keenest pangs of frost-bite. The cold and the night were now the conquerors, and the angry sunset-glow seemed to grudge the victory. The light rapidly faded, and the darkness, no longer seen in the strange contrast, subsided to its ordinary tones. The magic was gone; and it was in a commonplace though lovely summer night that we reached our resting-place at the Grands Mulets.

We felt that we had learnt some new secrets as to the beauty of mountain scenery, but the secrets were of that kind which not even the initiated can reveal. A great poet might interpret the sentiment of the mountains into song; but no poet could pack into any definite proposition or series of propositions the strange thoughts that rise in dif-ferent spectators of such a scene. All that I at last can say is that some indefinable mix-ture of exhilaration and melancholy pervades one's mind; one feels like a kind of cheerful Tithonus "at the quiet limit of the world," looking down from a magic ele-vation upon the

"dim fields about the homes
Of happy men that have the power to die."

One is still of the earth, earthy; for freezing toes and snow-parched noses are lively reminders that one has not become an immortal. Even on the top of Mont Blanc one may be a very long way from heaven. And yet the mere physical elevation of a league above the sea level seems to raise one by moments into a sphere above the petty interests of everyday life. Why that should be so, and by what strange threads of association the reds and blues of a gorgeous sunset, the fantastic shapes of clouds and shadows at that dizzy height, and the dramatic changes that sweep over the boundless region beneath your feet, should stir you like mysterious music, or, indeed,

193

why music itself should have such power, I leave to philosophers to explain. This only I know, that even the memory of that summer evening on the top of Mont Blanc has power to plunge me into strange reveries not to be analysed by any capacity, and still less capable of expression by the help of a few black remarks on white paper.

One word must be added. The expedition I have described is perfectly safe and easy, if, but only if, two or three conditions be scrupulously observed. The weather, of course, must be faultless; the snow must be in perfect order or a retreat may be difficult; and, to guard against unforeseen contingencies which are so common in high mountains, there should be a sufficient force of guides more trustworthy than the gentry who hang about Chamonix drinking-places. If these precautions be neglected, serious accidents would be easy, and at any rate there would be a very fair chance that the enthusiastic lover of scenery would leave his toes behind him.

—1871

Isabella L. Bird
from *A Lady's Life in the Rocky Mountains*

Isabella L. Bird (1831–1904) was one of the better-known nineteenth-century female travelers, and her memoirs provide an intimate portrait of frontier Colorado, before the frame house replaced the log cabin and the footprints of the elk and moose had disappeared. This passage describes her ascent of Long's Peak in the Rockies in the company of the gentlemanly ruffian Mountain Jim. Bird made no claim to any climbing skill, and her ascent of Long's Peak was one of slips, falls, bruises, and jaunts on the back of Mountain Jim. From her perspective, the peak seemed like an "American Matterhorn," though she realized that a serious mountaineer would have no difficulty in scaling it. Because of the time of year, all the water they encountered was frozen and the party, which also included two students, suffered from severe dehydration on the return trip. Bird trav-eled widely throughout the world in Persia, Scotland, the Sandwich Islands, Japan, and China. Her other travelogues include The Hawaiian Archipelago *(1875),* Unbeaten Tracks in Japan *(1883), and* Journeys in Persia and Kurdistan *(1891). Her behavior was somewhat unconven-tional and even scandalous for the time, and climbing and traveling provided Bird with a release from what she saw as a stultifying and repressive society for women.*

Letter VII.

"Personality" of Long's Peak—"Mountain Jim"—Lake of the Lilies—A Silent Forest—The Camping Ground—"Ring"—A Lady's Bower—Dawn and Sunrise—A Glorious View—Links of Diamonds—The Ascent of the Peak—The Dog's Lift—Suffering from Thirst—The Descent—The Bivouac.

Estes Park, Colorado, *October.*

As this account of the ascent of Long's Peak could not be written at the time, I am much disinclined to write it, especially as no sort of description within my powers could enable another to realise the glorious sublimity, the majestic solitude, and the unspeakable awfulness and fascination of the scenes in which I spend Monday, Tues-day, and Wednesday.

Long's Peak, 14,700 feet high, blocks up one end of Estes Park, and dwarfs all the surrounding mountains. From it on this side rise, snow-born, the bright St. Vrain, and the Big and Little Thompson. By sunlight or moonlight its splintered grey crest is the one object which, in spite of wapiti and bighorn, skunk and grizzly, unfailingly ar-rests the eye. From it come all storms of snow and wind, and the forked lightenings

Isabella L. Bird, *A Lady's Life in the Rocky Mountains* (New York: G. P. Putnam and Sons, 1879).

play round its head like a glory. It is one of the noblest of mountains, but in one's imagination it grows to be much more than a mountain. It becomes invested with a personality. In its caverns and abysses one comes to fancy that it generates and chains the strong winds, to let them loose in its fury. The thunder becomes its voice, and the lightenings do it homage. Other summits blush under the morning kiss of the sun, and turn pale the next moment; but it detains the first sunlight and holds it round its head for an hour at least, till it pleases to change from rosy red to deep blue; and the sunset, as if spell-bound, lingers latest on its crest. The soft winds which hardly rustle the pine needles down here are raging rudely up there round its motionless summit. The mark of fire is upon it; and though it has passed into a grim repose, it tells of fire and upheaval as truly, though not as eloquently, as the living volcanoes of Hawaii. Here under its shadow one learns how naturally nature worship, and the propitiation of the forces of nature arose in minds which had no better light.

Long's Peak, "the American Matterhorn," as some call it, was ascended five years ago for the first time. I thought I should like to attempt it, but up to Monday, when Evans left for Denver, cold water was thrown upon the project. It was too late in the season, the winds were likely to be strong, etc.; but just before leaving, Evans said that the weather was looking more settled, and if I did not get farther than the timber line it would be worth going. Soon after he left, "Mountain Jim" came in, and said he would go up as guide, and the two youths who rode here with me from Longmount and I caught at the proposal. Mrs. Edwards at once baked bread for three days, steaks were cut from the steer which hangs up conveniently, and tea, sugar, and butter were benevolently added. Our picnic was not to be a luxurious or "well-found" one, for, in order to avoid the expense of a pack mule, we limited our luggage to what our saddle horses could carry. Behind my saddle I carried three pair of camping blankets and a quilt, which reached to my shoulders. My own boots were so much worn that it was painful to walk, even about the park, in them, so Evans had lent me a pair of his hunting boots, which hung to the horn of my saddle. The horses of the two young men were equally loaded, for we had to prepare for many degrees of frost. "Jim" was a shocking figure; he had on an old pair of high boots, with a baggy pair of old trousers made of deer hide, held on by an old scarf tucked into them; a leather shirt, with three or four ragged unbuttoned waistcoats over it; an old smashed wideawake, from under which his tawny, neglected ringlets hung; and with his one eye, his one long spur, his knife in his belt, his revolver in his waistcoat pocket, his saddle covered with an old beaver-skin, from which the paws hung down; his camping blankets behind him, his rifle laid across the saddle in front of him, and his axe, canteen, and other gear hanging to the horn, he was as awful looking a ruffian as one could see. By way of contrast he rode a small Arab mare, of exquisite beauty, skittish, high-spirited, gentle, but altogether too light for him, and he fretted her incessantly to make her display herself.

Heavily loaded as all our horses were, "Jim" started over the half-mile of level grass at a hand-gallop, and then throwing his mare on her haunches, pulled up alongside of me, and with a grace of manner which soon made me forget his appearance, entered into a conversation which lasted for more than three hours, in spite of the manifold checks of fording streams, single file, abrupt ascents and descents, and other incidents of mountain travel. This ride was one series of glories and surprises, of "park" and glade, of lake and stream, of mountains on mountains, culminating in the rent pinnacles of Long's Peak, which looked yet grander and ghastlier as we crossed an attendant mountain 11,000 feet high. The slanting sun added fresh beauty every hour. There were dark pines against a lemon sky, grey peaks reddening and etherealising, gorges of deep and infinite blue, floods of golden glory pouring through canyons of enormous depth, an atmosphere of absolute purity, an occasional foreground of cotton-wood and aspen flaunting in red and gold to intensify the blue gloom of the pines, the trickle and murmur of streams fringed with icicles, and strange *sough* of gusts moving among the pine tops—sights and sounds not of the lower earth, but of the solitary, beast-haunted, frozen upper altitudes. From the dry, buff grass of Estes Park we turned off up a trail on the side of a pine-hung gorge, up a steep pine-clothed hill, down to a small valley, rich in fine, sun-cured hay about eighteen inches high, and enclosed by high mountains whose deepest hollow contains a lily-covered lake, fitly named "The Lake of the Lilies." Ah, how magical its beauty was, as it slept in silence, while *there* the dark pines were mirrored motionless in its pale gold, and *here* the great white lily cups and dark green leaves rested on amethyst-coloured water!

From this we ascended into the purple gloom of great pine forests which clothe the skirts of the mountains up to a height of about 11,000 feet, and from their chill and solitary depths we had glimpses of golden atmosphere and rose-lit summits, not of "the land very far off," but of the land nearer now in all its grandeur, gaining in sublimity by nearness—glimpses, too, through a broken vista of purple gorges, of the illimitable Plains lying idealised in the late sunlight, their baked, brown expanse transfigured into the likeness of a sunset sea rolling infinitely in waves of misty gold.

We rode upwards through the gloom on a steep trail blazed through the forest, all my intellect concentrated on avoiding being dragged off my horse by impending branches, or having the blankets badly torn, as those of my companions were, by sharp dead limbs, between which there was hardly room to pass—the horses breathless, and requiring to stop every few yards, though their riders, except myself, were afoot. The gloom of the dense, ancient, silent forest is to me awe-inspiring. On such an evening it is soundless, except for the branches creaking in the soft wind, the frequent snap of decayed timber, and a murmur in the pine tops as of a not distant waterfall, all tending to produce *eeriness* and a sadness "hardly akin to pain." There no lumberer's axe has ever rung. The trees die when they have attained their prime, and stand there, dead and bare, till the fierce mountain winds lay them prostrate. The pines grew smaller and more sparse as we ascended, and the last stragglers wore a tortured, warring look. The timber line was passed, but yet a little higher a slope of mountain meadow dipped to the south-west towards a bright stream trickling under

197

ice and icicles, and there a grove of the beautiful silver spruce marked our camping ground. The trees were in miniature, but so exquisitely arranged that one might well ask what artist's hand had planted them, scattering them here, clumping them there, and training their slim spires towards heaven. Hereafter, when I call up memories of the glorious, the view from this camping ground will come up. Looking east, gorges opened to the distant Plains, then fading into purple grey. Mountains with pine-clothed skirts rose in ranges, or, solitary, uplifted their grey summits, while close behind, but nearly 3,000 feet above us, towered the bald white crest of Long's Peak, its huge precipices red with the light of a sun long lost to our eyes. Close to us, in the caverned side of the Peak, was snow that, owing to its position, is eternal. Soon the afterglow came on, and before it faded a big half-moon hung out of the heavens, shining through the silver blue foliage of the pines on the frigid background of snow, and turning the whole into fairyland. The "photo" which accompanies this letter is by a courageous Denver artist who attempted the ascent just before I arrived, but, after camping out at the timber line for a week, was foiled by the perpetual storms, and was driven down again, leaving some very valuable apparatus about 3,000 feet from the summit.

Unsaddling and picketing the horses securely, making the beds of pine shoots, and dragging up logs for fuel, warmed us all. "Jim" built up a great fire, and before long we were all sitting round it at supper. It didn't matter much that we had to drink our tea out of the battered meat-tins in which it was boiled, and eat strips of beef reeking with pine smoke without plates or forks.

"Treat Jim as a gentleman and you'll find him one," I had been told; and though his manner was certainly bolder and freer than that of gentlemen generally, no imaginary fault could be found. He was very agreeable as a man of culture as well as a child of nature; the desperado was altogether out of sight. He was very courteous and even kind to me, which was fortunate, as the young men had little idea of showing even ordinary civilities. That night I made the acquaintance of his dog "Ring," said to be the best hunting-dog in Colorado, with the body and legs of a collie, but a head approaching that of a mastiff, a noble face with a wistful human expression, and the most truthful eyes I ever saw in an animal. His master loves him if he loves anything, but in his savage moods ill-treats him. "Ring's" devotion never swerves, and his truthful eyes are rarely taken off his master's face. He is almost human in his intelligence, and, unless he is told to do so, he never takes notice of any one but "Jim." In a tone as if speaking to a human being, his master pointing to me, said, "Ring, go to that lady, and don't leave her again to-night." "Ring" at once came to me, looked into my face, laid his head on my shoulder, and then lay down beside me with his head on my lap, but never taking his eyes from "Jim's" face.

The long shadows of the pines lay upon the frosted grass, an aurora leaped fitfully, and the moon-light, though intensely bright, was pale beside the red, leaping flames of our pine logs and their red glow on our gear, ourselves, and Ring's truthful face. One of the young men sang a Latin student's song and two negro melodies; the

198

other, "Sweet Spirit, hear my Prayer." "Jim" sang one of Moore's melodies in a singular falsetto, and all together sang "The Star-Spangled Banner" and "The Red, White, and Blue." Then "Jim" recited a very clever poem of his own composition, and told some fearful Indian stories. A group of small silver spruces away from the fire was my sleeping-place. The artist who had been up there had so woven and interlaced their lower branches as to form a bower, affording at once shelter from the wind and a most agreeable privacy. It was thickly strewn with young pine shoots, and these, when covered with a blanket, with an inverted saddle for a pillow, made a luxurious bed. The mercury at 9 P.M. was 12° below the freezing point. "Jim," after a last look at the horses, made a huge fire, and stretched himself out beside it, but "Ring" lay at my back to keep me warm. I could not sleep, but the night passed rapidly. I was anxious about the ascent, for gusts of ominous sound swept through the pines at intervals. Then wild animals howled, and "Ring" was perturbed in spirit about them. Then it was strange to see the notorious desperado, a red-handed man, sleeping as quietly as innocence sleeps. But, above all, it was exciting to lie there, with no better shelter than a bower of pines, on a mountain 11,000 feet high, in the very heart of the Rocky Range, under twelve degrees of frost, hearing sounds of wolves, with shivering stars looking through the fragrant canopy, with arrowy pines for bed-posts, and for a night lamp the red flames of a camp fire.

Day dawned long before the sun rose, pure and lemon-coloured. The rest were looking after the horses, when one of the students came running to tell me that I must come farther down the slope, for "Jim" said he had never seen such a sunrise. From the chill, grey Peak above, from the everlasting snows, from the silvered pines, down through mountain ranges with their depths of Tyrian purple, we looked to where the Plains lay cold, in blue grey, like a morning sea against a far horizon. Suddenly, as a dazzling streak at first, but enlarging rapidly into a dazzling sphere, the sun wheeled above the grey line, a light and glory as when it was first created. "Jim" involuntarily and reverently uncovered his head, and exclaimed, "I believe there is a God!" I felt as if, Parsee-like, I must worship. The grey of the Plains changed to purple, the sky was all one rose-red flush, on which vermilion cloud-streaks rested; the ghastly peaks gleamed like rubies, the earth and heavens were new-created. Surely "the Most High dwelleth not in temples made with hands!" For a full hour those Plains simulated the ocean, down to whose limitless expanse of purple, cliffs, rocks, and promontories swept down.

By seven we had finished breakfast, and passed into the ghastlier solitudes above, I riding as far as what, rightly or wrongly, are called the "Lava Beds," an expanse of large and small boulders, with snow in their crevices. It was very cold; some water which we crossed was frozen hard enough to bear the horse. "Jim" had advised me against taking any wraps, and my thin Hawaiian riding-dress, only fit for the tropics, was penetrated by the keen air. The rarefied atmosphere soon began to oppress our breathing, and I found that Evans's boots were so large that I had no foothold. Fortunately, before the real difficulty of the ascent began, we found, under a rock, a pair of small over-shoes, probably left by the Hayden exploring expedition, which just lasted for the day. As we were leaping from rock to rock, "Jim" said, "I was thinking in the night about your travelling alone, and wondering where you carried your Derringer, for I could see no signs of it." On my telling him that I travelled unarmed, he could hardly believe it, and adjured me to get a revolver at once.

On arriving at the "Notch" (a literal gate of rock), we found ourselves absolutely on the knife-like ridge or backbone of Long's Peak, only a few feet wide, covered with colossal boulders and fragments, and on the other side shelving in one precipitous, snow-patched sweep of 3,000 feet to a picturesque hollow, containing a lake of pure green water. Other lakes, hidden among dense pine woods, were farther off, while close above us rose the Peak, which, for about 500 feet, is a smooth, gaunt, inaccessible-looking pile of granite. Passing through the "Notch," we looked along the nearly inaccessible side of the Peak, composed of boulders and *débris* of all shapes and sizes, through which appeared broad, smooth ribs of reddish-coloured granite, looking as if they upheld the towering rock-mass above. I usually dislike bird's-eye and panormic views, but, though from a mountain, this was not one. Serrated ridges, not much lower than that on which we stood, rose, one beyond another, far as that pure atmosphere could carry the vision. Broken into awful chasms deep with ice and snow, rising into pinnacles piercing the heavenly blue with their cold, barren grey, on, on for ever, till the most distant range upbore unsullied snow alone. There were fair lakes mirroring the dark pine woods, canyons dark and blue-black with unbroken expanses of pines, snow-slashed pinnacles, wintry heights frowning upon lovely parks, watered and wooded, lying in the lap of summer; North Park floating off into the blue distance, Middle Park closed till another season, the sunny slopes of Estes Park, and winding down among the mountains the snowy ridge of the Divide, whose bright waters seek both the Atlantic and Pacific Oceans. There, far below, links of diamonds showed where the Grand River takes its rise to seek the mysterious Colorado, with its still unsolved enigma, and lose itself in the waters of the Pacific; and nearer the snow-born Thompson bursts forth from the ice to begin its journey to the Gulf of Mexico. Nature, rioting in her grandest mood, exclaimed with voices of grandeur, solitude, sublimity, beauty, and infinity, "Lord, what is man, that Thou art mindful of him? or the son of man, that Thou visitest him?" Never-to-be-forgotten glories they were, burnt in upon my memory by six succeeding hours of terror. You know I have no head and no ankles, and never ought to dream of mountaineering; and had I known that the ascent was a real mountaineering feat I should not have felt the slightest ambition to perform it. As it is, I am only humiliated by my success, for "Jim" dragged me up, like a bale of goods, by sheer force of muscle. At the "Notch" the real business of the ascent began. Two thousand feet of solid rock towered above us, four thousand feet of broken rock shelved precipitously below; smooth granite ribs, with barely foothold, stood out here and there; melted snow refrozen several times, presented a more serious obstacle; many of the rocks were loose, and tumbled down when touched. To me it was a time of extreme terror. I was roped to "Jim," but it was of no use my feet were paralysed and slipped on the bare rock, and he said it

200

was useless to try to go that way, and we retraced our steps. I wanted to return to the "Notch," knowing that my incompetence would detain the party, and one of the young men said almost plainly that a woman was a dangerous encumbrance, but the trapper replied shortly that if it were not to take a lady up he would not go up at all. He went on to explore, and reported that further progress on the correct line of ascent was blocked by ice; and then for two hours we descended, lowering ourselves by our hands from rock to rock along a boulder-strewn sweep of 4,000 feet, patched with ice and snow, and perilous from rolling stones. My fatigue, giddiness, and pain from bruised ankles, and arms half pulled out of their sockets, were so great that I should never have gone half-way had not "Jim," *nolens volens*, dragged me along with a patience and skill, and withal a determination that I should ascend the Peak, which never failed. After descending about 2,000 feet to avoid the ice, we got into a deep ravine with inaccessible sides, partly filled with ice and snow and partly with large and small fragments of rock, which were constantly giving way, rendering the footing very insecure. That part to me was two hours of painful and unwilling submission to the inevitable; of trembling, slipping, straining, of smooth ice appearing when it was least expected, and of weak entreaties to be left behind while the others went on. "Jim" always said that there was no danger, that there was only a short bad bit ahead, and that I should go up even if he carried me!

Slipping, faltering, gasping from the exhausting toil in the rarefied air, with throbbing hearts and panting lungs, we reached the top of the gorge and squeezed ourselves between two gigantic fragments of rock by a passage called the "Dog's Lift," when I climbed on the shoulders of one man and then was hauled up. This introduced us by an abrupt turn round the south-west angle of the Peak to a narrow shelf of considerable length, rugged, uneven, and so overhung by the cliff in some places that it is necessary to crouch to pass at all. Above, the Peak looks nearly vertical for 400 feet; and below, the most tremendous precipice I have ever seen descends in one unbroken fall. This is usually considered the most dangerous part of the ascent, but it does not seem so to me, for such foothold as there is it secure, and one fancies that it is possible to hold on with the hands. But there, and on the final, and, to my thinking, the worst part of the climb, one slip, and a breathing, thinking, human being would lie 3,000 feet below, a shapeless, bloody heap! "Ring" refused to traverse the Ledge, and remained at the "Lift" howling piteously.

From thence the view is more magnificent even than that from the "Notch." At the foot of the precipice below us lay a lovely lake, wood embosomed, from or near which the bright St. Vrain and other streams take their rise. I thought how their clear cold waters, growing turbid in the affluent flats, would heat under the tropic sun, and eventually form part of that great ocean river which renders our far-off islands habitable by impinging on their shores. Snowy ranges, one behind the other, extended to the distant horizon, folding in their wintry embrace the beauties of Middle Park. Pike's Peak, more than one hundred miles off, lifted that vast but shapeless summit which is the landmark of southern Colorado. There were snow patches, snow slashes,

201

snow abysses, snow forlorn and solid-looking, snow pure and dazzling, snow glistening above the purple robe of pine worn by all the mountains; while away to the east, in limitless breadth, stretched the green-grey of the endless Plains. Giants everywhere reared their splintered crests. From thence, with a single sweep, the eye takes in a distance of 300 miles—that distance to the west, north, and south being made up of mountains ten, eleven, twelve, and thirteen thousand feet in height, dominated by Long's Peak, Gray's Peak, and Pike's Peak, all nearly the height of Mont Blanc! On the Plains we traced the rivers by their fringe of cotton-woods to the distant Platte, and between us and them lay glories of mountain, canyon, and lake, sleeping in depths of blue and purple most ravishing to the eye.

As we crept from the lodge round a horn of rock, I beheld what made me perfectly sick and dizzy to look at—the terminal Peak itself—a smooth, cracked face or wall of pink granite, as nearly perpendicular as anything could well be up which it was possible to climb, well deserving the name of the "American Matterhorn."[1]

Scaling, not climbing, is the correct term for this last ascent. It took one hour to accomplish 500 feet, pausing for breath every minute or two. The only foothold was in narrow cracks or on minute projections on the granite. To get a toe in these cracks, or here and there on a scarcely obvious projection, while crawling on hands and knees, all the while tortured with thirst and gasping and struggling for breath, this was the climb; but at last the Peak was won. A grand, well-defined mountain-top it is, a nearly level acre of boulders, with precipitous sides all round, the one we came up being the only accessible one.

It was not possible to remain long. One of the young men was seriously alarmed by bleeding from the lungs, and the intense dryness of the day and the rarefaction of the air, at a height of nearly 15,000 feet, made respiration very painful. There is always water on the Peak, but it was frozen as hard as a rock, and the sucking of ice and snow increases thirst. We all suffered severely from the want of water, and the gasping for breath made our mouths and tongues so dry that articulation was difficult, and the speech of all unnatural.

From the summit were seen in unrivalled combination all the views which had rejoiced our eyes during the ascent. It was something at last to stand upon the storm-rent crown of this lonely sentinel of the Rocky Range, on one of the mightiest of the vertebrae of the backbone of the North American continent, and to see the waters start for both oceans. Uplifted above love and hate and storms of passion, calm amidst the eternal silences, fanned by zephyrs and bathed in living blue, peace rested for that one bright day on the Peak, as if it were some region

"Where falls not rain, or hail, or any snow,
Or ever wind blows loudly."

We placed our names, with the date of ascent, in a tin within a crevice, and descended to the Ledge, sitting on the smooth granite, getting our feet into cracks and against projections, and letting ourselves down by our hands, "Jim" going before me, so that I might steady my feet against his powerful shoulders. I was no longer giddy, and faced the precipice of 3,500 feet without a shiver. Repassing the Ledge and Lift, we accomplished the descent through 1,500 feet of ice and snow, with many falls and bruises, but no worse mishap, and there separated, the young men taking the steepest but most direct way to the Notch, with the intention of getting ready for the march home, and "Jim" and I taking what he thought the safer route for me—a descent over boulders for 2,000 feet, and then a tremendous ascent to the "Notch." I had various falls, and once hung by my frock, which caught on a rock, and "Jim" severed it with his hunting-knife, upon which I fell into a crevice full of soft snow. We were driven lower down the mountains than he had intended by impassable tracts of ice, and the ascent was tremendous. For the last 200 feet the boulders were of enormous size, and the steepness fearful. Sometimes I drew myself up on hands and knees, sometimes crawled; sometimes "Jim" pulled me up by my arms or a lariat, and sometimes I stood on his shoulders, or he made steps for me of his feet and hands, but at six we stood on the Notch in the splendour of the sinking sun, all colour deepening, all peaks glorifying, all shadows purpling, all peril past.

"Jim" had parted with his *brusquerie* when we parted from the students, and was gentle and considerate beyond anything, though I knew that he must be grievously disappointed, both in my courage and strength. Water was an object of earnest desire. My tongue rattled in my mouth, and I could hardly articulate. It is good for one's sympathies to have for once a severe experience of thirst. Truly, there was

> "Water, water, everywhere,
> But not a drop to drink"

Three times its apparent gleam deceived even the mountaineer's practised eye, but we found only a foot of "glare ice." At last, in a deep hole, he succeeded in breaking the ice, and by putting one's arm far down one could scoop up a little water in one's hand, but it was tormentingly insufficient. With great difficulty and much assistance I recrossed the "Lava Beds," was carried to the horse and lifted upon him, and when we reached the camping ground I was lifted off him, and laid on the ground wrapped up in blankets, a humiliating termination of a great exploit. The horses were saddled, and the young men were all ready to start, but "Jim" quietly said, "Now, gentlemen, I want a good night's rest, and we shan't stir from here to-night." I believe they were really glad to have it so, as one of them was quite "finished." I retired to my arbour, wrapped myself in a roll of blankets, and was soon asleep. When I woke, the moon was high shining through the silvery branches, whitening the bald Peak above, and glittering on the great abyss of snow behind, and pine logs were blazing like a bonfire in the cold still air. My feet were so icy cold that I could not sleep again, and getting some blankets to sit in, and making a roll of them for my back, I sat for two hours by the camp fire. It was weird and gloriously beautiful. The students were asleep not far off in their blankets with their feet towards the fire. "Ring" lay on one side of me with his fine head on my arm, and his master sat smoking, with the fire lighting up the handsome side of his face, and except for the tones of our voices, and an occasional crackle and splutter as a pine knot blazed up, there was no sound on the mountain side. The beloved stars of my far-off home were overhead, the Plough and Pole Star, with their steady light; the glittering Pleiades, looking larger than I ever saw them, and "Orion's studded belt" shining gloriously. Once only some wild animals prowled near the camp, when "Ring," with one bound, disappeared from my side; and the horses, which were picketed by the stream, broke their lariats, stampeded, and came rushing wildly towards the fire, and it was fully half an hour before they were caught and quiet was restored. "Jim," or Mr. Nugent, as I always scrupulously called him, told stories of his early youth, and of a great sorrow which had led him to embark on a lawless and desperate life. His voice trembled, and tears rolled down his cheek. Was it semi-conscious acting, I wondered, or was his dark soul really stirred to its depths by the silence, the beauty, and the memories of youth?

We reached Estes Park at noon of the following day. A more successful ascent of the Peak was never made, and I would not now exchange my memories of its perfect beauty and extraordinary sublimity for any other experience of mountaineering in any part of the world. Yesterday snow fell on the summit, and it will be inaccessible for eight months to come.

I. L. B.
—1879

Note

1. Let no practical mountaineer be allured by my description into the ascent of Long's Peak. Truly terrible as it was to me, to a member of the Alpine Club it would not be a feat worth performing.

Mark Twain
"The Ascent of the Riffelberg"

In this satiric piece excerpted from his travel novel A Tramp Abroad, *Samuel Langhorne Clemens (Mark Twain) (1835–1910) pokes fun at the Alpine Club–style summer holiday mountaineering trip. Twain mocks the excessive baggage, equipment, and unnecessary luxuries that were normally taken on an alpine climb and carried by the poor guides. He also satirizes the scientific experimentation sometimes carried out in the mountains. The Twain family's trip to Europe and the Black Forest in 1878–1879 provided background material for* A Tramp Abroad. *Four years later, Twain would write his immortal* Adventures of Huckleberry Finn *(1884). Twain had honed his travel writing skills as a correspondent for a number of U.S. newspapers, including* The Sacramento Union *and* The Alta California. *His experiences from these journeys formed the basis of another earlier travelogue,* The Innocents Abroad *(1869).*

CHAPTER XXXVII

After I had finished my reading, I was no longer myself; I was tranced, uplifted, intoxicated, by the almost incredible perils and adventures I had been following my authors through, and the triumphs I had been sharing with them. I sat silent some time, then turned to Harris and said,—

"My mind is made up."

Something in my tone struck him; and when he glanced at my eye and read what was written there, his face paled perceptibly. He hesitated a moment, then said,—

"Speak."

I answered, with perfect calmness,—

"I WILL ASCEND THE RIFFELBERG."

If I had shot my poor friend he could not have fallen from his chair more suddenly. If I had been his father he could not have pleaded harder to get me to give up my purpose. But I turned a deaf ear to all he said. When he perceived at last that nothing could alter my determination, he ceased to urge, and for a while the deep silence was broken only by his sobs. I sat in marble resolution, with my eyes fixed upon vacancy, for in spirit I was already wrestling with the perils of the mountains, and my friend sat gazing at me in adoring admiration through his tears. At last he threw himself upon me in a loving embrace and exclaimed in broken tones:

"Your Harris will never desert you. We will die together!"

Mark Twain, "The Ascent of the Riffelberg," *A Tramp Abroad* (Hartford: American Publishing Company, 1880).

I cheered the noble fellow with praises, and soon his fears were forgotten and he was eager for the adventure. He wanted to summon the guides at once and leave at two in the morning, as he supposed the custom was; but I explained that nobody was looking, at that hour; and that the start in the dark was not usually made from the village but from the first night's resting place on the mountain side. I said we would leave the village at 3 or 4 P.M. on the morrow; mean-time he could notify the guides, and also let the public know of the attempt which we proposed to make.

I went to bed, but not to sleep. No man can sleep when he is about to undertake one of these Alpine exploits. I tossed feverishly all night long, and was glad enough when I heard the clock strike half past eleven and knew it was time to get up for dinner. I rose jaded and rusty, and went to the noon meal, where I found myself the centre of interest and curiosity; for the news was already abroad. It is not easy to eat calmly when you are a lion, but it is very pleasant, nevertheless.

As usual, at Zermatt, when a great ascent is about to be undertaken, everybody, native and foreign, laid aside his own projects and took up a good position to observe the start. The expedition consisted of 198 persons, including the mules; or 205, including the cows. As follow:

Chiefs of Service.	Subordinates.
Myself.	1 Veterinary Surgeon.
Mr. Harris.	1 Butler.
17 Guides.	12 Waiters.
4 Surgeons	1 Footman.
1 Geologist.	1 Barber.
1 Botanist.	1 Head Cook.
3 Chaplains.	9 Assistants.
2 Draftsmen.	4 Pastry Cooks.
15 Barkeepers.	1 Confectionery Artist.
1 Latinist.	

Transportation, etc.

27 Porters.	3 Coarse Washers and Ironers.
44 Mules.	1 Fine ditto.
44 Muleteers.	7 Cows.
	2 Milkers.

Total, 154 men, 51 animals. Grand Total, 205.

Rations, etc.	Apparatus.
16 Cases Hams.	25 Spring Mattresses.
2 Barrels Flour.	2 Hair ditto.

22 Barrels Whiskey.	Bedding for same.
1 Barrel Sugar.	2 Mosquito Nets.
1 Keg Lemons.	29 Tents.
2,000 Cigars.	Scientific Instruments.
1 Barrel Pies.	97 Ice-axes.
1 Ton of Pemmican.	5 Cases Dynamite.
143 Pair Crutches.	7 Cans Nitro-glycerine.
2 Barrels Arnica.	22 40-foot Ladders.
1 Bale of Lint.	2 Miles of Rope.
27 Kegs Paregoric.	154 Umbrellas.

It was full four o'clock in the afternoon before my cavalcade was entirely ready. At that hour it began to move. In point of numbers and spectacular effect, it was the most imposing expedition that had ever marched from Zermatt.

I commanded the chief guide to arrange the men and animals in single file, twelve feet apart, and lash them all together on a strong rope. He objected that the first two miles was a dead level, with plenty of room, and that rope was never used except in very dangerous places. But I would not listen to that. My reading had taught me that many serious accidents had happened in the Alps simply from not having the people tied up soon enough; I was not going to add one to the list. The guide then obeyed my order.

When the procession stood at ease, roped together, and ready to move, I never saw a finer sight. It was 3,122 feet long—over half a mile; every man but Harris and me was on foot, and had on his green veil and his blue goggles, and his white rag around his hat, and his coil of rope over one shoulder and under the other, and his ice-axe in his belt, and carried his alpenstock in his left hand, his umbrella (closed), in his right, and his crutches slung at his back. The burdens of the pack mules, and the horns of the cows, were decked with the Edelweiss and the Alpine rose.

I and my agent were the only persons mounted. We were in the post of danger in the extreme rear, and tied securely to five guides apiece. Our armor-bearers carried our ice-axes, alpenstocks and other implements for us. We were mounted upon very small donkeys, as a measure of safety; in time of peril we could straighten our legs and stand up, and let the donkey walk from under. Still, I cannot recommend this sort of animal,—at least for excursions of mere pleasure,—because his ears interrupt the view. I and my agent possessed the regulation mountaineering costumes, but concluded to leave them behind. Out of respect for the great numbers of tourists of both sexes who would be assembled in front of the hotels to see us pass, and also out of respect for the many tourists, whom we expected to encounter on our expedition, we decided to make the ascent in evening dress.

At fifteen minutes past four I gave the command to move, and my subordinates passed it along the line. The great crowd in front of the Monte Rosa hotel parted in twain, with a cheer, as the procession approached; and as the head of it was filing

207

by I gave the order,—"Unlimber—make ready—HOIST!"—and with one impulse up went my half mile of umbrellas. It was a beautiful sight, and a total surprise to the spectators. Nothing like that had ever been seen in the Alps before. The applause it brought forth was deeply gratifying to me, and I rode by with my plug hat in my hand to testify my appreciation of it. It was the only testimony I could offer, for I was too full to speak.

We watered the caravan at the cold stream which rushes down a trough near the end of the village, and soon afterward left the haunts of civilization behind us. About half past five o'clock we arrived at a bridge which spans the Visp, and after throwing over a detachment to see if it was safe, the caravan crossed without accident. The way now led, by a gentle ascent, carpeted with fresh green grass, to the church of Winkelmatten. Without stopping to examine this edifice, I executed a flank movement to the right and crossed the bridge over the Findelenbach, after first testing its strength. Here I deployed to the right again, and presently entered an inviting stretch of meadow land which was unoccupied save by a couple of deserted huts toward its furthest extremity. These meadows offered an excellent camping place. We pitched our tents, supped, established a proper guard, recorded the events of the day, and then went to bed.

We rose at two in the morning and dressed by candle light. It was a dismal and chilly business. A few stars were shining, but the general heavens were overcast, and the great shaft of the Matterhorn was draped in a sable pall of clouds. The chief guide advised a delay; he said he feared it was going to rain. We waited until nine o'clock, and then got away in tolerably clear weather.

Our course led up some terrific steeps, densely wooded with larches and cedars, and traversed by paths which the rains had guttered and which were obstructed by loose stones. To add to the danger and inconvenience, we were constantly meeting returning tourists on foot or horseback, and as constantly being crowded and battered by ascending tourists who were in a hurry and wanted to get by.

Our troubles thickened. About the middle of the afternoon the seventeen guides called a halt and held a consultation. After consulting an hour they said their first suspicion remained intact,—that is to say, they believed they were lost. I asked if they did not *know* it? No, they said, they *couldn't* absolutely know whether they were lost or not, because none of them had ever been in that part of the country before. They had a strong instinct that they were lost, but they had no proofs,—except that they did not know where they were. They had met no tourists for some time, and they considered that a suspicious sign.

Plainly we were in an ugly fix. The guides were naturally unwilling to go alone and seek a way out of the difficulty; so we all went together. For better security we moved slow and cautiously, for the forest was very dense. We did not move up the mountain, but around it, hoping to strike across the old trail. Toward nightfall, when we were about tired out, we came up against a rock as big as a cottage. This barrier took all the remaining spirit out of the men, and a panic of fear and despair ensued.

They moaned and wept, and said they should never see their homes and their dear ones again. Then they began to upbraid me for bringing them upon this fatal expedition. Some even muttered threats against me.

Clearly it was no time to show weakness. So I made a speech in which I said that other Alp-climbers had been in as perilous a position as this, and yet by courage and perseverance had escaped. I promised to stand by them, I promised to rescue them. I closed by saying we had plenty of provisions to maintain us for quite a siege,—and did they suppose Zermatt would allow half a mile of men and mules to mysteriously disappear during any considerable time, right above their noses, and make no inquiries? No, Zermatt would send out searching-expeditions and we should be saved.

This speech had a great effect. The men pitched the tents with some little show of cheerfulness, and we were snugly under cover when the night shut down. I now reaped the reward of my wisdom in providing one article which is not mentioned in any book of Alpine adventure but this. I refer to the paregoric. But for that beneficent drug, not one of those men would have slept a moment during that fearful night. But for that gentle persuader they must have tossed, unsoothed, the night through; for the whisky was for me. Yes, they would have risen in the morning unfitted for their heavy task. As it was, everybody slept but my agent and me,—only we two and the barkeepers. I would not permit myself to sleep at such a time. I considered myself responsible for all those lives. I meant to be on hand and ready, in case of avalanches. I am aware now, that there were no avalanches up there, but I did not know it then.

We watched the weather all through that awful night, and kept an eye on the barometer, to be prepared for the least change. There was not the slightest change recorded by the instrument, during the whole time. Words cannot describe the comfort that that friendly, hopeful, steadfast thing was to me in that season of trouble. It was a defective barometer, and had no hand but the stationary brass pointer, but I did not know that until afterward. If I should be in such a situation again, I should not wish for any barometer but that one.

All hands rose at two in the morning and took breakfast, and as soon as it was light we roped ourselves together and went at that rock. For some time we tried the hook-rope and other means of scaling it, but without success. That is without perfect success. The hook caught once, and Harris started up it hand over hand, but the hold broke and if there had not happened to be a chaplain sitting underneath at the time Harris would certainly have been crippled. As it was, it was the chaplain. He took to his crutches, and I ordered the hook-rope to be laid aside. It was too dangerous an implement where so many people were standing around.

We were puzzled for a while; then somebody thought of the ladders. One of these was leaned against the rock, and the men went up it tied together in couples. Another ladder was sent up for use in descending. At the end of half an hour everybody was over, and that rock was conquered. We gave our first grand shout of triumph. But the joy was short-lived, for somebody asked how we were going to get the animals over.

This was a serious difficulty; in fact it was an impossibility. The courage of the men began to waver immediately; once more we were threatened with a panic. But when the danger was most imminent, we were saved in a mysterious way. A mule which had attracted attention from the beginning by its disposition to experiment, tried to eat a five-pound can of nitro-glycerine. This happened right along-side the rock. The explosion threw us all to the ground, and covered us with dirt and débris; it frightened us extremely, too, for the crash it made was deafening, and the violence of the shock made the ground tremble. However, we were grateful, for the rock was gone. Its place was occupied by a new cellar, about thirty feet across, by fifteen feet deep. The explosion was heard as far as Zermatt; and an hour and a half afterward, many citizens of that town were knocked down and quite seriously injured by descending portions of mule meat, frozen solid. This shows, better than any estimate in figures how high the experimenter went.

We had nothing to do, now, but bridge the cellar and proceed on our way. With a cheer the men went at their work. I attended to the engineering, myself. I appointed a strong detail to cut down trees with ice-axes and trim them for piers to support the bridge. This was a slow business, for ice-axes are not good to cut wood with. I caused my piers to be firmly set up in ranks in the cellar, and upon them I laid six of my forty-foot ladders, side by side, and laid six more on top of them. Upon this bridge I caused a bed of boughs to be spread, and on top of the boughs a bed of earth six inches deep. I stretched ropes upon either side to serve as railings, and then my bridge was complete. A train of elephants could have crossed it in safety and comfort. By nightfall the caravan was on the other side and the ladders taken up.

Next morning we went on in good spirits for a while, though our way was slow and difficult, by reason of the steep and rocky nature of the ground and thickness of the forest; but at last a dull despondency crept into the men's faces and it was apparent that not only they, but even the guides were now convinced that we were lost. The fact that we still met no tourists was a circumstance that was but too significant. Another thing seemed to suggest that we were not only lost, but very badly lost: for there must surely be searching-parties on before this time, yet we had seen no sign of them.

Demoralization was spreading; something must be done, and done quickly, too. Fortunately, I am not unfertile in expedients. I contrived one now which commended itself to all, for it promised well. I took three-quarters of a mile of rope and fastened one end of it around the waist of a guide, and told him to go and find the road, whilst the caravan waited. I instructed him to guide himself back by the rope, in case of failure; in case of success, he was to give the rope a series of violent jerks, whereupon the Expedition would go to him at once. He departed, and in two minutes had disappeared among the trees. I payed out the rope myself, while everybody watched the crawling thing with eager eyes. The rope crept away quite slowly, at time, at other times with some briskness. Twice or thrice we seemed to get the signal, and a shout was just ready to break from the men's lips when they perceived it was a false alarm. But at last, when over half a mile of rope had slidden away it stopped gliding and stood absolutely still,—one minute,—two minutes,—three,—while we held our breath and watched.

Was the guide resting? Was he scanning the country from some high point? Was he inquiring of a chance mountaineer? Stop,—had he fainted from excess of fatigue and anxiety?

This thought gave us a shock. I was in the very act of detailing an expedition to succor him, when the cord was assailed with a series of such frantic jerks that I could hardly keep hold of it. The huzza that went up, then, was good to hear. "Saved! saved!" was the word that rang out, all down the long rank of the caravan.

We rose up and started at once. We found the route to be good enough for a while, but it began to grow difficult, by and by, and this feature steadily increased. When we judged we had gone half a mile, we momently expected to see the guide; but no, he was not visible anywhere; neither was he waiting, for the rope was still moving, consequently he was doing the same. This argued that he had not found the road, yet, but was marching to it with some peasant. There was nothing for use to do but plod along,—and this we did. At the end of three hours we were still plodding. This was not only mysterious, but exasperating. And very fatiguing, too; for we had tried hard, along at first, to catch with the guide, but had only fagged ourselves, in vain; for although he was traveling slowly he was yet able to go faster than the hampered caravan over such ground.

At three in the afternoon we were nearly dead with exhaustion,—and still the rope was slowly gliding out. The murmurs against the guide had been growing, steadily, and at last they were becoming loud and savage. A mutiny ensued. The men refused to proceed. They declared that we had been traveling over and over the same ground all day, in a kind of circle. They demanded that our end of the rope be made fast to a tree, so as to halt the guide until we could overtake him and kill him. This was not an unreasonable requirement, so I gave the order.

As soon as the rope was tied, the Expedition moved forward with that alacrity which the thirst for vengeance usually inspires. But after a tiresome march of almost half a mile we came to a hill covered thick with a crumbly rubbish of stones, and so steep that no man of us all was now in a condition to climb it. Every attempt failed, and ended in crippling somebody. Within twenty minutes I had five men on crutches. Whenever a climber tried to assist himself by the rope, it yielded and let him tumble backwards. The frequency of this result suggested an idea to me. I ordered the caravan to 'bout face and form in marching order; I then made the tow-rope fast to the rear mule, and gave the command,—

"Mark time—by the right flank—forward—march!"

211

The procession began to move, to the impressive strains of a battle-chant, and I said to myself, "Now, if the rope don't break I judge *this* will fetch that guide into the camp." I watched the rope gliding down the hill, and presently when I was all fixed for triumph I was confronted by a bitter disappointment: there was no guide tied to the rope, it was only a very indignant old black ram. The fury of the baffled Expedition exceeded all bounds. They even wanted to wreak their unreasoning vengeance on this innocent dumb brute. But I stood between them and their prey, menaced by a bristling wall of ice-axes and alpenstocks, and proclaimed that there was but one road to this murder, and it was directly over my corpse. Even as I spoke I saw that my doom was sealed, except a miracle supervened to divert these madmen from their fell purpose. I see that sickening wall of weapons now; I see that advancing host as I saw it then, I see the hate in those cruel eyes; I remember how I dropped my head upon my breast, I feel again the sudden earthquake shock in my rear, administered by the very ram I was sacrificing myself to save, I hear once more the typhoon of laughter that burst from the assaulting column as I clove it from van to rear like a Sepoy shot from a Rodman gun.

I was saved. Yes, I was saved, and by the merciful instinct of ingratitude which nature had planted in the breast of that treacherous beast. The grace which eloquence had failed to work in those men's hearts, had been wrought by a laugh. The ram was set free and my life was spared.

We lived to find out that that guide had deserted us as soon as he had placed a half mile between himself and us. To avert suspicion, he had judged it best that the line should continue to move; so he caught that ram, and at the time that he was sitting on it making the rope fast to it, we were imagining that he was lying in a swoon, overcome by fatigue and distress. When he allowed the ram to get up it fell to plunging around, trying to rid itself of the rope, and this was the signal which we had risen up with glad shouts to obey. We had followed this ram round and round in a circle all day—a thing which was proven by the discovery that we had watered the Expedition seven times at one and the same spring in seven hours. As expert a woodman as I am, I had somehow failed to notice this until my attention was called to it by a hog. This hog was always wallowing there, and as he was the only hog we saw, his frequent repetition, together with his unvarying similarity to himself, finally caused me to reflect that he must be the same hog, and this led me to the deduction that this must be the same spring, also,—which indeed it was.

I made a note of this curious thing, as showing in a striking manner the relative difference between glacial action and the action of the hog. It is now a well established fact, that glaciers move; I consider that my observations go to show with equal conclusiveness, that a hog in a spring does not move. I shall be glad to receive the opinions of other observers upon this point.

To return, for an explanatory moment, to that guide, and then I shall be done with him. After leaving the ram tied to the rope, he had wandered at large a while, and then happened to run across a cow. Judging that a cow would naturally know more than a guide, he took her by the tail and the result justified his judgment. She nibbled her leisurely way down hill till it was near milking time, then she struck for home and towed him into Zermatt.

—1880

John Muir

from *The Mountains of California*

Known primarily as the father of the American conservation movement and a founder of the Sierra Club, John Muir (1838–1914) was also an avid mountain climber and served as president of the American Alpine Club from 1908 to 1911. Born in Scotland, Muir's family emigrated to Wisconsin in 1849. His book A Thousand-Mile Walk to the Gulf *(1916) describes the walking tour he made from the northern states to Florida. He was instrumental in promoting forest conservation in the United States and aided in the establishment and preservation of Yosemite and Sequoia National Parks. His favorite mountains were the Sierra Nevadas and he wrote about every aspect of them in his first book* The Mountains of California *(1894). Muir wrote several other books and essays on mountains, nature, and conservation, thus establishing himself as one of America's first environmentalist writers. In this passage, Muir describes the mountain passes and reflects on what the Sierras mean to him.*

THE PASSES

The sustained grandeur of the High Sierra is strikingly illustrated by the great height of the passes. Between latitude 36° 20´ and 38° the lowest pass, gap, gorge, or notch of any kind cutting across the axis of the range, as far as I have discovered, exceeds nine thousand feet in height above the level of the sea; while the average height of all that are in use, either by Indians or whites, is perhaps not less than eleven thousand feet, and not one of these is a carriage pass.

Farther north a carriage road has been constructed through what is known as the Sonora Pass, on the head waters of the Stanislaus and Walker's Rivers, the summit of which is about ten thousand feet above the sea. Substantial wagon roads have also been built through the Carson and Johnson passes, near the head of Lake Tahoe, over which immense quantities of freight were hauled from California to the mining regions of Nevada, before the construction of the Central Pacific Railroad.

Still farther north a considerable number of comparatively low passes occur, some of which are accessible to wheeled vehicles, and through these rugged defiles during the exciting years of the gold period long emigrant trains with footsore cattle wearily toiled. After the toil-worn adventures had escaped a thousand dangers and had crawled thousands of miles across the plains the snowy Sierra at last loomed in sight, the eastern wall of the land of gold. And as with shaded eyes they gazed

John Muir, *The Mountains of California* (New York: Century, 1894).

through the tremulous haze of the desert, with what joy must they have described the pass through which they were to enter the better land of their hopes and dreams!

Between the Sonora Pass and the southern extremity of the High Sierra, a distance of nearly 160 miles, there are only five passes through which trails conduct from one side of the range to the other. These are barely practicable for animals; a pass in these regions meaning simply any notch or cañon through which one may, by the exercise of unlimited patience, make out to lead a mule, or a sure-footed mustang; animals that can slide or jump as well as walk. Only three of the five passes may be said to be in use, namely, the Kearsarge, Mono, and Virginia Creek; the tracks leading through the others being only obscure Indian trails, not graded in the least, and scarcely traceable by white men; for much of the way is over solid rock and earthquake avalanche taluses, where the unshod ponies of the Indians leave no appreciable sign. Only skilled mountaineers are able to detect the marks that serve to guide the Indians, such as slight abrasions of the looser rocks, the displacement of stones here and there, and bent bushes and weeds. A general knowledge of the topography is, then, the main guide, enabling one to determine where the trail ought to go *must* go. One of these Indian trails crosses the range by a nameless pass between the head waters of the south and middle forks of the San Joaquin, the other between the north and middle forks of the same river, just to the south of "The Minarets"; this last being about nine thousand feet high, is the lowest of the five. The Kearsarge is the highest, crossing the summit near the head of the south fork of King's River, about eight miles to the north of Mount Tyndall, through the midst of the most stupendous rock scenery. The summit of this pass is over twelve thousand feet above sea-level; nevertheless, it is one of the safest of the five, and is used every summer, from July to October or November, by hunters, prospectors, and stock-owners, and to some extent by enterprising pleasure-seekers also. For, besides the surpassing grandeur of the scenery about the summit, the trail, in ascending the western flank of the range, conducts through a grove of the giant sequoias, and through the magnificent Yosemite Valley of the south fork of King's River. This is, perhaps, the highest traveled pass on the North American continent.

The Mono Pass lies to the east of Yosemite Valley, at the head of one of the tributaries of the south fork of the Tuolumne. This is the best known and most extensively traveled of all that exist in the High Sierra. A trail was made through it about the time of the Mono gold excitement, in the year 1858, by adventurous miners and prospectors—men who would build a trail down the throat of darkest Erebus on the way to gold. Though more than a thousand feet lower than the Kearsarge, it is scarcely less sublime in rock-scenery, while in snowy, falling water it far surpasses it. Being so favorably situated for the stream of Yosemite travel, the more adventurous tourists cross over through this glorious gateway to the volcanic region around Mono Lake. It has therefore gained a name and fame above every other pass in the range. According to the few barometrical observations made upon it, its highest point is 10,765 feet above the sea. The other pass of the five we have been

215

considering is somewhat lower, and crosses the axis of the range a few miles to the north of the Mono Pass, at the head of the southernmost tributary of Walker's River. It is used chiefly by roaming bands of the Pah Ute Indians and "sheep-men."

But, leaving wheels and animals out of the question, the free mountaineer with a sack of bread on his shoulders and an axe to cut steps in ice and frozen snow can make his way across the range almost everywhere, and at any time of year when the weather is calm. To him nearly every notch between the peaks is a pass, though much patient step-cutting is at times required up and down steeply inclined glaciers, with cautious climbing over precipices that at first sight would seem hopelessly inaccessible.

In pursuing my studies, I have crossed from side to side of the range at intervals of a few miles all along the highest portion of the chain, with far less real danger than one would naturally count on. And what fine wilderness was thus revealed—storms and avalanches, lakes and waterfalls, gardens and meadows, and interesting animals—only those will ever know who give the freest and most buoyant portion of their lives to climbing and seeing for themselves.

To the timid traveler, fresh from the sedimentary levels of the lowlands, these highways, however picturesque and grand, seem terribly forbidding—cold, dead, gloomy gashes in the bones of the mountains, and of all Nature's ways the ones to be most cautiously avoided. Yet they are full of the finest and most telling examples of Nature's love; and though hard to travel, none are safer. For they lead through regions that lie far above the ordinary haunts of the devil, and of the pestilence that walks in darkness. True, there are innumerable places where the careless step will be the last step; and a rock falling from the cliffs may crush without warning like lightning from the sky; but what then? Accidents in the mountains are less common than in the lowlands, and these mountain mansions are decent, delightful, even divine, places to die in, compared with the doleful chambers of civilization. Few places in this world are more dangerous than home. Fear not, therefore, to try the mountain passes. They will kill care, save you from deadly apathy, set you free, and call forth every faculty into vigorous, enthusiastic action. Even the sick should try these so-called dangerous passes, because for every unfortunate they kill, they cure a thousand.

All the passes make their steepest ascents on the eastern flank. On this side the average rise is not far from a thousand feet to the mile, while on the west it is about two hundred feet. Another marked difference between the eastern and western portions of the passes is that the former begin at the very foot of the range, while the latter can hardly be said to begin lower than an elevation of from seven to ten thousand feet. Approaching the range from the gray levels of Mono and Owen's Valley on the east, the traveler sees before him the steep, short passes in full view, fenced in by rugged spurs that come plunging down from the shoulders of the peaks on either side, the courses of the more direct being disclosed from top to bottom without interruption. But from the west one sees nothing of the way he may be seeking until near the summit, after days have been spent in threading the forests growing on the main dividing ridges between the river cañons.

It is interesting to observe how surely the alp-crossing animals of every kind fall into the same trails. The more rugged and inaccessible the general character of the topography of any particular region, the more surely will the trails of white men, Indians, bears, wild sheep, etc., be found converging into the best passes. The Indians of the western slope venture cautiously over the passes in settled weather to attend dances, and obtain loads of pine nuts and the larvae of a small fly that breeds in Mono and Owen's Lakes, which, when dried, forms an important article of food; while the Pah Utes cross over from the east to hunt the deer and obtain supplies of acorns; and it is truly astonishing to see what immense loads the haggard old squaws make out to carry barefooted through these rough passes, oftentimes for a distance of sixty or seventy miles. They are always accompanied by the men, who stride on, unburdened and erect, a little in advance, kindly stooping at difficult places to pile stepping-stones for their patient, pack-animal wives, just as they would prepare the way for their ponies.

Bears evince great sagacity as mountaineers, but although they are tireless and enterprising travelers they seldom cross the range. I have several times tracked them through the Mono Pass, but only in late years, after cattle and sheep had passed that way, when they doubtless were following to feed on the stragglers and on those that had been killed by falling over the rocks. Even the wild sheep, the best mountaineers of all, choose regular passes in making journeys across the summits. Deer seldom cross the range in either direction. I have never yet observed a single specimen of the mule-deer of the Great Basin west of the summit, and rarely one of the black-tailed species on the eastern slope, notwithstanding many of the latter ascend the range nearly to the summit every summer, to feed in the wild gardens and bring forth their young.

The glaciers are the pass-makers, and it is by them that the courses of all mountaineers are predestined. Without exception every pass in the Sierra was created by them without the slightest aid or predetermining guidance from any of the cataclysmic agents. I have seen elaborate statements of the amount of drilling and blasting accomplished in the construction of the railroad across the Sierra, above Donner Lake; but for every pound of rock moved in this way, the glaciers which descended east and west through this same pass, crushed and carried away more than a hundred tons.

The so-called practicable road passes are simply those portions of the range more degraded by glacial action than the adjacent portions, and degraded in such a way as to leave the summits rounded, instead of sharp; while the peaks, from the superior strength and hardness of their rocks, or from more favorable position, having suffered less degradation, are left towering above the passes as if they had been heaved into the sky by some force acting from beneath.

The scenery of all the passes, especially at the head, is of the wildest and grandest description,—lofty peaks massed together and laden around their bases with ice and snow; chains of glacier lakes; cascading streams in endless variety, with glorious views, westward over a sea of rocks and woods, and eastward over strange ashy plains, volcanoes, and the dry, dead-looking ranges of the Great Basin. Every pass, however, possesses treasures of beauty all its own.

217

Having thus in a general way indicated the height, leading features, and distribution of the principal passes, I will now endeavor to describe the Mono Pass in particular, which may, I think, be regarded as a fair example of the higher alpine passes in general.

The main portion of the Mono Pass is formed by Bloody Cañon, which begins at the summit of the range, and runs in a general east-northeasterly direction to the edge of the Mono Plain.

The first white men who forced a way through its somber depths were, as we have seen, eager gold-seekers. But the cañon was known and traveled as a pass by the Indians and mountain animals long before its discovery by white men, as is shown by the numerous tributary trails which come into it from every direction. Its name accords well with the character of the "early times" in California, and may perhaps have been suggested by the pre-dominant color of the metamorphic slates in which it is in great part eroded; or more probably by blood-stains made by the unfortunate animals which were compelled to slip and shuffle awkwardly over its rough, cutting rocks. I have never known an animal, either mule or horse, to make its way through the cañon either in going up or down, without losing more or less blood from wounds on the legs. Occasionally one is killed outright—falling head-long and rolling over precipices like a boulder. But such accidents are rarer than from the terrible appearance of the trail one would be led to expect; the more experienced when driven loose find their way over the dangerous places with a caution and sagacity that is truly wonderful. During the gold excitement it was at times a matter of considerable pecuniary importance to force a way through the cañon with pack-trains early in the spring while it was yet heavily blocked with snow; and then the mules with their loads had sometimes to be let down over the steepest drifts and avalanche beds by means of ropes.

A good bridle-path leads from Yosemite through many a grove and meadow up to the head of the cañon, a distance of about thirty miles. Here the scenery undergoes a sudden and startling condensation. Mountains, red, gray, and black, rise close at hand on the right, whitened around their bases with banks of enduring snow; on the left swells the huge red mass of Mount Gibbs, while in front the eye wanders down the shadowy cañon, and out on the warm plain of Mono, where the lake is seen gleaming like a burnished metallic disk, with clusters of lofty volcanic cones to the south of it.

When at length we enter the mountain gateway, the somber rocks seem aware of our presence, and seem to come thronging closer about us. Happily the ouzel and the old familiar robin are here to sing us welcome, and azure daisies beam with trustfulness and sympathy, enabling us to feel something of Nature's love even here, beneath the gaze of her coldest rocks.

The effect of this expressive outspokenness on the part of the cañon-rocks is greatly enhanced by the quiet aspect of the alpine meadows through which we pass just before entering the narrow gateway. The forests in which they lie, and the mountain-tops

218

rising beyond them, seem quiet and tranquil. We catch their restful spirit, yield to the soothing influences of the sunshine, and saunter dreamily on through flowers and bees, scarce touched by a definite thought; then suddenly we find ourselves in the shadowy cañon, closeted with Nature in one of her wildest strongholds.

After the first bewildering impression begins to wear off, we perceive that it is not altogether terrible; for besides the reassuring birds and flowers we discover a chain of shining lakelets hanging down from the very summit of the pass, and linked together by a silvery stream. The highest are set in bleak, rough bowls, scantily fringed with brown and yellow sedges. Winter storms blow snow through the cañon in blinding drifts, and avalanches shoot from the heights. Then are these sparkling tarns filled and buried, leaving not a hint of their existence. In June and July they begin to blink and thaw out like sleepy eyes, the carices thrust up their short brown spikes, the daisies bloom in turn, and the most profoundly buried of them all is at length warmed and summered as if winter were only a dream.

Red Lake is the lowest of the chain, and also the largest. It seems rather dull and forbidding at first sight, lying motionless in its deep, dark bed. The cañon wall rises sheer from the water's edge on the south, but on the opposite side there is sufficient space and sunshine for a sedgy daisy garden, the center of which is brilliantly lighted with lilies, castilleias, larkspurs, and columbines, sheltered from the wind by leafy willows, and forming a most joyful outburst of plant life keenly emphasized by the chill baldness of the onlooking cliffs.

After indulging here in a dozing, shimmering lake rest, the happy stream sets forth again, warbling and trilling like an ouzel, ever delightfully confiding, no matter how dark the way; leaping, gliding, hither, thither, clear of foaming: manifesting the beauty of its wildness in every sound and gesture.

One of its most beautiful developments is the Diamond Cascade, situated a short distance below Red Lake. Here the tense, crystalline water is first dashed into coarse, granular spray mixed with dusty foam, and then divided into a diamond pattern by following the diagonal cleavage joints that intersect the face of the precipice over which it pours. Viewed in front, it resembles a strip of embroidery of definite pattern, varying through the seasons with the temperature and the volume of water. Scarce a flower may be seen along its snowy border. A few bent pines look on from a distance, and small fringes of cassiope and rock-ferns are growing in fissures near the head, but these are so lowly and undemonstrative that only the attentive observer will be likely to notice them.

On the north wall of the cañon, a little below the Diamond Cascade, a glittering side stream makes its appearance, seeming to leap directly out of the sky. It first resembles a crinkled ribbon of silver hanging loosely down the wall, but grows wider as it descends, and dashes the dull rock with foam. A long, rough talus curves up against this part of the cliff, overgrown with snow-pressed willows, in which the fall disappears with many an eager surge and swirl and splashing leap, finally beating its way down to its confluence with the main cañon stream.

Below this point the climate is no longer arctic. Butterflies become larger and more abundant, grasses with imposing spread of panicle wave above your shoulders, and the summery drone of the bumblebee thickens the air. The dwarf pine, the tree mountaineer that climbs highest and braves the coldest blasts, is found scattered in stormbeaten clumps from the summit of the pass about halfway down the cañon. Here it is succeeded by the hardy two-leaved pine, which is speedily joined by the taller yellow and mountain pines. These, with the burly juniper, and shimmering aspen, rapidly grow larger as the sunshine becomes richer, forming groves that block the view; or they stand more apart here and there in picturesque groups, that make beautiful and obvious harmony with the rocks and with one another. Blooming underbrush becomes abundant,—azalea, spiraea, and the brier-rose weaving fringes for the streams, and shaggy rugs to relieve the stern, unflinching rock-bosses.

Through this delightful wilderness, Cañon Creek roves without any constraining channel, throbbing and wavering; now in sunshine, now in thoughtful shade; falling, swirling, flashing from side to side in weariless exuberance of energy. A glorious milky way of cascades is thus developed, of which Bower Cascade, though one of the smallest, is perhaps the most beautiful of them all. It is situated in the lower region of the pass, just where the sunshine begins to mellow between the cold and warm climates. Here the glad creek, grown strong with tribute gathered from many a snowy fountain on the heights, sings richer strains, and becomes more human and lovable at every step. Now you may by its side find the rose and homely yarrow, and small meadows full of bees and clover. At the head of a low-browed rock, luxuriant dogwood bushes and willows arch over from bank to bank, embowering the stream with their leafy branches; and drooping plumes, kept in motion by the current, fringe the brow of the cascade in front. From this leafy covert the stream leaps out into the light in a fluted curve thick sown with sparkling crystals, and falls into a pool filled with brown boulders, out of which it creeps gray with foam bells and disappears in a tangle of verdure like that from which it came.

Hence, to the foot of the cañon, the metamorphic slates give place to granite, whose nobler sculpture calls forth expressions of corresponding beauty from the stream in passing over it,—bright trills of rapids, booming notes of falls, solemn hushes of smooth-gliding sheets, all chanting and blending in glorious harmony. When, at length, its impetuous alpine life is done, it slips through a meadow with scarce an audible whisper, and falls asleep in Moraine Lake.

This water-bed is one of the finest I ever saw. Evergreens wave soothingly about it, and the breath of flowers floats over it like incense. Here our blessed stream rests from its rocky wanderings, all its mountaineering done,—no more foaming rock leaping, no more wild, exulting song. It falls into a smooth, glassy sleep, stirred only by the night wind, which, coming down the cañon, makes it croon and mutter in ripples along its broidered shores.

Leaving the lake, it glides quietly through the rushes, destined never more to touch the living rock. Henceforth its path lies through ancient moraines and reaches of ashy sage plain, which nowhere afford rocks suitable for the development of cascades or sheer falls. Yet this beauty of maturity, though less striking, is of a still higher order, enticing us lovingly on through gentian meadows and groves of rustling aspen to Lake Mono, where, spirit-like, our happy stream vanishes in vapor, and floats free again in the sky.

Bloody Cañon, like every other in the Sierra, was recently occupied by a glacier, which derived its fountain snows from the adjacent summits, and descended into Mono Lake, at a time when its waters stood at a much higher level than now. The principal characters in which the history of the ancient glaciers is preserved are displayed here in marvelous freshness and simplicity, furnishing the student with extraordinary advantages for the acquisition of knowledge of this sort. The most striking passages are polished and striated surfaces, which in many places reflect the rays of the sun like smooth water. The dam of Red Lake is an elegantly modeled rib of metamorphic slate, brought into relief because of its superior strength, and because of the greater intensity of the glacial erosion of the rock immediately above it, caused by a steeply inclined tributary glacier, which entered the main trunk with a heavy down-thrust at the head of the lake.

Moraine Lake furnishes an equally interesting example of a basin formed wholly, or in part, by a terminal moraine dam curved across the path of a stream between two lateral moraines.

At Moraine Lake the cañon proper terminates, although apparently continued by the two lateral moraines of the vanished glacier. These moraines are about three hundred feet high, and extend unbrokenly from the sides of the cañon into the plain, a distance of about five miles, curving and tapering in beautiful lines. Their sunward sides are gardens, their shady sides are groves; the former devoted chiefly to eriogonae, compositae, and graminae; a square rod containing five or six profusely flowered eriogonums of several species, about the same number of bahia and linosyris, and a few grass tufts; each species being planted trimly apart, with bare gravel between, as if cultivated artificially.

My first visit to Bloody Cañon was made in the summer of 1869, under circumstances well calculated to heighten the impressions that are the peculiar offspring of mountains. I came from the blooming tangles of Florida, and waded out into the plant-gold of the great valley of California, when its flora was as yet untrodden. Never before had I beheld congregations of social flowers half so extensive or half so glorious. Golden compositae covered all the ground from the Coast Range to the Sierra like a stratum of curdled sunshine, in which I reveled for weeks, watching the rising and setting of their innumerable suns; then I gave myself up to be borne forward on the crest of the summer wave that sweeps annually up the Sierra and spends itself on the snowy summits.

At the Big Tuolumne Meadows I remained more than a month, sketching, botanizing, and climbing among the surrounding mountains. The mountaineer with whom I then happened to be camping was one of those remarkable men one so frequently meets in California, the hard angles and bosses of whose characters have been brought into relief by the grinding excitements of the gold period, until they resemble glacial landscapes. But at this late day, my friend's activities had subsided, and his craving for rest caused him to become a gentle shepherd and literally to lie down with the lamb.

Recognizing the unsatisfiable longings of my Scotch Highland instincts, he threw out some hints concerning Bloody Cañon, and advised me to explore it. "I have never seen it myself," he said, "for I never was so unfortunate as to pass that way. But I have heard many a strange story about it, and I warrant you will at least find it wild enough."

Then of course I made haste to see it. Early next morning I made up a bundle of bread, tied my notebook to my belt, and strode away in the bracing air, full of eager, indefinite hope. The plushy lawns that lay in my path served to soothe my morning haste. The sod in many places was starred with daises and blue gentians, over which I lingered. I traced the paths of the ancient glaciers over many a shining pavement, and marked the gaps in the upper forests that told the power of the winter avalanches. Climbing higher, I saw for the first time the gradual dwarfing of the pines in compliance with climate, and on the summit discovered creeping mats of the arctic willow overgrown with silky catkins, and patches of the dwarf vaccinium with its round flowers sprinkled in the grass like purple hail; while in every direction the landscape stretched sublimely away in fresh wildness—a manuscript written by the hand of Nature alone.

At length, as I entered the pass, the huge rocks began to close around in all their wild, mysterious impressiveness, when suddenly, as I was gazing eagerly about me, a drove of gray, hairy beings came in sight, lumbering toward me with a kind of boneless, wallowing motion like bears.

I never turn back, though often so inclined, and in this particular instance, amid such surroundings, everything seemed singularly unfavorable for the calm acceptance of so grim a company. Suppressing my fears, I soon discovered that although as hairy as bears and as crooked as summit pines, the strange creatures were sufficiently erect to belong to our own species. They proved to be nothing more formidable than Mono Indians dressed in the skins of sage-rabbits. Both the men and the women begged persistently for whiskey and tobacco, and seemed so accustomed to denials that I found it impossible to convince them that I had none to give. Excepting the names of these two products of civilization, they seemed to understand not a word of English; but I afterward learned that they were on their way to Yosemite Valley to feast awhile on trout and procure a load of acorns to carry back through the pass to their huts on the shore of Mono Lake.

Occasionally a good countenance may be seen among the Mono Indians, but these, the first specimens I had seen, were mostly ugly, and some of them altogether hideous. The dirt on their faces was fairly stratified, and seemed so ancient and so undisturbed it might almost possess a geological significance. The older faces were, moreover, strangely blurred and divided into sections by furrows that looked like the cleavage joints of rocks, suggesting exposure on the mountains in a castaway condition for ages. Somehow they seemed to have no right place in the landscape, and I was glad to see them fading out of sight down the pass.

Then came evening, and the somber cliffs were inspired with the ineffable beauty of the alpenglow. A solemn calm fell upon everything. All the lower portion of the cañon was in gloaming shadow, and I crept into a hollow near one of the upper lakelets to smooth the ground in a sheltered nook for a bed. When the short twilight faded, I kindled a sunny fire, made a cup of tea, and lay down to rest and look at the stars. Soon the night wind began to flow and pour in torrents among the jagged peaks, mingling strange tones with those of the waterfalls sounding far below; and as I drifted toward sleep I began to experience an uncomfortable feeling of nearness to the furred Monos. Then the full moon looked down over the edge of the cañon wall, her countenance seemingly filled with intense concern, and apparently so near as to produce a startling effect as if she had entered my bedroom, forgetting all the world, to gaze on me alone.

The night was full of strange sounds, and I gladly welcomed the morning. Breakfast was soon done, and I set forth in the exhilarating freshness of the new day, rejoicing in the abundance of pure wildness so close about me. The stupendous rocks, hacked and scarred with centuries of storms, stood sharply out in the thin early light, while down in the bottom of the cañon grooved and polished bosses heaved and glistened like swelling sea waves, telling a grand old story of the ancient glacier that poured its crushing floods above them.

Here for the first time I met the arctic daisies in all their perfection of purity and spirituality,—gentle mountaineers face to face with the stormy sky, kept safe and warm by a thousand miracles. I leaped lightly from rock to rock, glorying in the eternal freshness and sufficiency of Nature, and in the ineffable tenderness with which she nurtures her mountain darlings in the very fountains of storms. Fresh beauty appeared at every step, delicate rock ferns, and groups of the fairest flowers. Now another lake came to view, now a waterfall. Never fell light in brighter spangles, never fell water in whiter foam. I seemed to float through the cañon enchanted, feeling nothing of its roughness, and was out in the Mono levels before I was aware.

Looking back from the shore of Moraine Lake, my morning ramble seemed all a dream. There curved Bloody Cañon, a mere glacial furrow two thousand feet deep, with smooth rocks projecting from the sides and braided together in the middle, like bulging, swelling muscles. Here the lilies were higher than my head, and the sunshine was warm enough for palms. Yet the snow around the arctic willows was plainly visible only four miles away, and between were narrow specimen zones of all the principal climates of the globe.

On the bank of a small brook that comes gurgling down the side of the left lateral moraine, I found a camp-fire still burning, which no doubt belonged to the gray Indians I had met on the summit, and I listened instinctively and moved cautiously forward, half expecting to see some of their grim faces peering out of the bushes.

Passing on toward the open plain, I noticed three well-defined terminal moraines curved gracefully across the cañon stream, and joined by long splices to the two noble laterals. These mark the halting-places of the vanished glacier when it was retreating into its summit shadows on the breaking-up of the glacial winter.

Five miles below the foot of Moraine Lake, just where the lateral moraines lose themselves in the plain, there was a field of wild rye, growing in magnificent waving bunches six to eight feet high, bearing heads from six to twelve inches long. Rubbing out some of the grains, I found them about five-eighths of an inch long, dark-colored, and sweet. Indian women were gathering it in baskets, bending down large handfuls, beating it out, and fanning it in the wind. They were quite picturesque, coming through the rye, as one caught glimpses of them here and there, in winding lanes and openings, with splendid tufts arching above their heads, while their incessant chat and laughter showed their heedless joy.

Like the rye-field, I found the so-called desert of Mono blooming in a high state of natural cultivation with the wild rose, cherry, aster, and the delicate abronia; also innumerable gilias, phloxes, poppies, and bush compositae. I observed their gestures and the various expressions of their corollas, inquiring how they could be so fresh and beautiful out in this volcanic desert. They told as happy a life as any plant company I ever met, and seemed to enjoy even the hot sand and the wind.

But the vegetation of the pass has been in great part destroyed, and the same may be said of all the more accessible passes throughout the range. Immense numbers of starving sheep and cattle have been driven through them into Nevada, trampling the wild gardens and meadows almost out of existence. The lofty walls are untouched by any foot, and the falls sing on unchanged; but the sight of crushed flowers and stripped, bitten bushes goes far toward destroying the charm of wildness.

The cañon should be seen in winter. A good, strong traveler, who knows the way and the weather, might easily make a safe excursion through it from Yosemite Valley on snowshoes during some tranquil time, when the storms are hushed. The lakes and falls would be buried then; but so, also, would be the traces of destructive feet, while the views of the mountains in their winter garb, and the ride at lightning speed down the pass between the snowy walls, would be truly glorious.

—1894

224

A. F. Mummery

"The Pleasures and Penalties of Mountaineering"

Albert F. Mummery (1855–1895) was widely respected for his rock climbing skill, which allowed him to ascend peaks and rock walls previously thought to be impassable in the nineteenth century, including the Zmutt Ridge on the Matterhorn. Mummery helped to define the very nature and ambitions of late-nineteenth-century climbing. He began the practice of guideless climbing in the Alps. His early successes and personal rivalries with other climbers prevented him from becoming an Alpine Club member, however, until 1888. Several difficult routes and features have been christened with his name, such as the "Mummery Crack" on the Grépon. Mummery disappeared mysteriously on Nanga Parbat in 1895 along with two Ghurkas, and his body was never recovered. His death was nationally mourned—similar to the disappearance of Mallory and Irvine on Everest in 1924. One of the deadliest mountains of the world, Nanga Parbat later claimed sixteen lives in a single 1937 avalanche. In this selection, Mummery reflects on why men climb mountains. For Mummery, the dangers of mountain climbing allowed "a man to know that he is not clean gone to flesh pots and effeminacy."

Well-known climbers, whose opinions necessarily carry the greatest weight, have recently declared their belief that the dangers of mountaineering no longer exist. Skill, knowledge, and text-books have hurled them to the limbo of exploded bogies. I would fain agree with this optimistic conclusion, but I cannot forget that the first guide to whom I was ever roped, and one who possessed—may I say it?—more knowledge of mountains than is to be found even in the Badminton library, was none the less killed on the Brouillard Mont Blanc, and his son, more recently, on Koshtantau. The memory of two rollicking parties, comprising seven men, who one day in 1879 were climbing on the west face of the Matterhorn, passes with ghost-like admonition before my mind and bids me remember that of these seven, Mr. Penhall was killed on the Wetterhorn, Ferdinand Imseng on the Macugnaga Monte Rosa, and Johann Petrus on the Fresnay Mont Blanc. To say that any single one of these men was less careful and competent, or had less knowledge of all that pertains to the climber's craft, than we who yet survive, is obviously and patently absurd. Our best efforts must sometimes be seconded by the great goddess of Luck; to her should the Alpine Club offer its vows and thanksgivings.

A. F. Mummery, "The Pleasures and Penalties of Mountaineering," *My Climbs in the Alps and Caucasus* (London: Unwin, 1895).

Indeed, if we consider for a moment the essence of the sport of mountaineering, it is obvious that it consists, and consists exclusively, in pitting the climber's skill against the difficulties opposed by the mountain. Any increase in skill involves, *pari passu* an increase in the difficulties grappled with. From the Breuil ridge of the Matterhorn we pass on to the Dru, and from the Dru to the Aiguille de Grépon: or to take a yet wider range, from the Chamonix Mont Blanc to the same mountain by way of the Brenva glacier and the Aiguille Blanche de Peuteret. It can scarcely be argued that Bennen and Walters were less fit to grapple with the cliff above the "Linceul" than we moderns to climb the Grépon "crack"; or than Jacques Balmat was less able to lead up the "Ancien passage" than Emile Rey to storm the ghastly precipices of the Brenva Peuteret. But if it be admitted that the skill of the climber has not increased relatively to the difficulties grappled with, it would appear to necessarily follow that climbing is neither more nor less dangerous than formerly.

It is true that extraordinary progress has been made in the art of rock climbing, and that, consequently, any given rock climb is much easier now than thirty years since, but the essence of the sport lies, not in ascending a peak, but in struggling with and overcoming difficulties. The happy climber, like the aged Ulysses, is one who has "Drunk delight of battle with his peers," and this delight is only attainable by assaulting cliffs which tax to their utmost limits the powers of the mountaineers engaged. This struggle involves the same risk, whether early climbers attacked what we now call easy rock, or whether we moderns attack formidable rock, or whether the ideal climber of the future assaults cliffs which we now regard as hopelessly inaccessible. Doubtless my difference with the great authorities referred to above is, in the main, due to a totally different view of the *raison d'être* of mountaineering. Regarded as a sport, some danger is, and always must be, inherent in it; regarded as a means of exercise amongst noble scenery, for quasi-scientific pursuits, as the raw material for interesting papers, or for the purposes of brag and bounce, it has become as safe as the ascent of the Rigi or Pilatus was to the climbers of thirty years since. But these pursuits are not mountaineering in the sense in which the founders of the Alpine Club used the term, and they are not mountaineering in the sense in which the elect—a small, perchance even a dwindling body—use it now. To set one's utmost faculties, physical and mental, to fight some grim precipice, or force some gaunt, ice-clad gully, is work worthy of men; to toil up long slopes of screes behind a guide who can "lie in bed and picture every step of the way up, with all the places for hand and foot," is work worthy of the fibreless contents of fashionable clothes, dumped with all their scents and ointments, starched linen and shiny boots, at Zermatt by the railway.

The true mountaineer is a wanderer, and by a wanderer I do not mean a man who expends his whole time in travelling to and fro in the mountains on the exact tracks of his predecessors—much as a bicyclist rushes along the turnpike roads of England—but I mean a man who loves to be where no human being has been before, who delights in gripping rocks that have previously never felt the touch of human fingers, or in hewing his way up ice-filled gullies whose grim shadows have been sacred to the mists and avalanches since "Earth rose out of chaos." In other words, the true mountaineer is the man who attempts new ascents. Equally, whether he succeeds or fails, he delights in the fun and jollity of the struggle. The gaunt, bare slabs, the square, precipitous steps in the ridge, and the black, bulging ice of the gully, are the very breath of life to his being. I do not pretend to be able to analyse this feeling, still less to be able to make it clear to unbelievers. It must be felt to be understood, but it is potent to happiness and sends the blood tingling through the veins, destroying every trace of cynicism and striking at the very roots of pessimistic philosophy.

Our critics, curiously enough, repeat in substance Mr. Ruskin's original taunt, that we regard the mountains as greased poles. I must confess that a natural and incurable denseness of understanding does not enable me to feel the sting of this taunt. Putting aside the question of grease, which is offensive and too horrible for contemplation in its effects on knickerbockers—worse even than the structure-destroying edges and splinters of the Grépon ridge—I do not perceive the enormity or sin of climbing poles. At one time, I will confess, I took great delight in the art, and, so far as my experience extends, the taste is still widespread amongst English youth. It is possible, nay even probable, that much of the pleasure of mountaineering is derived from the actual physical effort and from the perfect state of health to which this effort brings its votaries, and, to this extent, may plausibly be alleged to be the mere sequence and development of the pole and tree climbing of our youth. The sting of the taunt is presumably meant to lurk in the implication that the climber is incapable of enjoying noble scenery; that, in the jargon of certain modern writers, he is a *"mere gymnast."* But why should a man be assumed incapable of enjoying aesthetic pleasures because he is also capable of the physical and non-aesthetic pleasures of rock climbing?

A well-known mountaineer asserts that the fathers of the craft did not regard "the overcoming of physical obstacles by means of muscular exertion and skill" as "the chief pleasure of mountaineering." But is this so? Can any one read the great classic of mountaineering literature, "The Playground of Europe," without feeling that the overcoming of these obstacles was a main factor of its author's joy? Can any one read "Peaks, Passes, and Glaciers" and the earlier numbers of the Alpine Journal without feeling that the various writers gloried in the technique of their craft? Of course the skillful interpolation of "chief" gives an opening for much effective dialectic, but after all, what does it mean? How can a pleasure which is seated in health and jollity and the "spin of the blood" be measured and compared with a purely aesthetic feeling? It would appear difficult to argue that as a man cultivates and acquires muscular skill and knowledge of the mountains, he correspondingly dwarfs and impairs the aesthetic side of his nature. If so, we magnify the weak-kneed and the impotent, the lame, the halt and the blind, and brand as false the Greek ideal of the perfect man. Doubtless a tendency in this direction may be detected in some modern thought, but, like much else similarly enshrined, it has no ring of true metal. Those who are so completely masters of their environment that they can laugh and rollick on the ridges, free from all constraint of ropes or fear of danger, are far more able to appreciate the glories of the "eternal hills" than those who can only move in constant terror of their lives, amidst the endless chatter and rank tobacco smoke of unwashed guides.

The fact that a man enjoys scrambling up a steep rock in no way makes him insensible of all that is beautiful in nature. The two sets of feelings are indeed wholly unconnected. A man may love climbing and care naught for mountain scenery; he may love the scenery and hate climbing; or he may be equally devoted to both. The presumption obviously is that those who are most attracted by the mountains and most constantly return to their fastnesses, are those who to the fullest extent possess both these sources of enjoyment—those who can combine the fun and frolic of a splendid sport with that indefinable delight which is induced by the lovely form, tone, and colouring of the great ranges.

I am free to confess that I myself should still climb, even though there were no scenery to look at, even if the only climbing attainable were the dark and gruesome pot-holes of the Yorkshire dales. On the other hand, I should still wander among the upper snows, lured by the silent mists and the red blaze of the setting sun, even though physical or other infirmity, even though in after aeons the sprouting of wings and other angelic appendages, may have sunk all thought of climbing and cragsmanship in the whelming past.

It is frequently assumed, even by those who ought to know better, that if mountaineering involves danger of any sort, it should never be indulged in—at all events by such precious individuals as the members of the English Alpine Club. Before considering this most pernicious doctrine, it is well to remember, that though the perils of mountaineering may not have been wholly dissipated into space by the lightning-like flashes of the Badminton and All England series, yet, nevertheless, these perils are not very great. With a single exception, the foregoing pages contain an account of every difficulty I have experienced which has seemed to render disaster a possible contingency. As my devotion to the sport began in 1871, and has continued with unabated vigour ever since, it will be evident that the climber's perils—in so far as a modest individual may regard himself as typical of the class—are extremely few and very rarely encountered. Such, however, as they have been, I would on no account have missed them. There is an educative and purifying power in danger that is to be found in no other school, and it is worth much for a man to know that he is not "clean gone to flesh pots and effeminacy." It may be admitted that the mountains occasionally push things a trifle too far, and bring before their votaries a vision of the imminence of dissolution that the hangman himself with all his paraphernalia of scaffold, gallows, and drop, could hardly hope to excel. But grim and hopeless as the cliffs may sometimes look when ebbing twilight is chased by shrieking wind and snow and the furies are in mad hunt along the ridges, there is ever the feeling that brave companions and a constant spirit will cut the gathering web of peril, "forsan et haec olim meminisse juvabit."

The sense of independence and self-confidence induced by the great precipices and vast silent fields of snow is something wholly delightful. Every step is health,

228

fun, and frolic. The troubles and cares of life, together with the essential vulgarity of a plutocratic society, are left far below—foul miasmas that cling to the lowest bottoms of reeking valleys. Above, in the clear air and searching sunlight, we are afoot with the quiet gods, and men can know each other and themselves for what they are. No feeling can be more glorious than advancing to attack some gaunt precipitous wall with "comrades staunch as the founders of our race." Nothing is more exhilarating than to know that the fingers of one hand can still be trusted with the lives of a party, and that the lower limbs are free from all trace of "knee-dissolving fear," even though the friction of one hobnail on an outward shelving ledge alone checks the hurtling of the body through thin air, and of the soul (let us hope) to the realms above.

I am of course aware that it is an age which cares little for the more manly virtues, and which looks askance at any form of sport that can, by any stretch of extremest imagination, be regarded as dangerous: yet since we cannot all, for most obvious reasons, take our delight "wallowing in slimy spawn of lucre," something may surely be urged in favour of a sport that teaches, as no other teaches, endurance and mutual trust, and forces men occasionally to look death in its grimmest aspect frankly and squarely in the face. For though mountaineering is not, perhaps, more dangerous than other sports, it undoubtedly brings home to the mind a more stimulating sense of peril; a sense, indeed, that is out of all proportion to the actual risk. It is, for instance, quite impossible to look down the tremendous precipices of the Little Dru without feeling in each individual nerve the utter disintegration of everything human which a fall must involve; and the contingency of such a fall is frequently brought before the mind—indeed, throughout the ascent, constant and strenuous efforts are needed to avoid it. The love of wager, our religious teachers notwithstanding, is still inherent in the race, and one cannot find a higher stake—at all events in these materialistic days, when Old Nick will no longer lay sterling coin against the gamester's soul—than the continuity of the cervical vertebrae; and this is the stake that the mountaineer habitually and constantly wagers. It is true the odds are all on his side, but the off-chance excites to honesty of thought and tests how far decay has penetrated the inner fibre. That mountaineering has a high educational value, few, who have the requisite knowledge to form a fair judgment, would deny. That it has its evil side I frankly admit. None can look down its gloomy death-roll without feeling that our sport demands a fearful price.

Mountaineering being a sport not wholly free from danger, it behoves us to consider the directions from which this danger may come, and the methods by which it may usually be met and conquered. Amongst the mountains, as elsewhere, "the unexpected always happens." It is the momentary carelessness in easy places, the lapsed attention, or the wandering look that is the usual parent of disaster. It may appear that to this extent dangers are avoidable, and the high authorities referred to above justified in their optimism. But which of us can boast that his attention to the slope and his companions never flags, that his eyes are always on the watch for falling stones, for loose rocks, for undercut ice, and all the traps and pitfalls that

229

Madame Nature scatters with such profusion among the "lonely hills"? The chief source of danger is this need for incessant care, the unvarying readiness of ice, snow, and rock to punish relentlessly an instant's forgetfulness, or the most trifling neglect. The first lesson the novice has to learn is to be ever on his guard, and it is one that the oldest climber rarely fully masters. Unfortunately it is one which the beginner must find out for himself, it is a habit that must be acquired, and to which no road, other than constant practice, will ever lead him. It wants long experience to impress upon the mind that the chief danger of extremely difficult climbing is to be found on the easy places by which it is followed; that it lies less in the stress of desperate wrestling with the crags than in the relaxed attention which such work is apt to induce on the return to comparatively easy ground. Nothing is more usual than to hear a man say after some very formidable ascent—it may even be read in the Alpine Journal—that on the way up, certain preliminary rocks appeared distinctly difficult, but on the way down, after the terrible grapple with the cliffs above, these same rocks appeared "ridiculously easy." It is the delusive appearance of safety presented by these "ridiculously easy rocks" that swells the list of Alpine victims. There are few, even of the oldest and most cunning climbers, who do not have to struggle against the feeling that the difficulties are over and care is no longer essential. Twice have I seen incipient accidents arise from this cause, and on each occasion none but the fair goddess of luck could have rescued a friend from disaster.

There is, again, the impossibility of learning, except by actual experience, the length of time during which the nervous system may be relied on. The protracted strain of a long ice slope tells on men in wholly different ways. To some it means merely the sharpening of their faculties, and with every hour they get steadier and safer in their steps; with others it means utter exhaustion and collapse. It is distinctly unpleasant when a companion, whom you think is enjoying himself, suddenly informs you that he is doubtful of his power to stand in the steps, that his knees are wobbling, and that he may be expected to slip at any moment. At such times nothing but the fact that one has been brought up surrounded by the best religious influences, prevents the ejaculation of the strongest and most soul-satisfying expletives known to the English tongue. It may be said that such a man should not go climbing; but how is he to know that he is affected in this way till he has so gone? A man can never know his capabilities till he has tried them, and this testing process involves risk. Going over ground where a slip would not be serious is of no use; so long, as this is the case he may be as good or better than his companions. It is the knowledge that he holds the lives of the party in his hand that masters and conquers him, not the mere technical difficulties of the slope, which, to a man who has good steps cut for him, may be practically nil.

It will be evident that all these dangers press on the novice far more than on the old and seasoned mountaineer. Those who have learnt the craft, and spent fifteen or twenty summers amongst the mountains, are scarcely likely to be unaware of their own failings and weaknesses, and may be trusted to be generally on the alert. The dangers to which such "old hands" are subject come in the main from other directions, and are chiefly connected with "new expeditions." In the Alps, such ascents can only be found on previously unclimbed sides of peaks, and the mountaineer usually has the knowledge that if he reaches the top he can descend by an easy and well-known route. The temptation to persevere in an ascent, especially if anything very formidable has already been passed, is extremely great, and a party may even be urged forward by the fear of retreat. This fear should, however, never be yielded to; it may easily result in forcing the party into difficulties from which they have neither the time nor the ability to extricate themselves. If a place cannot be descended it should never be climbed.

A somewhat similar and still more deceitful peril is involved by the ascent in the early morning of gullies, which, though fairly safe at that hour, are known to be the channel of avalanches and falling stones in the afternoon. Should any unforeseen cause stop the party high up on the mountain, no safe line of retreat is open. In this way, when Herren Lammer and Lorria, foiled by the ice-glazed rocks of the western face of the Matterhorn, were forced to return, they found the great couloir ceaselessly swept by stones and snow. Persisting, none the less, in the descent, they were carried down by an avalanche, and though, by extraordinary luck, they both escaped with their lives, they suffered very serious injuries. Unless, therefore, the climber is absolutely certain that the ascent can be completed, it is in the highest degree perilous to enter such gullies, and those who do so should clearly recognise that they are running very serious risks. If, however, the risk has been run and the party is checked high up on the mountain, it is usually the better course to spend the night on the rocks, and wait till frost has sealed up the loose stones, snow and ice. This expedient has been adopted more than once by my old guide, Alexander Burgener. On the memorable descent of the Col du Lion, it undoubtedly saved both Dr. Güssfeldt's life and his own.[1] I am aware that his procedure involves some slight risk from adverse changes in the weather, and extreme discomfort from cold, and possibly hunger, but these latter are mere trifles to strong men, properly clad; and as for the former, such places as the great couloir of the western Matterhorn are far safer in a snowstorm than when the setting sun is blazing on the great slopes above. Indeed, when snow falls at a low temperature it instantly dries up the trickles of water, stops the melting of the great pendent icicles, and generally checks the fall of missiles, thus rendering slopes and couloirs, which one dare not climb in fine weather, fairly safe. On the other hand, a summer snow squall followed by a wind above freezing point (a not infrequent phenomenon), will convert rock slopes, usually innocent, into cascades of water, armed and rendered terrible by stones and dislodged crags. It will this be seen that most accurate judgment is necessary, and the requisite knowledge for this judgment is hardly to be obtained till the climber has learnt, by dangerous experience, to grasp the exact nature of the storm, and the effect it is likely to have on the slope he is dealing with.

Climbers sometimes write as though it were possible to avoid all slopes down which stones or ice can ever fall. In actual fact, though such slopes may, to some extent, be avoided on the days and at the hours when such falls may be most expected, it is impossible to keep wholly clear of them.

Mountaineers of the wildest experience and most approved prudence, even presidents and ex-presidents of the Alpine Club, have been known to descend, for hours on end, shelterless slopes of rock and ice, liable at any moment to be raked from top to bottom by falling stones and ice. The orthodox critic may protest, but none the less those who seek to effect new passes will occasionally find themselves in positions which leave them no endurable alternative. The pseudo mountaineer can, it is true, almost wholly avoid these dangers. Accompanied by guides who know every step of the way, he is led by a fairly sheltered route, or, if none such exists, he is told this fact before he starts, and can alter his plans accordingly. But the repetition of an accurately timed and adjusted performance, under the rigid rule of a guide as stage manager, does not commend itself to the real mountaineer. His delight and pleasure in the sport are chiefly derived from the very uncertainty and difficulties which it is the main function of such a guide to eliminate. Even if the pass is not exactly new, he likes to encounter it without the exact knowledge of the route which reduces it to a mere tramp of so many hours duration, and as a consequence he cannot invariably avoid all risk.

As a matter of fact, very few of the usual and customary ascents are quite free from ice and rock falls. Even the Chamonix route up Mont Blanc passes one place where the track is sometimes swept by stones from the Aiguille du Midi, and a second, where ice avalanches from the Dôme du Gouter threaten, and sometimes slay, the traveller. There is, in fact, no absolute immunity from this danger, and it is desirable, therefore, that the young mountaineer should learn the various methods by which it may most suitably be grappled. To acquire the art of watching a falling stone, and, at the critical moment, to remove oneself from the line of fire, is essential to the cragsman. To attain the knowledge requisite to judge where and when ice and snow avalanches may be expected to fall, is equally necessary for the safe guidance of a party. It requires, however, the best teaching that the oldest and steadiest guides can give, combined with a long experience of the upper snows. Those who aspire to lead a party cannot devote too great attention to this subject, and should be able to judge, with tolerable certainty, the effects which new snow on the one hand, or persistently fine weather on the other, has caused in the séracs towering above the lower glacier. Beginners are apt to forget that at no time is falling ice more greatly to be feared than when protracted sunshine has wrought havoc amongst the leering monsters poised above their track. To adapt the expedition to the weather is frequently of critical importance, and may make not merely the difference between success and failure, but even between health and jollity, and irremediable disaster.

In this connection it is desirable to notice that an unroped party is safer than a roped one, and that its chances of escape from the missiles at the mountain's disposal vary, at the very least, inversely with its size. With three on the rope the middle man is more or less of a fixture, and has very little chance of saving himself from falling stones unless cover is close at hand. If no cover is available, the fact that the party is spread over a considerable extent of rock renders it highly probable that the true line of escape for its first and last members will lie in opposite directions. Should this be the case no movement is immediately possible, and the middle man occupies a most unenviable position. Personally I much prefer discarding the rope in all such places, and if this is not desirable, consider two quite the maximum permissible. I may add that this opinion is shared by such men as Alex. Burgener and Emile Rey. I have known each of them object to add a third to the party, on the ground that it would prevent rapidity of movement in places where such rapidity might be desirable. There is also the very serious risk of stones upset by the leader, and which may acquire very dangerous velocity before they pass the lowest man when several climbers are on the slope. During the first ascent of the Rothhorn from Zermatt, disaster was narrowly escaped from this very cause.[2]

There are many gullies in which it is absolutely impossible to avoid dislodging stones, and as a consequence large parties are forced to "close up." Whilst this, to some extent, obviates the risk from falling stones, it negatives any advantage from the rope, and frequently compels all but the first man to be simultaneously on bad ground. Even then I have, more than once, seen a man badly hurt by such stones, and it is difficult to avoid the conclusion that some unexplained accidents may have resulted from a dislodged stone knocking a companion out of his steps, and his fall dragging the members of a "closed up" party, one after another, from their hold. On very steep ice, again, the leader is sometimes seriously hampered by the existence of a large party below him, and the consequent necessity of only cutting small pieces of ice with each stroke of the axe, and absolutely to avoid, on reaching rocks, any endeavour to clear the ice from them; the chance of detaching a fragment sufficiently large to knock a companion seventy or eighty feet below from his steps, being greater than the advantage of getting reliable footing.

These considerations of roping and numbers apply with even greater force to any danger arising from ice avalanches. Every additional man on the rope means a serious decrease of the extreme speed at which the party can move, and it is in speed, and in speed alone, that a party so surprised can hope for safety. In 1871 Mr. Tuckett's party were nearly swept away by a great avalanche falling from the Eiger, and he attributes his escape, in no small measure, to the fact that the party was not roped, and had, in consequence, much greater power of rapid movement than would otherwise have been the case.[3]

Of course if an incompetent man is included, the rope must be worn constantly, and at least two sound and reliable mountaineers must be watching over his idiosyncrasies; but parties so hampered should avoid such gullies as that ascended on the way up the Schreckhorn, or the pitiless slopes of the Italian side of the Col des Hirondelles.

There is one other condition in which the rope seriously increases the risks of competent mountaineers. In the event of an avalanche being started, a roped party is almost helpless. It may be frequently possible for any one of the party to escape from the seething snow, but he is, if roped, of necessity dragged back by his companions. In such a case escape from the avalanche is only possible if all can jump from the sliding snow on the same side and at the same moment, and even then only if they can free the rope from the wet masses of snow in which it is certain to have become somewhat involved. It is obvious, that under circumstances which may afford each single member of the party a dozen chances of escape, it will be highly improbable that all of them will get a simultaneous chance, and the rope in such a case is a veritable death-trap. In larger avalanches, where the utmost the climber can do is to keep his head above the crest of the wave, the roped climber is hampered, as a swimmer in a furious surf would be hampered, by the entanglement of his companions. One has only to read the account of the death of Bennen to realise how disastrous a rope may be.[4]

I have no wish to advocate the disuse of the rope, but merely to point out certain well-known facts that have been lost sight of in recent contributions to the literature of mountaineering. As a general rule it is of the utmost value, and where climbers are of unequal skill and experience, its constant use is demanded by the primary feelings of comradeship and good faith. There is, however, some danger of its being regarded as a sort of Providence, always ready to save the reckless and incompetent, no matter how slight their experience, no matter how little they may be fitted for the expeditions they undertake. Though I have dwelt at some length on the occasional disadvantages the rope entails, and said but little about the safety it so constantly assures, this is merely because there seems no danger of the latter being overlooked, and much that the former will be wholly forgotten. It is, moreover, to be remembered that the conduct of guideless parties has been chiefly in view. Since each member of such a party should be absolutely certain never to slip, the monotony of this precaution may in many places be relaxed with safety, and sometimes even with advantage.

I am, of course, aware that high authorities assert that a party should always be roped, and that it should never consist of less than three—does not the All England series tell that "whatever number may be right, two is wrong"? I must, however, confess that I fail to apprehend the reasons which have led to this unqualified dictum. It would rather appear that the best number depends on a variety of conditions, which vary with the expedition in view. For instance, on the Col du Lion, two is undoubtedly the best and safest number. Not merely is it desirable to reduce to the smallest dimensions the target offered to the mountain musketry and big guns, but it is also essential to move with the utmost speed attainable. Wherever this is the case each additional man is a source of danger.

Much recent writing on this question assumes that on steep slopes or cliffs three men are safer than two. It would, however, appear obvious that this is an error. If the leader slips, it almost of necessity involves the destruction of the party. In any case the whole impact of his fall must come on the man next him in the line, and if this man is dragged from his hold it is absurd to suppose that the third will be able to support the shock of the two men falling. Exactly the same may be said of a traverse; if

234

the leader slips he must be held, if he is held at all, by the man next him in the line. No matter how many may be behind, they will, of necessity, be dragged, one after another, from their hold. It is obvious that if the leader is held by the man next him in the line, two are sufficient for safety; if he is not so held, then three, or any greater number, are equally doomed to destruction. Writers on this subject seem to assume that a party of three or more have no ends to the rope—that each member of the party is between two others—in which case, doubtless, fairly efficient help could be given. It is needless to point out, however, that this is impossible. In every party there are two men, the slip of either of whom, on a steep traverse, is extremely dangerous, if not fatal. The insertion of a third climber, between these two, in no way reduces or diminishes this danger, though, in circumstances which can readily be imagined, it may gravely add to it.

The truth would appear to be, that if from a party of three you remove the worst climber, the two remaining men will, on steep slopes, be distinctly safer than the whole party. If, on the other hand, from the party of three you remove either of the more competent men, then the remaining two will be very much less safe. It must be remembered that I am not arguing in favour of a party consisting of one mountaineer and a duffer, but of two men, equally competent and skilled in all that pertains to the climber's craft.

A careful consideration of the various possibilities that can assail the mountaineer on the steeper slopes would appear to lead to the conclusion that a party of three or four is as often too many, as a party of two is too few. The loss of time and the danger of upset stones, and even of ice and snow hewn out in the process of step cutting appear to fairly balance the advantages of a greater number.

These advantages are chiefly, that in places where the second man is giving the leader a shoulder, a third man may be able to anchor the party with a hitched rope; or where the upper lip of a Schrund is almost out of reach, a third man can materially aid in the work of lifting and holding the leader on the shoulders of his companion whilst the necessary steps are being cut. It is also desirable, in all expeditions where much backing up is required, that the second man should be free from the encumbrance of the knapsack, spare rope, etc., and this, necessarily, involves a third to act as porter. It would appear then, that so far as the steeper slopes are concerned, the number of the party should be adapted to the nature of the expedition, and no attempt should be made to lay down any hard and fast rule.

The main strength of the objection to two men climbing alone is, perhaps, to be found in the common belief that if one man falls into a crevasse, his companion will be unable to pull him out. With regard to this extremely unpleasant supposition, it may be pointed out that there is no particular reason for him to fall in. Why any one should wish to dangle on the rope, in a dark and chilly chasm, is one of those profound and inscrutable mysteries which may be regarded as past all finding out. It is, of course, a quite unnecessary incident, and one which is not, perhaps, nearly so frequently indulged in as some people imagine. Once only have I been near falling into a crevasse, but on that occasion, being unroped, I felt it desirable to abandon such pleasure as this proceeding may afford.

A crevasse, except immediately after fresh snow, is always visible to any one who takes the trouble to look for it; and even if the leader is careless and does break through, the rope, if used with any readiness and skill, ought to check his going in beyond his waist.

It is a curious fact, that, from the very earliest days of mountaineering, two guides, dismissed after crossing a pass, have been in the habit of returning home by themselves. So far as I have been able to learn, no single crevasse accident has ever happened to them. When it is remembered that such extensive and fissured fields of névé, as those traversed by the routes over the Col du Géant, the Mönch Joch, the Weiss Thor, the Col d'Hérens and the Brèche de la Meije, are amongst those which have been habitually crossed by two guides alone, it would appear that the danger to such parties is almost or quite non-existent. It is, indeed, obvious that if such parties *were* exposed to the danger alleged, it would be little short of criminal to take two men across an ice pass and dismiss them under conditions which practically involve their climbing two on a rope. To permit guides to run risks, which their employer is warned on no account to face, would be, to say the least of it, contrary to the traditions of Englishmen at large and the Alpine Club in particular.

The difficulty of reconciling practice and teaching on this point leads me to suppose that, possibly, these denunciations are levelled, not against parties of two mountaineers, but against parties of one mountaineer and one duffer. Politeness, that arch-corrupter of truth, has, perchance, led our teachers to say "a party should never consist of less than three, of whom two should be guides," in preference to say that "a party should always consist of two mountaineers, with or without one or more pieces of animate luggage." It would, indeed, be passing strange, if my old friends Alex. Burgener and Emile Rey, being seized with a desire to cross the Col du Géant, were compelled to obtain the help of some weakly school girl, or decrepit tourist, before being able to face the perils of the pass! Yet this is the conclusion to which the doctrines of our prophets necessarily lead! Truly those who aspire to walk with the "quiet gods" on more than Olympian heights should shun the formal politeness which conceals truth and say their whole meaning, regardless of the feelings of the incompetent and the duffer. Two friends of mine once wished to cross an extensive Norwegian snow field; being learned in the written wisdom of the mountains, they felt that a third man was essential to their safety. They found him, and during the succeeding two days were able to rejoice in the security so afforded! Not only did he cause them to go so slowly that they were benighted in the most inconvenient quarters, not only did he do his best to drag them off the rocks whenever there was any possibility of his efforts being rewarded with success, but I am assured, on authority which is absolutely indisputable, that he indulged, at times, in the most profane and unbecoming language! From that time forth my friends have been firm converts to the doctrine, that if from a party of three you abstract the weakest member, the party is very materially strengthened and improved, and that two competent climbers constitute a far safer and better party than the two guides and a traveller, so dear to the orthodox authorities on mountaineering.

Since, however, it is conceivable that an extensive snow bridge might give way, and let the leader fall some distance before the rope could come into play, it may be of advantage to describe a method of using the rope by which, even in this case, a party of two should still be able to work out their own salvation. It is a fairly well known fact, attested by a considerable number of involuntary experiments, that one man can hold a companion who has fallen some distance into a crevasse. The friction of the rope on the edge of the crevasse, and the splendid holding ground which the soft, level snow affords, enables the fall to be checked without very grave difficulty. The crucial point is, however, to get your companion out again. This, with the rope used in the customary manner, is impossible. Ferdinand Imseng[1] and other of the experimenters referred to above have tried it and failed, and their experience may, I think, be taken as conclusive. If, however, instead of the usual rope, a rope of half its weight and strength be used *doubled*, the problem is easily solved. One of these ropes is provided with two loops, one close to each climber. In the event of a bridge breaking, and as soon as the fall has been checked, the remaining climber drives his axe into the snow, cuts himself free from the looped rope and slips this loop over the axe head. The position of affairs is now as follows. The man in the crevasse has hold of a rope fast to the ice-axe; round his waist is a second rope, also round his companion's waist and held by him. The man in the crevasse pulls on the rope fast to the axe, and the man outside pulls on the rope round his companion's waist: in other words two men are engaged in lifting one. Every advance is made secure and permanent by the man outside, who holds no slack in his hands but pushes his way back from the crevasse, step by step, as his companion nears the lip. Arrived at this point, where the ropes will have cut deep into the snow, the engulfed man has only to rest his whole weight on the rope round his waist, and he can then jerk the other rope free from the snow, and get fresh hold higher up, and little by little extricate himself.

Whilst the rope so used is a fairly effective safeguard against this danger—as efficient perhaps as the rope used in the ordinary way by a party of three—it may be admitted that those who have a constant and irresistible impulse to plunge into the blue depths of crevasses would be wise to travel with two or more companions. A light and portable windlass would, perhaps, be a judicious investment for any spare carrying power such a party might possess. Those, however, who have the fortitude to resist the blandishments of the crevasse, whose ears are stuffed with wax and do not hear the sirens singing in their depths, may adopt the precaution of the doubled rope and feel fairly assured of its efficacy. It ought, however, to be remembered that at least fifty feet should be put between two men, when they are on a glacier by themselves.

The habit of climbing alone is open to far other and more serious objections. It is true that under very exceptional circumstances, when, for instance, settled fine weather has rendered every crevasse visible, snow fields may be crossed in the early morning without much risk. At such times I have strolled over the Trift Joch, the Weiss Thor, the Col du Géant and other passes without experiencing any symptom of danger; but the sense of loneliness, a sense which, when fog and mists curl round the ridges, becomes almost painful, is apt to affect a man's steadiness and resource. It is certainly undesirable to push such solitary wanderings beyond very narrow limits.

On the other hand, nothing develops a man's faculties so rapidly and completely. No one detects a crevasse so readily as the man who is accustomed to traverse snow fields by himself. No one takes such careful note of the line of ascent as the cragsman who has got to find his way back alone. The concentration of all responsibility and all the work on a single individual forces him to acquire an all-round skill which is hardly to be gained in any other way. Climbing in parties is apt to develop one-sidedness. On man cuts the steps, another climbs the rocks, and a third always knows the way. Division of labour is doubtless excellent, and perchance deserves all that Adam Smith has said in its favour, but it does not develop the ideal mountaineer. In this department of human duty Mr. William Morris gives sounder advice. Of course this is merely another way of saying that the chamois hunter—i.e., the solitary moun-taineer—is the best raw material for a guide. The fact that a man has been in the habit of climbing alone, means that the law of the survival of the fittest has had full and ample opportunity of eliminating him should he be, in any way, a careless or inca-pable mountaineer.

From the individual's point of view this elimination may not, perhaps, appear wholly desirable. Yet, judging from his habits, the faithful climber, carried away by altruistic feelings and thinking merely of the welfare of future companions, prefers that the law of the survival of the fittest should have full scope and should pass him through its searching fires. Possibly critics may suggest other and less pleasing mo-tives, perhaps I could even do so myself, but wherefore filch from the lurking foe the joy of a trenchant onslaught? Any way, no matter what his motive may have been, the man so proved is quite independent of the rope, and moves as freely, or more freely, without it than with. He suggests at every step that he adds to the pool of safety that may be regarded as embodied in it. Those, on the other hand, who are imbued with the text books, and fear to move hand or foot when free from the trammels of loops and knots, insensibly suggest that they subtract from this same pool of safety.

It must not be supposed that I am an advocate of solitary climbing. It requires but a trifling knowledge of the average amateur to feel assured that at least nine out of every ten will break their necks if they seriously attempt it. All that is desirable to do, is to point out to those who wish to go without guides, the direction in which they may seek for reliable companions. The more orthodox method of ascending peaks, between two good guides, has much to recommend it, but its votaries had best be avoided by those who aspire to face the great ridges, trusting exclusively in their own right arms and slowly won experience.

The rope should, indeed, be regarded by each member of the party, exclusively as an aid and protection to his companions. Those who feel its constant use essential to their own comfort, should regard this as indisputable evidence that they are engaging in expeditions too difficult for them; a practice which will never make good and self-reliant climbers. To be able to move safely and freely on a mountain slope should be the one object which the young mountaineer sets before himself. At occasional "mauvais pas" he may legitimately ask his companions to look after him and either give actual help, or rescue him from disaster should he slip, but this help should be quite exceptional. If he finds on any expedition that this protection is constantly required, he should frankly recognise that he is attempting work for which he is unfit.

The Matterhorn gives a curious illustration of the way in which the modern amateur is deteriorating. The early climbers roped at the "shoulder." In 1873 they roped at the old hut. In 1886 they roped some distance below the old hut. Now they rope at the new hut, and the exploits of a gentleman in 1893 render it not impossible that future climbers will rope at the Hörnli. Yet these unfortunates fail to recognise that they are attempting work altogether beyond their powers, and are being nursed and coddled by their guides in a way that is destructive of all proper self-respect and of every feeling of self-reliant manliness. Whilst the true mountaineer is undoubtedly

". . . the noblest work of God,"

a thing that is pushed and hustled up peaks by Swiss peasants, and which is so wholly unable to take care of itself that it cannot be trusted to sit on a crag unroped, is as contemptible an object as may easily be imagined. A man should never knowingly and deliberately thrust himself into places where he is hopelessly mastered and dominated by his environment. He who does this is regarded by his guides as a sort of "vache au lait," a convenient source of tariffs and Trinkgeld; a butt for small jokes and witticisms; an object to smear with grease, to decorate with masks and veils, and to button up in strange, chain-clad gaiters; a thing to be wound up with wine and brandy, and which must never be lost sight of till safely handed over to the landlord of an inn. It is difficult to apprehend how men, who in other departments of life are not wanting in a sufficient sense of their own personal dignity, should consent to be treated in this way. It is not, even, as if it were the only form of mountain expedition open to them. Work within the powers of the least competent is abundant in every Alpine valley, much of it surrounded by the noblest scenery both of ice and now. The art of mountaineering consists in being able to climb easily and securely, in being able to relate one's skill to the difficulties of the slopes above and around, and it may, to some extent, be practised and enjoyed, consistently with reasonable safety and self-respect, by every man, no matter how slight his natural aptitude and training may be. It is merely necessary that he should recognise the limits so imposed.

High proficiency in the sport is only attainable when a natural aptitude is combined with long years of practice, and not without some, perhaps much, danger to life and limb. Happily, the faithful climber usually acquires this skill at an age when the responsibilities of life have not yet laid firm hold upon him, and when he may fairly claim some latitude in matters of this sort. On the other hand he gains a knowledge of himself, a love of all that is most beautiful in nature, and an outlet such as no other sport affords for the stirring energies of youth; gains for which no price is, perhaps, too high. It is true the great ridges sometimes demand their sacrifice, but the mountaineer would hardly forego his worship though he knew himself to be the destined victim. But happily to most of us the great brown slabs bending over into immeasurable space, the lines and curves of the wind-moulded cornice, the delicate undulations of the fissured snow, are old and trusted friends, ever luring us to health and fun and laughter, and enabling us to bid a sturdy defiance to all the ills that time and life oppose.

—1895

Notes

1. "In den Hochalpen," pp. 269, 270.
2. "Above the Snow Line," pp. 49, 50.
3. *Alpine Journal*, vol. ii, p. 342 *et seq*.
4. "Hours of Exercise in the Alps," pp. 204, 215.
5. Happily on each of these occasions another party was within hail, and by its assistance the entombed climber's rescue was effected.

Robert Dunn

from *The Shameless Diary of an Explorer*

A Harvard graduate from a genteel New England family, Robert Dunn (1877–1955) distinguished himself as an outdoor adventurer, writer, and newspaper reporter much like his friend Jack London. His journeys and military service during both World Wars took him to the Aleutian Islands, Alaska, Siberia, and Constantinople. He worked with editor Lincoln Steffens, who was instrumental in getting Dunn a spot on arctic explorer Frederick Cook's expedition to Mt. McKinley in Alaska, which remained unclimbed until Hudson Stuck's successful climb (see the selection from Hudson in this volume). In a sometimes uncompromising style, in which no one, including himself, escapes close critical scrutiny, Dunn detailed the physical and psychological challenges of Alaska's back country at the turn of the twentieth century. The most persistent foe of the expedition were the bloodthirsty mosquitoes that almost stripped the flesh from their pack horses. Dunn wrote several autobiographical novels about his travel adventures and war correspondence, and died at his birthplace in Newport, Rhode Island, in 1955.

CHAPTER XVI

WHAT IS COURAGE?

August 29.—To-day we did not quite wait for the sun, and by ten o'clock were discarding the superfluities which your expert in "traveling light" always lugs to the very highest point to throw away. I left my binoculars (the Professor wanted me to quit my camera. Not I, as I think all his films are over-exposed) and the others abandoned enough wool underwear for a winter camp. "We need to concentrate on food, not clothing," announced the Professor, throwing away a sweater; and we started to break trail in the blazing, non-thawing sun, through eight inches of soft snow, toward the foot of this great spur of bergschrunds jutting from below the steep southwestern shoulder of McKinley.

The Professor says he is sure that its steepness must relax on its far, or eastern side, hidden from us by the spur. This seems plausible, and gives me hope, even considering how height and distance in this cold, dustless air, where 6,000 feet look like 60, and a doorstep may be a half-mile cliff, knock imagination into a cocked hat. Of course we should have reconnoitered the slope, but how could we, with winter coming on, and our one sack of beans and one of flour five hundred miles from the coast? We have provisions for ten days, half of which was to be cached at to-night's camp, which was to

Robert Dunn, *The Shameless Diary of an Explorer: A Story of Failure on Mt. McKinley* (New York: The Outing Publishing Company, 1907).

be just below the steep place, at 10,000 feet, the Professor was certain; to serve as our base for the final attack and as a refuge in case we are driven back. Idle dreamer! You see, his programme is to reach the summit in about five days, returning in two or three.

The slope began easily, up the rough path of an old avalanche, but the packs were the sort that make you wonder how you can stagger on another ten minutes. We broke trail in turn; fifty paces each, then a rest, then, as we got used, seventy-five paces, and in an hour or so, a hundred. No one had spoken. Fred's "pass" to the Sushitna still gaped into blue sky, and the sheer 1,000 feet we'd risen above Peters seemed 200. Resting, we stamped a foot-hold in the névé, turned our backs skittishly to the slope, leaning against it on our packs; and once, doing so, came our first warning. Simon lost balance, and began to slip, slip, slip, as Fred caught him, and maneuvered him to safety, *i.e.*, saved his life. We all looked at each other and laughed, even Simon, all wiping the sweat from our burning faces with our arms; looked at our black-goggled eyes, which transform each fellow creature into a stranger; Fred a severe person, the Professor a funny big man, and Simon an aged clown.

Furtively, imperceptibly, the steepness had stolen a march on us. Névé ridges and humps of avalanche gave the only footing. As one line of foot-holds gave out, we had to sidle dexterously to another. In time the slides had scattered none at all. The steeper slope was swept clear and hard. Steps had to be cut.

Fred was ahead. He cut, cut, cut, with the cross-headed axe, slowly; laboriously balanced on one leg, trying the hole in the hard névé with the other foot; a new game for him, for us all; hole after hole, foot after foot. The slope braced upward into the bulging, overhanging walls of a huge bergschrund suspended over our abyss; higher, more of them hung, ending in two gigantic balconies, foreshortened against the sky. At last we could cut either to the right (southeast) toward the rocks which Fred had wanted to climb at the end of the spur (we've been going up its face), or to the left (northeast). We agreed, with no discussion, on the left.

We have only three ice-axes. Never giving them a thought this morning, all were gobbled up when we started, and I was left with the long willow tent-pole. It was never meant to balance you in half-cut steps that may or may not hold your toe, nor to clean out the granular stuff doused into one by Simon's laboriously lifted, stocking-stuffed hind leg. At the first shifts in cutting, no one wanted to trade an axe for the pole so I could cut. When at last I palmed it off on Simon, I wasn't too dexterous with the iron on the growing steepness. Soon they complained that I cut too far apart.

Yet we had risen. At last! A mountain looming through Fred's pass. "Foraker," said the Professor, though so small, distant, and snowless. It was two o'clock, the barometer only in the eight thousands, and it seemed you could spit into the tromped circle of last night's camp, and its black speck of superfluities. Some one said "Lunch," and when each had caught up, turned and staggered into his foot-shelf, I produced one of the red cheeses. The Professor cut it, and each mouth spit out its first bite—saltier than salt salmon, it is, here where water is worth its price in—oil. But

242

each cached his piece in his red bandanna, and turned to pemmican, which pleased Fred, as the chunk in use is wrapped in a towel in his pack.

The Professor sighed—and led on. Now we cut steps in regular turn, the leader waiting after a hundred steps or so till the others had filed past, the man behind him cutting, as he fell to the rear, and so on, etc. Slowly we were forced to the sheer west edge, under the upper balconies. Should we try the narrow shelves that might run along its brow, or still zigzag up the steepening slope among the bergschrunds?—which last was chosen to be done, as nervelessly and carelessly as before. Fred settled it by saying, as he pointed to the right, "Hadn't we better take that swag?" as if we were driving horses on the tundra. He can't swallow, nor can I, these technical terms of alpining; a rucksack we call a backpack; sérac, he daren't pronounce, it's "that steep place," and a bergschrund is "them overhanging humps."

The swag started all right, then led straight up over the back of a big hump. The Professor led, cutting very slowly, shouting back how to avoid a hidden crevasse. Looking downward, the sheerness appeared poisonous to me, and I tried to think that I'd stick, in falling, on the fractional level just below, where loose masses of snow from the last slide from this very place still hung.

As the steps changed from a stairway to a step-ladder, the other three betrayed no excitement, no uneasiness. Neither did I at first, but I felt both; not dizziness, not vertigo, but simply the lightning, kaleidoscopic force of imagination, looking down the sheer two thousand feet, from where we clung by our toes, resistlessly told over how it would feel, how long it would last, what the climax in sensation would be, were I to fall. As hour succeeded hour, I lived each minute only to make the false step, cursing inwardly, but only at what then would be said by our civilized friends, their pitiful comments on this party, that with no alpine experience just butted blindly in to the highest mountain on the continent. Thought of that angered me. Cold feet, you say? Perhaps. But the personal test is yet to come. Courage is only a matter of self-control, anyway—and the tyranny of imagination. . . .

Climbing McKinley with a tent-pole! Sometimes I boiled in those dizzy, anxious places that I had put myself in such a position with such men. My blind neglect of the Professor's silence on alpining now reproaches in another way. It's not bringing out his lack of staying power, as I thought, but his foolhardiness. Yet I must reap my own sowing. Once I asked if it wasn't customary to rope on such steep slopes, but no one but Fred answered, and he, "Y'aint goin' to ketch me tied up to no one. A man don't want to take chances with any one but himself, haulin' him down from these places." And right he is. . . .

One requisite of the explorer—besides aversion to soap and water—is insensitiveness. I understand now why their stories are so dry. They can't see, they can't feel; they couldn't do these stunts if they did. But the sensitive ones can't have their cake and eat it, too. They feel, but they can't *do*. As for me, is the doing of a thing to be no longer its end, as was in the old adventurous days? The telling of it the end instead? So I can't help admiring Simon and the Professor and their callousness, which is not

243

bravery, not self-control. Their brains do not burn, horrifying the present with visions of the supreme moments of life. But it's better so. Where would we be, if there was another fool like me along? . . .

The Professor has been a real companion the last two days; intelligent and sympathetic. Probably he realizes that this is the final effort, and is making a grand play to come up to scratch. At any rate, to-night I'm convinced that he's really trying for all he's worth to get up McKinley; that this is the actual bluff I promised myself to make on the mountain. Even if we fail, the worst suffering will be over—the days following the first repulse—and then, Oh! how I shall feel for him, perhaps an undeserved pity, but it will turn all the tables of my regard. I shan't be able to help that. We are trying, damnably trying. . . . And all my righteous disgust and revulsion of race toward Simon have vanished. To-day we exchanged the brotherhood that civilized people do *not* fool themselves into believing is always the heroism of explorers in a tight place. I know it's hollow and meaningless; take away the danger, and all will be as before. But it's heroic while it lasts. And I've often felt I'd die for the semblance of such a thing in this life. . . . Forward and back, into the future and past, you can't see very clearly in these places. The brain works too fast, and your capacity to bear cold and hunger appals. . . .

I am morbid? Perhaps—but this is no place for cold sanity, for me, at least; though Fred and I on reaching this camp had a boxing-match—for warmth.

It was five o'clock and we were right under those balconies of the sky. One way led up, straight over the shoulder of a bergschrund, jutting like a gargoyle from a skyscraper. We climbed it; there seemed no lead further. The Professor said, "Camp anyhow, and we'll see."

We have camped, and on not ten square feet of primeval level. We've dug into the névé wall to get enough flatness to spike the tent, and contorted ourselves to place within again, I still on the windy side. And the wind is rising from the darkening white ridges and each unplanetary depth. The silk overhead shivers like cobweb, and I jam down my head and cover up as I can in the soft snow, it steals through and stabs. Even in our warmth we're numb, tired, disappointed. We have come only half as high as the Professor hoped; we are only halfway to the top of the great snow spur, to the base of the doubtful rocks, to the camp for the final climb where the cache is to be made. So this brood of the Professor's chickens does hatch out dead.

"Tea or pea soup?" some one has just laughed. That will be the tag by which we will recall and laugh over this adventure. Simon has just remarked this. Thus, you see, self-consciousness is inseparable even from this sort of heroism. Perhaps after all it were best for us to slide off this gargoyle quietly as we sleep—as it keeps haunting me we shall—or better, that this ugly white beak shall fall with us senselessly in the night. I have just touched on the possibility of this, aloud, and Simon remonstrated, adding, "We don't want to speak of such things, even if we feel them!" What sickening insincerity, as if that could make the snow any firmer!—to choke the dizzy sense of danger, which is the very thing that's brought us here—

244

as if in this quivering suspension over the vast polar world, it were not criminal to be acting a part. . . .

Fred watches Simon fussing with the stove, much annoyed. The Professor is scribbling in his notebook—inches, feet, and degrees I suppose. How warmly the tea went down!—with dirty chunks of the crumbled zwieback, which the Professor draws from a white bag and throws at us with a "Here's your ration, Dunn." Two cups each; first you dip it out of the pot, then when it's low enough, you pour, spilling it on the sleeping-bags. Fred has corralled the empty milk can from Simon. We can't afford to melt snow for a "squeeze." Then the pemmican—all you want. It's scraping the roof of my mouth sore. Simon is telling how to run an auto. We are all laughing now. This is all a great joke; there's something very devilish about just being here. Every one is in a bully humor, more tolerant of his fellows than ever before on the whole trip. For aren't we the only ones in all this dastardly white world? How would it pay for the only four creatures in the universe to be the least at odds? We depend on one another. And yet, perhaps our devotion is— only the warm tea. . . .

I have been outside, forgetting to undo the safety pin that holds the flap, and nearly tearing down the tent—as Fred almost just did. The finnsku do not give a sanded footing, and you slip around on the inches of the gargoyle, expecting to be floating down through mid-air, your stomach feeling inside out. . . . Not an acre of the forbidden tundra was to be seen. Through Fred's gap, which leads even west of Foraker, and circling the dead, whitish granite of the front range and its three crocodilian glaciers, sleeps a billowy floor of summer cloud, into which the sun is blazing a vermilion trail, lighting the gentle Siwashes of Bristol Bay far west, perhaps, or a slow-smoking island off the coast of Asia. That vast, glimmering floor of cloud! At last, the silvery lining for us of what may be gloom to all the world, an enchanted plane cutting the universe, soft and feathery, yet strong and bright like opal—for us and us alone; veined and rippled, dyed with threads of purple, rose, and blue, where Foraker rises pale with late sunlight, like the ramparts of a new-created heaven, blushing a moment for us alone. . . .

I can feel the death-like silence. No one is asleep, yet no one dares move, lest he tell his neighbor he's awake. A cold blue from the nether world forms with the awful twilight a sort of ring about the tent, which magnifies the texture of the silk, and rises and falls as I lift my heard from its pillow of trousers and pack. It is a sort of corrupted rainbow, or what the halo of a fallen angel might be like, I think—the colors burned and wearied out. The world below is swinging on through space quite independently of us, at least. I am not cold, but I shiver, and shiver; think and think of everything I have thought and feared to-day, and the little of it put down here. And if I doze I seem to be at the very instant of slipping off the gargoyle in the finnsku. . . .

We hang our snow-glasses on the tent-pole, knotting the strings around it, so they dangle down. They look very funny up there, motionless above me—four of them, mine the lowest.

245

CHAPTER XVII

PUTTING YOUR HOUSE IN ORDER

August 30.—Not a word as we crawled from the tent toward nine this morning, and draped the gargoyle with tarpaulins wet from underneath, and sleeping-bags wet from feet and breath. Fred and I were awake, as usual, from a small hour, shooting anxious glances at the Professor, knowing it was no use to rouse his sigh—till I remarked aloud that the sun wouldn't reach our shelf till 4 P.M., so he turned over, threw us our pemmican, Simon lit the stove, and we told our dreams.

Just an "I suppose" from Fred, starting ahead, settled our direction, straight up, a bit to the right (S.E.)—Oh, yes, steeper than anything yesterday—houses are not built with such sheer walls as that slope began with, only began. Packs were the same, numb shoulders ached the same under weight of the deadly cheeses, for what use was a depot on that snow clothes-peg? We crawled along a crack in the névé, where you had to punch holes for your frozen hands to hold you there in the crumbly stuff, and looked down a clear 3,000 feet.

Whew! Those next four hours! I had the tent-pole, of course—no one would touch it on this stretch. All yesterday's torture in fears, regrets, from this life-blighting imagination reassailed me on the quivering brink of the END. We stopped, staggered with set faces, crawling around each step-cutter to let him gain the rear; so slowly leaned back to rest, carefully fitting heels into toe-nicks, backing upright against our ponchos; but more often rested with face to the slope, bowing down heads flat over the abyss, to let the packs bear straight down and ease shoulders, so the nether white glare swam upside down between your legs. . . . A hundred times I concluded (and am still convinced) that I was not meant to climb mountains; a hundred times more I called myself a fool, seeing the awkward rears of Simon and the Professor; clutching the tent-pole, again and again I turned just for the delicious suffering of seeing the hateful Below spring upward, as in desperation you pound a hurt to kill yourself with pain—to make the worst seem WORSE, knowing that THIS is not the moment when I must slip, but this, the NEXT, MUST BE; with Foraker leaping like a rocket into the sky, the far, pond-spattered tundra sweeping skyward in waves, a sort of dullness before the snow chokes off ALL . . .

And yet time passed like lightning. I could not believe the man who said that it was 2:20 P.M. The Professor was in the lead. It was my turn to cut, but he did not seem inclined to take the tent-pole and give me the axe. I offered and offered the pole, but couldn't tell if he withheld the axe because he thought I'd rather stay behind, or didn't want to give it up. I was content enough behind, but I felt he thought that he was sort of sacrificing himself to me. "It's all ice here. Look out," he would say calmly between most deliberate steps, and stopping to hack a little deeper. "Are they too far apart?"—just the things that I should say ahead there, *but I was not saying them;* that made me feel guilty; words of big consolation; I admired him mightily. Fred and Simon never spoke, except at rests, and then horrible little commonplaces.

Everything was ice, not an inch of névé. It seemed to take ten minutes to cut each step, which then held one toe, or one inch of a mushy, in-trod boot-sole. Nothing for mittened hands to grip. I asked Fred what he thought of climbing with the tent-pole. "Yer couldn't make me use it on these ice places," he said. And Simon—think of it— said, "The man with the tent-pole oughtn't to have to cut steps at all." But we kept on as before. "It's getting a little leveler," said the Professor. It was. And then I would ply him with questions about that leveling, laughingly fishing for more assurances. "Rocks ahead, the edge of a ridge, something, see them," he said. So there were. "Thank you, thank you," I said, as if that were all the Professor's doing. "God! I admire the way you take this slope," I'd exclaim. And by heaven, with all these mean pages behind, I still do.

We could dig a seat now, on the corniced brow of Fred's rock ridge, 1,000 feet sheer down, then down 1,500 of black porcupine-like spires. Lunch? No, no one was hungry. As usual we asked for the barometer. As usual, the Professor said, "It can't have responded yet," drawing it from his belt. It was not quite 10,000 feet.

I led at last with Simon's axe, straight up toward the objective rock slope (N.W.). We were above the balconies over last night's camp. Soon the snow softened to let you step sometimes without cutting, then again all was steep as ever. On the east, a huge ridge paralleled ours, depressed in the middle with a squarish gap, through which a dark, greenish line wavered in the sunlit haze—low peaks of the Sushitna valley flecking the horizon. So we could see on the great range's other side. Then toward Foraker, through that gap, gathering all the southern ridges about the final bend in Peters, and yet beyond all, rose and rose a turret-like summit, smooth, white, specked with huge bergschrunds, to a terrifying height. "There's a high mountain[1] over there," I shouted, "just appearing. You can't see it yet. A new one!" "Yes sir, yes," said Fred, catching up, and we sat down to gaze and gnaw pemmican.

In half an hour we stood here on the narrow knife of the spur-top, facing failure. Ahead, the zenith suddenly petrified into a big, pinkish-yellow strip of rock, offending the sight as a thunder-clap might have deafened. The Professor dropped his pack and ran on, mumbling an order to camp at the first flat spot, dashing through the deep snow toward our coveted ridge, now so black and puny. I saw it was hopeless.

The yellow strip shot downward, between ours and the Sushitna ridge; down, down, like a studded bronze door, straight into the reversed head of Peters—three thousand feet down, three thousand feet above; a double door, for a straight gorge cut it in twain, a split not glacier-made, but as if this apex of the continent were cracked like an old plate. Slides roared, the whole swam in snow-mist, and two turret-like summits far and high to the east, grew gold in the late light.

Here, where the black ridge leading to the top of the pink cliffs should have flattened, all was absolutely sheer, and a hanging glacier, bearded and dripping with bergschrunds, filled the angle between. . . . To-morrow? Here in the tent, not a word has been said. I wonder, has any one admitted to himself that we're checkmated, or

247

would, if he realized it? How sure is the Professor of spending a night on the summit? Looks like another brood of dead chickens. . . .

The old cooking, squirming, changing-sock game is on. I am digging névé to melt—"finest imported névé," we laughingly call it—from a snow hole at my head, where the kerosene has not spilt to flavor it. Fred glum. Simon at the stove. The barometer has adjusted itself, but only to 10,800 feet. . . .

The Professor has just come in from a long meditation outside. "Never, never," he says, "have I seen anything so beautiful." That from him! The Spirit of the North, like Moses, has struck water from the rock. But it's so. I've seen it. No cloud-floor hides the forbidden tundra, no mist softens the skeleton angles of these polar alps; only a wan red haze confuses the deeps of the universe, warning that they, and we, and life at last, is of another world. The tundra dazes; its million lakes, lifted by refraction mid-high on the front range, are shapeless, liquid disks ablaze; and the crazy curves of their shores far below, which may be the dark and sleepless land—no eagle could tell—are walled by pillars of smoky violet, verily from against the sea. . . .

Last night I tried to hide my fear with sophistry. Now to be honest, I dread the descent more than the climb. I believe that there's too much ahead in living to have it all cut suddenly off against your will in a fool business; and if it must be, there's no use shivering about it. If I had any beliefs, I'd put my house in order. Where this sort of thing leads a man, God only knows. Anyhow, we're not on a shelf that may break off. Good night. Pleasant dreams, and hear me whine in my sleep to the Professor— if I sleep.

———

August 31.—Alone in the tent. It's about noon, and the sun is blinding over the yellow wall. No one stirred till late. After breakfast, orders were given not to pack up. Fred and the Professor walked toward the cliffs. . . . I can see them now, sitting on a cornice where the ridge narrows. They are no longer staring at the yellow wall.

Simon and I have been talking. This is how I did put my house in order: "Simon," I said, "I want to apologize to you for everything unkind or offensive that I've done or said to you on this whole trip." He laughed, looked away, and said, "Oh, that's all right." Tears came to my eyes. Then I felt ashamed, then angry. Then we talked as if we'd been brought up together; he of dangers of ships in the polar sea, I of old days in Alaska. I said that I was certain we could get no further. He changed the subject.

Fred and the Professor have just returned. Neither spoke till right near the tent, and looks lie through snow-glasses. "Make tea, and put a whole can of milk into it," said the Professor. While taking in the bags and tarpaulins from the sun, I heard Fred say, "It ain't that we can't find a way that's possible, takin' chances. There ain't *no* way. . . . We thought it might be managed on that hangin' glacier first." Simon burst out in surprise. "Professor-r-r, you're not going to give it up, are you?" and began pointing to ridges and glaciers right and left, saying that of course we must go down and then up by them. The Professor tried to reason with him. Simon seemed strain-

248

ing points, but I was shamefacedly admiring his determination, when Fred came into the tent, and said, "A holler like that makes me sick." Is it a holler? I guess it is, which makes me feel smaller than ever. It doesn't matter. We're going to start down. . . . Something besides courage and determination is needed to climb a mountain like this. Forgive me, if I call it intelligence. . . .

Simon pretended that he wanted to lug down the twenty-pound tin of pemmican, but we kicked it off the ridge, and started descending on the run. How I got over the ice above Fred's rocks, don't ask. I've heard of persons sweating blood, and red stuff kept dripping from my forehead, as step by step, face outward into the dancing gulf, we tottered over the ice ladder of two days' cutting. I talked incessantly to the Professor of the various sorts of courage; how easy it had been for me to stand on the crater-edge of Mount Pelee, just after St. Pierre had been destroyed, because life or death there *was not in my own hands*, as here; and so new problems bothered me about cowardice and responsibility, which I've not solved yet. Half way down, the Professor insisted on my taking his axe for the tent-pole, for which I put him forever on Olympus, between Leonidas and Brutus. Thus at last we strung along Peters, each stopping dazedly in his tracks now and then to gaze back and upward. Now at the Professor's and my lone camp of the week ago, we are in our eiderdown, on the ice just above the sĕrac, in the messy disorder that it seems we've been living in forever.

—1907

Note

1. Mt. Hunter, about 15,000 feet.

Filippo de Filippi, Duke of Abruzzi

Ruwenzori

Luigi Amedeo Giuseppe Maria Ferdinando Francesco, Duke of Abruzzi (1873–1933), led a number of large expeditions to the world's unexplored mountain ranges, including Mt. St. Elias in Alaska (making the first ascent), the Karakoram, and the Ruwenzori (or "Mountains of the Moon") on the border between Uganda and the Congo. First mentioned in Ptolemy's Geography, the Ruwenzori rise over 16,000 feet above sea level and the duke was the first to explore this region extensively while making astronomical, geodetic, and sociological observations. In 1899 he made a notable attempt at reaching the North Pole. The account of the Ruwenzori expedition, illustrated with Vittorio Sella's stunning photographic prints reminiscent of Ansel Adams, provides a gold mine of information on colonial Africa at the turn of the century. In this excerpt, Filippi describes the climbs in the Bujongolo region, including Mt. Stanley and Sella Peak. A mountain leopard stalked the party the entire time; on the final day the cook laid a trap for the animal and shot it dead in an ambush.

FURTHER ASCENTS ON MTS. STANLEY, LUIGI DI SAVOIA, AND BAKER. WORK AT BUJONGOLO.

THREE MORE ASCENTS OF THE ALEXANDRA PEAK—ASCENT OF MOEBIUS PEAK—CROSSING OF THE CENTRAL COL OF MT. STANLEY—A WEEK OF BAD WEATHER ON THE FRESHFIELD PASS—ASCENT OF THE EDWARD PEAK BY THE SOUTH RIDGE—ASCENT OF THE SELLA PEAK—WORK AT BUJONGOLO—PREPARATION OF A BASE LINE—H.R.H. RETURNS TO THE EDWARD PEAK—ASCENT OF THE CAGNI PEAK—PANORAMA TAKEN FROM THE EDWARD PEAK—ASCENT OF PEAKS WOLLASTON AND MOORE—THE DEATH OF THE LEOPARD—GENERAL PLAN OF RETURN.

The history of an expedition divided into groups with distinct special aims, and busy simultaneously with their several labours in different places, is necessarily disconnected, and must now and again go back to take up another thread, and so follow the course of each separate section individually.

We must therefore beg the reader to return to the 22nd of June, when the Duke left Camp IV on the Scott Elliot Pass to descent into the Bujuku Valley and penetrate to the northern mountains. At this date Commander Cagni and Dr. Cavalli, and the guide Brocherel, were ascending the Alexandra Peak in a dense fog. During the three

Filippo de Filippi, *Ruwenzori: An Account of the Expedition of H. R. H. Prince Luigi Amedeo of Savoy* (New York: E.P. Dutton, 1908).

hours they spent on the summit they had a few glimpses of clear sky and were able to discern the neighbouring Margherita Peak and to repeat certain compass observations of the surrounding mountains. On their way back they had to wade through soft snow to the knee.

Vittorio Sella had left at daybreak with his photographic equipment and succeeded in getting a few views of the peaks from the ridges around the camp, while Roccati was collecting geological data and mineralogical specimens.

During the 23rd and the 24th the same storm which had rendered useless the Duke's first ascent to Vittorio Emanuele Peak and had kept him a prisoner in Camp V for two whole days, prevented Vittorio Sella and Roccati from accomplishing any sort of work outside of the tent.

As to Cagni, he was in a hurry to get back to Bujongolo as soon as might be, in order to lose no time in starting his magnetic observations and in calculating the formation of a base line, which was necessary to complete the triangulation. He left Camp IV on the 23rd with Dr. Cavalli, and the very same evening crossed the Freshfield Pass, and reached Bujongolo under pouring rain. He left deposits of rations along the way for the use of those who had remained behind. Dr. Cavalli remained at Camp III, at the foot of the western slope of Mt. Baker, to collect botanical specimens, and only reached Bujongolo on the following day, also in a completely soaked condition.

He found Cagni busy with all sorts of occupations. He had been working at organization, paying porters, etc., and was now engaged in sending off small parties of natives to provide the Duke's party with rations in the far valleys to the west of Mt. Speke. Several Bakonjo had bruised their feet and stood in need of the doctor's care. Profiting by the absence of the greater part of the tents, they proceeded with the work of improving the camp, enlarging the platforms already existing and forming new ones, filling up holes, moving blocks of rock and cutting down trees to increase the level space at their disposal.

The fearful weather prevented them from taking any observations. During a whole week Commander Cagni was not able to see the sun for a single continuous hour. The rainfall was slight but almost incessant, and the fog was so dense as to make it impossible to see the further side of the valley.

In spite of all this, Commander Cagni was able to take a few astronomical observations during fugitive moments of clear weather on the 25th, 27th, and 28th of June.

On the 25th, Vittorio Sella, taking advantage of a slight improvement in the weather, started from Camp IV with Roccati, Brocherel, and Botta and accomplished the ascent of the Moebius Peak, the only one of Mt. Stanley which had not yet been ascended. He then made a short excursion on the serpentine rocks of the western slopes, crossing the ridge after demolishing the great snowy cornice with the ice-axes. Here they had a view of two good-sized lakes in the valley to the west. They came back to camp under a heavy snowfall, but the day had not been wasted.

He set forth again on the following morning, by daybreak, with Brocherel and Botta. From the ice plain they saw the Duke on the summit of the Vittorio Emanuele Peak.

251

They took photographs between one drift of mist and another, and in due time reached the summit of Alexandra Peak. The snow began to fall again as they returned to camp.

The 27th was an even more successful day for Vittorio Sella, who, accompanied by Roccati, first re-ascended Alexandra Peak, which was thus climbed for the fifth time, then returned to the Stanley plateau, and with Brocherel and Botta crossed the col between Alexandra and Moebius Peaks, and went about 1,300 feet down the broken western glacier. From a rocky spur projecting between the glaciers which descend from Moebius Peak and those which descend from Alexandra Peak he was able to take several photographs of the western slopes, thus getting a complete series of views of Mt. Stanley from every side.[1]

Thence he re-ascended to the ridge and to the plateau, and returned with Roccati to the camp.

On the following day, in a storm of snow and hail, they struck camp with the assistance of the porters newly arrived from Bujongolo, and descended to the lakes to the west of Mt. Baker. On the 29th they again set up their tent on the Freshfield Pass. On the very same day the photographic camera was planted high on the south ridge of the Edward Peak, near to the edge of the glacier. After three hours of vain waiting under rain and sleet, they finally came down to the tent, leaving the camera where it stood. The whole of the following day was spent upon the ridge, crouching under the snowfall close to the camera. Even on the pass so much snow had fallen that it had brought down the tent. The firewood was soaked through and through, and in spite of copious libations of petroleum it was extremely difficult to kindle.

By the 1st of July, Roccati had finished his collection of minerals and rocks around this pass and the neighbouring glaciers. He therefore descended to Bujongolo, leaving Vittorio Sella alone with Brocherel and Botta, obstinately determined not to give up the struggle. In the afternoon the Duke also crossed the pass, returning from the far distant Mt. Emin and proceeding directly to Bujongolo.

On the following morning, in most unpromising weather, Vittorio Sella, with the two guides, climbed the Edward Peak directly from the col by the southern ridge. He was able to take an occasional photograph and an incomplete panorama. On the way down he was overtaken by a violent recrudescence of the storm, which lasted the whole of the next day with alternate snow and hail.

The spectacle presented by storms at that altitude (above 14,000 feet) is surpassingly grand. Heavy cumulus clouds hang over the Semliki River, which winds far off in the valley like a streak of silver. Huge bodies of whirling vapours rise from the eastern and western valleys and strike one another with an incessant explosion of lightning and thunder, dissolving only to be replaced by fresh supplies from below.

Often of an evening after a day of fog, rain, snow and hail, the sky clears up. Through the moist atmosphere, as transparent as glass, the sinking sun appears like a vast globe of fire, suffusing the valleys, glaciers and snows to the westward with vivid flame colour.

On the morning of the 4th of July, Vittorio Sella with his two companions again left the tent to climb to the central peak of Mount Luigi di Savoia which now bears his name. Crossing the head of the valley to the west of the Freshfield Pass he reached a depression of the ridge. It was extremely difficult to find the way in the mist. Numerous aiguilles of rock obliged them to cross a steep névé to the south of the ridge and then to return to the north side under the summit, which they reached by a rocky gully. The Sella Peak, 15,286 feet, is rocky and dotted with numerous fulgurites. The edges of the slabs are here and there perforated to a depth of some inches and look as if they were worm-eaten. They spent several hours upon the summit without the chance of taking a single photograph. They were scarcely able, during a momentary clearing of the mist, to distinguish the Weismann Peak to the south-west at the end of a long snowy ridge. On their return they descended straight to the bottom of the valley, which was full of watery and muddy spots, with the usual vegetation of senecio, and reached the tent after nightfall with fine moonlight.

Vittorio Sella finally rejoined the rest of the expedition at Bujongolo on the 5th of July, after a whole week spent upon the Freshfield Pass in fruitless expeditions up the ridges, and hours and hours of waiting beside his camera in the storms. For all his tenacity and energy he had not succeeded in getting a complete panorama from the Edward Peak as he had proposed to do.

The party at Bujongolo had not meantime remained idle. Commander Cagni had vainly attempted to take magnetic observations, but was prevented by the abundance of minerals containing iron in the rocks around Bujongolo. This influence was so considerable that it could be felt even when the inclinometer was placed at a height of some yards above the earth upon a wooden frame-work constructed for the purpose.

The greatest difficulty, however, was in finding a stretch of ground level enough and wide enough to allow of measuring a base line whose extremities were to be connected with two of the peaks forming a part of the network of angles measured by the Duke from the different mountains which he ascended.

There was a level place some distance back, above the cliff, at the foot of which stood the Camp of Bujongolo. But from this level space they could only see the Edward and Cagni Peaks which had not been connected with the others. Another place higher up on the path leading to the Freshfield Pass, which the rains and the going to and fro of the porters had now reduced to the condition of a ditch full of mud, offered no better opportunities. The Duke and Cagni became convinced of this after spending a whole day there in the rain.

They accordingly planned to prepare a base line on the first-mentioned level behind Bujongolo. The Duke was then to re-ascend the Edward Peak, while Cagni was to climb the mountain which bears his name, and from these two they were to measure the angles of the other peaks. Everything now depended upon the good luck of getting a few hours of clear weather upon these two summits.

Meantime, on the 2nd of July, the Duke made a recognizance in the valley which runs between Mts. Baker and Cagni and comes out opposite Bujongolo. This valley he found to be barred by great steep slabs of rock, extremely slippery and certainly impassable for the native porters. The weather continued bad. Mt. Baker was completely covered with fresh snow. In the valley the rain had turned the whole ground into one mass of deep mud. On the 4th of July, between the showers, they succeeded, by taking advantage of every break in the fog, in tracing the base line upon the level tract above the camp, which consisted of a carpet of moss upon a muddy soil, dotted with senecios dripping with rain. In order to mount the theodolite at the extremities of the base line, they were obliged to build real foundations, sinking tree trunks into the mud more than six feet down to serve as piles.

Hardly had they taken these preparatory measures before the weather began to improve. On the 5th of July, on a perfectly clear and very cold morning, the Duke again went up to the Freshfield Pass. Roccati, who had accompanied him so far, here re-descended to Bujongolo with Sella, while H.R.H. proceeded directly to the Edward Peak, following the southern crest along which Sella had made the ascent three days before. The mists returned before he reached the summit. It was only late in the afternoon that he was able to take a few angles in a brief moment of clear sky.

The Duke returned to the camp at nightfall. On the 6th of July the weather was again completely overcast and no work was possible, but on the 7th he returned early in the morning to the summit and was able to complete all the measurements.

On the following morning he ascended the Stairs Peak of Mt. Luigi di Savoia before returning to Bujongolo.

Commander Cagni in the meantime had left Bujongolo on the 6th with Joseph Petigax, Brocherel and a few natives to ascend the rocky peak to the north of the camp, which was to be connected on one hand with one extremity of the base line, and on the other with the net of angles of the different peaks.

The Cagni Peak, as may be seen upon the map, rises at the southern extremity of a buttress which runs between Mt. Baker and the South Portal Peak, flanked by two little valleys containing small lakes and tributary streams of the Mobuku.

Wishing to avoid the slabs of rock which had prevented the Duke in his recognizance of the 2nd of July from entering the valley to the west of the peak, and likewise to avoid crossing the Mobuku Valley below Bujongolo in the deep mire and through the dense heath forest, Cagni had decided to go up the slopes of Mt. Baker and thence to traverse under Wollaston and Moore Peaks, towards the Cagni Peak.

Accordingly the party turned its steps first towards Grauer's Camp near to the Moore Glacier, and thence skirted the eastern slopes of Mt. Baker, intending to reach the col to the east of the Moore Peak. But their eternal enemy the fog obliged them to stop on the steep slope in the snow, stones and mud.

On the following day it became plain that it was impossible to pursue this route. It was necessary to go down to the narrow gorge between Wollaston Peak and Mt. Cagni. This was no easy task, and in more places than one they were obliged to let down the loads by a rope, and even to let down the porters as if they were parcels. Once at the foot of the south-west side of the Cagni Peak, which was quite perpendicular to the very bottom of the little valley, they ascended this latter as far as its head, through a dense wood of heath, and set up their tents immediately under the col.

From this point, on July 8th, they followed the spur which bears the Cagni Peak at its end along its whole length from north to south, keeping upon its western slope. In this way they reached the terminal cone, where they left their equipment, and after a short climb in the mist, about 3:30 P.M. they reached a small platform, which they took for the summit. The camp theodolite was at once set up upon its tripod. Suddenly through the mist they perceived to the south the real peak, which the refraction of the mist caused them to see as if at a very great height over their heads. The theodolite was immediately taken down, they descended from the little point which they had reached, and after a real Alpine climb up a very narrow ridge over a difficult bit of *arête*, about 12 feet high with insufficient handholds, and skirting round rocky *gendarmes* on their smooth, steep sides, they reached the real summit about six in the evening.

The mist had entirely disappeared, but nightfall was very near. Commander Cagni had scarcely time to take observations of all the peaks with the compass. They came down in the dark.

On the following morning by sunrise, the weather being perfectly clear, Cagni was once more on the summit, and was able to take measurements of all the angles with the theodolite and with the compass. They set up a stone man, and by eight o'clock they were preparing to return when the first mists began to rise. They came back by the same way, along the spur to the north of the peak and then down into the little valley to the west of it, which they now descended to the point where it opens into the Mobuku Valley. Here the mist, which had become dense, was added to all the other difficulties of crossing the tangled forest, which was very similar to the one above Kichuchu. They reached Bujongolo the same evening.

Sella was there alone, waiting for Cagni's Alpine tent to set forth upon a new photographic expedition. The Duke had gone up to Camp I upon Mt. Baker that very day. From this point on the following day, July 10th, through a gully to the east and then along the south ridge, he reached the Wollaston Peak, 15,286 feet, which had not as yet been ascended by any member of the expedition. The rocks were covered with ice. The weather was clear, and he was able to take observations for two whole hours. Next, following the high ridge, he traversed to the Moore Peak, whence he came down along the ridge which had already been climbed by Vittorio Sella, to the Grauer Col, and so back to Bujongolo.

Vittorio Sella had set forth in the morning with Botta and a few natives, and had returned to the Freshfield Pass. He did not return again to Bujongolo. On the 11th of July he was again upon the Edward Peak at sunrise, and was at last enabled to take the complete panorama of the chain for which he had once waited a whole week in vain on the Freshfield Pass. On the way back he paid a visit to the little knob somewhat lower down, which had been climbed twice by Wollaston, whose card he now found with the following inscriptions: "A. F. R. Wollaston, R. B. Woosnam, 17th February, 1906. Height by aneroid 16,050 feet."

"A. F. R. Wollaston (Alpine Club), R. B. Woosnam, D. Carruthers of the British Museum Expedition to Ruwenzori. Five hours from Bujongolo. Water boil. 183.6; temp of air 39.7; aneroid 16,150 feet, 3rd April, 1906."

On the 12th of July, the weather remaining fair, Sella again ascended the Stairs Peak, where he took some good photographs.

In the meantime Commander Cagni had done two days' work in finishing the mensuration of the base line and connecting it with Edward and Cagni Peaks, and was able to complete an occultation, fixing the longitude and the latitude of one of its extremities.

In order to follow the intense activity of all the different members of the expedition occupied in such various ways and yet directed to one common aim, our story has necessarily become little more than a simple list of facts and of dates.

After the return of the expedition to Bujongolo, the leopard had resumed his daring visits to the camp, killing sheep and coming close to the fires among the native porters to steal the meat. Everyone was too busy to heed him. But the cook, Igini, with Bulli, planned an ambush with two rifles and a piece of meat. One night the splendid animal fell into this trap and was killed on the spot with two balls through its skull.

On the 12th of July, the Prince was able to consider the work of the expedition as ended. On the 7th, Roccati, who had again returned to the Mobuku Glacier to put marks of red paint on the rocks at the limit where the ice stopped, and who had finished arranging all his collections, had already left Bujongolo with Cavalli and with a party of Bakonjo porters carrying a portion of the equipment, bound for Ibanda, the lowest camp in the Mobuku Valley.

One mountain alone remained unclaimed, namely, Mt. Gessi, and the Duke was not in a mood to leave it unattempted, all the more so as this ascent would be connected with an exploration of the Bujuku Valley as yet absolutely unknown and worth traversing in its whole length. A party of Bakonjo had started from the point where the Bujuku Valley opens into the Mobuku Valley opposite Nakitawa, and had already cut a rough track as far as the head of the Valley.

The plan was now for the Duke to descend the Bujuku Valley with Sella, while Cagni was to direct the transport of all the portion of the equipment which was till at Bujongolo down the Mobuku Valley, and was then to meet Cavalli and Roccati at Ibanda and there wait for the Duke. Thus Ibanda became the general rendezvous for the whole expedition.

—1908

Note

1. The rocky spur at the foot of the western glaciers of Mt. Stanley, which was climbed by Vittorio Sella, comes out quite clearly in Stuhlmann's plate. The photographs taken by Vittorio Sella on this occasion are those which have enabled us to identify with Mt. Stanley the mountain represented in the above-mentioned plate.

Annie Peck

from *A Search for the Apex of America*

Professor Annie Peck (1850–1935) of Smith College set the women's altitude record of about 22,000 feet in 1908 by her ascent of Huascarán in the Peruvian Andes. She was bitterly disappointed, however, that against her express orders one of her guides, Rudolf Taugwalder, climbed ahead to reach the summit first. Taugwalder later suffered amputations of his hands from frostbite. The north peak of Huascarán has been designated Cumbre Aña Peck to honor her achievements. A graduate of the University of Michigan in classics, she taught Latin at both Purdue University and Smith College. From the 1880s into the early twentieth century, Peck climbed in the Alps and the Americas, with a notable ascent of the Matterhorn in 1895. She also lectured on her exploits to audiences throughout the United States. During her climbing career, she engaged in a personal, intensely competitive battle with Fanny Workman for fame and glory among the small group of women climbers at the turn of the twentieth century. Peck wrote three other books arising from her South American climbs and travels: The South American Tour *(1913),* Industrial and Commercial South America *(1922), and* Flying over South America—20,000 Miles by Air *(1932). She continued to climb well into her eighties.*

VICTORY AT LAST!
THE FIRST ASCENT OF HUASCARÁN

A day's rest and preparations were renewed. "What, again!" they said. "*Pobre* Miss Peck! *Pobrecita!*" "do you want to go again?" they inquired. "No, indeed!" I replied. "I don't *want* to go. I *must* go!" Consultation with the guides proved them ready for another attempt, that is, after a few day's rest, Gabriel said, the time in any case being needful for preparation. Telegrams and messengers were sent to mines and to neighbouring towns to procure, if possible, heavy shoes, woollen stockings, and flannel shirts, for the two additional porters that seemed necessary; above all, for an alcohol or kerosene stove. After some delay, I procured from the neighbouring town of Caraz, a good Norwegian stove which burned kerosene with a gas flame in a manner similar to the one I had before, but a better article, probably the only one in the valley. I rejoiced indeed that my whole expedition had not been rendered abortive, through my inability to replace the cooking utensil, absolutely essential for food and drink. It was the merest chance that all my toil was not in vain. I made two more pairs of *unmentionables*, I developed films to find all that I had taken with my new camera worthless. Quickly ten days passed, for me mostly spent in labour, until again, for the sixth and happily the last time, Friday, August 28, I set out for my long desired goal.

Annie Peck, *A Search for the Apex of America* (New York: Dodd, Mead, 1911).

257

It was now far later in the year than I ever expected to climb the mountain. June I believed would be the best month, soon after the close of the wet season, when sufficient time had elapsed by thawing and freezing to bring the snow into good condition, yet not so much as to make the crevasses wide and open as in 1904. I had hoped to make the climb at least early in July. Now it was almost September, hardly a month in advance of my first visit in 1904. But fortunately the mountain was in vastly better condition than then, better even than in July, 1906. The precipitation the preceding season had been unusually great and the present dry season cold; thus the glacier this year was better covered with snow than I had ever seen it before, which was greatly to our advantage. The weather should at this time have been growing warmer; instead it was colder, although the sky was more cloudy, and for a day or two the mountain had been thickly veiled.

On my last ride to the mine, Matarao, I set out at 3:20 P.M. The Indians had arrived a little before three, so late that I had given them up. Señor Jaramillo with the horses was later still, but by fast riding and, at the end, taking a new route we arrived before six. The ride, if one were not in a hurry or tired, as was always my case, is delightful. For an hour the route follows to the town of Mancos the highway leading up the valley. There are houses here and there along the road, cultivated fields at the right down towards the river, many also at the left on the rounded slopes and hilltops up towards Huascarán; and except on this occasion, there was, in the afternoon sunlight, a varying and glorious view of that radiant majestic mountain, which, with the completion of the railroad up the valley, will annually attract thousands of visitors. The road is lined with walls of stone or adobe, there are gurgling brooks, and the air is fragrant with the perfume of many blossoms; yellow broom, blue larkspur, and white everlasting were some of the flowers I recognized.

From the paved plaza of Mancos, one turns directly east towards Huascarán, at first along a narrow paved and walled pathway, among numerous houses which gradually become more scattered. The homes for pigs and people closely resemble each other. There are fields of wheat, corn, peas, beans, and alfalfa, with grassy meadows supplying all shades of green and brown. There are peach trees, poplars, and willows, some trees that resemble the orange but are larger. The land is well tilled and supports many people. It is a beautiful country, even without the great mountain confronting us. There is a gorge below on our right, presently on the other side of a high brown bluff, in which are coal mines now useless for lack of transportation. The path is rough, sometimes with steps hewn out of rocks. The Indians we meet are badly dressed, most of them look old and bent. They have no ambition for anything beyond the absolute necessities of life.

Señor and Señora Campos, who were expecting us at the mine, were our cordial hosts as before. Both had been ill with colds but were now improving. The Señor had a particularly weak throat, which, he said, he had learned to strengthen by taking a cold bath every morning. This was unheard-of rashness on the part of a Peruvian, and I exclaimed, "What! a whole cold bath!" "Well, no," he said, "but to his waist";

even this, he agreed, was amazing to all his friends, who thought it would be his death; he assured me, however, that it had proved beneficial and I encouraged him to continue the operation, telling him that in our colder climate people indulge daily baths to advantage.

As the Indians with our baggage did not appear, cotton cloth in the piece was spread as a bed for me. Further, Señor Jaramillo supplied a heavy poncho, Señora C— a shawl, with which I managed to be comfortable, but for some reason I could not sleep. During the night the Indians arrived, with everything safe, but in the morning, as it was still cloudy on the mountains, I decided that a day's delay might be wise. There was sure to be fresh snow on the glacier, which needed a day or two of sun and nightly freezing to bring it into good condition. On departing with the horses for Yungay, Señor Jaramillo inquired when I thought we should be back. After a moment's hesitation, I replied, "Next Saturday," as we were. A heavy poncho, which had been used on my saddle on the way out, Señor J—said he would leave, so that I could have it on my return; a most fortunate accident, as without that poncho I should doubtless have come back, if at all, with the ultimate loss of my left hand.

For some unaccountable reason, possibly over-work, I was not feeling very well this morning, for an instant a little faint, which had the more inclined me to wait over a day. The hospitable Señora, inquiring what I would like for *almuerzo*, the noon meal, I replied, "*Caldo* (a soup), and boiled eggs," which I knew could be easily provided. (An extensive menu or much variety was not to be had on the mountain side.) These were supplied and in addition, beefsteak and rice, coffee and tea. Tea was served again at three, but none for me. I took a needed nap in the forenoon, and a short walk in the afternoon, looking into the houses both of an Indian and of the administrador. The indians use their houses very little except for sleeping, and storing what few goods they possess. Many things were hung up. The cooking was done outside, the sewing as well. There were no chairs. In the house of the administrador, the chairs were few and rickety. The adobe floor of the dining room, which was living room as well, was very uneven, dishes were not many, but the genuine hospitality was large.

Sunday morning, about eight o'clock, we set out for the snow line, Señor Jaramillo's poncho being added to our baggage. Though he had not left it for that purpose, I thought he would not object, and that it would help out our supply of bedding which was rather scanty. It soon appeared that we three, the Swiss guides and myself, were in better condition than before, and going by the proper route from the ridge into the gully where there was water for luncheon, we continued to the camping place which I indicated, arriving at the extraordinarily early hour of quarter past two. Thus we had ample time to set up the tent, collect firewood, make soup and tea before dark and get early to bed. Our new men, who at first seemed a trifle less willing and intelligent than the others, later proved entirely satisfactory.

Domingo and Anacreo, whom we wished to have accompany us, had been unable to do so, not yet having recovered from their arduous labours, especially on the descent; the climax of which had been the insistence of Señor Jaramillo that they on foot keep up with us on horseback on our way from the mine back to Yungay. To do this they were obliged to trot down the hill and along the road (a really cruel proceeding in their fatigued condition, though they were not then carrying the packs), merely to please their master by our all returning together. Finally upon my protest he allowed them to lag in the rear.

On Monday after an early breakfast of soup, improving in this way our last opportunity for a wood fire, at the early hour of 7:15 we entered upon the glacier, the four Indians all wearing climbing irons, as enough had been made so that each of us had a pair. The Swiss guides, however, preferred to dispense with them, and I as well, unless they should provide absolutely necessary, for after my return to Yungay, I had discovered that two toes and the whole top of my right foot had been frost-bitten, on account of one strap, which was a little short, having been drawn so tight as to impede the circulation in that foot. Gabriel also had had two of his toes frost-bitten, but not severely.

During Saturday forenoon the clouds had left the mountain so that, with two days of sunshine on the fresh snow and the nightly freezing, we found the glacier in better condition than ever before. Going straight up from our more favourable starting point, in two hours we arrived at the site of our previous first camp. After a brief halt we pushed on to our second camp, where we had luncheon. Under the excellent conditions, with four good porters, and no double work, we continued in the afternoon almost up to the site of our fourth camp. Pausing about four o'clock, well pleased with our day's work, we pitched our tent in a sheltered spot, well up in the saddle, at the foot of a more than vertically inclined snow wall.

In spite of our favourable position, the night was windy and the morning cold, but soon after eight we were on our way. Having safely negotiated the steep ascent concluded by the perpendicular bit of blue ice (which we reached by going up in zigzags farther to the right outside of the picture, then walking along the ledge to the place where Gabriel is cutting steps), we were soon near the foot of the great wall, in the midst of séracs, crevasses, caverns, and every variety of difficulties. The way we had previously taken was blocked by the disappearance of a snow bridge, but Gabriel found another route, threading this way among hollows and immense crevasses till we came to the more solid part of the wall with an angle of approximately 80° or 85°. We went up in two divisions, as we had been climbing previously, Gabriel leading one and Rudolf the other. Thankful was I to reach the top in safety and throw myself down for rest and luncheon, knowing that the remainder of the way to the top of the saddle was comparatively easy.

Yet in this easy part we had an adventure, which was the more surprising. A crevasse extending nearly all the way across the saddle was spanned by a bridge of so doubtful appearance that Rudolf who was leading went over on hands and knees. I, being in the middle of the rope and also much lighter, walked carefully across, while Rudolf was sitting on the farther slope with the rope around his ice axe. Taking a position above him in the same manner, I re-enforced his strength with mine; Lucas at

260

the end of the rope then followed, walking, as on account of his pack it would have been impossible for him to crawl.

Suddenly there was a cry. Lucas had disappeared. Of course the alpen rope was strong and our hold was good. Rudolf admitted later that my help was of real value. My wrists, it happens, are disproportionately strong. Lucas, though uncomfortable, was probably in no danger. Gabriel at the head of the second rope, exhorted the other three men to untie quickly, this more by motion than by speech, for neither of the Swiss had picked up much Spanish; he then threw down one end of the rope to Lucas, who, luckily, was the most intelligent of the Indians, and preserved his coolness. Though he had fallen head down, as is usual, he was able to right himself and tie this rope to the one about his waist. Then the men below and Rudolf and I above pulled him up to the surface, when he got out on the lower side, naturally without his pack, which, with many other articles, again contained the stove. As without this further advance was impossible, when the men had made the crossing at a point farther north, and Lucas had declined the honour, Gabriel undertook its recovery. The crevasse luckily was neither very wide nor deep, so Gabriel, at the end of the rope which was held carefully by the others, climbed down where they had crossed to a depth of thirty feet, walked along the bottom to the broken bridge, and after some minutes of suspense appeared again with the rescued baggage. Such an effort at this altitude, over 19,000 feet, was doubly severe, and Gabriel paused a few moments, leaning over with this head on his ice axe, before he was able to proceed. I, meanwhile, remaining where Rudolf and I had crossed, had improved my time by taking photographs of the crevasse. Afterwards, at the top of the very last wall, Adrian stumbled and almost fell backwards, dropping his alpenstock, which happily lodged not far down and was recovered again by Gabriel.

In fairly good season we encamped that night on the plain at the top of the saddle, in two days from the snow line, a feat which I had previously hoped with Swiss guides to be able to accomplish. The exceptionally cold day, the coldest I had experienced in my six efforts on this mountain, was followed by a high wind at night—an unpleasant contrast to our previous experience here, when all three nights had been almost windless. In the early morning, I thought it wiser to postpone our final effort till the fierce winds should abate; we should also be in better condition following a rest from two long and hard day's labour. Had I expected to make the attempt on this day I should have insisted upon an earlier start. Both guides, however, though not anxious to set out early, were in favour of going, asserting that we might find less wind higher up, if not that we could turn back. On the contrary, unless the wind died down altogether, it was more likely to be worse above, and it was against my better judgment that I yielded to their wishes.

At the late hour, for such a climb, of eight o'clock, we set forth, myself and the two guides only, as with the two Swiss the Indians would not add to the safety of the party, probably the reverse. For the cold ascent, I was wearing every stitch of clothing that I had brought:—three suits of light weight woollen underwear, two pairs of tights, canvas knickerbockers, two flannel waists, a little cardigan jacket, two sweaters, and four pairs of woollen stockings; but as most of the clothing was porous it was inadequate to keep out the wind, for which I had relied upon the eskimo suit now at the bottom of a crevasse. I had not really needed it before, nor worn it except at night. Now when I wanted it badly, it was gone. I am often asked if my progress is not impeded by the weight of so much clothing, to which I answer, No. All of the articles were light, and garments which cling closely to the body are not burdensome. I never noticed the weight at all. A skirt, on the contrary, however short and light, anything depending from the waist or shoulders, is some hindrance to movement and of noticeable weight. I had not an ounce of strength to spare for superfluities, neither do I consider that an abbreviated skirt would add to the gracefulness of my appearance, or if it did, that this, upon the mountain, would be of the slightest consequence: while in rock climbing the shortest skirt may be an added source of danger.

A woollen face and head mask, which I had purchased in La Paz, provided with a good nose piece as well as eye-holes, mouth-slit, and a rather superfluous painted mustache, protected my head, face, and neck from the wind. An extra one, which I had brought along, a rather better article except that it left the nose exposed, I offered to Gabriel, Rudolf having brought a hood of his own. Somewhat to my surprise, as the guides had seemed always to despise the cold and to regard my warnings as superfluous, this offer was accepted with alacrity. My hands were covered with a pair of vicuña mittens made for me in La Paz with two thicknesses of fur, one turned outside and one in. For these, until the day before, I had had no use; they now kept even my cold hands comfortable. In fact, as the sun rose higher, they became too warm and were exchanged for two pairs of wool mittens, one of which, however, did not cover the fingers. The fur mittens, being too large to go into my pocket or leather bag, were handed over to Rudolf, who was next to me, to put into his rück-sack.

I had repeatedly warned the men of the great danger of freezing above, not so much from the actual cold as from the rarity of the air, telling them how Pelissier (one of Conway's guides), with two pairs of stockings, had had his feet frozen on Aconcagua so that they turned black, and he barely escaped losing them; how Zurbriggan, Maquignaz, and others had been frost-bitten on Aconcagua and Sorata. In spite of this, they hardly seemed to realize the necessity of so much care. They stated that their shoes would admit of but one pair of their heavy woollen stockings and seemed quite unconcerned as to the possibilities of freezing.

The men carried food and tea for luncheon (the latter I had sat up to make the night before, after the rest had gone to bed), the hypsometer to take observations, and my camera. The mercurial barometer I had left in Yungay, from misgivings that I might have to carry it if it was brought along. As there was no extra clothing of mine to transport, since I had put it all on, I ventured to ask if one of the guides could carry up the warm poncho, fearing that I might need it when we paused for luncheon or on the summit. It was rather heavy and a considerable burden at that altitude, but Gabriel said he could take it; to the fact of my extreme, apparently superfluous caution, and of Gabriel's willingness and strength, I certainly owe the possession and soundness of all my limbs, as I also owe Gabriel my life. The canteen of alcohol, which was used to light the fire of our kerosene stove, and from which also a small draught night and morning was given to the Indians, was carried some distance from the tent lest the temptation to drink this in our long absence should prove too much for them. When the can was deposited in the snow, with which it was half covered to make sure that it would not blow away, I inquired, "Are you sure you can find this on our return?" Both men replied that they certainly could.

Considering the altitude our progress seemed rapid. On the slope above the camp no steps were needed, but when, after an hour or less, we turned to the left, making a long traverse among great crevasses, walls, and appalling downward slopes, it was necessary that steps should be cut all of the time. The snow was in a worse condition than before. It had been hard enough then (though softer in the middle of the day), but not so smooth. Now the severe cold had made it harder still, while the high wind had blown from the exposed slopes all of the lighter particles, leaving a surface smooth as glass, such as Gabriel said he had never seen in Switzerland except in small patches.

Coming out at length upon a ridge where we were more exposed to the wind I felt the need of my vicuña mittens which had seemed too warm below. I delayed asking for a while, hoping to come to a better standing place; but as none appeared, calling a halt I approached Rudolf, who continually held the rope for me, while Gabriel was cutting the steps, so that the delays necessary on the previous ascent were avoided. Rudolf, taking the mittens from his rück-sack with some black woven sleeves I had earlier worn on my forearms, tucked the former under one arm saying, "Which will you have first?" I had it on the end of my tongue to exclaim, "Look out you don't lose my mittens!" But like most men, the guides were rather impatient of what they considered unnecessary advice or suggestions from a woman, even an employer; so, thinking, he surely will be careful of my mittens, I refrained and said, "Give me the armlets!" A second later Rudolf cried, "I have lost one of your mittens!" I did not see it go, it slipped out at the back, but anything dropped on that smooth slope, even without the high wind, might as well have gone over a precipice.

I was angry and alarmed at his inexcusable carelessness, but it was useless to talk. I could do that after we got down, though under subsequent circumstances I never did. I hastily put my two brown woollen mittens and one red mitt on my left hand, the vicuña fur on my right which generally held the ice axe and was therefore more exposed. Onward and upward for hours we pressed, when at length we paused for luncheon being too cold and tired to eat the meat which had frozen in the rück-sack, and the almost equally hard bread; though we ate Peter's chocolate and raisins, of which we had taken an occasional nibble, each from his own pocket, all along the way. (I had found a few raisins in one of the stores and bought all they had.) The tea, too, was partially frozen in Rudolf's canteen. About two o'clock, Taugwalder declared himself unable to proceed. I was for leaving him there and going on with

Gabriel, but the latter urged him onward, suggesting that by leaving his rück-sack, he might be able to continue with us. This, after a short rest, he did, finding that we were going on any way. Gabriel now carried the camera and hypsometer, in addition to the poncho, besides cutting the steps.

The latter part of the climb was especially steep. All, suffering from cold and fatigue, required frequent brief halts, though we sat down but twice on the way up and not at all at the top. At last we were approaching our goal. Rounding the apparent summit we found a broad way of the slightest grade leading gently to the northern end of the ridge, though from below, the highest point had appeared to be at the south. On the ridge, the wind was stronger than ever, and I suddenly realized that my left hand was insensible and freezing. Twitching off my mittens, I found that the hand was nearly black. Rubbing it vigorously with snow, I soon had it aching badly, which signified its restoration; but it would surely freeze again (it was now three o'clock) in the colder hours of the late afternoon and night. My over-caution in having the poncho brought up now proved my salvation. This heavy shawl or blanket, with a slit in the middle, slipped over my head, kept me fairly warm to the end, protecting my hand somewhat, as well as my whole body. At the same time, it was awkward to wear, reaching nearly to my knees, and was the cause of my slipping and almost of my death on the way down. But for the loss of my fur mitten I should not have been compelled to wear it except, as intended, on the summit.

A little farther on, Gabriel suggested our halting for the observations, as the wind might be worse at the extremity of the ridge. The slope, however, was so slight that there was probably no difference. Rudolf now untied and disappeared. I was so busy over the hypsometer that I did not notice where he went, realizing only that he was not there. While, careful not to expose too much my left hand, I shielded the hypsometer from the wind as well as I was able with the poncho, Gabriel struck match after match in vain. Once he lighted the candle, but immediately it went out. After striking twenty matches, Gabriel said, "It is useless; we must give it up." With Rudolf's assistance in holding the poncho we might have done better. But it was past three. That dread descent was before us. Sadly I packed away the instrument, believing it better to return alive, if possible, than to risk further delay. It was a great disappointment not to make the expected contribution to science; perhaps to have broken the world's record, without being able to prove it; but to return alive seemed still more desirable, even though in ignorance of the exact height to which we had attained.

Rudolf now appeared and informed me that *he* had been on to the summit, instead of remaining to assist with the hypsometer. I *was* enraged. I had told them, long before, that, as it was my expedition, I should like, as is customary, to be the first one to place my foot at the top, even though I reached it through their instrumentality. It would not lessen their honour and I was paying the bills. I had related how a few feet below the top of Mt. St. Elias, Maquignaz had stepped back and said to the Duke of the Abruzzi, "Monsieur, à vous la glorie!" And Rudolf, who with little grit had on the first attempt turned back at 16,000 feet, compelling me to make this weary climb over again, who this time had not done half so much work as Gabriel, who had wished to give up an hour below the summit, instead of remaining here with us to render assistance with the observations, had coolly walked on to the highest point! I had not *dreamed* of such an act. The disappointment may have been trivial. Of course it made no real difference to the honour to which I was entitled, but of a certain personal satisfaction, long looked forward to, I had been robbed. Once more I resolved, if ever we got down again, to give that man a piece of my mind, a large one; but after all I never did, for then he had troubles enough of his own, and words would not change the fact. Now, without a word, I went on.

Though the grade was slight, I was obliged to pause several times in the fierce wind, once leaning my head on my ice axe for a few seconds before I could continue to the goal. Gabriel stopped a short distance from the end, advising me not to go too near the edge, which I had no inclination to do, passing but a few feet beyond him. I should like to have looked down into the Llanganuco Gorge, whence I had looked up at the cliff and the thick overhanging cornice, such as impended above the east and west cliffs also. We had, therefore, kept in the center of the broad ridge, at least 40 feet wide, it may have been more: it seemed wider than an ordinary city street. Had it been earlier in the day, being particularly fond of precipices, and this would have been the biggest I had ever looked down, I should have ventured near the north edge with Gabriel holding the rope; but now I did not care to hazard delay from the possibility of breaking through the cornice.

My first thought on reaching the goal was, "I am here at last, after all these years; but shall we never get down again?" I said nothing except: "Give me the camera," and as rapidly as possible took views towards the four quarters of the heavens, one including Gabriel. The click of the camera did not sound just right, and fearing that I was getting no pictures at all, I did not bother to have Gabriel try to take a photograph of me. This I afterwards regretted, as I should like to have preserved such a picture for my own pleasure. But in later days I was thankful indeed that in spite of high wind and blowing snow the other pictures did come out fairly; for it is pictures *from* the summit that tell the tale, and not the picture of some one standing on a bit of rock or snow which may be anywhere.

The view was nothing unless I could have gone to the edge of the broad surface. The other twin peak at the south, obviously a little higher, as I had always maintained, shut out the rest of the range in that direction, as we were so much above the mountains at the north that not going quite to the end, I did not see even Huandoy on the other side of the Gorge. The Cordillera Negra I had long been familiar with from the valley below and all the way up, while the view of the snow mountains towards the east, which I particularly desired to see, was cut off by our distance from the edge, save at the southeast where some peaks far below were visible.

There was no pleasure here, hardly a feeling of triumph, in a view of my disappointment over the observations, and my dread of the long and terrible descent. If ever I were safely down, there would be plenty of time to rejoice. It was half past three, and soon would be dark. Seven hours coming up! Would it take us as long to return? Steep rocks and icy slopes are far more dangerous to descend, and especially perilous after dark; with those small steps, the prospect was indeed terrifying: so without a moment's rest we began our retreat. The summit ridge, at least a quarter of a mile in length, was quickly traversed, at that altitude a slight change in grade making as much difference as in bicycling.

Gabriel had led nearly all the way up, cutting most, if not all, of the steps. Rudolf had been second, in order to hold the rope for me, avoiding all possible delay. Going down I was roped in the middle, the more usual position for the amateur, Rudolf at first taking the lead and Gabriel occupying the more responsible place in the rear; for in descending, the rear is the post of honour, as that of leader in the ascent; since the strongest of a party must be above, holding the rope in case of a slip on the part of the amateur in front. A guide, of course, is never expected to slip and a good one practically never does. If the rear guard goes, as a rule all are lost.

The guides' shoes being well studded with nails they had not cared to wear the climbing irons, to which they were unaccustomed, and which by impeding the circulation would have made their feet colder. My shoes were more poorly provided, as it was impossible to procure in New York such nails as are employed in the Alps. I had intended to wear the crampons which would have made them unnecessary, but on Gabriel's advice had left them below, lest my feet should be frozen, as the one previously touched by the frost would have greater liability.

At the end of the ridge difficulties began. A smooth slope of 60° is never pleasant. From the beginning of the descent I greatly feared the outcome, but we had to go down and the faster we could go, yet carefully, the better. Presently I saw something black fly away: one of Rudolf's mittens. One might suppose that after losing mine he would have been the more careful of his own. When I inquired afterwards how he came to lose it, he said he laid it down on that icy slope to fasten his shoe. Of course the wind blew it away. Later I learned that after dark he lost the second mitten. This he said was in trying to change from one hand to the other. He thought he had hold of it, but his hand being numb, he could not feel it, and this went also. If he had spoken we should have halted, so that he could make sure. His carelessness seems incredible and inexcusable, and brought disastrous consequences to himself and nearly to us all, almost costing our lives. Probably I should not have slipped, had I not been obliged on account of the loss of my fur mittens to wear the poncho which occasionally prevented my seeing the steps. Certainly Rudolf himself would not have slipped any more than Gabriel, if his hands had not been frozen and himself chilled through, so that one foot froze also; thus his footing was insecure and his grip on his ice axe less firm. It seems almost a miracle that he slipped only once and that we at last got down alive. His carelessness may perhaps be explained by the fact of his being so much affected by the altitude that it rendered him stupid, as below he had seemed as thoughtful and as careful as Gabriel. The latter, however, I had regarded as a trifle the more intelligent, as he was evidently the stronger.

On this steep slope, I deeply regretted the absence of my climbing irons, for the steps were small indeed. On the Jungfrau those made by my guide Baumann were very large, requiring from ten to twenty blows; but this would never do on the much longer slope of Huascarán. Two or three hacks for each were all that Gabriel could give, so they were not half as large as his shoes, little more than toe-holes. They did well enough going up but not on the way down. While zigzagging I missed a step, sat down and slid a few feet, but Gabriel above was holding the rope tight and I easily regained my footing.

Some time after dark it seemed advisable for Gabriel to take the lead (such matters of course I left to them), perhaps because he was more familiar with the way or could see better on the long sloping traverse across the wide face of the mountain in the midst of caverns, crevasses, and those dreadful slopes and precipices; yet as a slide anywhere would have been fatal, one place was just as bad as another, except as some parts were steeper. Gabriel estimated the incline as from 40° to 60° through the greater part of the distance. I had brought with me a clinometer, but never had time and strength to use it. I had been on measured slopes of 42° and 53° on my first mountain, and judging from these, had never afterwards over-estimated any that had been capable of verification. My opinion here coincides with Gabriel's. If anyone should not accept it, the matter is of little consequence as compared with the altitude, which unfortunately I had been obliged to leave unmeasured. But that could be determined at a later date. Whatever it might be, the *fact* of my ascent would stand.

My recollection of the descent is as of a horrible nightmare, though such I never experienced. The little moon seemed always at my back, casting a shadow over the place where I must step. The poncho would sway in the wind, and, with my motion as I was in the act of stepping, would sometimes conceal the spot where my foot should be placed. Although my eye for distance is good, my foot once missed the step, slipping then on the smooth slope so that I fell, as usual in a sitting posture, crying out at the same time to warn the guides. I expected nothing serious, but to my horror, I did not remain where I was. Still sitting I began to slide down that glassy, ghastly incline. As we were all nearly in the same line, I slid at least fifteen feet before coming to a halt, when checked by the rope. Now to get back! The guides called to me to get up, but being all in a heap, with the rope tight around my waist, I was unable to move. The guides therefore came together just above and hauled me up the slope. Thankful again to be in the line of the steps, though more alarmed than ever, I went onward, resolved to be more careful. But again I slipped, and again slid far below. While from the beginning of the descent, I had greatly feared the outcome, after these slips my terror increased. Several times I declared that we should never get down alive. I begged Gabriel to stop for the night and make a cave in the snow, but, saying this was impossible, he continued without a pause. The snow indeed was too hard, yet in some cavern or crevasse I thought we could find shelter from the wind. Gabriel afterwards asserted that if we had stopped we should all have frozen to death.

Again and again I slipped, five or six times altogether, but always Gabriel held his ground firmly. Always, too, I clung to my ice axe; so to his shout, "Have you your axe?" I could respond in the affirmative, and sometimes with it could help myself back again. Once when I had slipped, I was astonished to see Rudolf dart by me, wondering how he could help me by running far below. Afterwards I learned, that with my pull he, too, had slipped and Gabriel's strong arm alone saved us all from destruction. Had he given way, after sliding some distance we should all have dropped off thousands of feet below. When he saw Rudolf go, Gabriel thought for a moment that we were all lost; but this axe was well placed with the rope around it, and although two fingers were caught between the rope and ice axe, knowing it was life or death he stood firm until Rudolf recovered himself. Otherwise, Gabriel said afterwards, he never despaired but thought only of going on. Rudolf, however, to my great astonishment, for I had supposed I was the only one who was frightened, confessed later that he never expected to get down alive.

The cold and fatigue, the darkness and shadow, the poncho blowing before me, the absence of climbing irons, the small steps, the steep glassy slopes, presented an extraordinary combination of difficulties. It seemed that the way would never end. I tried to comfort myself with the reflection that accidents do not run in our family, that nothing serious, more than broken ribs or knee-pan—these not in climbing—ever *had* happened to me; but also I was aware that people do not generally die but once. I said to myself, for the first time in my life, I *must* keep cool and do my best, and so I did; but after several of those horrible slides—Well, there was nothing to do but to plod along.

At last, at last—! Before I was aware that we had emerged from among those terrible abysses to the slope above the tent, Gabriel said "Now we are safe; and if you like you can slide." What a tremendous relief! I sat down happily, Gabriel walking ahead and guiding me with the rope. At first it was fun, then I went too fast, bobbing here and there, bumping, floundering, finally turning around, sliding on my back, and giving my head a hard whack before I came to a halt. However, we were nearly down and walked on to the tent where we arrived at half past ten, thankful for rest and shelter. There was nothing to drink, we were too tired to eat or sleep, but glad indeed to sit down in safety, too fatigued at first even to lie down.

Poor Rudolf! His hands were badly frozen, his fingers black, the left hand worse than the right. He was rubbing them weakly with snow, first one, then the other. I told him he should rub them harder to get up circulation; I felt I ought to do it myself, but somehow sat there and did not. Gabriel did not offer to, either. He no doubt was thoroughly worn out, too. One of the Indians might have done it, but after greeting us, they huddled up on their own side of the tent and went to sleep again, and no one asked them. There was not room in the tent for seven persons to lie down, so we three had one side of the pole, the four Indians the other. They curled up in their ponchos, two with heads one side and two the other, half sitting, with feet toward the middle. I was unable to use my sleeping bag properly on this trip, for there would have been no room left for the guides. I had therefore taken the blankets from the canvas cover and spread them out with other blankets brought from the Vinatéas, and we had managed to be fairly comfortable. Heretofore I had taken the inside as being warmer, but to-night after sitting awhile, I took the outside, leaving the place in the center for Rudolf.

The wind continued to blow hard all night and the next day. We did not rise early and no one proposed descending, though I felt that Rudolf ought to get down as soon as possible. Gabriel went up for the can of alcohol, looking at the same time for a leather bag which had been attached to my belt and which had disappeared, doubtless in one of those terrible earlier slides, rather than on the last, since it was nowhere to be found. Also, as I had feared, the can of alcohol did not appear; whether covered by blowing snow or whether the Indians had gone up and drunk it, then concealing the can (though of this they gave no sign), or what became of it we could not tell. Being without fire we had no water, soup, or tea. I tried for an hour or more by burning matches to heat and ignite some oil in the place where the alcohol should have gone. Once I had it burning for a moment, but after using a whole box of matches, I gave it up. Quinua meal with snow and sugar, or the last two alone were our best substitutes for water.

Friday we were somewhat rested, the wind abated, and we started down. Soon we came to another icy slope, not very steep, where the Indians with their climbing irons passed easily, but where I began to slide standing. Gabriel appeared rather vexed with me, but I did not see how I could help it. The guides weighed much more than I, and with the heavy nails on their boots doubtless made indentations which I could not do. However, by going slowly, with care and with the aid of the rope, I passed the glassy surface safely.

At the top of the great wall, I decided to put on my crampons, preferring on the whole to risk freezing my toes rather than losing my life. Gabriel had proposed that all descend together. I said "No, one at a time, if it does take longer." I had climbed my mountain at last and did not wish to be killed on the way down. Our three ropes being tied together, the others descended one by one, Rudolf first, then the Indians, while Gabriel, aided by Lucas, lowered the rope from above and then hauled it up for the next man. The rope reached but part way down to a convenient ledge of snow, where the men waited in the midst of crevasses until all had come down. Gabriel had estimated the entire wall at 300 feet. After my return to Yungay, I took the trouble to measure the ropes; the total being 180 feet, it seemed that his judgment was fairly accurate. I should not have ventured a guess myself, not being used to making estimates of that nature. While descending this upper part of the wall, one of the Indians slipped, falling, he said, *dos cuadras*—two blocks—an evident exaggeration, as the rope was held above; but it was fortunate we were not together, or his slip might have proved fatal to all.

I was the last to go down except Gabriel and Lucas. For a time all was well. Of course we went backwards as on a ladder. Then for some reason I moved a little more

269

slowly, while the men seemed to lower the rope more rapidly. I did not like to proceed with the rope so loose; as there was a deep crevasse in the wall close by, the upper outside edge of which gave a seat, with a resting place for one foot below, I sat down there, hoping that the men might perceive that the rope was not taut and draw it part way up again. As they did not, I untied and threw if off, shouting to them to pull it up. Evidently they could not hear and continued to lower it farther, the end going down into the crevasse behind me. At last they pulled it up and there I sat perched half way on the wall, unable to see the men above or those below, and obliged to remain motionless on my icy seat, where a fall backwards would precipitate me into a black and profound abyss, and a slip forward to a greater depth down the face of the wall into some immense cavern or *bergschrund* at the bottom. So long as I sat still, I was safe, though when at last Lucas came down, I had to crowd myself into the smallest possible space in order to give him room to pass by. Gabriel came last; he did not need anyone to hold the rope for him. I was glad to see him, though I expected a scolding for having untied and being left here halfway; but he was unexpectedly amiable, and tying me to the rope of which he had kept the upper end, I went down without any trouble till we came to the men below. Such an array of *bergschründe* and caverns, a perfect medley of enormous hollows, great snow masses, and precipices, I never elsewhere witnessed: a wonderful sight which would delight the heart of any mountaineer. From here we went on together. It would seem that in this section at some time there must be tremendous snow falls, great masses splitting off from the side slopes above; but at this season there was no sign of snow avalanches, except as overhanging ice walls and immense irregular masses below, gave evidence that at some seasons great operations were here conducted. The wall was not of hard ice but of solid snow or névé, the space between the two peaks being filled in with snow, obviously hundreds of feet deep. Here in the middle of the saddle, a rock wall beneath has evidently caused a tremendous mass of snow to break off nearly all the way across, leaving a snow wall the solid part of which was about the length of our united ropes, 180 feet, with 100 feet more of irregular cavernous and crevassed descent. The solid part in places lacked little of the perpendicular, equalling the angle of the cliff of the Fünf-fingerspitze above the Daumen-scharte.

After descending, also one at a time, the shorter ice wall farther down, we could go more rapidly, except for delay on a steep traverse, where first one of the *peónes*, then another, slide twenty or thirty feet. At length all dangers were over; we passed one old camp after another, eager to reach the rocks where we could have fire and water, of which we had been destitute for more than forty-eight hours.

At the edge of the glacier, before sunset, the men paused where a few streams trickled, and drank and drank, while I sat patiently waiting till they had their fill and one of them was ready to bring a bucket of water from a larger stream at a distance. Within the next five minutes, I drank four tin cupfuls, a greater quantity at once than ever before in my life. Presently we had soup and tea. It was a quiet moonlight evening and with the Indians preferring to sleep outside the tent, we should have been very comfortable and happy had it not been for Rudolf's frozen hands and foot. He dared not take off one boot lest he should be unable to put it on again in the morning.

Soon after sunrise on Saturday we started down, as I was anxious to get Rudolf to Yungay and a physician. This time, descending by the proper route, we arrived about ten o'clock at the mine, where we found Señor Jaramillo with the horses, this being the appointed day. After breakfast we hastened on to Yungay, I at least rejoicing that I should not have to come that way again; though the sad condition of Rudolf, then and always, greatly marred the satisfaction of my triumph. His misfortune seemed indeed to outweigh any benefit derived from the ascent, my only consolation being that it was his own fault and not a necessary consequence of the climb, as the soundness of myself and Gabriel proved. I learned afterwards that Rudolf, in spite of all I had said about the cold, had even left an extra flannel shirt in the tent at the saddle while he went to the top. This, by keeping his body warmer, might have slightly lessened his calamity. Also there were four pairs of mittens in the tent, some of which might have been carried, if one had supposed that any would be lost.

As I rode along the valley and looked up at that great magnificent mountain conquered at last, after so many years of struggle, days and weeks of hardship, and now at such cost, I felt almost like shaking my fist at it and saying, "I have beaten you at last and I shall never have to go up there again," but I didn't.

Immediately upon our arrival, without waiting for congratulations, I sent for the only physician in the place who, soon after a second summons, arrived. He expressed himself as doubtful of the result but said he would do his best. Cotton was procured and a proper solution for bathing the injured members, in the method of which I was duly instructed. For the next twenty-four hours, this operation which consumed about ten minutes was repeated every quarter of an hour, so that there was very little intermission in one's labours. I had expected to share the night with Gabriel, but finding that a nurse could be procured, a cholo woman, I was glad to leave the night work to her. The second day, once in half an hour was sufficient. Other treatment followed. After a day or two the doctor said it would be a fortnight before he could tell whether amputation would be required, perhaps longer; if so, it would be two months before Rudolf would be able to travel. As there was nothing that I could do, since Gabriel would remain with him to assist and to keep him company, I decided to leave them both there, Rudolf without the use of his hands being unable to travel on horseback to the seashore. I was assured that the physician was perfectly able to attend him and to perform any needed operation, he was the only one to be had within thirty miles; so with a promise from the Vinatéas and Señor Handabaka that he should be well looked after, I went on to Lima to improve my time in the country by visits to other sections.

Before my departure the men had been removed to a hospital conducted by a society of the good people of Yungay, of which Señor Handabaka was president. For attendance upon Taugwalder no charge was made; for the board of Zumtaugwald but a modest sum. Having provided in advance for all their expenses and arranged for their transportation to the coast, about a week after my ascent of the mountain I bade farewell to Yungay, and to the hospitable family that had so long entertained me. I had previously planned to go over land with my guides to Cerro de Pasco, pausing on the way at Chiquián, and if it looked at all feasible, attempting the ascent of the great mountain near by, La Viuda, the highest in that part of the Cordillera, northwest of Cerro, to which place we should then proceed, perhaps if time permitted afterwards trying the high mountain to the northeast. Also I had had in view an ascent of Coropuna. At least one or more of these ascents might have been accomplished, had it not been first, for Rudolf's illness on our first attempt, which occasioned a loss of two or three weeks, and then, for his sad accident which prevented any further mountain climbing.

I was greatly grieved to learn afterwards in Lima that it was finally necessary to amputate most of Taugwalder's left hand, a finger of his right, and half of one foot. He was unable to travel until December, when the men rode down to Samanco and sailed to Callao, where they took the steamer for Panama and New York, returning in January to their homes in Zermatt. The well-known surgeon, Dr. William Tod Helmuth, kindly examined Rudolf in New York City, and I was glad to hear him say that undoubtedly he had received suitable attention and that the operations, especially the very difficult one on his foot, had been excellently performed.

Concerning the altitude of Mt. Huascarán, in regard to which there has been a rather one-sided controversy, a few words must be said. That I ever asserted the height of the mountain to be 24,000 feet is a deliberate misstatement, to which my articles published in *Harper's Magazine* for January, 1909, and in the *Bulletin of the American Geographical Society* for June of the same year bear witness. Following is a precise presentation of the facts.

The day after we reached the summit of the north peak, I requested the guides separately to estimate its height above the saddle, taking into consideration the angle of the slope, our rate of progress, and the number of hours occupied in the ascent. After a few moments' thought they said that they had formed an opinion. Rudolf's estimate was from 4,000 to 5,000 feet, Gabriel's from 3,800 to 4,200 feet. Comparing in my own mind this ascent with that of Orizaba where, in about the same length of time, an altitude of 4,000 feet had been gained, remembering that the incline here was greater and the halts fewer, aside from the momentary pauses for step cutting, 4,000 feet then seemed a fairly reasonable estimate. Furthermore, in the photographs, as well as when viewed from the hills in front, the height of the peaks above the saddle appears hardly inferior to the distance from the snow line to the saddle, which is approximately 5,000 feet. I was aware that the north peak sets farther forward than the top of the saddle, for which I made some allowance, apparently not enough. I *thought* the mountain would reach the height of 23,000 feet and stated that *if* it should prove to be 24,000, my ascent would be the world's record for men as well as for women; the greatest height previously attained being the ascent of Kabru to a trifle less altitude by W. W. Graham, twenty-five years earlier, an achievement which I never saw any good reason to doubt. I naturally expected one to take an estimate as authority and said so.

From my observations at the saddle with hypsometer and mercurial barometer compared with hypsometric observations made at the same time in Yungay by Mr. Handabaka, the height of the saddle or *col* between the peaks was calculated by Prof. C. F. Marvin of the United States Weather Bureau, and by Prof. H. C. Parker of Columbia University to be 19,600 feet, a trifle less than I had hoped, but not enough to preclude the possibility of a total altitude for Huascarán of from 23,000 to 24,000 feet when that should be accurately determined from later observations on some other ascent or from triangulation. Whatever the result might be, the *fact* of my attaining the summit, happily attested by photographic evidence, would stand.

The triangulation was not long delayed. Solely in the interest of science, it is said, an expedition of three French engineers was sent from Paris to Peru to secure the altitude of this one mountain. Apparently the work was done with an extreme care which presupposes accurate measurement; yet $13,000 seems a large sum to spend for the triangulation of a single mountain which it cost but $3,000 to climb. With $1,000 more for my expedition, I should have been able with an assistant to triangulate the peak myself. With $12,000 additional I could have triangulated and climbed many mountains and accomplished other valuable exploration. The figures given as the result of this triangulation are 21,812 feet for the north peak and 22,187 for the south. Though it would thus appear that Huascarán is not so lofty as I had hoped, my ten long years of effort had culminated in the conquest of a mountain at least 1,500 feet higher than Mt. McKinley, and 2,500 feet higher than any man residing in the United States had climbed. With this I must be content until opportunity is offered to investigate some other possibilities in regard to the Apex of America.

—1911

Hudson Stuck

from *The Ascent of Denali (Mt. McKinley)*

The first confirmed ascent of Denali followed Dr. Frederick A. Cook's alleged expedition to the summit in 1903. Cook's account, published in To the Top of the Continent, *was greeted with widespread skepticism, and his "summit photograph" was later proved by Belmore Browne and Robert M. Bryce to depict a point much lower down on the mountain. Hudson Stuck's (1863–1920) party took three months to reach the top of Denali due to the remoteness of the mountain, and they relied on hunting and scavenging for food after an accidental fire burned up some of their supplies and tents. Stuck's account provides a detailed description of the equipment, techniques, and psychology of back-woods mountain climbing written in a reflective, philosophical style. Stuck later served as archdeacon of the Yukon.*

THE ULTIMATE HEIGHT

We lay down for a few hours on the night of the 6th June, resolved to rise at three in the morning for our attempt upon the summit of Denali. At supper Walter had made a desperate effort to use some of our ten pounds of flour in the manufacture of "noodles" with which to thicken the stew. We had continued to pack that flour and had made effort after effort to cook it in some eatable way, but without success. The sour dough would not ferment, and we had no baking-powder. *Is* there any way to cook flour under such circumstances? But he made the noodles too large and did not cook them enough, and they wrought internal havoc upon those who partook of them. Three of the four of us were unwell all night. The digestion is certainly more delicate and more easily disturbed at great altitudes than at the lower levels. While Karstens and Tatum were tossing uneasily in the bed-clothes, the writer sat up with a blanket round his shoulders, crouching over the primus stove, with the thermometer at –21°F. outdoors. Walter alone was at ease, with digestive and somnolent capabilities proof against any invasion. It was, of course, broad daylight all night. At three the company was aroused, and, after partaking of a very light breakfast indeed, we sallied forth into the brilliant, clear morning with not a cloud in the sky. The only packs we carried that day were the instruments and the lunch. The sun was shining,

Hudson Stuck, *The Ascent of Denali (Mt. McKinley): A Narrative of the First Complete Ascent of the Highest Peak in North America* (New York: Scribner, 1914).

but a keen north wind was blowing and the thermometer stood at –4°F. We were rather a sorry company. Karstens still had internal pains; Tatum and I had severe headaches. Walter was the only one feeling entirely himself, so Walter was put in the lead and in the lead he remained all day.

We took a straight course up the great snow ridge directly south of our camp and then around the peak into which it rises; quickly told but slowly and most laboriously done. It was necessary to make the traverse high up on this peak instead of around its base, so much had its ice and snow been shattered by the earthquake on the lower portions. Once around this peak, there rose before us the horseshoe ridge which carries the ultimate height of Denali, a horseshoe ridge of snow opening to the east with a low snow peak at either end, the centre of the ridge soaring above both peaks. Above us was nothing visible but snow; the rocks were all beneath, the last rocks standing at about 19,000 feet. Our progress was exceedingly slow. It was bitterly cold; all the morning toes and fingers were without sensation, kick them and beat them as we would. We were all clad in full winter hand and foot gear—more gear than had sufficed at 50° below zero on the Yukon trail. Within the writer's No. 16 moccasins were three pairs of heavy hand-knitted woollen socks, two pairs of camel's-hair socks, and a pair of thick felt socks; while underneath them, between them and the iron "creepers," were the soles cut from a pair of felt shoes. Upon his hands were a pair of the thickest Scotch wool gloves, thrust inside huge lynx-paw mittens lined with Hudson Bay duffle. His moose-hide breeches and shirt, worn all the winter on the trail, were worn throughout this climb; over the shirt was a thick sweater and over all the usual Alaskan "parkee" amply furred around the hood; underneath was a suit of the heaviest Jaeger underwear—yet until high noon feet were like lumps of iron and fingers were constantly numb. That north wind was cruelly cold, and there can be no possible question that cold is felt much more keenly in the thin air of nineteen thousand feet than it is below. But the north wind was really our friend, for nothing but a north wind will drive all vapor from this mountain. Karstens beat his feet so violently and so continually against the hard snow to restore the circulation that two of his toe-nails sloughed off afterward. By eleven o'clock we had been climbing for six hours and were well around the peak, advancing toward the horseshoe ridge, but even then there were grave doubts if we should succeed in reaching it that day, it was so cold. A hint from any member of the party that his feet were actually freezing—a hint expected all along—would have sent us all back. When there is no sensation left in the feet at all it is, however, difficult to be quite sure if they be actually freezing or not—and each one was willing to give the attempt upon the summit the benefit of the doubt. What should we have done with the ordinary leather climbing boots? But once entirely around the peak we were in a measure sheltered from the north wind, and the sun full upon us gave more warmth. It was hereabouts, and not, surely, at the point indicated in the photograph in Mr. Belmore Browne's book, that the climbing party of last year was driven back by the blizzard that descended upon them when close to their goal. Not until we had stopped for lunch and had drunk the scalding tea from the thermos bottles, did we all begin to have confidence that this day would see the completion of the ascent. But the writer's shortness of breath became more and more distressing as he rose. The familiar fits of panting took a more acute form; at such times everything would turn black before his eyes and he would choke and gasp and seem unable to get breath at all. Yet a few moments' rest restored him completely, to struggle on another twenty or thirty paces and to sink gasping upon the snow again. All were more affected in the breathing than they had been at any time before—it was curious to see every man's mouth open for breathing—but none of the others in this distressing way. Before the traverse around the peak just mentioned, Walter had noticed the writer's growing discomfort and had insisted upon assuming the mercurial barometer. The boy's eager kindness was gladly accepted and the instrument was surrendered. So it did not fall to the writer's credit to carry the thing to the top as he had wished.

The climbing grew steeper and steeper; the slope that had looked easy from below now seemed to shoot straight up. For the most part the climbing-irons gave us sufficient footing, but here and there we came to softer snow, where they would not take sufficient hold and we had to cut steps. The calks in these climbing-irons were about an inch and a quarter long; we wished they had been two inches. The creepers are a great advantage in the matter of speed, but they need long points. They are not so safe as step-cutting, and there is the ever-present danger that unless one is exceedingly careful one will step upon the rope with them and their sharp calks sever some of the strands. They were, however, of great assistance and saved a deal of laborious step-cutting.

At last the crest of the ridge was reached and we stood well above the two peaks that mark the ends of the horseshoe.[1]

Also it was evident that we were well above the great North Peak across the Grand Basin. Its crest had been like an index on the snow beside us as we climbed, and we stopped for a few moments when it seemed that we were level with it. We judged it to be about five hundred feet lower than the South Peak.

But still there stretched ahead of us, and perhaps one hundred feet above us, another small ridge with a north and south pair of little haycock summits. This is the real top of Denali. From below, this ultimate ridge merges indistinguishably with the crest of the horseshoe ridge, but it is not a part of it but a culminating ridge beyond it. With keen excitement we pushed on. Walter, who had been in the lead all day, was the first to scramble up; a native Alaskan, he is the first human being to set foot upon the top of Alaska's great mountain, and he had well earned the lifelong distinction. Karstens and Tatum were hard upon his heels, but the last man on the rope, in his enthusiasm and excitement somewhat overpassing his narrow wind margin, had almost to be hauled up the last few feet, and fell unconscious for a moment upon the floor of the little snow basin that occupies the top of the mountain. This, then, is the actual summit, a little crater-like snow basin, sixty or sixty-five feet long and twenty to twenty-five feet wide, with a haycock of snow at either end—the south one a little higher than the north. On the southwest this little basin is much corniced, and the whole thing looked as though every severe storm might somewhat change its shape.

276

So soon as wind was recovered we shook hands all round and a brief prayer of thanksgiving to Almighty God was said, that He had granted us our hearts' desire and brought us safely to the top of His great mountain.

This prime duty done, we fell at once to our scientific tasks. The instrument-tent was set up, the mercurial barometer, taken out of its leather case and then out of its wooden case, was swung upon its tripod and a rough zero established, and it was left awhile to adjust itself to conditions before a reading was attempted. It was a great gratification to get it to the top uninjured. The boiling-point apparatus was put together and its candle lighted under the ice which filled its little cistern. The three-inch, three-circle aneroid was read at once at 13.2 inches, its mendacious altitude scale confidently pointing at 23,300 feet. Half an hour later it had dropped to 13.175 inches and had shot us up another one hundred feet into the air. Soon the water was boiling in the little tubes of the boiling-point thermometer and the steam pouring out of the vent. The thread of mercury rose to 174.9° and stayed there. There is something definite and uncompromising about the boiling-point hypsometer; no tapping will make it rise or fall; it reaches its mark unmistakably and does not budge. The reading of the mercurial barometer is a slower and more delicate business. It takes a good light and a good sight to tell when the ivory zero-point is exactly touching the surface of the mercury in the cistern; it takes care and precision to get the vernier exactly level with the top of the column. It was read, some half-hour after it was set up, at 13.617 inches. The alcohol minimum thermometer stood at 7°F. all the while we were on top. Meanwhile, Tatum had been reading a round of angles with the prismatic compass. He could not handle it with sufficient exactness with his mitts on, and he froze his fingers doing it barehanded.

The scientific work accomplished, then and not till then did we indulge ourselves in the wonderful prospect that stretched around us. It was a perfectly clear day, the sun shining brightly in the sky, and naught bounded our view save the natural limitations of vision. Immediately before us, in the direction in which we had climbed, lay—nothing: a void, a sheer gulf many thousands of feet deep, and one shrank back instinctively from the little parapet of the snow basin when one had glanced at the awful profundity. Across the gulf, about three thousand feet beneath us and fifteen or twenty miles away, sprang most splendidly into view the great mass of Denali's Wife, or Mount Foraker, as some white men misname her, filling majestically all the middle distance. It was our first glimpse of her during the whole ascent. Denali's Wife doe not appear at all save from the actual summit of Denali, for she is completely hidden by his South Peak until the moment when his South Peak is surmounted. And never was a nobler sight displayed to man than that great, isolated mountain spread out completely, with all its spurs and ridges, its cliffs and its glaciers, lofty and mighty and yet far beneath us. On that spot one understood why the view of Denali from Lake Minchúmina is the grand view, for the west face drops abruptly down with nothing but that vast void from the top to nigh the bottom of the mountain. Beyond stretched, blue and vague to the southwest, the wide valley of the Kuskokwim, with an end of all mountains. To the north we looked right over the North Peak to the foot-hills below, patched with lakes and lingering snow, glittering with streams. We had hoped to see the junction of the Yukon and Tanana Rivers, 150 miles away to the northwest, as we had often seen the summit of Denali from that point in the winter, but the haze that almost always qualifies a fine summer day inhibited that stretch of vision. Perhaps the forest-fires we found raging on the Tanana River were already beginning to foul the northern sky.

It was, however, to the south and the east that the most marvellous prospect opened before us. What infinite tangle of mountain ranges filled the whole scene, until gray sky, gray mountain, and gray sea merged in the ultimate distance! The nearby peaks and ridges stood out with dazzling distinction, the glaciation, the drainage, the relation of each part to the others all revealed. The snow-covered tops of the remoter peaks, dwindling and fading, rose to our view as though floating in thin air when their bases were hidden by the haze, and the beautiful crescent curve of the whole Alaskan range exhibited itself from Denali to the sea. To the right hand the glittering, tiny threads of streams draining the mountain range into the Chulitna and Sushitna Rivers, and so to Cook's Inlet and the Pacific Ocean, spread themselves out; to the left the affluents of the Kantishna and the Nenana drained the range into the Yukon and Bering Sea.

Yet the chief impression was not of our connection with the earth so far below, its rivers and its seas, but rather of detachment from it. We seemed alone upon a dead world, as dead as the mountains on the moon. Only once before can the writer remember a similar feeling of being neither in the world or of the world, and that was at the bottom of the Grand Cañon of the Colorado, in Arizona, its savage granite walls as dead as this savage peak of ice.

Above us the sky took a blue so deep that none of us had ever gazed upon a midday sky like it before. It was a deep, rich, lustrous, transparent blue, as dark as a Prussian blue, but intensely blue; a hue so strange, so increasingly impressive, that to one at least it "seemed like special news of God," as a new poet sings. We first noticed the darkening tint of the upper sky in the Grand Basin, and it deepened as we rose. Tyndall observed and discussed this phenomenon in the Alps, but it seems scarcely to have been mentioned since.

It is difficult to describe at all the scene which the top of the mountain presented, and impossible to describe it adequately. One was not occupied with the thought of description but wholly possessed with the breadth and glory of it, with its sheer, amazing immensity and scope. Only once, perhaps, in any lifetime is such vision granted, certainly never before had been vouch-safed to any of us. Not often in the summertime does Denali completely unveil himself and dismiss the clouds from all the earth beneath. Yet we could not linger, unique though the occasion, dearly bought our privilege; the miserable limitations of the flesh gave us continual warning to depart; we grew colder and still more wretchedly cold. The thermometer stood at 7° in the full sunshine, and the north wind was keener than ever. My fingers were so cold that I would not venture to withdraw them from the mittens to change the film in the camera, and the other men were in like case; indeed, our hands were by this time so numb as to make it almost impossible to operate a camera at all. A number of photographs had been taken, though not half we should have liked to take, but it is probable that, however many more exposures had been made, they would have been little better than those we got. Our top-of-the-mountain photography was a great disappointment. One thing we learned: exposures at such altitude should be longer than those below, perhaps owing to the darkness of the sky.

When the mercurial barometer had been read the tent was thrown down and abandoned, the first of the series of abandonments that marked our descent from the mountain. The tent-pole was used for a moment as a flagstaff while Tatum hoisted a little United States flag he had patiently and skillfully constructed in our camps below out of two silk handkerchiefs and the cover of a sewing-bag. Then the pole was put to its permanent use. It had already been carved with a suitable inscription, and now a transverse piece, already prepared and fitted, was lashed securely to it and it was planted on one of the little snow turrets of the summit—the sign of our redemption, high above North America. Only some peaks in the Andes and some peaks in the Himalayas rise above it in all the world. It was of light, dry birch and, though six feet in length, so slender that we think it may whether many a gale. And Walter thrust it into the snow so firmly at a blow that it could not be withdrawn again. Then we gathered about it and said the Te Deum.

It was 1:30 P.M. when we reached the summit and two minutes past three when we left; yet so quickly had the time flown that we could not believe we had been an hour and a half on top. The journey down was a long, weary grind, the longer and the wearier that we made a détour and went out of our way to seek for Professor Parker's thermometer, which he had left "in a crack on the west side of the last boulder of the northeast ridge." That sounds definite enough, yet in fact it is equivocal. "Which is the last boulder?" we disputed as we went down the slope. A long series of rocks almost in line came to an end, with one rock a little below the others, a little out of the line. This egregious boulder would, it seemed to me, naturally be called the last; Karstens thought not—thought the "last boulder" was the last *on* the ridge. As we learned later, Karstens was right, and since he yielded to me we did not find the thermometer, for, having descended to this isolated rock, we would not climb up again for fifty thermometers. One's disappointment is qualified by the knowledge that the thermometer is probably not of adequate scale, Professor Parker's recollection being that it read only to 60° below zero, F. A lower temperature than this is recorded every winter on the Yukon River.

A thermometer reading to 100° below zero, left at this spot, would, in my judgment, perhaps yield a lower minimum than has ever yet been authentically recorded on earth, and it is most unfortunate that the opportunity was lost. Yet I did not leave my own alcohol minimum—scaled to 95° below zero, and yielding, by estimation, perhaps ten degrees below the scaling—there, because of the difficulty of giving explicit

279

directions that should lead to its ready recovery, and at the close of such a day of toil as is involved in reaching the summit, men have no stomach for prolonged search. As will be told, it is cached lower down, but at a spot where it cannot be missed.

However, for one, the writer was largely unconscious of weariness in that descent. All the way down, my thoughts were occupied with the glorious scene my eyes had gazed upon and should gaze upon never again. In all human probability I would never climb that mountain again; yet if I climbed it a score more times I would never be likely to repeat such vision. Commonly, only for a few hours at a time, never for more than a few days at a time, save in the dead of winter when climbing is out of the question, does Denali completely unveil himself and dismiss the clouds from all the earth beneath him. Not for long, with these lofty colds contiguous, will the vapors of Cook's Inlet and Prince William Sound and the whole North Pacific Ocean refrain from sweeping upward; their natural trend is hitherward. As the needle turns to the magnet so the clouds find an irresistible attraction in this great mountain mass, and though the inner side of the range be rid of them the sea side is commonly filled to overflowing.

Only those who have for long years cherished a great and almost inordinate desire, and have had that desire gratified to the limit of their expectation, can enter into the deep thankfulness and content that filled the heart upon the descent of this mountain. There was no pride of conquest, no trace of that exultation of victory some enjoy upon the first ascent of a lofty peak, no gloating over good fortune that had hoisted us a few hundred feet higher than others who had struggled and been discomfited. Rather was the feeling that a privileged communion with the high places of the earth had been granted; that not only had we been permitted to lift up eager eyes to these summits, secret and solitary since the world began, but to enter boldly upon them, to take place, as it were, domestically in their hitherto sealed chambers, to inhabit them, and to cast our eyes down from them, seeing all things as they spread out from the windows of heaven itself.

Into this strong yet serene emotion, into this reverent elevation of spirit, came with a shock a recollection of some recent reading.

Oh, wisdom of man and the apparatus of the sciences, the little columns of mercury that sling up and down, the vacuum boxes that expand and contract, the hammer that chips the highest rocks, the compass that takes the bearings of glacier and ridge—all the equipage of hypsometry and geology and geodesy—how pitifully feeble and childish it seems to cope with the majesty of the mountains! Take them all together, haul them up the steep, and as they lie there, read, recorded, and done for, which shall be more adequate to the whole scene—their records?—or that simple, ancient hymn, "We praise Thee, O God!—Heaven and earth are full of the majesty of Thy Glory!" What an astonishing thing that, standing where we stood and seeing what we saw, there are men who should be able to deduce this law or that from their observation of its working and yet be unable to see the Lawgiver!—who should be able to push back effect to immediate cause and yet be blind to the Supreme Cause of All Causes; who can say, "This is the glacier's doing and it is marvellous in our eyes," and not see Him "Who in His Strength setteth fast the mountains and is girded with power," whose servants the glaciers, the snow, and the ice are, "wind and storm fulfilling His Word"; who exult in the exercise of their own intelligences and the play things those intelligences have constructed and yet deny the Omniscience that endowed them with some minute fragment of Itself! It was not always so; it was not so with the really great men who have advanced our knowledge of nature. But of late years hordes of small men have given themselves up to the study of the physical sciences without any study preliminary. It would almost seem nowadays that whoever can sit in the seat of the scornful may sit in the seat of learning.

A good many years ago, on an occasion already referred to, the writer roamed through the depths of the Grand Cañon with a chance acquaintance who described himself as "Herpetologist to the Academy of Sciences" in some Western or Mid-Western State, and as this gentleman found the curious little reptiles he was in search of under a root or in a cranny of rock he repeated their many-syllabled names. Curious to know what these names literally meant and whence derived, the writer made inquiry, sometimes hazarding a conjectural etymology. To his astonishment and dismay he found this "scientist," whom he had looked up to, entirely ignorant of the meaning of the terms he employed. They were just arbitrary terms to him. The little hopping and crawling creatures might as well have been numbered, or called x, y, z, for any significance their formidable nomenclature held for him. Yet this man had been keenly sarcastic about the Noachian deluge and had jeered from the height of his superiority at hoary records which he knew only at second-hand reference, and had laid it down that if the human race became extinct the birds would stand the best chance of "evolving a primate"! Since that time other "scientists" have been encountered, with no better equipment, with no history, no poetry, no philosophy in any broad sense, men with no letters—illiterate, strictly speaking—yet with all the dogmatism in the world. Can any one be more dogmatic than your modern scientist? The reproach has passed altogether to him from the theologian.

The thing grows, and its menace and scandal grow with it. Since coming "outside" the writer has encountered a professor at a college, a Ph.D. of a great university, who confessed that he had never heard of certain immortal characters of Dickens whose names are household words. We shall have to open Night-Schools for Scientists, where men who have been deprived of all early advantages may learn the rudiments of English literature. One wishes that Dickens himself might have dealt with their pretensions, but they are since his day. And surely it is time some one started a movement for suppressing illiterate Ph.D.'s.

Of this class, one feels sure, are the scientific heroes of the sensational articles in the monthly magazines of the baser sort, of which we picked up a number in the Kantishna on our way to the mountain. Here, in a picture that seems to have obtruded itself bodily into a page of letterpress, or else to have suffered the accidental irruption of a page of letterpress all around it, you shall see a grave scientist looking anxiously down a very large microscope, and shall read that he has transferred a kidney from a cat to a dog, and therefore we can no longer believe in the immortality of the soul; or else that he has succeeded in artificially fertilizing the ova of a starfish—or was it a jellyfish?—and therefore there is no God; not just in so many bald words, of course, but in unmistakable import. Or it may be—so commonly does the crassest credulity go hand in hand with the blankest scepticism—he has discovered the germ of old age and is hot upon the track of another germ that shall destroy it, so that we may all live virtually as long as we like; which, of course, disposes once for all of a world to come. The Psalmist was not always compliant or even temperate in his language, but he lived a long time ago and must be pardoned; his curt summary stands: "Dixit insipiens!" But the writer vows that if he were addicted to the pursuit of any branch of physical knowledge he would insist upon being called by the name of that branch. He would be a physiologist or a biologist or an anatomist or even a herpetologist, but none should call him "scientist." As Doll Tearsheet says in the second part of "King Henry IV": "These villains will make the word as odious as the word 'occupy'; which was an excellent good word before it was ill-sorted." If Doctor Johnson were compiling an English dictionary to-day he would define "scientist" something thus: "A cant name for an experimenter in some department of physical knowledge, commonly furnished with arrogance and dogmatism, but devoid of real learning."

Here is no gib at the physical sciences. To sneer at them were just as foolish as to sneer at religion. What we could do on this expedition in a "scientific" way we did laboriously and zealously. We would never have thought of attempting the ascent of the mountain without bringing back whatever little addition to human knowledge was within the scope of our powers and opportunities. Tatum took rounds of angles, in practice against the good fortune of a clear day on top, on every possible occasion. The sole personal credit the present writer takes concerning the whole enterprise is the packing of that mercurial barometer on his back, from the Tanana River nearly to the top of the mountain, a point at which he was compelled to relinquish it to another. He has always had his opinion about mountain climbers who put an aneroid in their pocket and go to the top of a great, new peak and come down confidently announcing its height. But when all this business is done as closely and carefully as possible, and every observation taken that there are instruments devised to record, surely the soul is dead that feels no more and sees no further than the instruments do, that stirs with no other emotion than the mercury in the tube or the dial at its point of suspension, that is incapable of awe, of reverence, of worshipful uplift, and does not feel that "the Lord even the most mighty God hath spoken, and called the world from the rising of the sun even to the going down of the same," in the wonders displayed before his eyes.

We reached our eighteen-thousand-foot camp about five o'clock, a weary but happy crew. It was written in the diary that night: "I remember no day in my life so full of toil, distress, and exhaustion, and yet so full of happiness and keen gratification."

—1914

282

Note

1. The dotted line on the photograph opposite page 346 of Mr. Belmore Browne's book, "The Conquest of Mt. McKinley," does not, in the writer's opinion, represent the real course taken by Professor Parker, Mr. Belmore Browne, and Merl Le Voy in their approach to the summit, and it is easy to understand the confusion of direction in the fierce storm that descended upon the party. If, as the dots show, the party went to the summit of the right-hand peak, they went out of their way and had still a considerable distance to travel. "Perhaps five minutes of easy walking would have taken us to the highest point," says Mr. Browne. It is probably more than a mile from the summit of the snow peak shown in the picture to the actual summit of the mountain. One who took that course would have to descend from the peak and then ascend the horseshoe ridge, and the highest point of the horseshoe ridge is perhaps two hundred feet above the summit of this snow peak. In the opinion that Professor Parker expressed to the writer, the dotted lines should bear much more to the left, making directly for the centre of the horseshoe ridge, which is the obvious course. But it should again be said that men in the circumstances and condition of this party when forced to turn back, may be pardoned for mistaking the exact direction in which they had been proceeding.

Douglas William Freshfield

"The Song of the Himalayan Faeries" and "Ad Alta"

These lyrics are drawn from Douglas William Freshfield's (1845–1934) collection of travel and mountaineering poetry. President of both the Alpine Club (1893–1895) and the Royal Geographical Society (1914–1917), Freshfield was perhaps the most experienced and far-ranging climber in the nineteenth and early twentieth centuries. He pioneered exploration in the Alps, Himalaya, and the Caucasus in Russia. He wrote the standard work on Russian mountains in The Exploration of the Caucasus *(1896) with photographs by Vittorio Sella.*

"THE SONG OF THE HIMALAYAN FAERIES"

Far from the dusky alleys
Of the many-tongued Bazaar,
Beyond the shadowy valleys
Where the Lamaseries are,
Here, where no springtime varies
The frost's eternal span,
We dwell, the Mountain Fairies,
Since first the world began.

The glacier's winding river
Is our familiar road,
Through frozen waves that shiver
We sweep to our abode,
The foam-flakes on our horses
Are sheets of driven snow,
The goal of their wild courses
Only the winds may know.

The tribesmen, bent on plunder,
Who crawl in troops, like mice,
Where keen peaks, rent asunder,

Douglas William Freshfield, "The Song of the Himalayan Faeries" and "Ad Alta," *Unto the Hills* (London: Edward Arnold, 1914).

Gird hidden seas of ice,
Hear, as the shadows thicken,
Clear through the crystal air,
Sounds that the silence quicken,
Our evening call to prayer.

Then grows in ears that listen,
Beyond the dim crevasse,
The pulse of wings that glisten,
The beat of hosts that pass,
As round earth's loftiest steeples,
In shrines by man untrod,
The sky's primaeval peoples
Assemble unto God.

From our far-shining stations,
Where Death finds nought to slay,
We watch the way-worn nations
Toil upward from their clay;
We wait on our white islands
Of everlasting light
For souls who love the Highlands,
That soar above the Night.

For them we weave strange dances,
Like cloudlets "lightly curled,"
We whisper them in trances
The Secret of the World;
Those whom we show our faces
Are fain with us to dwell
In the elemental spaces,
Remote from Heaven or Hell.

BECAUSE IT'S THERE

"AD ALTA"

There are who love the silver heights,
The silver heights above the lawn,
Who spurn the lowland's tame delights,
Sworn fellow-travellers with the dawn;
Pursuers of no earthly goal,
They leave the slopes of maize and vine,
Outclimbing pasturage and pine
To seek beyond the mountain line
That fabled country, dim, divine,
Where Life is whole.

Not as on Mecca's pilgrimage
In one long, bright, unbroken stream
These pilgrims of our modern age
Their march pursue; to crowds who dream
As dreamt our fathers long ago

They yield the broad, the common round,
Daring their fate, beyond the bound
Of mortal sense, on that high ground
Whence Truth and Knowledge, star-encrowned,
Watch ages flow.

They strive, they strain, to reach the pass
Where the white peaks asunder swerve
To frame the Heaven's blue. Alas!
Of all that reach that shining curve
not one returns—not one to tell
What lies beyond—a void abyss,
Or summer-lands where those we miss,
Those gone before, join hands and kiss,
Before they mount through spheres of bliss
With God to dwell.

Yet some, who leave a vacant hearth,
And, grief for guide and comrade, scale
Heights that within our fate-fixed garth
Yet half o'erlook its bounding pale;
These in the all-embracing skies
Watch, through the gates of quiet snow

286

Where Death sits warder, far and low,
On earth's horizon pulsing slow,
The gleam of Deathless Love, the glow
Of Paradise.

To their high silence human strife
Comes as the torrent's muffled roar;
The clouds that roof the Plains of Life
For them are Heaven's golden floor;
The lights that all about them fly
Are God's own shadow; in their ears
The Soul that makes and moves the spheres,
That is in all that here appears,
Whispers the secret of the years:
Life cannot die.

—1914

George L. Mallory

from *The Assault on Mount Everest 1922*

The first major attempt on Everest was led by Brigadier General Charles Glanville Bruce (1866–1939), who had served on Martin Conway's Karakoram climbs and on Mummery's 1895 Nanga Parbat expedition, which claimed Mummery's life. Charles Howard-Bury had led a reconnaissance mission to the mountain in 1921 with some of the same team members who would later return to the mountain in 1922. Bottled oxygen equipment was first used extensively on this expedition, despite complaints from some prominent climbers that the use of such artificial aid was unethical and unsporting. George Leigh Mallory (1886–1924), T. H. Somervell, and Edward Norton reached 26,800 feet without oxygen on their first attempt. Immediately after, C. G. Bruce and George Finch achieved a world height record of 27,300 feet using bottled oxygen. A third attempt by Mallory and Somervell ended in the death of seven Sherpas in an avalanche. This selection, written by George Leigh Mallory, who had serious ambitions as a writer, describes the highest point attained in the first attempt. Mallory disappeared two years later on Everest with Sandy Irvine. Mallory's body was discovered in 1999.

THE HIGHEST POINT

My first recollection of the morning of May 20 is of shivering outside the porters' tents. It is not an enviable task at 23,000 feet, this of rousing men from the snugness of their sleeping-bags between 5 and 6 A.M. One may listen in vain for a note of alertness in their response; the heard notes will not echo the smallest zest for any enterprise. On this occasion the replies made to my tender inquiries and encouragements were so profoundly disappointing that I decided to untie the fastenings of the tent, which were as nearly as might be hermetically sealed. In the degree of somnolence and inertia prevailing I suspected the abnormal. Soon I began to make out a tale of confused complaints; the porters were not all well. The cause was not far to look for; they had starved themselves of air during the night. The best chance of a remedy was fresh air now and a brew of tea, which could easily be managed.

Meanwhile Norton had been stirring, and while I retired to "dress" he began to busy himself with preparations for our own breakfast. Tea of course was intended for us too, and further two tins of spaghetti had been reserved to give us the best possible start for the day. But one small thing had been forgotten. Those precious tins had lain

C. G. Bruce et alia, *The Assault on Mount Everest 1922* (London: Edward Arnold, 1923).

all night in the snow; they should have been cuddled by human bodies, carefully nursed in the warmth of sleeping-bags. Now their contents were frozen stiff and beyond extraction even by an ice-axe. Even so it might be supposed a little boiling water would put all to rights. Had a little sufficed I should omit to tell the doleful tale. Only very gradually were the outer surfaces thawed, permitting the scarlet blocks (tomato sauce was an ingredient) to be transferred to another saucepan, where they had still to be thawed to homogenous softness and afterwards heated to the point required for doing justice to the genius of Mr. Heinz. As the expenditure of treasured hot water merely for thawing spaghetti involved more melting of snow to water and boiling of water for indispensable tea, the kitchen-maid's task was disagreeably protracted; and the one among us, Norton, who most continuously and stubbornly played the man's part of kitchen-maid, sitting upon the snow in the chill early morning became a great deal colder than anyone should be with a day's mountaineering in front of him.

Of our nine porters it was presently discovered that five were mountain-sick in various degrees; only four were fit to come on and do a full day's work carrying up our camp. The whole of our reserve was already exhausted before we had advanced a single step up the North Ridge. But pessimism was not in the air this morning. We had won through our various delays and difficulties, we had eaten and enjoyed our wonderful breakfast, and after all we were able to make a start about 7:30 A.M. The reserve had already been of use; without it we should have been obliged to remain in camp, waiting for sick porters to recover, and counting our stores. Morshead, who by the testimony of good spirits seemed the fittest of us all, was set to lead the party; I followed with two porters, while Norton and Somervell shepherded the others on a separate rope. In a short half-hour we were on the North Col itself, the true white neck to the South of those strange blocks of ice, and looking up the North Ridge from its foot.

The general nature of what lay ahead of us can readily be appreciated from this point of view. To the right, as you look up, the great Northern slopes of Mount Everest above the main Rongbuk Glacier are slightly concave; the North-eastern face to the left is also concave, but much more deeply, and especially more deeply in a section of about 1,500 feet above the North Col. Consequently the ground falls away more suddenly on that side below the ridge. The climber may either follow the crest itself or find a parallel way on the gently receding face to right of it. The best way for us, we soon saw, was not to follow the crest of snow or even the snow-slopes immediately to the right; for these were merged after a little interval in the vast sweep of broken rocks forming the North face of the mountain, and at the junction between snow and rocks was an edge of stones stretching upwards for perhaps 1,500 feet at a convenient angle. Loose stones that slip as he treads on them are an abomination to the climber's feet and only less fatiguing than knee-deep sticky snow. We presently found those stones agreeably secure; enough snow lay among them to bind and freeze all to the slope; we were able to tread on firm, flat surfaces without the trouble of kicking our feet into snow; no sort of ground could have taken us more easily up the mountain. The morning, too, was calm and fine. Though it can hardly be said that we enjoyed the exercise

289

of going up Mount Everest, we were certainly able to enjoy the sensation so long as our progress was satisfactory. But the air remained perceptibly colder than we could have wished; the sun had less than its usual power; and in the breeze which sprang up on our side, blowing across the ridge from the right, we recognized an enemy, "the old wind in the old anger," the devastating wind of Tibet. The wolf had come in lamb's clothes. But we were not deceived. Remembering bitter experiences down in the plains now 10,000 feet below us, we expected little mercy here, we only hoped for a period of respite; so long as this gentle mood should last we could proceed happily enough until we should be obliged to fight our way up.

We had risen about 1,200 feet when we stopped to put on the spare warm clothes which we carried against such a contingency as this. For my part, I added a light shetland "woolly" and a thin silk shirt to what I was wearing before under my closely woven cotton coat. As this outer garment, with knickers to match, was practically windproof, and a silk shirt too is a further protection against wind, with these two extra layers I feared no cold we were likely to meet. Morshead, if I remember right, troubled himself no more at this time than to wrap a woollen scarf round his neck, and he and I were ready and impatient to get off before the rest. Norton was sitting a little way below with his rucksack poised on his lap. In gathering up our rope so as to have it free when we should move on I must have communicated to the other rope some small jerk—sufficient, at all events, to upset the balance of Norton's rucksack. He was unprepared, made a desperate grab, and missed it. Slowly the round, soft thing gathered momentum from its rotation, the first little leaps down from one ledge to another grew to excited and magnificent bounds, and the precious burden vanished from sight. For a little interval, while we still imagined its fearful progress until it should rest for who knows how long on the snow at the head of the Rongbuk Glacier, no one spoke. "My rucksack gone down the kudh!" Norton exclaimed with simple regret. I made a mental note that my warm pyjama-legs which he had borrowed were inside it, so if I were to blame I had a share in the loss. A number of offers in woollen garments for the night were soon made to Norton; after which we began to explain what each had brought for comfort's sake, and I wondered whether my companions' system of selection resembled mine;—as I never can resolve in cold blood to leave anything behind, when each article presents itself as just the one I may particularly want, I pack them all into a rucksack and then pull out this and that more or less at random until the load is not greater than I can conveniently carry; even so I almost invariably find that I have more clothing in reserve than I actually use.

However, we had no time to spare for discussing the dispensation of absolute justice between the various claims of affection and utility among a man's equipment. We were soon plodding upwards again, and had we been inclined to tarry the bite of the keen air would have hurried us along. The respite granted us was short enough. The sun disappeared behind a veil of high clouds; and before long grey tones to match the sky replaced the varied brightness of snow and rocks, and soon now we were struggling to keep our breath and leaning our bodies against a heavy wind. We had not the experience to reckon exactly the dangers associated with these conditions. We could only look to our senses for warning, and their warning soon became obvious enough. Fingertips and toes and ears all began to testify to the cold. By continuing on the windward flank of the ridge just where we were most exposed we should incur a heavy risk of frostbite and the whole party might be put out of action. It was clear that something must be done, and without delay. The best chance was to change our direction. Very likely we should find less wind, as is often the case, on the crest itself, and in any case we must reach shelter on the leeward side at the earliest possible moment.

While Morshead stopped, at last submitting so far as to put on a sledging suit, which is reputed to be the best possible protection, I went ahead, abandoned the rocks, and steered a slanting course over the snow to the left. Unlike the softer substance we had met in the region of the North Col, the surface here was hard; on this smooth slope the blown snow can find no lodgment, cannot stay to be gathered into drifts, and the little that falls there is swept clean away. The angle soon became steeper, and we must have steps to tread in. A strong kick was required to make the smallest impression in the snow. It was just the place where we could best be served by crampons and be helped up by their long steel points without troubling ourselves at all about steps. Crampons of course had been provided among our equipment, and the question of taking them with us above Camp IV had been considered. We had decided not to bring them: we sorely needed them now. And yet we had been right to leave them behind; for with their straps binding tightly round our boots we should not have had the smallest chance of preserving our toes from frostbite. The only way was to set to work and cut steps. The proper manner of cutting one in such a substance as this is to take but one strong blow, tearing out enough snow to allow the foot to finish the work as it treads in the hold. Such a practice is not beyond the strength and skill of an amateur in the Alps. But even if he can muster the power for this sort of blow at a great altitude, he will soon discover the inconvenience of repeating it frequently; he will be out of breath and panting and obliged to wait, so that no time has been gained after all. The alternative is to apply less force; three gentle strokes, as a rule, will be required for each step. To cut a staircase in this humble manner was by no means impossible, as was proved again on the descent, up to 25,000 feet. But the same rules and limitations determine this labour as every other up here. The work can be done and the worker will endure it provided sufficient time is allowed. It is haste that induces exhaustion. On this occasion we were obliged to hurry; our object was to reach shelter as soon as possible. In a wind like that on a bare snow-slope a man must take his axe in both hands to meet the present need; future contingencies will be left to take care of themselves. The slope was never steep; the substance was not obdurate; but when at length we lay on the rocks and out of the wind I computed our staircase to be 300 feet, and at least one of us was very tired.

I cannot say precisely how much time passed on this arduous section of our ascent. It was now 11.30 A.M. The aneroid was showing 25,000 feet compared with a reading 23,000 on the North Col; the rise of 2,000 feet had taken us in all three and one-half hours.

For some reason Morshead had been delayed with two or three of the porters, and as the rest of us now sat waiting for them we began to discuss what should be done about fixing our camp. It had been our intention to reach 26,000 feet before pitching the tents. But it was evident that very few places would accommodate them. We had already seen enough to realise how steeply the rocks of this mountain dip towards the North, with the consequence that even where the ground is broken the ledges are likely to prove too steep for camping. We must pass the night somewhere on this leeward side, and we had little hopes of finding a place above us. However, at about our present level, well marked as the point of junction between snow and rocks, we had previously observed from Camp III some ground which appeared less uncompromising than the rest. A broken ledge offered a practicable line towards this same locality.

Whether the decisions we came to at this crisis of our fortunes were right or wrong, I cannot tell, and I hardly want to know. I have no wish to excuse our judgment. Who can tell what might have happened had we decided otherwise? And who can judge? Then why should I be at the pains to analyse the thoughts which influenced our decision? It is perhaps a futile inquiry. Nevertheless it is such decisions that determine the fate of a mountaineering enterprise, and the operative motives or contending points of view may have an interest of their own. Among us there was deliberation often enough, but never contention. There never was a dissentient voice to anything we resolved to do, partly, I suppose, because we had little choice in the matter, more because we were that sort of party. We had a single aim in common and regarded it from common ground. We had no leader within the full meaning of the word, no one in authority over the rest to command as captain. We all knew equally what was required to be done from first to last, and when the occasion arose for doing it one of us did it. Some one, if only to avoid delay in action, had to arrange the order in which the party or parties should proceed. I took this responsibility without waiting to be asked; the rest accepted my initiative, I suppose, because I used to talk so much about what had been done on the previous Expedition. In practice it amounted only to this, that I would say to my companions, "A, will you go first? B, will you go second?" and we roped up in the order indicated without palaver. Apart from this I never attempted to inflict my own view on men who were at least as capable as I of judging what was best. Our proceedings in any crisis of our fortunes were informally democratic. They were so on the occasion from which I have so grievously digressed.

It must not be forgotten that we had just come through a trying ordeal. Nothing is more demoralising than a severe wind, and it may be that our *morale* was affected. But I don't think we were demoralised, or not in any degree so as to affect our judgment. The impression I retain from that remote scene where we sat perched in discussion crowding under a bluff of rocks is of a party well pleased with their performance, rejoicing to be sheltered from the wind, and every one of them quite game to go higher. Perhaps the deciding influence was the weather. A mountaineer judges of the weather conditions almost by instinct; and apart from our experience of the wind, which had already been sufficiently menacing, we knew, so far as such things can be known, that the weather would get worse before it got better. But we could not imagine what might be coming without thinking definitely about the porters. It would be their lot, wherever our new camp was fixed, to return this same day to Camp IV. It was no part of our design to risk even the extremities of their limbs, let alone their lives; apart from any consideration of ethics it would not be sensible; no one supposed that this attempt on Mount Everest would be the last of the season, even for ourselves, and if the porters who first completed this stage were to suffer nothing worse than severe frostbite the moral effect of that injury alone might be an irreparable disaster. The porters must be sent down before the weather grew worse, and the less they were exposed to the cold wind the better. It was 12.30 P.M. before the stragglers who had joined us had rested sufficiently to go on. To fix a camp 1,000 feet higher would probably require, granted reasonably good fortune in finding a site, another three hours; and if snow began to fall or the ridge were enveloped in mist it would be necessary to provide an escort for the porters. Had we supposed a place might be found anywhere above us within range on this lee-side of the ridge, we might conceivably have accepted these hard conditions and pushed on. Deliberately to choose a site on the ridge with such a wind blowing and in defiance of every threat in the sky was a folly not to be contemplated, and our suppositions as to the lee-side above us (they were afterwards proved correct) were all unfavourable to going higher. The plan of encamping somewhere near at hand, not lower than 25,000 feet, still left plenty to hope for this time besides building the best foundation for a second attempt. In my opinion no other alternative was sanely practicable; and I believe this conviction was shared by all when at length we left our niche, having conceded so much already to the mountain.

As the broken ledges we now followed presented no special difficulties the party was able to explore more than one level in search of some place sufficiently flat and sufficiently commodious. The nature of the ground and the presence of cloud, though we were never thickly enveloped, prevented any sort of extensive view. Many suggestions were mooted and rejected; a considerable time elapsed and still we had found no site that would serve. At about 2 P.M. Somervell and some porters shouted the news that one tent could be pitched in the place where they were. On the far side of a defined rib slanting up to the ridge we had left they had discovered some sort of a platform. It was evident that work would be required to extend and prepare it for the tent, and they at once set about building a supporting wall and levelling the ground. It remained to find a place near at hand for the other tent. We could see no obvious shelf, but the constructional works undertaken by Somervell seemed to contain such a promising idea that Norton and I in separate places each started works of our own. Each of us very soon reached the same conclusion, that nothing could be done where he was. We moved away and tried again; but always with the same result; the ground was everywhere too steep and too insecure. One soon tires of heaving up big stones when no useful end is served. Eventually coming together, we resolved to agree on the least unlikely site and make the best of it. We chose the foot of a long sloping slab—at all events it was part of the mountain and would not budge—and there built up the ground below it with some fine stones we found to hand. Our tent was pitched at last with one side of the floor lying along the foot of the sloping slab and the other half on the platform we had made. It was not a situation that promised for either of us a bountiful repose, for one would be obliged to lie along the slope and the only check to his tendency to slip down would be the body of the other. However, there it was, a little tent making a gallant effort to hold itself proudly and well.

Before we had concluded these operations the porters had been sent down about 3 P.M. and kitchen had been instituted, and a meal was already being prepared. Presumably because their single tent would have to accommodate the four of us (ours was too far away), when we set ourselves down to eat and be warm, Somervell and Morshead had arranged the kitchen outside it. Somervell had appointed himself chief in this department and it remained only for the rest of us to offer menial service. But so great had been his energy and perseverance, sheltering the flame from the cold draught and by every device encouraging the snow to melt, that almost all such offers were rejected. Like a famous pretender, I would have gladly been a scullion, but I was allowed only to open one or two tins and fill up a pot with snow. I have no recollection of what we ate; I remember only a hot and stimulating drink, Brand's essence of bovril or something of the sort. We did not linger long over this meal. We wanted to go to bed still warm. Norton and I soon left the others in possession of their tent and began to make our dispositions for the night.

To the civilised man who gets into bed after the customary routine, tucks himself in, lays his head on the pillow, and presently goes to sleep with no further worry, the dispositions in a climber's tent may seem to be strangely intricate. In the first place, he has to arrange about his boots. He looks forward to the time when he will have to start next morning, if possible with warm feet and in boots not altogether frozen stiff. He may choose to go to bed in his boots, not altogether approving the practice, and resolving that the habit shall not be allowed to grow upon him. If his feet are already warm when he turns in, it may be that he can do no better; his feet will probably keep warm in the sleeping-bag if he wears his bed-socks over his boots, and he will not have to endure the pains of pulling on and wearing frozen boots in the morning. At this camp I adopted a different plan—to wear moccasins instead of boots during the night and keep them on until the last moment before starting. But if one takes his boots off, where is he to keep them warm? Climbing boots are not good to cuddle, and in any case there will be no room for them with two now inside a double sleeping-bag. My boots were happily accommodated in a rucksack and I put them under my head for a pillow. It is not often that one uses the head for warming things, and no one would suspect one of a hot head; nevertheless my boots were kept warm enough and were scarcely frozen in the morning.

It was all-important besides to make ourselves really comfortable, if we were to get to sleep, by making experiments in the disposition of limbs, adjusting the floor if possible and arranging one's pillow at exactly the right level—which may be difficult, as the pillow should be high if one is to breathe easily at a great altitude. I had already found out exactly how to be comfortable before Norton was ready to share the accommodation. I remarked that in our double sleeping-bag I found ample room for myself but not much to spare. Norton's entrance was a grievous disturbance. It was doubtful for some time whether he would be able to enter; considering how long and slim he is, it is astonishing how much room he requires. We were so tightly pressed together that if either was to move a corresponding manoeuvre was required of the other. I soon discovered, as the chief item of interest in the place where I lay, a certain boulder obstinately immovable and excruciatingly sharp witch came up between my shoulder-blades. How under these circumstances we achieved sleep, and I believe that both of us were sometimes unconscious in a sort of light, intermittent slumber, I cannot attempt to explain. Perhaps the fact that one was often breathless from the exhaustion of discomfort, and was obliged to breathe deeply, helped one to sleep, as deep breathing often will. Perhaps the necessity of lying still because it was so difficult to move was good for us in the end. Norton's case was worse than mine. One of his ears had been severely frostbitten on the way up; only one side was available to lie on; and yet the 'blessed sleep' we sometimes sigh for in easy beds at home visited him too.

The party had suffered more than at first we realized from exposure in the wind on the way up. The damage to Norton's ear was not all. I noticed when my hands got warm in bed that three finger-tips appeared to be badly bruised; the symptom could only point to one conclusion, and I soon made out how they had come to be frostbitten. At the time when the step-cutting began I had been wearing a pair of lined leather gloves, motor-drivers' gloves well suited to the occasion, and my hands had been so warm that I thought it safe to change the glove on my right hand for a woollen one with which it was easier to grasp the axe. But wool is not a good protection against wind, and in grasping the axe I must have partially stopped the circulation in these finger-tips. The injury, though not serious, was inconvenient. And Morshead had felt the cold far more than I. It is still uncertain whether he had yet been frostbitten in toes and fingers, but though he made no complaint about them until much later I have little doubt they were already touched, if not severely frozen. At all events, he had been badly chilled on the way up; he was obliged to lie down when we reached our camp and was evidently unwell.

When all is said about our troubles and difficulties, the night, in spite of everything, was endurable. For distraction to pass the sleepless intervals engaging thoughts were not far to seek; we had still our plans for to-morrow; the climax was to come; and, might we not get so high by such a time? Then, might not the remaining hours be almost, even quite enough? Besides, we had accomplished something, and though the moments following achievement are occupied more often in looking forward than in looking back, we perhaps deliberately encouraged in ourselves a certain complacency on the present occasion; we were able to feel some little satisfaction in the mere existence of this camp, the two small tents perched there on the vast mountain-side of snow-bound rocks and actually higher, at 25,000 feet, than any climbing party had been before. "Hang it all!" we cooed, "it's not so bad."

The worst of it in dimly conscious moments was still the weather. The wind had dropped in the evening, as it often does, and nothing was to be deduced from that; but the hovering clouds had not cleared off and the night was too warm. I'm not meaning that we complained of the warmth; but for fine weather we must have a cold night, and it was no colder here than we had often known it at Camp III.[1] Occasionally stars were visible during the night; but they shone with a feeble, watery light, and in the early morning we were listening to the musical patter of fine, granular snow on the roofs of our tents. A thick mist had come up all about us, and the stones outside were white with a growing pall of fresh snow. We were greatly surprised under these conditions when, at about 6:30 A.M., a perceptible break appeared in the clouds to the East of us, the "weather quarter," and this good sign developed so hopefully that we were soon encouraged to expect a fair day. It was even more surprising perhaps that some one among us very quickly discovered this conscience: "I suppose," he said with a stifled yawn, in a tone that reminded one of Mr. Saltena rolling over in his costly bed, "It's about time we were getting up." No one dissented—how could one dissent? "I suppose we ought to be getting up," we grunted in turn, and slowly we began to draw ourselves out from the tight warmth of those friendly bags.

I do not propose to emphasise the various agonies of an early-morning start or to catalogue all that may be found for fumbling fingers to do; but one incident is worth recording. A second rucksack escaped us, slipping from the ledge where it was perched, and went bounding down the mountain. Its value, even Norton will agree, was greater than that of the first; it contained our provisions; our breakfast was inside it. From the moment of its elusion I gave it up for lost. What could stop its fatal career? What did stop it unless it were a miracle? Somehow or another it was hung up on a ledge 100 feet below. Morshead volunteered to go and get it. By slow degrees he dragged up the heavy load, and our precious stores were recovered intact.

At 8 A.M. we were ready to start and roped up, Norton first, followed by myself, Morshead and Somervell. This bald statement of fact may suggest a misleading picture; the reader may imagine the four of us like runners at the start of a race, greyhounds straining at the leash, with nerves on the stretch and muscles aching for the moment when they can be suddenly tight in strong endeavor. It was not like that. I suppose we had all the same feelings in various degrees, and even our slight exertions about the camp had shown us something of our physical state. In spite of the occasional sleep of exhaustion it had been a long, restless night, scarcely less wearisome than the preceding day; we were tired no less than when we went to bed, and stiff from lying in cramped attitudes. I was clear about my own case. Struggling across with an awkward load from one tent to the other, I had had been forced to put the question, Is it possible for me to go on? Judging from physical evidence, No; I hadn't the power to lift my weight repeatedly step after step. And yet from experience I knew that I should go on for a time at all events; something would set the machinery going and somehow I should be able to keep it at work. And when the moment of starting came I felt some little stir of excitement. If we were not going to experience "the wild joy of living, the leaping from rock up to rock," on the other hand this was not to be a sort of funeral procession. A certain keenness of anticipation is associated merely with tying on the rope. We tied it on now partly for convenience, so that no one would be obliged to carry it on his back, but no less for its moral effect; a roped party is more closely united; the separate wills of individuals are joined into a stronger common will. Our roping-up was the last act of preparation. We had "got ourselves ready," lacing up our boots so as to be just tight enough but not too tight, disposing puttees so that they would not slip down, attending to one small thing or another about our clothing for warmth and comfort's sake, possibly even tightening a buckle or doing up a button simply for neatness, and not forgetting to arrange the few things we wanted to take with us, some in rucksacks, some nearer to hand in pockets. Two of us, Norton and I, as Somervell's photograph proves, appeared positively dainty; the word seems hardly applicable to Somervell himself: but at all events we were all ready; we felt ready; and when all these details of preparation culminated in tying on the rope we felt something more, derived from the many occasions in the past when readiness in mind and body contained the keen anticipation of strenuous delights.

How quickly the physical facts of our case asserted their importance! We had only moved upwards a few steps when Morshead stopped. "I think I won't come with you any farther," he said. "I know I should only keep you back." Considering his condition on the previous day I had not supposed Morshead would get very much higher; but this morning he had so made light of his troubles, and worn so cheerful a countenance, that we heard this statement now with surprise and anxiety. We understood very well the spirit of the remark; if Morshead said that, there could be no longer a question of his coming on, but we wondered whether one of us should not stay behind with him. However, he declared that he was not seriously unwell and was perfectly capable of looking after himself. Somervell's judgment as a doctor confirmed him, and it was decided he should remain in camp while we three went on without him.

Our first object was to regain the crest of the North Ridge, not by retracing our steps to the point where we had left it yesterday, but slanting up to meet it perhaps 800 feet above us. Ascent is possible almost everywhere on these broken slopes; a steeper pitch can usually be avoided, and the more difficult feats of climbing need not be performed. In fact, the whole problem for the mountaineer is quite unlike that presented by the ridge of any great mountain in the Alps, which, if it is not definitely a snow ridge like that from the Dômedu Gouter to the summit of Mont Blanc, will almost invariably present a sharper edge and a more broken crest. On the North Ridge of Everest one has the sensations rather of climbing the face than the ridge of a mountain; and it is best thought of as a face-climb, for one is actually on the North face, though at the edge of it. I can think of no exact parallel in the Alps—the nearest perhaps would be the easier parts on the Hornli Ridge of the Matterhorn, if we were to imagine the stones to be fewer, larger and more secure. Somervell's photographs will convey more to the trained eye of a mountaineer than any words of mine, and it will readily be understood that there was no question for us of gymnastic struggles and strong armpulls, wedging ourselves in cracks and hanging on our finger-tips. We should soon have been turned back by difficulties of that sort. We could allow ourselves nothing in the nature of a violent struggle. We must avoid any hasty movement. It would have exhausted us at once to proceed by rushing up a few steps at a time. We wanted to hit off just that mean pace which we could keep up with out rapidly losing our strength, to proceed evenly with balanced movements, saving effort, to keep our form, as oarsmen say, at the end of the race, remembering to step neatly and transfer the weight from one leg to the other by swinging the body rhythmically upwards. With the occasional help of the hands we were able to keep going for spells of twenty or thirty minutes before halting for three or four or five minutes to gather potential energy for pushing on again. Our whole power seemed to depend on the lungs. The air, such as it was, was inhaled through the mouth and expired again to some sort of tune in the unconscious mind, and the lungs beat time, as it were, for the feet. An effort of will was required not so much to induce any movement of the limbs as to set the lungs to work and keep them working. So long as they were working evenly and well the limbs would do their duty automatically, it seemed, as though actuated by a hidden spring. I remember one rather longer halt. In spite of all my care I found that one of my feet was painfully cold, and fearing frostbite I took off my boot. Norton rubbed my foot warm. I had been wearing four thick socks, and now put back on this foot only three. As it remained warm for the rest of the day I have no doubt that the boot was previously too tight. Once again I learned the futility of stopping the circulation by wearing one layer of wool too many.

It was our intention naturally in setting out this day to reach the summit of Mount Everest. Provided we were not stopped by a mountaineering difficulty, and that was unlikely, the fate of our Expedition would depend on the two factors, time and speed. Of course, we might become too exhausted to go farther before reaching our goal; but the consideration of speed really covers that case, for provided one were capable of moving his limbs at all he would presumably be able to crawl a few steps only so slowly that there would be no point in doing so. From the outset we were short of time; we should have started two hours earlier; the weather prevented us. The fresh snow was an encumbrance, lying everywhere on the ledges from 4 inches to 8 inches deep; it must have made a difference, though not a large one. In any case, when we measured our rate of progress it was not satisfactory, at most 400 feet an hour, not counting halts, and diminishing a little as we went up. It became clear that if we could go no farther—and we couldn't without exhausting ourselves at once— we should still at the best be struggling upwards after night had fallen again. We were prepared to leave it to braver men to climb Mount Everest by night.

By agreeing to this arithmetical computation we tacitly accepted defeat. And if we were not to reach the summit, what remained for us to do? None of us, I believe,

298

cared much about any lower objective. We were not greatly interested then in the exact number of feet by which we should beat a record. It must be remembered that the mind is not easily interested under such conditions. The intelligence is gradually numbed as the supply of oxygen diminishes and the body comes nearer to exhaustion. Looking back on my own mental processes as we approached 27,000 feet, I can find no traces of insanity, nothing completely illogical; within a small compass I was able to reason, no doubt very slowly. But my reasoning was concerned only with one idea; beyond its range I can recall no thought. The view, for instance—and as a rule I'm keen enough about the view—did not interest me; I was not "taking notice." Wonderful as such an experience would be, I had not even the desire to look over the North-east ridge; I would have gladly got to the North-east shoulder as being the sort of place one ought to reach, but I had no strong desire to get there, and none at all for the wonder of being there. I dare say the others were more mentally alive than I; but when it came to deciding what we should do, we had no lively discussion. It seemed to me that we should get back to Morshead in time to take him down this same day to Camp IV. There was some sense in this idea, and many mountaineers may think we were right to make it a first consideration. But the alternative of sleeping a second night at our highest camp and returning next day to Camp III was never mentioned. It may have been that we shrank unconsciously from another night in such discomfort; whether the thought was avoided in this way, or simply was not born, our minds were not behaving as we would wish them to behave. The idea of reaching Camp IV with Morshead before dark, once it had been accepted, controlled us altogether. It was easy to calculate from our upward speed, supposing that we could treble this on the descent at what time we ought to turn; we agreed to start down at 2:30 P.M., but we would maintain our rate of progress as best we could until that time approached.

At 2:15 we completed the ascent of a steeper pitch and found ourselves on the edge of an easier terrain, where the mountain slopes back towards the North-east shoulder. It was an obvious place for a halt: we were in need of food; and we lay against the rocks to spend the remaining fifteen minutes before we should turn for the descent according to our bond. None of us was altogether "cooked" we were not brought to a standstill because our limbs would carry us no farther. I should be very sorry to reach such a condition at this altitude; for one would not recover easily; and a man who cannot take care of himself on the descent will probably be the cause of disaster to his companions, who will have little enough strength remaining to help themselves and him. It is impossible to say how much farther we might have gone. In the light of subsequent events it would seem that the margin of strength to deal with an emergency was already small enough. I have little doubt that we could have struggled up perhaps in two hours more to the North-east shoulder, now little more than 400 feet above us. Whether we should then have been fit to conduct our descent in safety is another matter.

While we ate such food as we had with us, chiefly sugar in one form or another, chocolate, mintcake, or acid-drops, and best of all raisins and prunes, we now had leisure to look about us. The summit of Everest, or what appeared to be the summit (I doubt if we saw the ultimate tip), lying back along the North-east ridge, was not impressive, and we were too near up under this ridge to add anything to former observations as to the nature of its obstacles. The view was necessarily restricted when Everest itself hid so much country. But it was a pleasure to look westwards across the broad North face and down it towards the Rongbuk Glacier; it was satisfactory to notice that the North Peak which, though perceptibly below us, had still held, so to speak, a place in our circle when we started in the morning, this same Changtse had now become a contemptible fellow beneath our notice. We saw his black plebeian head rising from the mists, mists that filled all the valleys, so that there was nothing in all the world as we looked from North-east to North-west but the great twins Gyachung Kang and Chö Uyo; and even these, though they regarded us still from a station of equality, were actually inferior. The lesser of them is 26,000 feet, and we could clearly afford to despise him; the greater Chö Uyo we had to regard respectfully before we could be sure; his triangulated height is 26,870, whereas our aneroid was reading only 26,800; it seemed that we were looking over his head, but such appearances are deceptive, and we were glad to have the confirmation of the theodolite later proving that we had reached 26,985 feet—higher than Chö Uyo by 100 feet and more.

The beneficent superiority with which we now regarded the whole world except Mount Everest no doubt helped us to swallow our luncheon—or was it dinner?—a difficult matter, for our tongues were hanging out after so much exercise of breathing. We had no chance of finding a trickle here as one often may in the blessed Alps; and medical opinion, which knew all about what was good for us, frowned upon the notion of alcoholic stimulant for a climber in distress at a high altitude. And so, very naturally, when one of us (Be of good cheer, my friend, I won't give you away!) produced from his pocket a flask of Brandy—each of us took a little nip. I am glad to relate that the result was excellent; it is logically certain therefore that the Brandy contained no alcohol. The non-alcoholic Brandy, then, no doubt by reason of what it lacked, had an important spiritual effect; it gave us just the mental fillip which we required to pull ourselves together for the descent.

Happily inspired by our "medical comfort," I announced that I would take the lead. Norton and I changed places on the rope. I optimistically supposed that I should find an easier way down by a continuous snow-slope to the West of the ridge. Somervell, also moved by inspiration, suggested that he should remain behind to make a sketch and hurry down our tracks to catch us up later. He says that I found it difficult to understand that he would only require a few minutes, and that I replied irritably. I can hardly believe that my tone just then was anything but suave, but I have no doubt I was glad to have him with us to be our sheet-anchor, and particularly so a little later, for we were in difficulties almost at once. We found more snow on this new line, as I had supposed; but it was not to our liking; it lay not on a continuous slope, but covering a series of slabs and only too ready to slide off. We were obliged to work back to the ridge itself and follow it down in our morning's tracks.

300

At 4 P.M. we reached our camp, where Morshead was waiting. He was feeling perfectly well, he reported, and ready to come down with us to Camp IV. After collecting a few of our possessions which we did not wish to abandon to the uncertain future, we roped up once more to continue our descent. So far our pace going down had been highly satisfactory. In the Alps one usually expects to descent on easy ground twice as fast as one would go up. But we had divided our time of ascent by four, and in an hour and a half had come down 2,000 feet. Under normal conditions at lower altitudes even this pace would be considered slow; it would not be an exceptionally fast pace for going up these slopes; and yet the image that stays in my memory is of a party coming down quite fast. It is evident that the whole standard of speed is altered. On the ascent, too, I had the sensation of moving about twice as fast as we actually were. I imagine that the whole of life was scaled down, as it were, that we were living both physically and mentally at half, or less than half, the normal rate. However that may be we had now to descend only 2,000 feet to Camp IV, and with more than three hours' daylight left we supposed we should have no difficulty in reaching our tents before dark.

Meditating after the event about the whole of our performance this day, I have often wondered how we should have appeared at various stages to an unfatigued and competent observer. No doubt he would have noted with some misgiving the gradually diminishing pace of the party as it crawled upwards; but he would have been satisfied, I think, that each man had control of his limbs and a sure balance, and as we were moving along together over ground where the rope will very easily be caught under the points of projecting rocks and thereby cause inconvenience and delay while it is unhitched, this observer, watching the rope, would have noticed that in fact it almost never was caught up. The party at all events were "keeping their form" to the extent of managing the rope as it ought to be managed. For a moment when they were in difficulties after turning back, he might have thought them rather shaky; but even here they were able to pull themselves together and proceed with proper attention and care. Whether he would have noticed any difference when they started off again I cannot say. A certain impetus of concentration, a gathering of mental and physical energy, a reserve called up from who knows where when they turned to face the descent, had perhaps spent its force; and though the party was a stage nearer to the end of the journey, it was also a stage nearer to exhaustion and to that state where carelessness so readily slips in unperceived. It may be supposed we were a degree less alert, all the more because we foresaw no difficulty; we had not exercised the imagination to figure difficulties on the descent, and we now came upon them unexpectedly.

The fresh snow fallen during the night had so altered appearances that we could not be certain, as we traversed back towards the ridge again, that we were exactly following the line by which we had approached our camp the day before. My impression is that we went too low and missed it. We were soon working along broken ground above a broad snow slope. Fresh snow had to be cleared away alike from protruding rocks where we wished to put our feet and from the old snow where we

301

must cut steps. It was not a difficult place and yet not easy, as the slope below us was dangerous and yet not very steep, not steep enough to be really alarming or specially to warn the climber that a slip may be fatal. It was an occasion when the need for care and attention was greater than obviously appeared, just the sort to catch a tired party off their guard. Perhaps the steps were cut too hastily, or in one way and another were taking small risks that we would not usually take. The whole party would not necessarily have been in grave danger because one man lost his footing. But we were unprepared. When the third man slipped the last man was moving, and was at once pulled off his balance. The second in the party, though he must have checked these two, could not hold them. In a moment the three of them were slipping down and gathering speed on a slope where nothing would stop them until they reached the plateau of the East Rongbuk Glacier, 3,500 feet below. The leader for some reason had become anxious about the party a minute or two earlier, and though he too was moving when the slip occurred and could see nothing of what went on behind him, he was on the alert; warned now by unusual sounds that something was wrong, he at once struck the pick of his axe into the snow, and hitched the rope round the head of it. Standing securely his position was good, and while holding the rope in his right hand beyond the hitch, he was able to press with the other on the shaft of the axe, his whole weight leaning towards the slope so as to hold the pick of the axe into the snow. Even so it would be almost impossible to check the combined momentum of three men at once. In ninety-nine cases out of a hundred either the belay will give or the rope will break. In the still moment of suspense before the matter must be put to the test nothing further could be done to prevent a disaster one way or the other. The rope suddenly tightened and tugged at the axe-head. It gave a little as it gripped the metal like a hawser on a bollard. The pick did not budge. Then the rope came taut between the moving figures, and the rope showed what it was worth. From one of the bodies which had slid and now was stopped proceeded an utterance, not in the best taste, reproaching this fate, because he must now start going up hill again when he should have been descending. The danger had passed. The weight of three men had not come upon the rope with a single jerk. The two lengths between the three as they slipped down were presumably not stretched tight, and the second man had been checked directly below the leader before the other two. Probably he also did something to check those below him, for he was partly held up by projecting rocks and almost at once recovered his footing. We were soon secure again on the mountain-side, and—not the least surprising fact—no one had been hurt.

I suppose we must all have felt rather shaken by an incident which came so near to being a catastrophe. But a party will not necessarily be less competent or climb worse on that account. At all events we had received a warning and now proceeded with the utmost caution, moving one at a time over the snow-covered ledges. It was slow work. This little distance which with fair conditions could easily be traversed in a quarter of an hour must have taken us about five times as long. However, when we reached the ridge and again looked down the snow where we had come up the day before, though it was clear enough we must waste no time, we did not feel greatly pressed. Our old tracks were, of course, covered, and we looked about for a way to avoid this slope; but it seemed better to go down by the way we knew, and we were soon busy chipping steps. It was a grim necessity at this hour of the day. I felt one might almost have slipped down checking himself with the axe. We were distinctly tempted. But after all, we were not playing with this mountain; it might be playing with us. There was a clear risk, and we were not compelled to accept it. We must keep on slowly cutting our steps. The long toil was shared among us until the slope eased off and we had nothing more to fear. We looked down to the North Col below us. No difficulty could stop our descent. We had still an hour of daylight. After all, with ordinary good fortune, we should be back in our tents before dark.

I had been aware for some time that Morshead, though he was going steadily and well, was more tired than the rest of us. His long halt at our high camp can have done him little good. He had not recovered. His strength had just served to keep him up where it was urgently necessary that he should preserve his balance; but it was now exhausted; he had quite come to the end of his resources, and at best he could move downwards a few steps at a time. It was difficult to see what could be done for him. There were places where we might sit down and rest, and we should be obliged not only to stop often for two or three minutes, but also to stay occasionally for perhaps ten minutes or a quarter of an hour. Anything like a longer halt must be avoided if possible, as the air was already cold, and an exhausted man would be particularly sensitive. Probably a longer rest would not have helped him, and we proceeded as best we could, so as to avoid delay as much as possible. One of us, and it was usually Norton, gave Morshead the support of his shoulder and an arm round his waist, while I went first, to pick out exactly the most convenient line, and Somervell was our rearguard in any steeper place. So we crawled down the mountain-side in the gathering darkness, until as I looked back from a few yards ahead my companions were distinguishable only as vague forms silhouetted against the snow. There were long hours before us yet, and they would be hours of darkness. Occasionally the flicker of lightning from distant clouds away to the West reminded us that the present calm might sometime be disturbed. Perhaps below on the cold, or it might be sooner, the old unfriendly wind would meet us once again. For the present it was fortunate that the way was easy; the great thing was to keep on the snow, and we found that the edge of rocks by which we had come up, and where it was now so much more difficult to get along, could be avoided almost everywhere. With the same edge of stones to guide us, we could not miss our way, and were still stumbling on in the dark without a lantern when we reached the North Col. But we had a lantern with us, and a candle too, in Somervell's rucksack, and we should now require a light. I was reminded once again of the most merciful circumstance, for the air was still so calm that even with matches of a Japanese brand, continually execrated among us, we had no difficulty in lighting our candle.

Two hundred yards, or little more in a direct line, now separated us from our tents, with the promise of safety, repose, and warmth in our soft eiderdown bags. Looking back, I never can make out how we came to spend so long in reaching them. We had but to go along the broken saddle of snow and ice where our tracks lay, and then drop down to our camp on the shelf. But the tracks were concealed, and not to be found; crevasses lay under the snow waiting for us. With nothing to guide us, we must proceed cautiously, and once among the confusing shapes of white walls and terraces and monticules and corridors, it was the easiest thing in the world to lose our way. Somervell, who had covered the ground once each way more often than any of us, held the helm, so to speak, against a sea of conflicting opinions. Even he, now our leader, was not always right, and we had more than once to come back along our tracks and take a cast in another direction. To avoid the possible trouble or disaster of having two men at once in a crevasse, we were obliged to keep our intervals on the ropes, so that Morshead had now to take care of himself. Perhaps the lower altitude had already begun to tell, for he was stronger now, and came along much better than was to be expected. At length we reached a recognisable landmark, a cliff of ice about 15 feet high, where we had jumped down over a crevasse on our first visit here in order to avoid a disagreeable long step over another crevasse on an alternative route. I was very glad we had come this way rather than the other, for though, looking down at the dimly lit space of snow which was to receive us, I boggled a little at the idea of this leap, the landing-place was sure to be soft, and it would be easy not to miss it.

I think each of us was just a little relieved when he found himself safely down, and I dimly remember congratulating, not Morshead, but Longstaff. I had already transposed the names several times, and he now protested; but it made no difference, as I could remember no other. "Longstaff" became an *idée fixe*, and though the entity of Morshead remained unconfused—I did not, for instance, give him Longstaff's beard—he was fixedly Longstaff until the following morning.

The agreeable change of finding ourselves together in that curious coign was hardly disturbed by Somervell's remark, "We're very near the end of our candle." We felt we were all very near the end of our journey, for we had dimly made out from the higher level we had just quitted the neat rank of our tents still standing on the shelf below and ready to welcome us. We had only to find the rope which had been fixed on the steep slope below us and we should be at the end of our troubles. But the rope was deeply buried, and we searched in vain, dragging the snow with our picks along the edge of the fall. We were still searching when the last of our candle burnt out. In the end we must do without the rope, and began the abrupt descent tentatively, dubiously, uncertain that we had hit off just the right place. The situation was decidedly disagreeable. Suddenly someone among us hitched up the rope from under the snow. It may be imagined we were not slow to grasp it. The blessed security of feeling the frozen but helpful thing firmly in our hands! We positively made some sort of a noise; unrecognisable, perhaps, it would have been to sober daylight beings who know how to produce the proper effect, but if a dim bat of the night were asked what this noise resembled, he might have indicated that distantly, but without mistake it was like a cheer. A few minutes more and then—then, at 11:30 P.M., and there on the good flat snow as we fumbled at the tent-doors, then and there at last we began to say, "Thank God."

Had we known what was yet in store for us, or rather what was not in store, we might have waited a little longer for so emphatic an exclamation. We were in need of food, and no solid food could be eaten until something had been done towards satisfying our thirst. It was not that one felt, at least I did not feel, a desire to drink; but the long effort of the lungs during the day in a rarefied atmosphere where evaporation is so rapid had deprived the body of moisture to such an extent that it was impossible to swallow, for instance, a ration biscuit. We must first melt snow and have water. But where were the cooking-pots? We searched the tents without finding a trace of them. Presumably the porters whom we had expected to find here had taken them down to Camp III in error. As we sat slowly unlacing our boots within the tents, it was impossible to believe in this last misfortune. We waited for a brain wave; but no way could be devised of melting the snow without a vessel. Still supperless, we wriggled into our sleeping-bags. And then something happened in Norton's head. In his visions of all that was succulent and juicy and fit to be swallowed with ease and pleasure there had suddenly appeared an ice-cream. It was this that he now proposed to us; we had the means at hand to make ice-creams, he said. A tin of strawberry jam was opened; frozen Ideal Milk was hacked out of another; these two ingredients were mixed with snow, and it only remained to eat the compound. To my companions this seemed an easy matter; their appetite for strawberry cream ice was hardly nice to watch. I too managed to swallow down a little before the deadly sickliness of the stuff disgusted me. My gratitude to Norton was afterwards cooled by disagreeable sensations. In the last drowsy moments before complete forgetfulness I was convulsed by shudderings which I was powerless to control; the muscles of my back seemed to be contracted with cramp; and, short of breath, I was repeatedly obliged to raise myself on my elbows and start again that solemn exercise of deep-breathing as though the habit had become indispensable.

The last stage of our descent to Camp III had still to be accomplished on the following morning of May 22. I imagine that a fresh man with old tracks to help him might cover the distance from Camp IV in about an hour and a quarter. But no sign was left of our old tracks, and the snow was deeper here than higher up. Only in the harder substance below the fresh surface could new steps be cut wherever the slope was steep; and as we began to understand that the way would be long and toilsome, another thought occurred to us—our sleeping-bags at Camp IV would now be required at Camp III, and porters must be sent to fetch them. Our tracks, therefore, must be made safe for them. Half our labour was in hewing so fine a staircase that the porters would be able to go up and down unescorted without danger. The wearisome descent, which began at 6 A.M., continued far into the morning; the sun pierced the vapoury mists and the heat was immoderate now as the cold had been higher up. The fatigued party regarded the conventions until the first man reached the snow at the foot of the final ice-slope. There, so far as I could understand, the van became possessed of the idea that it would be more companionable for all to finish together. I found myself deliberately pulled from my steps and slid about 80 feet down the ice until the pick of my axe pulled me up at the foot of the slope. I could have born the ignominy of my involuntary glissade had I not found Finch at the foot of the slope taking advantage of my situation with a kodak.

The presence of Finch was easily explained. Reinforcements had arrived at Camp III in our absence, and the transport had worked with such wonderful speed that the oxygen cylinders were already in action. Finch, whom we had last heard of in bed with dysentery at the Base Camp, had shown such energy that he was now testing the oxygen apparatus with Wakefield and Geoffrey Bruce. They were bound for the North Col with a party of porters, so the return of our sleeping-bags was easily arranged. The lesser injustices of fate are hard to forgive, and we regretted labour that might have been left to others. However, Wakefield now took us in charge and at noon we were at Camp III once more. Strutt and Morris had come out to meet us. Noel had stayed in camp, and, like a tormentor waiting for his disarmed victim, there we found the "movie" camera and him winding the handle.

However, our welcome in camp is a pleasing memory. The supply of tea was inexhaustible. Somervell confesses to having drunk seventeen mugfuls; he can hardly have been so moderate. Morshead probably needed to drink more than any of us; he ascribed his exhaustion on the mountain to want of liquid, and medical opinion was inclined to agree with the suggestion. However that may be, the night's rest at a lower elevation had largely restored his strength, and Morshead arrived at Camp III no more fatigued to all appearances than the rest of us. But he bore the marks of his painful ordeal. His condition had made him a prey to the cold, and we only began to realise how badly he had been frostbitten as we sat in camp while Wakefield bound up the black swollen fingers.

—1923

Note

1. The thermometer confirmed our senses and showed a minimum reading for the night of 7°F.

Edward F. Norton

from *The Fight for Everest: 1924*

Edward F. Norton's (1884–1954) book describes the unsuccessful 1924 British expedition to Everest (using closed circuit oxygen equipment) on which George Leigh Mallory and Andrew Irvine disappeared after possibly having reached the summit. Noel E. Odell last spotted the pair at 28,200 feet, climbing into the mist. Mallory was a well-known public figure and his death was greeted with shock in the world press. On May 1, 1999, Mallory's body was discovered at 27,000 feet by Conrad Anker, part of a special expedition mounted to find "an Old English dead" described by a Chinese climber in 1975.

MALLORY AND IRVINE'S ATTEMPT

Of all our long line of camps from the Base Camp to Camp VI, No. IV on the North Col was perhaps the most remarkable and the most distinctive in character. It was the only one in which we had perforce to forsake the warmth and dryness of a rock foundation and take to the dubious alternative of snow. The experience of at least two of us in the Arctic had taught us that, unless altogether impossible, it was worth while going to infinite trouble to pitch on rock. Snow may be delightful for a temporary siesta, if nature has provided one with a good hide and a low coefficient of thermal conductivity, but it is remarkable how soon it congeals to the consistency of the hardest rock, and how difficult it is to smooth out the relief of one's anatomy first impressed upon it! But there have been many worse camps on snow than that on the North Col at 23,000 feet; indeed, in my experience it was one of the best. Perched on an ice-ledge in about the same position as the camp of 1922, it had four tents: two for sahibs and two for porters. The ledge was a shelf of *névé* with a greatest breadth of about 30 feet, and a high wall of ice which rose above it on the western side gave comforting protection from the chilly winds that constantly blew from that direction. Indeed, had it not been for this natural screen the camp could never have been occupied for such long periods as it eventually was. To the east one looked out over the upper *névé* basin of the East Rongbuk Glacier, and beyond its high border and the Hlakpa La, to the distant rugged range of Gyankar outlying the wide depression of the Arun River: a commanding view which, when in addition the effulgence of sunrise touched and tinted the nearer rock spires of Chomo-Lönzo, formed a picture that made it worth while leaving the warmth of one's sleeping-bag at 4 A.M. to gaze upon in an ecstasy of adoration. During my eleven days' residence here I experienced all kinds of weather conditions, not the least remarkable being two days when the sun

Edward F. Norton, *The Fight for Everest: 1924* (New York: Longmans, Green, 1925).

temperature at midday was 105° F while the air temperature at the same time was only 29°. It is a question if the air temperature up here ever exceeds that of the freezing-point, and it is probable that the fallen snow wastes away entirely by direct evaporation. The snow was consequently very dry and unconsolidated, and in the complete absence of any running water supply, snow melting and water boiling was a rather protracted occupation of mine as camp cook. The ledge was fortunately extensive enough to allow of an ample area of clean snow being reserved for water supply, and the preservation of this and all the other little duties attendant on camp life fell to my lot while in charge. One is so often asked what it feels like living up at these altitudes, and the only reply that can be given is that after some degree of acclimatization one's sensations are really quite normal, and it is only when great exertion is necessary that one feels "like nothing on earth"! And certainly the adverse effect of high altitude on one's mentality has been exaggerated: the speed of one's mental processes may perhaps be slowed down, but their capacity is but little impaired. And this is not self-delusion, as some physiologists would wish to make out, from evidence derived from unacclimatized subjects!

To reach the actual saddle of the North Col, which lay nearer the foot of the North Ridge of Everest than the ledge on which the camp was situated, it had been necessary in 1922 owing to the presence of difficult schrunds to make a way up towards the North Peak and then back again along the crest of the Col. An annoying and time-wasting necessity this had proved to be, especially when tired climbers were returning from the mountain at dusk, and we were anxious at the outset to try and cut it out. And this we succeeded in doing, as on the occasion of our first reaching the site of Camp IV, on May 20, Mallory and I found it was just possible to force a somewhat complicated route from the southern end of the camp ledge direct up to the Col. This route, though a little treacherous from two doubtful snow-bridges, proved to be negotiable until the end.

On June 1 I had gone down to Camp III, and on getting back to IV next day with a fresh supply of stores, I had been surprised to see Mallory and Geof. Bruce returning from V, their attempt to get higher having been rendered abortive by the refusal of the porters to go on. Mallory was not a little disappointed and upset about this, and he took the view, possibly on account of the strained condition of Bruce's heart, that a further attempt should not be made except with the use of oxygen. He went down with Bruce and Irvine that same day to Camp III, intent on investigating afresh with Bruce's aid the question of available porterage. It was found just possible to collect together sufficient men, who were not indisposed, to carry up oxygen supplies for such an attempt. Irvine occupied himself meanwhile in putting the final touches to the recreated oxygen-breathing sets. I was still in charge of IV, and in the meanwhile with Hazard had been up to V in support of Norton and Somervells' wonderful attempt on the summit without oxygen, and to conduct their porters back to the North Col.

On the evening of June 4 Mallory and Irvine with a few coolies came up from III, the two former using oxygen. They were able to cover the distance in the fast time of two and a half hours, and seemed well pleased with a performance which had no doubt been prompted by the wish to demonstrate the real efficacy of oxygen. But in my opinion the demonstration was hardly justified, and Irvine's throat at any rate, that had already given him considerable discomfort from the cold dry air, that at these altitudes can reduce this delicate passage to the consistency of cardboard, was palpably aggravated by the effect of the oxygen. Mallory's throat was less affected, though it was undoubtedly causing him some little irritation; and, besides, his usual equanimity was perhaps a little disturbed by the feeling of responsibility consequent upon this being probably the turning-point in the success or failure of the campaign. Who with the fighting spirit of Mallory, or with the long-tried obsession of attainment of the greatest goal of his ideals, could be otherwise than impatient to be off on the culminating challenge of a lifetime, nay even of a whole generation of active mountaineers! And Irvine, though through youth without the same intensity of mountain spell that was upon Mallory, yet was every bit, if not more, obsessed to go "all out" on what was certainly to him the greatest course for "pairs" he would be ever destined to "row"! I had frequently shared a tent with Sandy Irvine in one or other of our glacier camps, but it was the previous year on our sledging journey across Spitzbergen that I had first got to know him intimately. The effects of high altitude somewhat enhanced his natural reserve, but he told me on more than one occasion how much he hoped he would have a real chance of "a shot at the summit." And careful and devoted though his work was on making the oxygen apparatus efficient for use, he did not hesitate to tell me that he would rather reach the foot of the final pyramid without the use of oxygen than the summit by means of its aid! He thought that if it were worth while doing at all, it was worth while doing without artificial means. Nevertheless when the call came from Mallory for this one last effort with every means at our disposal, he saw the necessity of foregoing any personal preference in the matter, and welcomed almost with boyish enthusiasm a chance that he had little thought would come his way.

It was late the same evening of Mallory and Irvine's arrival at Camp IV that the former and myself went up to meet Norton and Somervell returning from their record climb, the events of which have already been described. June 5 was spent quietly at the North Col, one and all of us feeling a sense of impotence at our inability to diminish the suffering that poor Norton was undergoing from his painful attack of snow-blindness, and Somervell on account of his severely relaxed throat. The latter, however, with his customary fortitude and resolution, announced that he was fit enough to go down to Camp III, and down to Camp III in the evening, of course, he went. Hazard was signaled for from Camp III by means of our usual code of blankets placed against the snow, and Irvine and I busied ourselves with re-testing and putting further final touches to the oxygen apparatus. It was a brilliant day with a maximum midday sun temperature of 105°, though the air temperature never rose above freezing. We had to darken the tent where Norton was lying by an outside covering of sleeping-bags. I took the precaution of wearing a sun helmet up here on the North

Col, and at times on the glacier below, though I could never get an authoritative opinion from either of our medical experts as to the necessity of such a procedure, so detached, or arbitrary, in their counsel can the advanced thinkers in that dignified profession become! But though blessed with a fairly thick skull, I was taking no risks, and while in respect of the sun considerations of latitude rather than altitude were perhaps uppermost in one's thoughts, yet the altitude and prevailing air temperature never allowed to go far out of mind the possibility of one's shaded side freezing!

I think most of the party, with perhaps the exception of the unfortunate Norton, slept well that night, though Irvine admitted his sorely sun-scorched face had caused him distinct discomfort at times. Hazard and I were up early the morning of the 6th, and soon had frizzling and crackling over the Primus stove a choice fry of sardines, to be served up in Mallory and Irvine's tent with biscuits and ample hot tea, or chocolate. On the announcement of this breakfast they seemed pleased enough, but I must admit that either owing to excitement or restlessness to be off they hardly did justice to the repast, or flattered the cooks! At 8:40 they were ready to start, and I hurriedly "snapped" them as they were loading up with the oxygen apparatus. Their personal loads consisted of the modified apparatus with two cylinders only and a few other small items such as wraps and a food ration for the day, amounting to not more than perhaps 25 lb. This may sound to many a very heavy load to carry at such altitudes, and in actual fact it is, but it is an easy load compared with the total of 40 lb. or more that the original breathing apparatus as well as the items of extra clothing, etc., that must be carried, amounted to. The eight porters, who accompanied them from Camp IV, carried provisions, bedding, and additional oxygen cylinders, but of course no breathing apparatus for their own use. It always amazed us how little on the whole our Sherpas were affected by moderate loads, though as a matter of fact at these altitudes we contrived to give them no more than 20 to 25 lb. to carry. The party moved off in silence as we bid them adieu, and they were soon lost to view amidst the broken ice-masses that concealed from view the actual saddle of the North Col and the lower part of the North Ridge of the mountain.

Though a brilliant morning, my diary records it as very cloudy in the afternoon and even snowing a little in the evening. It was at 9:45 that morning that Hingston arrived and conducted Norton in his sightless condition down to Camp III, Hazard going down as far as the rope ladder and then returning to me on the North Col. I occupied myself meanwhile with various camp duties and observations. That evening, soon after 5 o'clock, four of Mallory's porters returned from Camp V, where his party was spending the night, and brought me a note saying, "There is no wind here, and things look hopeful."

On the 7th Mallory's party was to go on up to Camp VI, and I that same day with Nema, who was the only porter of the two available at the North Col, followed up in support to Camp V. This method of support, a stage as it were behind, was rendered necessary by the limited accommodation at these two high camps, consequent upon the inadequate number of porters available to carry up sufficient tentage, etc. I had expected on my way up to Camp V to find a spare oxygen-breathing set that had been left there earlier, but discovered that Irvine the previous day had taken the mouth-piece from it for a spare, and so rendered it useless to me. However, I carried it on up to Camp V in case another mouthpiece were available there; but this was not so, though it did not bother me, since I found I was able to get along as well without its aid, and better without the bulky inconvenience of the whole apparatus. Not long af-ter my arrival Mallory and Irvine's four remaining porters returned from Camp VI, their advent having been heralded by stones falling unpleasantly near the tent, that had been unwittingly displaced by them during their descent of the steep slopes above. The exposure of Camp V in this respect had been borne in on me during my first visit with Hazard, when Norton and Somervell's returning porters had likewise unknowingly bombarded our frail tents with stones and struck a porter of ours, though fortunately with no severe results. Mallory's porters brought me the follow-ing message:

"DEAR ODELL,—
"We're awfully sorry to have left things in such a mess—our Unna Cooker rolled down the slope at the last moment. Be sure of getting back to IV to-morrow in time to evacuate before dark, as I hope to. In the tent I must have left a compass—for the Lord's sake rescue it: we are without. To here on 90 atmospheres[1] for the two days—so we'll probably go on two cylinders—but it's a—load for climbing. Perfect weather for the job!
"Yours ever,
"G. MALLORY."

Nema, my porter, was obviously much affected by mountain sickness, which made it very unlikely that he would be able to go higher next day, and consequently I decided to send him down that evening with the other four returning men. It is wonderful how soon that strange malady, so often described as "mountain sickness," seems to disap-pear not only with the descent, but when the decision to descend had been made: at any rate I have noticed it time and again with these native porters, if not with other climbers! When no further effort is to be called for, the psychological effect is such that a fresh stimulus to normality is given, and sickness and other effects disappear. And as the little party started down Nema seemed as active and fit as the rest of them. How-ever, I was not loath to let him go, as I knew by so doing I should be freer to the mor-row to wander about over the North Face and make a more thorough geological exam-ination of it on my way up to Camp VI. After a short search within the tent I duly found Mallory's missing prismatic compass. That evening as I looked out from the little rock ledge on which my tent was situated, the weather seemed most promising, and I knew with what hopeful feelings and exultant cheer Mallory and Irvine would take their last look around before closing themselves in their tiny tent at VI that night. My outlook,

311

situated though I was 2,000 feet lower down the mountain-side than they, was nevertheless commanding and impressive in the extreme, and the fact that I was quite alone certainly enhanced the impressiveness of the scene. To the westward was a savagely wild jumble of peaks towering above the upper Rongbuk Glacier and its many affluents, culminating in the mighty Cho-uyo (26,750 feet) and Gyachung Kang (25,910 feet), bathed in pinks and yellows of the most exquisite tints. Right opposite were the gaunt cliffs of Everest's North Peak, their banded structure pregnant with the more special and esoteric interest of their past primeval history, and in this respect not detracting by its impression from the vision of such as can behold with more than single eye. This massive pyramid of rock, the one near thing on God's earth, seemed only to lend greater distance to the wide horizon which it intercepted, and its dark bulk the more exaggerated the brilliant opalescence of the far northern horizon of Central Tibet, above which the sharp-cut crests of distant peaks thrust their purple fangs, one in particular rising supreme among them. To the eastward, floating in thin air, 100 miles away, the snowy top of Kanchenjunga appeared, and nearer, the beautifully varied outline of the Gyankar Range, that guards the tortuous passages of the Arun in its headlong plunge towards the lowlands of Nepal. It has been my good fortune to climb many peaks alone and witness sunset from not a few, but this was the crowning experience of them all, an ineffable transcendent experience that can never fade from memory.

A meal of "Force" and a little jam varied with macaroni and tomatoes completed my supper, and then by dint of two sleeping-bags and the adoption of a position to avoid the larger stones of the floor I stretched myself diagonally across the tiny tent in an endeavour to obtain what sleep I might pending a visit from the notorious Sukpas, or even the watchdogs of Chomolungma! For all I know none put in an appearance, and even the wind did not attain its usual boisterous degree, or threaten to start the somewhat precarious built-up platform on which the tent was perched from a glissade down the mountain-side. I kept reasonably warm and consequently had a fair amount of sleep. I was up at 6, but the great efforts necessitated and energy absorbed at these altitudes, by the various little obligations of breakfast and putting on one's boots, etc., prevented my starting off before eight o'clock. Carrying a rucksack with provisions in case of shortage at Camp VI, I made my solitary way up the steep slope of snow and rock behind Camp V and so reached the crest of the main North Ridge. The earlier morning had been clear and not unduly cold, but now rolling banks of mist commenced to form and sweep from the westward across the great face of the mountain. But it was fortunate that the wind did not increase. There were indications though that this mist might be chiefly confined to the lower half of the mountain, as on looking up one could see a certain luminosity that might mean comparatively clear conditions about its upper half. This appearance so impressed me that I had no qualms for Mallory and Irvine's progress upward from Camp VI, and I hoped by this time that they would be well on their way up the final pyramid of the summit. The wind being light, they should have made good progress and unhampered by their intended route along the crest of the north-east shoulder.

312

My plan was to make a rather circuitous route outwards over the northern face in order to examine the geological structure of the mountain. The lower part of it is formed of a variety of gneisses, and on these rest a mass of rocks, mainly highly altered limestones, which compose the greater part of its upper half, and here and there are to be seen in small amount light granitoid rocks which break across, or are interbedded with, all the other series. But for a fuller description I would direct the reader's attention to Part III, the above being sufficient to indicate roughly the general character of the rock met with. The whole series dips outwards from the mountain at about 30°, and since the general slope of this face, above 25,000 feet, is about 40° to 45°, the effect is to make a series of overlapping slabs nearly parallel with the slope, and presenting a number of little faces often up to 50 feet in height, which can be climbed, usually by an easy though sometimes steepish route, while most can be entirely circumvented. The rocks are not on the whole rotten in texture since they have been considerably hardened by the igneous intrusions of granitoid rocks. But the slabs are often sprinkled to a varying degree with débris from above, and when to this is added freshly fallen snow, the labour and toil of climbing at these altitudes may perhaps be imagined. It is not so much the technical difficulty as the awkwardness of a slope of uncertain footing not quite steep enough for the use of one's hands.

At about 26,000 feet I climbed a little crag which could possibly have been circumvented, but which I decided to tackle direct, more perhaps as a test of my condition than for any other reason. There was scarcely 100 feet of it, and as I reached the top there was a sudden clearing of the atmosphere above me and I saw the whole summit ridge and final peak of Everest unveiled. I noticed far away on a snow slope leading up to what seemed to me to be the last step but one from the base of the final pyramid, a tiny object moving and approaching the rock step. A second object followed, and then the first climbed to the top of the step. As I stood intently watching this dramatic appearance, the scene became enveloped in cloud once more, and I could not actually be certain that I saw the second figure join the first. It was of course none other than Mallory and Irvine, and I was surprised above all to see them so late as this, namely 12:50, at a point which, if the "second rock step," they should have reached according to Mallory's schedule by 8 A.M. at latest, and if the "first rock step" proportionately earlier. The "second rock step" is seen prominently in photographs of the North Face from the Base Camp, where it appears a short distance from the base of the final pyramid down the snowy first part of the crest of the North-east Arête. The lower "first rock step" is about an equivalent distance again to the left.[2] Owing to the small portion of the summit ridge uncovered I could not be precisely certain at which of these two "steps" they were, as in profile and from below they are very similar, but at the time I took it for the upper "second step." However, I am a little doubtful now whether the latter would not be hidden by the projecting nearer ground from my position below on the face. I could see that they were moving expeditiously as if endeavouring to make up for lost time. True, they were moving one at a time over what was apparently but moderately difficult ground, but one cannot definitely conclude from this that they were roped together—a not unimportant consideration in any estimate of what may have eventually befallen them. I had seen that there was a considerable quantity of new snow covering some of the upper rocks near the summit ridge, and this may well have caused delay in the ascent. Burdened as they undoubtedly would be with the oxygen apparatus, these snow-covered débris-sprinkled slabs may have given much trouble. The oxygen apparatus itself may have needed repair or readjustment either before or after they left Camp VI, and so have delayed them. Though rather unlikely, it is just conceivable that the zone of mist and clouds I had experienced below may have extended up to their level and so have somewhat impeded their progress. Any or all of these factors may have hindered them and prevented their getting higher in the time.

I continued my way up to Camp VI, and on arrival there about two o'clock snow commenced to fall and the wind increased. I placed my load of fresh provisions, etc., inside the tiny tent and decided to take shelter for a while. Within were a rather mixed assortment of spare clothes, scraps of food, their two sleeping-bags, oxygen cylinders, and parts of apparatus; outside were more parts of the latter and the duralumin carriers. It might be supposed that these were undoubted signs of reconstructional work and probable difficulties with the oxygen outfit. But, knowing Irvine's propensities, I had at the time not the slightest qualms on that score. Nothing would have amused him more—as it ever had, though with such good results—than to have spent the previous evening on a job of work of some kind or other in connection with the oxygen apparatus, or to have invented some problem to be solved even if it never really had turned up! He loved to dwell amongst, nay, revelled in, pieces of apparatus and a litter of tools, and was never happier than when up against some mechanical difficulty! And here to 27,000 feet he had been faithful to himself and carried his usual traits, though his workshop for the purpose would be decidedly limited, and could not have run to much more than a spanner and possibly a pair of pliers! But it was wonderful what he could do with these. I found they had left no note, which left me ignorant as to the time they had actually started out, or what might have intervened to cause delay. The snow continued, and after a while I began to wonder whether the weather and conditions higher up would have necessitated the party commencing their return. Camp VI was in rather a concealed position on a ledge and backed by a small crag, and in the prevailing conditions it seemed likely they would experience considerable difficulty in finding it. So I went out along the mountain-side in the direction of the summit and having scrambled up about 200 feet, and whistled and yodelled meanwhile in case they should happen to be within hearing, I then took shelter for a while behind a rock from the driving sleet. One could not see more than a few yards ahead so thick was the atmosphere, and in an endeavour to forget the cold I examined the rocks around me in case some new point of geological significance could be found. But in the flurry of snow and the biting wind even my accustomed ardour for this pursuit began to wane, and within an hour I decided to turn back, realizing that even if Mallory and Irvine were returning they could hardly yet be within call, and

314

less so under the existing conditions. As I reached Camp VI the squall, which had lasted not more than two hours, blew over, and before long the whole north face became bathed in sunshine, and the freshly fallen snow speedily evaporated, there being no intermediate melting phase as takes place at lower altitudes. The upper crags became visible, but I could see no signs of the party. I waited for a time, and then I remembered that Mallory had particularly requested me in his last note to return to the North Col as he specially wished to reach there, and presumably if possible evacuate it and reach Camp III that same night, in case the monsoon should suddenly break. But besides this the single small tent at Camp VI was only just large enough for two, and if I remained and they returned, one of us would have had to sleep outside in the open—a hazardous expedient in such an exposed position. I placed Mallory's retrieved compass that I had brought up from Camp V in a conspicuous place in the corner of the tent by the door, and after partaking of a little food and leaving ample provisions against their return, I closed up the tent. Leaving Camp VI therefore about 4:30, I made my way down by the extreme crest of the North Ridge, halting now and again to glance up and scan the upper rocks for some signs of the party, who should by now, it seemed to me, be well on their downward tracks. But I looked in vain: I could, at that great distance and against such a broken background, little hope to pick them out, except by some good chance they should be crossing one of the infrequent patches of snow, as had happened that morning, or be silhouetted on the crest of the North-east Arête, if they should be making their way back by that of their ascent, as seemed most likely. I was abreast of Camp V at 6:15, but there being no reason to turn aside to visit it, situated as it was a hundred yards or so off the main ridge eastward along the face, I hurried downwards. It was interesting to find, as I had earlier, that descending at high altitudes is little more fatiguing than at any other moderate altitudes, and of course in complete contrast to the extraordinarily exhausting reverse of it, and it seemed that a party that has not completely shot its bolt and run itself to a standstill, so to speak, on the ascent, and in any attempt on the summit, should find itself unexpectedly able to make fast time downward and escape being benighted. And as I shall mention later, the unnecessity of oxygen for the properly acclimatized climber seems never more evident than in this capability of quick descent. I was able to speed up my headlong descent upon the North Col by taking to the crest of the snow cornice to the leeward of the North Ridge, and finding the snow between 24,800 and 23,500 feet hard and conveniently steep, it was possible to indulge in a fast standing glissade that brought me to Camp IV by 6:45 P.M. It was rather surprising and withal useful to know that this distance between Camps IV and V, which upwards necessitated at any time three to four hours of arduous toil, could be covered in barely thirty-five minutes descending by means of a glissade; but it was a glissade that involved care and judgment to avoid the Scylla of the rocks on the one hand, and the Charybdis of the cornice edge on the other![3]

Hazard welcomed me at Camp IV, and right glad was I of his wonderful brew of hot soup made from a mixture of at least six varieties of Maggi. Fortunately I am not

315

habitually cursed with thirst on a mountain, but I was rather surprised to find how little Everest with its excessive dryness affects me in that way. However, whatever necessary moisture had been evaporated from my constitution during the last two days was now speedily replaced from the amazing quantities of soup and tea put in front of me by Hazard. And what a two days had it been—days replete with a gamut of impressions that neither the effects of high altitude, whatever this might be, nor the grim events of the two days that were to follow could efface from one's memory! A period of intensive experiences, alike romantic, aesthetic, and scientific in interest, these each in their various appeals enabling one to forget even the extremity of upward toil inherently involved, and ever at intervals carrying one's thoughts with expectancy to that resolute pair who might at any instant appear returning with news of final conquest. They would be late, for were they not behind their scheduled time when last seen! And hence they would succeed in reaching Camp VI only, or Camp V possibly, before darkness. The evening was a clear one, and we watched till late that night for some signs of Mallory and Irvine's return, or even an indication by flare of distress. The feeble glow that after sunset pervaded the great dark mountain face above us was later lost in filtered moonlight reflected from high summits of the West Rongbuk. We hoped that this would aid them if perchance some incident had precluded their return as yet to Camp V or VI.

Next morning we scrutinized through field-glasses the tiny tents of those camps far up above us, thinking they must be at one or other, and would not as yet have started down. But no movement at all could be seen, and at noon I decided to go up in search. Before leaving, Hazard and I drew up a code of signals so that we could communicate to some extent in case of necessity: this was by fixed arrangement of sleeping-bags placed against the snow for day signals, and as far as I was concerned Hazard was to look out for them at stated times at either of the upper camps. Answering signals from him were also arranged. For use after dark we arranged a code of simple flash signals, which included, of course, in case of need, the International Alpine Distress Signal. We had by this time three porters at the North Col Camp, and two of these I managed after some difficulty to persuade to come with me. We started off at 12:15, and on our way up the North Ridge we encountered that bitter cross-wind from the west that almost always prevails, and which had really been the means of rendering abortive Mallory and Bruce's earlier attempt. I found my two Sherpas repeatedly faltering, and it was with difficulty that one in particular could be persuaded to proceed. We reached Camp V, however, where the night was to be spent, in the fairly good time of three and a quarter hours. I hardly expected, I must admit, to find that Mallory and Irvine had returned here, for if they had, some movement must have been seen from below. And now one's sole hopes rested on Camp VI, though in the absence of any signal from here earlier in the day, the prospects could not but be black. And time would not allow, even if I could have induced my men to continue in the conditions, of our proceeding on to Camp VI that evening. We made ourselves as comfortable at V as the boisterous wind would permit, but gusts sweeping over the North

316

Ridge would now and again threatened to uproot our small tents bodily from the slender security of the ledges on which they rested, and carry them and us down the mountain-side. Fleeting glimpses of stormy sunset could at intervals be seen through the flying scud, and as the night closed in on use the wind and cold increased. The porters in their tent below mine were disinclined for much food, and were soon curled up into their sleeping-bags, and I went down and added a stone or two to the guys for the security of their tent. I did likewise to mine and then repaired inside, and fitted up for use next day the oxygen apparatus that had lain idle here since I brought it from the ridge two days previously: having with me another mouthpiece, it was now ready for use. I managed to cook a little macaroni and tomatoes on the Meta stove, and that with tea and "Force" comprised my meal. The cold was intense that night and aggravated by the high wind, and one remained chilled and unable to sleep—even inside two sleeping-bags and with all one's clothes on.

By morning the wind was as strong and bitter as ever, and on looking in at the porters' tent I found them both heavy and disinclined to stir. I tried to rouse them, but both seemed to be suffering from extreme lassitude or nausea. After partaking of a little food myself I indicated that we must make a start, but they only made signs of being sick and wishing to descend. The cold and stormy night and lack of sleep had hardly been conducive to their well-being, and to proceed under these conditions was more than they could face. I told them, therefore, to return without delay to Camp IV, and seeing them well on their way downwards I then set off for Camp VI. This time with an artificial oxygen supply available I hoped to make good time on my upward climb. But the boisterous and bitter wind, blowing as ever from the west part of the ridge, was trying in the extreme, and I could only make slow progress. Now and then I had to take shelter behind rocks, or crouch low in some recess to restore warmth. Within an hour or so of Camp VI, I came to the conclusion that I was deriving but little benefit from the oxygen, which I had been taking only in moderate quantities from the single cylinder that I carried. I gave myself larger quantities and longer inspirations of it, but the effect seemed almost negligible: perhaps it just allayed a trifle the tire in one's legs. I wondered at the claims of others regarding its advantages, and could only conclude that I was fortunate in having acclimatized myself more thoroughly to the air of these altitudes and to its small percentage of available oxygen. I switched the oxygen off and experienced none of those feelings of collapse and panting that one had been led to believe ought to result. I decided to proceed with the apparatus on my back, but without the objectionable rubber mouthpiece between my lips, and depend on direct breathing from the atmosphere. I seemed to get on quite as well, though I must admit the hard breathing at these altitudes would surprise even a long-distance runner.

On reaching the tent at Camp VI, I found everything as I had left it: the tent had obviously not been touched since I was there two days previously: one pole had, however, given way in the wind, though the anchorages had prevented a complete collapse. I dumped the oxygen apparatus and immediately went off along the probable route Mallory and Irvine had taken, to make what search I could in the limited time available. This upper part of Everest must be indeed the remotest and least hospitable spot on earth, but at no time more emphatically and impressively so than when a darkened atmosphere hides its features and a gale races over its cruel face. And how and when more cruel could it ever seem than when balking one's every step to find one's friends? After struggling on for nearly a couple of hours looking in vain for some indication or clue, I realized that the chances of finding the missing ones were indeed small on such a vast expanse of crags and broken slabs, and that for anymore expensive search towards the final pyramid a further party would have to be organized. At the same time I considered, and still do consider, that wherever misfortune befell them some traces of them would be discovered on or near the ridge of the North-east Arête: I saw them on that ridge on the morning of their ascent, and presumably they would descend by it. But in the time available under the prevailing conditions, I found it impossible to extend my search. Only too reluctantly I made my way back to Camp VI, and took shelter for a while from the wind, which showed signs of relenting its force. Seizing the opportunity of this lull, with a great effort I dragged the two sleeping-bags from the tent and up the precipitous rocks behind to a steep snow-patch plastered on a bluff of rocks above. It was the only one in the vicinity to utilize for the purpose of signalling down to Hazard at the North Col Camp the results of my search. It needed all my efforts to cut steps out over the steep snow slope and then fix the sleeping-bags in position, so boisterous was the wind. Placed in the form of a T, my signal with the sleeping-bags conveyed the news that no trace of the missing party could be found. Fortunately the signal was seen 4,000 feet below at the North Col, though Hazard's answering signal, owing to the bad light, I could not make out. I returned to the tent, and took from within Mallory's compass that I had brought up at his request two days previous. That and the oxygen set of Irvine's design alone seemed worth while to retrieve. Then, closing up the tent and leaving its other contents as my friends had left them, I glanced up at the mighty summit above me, which ever and anon deigned to reveal its cloud-wreathed features. It seemed to look down with cold indifference on me, mere puny man, and howl derision in wind-gusts at my petition to yield up its secret—this mystery of my friends. What right had we to venture thus far into the holy presence of the Supreme Goddess, or, much more, sling at her our blasphemous challenges to "sting her very nose-tip?" If it were indeed the sacred ground of Chomo-lungma—Goddess Mother of the Mountain Snows, had we violated it—was I now violating it? Had we approached her with due reverence and singleness of heart and purpose? And yet as I gazed again another mood appeared to creep over her haunting features. There seemed to be something alluring in that towering presence. I was almost fascinated. I realized that no mere mountaineer alone could but be fascinated, that he who approaches close must ever be led on, and oblivious of all obstacles seek to reach that most sacred and highest place of all. It seemed that my friends must have been thus enchanted also: for why else should they tarry? In an effort to suppress my feelings, I turned my gaze downwards to the North Col far below, and I remembered that other of my companions would be

318

anxiously awaiting my return, eager to hear what tidings I carried. How then could I justify my wish, in face of such anxiety, to remain here the night, and prolong my search next day. And what hope, if I did, of finding them yet alive?

Alone and in meditation I slowly commenced my long descent. But it was no place for silent contemplation, for buffeted by storm-blasts that seemed to pierce one through, it needed all one's attention and calculation to negotiate safely the exposed slabs of the ridge and prevent a slip on their débris-sprinkled surfaces. Hampered as I was with the unwieldy oxygen outfit, which I had no need to use but wished to recover, these slabs were in places, under these conditions, decidedly awkward. I quickened my pace on the easier ground farther down, but at times found it necessary to seek protection from the biting gale in the lee of rocks and reassure myself that no symptoms of frostbite were imminent. Hazard had seen me coming, and sent his one remaining Sherpa to welcome me at the foot of the ridge. Arrived at the North Col Camp I was pleased to find a note from Norton and to discover that I had anticipated his wishes that I should return and not prolong my search on the mountain, seeing that the monsoon seemed likely to break at any moment. Next day Hazard, the porter and myself, leaving the tents standing and loading ourselves up with all we could save, evacuated the North Col Camp, and went down in good weather, and in quick time, by the "avalanche route" to Camp III, where we found the rest of the party gone, save Hingston and Shebbeare who were about to evacuate it. After a rest and good meal here, we proceeded on down the changed and wasted glacier to Camp II, where we spent the night, and the following day rejoined the main party at the Base Camp, to revel in the joys of opening spring, so long withheld and now let loose on us in all their glory of flower and insect life, as we plunged forth from our erstwhile Arctic environment.

I have already mentioned the possible reasons why Mallory and Irvine were so late in reaching the point at which they were last seen, which if the "second rock step," as referred to earlier, would be an altitude of about 28,230 feet, as determined by theodolite from the Base Camp by Hazard; if the "first rock step," then not more than 28,000 feet. And in the latter event we must assuredly and deservedly attribute the *known* altitude record, the greatest mountain height definitely attained by man, to Norton, who reached not less than 28,100 feet. I propose, therefore, very briefly just to speculate on the probable causes of their failure to return. From the "second step" they had about 800 feet of altitude to surmount, and say 1,600 feet of ground to cover, to reach the top, and if no particularly difficult obstacle presented itself on the final pyramid they should have got to the top at about 3 to 3:30. Before, however, he left Camp VI Mallory had sent a note to Noel at Camp III saying he hoped to reach the foot of the final pyramid (about 28,300 feet odd) by 8 A.M. So on this schedule they would be perhaps five or six hours late in reaching the top, and hence they would find it almost impossible to get down to Camp VI before nightfall, allowing five or six hours for the return. But at the same time it must be remembered there was a moon, though it rose rather late, and that evening it was fine and the mountain clear of mist as far as could be seen. In spite of this they may have missed their way and failed to find Camp VI, and in their overwrought condition sought shelter till daylight—a danger that Mallory, experienced mountaineer that he was, would be only too well aware of, but find himself powerless to resist. Sleep at that altitude and in that degree of cold would almost certainly prove fatal. Norton, I know, finds it difficult to reconcile this explanation with the fact that no light was seen on the mountain after dark, and I am well aware it is a potent argument against it. But to me it is by no means conclusive since anything might have happened, in the way of damage or loss of their lantern or flash-light, to have prevented their showing a light. And the same applies to the magnesium flares which we supposed that they carried. In the tent at Camp VI I found one or two of the latter, which indicates the possibility of their having forgotten them the morning of their departure.

The other likely possibility, that many will not unnaturally subscribe to, is that they met their death by falling. This implies that they were roped together, a suggestion that I have mentioned earlier need not necessarily be inferred from their observed movements when last seen. It is at the same time just possible that though unroped they may have been climbing, on the ascent or descent, on some steepish pitch in close order, and the one above fallen on the lower and knocked him off. But it is difficult for any who knew the skill and experience of George Mallory on all kinds and conditions of mountain ground to believe that he fell, and where the difficulties to him would be so insignificant. Of Sandy Irvine it can be said that although less experienced than Mallory, he had shown himself to be a natural adept and able to move safely and easily on rock and ice. He could follow, if not lead, anywhere. Such had been my experience of him in Spitzbergen, Norway, and on our own home mountains. They were, of course, hampered by the oxygen apparatus—a very severe load for climbing with, as Mallory had mentioned in his last note to me. But could such a pair fall, and where technically the climbing appeared so easy? Experts nevertheless have done so, under stress of circumstances or exhaustion. Following what we called the "ridge route," i.e. by the crest of the North-east Arête, there seemed to be only two places which might in any way cause them trouble. The first was the "second step," already referred to more than once. This seemed steep, though negotiable at any rate on its north side. And if it were this step, as I thought at the time it was, that I saw the first figure (presumably Mallory) actually surmount within the five minutes of my last glimpse of them, then we had been deceived as to its difficulties, as at the distance we might well be. The only other part of the ascent that might have presented any difficulty, and probably not more than awkwardness, is the very foot of the final pyramid, where the slabs steepen before the relatively easy-looking ridge to the final summit can be attained. Norton at his highest point was close below this section, and he expressed the opinion that these slabs, sprinkled with snow, might constitute a considerable source of danger in the case of a slip. But with all due deference to Norton's actual view of this place, from what can be seen of the local detail both in Somervell's photograph taken at 28,000 feet and in Noel's wonderful telephotograph of the final pyramid taken from above Camp III, the difficulties here look decidedly as if they could be circumvented by a nearly horizontal traverse to the right to the actual foot of the ridge of the final pyramid. In any case to a leader of Mallory's experience and skill such moderate difficulties, as these would present, cannot long have detained him, much less defeated him, and during the descent such place as the above, and the probable consequences of a slip thereon, would be so impressed upon him, as well of course as on Irvine, that the greatest care and attention would be exercised.

Again, it has been suggested that the oxygen apparatus may have failed and thereby rendered them powerless to return. I cannot accept the validity of this argument, for from my own personal experience, to be deprived of oxygen—at any rate when one has not been using it freely—does not prevent one from continuing and least of all getting down from the mountain. On my second journey up to Camp VI, as related earlier, when I was using oxygen, I switched it off at about 26,000 feet and continued on, and returned, without it. Mallory in his last note to me said they were using little oxygen, and that they hoped to take only two cylinders each, instead of the full load of three each, from Camp VI. But even if later they were using much oxygen, they had both during the previous weeks spent adequate time at extreme altitudes, namely 21,000 feet and over, to become sufficiently acclimatized and not liable to collapse in the event of the oxygen failing. The importance of this factor of acclimatization is discussed elsewhere.

Hence I incline to the view first expressed that they met their death by being benighted. I know that Mallory had stated he would take no risks in any attempt on the final peak; but in action the desire to overcome, the craving for the victory that had become for him, as Norton has put it, an obsession, may have been too strong for him. The knowledge of his own proved powers of endurance, and those of his companion, may have urged him to make a bold bid for the summit. Irvine I know was willing, nay, determined, to expend this last ounce of energy, to "go all out," as he put it, in an utmost effort to reach the top: for had not his whole training in another hardy pursuit been to inculcate the faculty of supreme final effort? And who of us that has wrestled with some Alpine giant in the teeth of a gale, or in a race with the darkness, could hold back when such a victory, such a triumph of human endeavour, was within our grasp?

The question remains, "Has Mount Everest been climbed?" It must be left unanswered, for there is no direct evidence. But bearing in mind all the circumstances that I have set out above, and considering their position when last seen, I think myself there is a strong probability that Mallory and Irvine succeeded.

Notes

1. This refers to the pressure, and consequent amount, of oxygen they had been using. For full supply, the pressure stood at 120 atmospheres.

2. *Vide* diagram in *Geographical Journal*, Vol. LXIV, No. 6, p. 457.

3. The place is well seen, though foreshortened, in the background of the frontispiece of the *Assault on Mount Everest*, 1922.

Geoffrey Winthrop Young
from *On High Hills*

Not only did Geoffrey Winthrop Young (1876–1958) consolidate and standardize twentieth-century mountain climbing techniques in his classic textbook Mountaincraft (1920), *he also helped to found the British Mountaineering Council in 1944. His poetic introspections into the effects of mountains on the human soul have established him as one of mountaineering's most enduring poets. He made numerous superb rock climbs throughout the Alps with his guide Josef Knubel, and the two solved traverse, chimney, and face problems that had defeated the great Mummery himself. In the early twentieth century, Young set new mountain and rock climbing standards. His most lasting achievements were the east face of the Grépon, climbed in 1911, and a 1906 ascent of the Täschhorn wall, again with Josef Knubel along with Josef and Franz Lochmatter, and V. J. E. Ryan. In this passage, Young reflects on the suspense that seizes mountaineers and the colors of the mountains and their moods, which are indelibly impressed upon the memory.*

SUSPENSE AND COLOUR

In this short span
between my fingertips on the smooth edge
and these tense feet cramped to the crystal ledge
I hold the life of man.
. . . .
In these two eyes
that search the splendour of the earth, and seek
the light-born mysteries on plain and peak,
all vision wakes and dies.

It is the uncertainty of its result which makes an adventure attractive. The feeling of suspense, so long as we are free to take action to end it, adds zest. Only when we are forced to remain inactive during our suspense does the feeling become disagreeable. And when a feeling is recognized as disagreeable it ceases to be profitable to us, because definite feelings of pain, or of pleasure, grow commonplace with their repetition or their persistence, and so lose their power to stimulate us.

Geoffrey Winthrop Young, *On High Hills* (London: Methuen, 1927). © 1927 by Geoffrey Winthrop Young. Text from pages 191–220 of *On High Hills*. Included by permission of Jocelin Winthrop Young. Originally published in London by Methuen.

But the feeling of suspense, so long as we ourselves are free to take action to end it, belongs to an order of neutral emotions which are not only fascinating in themselves, but which remain provocative of fresh enterprise. Our sensation, for instance, at the sound of good music, at the sight of big waves, or at the start of a fateful voyage, is undetermined, but exciting. We cannot be sure whether it is pain or pleasure that we are experiencing, in their accepted sense. We remain for its duration in a condition of enlivening suspense.

Of course it is in our nature, and in the nature of the provocative emotion we are experiencing, that we should feel driven to put an end to these uncertainties as they occur. The suspense may be of a kind that calls for bodily action on our part, to prevent it from defining itself as pain to ourselves in the issue. Or, again, it may be the ambiguous emotion produced in us by a sight or a sound of neutral character; when we shall feel no less compelled to make the effort designed to turn its effect upon us definitely to our advantage, that is, to determine it as a feeling of pleasure in ourselves. By so doing, indeed, by terminating our period of suspense physically or by determining it mentally, we shall put an end to the stimulus which it had for us so long as it remained an unresolved uncertainty. But its provocative purpose will have been sufficiently served. Our moment of suspense will have incited us successfully to action, of the limbs or of the mind, urged us further along the path of new adventure, towards new and attractive uncertainties.

Mountaineering is rich in a type of suspense not easily definable as a pleasurable sensation, nor yet always certainly terminable by action to our advantage,—and therefore the more enduringly stimulating. As one example—for every class of mountaineer a corresponding grade of peak can provide some degree of uncertainty in its overcoming. In like manner, as we improve in skill, we have only to seek increasingly difficult ways of ascent, in order to be able always to renew our wholesome diffidence, to multiply the occasions for undefined impression, and to prolong our periods of stimulating doubt. To have attained a summit too readily, is to have neglected most of its opportunity. We shall have sacrificed for one instant of brief-lived gratification the countless possibilities that might have lived on for us, undetermined and enticing, in its less certain emprise.

Not that we should have deigned to pursue consciously such an abstraction as "suspense" in our active years: a tangible mountain was then what we set out each day to climb. But, when we look back, we are tempted to search for some motive or feature that may be common to all our clearest memories. And we find then that it is our moments of uncertainty as to the issue of some event, or again the moments when we were experiencing feelings inexplicable as ordinary pleasure or pain, which return most constantly to mind, and which seem to have contributed most towards keeping the allure of climbing always new.

The more common type of suspense was the sensation we experienced during times of doubt as to the issue of some active incident. I believe that these moments impressed us exceptionally because, for their duration, the *timing* of the action of a scene was altered. Our suspense might retard or it might hurry the movement, as in a film: never could it leave the current of incident or of feeling normal. Consequently we received the impressions exceptionally at the time; and we remember them afterwards with abnormal clearness. In this way the single recollection of our hesitation in the face of some dubious passage can re-create for us the whole atmosphere of one past climbing day. The recall of a fateful indecision as to the route, or our anxiety as to the measure of daylight still left to us, colours all the happenings of another.

The times when we were conscious of experiencing what I have called a neutral emotion, some state of feeling neither to be classed as enjoyment nor as its opposite, were less frequent; but perhaps even more tenacious as memories. Probably the picture-scenes to which we mountaineers return most often, and which can reawaken in any later year all our pristine unsatisfiable longing for the hills, are those of our alpine starts before dawn, up the cold greyness of the first glaciers, with the last stars paling above the suspended life of the white peaks. Why are these nocturnes so deeply etched? Our feeling at the time was certainly neither definite pleasure nor its opposite. It was neutral, undefined; and therefore memorable. For at these moments we were free of all but one small certainty, that of our unfulfilled purpose for the day; and we were fresh to feel the long suspense of the whole doubtful day before us quivering in the spellbound silence, quivering in every raw particle of our expectant energy, and inciting our eager hopes and fears to a very fever of impatient uncertainty.

If this be a true explanation, it may give us also the reason why a number of mountain ascents seem to lose their brilliance in recollection. They were too successful, too swiftly satisfying at the moment. Their uncertainty faded too early, or their moments of suspense were too lightly resolved.

The new ascent of the Zinal Rothhorn from the west ought, for example, to have had every mountaineering claim to remembrance. For the attempt was based, without reconnoitering, upon a flattering chain of reasoning. We found one day that an unusual coating of hard snow enabled us to scamper about over the unchancy slabs of the west face of the Dent Blanche. We reminded ourselves that the west face of the Rothhorn had remained unclimbed by reason of a similar slope of slab; and we argued that the same aspect and structure should be susceptible of the same snow condition. A few days later, accordingly, we crossed the Trifthorn from Zermatt, ran down the snow dunes to the western base of the Rothhorn, and found our prediction triumphantly vindicated:—there above us shone a gleaming wall of hard snow, mounting from bergschrund to summit ridge.

But of all the easy gratification of that ascent only two moments survive: and they were intrusions of suspense foreign to the smooth progress of the climb. As we chatted and chipped our steps steeply up the immense snow curtain, a sound startled us, the sibilant hoot of a stone spinning over our heads. Some thousands of feet above a midget party could just be distinguished upon the rocky skyline, the ordinary way of ascent from Zermatt. We shouted; but at the same instant another fragment appeared, rocketing and wheezing down the centre of the white wall, straight for our zigzag of steps. We watched it, and watched it. It took an hour of suspense to fall; and leap by leap every tract of the featureless snow-slope over which it descended is printed upon memory, in a succession of instantaneous pictures which survive only because they made a background for the duration of the rock menace. It missed us, and the moving pictures end.

As a matter of fact a small astute pilot-fish of a pebble, no larger than a button, did hit Josef on the hat, flatly, stunning him so that I had for a time to hold him up in his steps. But the suspense was by then ended; and even that incident would probably have been forgotten had it not suggested a more lingering speculation as to how so small a stone could smite so hard a blow without breaking the skin.

A second little flashlight of suspense has picked out for remembrance a chance impression of the finish of our snow wall:—although there must have been much of greater interest at the time in our intervening flight up the precipitous slabs. We had reached the foot of a rock outcrop not far below the summit ridge. From a step on the steep ice-collar that surrounded the rock Josef had climbed on to it, and glad of the pleasant change to good holds and arm-work I started the machinery for a swing-up.

Possibly my muscles were stiffened, or the mere easiness of the movement encouraged my attention to wander before I had seen it through. Anyhow, as my feet reached the sloping shelf, and I was straightening up into balance—I realized agonizingly that I was short of momentum. With infinite slowness I began to sway backward again over the edge. The suspense seemed endless. I had time, first, to notice that Josef was moving and not looking back—it was a very insignificant passage; to picture him jerked from his holds, both of us falling and dragging Marcus Heywood from his ice-steps below; and to imagine all that would be conjectured afterwards about wrong reasons for the accident. Then, or perhaps simultaneously, came a flush of anger with myself: this was the first blunder I could recollect making, and I had been trapped into it on a most unworthy passage of rock. Then, a rush of resentment with fate, which had staged the blunder at a place and in a moment when it would not be expected, and when, therefore, it could not be retrieved by the precautions usual in our combined climbing:—all this, in a single scorching sight of the arena of ice and rock about and above us, which seared every detail indelibly upon the eyeballs of memory.

And then, for some equally trivial reason—possibly some excrescence under the downward pressure of a heel as I moved—the back-sway ended, and I balanced slowly forward again, erect. Whereupon the flaring of suspense died down, and the rest of the day's doings have passed into oblivion. But I may add that I never forgot the warning; and although I was often afterwards beaten upon a mountain by what I could not climb, I do not think I ever again made an inattentive movement in climbing what I could.

The first ascent of the east face of the same Rothhorn might have left much to recall, for it was an exceptionally faultless and happy day. But for that very reason, as I think, I look back on it now as into a bright nebula, wherein all detail is lost. I have sometimes wondered why this has not become one of the more regular Zermatt ascents. It substitutes for the slight monotony of an ascent and descent of the Rothhorn by the same southern ridge an ambit through noble scenery, and includes the traverse of the red towers of the north arête, usually only to be enjoyed by descending upon Zinal. The approach which it makes for us to the mountain, across the low east shoulder in the dark hours, and over the undulating plateau of the secluded Hohlicht glacier where the white recesses creep in and out among the brown bases of the cliffs under an overhang shadowing enormously against the sky, is as impressive as anything in the Pennines.

This overhang under the summit appeared to us certainly unclimbable: equally so the higher part of the great couloir leading up from the glacier to the overhang. But the telescope suggested some attractive uncertainties for our day. We could see a great sabre-slash of a cleft down the rock nose forming the north wall of the couloir. Could we reach the lower end of this cleft by a traverse out of the couloir? And, if so, was the cleft itself climbable?

Happily for our success, but disastrously for its recollection, our uncertainty was only short-lived. We bestrode the Rothhorn and Hohlicht glaciers, engulfed ourselves in the great central couloir, and followed it upward, with reaches of step-cutting on its steep ice-shoot, until we were blocked by an overhead obstruction of grey rock. So far doubt had endured, and it has served to keep the mirror of detail clear. But then, a broad snow band joined the couloir from the left, by which we might if we liked have reached the conspicuous shoulder on the north-east arête; and we saw for certain that its continuation upon the right of the couloir, more faintly marked, would enable us to traverse out on to the profile of our intended rib, at just the right point to admit us to the lower end of the deep slash up the nose.

With a laughing certainty which has covered recollection like a uniform colour-wash we swarmed out of the couloir, and up the slash, and up the subsequent rugosities of the rib: until its sequence of forgotten incidents was interrupted by an uncompromising "step." An attempt to scale this step direct ended in our repulse, and in our re-descent from it with the help of a doubled rope. So we traversed off the rib and out to the right again, into an open slabby funnel; and zigzagged up snowy slabs, first to the right and then back to the left, until we found ourselves upon a slim horizontal spar of rock, the lower and retaining wall of small glacier. The baby glacier impends from the cornice of 'le Blanc'; and our embryonic rock spine, had it ever grown up, might have been acknowledged as the true backbone between the Rothhorn and the Mominghorn. We followed it back to our left, turned directly up the steep east face of the pack again, and by way of some accommodating granite slabs came out on to the main north arête of the mountain under the ear-lobe of its second big tower, and twenty minutes distant from the summit.

But of all this last over-generous passage one picture-memory alones survives. Before we broke out into the west wind over the main north ridge, we paused to eat, standing upon snow-frosted ledges, and roped together. Over our heads and about us icicle-spears of a man's length fringed a cluster of shallow stoops and niches: icicles flashing wet in the sun with sea-pearl and chrysoprase, and snapping at our touch or in the brawling of the gusts. The red overhang of the east face boomed out above on the moving sky, and seemed to be moving with us outward and over the hollow plain of glacier. And then Donald Robertson began to recite sonorously a long roll of Æschylean chorus. The chant blended with and echoed astonishingly the roar of the wind, the ice-clatter and the uneasiness of space.

We coiled up our rope on the summit that day; and came down as free-companions. Possibly the absence of the rope on the descent may account for my recollecting a dim revival of suspense where we turned down the west wall on very faulty ice-steps, and in the teeth of the gale. But the rest of our doings remain only rattle and vague pleasure and—the unicoloured mist.

———

Face-climbs in the Alps had for me, and may for others still retain, more of this charm of uncertainty than ascents by the more obvious ridges. A part of this they owed to the fact that they remained unclimbed, and therefore un-ascertained, to a later period; a part to their supposed uncertain temper, to their spasmodic fashion of defence by rock-avalanche and stone-discharge. In our effort, therefore, to restore the romance of adventure, to prolong doubt and defeat the local cocksureness of the guide who knew his Alps, and in whose sophisticated mind the details of familiar climbs were all salted down and labelled with "Here I haul the Herr" and "Here I haul him harder," face-climbs played a leading conspirator's part. Their uncertainties and traditional insecurity helped us to readorn the ascents of historic Pennine peaks with something of an earlier glitter of pomp and circumstance.

It was Giraldus Cambrensis who first remarked—"It is wonderful that when, after diligent search, all the stones have been removed from the mountains, and no more can be found, a few days after they reappear in greater quantities to those who seek them." Giraldus's experience of this discomfort will be confirmed by anyone who has slept out on a mountain side, and whose nature has not been hardened to the point of boasting with Goldsmith's Traveller that he finds where

—the rocky summits frown
These rocks, by custom, turn to beds of down.

But when we come to climb such mountains, since we cannot even attempt to "remove all the stones" as a precaution, we have to learn a new science of their fashion of falling and make a new art of our manner of evading them.

In these ways face-climbs opened before us a fair field of study and experiment. There are, of course, good rock faces and bad rock faces; but nearly every face has its sound points and salient ribs free from the defects of its general character. It remains for us to distinguish these "safeties." Now a rock face seen from in front looks evenly

327

"exposed" all over; and a side view of it is as often misleading, revealing nothing but the general angle, and suggesting a false rib with every new profile as we shift. But the stones themselves prefer to fall down the real depressions. They can be trusted to betray the true modeling. The more pronounced the stone-fall, the easier it will be for the seeing eye to trace the real ribs and wrinkles. There remains, indeed, a less locatable risk from flanking fire, from rocks which burst and scatter as they strike. But this is a peril incidental also to many classic "ridge" climbs. Such cross-fire is in any case short, and the dominant lines of the slope may be trusted soon to regulate the traffic within its proper channels again. The very steepness of rock precipices is also our protection. A slight projection makes cover for a considerable distance below it; and often the angle of a cliff of itself boars all but very fancy "drop" shots. The single stealthy block which stalks us at noonday is of course an importunist common to all types of ascent.

Face-climbs, further, have the merit of offering us lateral escapes on to alternative lines. It is true that we would rather not be driven to cross exposed couloirs on faces, just as we would rather not walk upon corniced ridges or drive over the toes of policemen at street crossings. But the risks involved in all these three instances are at least localized and quickly passed. Their short interference concentrates for us within almost negligible compass the terrors of incalculable laws of motion such as were never intended for the purposes for which we break them. Foresight, caution, and above all pace, are a rule of three which can solve the problems of fractions which fall upon faces as surely as those of the squared roots—or boots—of gendarmes standing upon ridges, or upon point-duty.

A new ascent of the Rimpfischhorn from the east was one of the face-climbs undertaken in this spirit; with the double intention of finding a worthy way up a dignified but somewhat hackneyed peak, and of clearing the character of its less-visited rock aspect. We cross the Adler pass, and circled round the foot of the black precipices, to a point a little north-east of the summit. An inquisitive sun sharpened the features of the face, and discovered to our reconnaissance a blunt, abrupt rib. It rests upon a broad band of snow which crosses the cliffs some two hundred feet above their base, and it forms the northern wall of a depression which is marked at half its height by a yawning ice-toothed cave. If any line was to be found free of stone-hap up the exceedingly steep face, we decided that it must lie upon this rib.

Some overhanging crags sheltered us in the start of our race with sunshine, already at its agitating work above. One dawdling block did pass within hail; and its deliberate excursion and alarum played a useful part. For I owe to it my one vivid memory of the whole look of that wall:—a wide front of somber and unstable precipice, steepening below over the snows of pass and glacier, steepening above into a harrow of white-pronged pinnacles, clogged with wind-snow out of a cold blue sky. How unpleasant these solitary stone-threats seemed at the time! And yet how much memory owes to them, in the deep etching of every line and form which chanced upon sight during the suspense of their passage. Moments which threaten extinction, like moments of creation, possess the power of intensifying our consciousness, of heightening the quality of our instants of living, and unforgettably.

We crossed the snow band; and the neighbourliness of the couloir helped us, after one false start, to a lodgment upon the butt of the chosen rib. Its rock had seen better days, and the holds were fractious and secretive. I surveyed our leader's quarrels with it, sheer and far above my head, for a length of doubt that has guarded the scene—even the words of his unconsidered speech. Some few hundred feet higher the angle and testiness of the rock abated; and our hope drew breath. And again a few hundred feet, and the whole face of the rocks smiled: the smile widening out into a broad "breakfast" platform, and a boss of yellow rock, at the foot of a benign couloir. Thereafter assured success flooded in about us; and it has washed out all features from our ascent of the iced couloir, and from that of the upright rock chimney which smuggled us out through the cornice on to the snow-capped main ridge, a few blustering minutes north of the highest point.

Two pictures from those last few minutes on the ridge stand out more clearly. One, a vignette of two of us, embracing each a spiked snowy prong upon the frosted crest; while the man between us danced angrily in the air upon the tight rope, and the small cornice that had betrayed him splurged and grumbled down the emptiness of the great east wall under our feet. And the other, of our short-roped party, as we swung off the mountain, down the insufferable glare of the long glacier. Monotony and the heat soon reduced me to the usual snow-plodding automaton. Suddenly a small snow crack or crevice revealed itself behind the heels of the man in front of me. Instinct warned me that my stride would take my foot exactly into, and not over it. On such mechanical trudges to break step is exasperating. To shorten step I knew must jerk the man in front and myself; to lengthen it or jump must jerk the man behind, and likewise myself. Whole dark ages seemed to pass, of suspense and indecision. Time ceased. The white glare whelmed in about me, maddeningly, unendingly. The men behind and in front waxed, in my consciousness of them, to immensities of hatefulness. The awful instant of passage arrived. My foot began to move out despairingly over all space. Some slight muscular adjustment—probably the extension of a leg-muscle, but magnified in feeling to a cosmic convulsion—syncopated the rhythm of the universe:—and the picture ends, and with it all the rest of the day.

The first ascent of the south face of the Dom was undertaken in a like quixotic spirit. As I noted at the time—"it was desirable that one at least of its aspects should be discharged without a stone upon its character." There was a further reason. The twin pyramidal faces of the Dom and the Täschhorn challenge the view from Zermatt in an indissociable kinship of height. The face of the Täschhorn had given us, as is told elsewhere, more than enough of grim and memorable suspense. To have neglected the defiance of its yet loftier brother, the Dom, might have introduced a discordant note between them, and have missed for ourselves what in a more chivalrous age would have been termed a very gentle opportunity for advancement.

329

Josef Knubel was once again handicapped by an injury to his knee, not acquired in the way of climbing but as the result of some impatience with a tin of raspberry-jam on the Weisshorn. Hinc illi Lochrimatteri!—for Gabriel Lochmatter came in his place, with Robin Mayor and myself. To reach the Dom hut consumed all our impatience. It is impossible upon sunbaked westward slopes at evening to keep the mounting shadow of heights behind us always between us and the sun. Some unthinking pass is sure to let a leak of hot rays through upon our back, and usually on the most treeless zigzags. As some solace, in the hut, we had the starlight, and the straw, to ourselves.

The ascent contented itself, humorously, with contradicting in every point of angle, difficulty and sensation the expectations grounded upon our memory of the corresponding precipice of the Täschhorn. We put on the rope prematurely, in order to try to recall the highest of Swiss peaks to some sense of its family dignity. But the very core of the southern face could never even rise—or sink—to the distinction of a recognizable central couloir; its best effort seeming no more than a neutral depression between bumptious intrusions of rock from the western and southern ridges of the mountain.

We skirted up the depression, following a trimmed and tidy necklet of ridge depending from near the Domjoch. The neck bridled, arched itself off the face, and shook a mane of loose pinnacles. Whereupon we slid off it on the left; and again skirted up the sloping strata of the central scoop; until this opened out into a great rough-backed amphitheatre, the cloaca maxima of a number of higher gullies. This was our one cautionary section. The mouth of the gullies gaped above us with the possibility of falling stones: and we must remain exposed to their chance until we could reach the lower end of one of the ribs dividing the gullies.

We collected our breath, and took the danger-zone at a hand and foot gallop. The end of the most prominent rib, descending in a line with the summit, met us on the bound; and we skimmed up its corrugations into safety, to our first halt, and to breakfast. For on principle, and on such sunswept stoneslopes, I had hitherto negatived all suggestions of a pause. But now we were well ahead of time, and free from all external risks. We could eat, and enjoy at leisure, framed in the supreme height of the enclosing walls, our view of the opposite snows of the Täschhorn shuddering bleakly in the first chill of morning light, and of the Rimpfischhorn as it towered in frosty isolation over the nearer chequered curve of the Domjoch and reveled in its unusual divorce from the virtuous commonplaceness of the Strahlhorn.

On a day which soon became the hottest in an exceptional year, on a dry rock which courted our hands and feet with firm and fulsome holds, we were almost compelled to invent a new interest for the final rib. The two sky-ridges were now racing in upon us from either hand, clashing above our heads into the apex of the great pyramid. It became a point of honour with us to keep to the exact centre of the face, to arrive precisely upon the summit. The formality imposed upon us some intensified gymnastics up the last overhanging and dissolute red crags. Where the meeting of the two snow crests above the rock precipice jetted a little confusingly at the last, our solemnity declined to move until Gabriel, pulling himself up tentatively here and there and peeping over the edge, was able to assure us that our bearing upon the final snow cone was absolutely true. Then we issued, gravely, in a state entry upon the summit.

Of several sights of the impeccable panorama from the Dom I have never succeeded in remembering anything but the little dollops of unlovely cloud, flat-bottomed, fuzzy-topped and dingy, which seem invariably to smudge the low modelling of the bird's-eye ranges. But the descent that day! The Festi glacier was under some burning-glass of sun haze. Its white heat seethed and smoked about us and we stewed and suffocated, dry-shrivelled within and steaming without. Faster and faster we fell down, over snow and track, goaded by new blasts of the fiery heat. It took me two hours and thirty-five minutes to escape from the top to the door of the Randa bathroom; and I noted the fact because of the coincidence that exactly the same length of time was recorded for our passage through its consolations to the tea-table.

Knubel had always a prejudice against climbing the Breithorn. It is a patrician peak as it stares haughtily down the Zermatt valley from under its Cæsarean wreath of white laurel; but it has a plebeian backstairway of snow which makes a crowded thoroughfare of its stooping shoulders and bald crown. Up the north face suggested itself as the only worthy approach; and yet the one route known upon it—that by the Triftje ridge—was swept by occasional ice-avalanches. Knubel shuddered again at the thought of having the word 'Breithorn' inscribed upon his monument. In a happy moment I called his attention to the eastern end of the long serrated summit ridge, from which descends yet another rib, the Klein Triftje. It is a reticulated high-stepping ridge of most alpine promise, subtended by ice-cliffs and vanishing above upon the fan-face of a great belfry-tower of rock and ice. By starting from the Gandegg hut on the Thèodule, and crossing the base of the Triftje rib on to the pleasant glacial terraces of the north face, we could clearly reach, almost without loss of height, the springing start of the Klein Triftje rocks.

With Mayor, Robertson and a porter we made the adventure. We crossed the Triftje by an easy descending chimney, raced along the glacier plateau, mounted the start of the our rib and were welcoming the steepness of its first few hundred feet,—when a valley snow-storm emptied its darkness over us, and worried us back to the Gandegg.

The postponement was intriguing: it made for uncertainty. We returned next day all the more keenly and rejoined the ridge, using the ice-steps by which we had been forced to leave it the day before. It set us to work at once, upon a narrow rising snow-crest mottled with ice. When we grew tired of step-cutting and of nice balancing upon it, it made horns of rock at us, and then discovered crimp little upward traverses, by which to turn the horns. I had hopes that the most noticeable barrier upon the ridge, a pugnacious stack of rock, might live up to its distant promise. It gave us a stimulating scramble, but no memorable check. The recording light of uncertainty only began to play about us again where the last, almost upright, edge of snow frilled out against the fanface of the belfry tower above us. A direct ascent of the belfry wall looked hopeless. We drove our axes into the vanishing point of snow, and watched Josef traverse out to the right across the face, scraping toe-holds upon gleening slabs. He made three precarious attempts upon an ugly cold-shoulder of a corner, before he could force his way up over it, and pack himself into a glazed crack. The crack was almost as unsociable as the corner; but it acknowledged a remote connexion with the main ridge, which we could now see tossing a brilliant ice-crest against the sky above our heads.

For another reason my recollection of this passage is not as distinct as our moment of doubt should have made it. In a later year, during a troublesome descent of the great Moine ridge of the Aiguille Verte, I had to watch, with all the responsible anxiety of last man, a magnified repetition of the same manoeuvres: a skirmish of Josef's across a sun-treacherous traverse, and up an ice-bolstered corner. The ice-glaze, globular and sweltering, which covered the precipitous slabs was in that indescribable condition when not only does it offer no hold, but boasts to the eye that by no ingenuity of axe or attachment can any safe hold be fashioned upon it. My feelings, as it happened, upon these two occasions were so alike that their resemblance has confused the details of the similar feats which evoked them.

The overhang of the Breithorn crack nodded us cavalierly up to the brilliant cornice; and the cornice bowed us stiffly on to the crest of the main ridge. This easterly prolongation of the Breithorn summit is all admirable rock and firmly modulated crests of snow. There is nothing better in the district; and it is, or used to be, all too seldom visited. We spread ourselves over its varied support; and passed for the time into the cloud of confident pleasurable action which leaves so indefinite a memory.

But on the final snow spine up to the summit a more real and very thick white mist crept down to envelop us, and framed an enduring shadow-picture. Snow-footing and mist-wrap were all one and the same white opacity, indistinguishable from each other. Josef, a formless darkening of mist just above me, was moving upwards through a lighter obscurity, flogging with single swings of his axe foot-holds of whitish vapour upon the denser edge of vapour between his feet. In such an envelope, uniform and featureless, we can feel no certainty whether we are going up or down, standing erect or toppling over. The uncertainty produces suspense, of an unusual kind. And the more unreal Josef looked, a wraith gesturing in white fog, the more intently I had to watch and follow him; until the grey-white nothingness under his feet no longer seemed to arrest the swing-through of his axe, and we discovered by the absence of touch in the mist ahead that we were standing upon the clouded summit.

Of the dull snow descent that always un-distinguishes the backstairs of the Breithorn I should have kept no memory, but for a brighter impression of it, borrowed from a later year. Not long before the war, with Laurence and Eleanor Slingsby, a party whose united ages about equalled my own, we had walked up the October loveliness of the Zermatt valley, watching almost hour by hour the last breadths of its

332

summer mourning softening with all the colours of the first night frosts. On the next day we turned off the Thèodule up the new snow of the Breithorn, for no other reason, I think, than to prolong that unsurpassable view of the Matterhorn. The mountains lay under white sunlight, and in a windless wintry cold so secret and severe that we had already spent two evening hours in the hut restoring life to Laurence's frost-nipped fingers. Upon those endless Breithorn slopes the affliction returned; and there is no boredom like the boredom of unrelieved snowfields. We dawdled, and looked at the Matterhorn; and then crawled, and looked back at it longer. Finally, half an hour from the top, we turned round with one consent, and fled heartily to the valley.

The autumn foliage of trees flooded up to meet us. The warmth of it, dividing like a miracle, for our exodus, the white seas of snow and ice, linked the promised land of Italy to our coloured memory of the Swiss forests. Among the vines and creepers of Valtournanche that night the peasants, with the sociability which revisits them in the fall, made fiesta for us, with dancing and music and tinted lamps under the trellises. Was it the contrast of these valley colours, on this side and on that isolating our white desert hours upon the Breithorn, which has kept that last picture of the mountain so distinct? Or because its image stands upon the edge of the long shadow of war-suspense which followed so soon?

From that day, as from a milestone set between the years, the fairway of memory travels backward into the past. From it again the way winds forward—to the turning that ended for one of us three so swiftly in deeper shadow, and for the other two began again under such unlooked-for sunshine.

––––––

Suspense I have suggested may have much to say in the selection of pictures for our gallery of memory. But at least when our interludes of fear or of doubt are in question we ourselves can exercise some indirect supervision of their action as our collecting-agents. Our nerves are our own. It is for us to control them more or less; and in this way we can secure that the moments they select to perpetuate shall at least have had some importance for ourselves at the time.

But there is another and very independent category of impressions, an agency which is as active in adding to our collection, and that is Colour,—the accident of colour in objects we see great or small, the lighting of a scene in general or in detail.

Now over colour we have no control; it is solely of nature's contriving; and it all too often takes advantage of its independence to give permanence to the most trivial sights or seconds regardless of any preference or discretion of our own. We all know how irresponsibly it may act in any attempt we make to recover our earliest childish memories. Of most of our infancy we can never re-create more than an external or spectator's point of view. We can reproduce portraits of ourselves in certain remembered surroundings; but we cannot return *into* ourselves, inside our personalities as we were then; for the reason that with every widening of our horizon we have replaced something of an old self with something of a new.

But we all know, also, how a chance reminder of a particular colour, or touch or smell, may serve if only for one instant of time to re-identify us with the inside reality of some forgotten stage in our lives. I remember that as very small boys a younger brother and I were allowed to paint a garden seat, with large and dripping brushes. At some point it seemed to us a matter of greater moment to paint each other, gravely and amply. The sheen of thick wet gloss upon glowing terra-cotta paint, as I saw it then upon his curls and smock-frock, rounded off into an entirely memorable sensation by the smell and the stiff touch of the same colour upon my own face, has kept the power, whenever I see it again, of putting me back in mind and feeling inside my whole sentient and satisfied self of that period. Through no other remembered experience can I resume my whole feeling and thinking self, within and without, so far back in time.

It is said that few of us can dream colours; and perhaps this is why so many of us find the colourless chiaroscuro of high Alps the most suitable material for our mature day-dreaming. But all the more violently does our masterless collecting-agency of memory pounce upon and cling to the unexpected notes of colour or lighting which nature may arbitrarily discover to us among our hills. A green tuft of pine through the remains of a winter avalanche, the aquamarine thumb-marks on a crevasse-wall, the last rim of fire between darkness and snow at sunset, the crimson scarf of a workman passing us on the glacier path, or that most constant relief, the chromatic blues of water changing within their encirclement of ice or snow or across their rock reflections,—these are accidents of colour which stay with us, sometimes detached from any context, sometimes as magic clues which can lead us back over forgotten tracks of experience, into lost phases of personality.

To the colour of one glacial pool I owe the memory of one of the brightest of long alpine days, and the recall of a whole year of myself as I was.

The ascent of the north-west face of the Dent d'Hérens was designed as a new approach for an impressive peak. That our way proved only to be new in part detracted nothing from our pleasure in it at the time, and added to it afterwards: since a good thing only gains from multiplied appreciation of the right kind. The Schönbuhl hut above the Z'Mutt glacier had just been formally opened by Edward Whymper—whose characteristic remark upon the occasion was still in our ears—and it offered us a more sheltered base than the rather jaded hollow upon the Stockje rocks.

The crevasses of the Tiefenmatten glacier were enjoying a close season; and we were jealous not to disturb them, flitting through them in the dark hours on light and early feet. Above us, upon our face of the Dent d'Hérens, the wrinkled bolsters of ice and snow, heaped high one upon the other up the triangular wall, had been smoothed out for us by the hand of a kindly summer. We wheeled straight up the central ice of the wall; and then, instead of bearing away to the right on to the accessible west ridge, the line followed as we learned later by our predecessors, we yielded to the direct temptation of the broken ice-cliffs above us.

Spits and ladders and corridors of ideal snow conspired to help us on, and prevented our spells of step-cutting upon the cliffs from ever becoming earnest. The last

334

ice barrier, a moat and wall rent and raised across the steep white face from ridge to ridge, gave away its own terrors even before we had had time to feel them. In the morning sun-blaze the moat or schrund flashed before our eyes its one and only bridge, a single and gigantic icicle, all but "perpendicular," which spanned both chasm and wall from indrawn lower to pouting upper ice-lip. Solid and semi-transparent, a pillar of green rock-salt, it was a column made for the display of showy and safe ice-work. In turn we embraced it, and by nick-steps and finger-notches swarmed up it. Snow spit and snow slope, steadily accelerating, piled themselves upward under our feet as we climbed; until we paused upon the junction of the west and northwest ridges, to take breath for the sort ridge-run to the summit.

Hill climbers may be, not unfairly, described as people who expend much energy in going somewhere, in order to look there from at something else. The privileged view of the Matterhorn to which it admits us should certainly justify many ascents of the often difficult and sometimes dangerous Dent d'Hérens. The Matterhorn is always the Matterhorn, massive and stable to the eye. But as we see it from here,—and there is nothing else in the picture—its mass soars into the sky above us with an inexpressible lightness. It seems to be borne upon air, balanced upon its structural lines, as upon wings. This effect is principally due to the profile line of the northern or Z'Mutt ridge, as we see it upon our left lifting against the sky. In two smooth gigantic curves this ridge springs from the glacier in support, and bears aloft the spire of the summit; and its two ascending curves, joined like outspread pinions, are tilted to resemble the flight of a bird as it slants in a swinging turn across the wind.

We were using ice-claws, and they served us well on the giant strides of the descent. For from the summit we literally leaped, in long bounds. The afternoon snow had softened to that fine consistency which accepts and steadies the forward drive of a straight leg, and yet springs it again into the air behind us with the resilience of india-rubber. The rope was no impediment; because Josef and I cantered in freedom at either end, and Marcus Heywood was young and long-legged enough to have his protests in the uncomfortable middle-distance disregarded. We cascaded harmoniously down the big icicle, skated the passages of ice-steps in combined figures, and were laughing ourselves back into breath upon the Tiefenmatten plateau in less than thirty minutes from the summit.

Uncertainty there may have been; stone suspense and incidence there certainly was, as we ran the usual risks down the Tiefenmatten icefalls. But neither conservative medium has succeeded in salving any details out of "the glory of speed and the glow."

All that I remember I owe to the presence of a small turquoise ice-pool below the Stockje promontory. At one end of it the shelving glacier slid in under the ripples, on a gradual incline of ice soft and silver-crusted to the feet. And to and fro along this, in sunlight and the after-glow of our torrid descent, we raced for an hour, perhaps more, in a rivalry of flying headers that reflected their own joy of motion upon a surface rapturously cold, serenely blue. More and more in retrospect the sky-colour of the pool has crept upon the panorama of the day, flooding over the drabness of the

Z'Mutt glacier, rising upon the lines of cliff and buttress, invading like a spring tide even the higher ice-bays and the black, squared precipices of the Dent d'Hérens itself. Until the whole climb has become merely an overture to the bathe; and I could almost think that we plunged headlong from the parching and snowy island-summit into an ocean of refreshing blue light.

Water, its many shades of interrupting colour, has stolen as many minutes of recollection out of the oblivion waiting for our care-free days, days of too little event or of too unrelieved a success. Of a devious and perhaps original variant up the westerly flank of the Blümlisalphorn, not a toilsome yard would have been remembered, but for one downward view which it gave us of the Oeschinensee. Set deeply, as in a carter, under its brows of cliff, the little circular lake stared up and past us at the contracted sky: a grey untroubled eye of the world, watching only to reflect the short greeting of sunlight or to borrow from darkness the transient gleaming of a star.

A fantasy of bottle-green ice, edged with olive crystals and still freezing in encrusted pillars of ice-drip on the weathered cheek-bones of a snow-crowned buttress of rock, alone reminds me that I did once succeed in climbing the Mönch. And in the thought of it I can feel over again the purgatory of two days' confinement by a blizzard in the Bergli hut, and subsequently of our seven hours' trudge to the foot of the green-garnished buttress, along all the weariness of the Ewig Schneefeld. That day the firn was a value of Siddim, a swamp of snow, with a crust on it that twisted each stumbling leg knee-deep, and then clung to it like a trap, with sharp dragging edges. For the fortitude of my companion, Arnold Lunn to whose old mountain injury every one of the many thousand rasping paces must have meant a new and painful wrench demanding from him a separate effort of will, I can feel as wondering an admiration now as then.

Yet another contrivance of strange ice that day did much to remove an old prejudice. As we looked back from the Ober Mönchjoch I could see the gallery-openings of the much-abused Jungfrau railway pricked blackly here and there upon the enormous brindled walls of the Eiger, each tiny puncture brought to the eye by a tapestry of discoloured ice. Seen in this perspective the trespass lost its offence. A shift of rock imperceptible to the eye, a year or so's neglect to keep the work in repair, and every trace of it would be gone. The courage of it challenged sympathy, almost a fellow-feeling. How little the impertinence differed, upon consideration, from our own in forcing ourselves for a few hours upon the wilderness of these great mountains, and calling our ephemeral track a "conquest."

I have but to think again of that ice-pointing to the pin-pricks on the Eiger wall, to suffer the same change of feeling among our own hills. If I turn now and look down from a height upon the winding of some raw and objectionable roadway, it looks no longer so arrogant an intruder; it has no more importance than the curl of apple-rind which we chuck over a shoulder and glance at momentarily for its fanciful pattern. The cars, too, that seemed to magnify the trespass upon the view into an insult to three senses at once, diminish with the thought to tardy grubs, absurdly in pursuit of each other's tails. Their insignificance, their movement upon sufferance along a line without breadth, stir a kind of compassion. The passing of a minute—as hills measure time—and the white thread of road may be lost under wild growth upon the hillside; and with it the sort trespass, human and mechanical, will have ended. From dislike to disregard, and from disregard to a humorous appreciation are the steps we make as we shift our point of view with wider experience, and see sights or people or ideas, which once shocked us as inappropriate, in better proportion. In scenery, as in our opinions, we can never know what we shall finally like or dislike until we have moved far enough off, on our feet or in thought, to find for them exactly the right perspective, and to see them, and ourselves, as part of a longer view.

Of a winter ascent of the Tschingelhorn, with the same good companion and Claude Elliott as pilots, memory only begins to take notice where, as we sped downward on ski over the edge of the Tschingelfirn, the hunting-green of the Lauterbrünnen valley broke upward through the sameness of white glaciers and made a truant of every thought and of every alternate glance. And the lawless inroad of colour brings back with it still the ache I felt behind inexpert knees after the hours of rough and tumble down snow-crusts of adamant.

In like manner the image of a ski-crossing of the Furggjoch, when late spring snow drifted us down over planes of white samite right into Breuil, begins to live where I looked back once, and saw the unexpected colours that sunlight was gleaning behind us upon the silken and winding trails of our ski. And it becomes active where the snow ran out upon a meadow, and a rainbow dance of spring flowers raced up round us, and tripped our feet.

Of several ascents of the Aiguille d'Argentière I can revive most easily one we made—possibly for the first time in its entirety—up the whole ridge-crest from the col du Chardonnet. And that owes its liveliness to some fanciful oppositions of colour. In the beginning, there is the picture of the first great snow wall above the pass, illuminated by the rubicund face of the guide who lost his temper upon it. At the end, the vision of the final ice-cone is preserved as a background for a certain sombre and sinuous expressiveness in the coloration and curving of Maynard Keynes's back, as he swerved, like a short dark ray, up the ivory wall above me. Finally, I can recover much of the sensation of fatigue and responsibility produced in me on that ascent by long hours of step-cutting in the lead, not from any memory of the step-cutting in progress, but from the short intervals of rest when I stopped working. For then, balanced on one leg in a step, I could turn my head for instants from the close and dazzling wall, and my eyes rested upon the evergreen pinetops in the valley with a sense of physical relief so acute that it can bring back with it a whole anthology of other feelings unconnected with it, and even the happenings they reflected.

A traverse of the neighbouring Aiguille du Chardonnet made a double bid for longer remembrance. Suspense the peak held over our heads throughout the day. For it threatened us with falling stones up most of the ascent by cliff and snow-chimney from the col du Chardonnet; and as we descended the solid-looking and steep rock flues of the northern wall, it threw earthenware slivers and plates after us with the

337

open-handedness of an angry kitchenmaid. We only escaped from our own anxiety at the point where the rocks ended, above a wild and stormy steep of snow descending through maroon shadows on to the glacier du Tour. There we flung suspense and tradition to the winds, after the stones, left an over-cautious young guide to make his own slow ladder of descending steps, and ourselves spun in a riotous glissade down the whole height of the hollowing wall to the glacier.

Then the Chardonnet fell back upon colour as its second string. As we halted upon the col du Passon, it confronted us suddenly with the cloistral vista of the glacier d'Argentière, a frosted and clouded lake of ice, dipping to its long centre, and lifting the length of its smooth borders against the bases of the white meditative peaks enclosing it. And in the slanting afternoon sunlight the shadows of these Aiguilles were descending and marching upon the glacial surface in armies of colour, like the invading Persian host for multitude and variety: in wedges, in squares, in crescent and in column making the white perspective live with wheeling masses of shade, violet and lavender and amethyst and gentian purple and blue—all the inadequate names we have to give to such effects and interruptions of light. For all I know we never came away from the col du Passon. The shadowy armies captured the day; and they have kept it prisoner.

In another year we made quite a difficult business of an ascent of the Dent du Géant: because we sternly refused even to see the fixed ropes which degrade the huge up-ended slabs. Perhaps I refused to see too much, for the climb only secured three impressions. I can see, as we approached the rocks, the sharp lance-headed image of the Dent thrown by sunrise across the snow to our feet: so boldly and tangibly modelled in shadow that it seemed to rest in high relief upon the snow, of a colour of dark ripe damsons, running more unripely red at the edges where it met the sun-glare. Again, and these were moments of suspense, I can re-enter very realistically into our struggles, as we successively fought our way up the famous V-cleft overhanging a mile of brown slab. It is the only place where the fixed rope has excuse; and we did look at it, as it tempted and impeded us there, but virtuously refrained in the end from using it. In the third memory, although its appearance is gone I can still feel the summit crag under my boots, because of what we saw from it. The Italian valleys were filled with their familiar swell and surf of cloud. And the sunlight had broken into the heart of the clouds, blowing them up into great bubbles of dull amber, each bubble with a whorl of darker gold inside it. The broken surf-edges and trailing wisps were charged with an incandescence that kept bursting their thinner mantle into flashes of yellow light, like the flaming of resin-dust puffed through candle-smoke. Into the shallower and inclined drifts of cloud lying far down upon the higher glaciers the sun's rays could not penetrate so luminously. The light was slipping over them fugitively, and they lay faintly a-glow between the harsh ridges and softer ridge-shadows: great petals of phosphorescent mist, of the colour and texture of early primroses as we see them in their rough setting between grey boulders and moss-green roots.

The comely Lötschenthaler Breithorn stands so satisfactorily, and is such a complete pleasure to look at, that the matter of climbing it—as in the case of several other Oberland peaks—seems altogether of small importance. But we must have done so, some-how and some time, because the view along the insecure steeples on the summit ridge stays an obstinate memory. They were top-heavy with snow, and webbed between with ice. So precariously did they project that I decided not to risk the crawl forward on to the last and reputedly highest. But I have clear impression of those further knobbly and black talons of rock, splitting at the top joints out of their ill-fitting icy webbing. And I suppose the clearness to be due not only to my moments of doubt, but to the dark con-trast which they made with the auburn beard of Sir William Ellis's guide, who was pre-ceding us. He insisted upon fighting his way through, rather than along, the unsub-stantial covering of the crest, to its last shred; and his bright beard burned refulgent, appearing to shrivel up the snow-frills as he embraced and struggled with them.

A like mystery envelops most of the story of our ascent of the south-eastern and rocky face of the Gabelhorn, which I made with Herbert V. Reade. I think we must have made some mistake in our line upon the great buttress, for I have an impression of dire and dangerous manoeuvres up snow-covered mantel-pieces, and of seeing a guided party pass us by on the other side, gloatingly. But reality begins where we stood on one horn of the summit, gazed longingly across at the other, and saw the "gabel" between the two filled by its notorious dilemma, the tormented ice-crest of a double cornice. A double cornice is an ice-wave which starts to fall one way, recollects itself with an upward wriggle, and decides to fall the other way. As I looked across the broad sagging swirl of ice leaning far out over space between the horns with a fringe of huge icicles under its drooping chin, I was reminded of a nursery picture of Sam-son in the temple at Gaza, with his shoulders locked about the two central columns, stooping and straining dizzily to bring them crashing down with him. But as I looked a second time down the vertical height of blue and scaly ice serpentining ponderously upward between the rock stacks, it suggested another and quite a different picture: that of the illustration in *Alice in Wonderland* of the unlucky Bill the Lizard, as he shoots into the air out of the White Rabbit's chimney-stack. And against the impassable ice, and for all I know perpetuating its memory, is painted the colour of Herbert's felt hat, and of the scarf by which its broad brims were tied down under his chin.

It is possible that both upon the Lötschenthaler Breithorn and the Gabelhorn the irruption of uncertainty at a moment when the climbs seemed all but over may have helped the conservative action of the beard and of the coloured scarf. Certainly from yet one more guideless ascent of the Weisshorn, which I made with Herbert Reade, and upon which from first to last there was no such moment of doubt, not even the image of the hat survives. Moreover, of the elegant precision of my companion's climbing I was too often a spectator during the twenty years of our association, for any instances of it upon these particular ascents to have remained distinctive, and so to have helped towards recollection.

As with colour so with light: bright contrasts have picked out their own assort-ment of scenes remembered. A crossing which we made of the Aiguille du Tacul passes from shadow into shadow—through a few shining seconds just after Josef and

I had left the top. For it happened that a cloud was whisking across the blunt edge of the arête below me, brushing with it over shadowy space frozen particles of snow-dust. And upon the blend of cloud and snow-speck there sparkled vivid shreds of rainbow, coming and going enchantingly like lights at sea, and still recalling those few instants of our descent out of forgetfulness.

A second traverse of the Aiguille Verte has no less its rainbow for remembrance. While we were descending the Moine ridge in sunshine, a local snow-storm covered our view of the Grandes Jorasses at the head of the glacier; and upon it there took shape a quarter rainbow of most startling complexion. The snow or sleet falling through, or behind, this exuberant gem-like colouring had the artificiality of a stage storm helped out by limelights. Of this descent, a little lower down, I have yet another glimpse; but seen through a window of suspense. I knew that two friends, eminent mountaineers, were to have ascended the ridge on the day before our traverse. So I was on the look out for their tracks. We had not found them as we descended the higher portion. Then, peering down over the heads of the descending line of towers, I saw a line of steps winding up along the intricate white crest far below us. We moved on down; more of the tracks came into sight; and with a catch of the breath I saw that the tracks ended abruptly at a black gaping hole in the narrow crest. The snowy fish-back of the ridge was not solid: it was in part a cornice hollow underneath; and a square chunk of it had dropped through, like an oubliette. We said nothing; but I saw Josef, a hundred feet below me, stop, and gaze very intently. We moved down again. More of the narrow white ridge came into sight, still far underneath us; and Josef turned and grinned up at me:— the line of tracks had again become visible, continuing, and safely upon our side of the oubliette. The trap therefore must have fallen during the few hours that followed the passing of our friends and that preceded our arrival. Even so, the sight of the black gape was grim and unforgettable. For, innocent as that length of snow-crest looked, to us as to them, they had passed for the whole length of it over the vaulting of a cornice so rotten that portions of it were ready to drop through of their own weight.

To climb the Little Dru, and from it scale the arrogant higher monolith of the Great Dru has always seemed to me the right mountaineering way to make acquaintance with these two magnificent Aiguilles. Twice I was driven back, by weather and by an embarrassing condition of the Charpoua glacier. But when the favourable day came, the double event accomplished itself so smoothly that its legacy is reduced to two flash-light pictures. From the little to the larger Dru we make a zigzag up a hopeless-looking wall; and where this overhangs bombastically we squirm up over its steep left-hand profile, and continue to the top by a miraculous groove up the very outside edge of impossibility. The season had filled this groove for us with a troublesome, round-backed snake of ice. The groove is of surpassing steepness, and suspended over more space than is even usual. So also was the ice-snake within it, up which we had to climb. Its slippery back was grit-speckled and water-marked, and, like a snake, it shone dull green or bright blue in the sunlight as we moved upwards upon it. Close to my face the cold wet ice winked and blinked, confusingly, and slimed away from my feet. So that, and again all too like a snake, it seemed to be actually shifting and elongating as much under my grasp as to my eyes. It could never be easy to forget a climb up the glimmering back of a python in agitation. Again, of all our fatiguing descent that day of precipices of the Great Dru, only one chimney with a particularly lowering and vacant expression comes back into mind. It was overhanging at the top: and since it fell to me to go down it last, I peered over into it with much concern, so as to make certain that there were really no holds on its gloomy walls. Every time I leaned over to look, a fractured corner of wet quart upon the lower, opposite wall of the chimney blazed up into my eyes all the colours of a kaleidoscope. I could not dodge it: it never missed its dazzle. At last I shuffled a leg over the edge, screened off the unerring foot-light with my boot, and started down into vacancy upon trust alone. It must have served; but with the quenching of the quartz-light the shadow returns upon the day.

Where colour is more varied in tone, and more general, as in the British hills, memory may have to wait more often upon these exaggerated contrasts, or upon some very conspicuous arrangement of light, for its trove of accidental pictures.

The jagged combs and rough-hewn corries of Skye I find return most clearly in glimpses; wheresoever, as might always happen, it chanced that they were seen vividly for a moment between sun and storm, against the rainbow halos around our own cloud "spectres," or printed upon some veil of moving shadow under-run at its lower trailing edges by startling wind-lights off the sea.

Of many scores of crossings which I have made of the Welsh Glydyrs one alone stays undimmed: when upon a snow shoulder we watched spell-bound through the whole course of a mid-winter sunset the rare phenomenon of the "blood-red sword"—a single bar of crimson light, bent upon the sky behind Snowdon, and reaching in even breadth from sea to zenith.

Late on a rainy afternoon Humphrey Jones and I once climbed out upon the top of Tryfan; and found ourselves looking out over a furrowed plain of cloud, which filled all the Nant Francon and sloped upwards against the higher summits of the Carnedds opposite. All this inclined surface was a turmoil of rainbow colours. Near at hand the curves and bands of the spectrum were brilliant and distinguishable. But as they continued ring beyond ring up the farther distance, the colouring became a chaos, subdued and broken tints melting upon each other in admired disorder over miles of tossing mist. Jones as a man of science tried to count and to record their number; but they were the better remembered for their lovely confusion.

Yet another climb upon Tryfan emerges from the many we had upon its good cliffs because of the singular storm-lighting which intimidated us. I had for some time been sensible of the ordinary darkening of the landscape under a thunder cloud. But, when I looked round from my busy climbing again, this had changed to an uncanny and lividgreen visibility, which was magnifying in unnatural colour and distinctness every detail upon the hillsides or in the valley-lengths lying under the electric pall. The corpselighting had a distressing nearness: it seemed to be a freak in my own eyes, as though I were looking at daylight under jaundiced lids or through tinted glasses. As the oppression of gloom overhead increased, descending and thickening foot by foot, the rugged spaces of hillside still showing beneath it appeared as if of themselves to be diffusing more and more of this lurid glare, altering, under growing obscurity, from ashen-green to sulphurous yellow, blotched like calcined copper. Shadow thickened upon shadow, lower and lower through the following minutes. Until, at last, the pall had sunk about us and beneath us on the face of the precipice; and I was looking out and down into a crater of sooty eddies, penetrated deep below by an under-glow as of molten lava. A quick, close flicker of lightning, when it began, came only as a relief; and we returned to normal unpleasantnesses, and lightened spirits, in a fierce squall of snow.

In high Alpine mountaineering much of every day is spent among the whiteness of snow and ice. And a white light either as a single reflection of sunshine or as general illumination might well have been expected, even more frequently than an occasional strange colour, to have formed the clairvoyant disk, the crystal that preserved for our gazing the incidents of some past climb. But I can only think of one vigorous day, that of our crossing of the col Tournanche, which survives as an image seen in a circle of unbroken light, in the filmy whiteness of fresh snow, the semi-transparency and again the dull ivory of ice, the silver of glacial reflections.

Its whiteness indeed owed something to contrast. Out of the shadow of tragedy at Courmayeur we had driven up to Valtournanche. Still with clouded minds we had walked on to Breuil; and in the dark hours, under a whisper of rain-mist, we wound over the wet meadows to the base of the unseen Matterhorn. We were well up under the cliffs of the Tête du Lion when the darkness, upon memory as upon the view, dispersed. An oblique, frosty sunrise carved out with a single sword-stroke the reality of the peaks about us; and upon their white mirror of new snow all the following course of the day shines clearly. Instantaneously the whole flashing height of the Matterhorn clanged into the sky above our heads, plated with metalline sheets of ice, with silvered flutings and giant pan-pipes of fantastic icicles. For a minute or so after the tearing of the mist veil the stillness remained unbroken, the armour of frost held proof against the blaze of the sun. Then there came a rustle from far overhead, and a shiver of falling; and another followed, and yet another, before the echoes had died away. Soon the vast mountain wall was tremulous with splintering shafts of light, and the air was trembling no less about our ears, as moonstone-shields and spears of steely ice began to flicker and crash like shattering glass down the southern precipices. The sight was enough to tell us that we should make no traverse of the Matterhorn that day; and more than enough, too, to console us for our loss by its sheer splendour.

We were, at the moment chosen for this apocalypse, engaged upon the delicate traverse in ice-steps round under the bulking cliffs of the Tête du Lion. It seemed a pity to turn our backs, before we must, upon the shining marvel of the peak. So I suggested that we might invent a line straight up the Lion crags above us, and only when we stood upon its head turn left-handed and follow the high skyline of snow back to the col Tournanche.

The col Tournanche is a real pass, with a personality. Many titular passes are not more than "slacks" between adjacent mountains, dead-points from which the ridges ascending to the heights upon either hand have stolen all individual character so as to add to their own length and symmetry. Wherefore a high snow pass between two strutting peaks often retains for itself no more significance than the white handkerchief dropped as a mark between two duellists, whose opposing legs and feet, as they front one another across it, encroach even upon its edges and modest compass. But the Matterhorn and the Dent d'Hérens treat the col Tournanche with punctilious respect. They stand far back, upon their own dignity of rock bases; so that the whole length of the beautiful snow curves between them belongs to the fall of the pass, not to their height. We feel instinctively that the mutual inclination of the ridges is leading our eye downward from either peak, to rest upon their white arc of union, the pass; not upward, in the more usual tribute of ridges to their parent mountains.

The Tête du Lion began to imitate its great neighbour, and to pelt us as we balanced in our steps with clinking plates and ice-brash. So we stopped watching and wondering, and clambered straight up its unprepared south wall. Mallory overwhelmed the first little overhang with wave like ease. His movement in climbing was entirely his own. It contradicted all theory. He would set his foot high against any angle of smooth surface, fold his shoulder to his knee, and flow upward and upright again on an impetuous curve. Whatever may have happened unseen the while between him and the cliff, in the way of holds or mutual adjustments, the look, and indeed the result, were always the same—a continuous undulating movement so rapid and so powerful that one felt the rock must either yield, or disintegrate. Hugh Pope came last. This was his first big alpine season. But as I watched throughout the day his familiar virtuosity upon rock surpassed by his mastery of complicated mountaineering, a former conviction strengthened, that his were a temperament, a skill and a physique that ought to produce the greatest amateur the mountains had yet seen. In such company I preferred the contemplative position and the subtle rhythm that can delight the middle-man on the rope, on a varied and difficult ridge.

We broke our way through the ice and rock entanglements on to the white sphinx head, and rested again to look at the great pyramid towering into sunshine above us. No simile can suggest the white radiance of that morning's Matterhorn: the thousand shapes and tones and shadows of whiteness which combined in its ascendant light. One would have to borrow an image from music and compare it to the thousand instruments of a great orchestra, sounding together the crescendo of an unknown chord. Only to stand upon one shining point in space and look up at another can give us a feeling for which we can find no words. Three minutes of what we see and feel there are worth three years of life.

We turned westward along the miles of narrow snow-crest and followed our shadows now on this side and now on that of its descending and glittering edge. Mallory's axe twinkled and clicked, and the hard chips from the steps rustled continuously and harshly downward over the steep snow crust. Below us, upon whichever

343

side we moved, the flawless white curve swept over into a mere feeling of depth. Beyond all depth, the white curve renewed itself, upon the level and lesser whiteness of the glaciers; and it returned upon our sight again almost blindingly from the mounting snow-walls of the opposite peaks. All too soon, for such a day, we dipped into the crescent of the pass. As we lay on the snow in its centre, the horns at either end of the silver arc cut off everything from me except the sky. A man riding between the horns of an old moon might not see the world very differently; nor could he feel a greater sense of height and of lonely illumination.

To the south, as I leaned over the rim, I gazed down with satisfaction upon the falling glaciers de Chérillon, whereon Josef and I had once spent two successive days of fog, and of struggles to reach this same pass. The glaciers had compassed us about with séracs of such nightmare difficulty that I doubted, afterwards, whether they had not been evil changelings of the mist. There, too, I had won a bottle of champagne from Josef, in a wager as to which of the glaciers we were really lost upon. That bottle also never gave proof of an existence separable from the fog.

On the north side of our moon, the planes of light poured downward, sliding and rounding one upon another much as the white plumage ruffles and resettles smoothly down the arched neck of a swan. They cascaded to the Tiefenmatten in a single span; and thence, in planes as white but less precipitate, to the Z'Mutt glacier. Over their hurrying brightness we were to make our more gradual descent.

The steep snow was firm, and we could use our feet for step-making as often as our axes. But the fluctuating white surface was shadowless and deceitful. Often after I had clung timidly down over the "vertical" smother of one frozen wave into the white trough above the next, the touch of my outstretched foot would upset every calculation of the eye, the snow would meet it on an unexpected curve bewildering to the balance. And then I would look upward from below at my vertical illusion and decide to reduce my estimate of the angle to a generous 45 degrees. Where there were genuine ice-breaks Hugh Pope was always below me, ready with his immense reach to make me a handrail of his axe and arm down any cliff of under twelve feet. It was a convenience that saved all the time and trouble I should otherwise have had to spend upon fixing a double rope for my descent.

As we came down among the lower glaciers, and out of the light of newer fallen snow, the irradiating whiteness of the day diminished; and with it memory grows indistinct. Both the whiteness and the pictures which return in it came to an end when we reached the dark August woods of the Zermatt valley; and I have no idea what happened to us afterwards. But the crystal of the day stays undimmed. I see it with its globe set against the sun; and within it all our movements and our impressions are reflected in light, as though they had been the scintillations of wind upon water or the lightness of snowfall upon sunlit snow.

—1927

Frank Smythe

"The Abominable Snowman"

Hugh Ruttledge (1884–1961) led an unparalleled team of Britain's climbing superstars—Frank Smythe (1900–1945), Eric Shipton, L. R. Wager, and Wyn Harris—on the 1933 expedition to Mt. Everest. Ruttledge published the official account of the expedition in Everest 1933. *Without oxygen, Harris and Wager climbed to 28,200 feet, and Smythe later reached about the same height before retreating from extreme fatigue. At 28,000 feet, Harris discovered an ice axe along the "Yellow Band" belonging to either Mallory or Irvine, who both perished in 1924. Smythe was a key figure in world climbing for his ascents of Kamet and the Brenva Face in the Alps, and his writing represents some of the most penetrating and insightful explorations of the psychology of mountaineering. He and Shipton joined forces again in 1938 for another unsuccessful attempt on Everest, led by Harold Tilman. In this passage, Smythe describes the "Abominable Snowman" or Yeti, which has been sighted in various remote mountain areas the world over.*

Since I had first seen that grand mountain named Nilgiri Parbat, 21,264 feet, by Lieutenant R. A. Gardiner of the Survey of India, I had on several occasions turned over in my mind the possibility of an ascent. I had examined the mountain from the west, south and east and from these directions there did not seem the least hope of an attempt proving successful. The sole remaining possibility was a route from the north or north-west. There were two possible lines of approach: one via the Bhyundar Pass and the Banke Glacier and the other via the snow pass, which I had already visited, and the glacier-filled valley which runs in its uppermost portion roughly parallel with the Bhyundar Valley. I decided on the last-named approach, as it at least involved the exploration of a valley the upper portion of which, as far as I knew, had not been visited by Europeans.

On July 16th I left the base camp, taking with me Wangdi, Pasang and Nurbu with light equipment and provisions for five days. The past week had seen many more flowers come into bloom, prominent among which was the *pedicularis*. This plant goes by the unpleasant popular name of lousewort, from the Latin *pediculus*, a louse, as one of the species, *Pedicularis palustris*, was said to infect sheep with a lousy disease; but it would be difficult to associate the beautiful pedicularis of the Bhyundar Valley with any disease, particularly the *Pedicularis siphonantha* with its light purple blooms. There were also many dwarf *geraniums* and the *saussurea*, which grows in an astonishing va-

Frank Smythe, *The Valley of Flowers* (London: Hodder and Stoughton, 1938). © 2000 by John Smythe, Tony Smythe, and Richard Smythe. "The Abominable Snowman" from *The Valley of Flowers* from *Frank Smythe: The Six Alpine/Himalayan Climbing Books*. Included by permission of the publishers, The Mountaineers, Seattle, WA.

riety of forms, varying from wide-spreading, flattish leaves with purple corn-flower-like blooms rising almost stalkless in the center, to curious balloon-shaped plants and little balls of silver-grey wool that grow high up above the snow-line.

Gentians, formerly conspicuous by their absence, with the exception of the ubiquitous *Gentiana aprica*, were also in bloom, and I came across a plant (*G. venusta*) like a small edition of that well-known denizen of the Alps, *G. acaulis*. It seems very shy of opening its petals and its little flower is almost stalkless. There was also growing in moist mossy places among the rocks *Primula reptans*, which rivals the *Primula minutissima* in delicacy. With so much beauty and interest attached to the ascent I scarcely noticed that I was walking uphill.

As we passed near some boulders, there was a sudden startled squawking and half a dozen or more young pheasants flew out from a small cave. Wangdi was greatly excited at this, and said that the birds would return to roost. I must confess that my mouth watered so much at the thought of roast pheasant as a change from sheep and goat that then and there I consented to a most nefarious expedition, which was planned to take place after dark.

In order to shorten the morrow's march we camped several hundred feet above our former camping place by the edge of a snow-drift amidst hundreds of *Primula denticulate*, many of which were still in bud. As I had found the same species of *primula* in seed five weeks previously, this struck me as remarkable. As late as October 7th I found flowering plants in ground where avalanche snow had recently melted. It would be interesting to know what process takes place in a plant that is covered for a year or more by avalanche snow, as must often occur in this country. Does it continue to live? Presumably it does, as even compacted avalanche snow contains an appreciable quantity of air. Small wonder that in England gardeners experience difficulty in growing a high Alpine or Himalayan plant, for these supposedly hardy plants are not really as hardy as plants that grow at much lower elevations, which are exposed to climatic conditions all the year round. It is nothing short of miraculous that a plant which lies dormant, protected by a covering of snow for six months of the year, should deign to grow in our bewildering climate.

It was almost completely dark when Wangdi poked his head in at the door of my tent and with a wicked grin announced himself as ready for the murder of the innocents. Together with Nurbu and Pasang, who were armed with blankets, we descended the boulder-clad hillside. A few yards from the cave Wangdi whispered to me to wait; then he and the other two conspirators crept forward as softly as cats. The next moment there was a concerted rush and both entrances to the cave were stopped by blankets. There was no answering scurry of startled birds, so Wangdi crawled under one of the blankets and groped about inside. There were no pheasants roosting there, and he retired into the open, saying things in Tibetan which doubtless exercised the nuances of that language, but at the meaning of which I could only guess. For a few moments I was as disappointed as he, then the humour of our attempted murder struck us both simultaneously and we burst into a roar of laughter.

Next morning we were away in excellent weather. Being lightly laden, I was well ahead of the men. On approaching the pass, I was surprised to notice some tracks in the snow, which I first took to be those of a man, though we had seen no traces of shepherds. But when I came up to the tracks I saw the imprint of a huge naked foot, apparently of a biped, and in stride closely resembling my own tracks. What was it? I was very interested, and at once proceeded to take some photographs. I was engaged in this work when the porters joined me. It was at once evident when they saw the tracks that they were frightened. Wangdi was the first to speak.

"Bad Manshi!" he said, and then "Mirka!" And in case I still did not understand, "Kang Admi" (Snowman).

I had already anticipated such a reply and to reassure him and the other two, for I had no wish for my expedition to end prematurely, I said it must be a bear or snow leopard. But Wangdi would have none of this and explained at length how the tracks could not possibly be those of a bear, snow leopard, wolf or any other animal. Had he not seen many such tracks in the past? It was the Snowman, and he looked uneasily about him.

I am not superstitious. The number thirteen even in conjunction with a Friday means nothing to me. I do not hesitate to walk under a ladder unless there is the danger of a paint-pot falling on my head. Crossed knives, spilt salt, sailors drowning when glasses are made to ring, black coats, new moons seen through glass, chimney-sweeps and such-like manifestations leave me unmoved. But here was something queer, and I must admit that Wangdi's argument and fear was not without its effect. The matter must be investigated. So I got out of my rucksack a copy of the "Spectator" and with a pencil proceeded to mark the size and stride of the track, while the men huddled together, a prey to that curious sullenness which in the Tibetan means fear.

About four inches of snow had fallen recently, and it was obvious that the tracks had been made the previous evening after the sun had lost its power and had frozen during the night, for they were perfect impressions distinct in every detail. On the level the footmarks were as much as 13 inches in length and 6 inches in breadth, but uphill they averaged only 8 inches in length, though the breadth was the same. The stride was from 18 inches to 2 feet on the level, but considerably less uphill, and the footmarks were turned outwards at about the same angle as a man's. There were the well-defined imprints of five toes, 1 ½ inch to 1 ¾ inch long and ¾ inch broad, which unlike human toes were arranged symmetrically. Lastly there was at first sight what appeared to be the impression of a heel, with two curious toe-like impressions on either side.

Presently the men plucked up courage and assisted me. They were unanimous that the Snowman walked with his toes behind him and the impressions at the heel were in reality the front toes. I was soon able to disprove this to my own satisfaction by discovering a place where the beast had jumped down from some rocks, making deep impressions where he had landed, and slithering a little in the snow. Superstition, however, knows no logic, and my explanation produced no effect whatever on Wangdi. At length, having taken all the photographs I wanted on the pass, I asked the men to accompany me and follow up the tracks. They were very averse to this at first, but eventually agreed, as they said, following their own "logic," that the Snowman had come from, not gone, in that direction. From the pass the tracks followed a broad, slightly ascending snow-ridge and, except for one divergence, took an almost straight line. After some 300 yards they turned off the ridge and descended a steep rock-face fully 1,000 feet high seamed with snow gullies. Through my monocular glass I was able to follow them down to a small but considerably crevassed glacier, descending towards the Bhyundar Valley, and down this to the lowermost limit of the new snow. I was much impressed by the difficulties overcome and the intelligence displayed in overcoming them. In order to descend the face, the beast had made a series of intricate traverses and had zig-zagged down a series of ridges and gullies. His track down the glacier was masterly, and from our perch I could see every detail and how cunningly he had avoided concealed snow-covered crevasses. An expert mountaineer could not have made a better route and to have accomplished it without an ice-axe would have been both difficult and dangerous, whilst the unroped descent of a crevassed snow-covered glacier must be accounted as unjustifiable. Obviously the "Snowman" was well qualified for membership of the Himalayan Club.

My examination in this direction completed, we returned to the pass, and I decided to follow the track in the reverse direction. The men, however, said that this was the direction in which the Snowman was going, and if we overtook him, and even so much as set eyes upon him, we should all drop dead in our tracks, or come to an otherwise bad end. They were so scared at the prospect that I felt it was unfair to force them to accompany me, though I believe that Wangdi, at least, would have done so had I asked him.

The tracks, to begin with, traversed along the side of a rough rock-ridge below the minor point we had ascended when we first visited the pass. I followed them for a short distance along the snow to one side of the rocks, then they turned upwards into the mouth of a small cave under some slabs. I was puzzled to account for the fact that, whereas tracks appeared to come out of the cave, there were none going into it. I had already proved to my own satisfaction the absurdity of the porters' contention that the Snowman walked with his toes behind him; still, I was now alone and cut off from sight of the porters by a mist that had suddenly formed, and I could not altogether repress a ridiculous feeling that perhaps they were right after all; such is the power of superstition high up in the lonely Himalayas. I am ashamed to admit that I stood at a distance from the cave and threw a lump of rock into it before venturing further. Nothing happened, so I went up to the mouth of the cave and looked inside; naturally there was nothing there. I then saw that the single track was explained by the beast having climbed down a steep rock and jumped into the snow at the mouth of the cave. I lost the track among the rocks, so climbed up to the little summit we had previously visited. The mist was now dense and I waited fully a quarter of an hour for it to clear. It was a curious experience seated there with no other human being within sight and some queer thoughts passed through my mind. Was there really a

Snowman? If so, would I encounter him? If I did an ice-axe would be a poor substitute for a rifle, but Wangdi had said that even to see a Snowman was to die. Evidently, he killed you by some miraculous hypnotism; then presumably gobbled you up. It was a fairy-tale come to life.

Then, at last, the mists blew aside. At first I could see no tracks coming off the rock island on which I was seated and this was not only puzzling but disturbing, as it implied that the beast might be lurking in the near vicinity. Then I saw that the tracks traversed a narrow and almost concealed ridge to another rock point, and beyond this descended a glacier to the east of our ascending route to the pass. Whatever it was, it lived in the Bhyundar Valley; but why had it left this pleasant valley for these inhospitable altitudes, which involved difficult and dangerous climbing, and an ascent of many thousands of feet?

Meditating on this strange affair I returned to the porters, who were unfeignedly glad to see me, for they had assumed that I was walking to my death. I must now refer to the subsequent history of this business.

On returning to the base camp some days later, the porters made a statement. It was witnessed by Oliver and runs as follows:

"We, Wangdi Nurbu, Nurbu Bhotia and Pasang Urgen, porters employed by Mr. F. S. Smythe, were accompanying Mr. Smythe on July 17th over a glacier pass north of the Bhyundar Valley when we saw on the pass tracks which we knew to be those of a Mirka or Jungli Admi (wild man). We have often seen bear, snow leopard and other animal tracks, but we swear that these tracks were none of these, but were the tracks of a Mirka.

"We told Mr. Smythe that these were the tracks of a Mirka and we saw him take photographs and make measurements. We have never seen a Mirka because anyone who sees one dies or is killed, but there are pictures of the tracks, which are the same as we have seen, in Tibetan monasteries."

My photographs were developed by Kodak Ltd. of Bombay under conditions that precluded any subsequent accusation of faking, and together with my measurements and observations, were sent to my literary agent, Mr. Leonard P. Moore, who was instrumental in having them examined by Professor Julian Huxley, Secretary of the Zoological Society, Mr. Martin A. C. Hinton, Keeper of Zoology at the Natural History Museum, and Mr. R. I. Pocock. The conclusion reached by these experts was that the tracks were made by a bear. At first, due to a misunderstanding as to the exact locality in which the tracks had been seen, the bear was said to be *Ursus Arctos Pruinosus*, but subsequently it was decided that it was *Ursus Arctos Isabellinus*, which is distributed throughout the western and central Himalayas. The tracks agreed in size and character with that animal and there is no reason to suppose that they could have been made by anything else. This bear sometimes grows as large, or larger, than a grizzly, and there is a well-grown specimen in the Natural History Museum. It also varies in colour from brown to silver-grey.

The fact that the tracks appeared to have been made by a biped, is explained by the bear, like all bears, putting its rear foot at the rear end of the impression left by its front foot. Only the side toes would show, and this explains the Tibetans' belief that the curious indentations, in reality superimposed by the rear foot, are the front toes of a Snowman who walks with his toes behind him. This also explains the size of the spoor, which when melted out by the sun would appear enormous. Mr. Eric Shipton describes some tracks he saw near the peak of Nanda Ghunti in Garhwal as resembling those of a young elephant. So also would the tracks I saw when the sun had melted them away at the edges.

How did the legend originate? It is known over a considerable portion of Tibet, in Sikkim and parts of Nepal, including the Sola Khombu Valley, the home of the Sherpas on the south side of the Himalayas. The reason for this probably lies in the comparative ease of communication on the Tibetan plateau, as compared with that in the more mountainous regions south of the Himalayan watershed, where it is known only to peoples of Buddhist faith, such as the Sherpas of Nepal and the Lepchas of Sikkim. The Snowman is reputed to be large, fierce, and carnivorous; the large ones eat yaks and the small ones men. He is sometimes white, and sometimes black or brown. About the female, the most definite account I have heard is that she is only less fierce than the male, but is hampered in her movements by exceptionally large pendulous breasts, which she must perforce sling over her shoulders when walking or running.

Of recent years, considerable force has been lent to the legend by Europeans having seen strange tracks in the snow, sometimes far above the permanent snowline, apparently of a biped. Such tracks had in all cases been spoiled or partially spoiled by the sun, but if such tracks were made by bears, then it is obvious that bears very seldom wander on to the upper snows, otherwise fresh tracks unmelted by the sun would have been observed by travelers. The movements of animals are incalculable, and there seems no logical explanation as to why a bear should venture far from its haunts of woodland and pasture. There is one point in connection with this which may have an important bearing on the tracks we saw, which I have omitted previously in order to bring it in at this juncture. On the way up the Bhyundar Valley from the base camp, I saw a bear about 200 yards distant on the northern slopes of the valley. It bolted immediately, and so quickly that I did not catch more than a glimpse of it, and disappeared into a small cave under an overhanging crag. When the men, who were behind, came up with me, I suggested that we should try to coax it into the open, in order that I could photograph it, so the men threw stones into the cave while I stood by with my camera. But the bear was not to be scared out so easily, and as I had no rifle it was not advisable to approach too near to the cave. Is it possible that we so scared this bear that the same evening it made up the hillside some 4,000 feet to the pass? There are two objections to this theory: firstly, that it appeared to be the ordinary small black bear, and too small to make tracks of the size we saw and, secondly, that the tracks ascended the glacier fully a mile to the east of the point where we saw the bear. We may, however, have unwittingly disturbed another and larger bear during our ascent to our camp. At all events, it is logical to assume that an animal would not venture so far from its native haunts without some strong motive to impel it. One last and very interesting point—The Sikh surveyor whom I had met in the Bhyundar Valley was reported by the Postmaster of Joshimath as having seen a huge white bear in the neighbourhood of the Bhyundar Valley.

It seems possible that the Snowman legend originated through certain traders who saw bears when crossing the passes over the Himalayas and carried their stories into Tibet, where they became magnified and distorted by the people of that superstitious country which, though Buddhist in theory, has never emancipated itself from ancient nature and devil worship. Whether or not bears exist on the Tibetan side of the Himalayas I cannot say. It is probable that they do in comparatively low and densely forested valleys such as the Kharta and Kharma Valleys east of Mount Everest, and it may be that they are distributed more widely than is at present known.

After my return to England I wrote an article, which was published by "The Times" in which I narrated my experiences and put forward my conclusions, which were based of course on the identifications of the zoological experts.

I must confess that this article was provocative, not to say dogmatic, but until it was published I had no idea that the Abominable Snowman, as he is popularly known, is as much beloved by the great British public as the Sea-serpent and the Loch Ness Monster. Indeed, in debunking what had become an institution, I roused a hornet's nest about my ears. It was even proposed by one gentleman in a letter to "The Times" that the Royal Geographical Society and the Alpine Club should send a joint expedition to the Himalayas in an attempt to prove or disprove my observations and conclusions. It was obvious that the writer hoped that this expedition, if it took place, would not only disprove them, but would prove the existence of the Abominable Snowman. I can only say in extenuation of my crime that I hope there is an Abominable Snowman. The tracks I saw were undoubtedly made by a bear, but what if other tracks seen by other people were made by Abominable Snowmen? I hope they were. In this murky age of materialism, human beings have to struggle hard to find the romantic, and what could be more romantic than an Abominable Snowman, together with an Abominable Snow-woman and, not least of all, an Abominable Snow-baby?

—1938

Eric Shipton

from *Blank on the Map*

Eric Shipton (1907–1977) was born in Ceylon in 1907, and his family traveled throughout India and Europe after the death of his father. Shipton climbed with all of the great British climbers of the 1930s, 1940s, and 1950s. Shipton accompanied Frank Smythe on the 1931 summiting of Kamet. The now unexplainably rare book Blank on the Map *details the 1937 mapping expedition led by Shipton and H. W. Tilman in the northern Karakoram around K2. Shipton, a key figure in the saga of Mt. Everest, also led a 1951 reconnaissance mission to Everest, and determined that the route over the Khumbu Glacier into the Western Cwm was feasible. This route allowed Edmund Hillary and Tenzing to reach the summit of Everest on the subsequent 1953 British expedition. Shipton was the obvious candidate to lead the 1953 British attempt on Everest, but in a black episode in the history of British climbing, the joint Himalayan Commitee of the Alpine Club and Royal Geographical Society passed over Shipton and instead chose John Hunt as the leader. The effect on Shipton was devastating. Shipton spent the last years before his death in 1977 from liver cancer exploring Patagonia and the southern Americas. This selection from* Blank on the Map *outlines Shipton's climbing philosophy. Diadem Press has collected Shipton's mountaineering books into a collection entitled* The Six Mountain-Travel Books.

OF THE REAL VALUE OF CLIMBING

Those days in London, before we had even packed our rucksacks, were very strenuous. There were formal permissions to be set in order, supplies to be bought, passages to be booked, and a mass of detail to be attended to that seemed to have little relation to the life we would lead in the mountains. Was all this effort worthwhile? Why should we go to such lengths to plunge ourselves into a life of discomfort and privation? To me it is worthwhile because of what it leads to. Every time I start an expedition I feel that I am getting back to a way of living which is now lost.

With a wistfulness, perhaps a little tinged with sentimentality, I think of the leisurely days of a few hundred years ago, before life was so mad a rush, before the countryside was spoiled by droves of people, and beauty itself exploited as a commercial proposition.

Eric Shipton, *Blank on the Map* (1938; Reprint, 1985, *The Six Mountain-Travel Books*, London: Diadem Books, Ltd., 1985). © 1985 by Nick Shipton. Text from "Blank on the Map" from *Eric Shipton: The Six Mountain Travel Books*. Included by permission of the publishers, The Mountaineers, Seattle, WA.

It is true that the very act of looking back seems to touch the past with gold. Probably the "good old days" were hard and uncomfortable, but they did foster individuality. Life had then an essential quality of reality which now we seem to have lost. We have become so accustomed to having everyday life made easy for us, that our energies are not absorbed in the art of living, but run riot in a craving for sensation. Individuality is swamped in the mass emotion of hurrying mobs of people whose thoughts are dragooned by the ready-made ideas of shallow press articles.

So many human activities have lost their power to refresh the spirit because people tend to do things for the wrong reasons—for publicity, for sensationalism, for money, or because it is the fashion to do them. A wrong attitude, based on an unreal sense of values, poisons our recreations no less than the more serious aspects of living. Reality should be the essential factor in sport as in life. Any other basic aim endangers the right attitude of mind without which there can be no real happiness nor the full enjoyment of any activity.

A man who is really keen about sailing is in the first place attracted by the sea with all its problems, hardships and beauties—by the very form of life which the sea offers. He sails because sailing teaches him the art of living in the environment which he loves. It gives him a larger, clearer view of the problems and difficulties of his craft; and so he comes to a realization of the true æsthetic value of the sea.

In the same way the skier wishes to become part of the country of snow-laden firs and winter mountains which means so much to him. He finds in his sport a way of identifying himself with this enchanting world. He cannot easily achieve this in the competitive social atmosphere of a crowded winter sports resort. He must go to the higher mountains, or to the silent forests of Norway. So it is with the fisherman and his lake and rivers; and with the big-game hunter and his jungles; and with the mountaineer and his peaks and glaciers.

But directly people allow the element of competition to rule their activities, and care more for trophies, or record-breaking, or acclamation, than for a real understanding of their craft, or even if they are content with short cuts to proficiency and superficial knowledge, they are in danger of losing the touchstone of genuine values which alone makes anything worthwhile.

The tendency nowadays to be artificial instead of genuine, and superficial instead of thorough, is caused partly by everyone being in such a hurry, and partly by things being made too easy for us. If a man has money to spend and feels that it would be exciting to go and shoot big game in East Africa, all he need do is to go to a travel agency and book his passage in a luxury liner. When he arrives, he engages the services of a "white hunter," relies on that man's marksmanship and knowledge of the bush, and returns a few months later with a number of tall stories and several crates of trophies. But he has not lived the real life of a hunter; nor has he made the experience a part of his own life. He has taken an easy short cut to vicarious adventure. The mountaineer who goes to the Alps for a season's climbing, with a desire to climb more peaks than other men, and be more difficult routes, misses the real value

353

of the experience—the love of mountains for their own sake. The real purpose of climbing, and of any other sport, should be to transmute it into a way of living, however temporary, in an environment which appeals to the individual.

Often when I have been climbing in the Alps I have thought how enthralling it must have been to see the Alps as De Saussure saw them, before they had been civilized out of their wild unspoiled beauty and tamed into a social asset. A hundred and fifty years ago men went to the Alps to investigate the phenomena of mountains. The result of their quest was the birth of the sciences of geology and glaciology, and the study of the rarefication of the atmosphere at high altitudes, together with its effect upon the human body and upon plants. But in addition to all these discoveries, De Saussure and his companions found in mountains not only the grim hostility which tradition had ascribed to them, but also infinite beauty, peace and solitude, and a recreation of spirit of which they had not dreamed. And just as hundreds of years before sailors had learned to love the sea though it confronted them with dangers and hardships, so these scientists and pioneer travellers came to love the mountains in spite of, or perhaps because of, their severity.

We, to-day, envy them the access they had to that unknown mountain world, and the unspoiled culture of its people. But even now the Alps themselves are potentially what they were, if only a man goes to them in the right spirit. Hilaire Belloc, in our own day, saw the Alps by the grace of his shaping imagination, as "peak and field and needle of intense ice, remote, remote from the world."

But it is useless to long for the past. We cannot put back the clock of Time. We cannot set out with Columbus and experience the thrill of finding America, nor sail with Captain Cook in search of the mythical continent of the South Pacific. We cannot share the mounting excitement of the men who first crossed the high pass from Zermatt to Breuil and saw Italy below them, and above them the curving spire of the unclimbed Matterhorn. Now, whether we like it or not, the Matterhorn is surrounded by hotels, and if we climb it we have the help of fixed ropes and the security of other men's experience.

But the greater mountain ranges of the world are still surprisingly little known. We now have the opportunity to see the Himalaya as De Saussure saw the Alps a hundred and fifty years ago. Its peaks and valleys are unexplored. Its people are leading natural lives, instead of feverishly exploiting their country for profit of doubtful value. The Himalaya provides an even greater field of opportunity than the Alps gave to De Saussure. It is so vast a range that it embraces many countries and different types of people. The peaks and glaciers present such difficulties to the pioneer that exploring them calls for a higher standard of mountaineering skill than at present exists.

Let us approach this great heritage in the right spirit, not impelled by ambition. Let us study its people and their culture. Let us explore its vast tangle of mountains and glaciers, penetrating the deep sunless gorges to find the hidden beauty which lies beyond, crossing unknown passes which lead us from one region of mystery to another. Let us climb peaks by all means, because their beauty attracts us; not because others have failed, nor because the summits stand 28,000 feet above the sea, nor in patriotic fervour for the honour of the nation, nor for cheap publicity. Let us approach the peaks with humility; and, having found the way to them for ourselves, learn to solve their problems. Let us not attack them with an army, announcing on the wireless to a sensation-loving world the news of our departure and the progress of our subsequent advance.

But it is not yet time to climb these great mountains. With so much of the vast Himalaya still a blank on the map, our first privilege is to explore rather than to climb. In two hundred years, when the Himalaya are known, then we may enjoy the range by climbing its peaks. In two thousand years time, when all the peaks are climbed, we shall look for more difficult routes by which to climb them, to recapture the feel of adventure, and perhaps to demonstrate our modern superiority!

It is unfortunately just as possible to go to the Himalaya, as to the Alps, with the wrong attitude of mind. Whether people realize that mountaineering is an inspiration, or condemn it as an insane risk of human life, it is obvious that its value lies in the motives of the climber. The ascent of Everest, like any other human endeavour, is only to be judged by the spirit in which it is attempted.

There is something fine in the desire to test human endurance against the deadening power of altitude, the difficulties of steep ice and rock, and the searching rigours of intense cold and wind; but the greatest value of the art of climbing, with its perfect co-ordination of mind and muscle, is that it teaches man a way of living in the beauty and solitude of high remote places.

And so—despite all the turmoil—the preparations of an expedition are for me so full of excitement that the irritation and delays only increase my longing to be off.

The voyage out to India was an interlude between a life and a life. We arrived at Bombay on April 22nd.

—1938

Maurice Herzog

from *Annapurna*

Maurice Herzog's (1919–) account of the first successful ascent of Annapurna in 1950 instantly became a mountaineering classic. Herzog's French team was the first party to conquer a Himalayan peak over 8,000 meters high. The team included almost every French climbing superstar of the period, including Louis Lachenal, Lionel Terray, and Gaston Rébuffat. Extensive experience on the north walls of the Alps, such as the Eigerwand and Walker Spur, had taught the French climbers to establish high base camps as soon as the adjustment to altitude allowed, and then burst to the summit before the effects of oxygen deprivation, fatigue, cold, and weather weakened the body and broke the spirit. The victory came at a great cost, however, with severe frostbite and a series of amputations for Herzog as his wounded body was carried from the mountain by porters through heavy monsoon rains. It is surprising that no one died on Annapurna, as several costly and fundamental mistakes of technique almost led to disaster: Herzog lost his gloves and his hands became useless masses of ice; both Terray and Rébuffat succumbed to snowblindness by neglecting their goggles and needed to be helped from the mountain by Sherpas. During the descent, the group fell into a crevasse and spent the night there. The selection below describes the harrowing descent from Annapurna and demonstrates the remarkable good fortune that blessed an expedition veering towards disaster at every turn.

Time passed, but we had no idea how long. Night was approaching, and we were terrified, though none of us made any complaint. Rébuffat and I found a way that we thought we remembered, but were brought to a halt by the extreme steepness of the slope—the mist turned it into a vertical wall. We were to find next day that at that moment we had been only thirty yards from the camp, and that the wall was the very one that sheltered the tent which would have been our salvation.

"We must find a crevasse."

"We can't stay here all night!"

"A hole—it's the only thing."

"We'll all die in it."

Maurice Herzog, *Annapurna: First Conquest of an 8,000-meter Peak*, trans. Nea Morin and Janet Adam Smith (New York: E. P. Dutton and Co., Inc., 1953). *Annapurna: First Conquest of an 8,000-meter Peak* by Maurice Herzog (translated by Nea Morin and Janet Adam Smith). © 1953 by Maurice Herzog. Originally published in New York by E. P. Dutton. Included by permission of Lyons Press.

Night had suddenly fallen and it was essential to come to a decision without wasting another minute; if we remained on the slope, we should be dead before morning. We would have to bivouac. What the conditions would be like, we could guess, for we all knew what it meant to bivouac above 23,000 feet.

With his axe Terray began to dig a hole. Lachenal went over to a snow-filled crevasse a few yards further on, then suddenly let out a yell and disappeared before our eyes. We stood helpless: should we, or rather would Terray and Rébuffat, have enough strength for all the maneuvers with the rope that would be needed to get him out? The crevasse was completely blocked up save for the one little hole which Lachenal had fallen through.

"Lachenal!" called Terray.

A voice, muffled by many thicknesses of ice and snow, came up to us. It was impossible to make out what it was saying.

"Lachenal!"

Terray jerked the rope violently; this time we could hear.

"I'm here!"

"Anything broken?"

"No! It'll do for the night! Come along."

This shelter was heaven-sent. None of us would have had the strength to dig a hole big enough to protect the lot of us from the wind. Without hesitation Terray let himself drop into the crevasse, and a loud "Come on!" told us he had arrived safely. In my turn I let myself go: it was a regular toboggan-slide. I shot down a sort of twisting tunnel, very steep, and about thirty feet long. I came out at great speed into the opening beyond and was literally hurled to the bottom of the crevasse. We let Rébuffat know he could come by giving a tug on the rope.

The intense cold of this minute grotto shriveled us up, the enclosing walls of ice were damp and the floor a carpet of fresh snow; by huddling together there was just room for the four of us. Icicles hung from the ceiling and we broke some of them off to make more head room and kept little bits to suck—it was a long time since we had had anything to drink.

That was our shelter for the night. At least we should be protected from the wind, and the temperature would remain fairly even, though the damp was extremely unpleasant. We settled ourselves in the dark as best we could. As always in a bivouac we took off our boots; without this precaution the construction would cause immediate frost-bite. Terray unrolled the sleeping-bag which he had had the foresight to bring, and settled himself in relative comfort. We put on everything warm that we had, and to avoid contact with the snow I sat on the movie camera. We huddled close up to each other, in our search for a hypothetical position in which the warmth of our bodies could be combined without loss, but we couldn't keep still for a second.

We did not open our mouths—signs were less of an effort than words. Every man withdrew into himself and took refuge in his own inner world. Terray massaged Lachenal's feet; Rébuffat felt his feet freezing too, but he had sufficient strength to rub

357

them himself. I remained motionless, unseeing. My feet and hands went on freezing, but what could be done? I attempted to forget suffering by withdrawing into myself, trying to forget the passing of time, trying not to feel the devouring and numbing cold which insidiously gained upon us.

Terray shared his sleeping-bag with Lachenal, putting his feet and hands inside the precious eiderdown. At the same time he went on rubbing.

Anyhow the frost-bite won't spread further, he was thinking.

None of us could make any movement without upsetting the others, and the positions we had taken up with such care were continually being altered so that we had to start all over again. This kept us busy. Rébuffat persevered with his rubbing and complained of his feet; like Terray he was thinking: We mustn't look beyond tomorrow—afterwards we'll see. But he was not blind to the fact that "afterwards" was one big question-mark.

Terray generously tried to give me part of his sleeping-bag. He had understood the seriousness of my condition, and knew why it was that I said nothing and remained quite passive; he realized that I had abandoned all hope for myself. He massaged me for nearly two hours; his feet, too, might have frozen, but he didn't appear to give the matter a thought. I found new courage simply in contemplating his unselfishness; he was doing so much to help me that it would have been ungrateful of me not to go on struggling to live. Though my heart was like a lump of ice itself, I was astonished to feel no pain. Everything material about me seemed to have dropped away. I seemed to be quite clear in my thoughts and yet I floated in a kind of peaceful happiness. There was still a breath of life in me, but it dwindled steadily as the hours went by. Terray's massage no longer had any effect upon me. All was over, I thought. Wasn't this cavern the most beautiful grave I could hope for? Death caused me no grief, no regret—I smiled at the thought.

After hours of torpor a voice mumbled "Daylight!"

This made some impression on the others. I only felt surprised—I had not thought that daylight would penetrate so far down.

"Too early to start," said Rébuffat.

A ghastly light spread through our grotto and we could just vaguely make out the shapes of each other's heads. A queer noise from a long way off came down to us—a sort of prolonged hiss. The noise increased. Suddenly I was buried, blinded, smothered beneath an avalanche of new snow. The icy snow spread over the cavern, finding its way through every gap in our clothing. I ducked my head between my knees and covered myself with both arms. The snow flowed on and on. There was terrible silence. We were not completely buried, but there was snow everywhere. We got up, taking care not to bang our heads against the ceiling of ice, and tried to shake ourselves. We were all in our stockinged feet in the snow. The first thing to do was to find our boots.

Rébuffat and Terray began to search, and realized at once that they were blind. Yesterday they had taken off their glasses to lead us down and now they were paying for it. Lachenal was the first to lay hands upon a pair of boots. He tried to put

358

them on, but they were Rébuffat's. Rébuffat attempted to climb up the chute down which we had come yesterday, and which the avalanche had followed in its turn.

"Hi, Gaston! What's the weather like?" called up Terray.

"Can't see a thing. It's blowing hard."

We were still groping for our things. Terray found his boots and put them on awkwardly, unable to see what he was doing. Lachenal helped him, but he was all on edge and fearfully impatient, in striking contrast to my immobility. Terray then went up the icy channel, puffing and blowing, and then at last reached the outer world. He was met by terrible gusts of wind that cut right through him and lashed his face.

Bad weather, he said to himself, this time it's the end. We're lost . . . we'll never come through.

At the bottom of the crevasse there were still two of us looking for our boots. Lachenal poked fiercely with an ice-axe. I was calmer and tried to proceed more rationally. We extracted crampons and an axe in turn from the snow, but still no boots.

Well—so this cavern was to be our last resting-place! There was very little room— we were bent double and got in each other's way. Lachenal decided to go out without his boots. He called frantically, hauled himself up on the rope, trying to get a hold or to wiggle his way up, digging his toes into the snow walls. Terray from outside pulled as hard as he could. I watched him go; he gathered speed and disappeared.

When he emerged from the opening he saw the sky was clear and blue, and he began to run like a madman, shrieking, "It's fine, it's fine!"

I set to work again to search the cave. The boots *had* to be found, or Lachenal and I were done for. On all fours, with nothing on my hands or feet I raked the snow, stirring it around this way and that, hoping every second to come upon something hard. I was no longer capable of thinking—I reacted like an animal fighting for its life.

I found one boot! The other was tied to it—pair! Having ransacked the whole cave I at last found the other pair. But in spite of all my efforts I could not find the movie camera, and gave up in despair. There was no question of putting my boots on—my hands were like lumps of wood and I could hold nothing in my fingers; my feet were very swollen—I should never be able to get boots on them. I twisted the rope around the boots as well as I could and called up the chute:

"Lionel . . . Boots!"

There was no answer, but he must have heard for with a jerk the precious boots shot up. Soon after the rope came down again. My turn. I wound the rope around me. I could not pull it tight so I made a whole series of little knots. Their combined strength, I hoped, would be enough to hold me. I had no strength to shout again; I gave a great tug on the rope, and Terray understood.

At the first step I had to kick a notch in the hard snow for my toes. Further on I expected to be able to get up more easily by wedging myself across the runnel. I wriggled up a few yards like this and then I tried to dig my hands and my feet into the wall. My hands were stiff and hard right up to the wrists and my feet had no feeling up to the ankles, the joints were inflexible and this hampered me greatly.

Somehow or other I succeeded in working my way up, while Terray pulled so hard he nearly choked me. I began to see more distinctly and so knew that I must be nearing the opening. Often I fell back, but I clung on and wedged myself in again as best I could. My heart was bursting and I was forced to rest. A fresh wave of energy enabled me to crawl to the top. I pulled myself out by clutching Terray's legs; he was just about all in and I was in the last stages of exhaustion. Terray was close to me and I whispered:

"Lionel . . . I'm dying!"

He supported me and helped me away from the crevasse. Lachenal and Rébuffat were sitting in the snow a few yards away. The instant Lionel let go of me I sank down and dragged myself along on all fours.

The weather was perfect. Quantities of snow had fallen the day before and the mountains were resplendent. Never had I seen them look so beautiful—our last day would be magnificent.

Rébuffat and Terray were completely blind; as he came along with me Terray knocked into things and I had to direct him. Rébuffat, to, could not move a step without guidance. It was terrifying to be blind when there was danger all around. Lachenal's frozen feet affected his nervous system. His behavior was disquieting—he was possessed by the most fantastic ideas:

"I tell you we must go down . . . down there . . ."

"You've nothing on your feet."

"Don't worry about that."

"You're off your head. The way's not there . . . it's to the left!"

He was already standing up; he wanted to go straight down to the bottom of the glacier. Terray held him back, made him sit down, and though he couldn't see, helped Lachenal put his boots on.

Behind them I was living in my own private dream. I knew the end was near, but it was the end that all mountaineers wish for—an end in keeping with their ruling passion. I was consciously grateful to the mountains for being so beautiful for me that day, and as awed by their silence as if I had been in church. I was in no pain, and had no worry. My utter calmness was alarming. Terray came staggering towards me, and I told him: "It's all over for me. Go on . . . you have a chance . . . you must take it . . . over to the left . . . that's the way."

I felt better after telling him that. But Terray would have none of it: "We'll help you. If we get away, so will you."

At this moment Lachenal shouted: "Help! Help!"

Obviously he didn't know what he was doing . . . Or did he? He was the only one of the four of us who could see Camp II down below. Perhaps his calls would be heard. They were shrieks of despair, reminding me tragically of some climbers lost in the Mont Blanc massif whom I had endeavored to save. Now it was our turn. The impression was vivid: we were lost.

I joined in with the others; "One . . . two . . . three . . . *Help!* One . . . two . . . three . . . *Help!*" We tired to shout together, but without much success; our voices could not

360

have carried more than ten feet. The noise I made was more of a whisper than a shout. Terray insisted that I should put my boots on, but my hands were dead. Neither Rébuffat nor Terray, who were unable to see, could help much, so I said to Lachenal: "Come and help me to put my boots on."

"Don't be silly, we must go down!"

And off he went once again in the wrong direction, straight down. I was not in the least angry with him; he had been sorely tried by the altitude and by everything he had gone through.

Terray resolutely got out his knife, and with fumbling hands slit the uppers of my boots back and front. Split in two like this I could get them on, but it was not easy and I had to make several attempts. Soon I lost heart—what was the use of it all anyway since I was going to stay where I was? But Terray pulled violently and finally he succeeded. He laced up my now gigantic boots, missing half the hooks. I was ready now. But how was I going to walk with my stiff joints?

"To the left, Lionel!"

"You're crazy, Maurice," said Lachenal, "it's to the right, straight down."

Terray did not know what to think of these conflicting views. He had not given up like me, he was going to fight; but what, at the moment, could he do? The three of them discussed which way to go.

I remained sitting in the snow. Gradually my mind lost grip—why should I struggle? I would just let myself drift. I saw pictures of shady slopes, peaceful paths, there was a scent of resin. It was pleasant—I was going to die in my own mountains. My body had no feeling—everything was frozen.

"Aah . . . aah!"

Was it a groan or a call? I gathered my strength for one cry: "They're coming!" The others heard me and shouted for joy. What a miraculous apparition! "Schatz . . . it's Schatz!"

Barely two hundred yards away Marcel Schatz, waist-deep in snow, was coming slowly towards us like a boat on the surface of the slope. I found this vision of a strong and invincible deliverer inexpressibly moving. I expected everything of him. The shock was violent, and quite shattered me. Death clutched at me and I gave myself up.

When I came to again the wish to live returned and I experienced a violent revulsion of feeling. All was not lost! As Schatz came nearer my eyes never left him for a second—twenty yards—ten yards—he came straight towards me. Why? Without a word he leaned over me, held me close, hugged me, and his warm breath revived me.

I could not make the slightest movement—I was like marble. My heart was overwhelmed by such tremendous feelings and yet my eyes remained dry.

"It is wonderful—what you have done!"

—1953

361

Gaston Rébuffat

from *Starlight and Storm*

The lyrical writings of famed French climber Gaston Rébuffat (1921–1985) signaled a change in mountaineering literature from the Victorian "siege" mentality of "conquering" and "assaulting" mountains toward an aesthetic of the appreciation of the beauty and serenity of the mountain environment. Rébuffat reveals the inner life of the climber in his writings. Rébuffat was known throughout France and the world as a top climber, and his exploits on the Piz Badile, Eiger, Grandes Jorasses, and Cima Grande di Lavaredo are legendary. He was an obvious choice for Maurice Herzog's successful expedition to Annapurna in 1950, the first 8,000-meter peak ever climbed. Although the Piz Badile does not reach above 11,000 feet, it was a technically difficult and stunning climb, described by Rébuffat below.

THE NORTH-EAST FACE OF PIZ BADILE

The Piz Badile is situated in the most enchanting cirque of mountains that one could imagine, the Bondasca Valley in the Ticino. Here everything is wonderfully ordered, from the depths of the valley to the slender summits of pale granite. And the villages of Promontogno and Bondo are real mountain villages, a mixture of Swiss orderliness and Italian fantasy: not ugly, hybrid growths of upstart towns, as is often the case with mountaineering and skiing centres.

The path which leads towards the summits cuts deeply through the dense, scented forest. When you have crossed the moss-clad ravines you reach a vast amphitheatre of mountains. Here peace reigns. The only sound, the only movement, is that of the torrents and waterfalls, born from the womb of the eternal glaciers as they go rushing down noisily through this world of silence, whose only life is the slow rhythm of the seasons. Wild gorges open up on either side: deep and twisted, worn and polished smooth each spring by the avalanches, they are sprinkled with dead trees tossed among the bushes that are reborn each summer. It is a romantic scene. Here you are tempted to sit and gaze and drink it in. The air is laden with a delicious scent of grass, of resin and of the keen breeze. Here a man forgets everything, even that he has come to climb.

The Piz Badile is of modest height, no more than 10,853 feet. It is not surrounded by huge glaciers, nor are the neighbouring summits imposing. But its north-east face presents a wall 3,000 feet high, smooth and straight and regular to perfection. Moreover, like many other mountain groups, the Piz Badile and its neighbours, the Piz Cengalo, Pizzi Gemelli and Aiguilles de Sciora, form the frontier between Switzerland to the north and Italy to the south. As is the case with the Grandes Jorasses, the north faces are as difficult as their sunlit southern flanks are easy and attractive.

———

Here again it was Riccardo Cassin who, after his great climbs in the Dolomites on the Torre Trieste and the western Cima (peak) di Lavaredo, was attracted by the wall of the Badile. After a first visit to reconnoitre the face Cassin and his climbing companions, Esposito and Ratti, made an attempt in earnest on the first day of fine weather, 13th July 1937. At the same time two young climbers from Como, Molteni and Valsecchi, were attempting the wall from a different starting-point. The two parties spent the night together on a little platform, and on the next day Molteni and Valsecchi showed signs of fatigue. During the rainy days that had preceded their attempt they had remained at the Sciora hut under difficult conditions, sleeping on the kitchen floor because they did not have the key to the dormitory, and eating sparingly so that they would be ready to start out at a moment's notice. Accordingly they joined on to Cassin's rope.

On the evening of the second day the climbers bivouacked at the foot of the big, light-coloured slab. It was a bad night, for a storm had risen, and on the next day the rocks were in very bad condition. At last, thanks to the determination and immense powers of resistance of Cassin, Esposito and Ratti, the five climbers emerged on the summit at 4 P.M. on the third day, in the teeth of a blizzard. Then they began the descent by the normal route, down the Italian side. This is quite simple in good conditions, but now the whirling snow and gusts of icy wind made it very hard going. Almost immediately Molteni died of exhaustion. The others continued their painful way, but when they had reached the last obstacle, a little rock wall, the visibility was so limited, the rocks so unrecognizable under their coating of snow, that Cassin hesitated, casting about for the right way. If they could only cross or get round this rock step they would be saved, for the Gianetti hut was very close. Cassin plunged out, then after a short while came back again. The four climbers stood together, and Valsecchi, who had not seen his friend's death, looked round for Molteni. He realized what had happened and burst into tears; then he too sank down and died. Like many another mountain, the Badile had seen to it that victory was dearly won.

For twelve years the north-east face of the Badile was abandoned. The great difficulty, the distance and the circumstances surrounding the first ascent scared mountaineers away. Why then was I attracted by it? There are ideas which link together, flow on and gradually impose themselves. Basically it is a question of wanting a thing enough; and if your desire is a worthy one it will be granted in the long run. But the ripe fruit must be plucked, and there is a special pleasure in savouring the fruit of desire gathered in due season. So it was with the Badile.

In 1945, on the Walker Spur of the Grandes Jorasses, I had followed a climb first made by Cassin; so it was again this time. On the former route I had known nothing whatever about the line he had taken. Again, here on the Badile, I knew almost nothing of the route he had followed; I had the benefit of a technical note, but was handicapped by the situation of the mountain, in a district isolated and unknown to me. Thus it became a matter of recapturing the spirit of Cassin himself at the foot of his great climb, his will to conquer and his love of the game. Given these qualities the rest follows, all the delights of climbing and the eventual triumph.

On the eve of a great climb, and especially before the Walker, I have often tried to recapture the feelings of a climber on the eve of a first ascent, simply for the hard, egotistical pleasure of pioneering; but first for the pleasure of prowling about at the foot of the great slabs, of looking at them with a kind of tenderness, making out their forms, knowing them, savouring them in advance. First the joy of anticipation, then the delight of action. All this there was. And yet in itself the prospect of the climbing would not have sufficed; for a good technique combined with fitness is all that is needed to overcome the difficulties. This time there was another pleasure to add to the rest: the chance to test the mastery of my craft and to observe the delight of my friend Bernard Pierre during the three days we would spend together on the Badile. "Right! Let's go." His look of relief had been sufficient reward for the long periods of deliberations and doubt, when I had to weigh carefully the difficulties of the climb, to balance desire against cold reason and conscience. Was it reasonable to tackle the central spur of the Jorasses north face with learners? Was it now sensible to take Bernard to the Badile, with his brief experience of mountains?

Originally there had been no such doubts, for I was to have made the attempt with Jean Deudon. It would have been a splendid symbol of our friendship. We would have gone, and together we would have looked upon, then loved these great slabs. We would have attacked; Jean would have taken the big sack and as usual would have given me a shoulder where necessary. What a fine pedestal those shoulders of his were! We would have bivouacked, and as usual we would have been rained on and stormed on, but I would not have dared to say anything, for as usual Jean would not have complained. He would only have asked for cigarettes to warm his enormous frame. Perhaps we would have talked; he would have said:

"You know, at Camp IV on Hidden peak . . ."[1]

———

On the next day we would have set off again, now one now the other leading, and I would have felt strong enough to climb pitches of the seventh or eighth degree of severity, having with me the indomitable Jean Deudon. But this time the weather had decided differently. I had to wait, then choose the moment, and as Jean was not there, what could be more natural than to take Bernard Pierre? At Easter we had traversed the Aiguilles du Diable.[2] And a short while before we had all three been on the rope together on the great face of the Aiguille de la Brenva.[3]

Only the previous evening at supper we had been wondering what to do in the fine weather which had at last begun three days before, during this particularly rainy summer. We felt the need for a big climb, something in the nature of an expedition even. It is amusing to recall the bubbling optimism which reigns over these evening meals. We had been depressed, but now the stars had come back and out we went to look at them, to receive their message. We came in again joyful, but scarcely were we seated than we were nervous once more: were they still shining? We went to sleep happy, and yet we would have liked to stay awake with these cold stars in which our hopes rested. The night was lightened by a new fire, and our awakening made happy by the thought of settled fine weather.

Off we go then!

During the morning I had to climb the Brévent[4] by the face, and in the early afternoon the Gaillands,[5] both with clients. As usual I only finished packing my sack as I started running for the *téléferique*. But I was in a good mood, and if the client was not a good goer, so much the worse for him! This hesitant client of mine was losing me precious time in this limited spell of fine weather!

Meanwhile Bernard had prepared the sacks, and there was the car waiting for us. Good-bye, Clocher-Clochertons, Brévent, Gaillands, on which I had been scrambling for the past week between the showers. I felt a kind of fatherly affection for them now. It was five o'clock as we drove off, without any notion where we would spend the night. But when you are happy that does not worry you overmuch. Nor, for that matter, could we foretell where we should be bivouacking in two and three days' time, tied to the wall of the Badile.

The evening before we were talking of nothing but the Matterhorn by the Furggen ridge; we did not so much as mention the Badile, for Promontogno seemed too distant and the fine weather too recent. But since waking up that morning I had felt good-humoured, my thoughts wandered, and I was happy; my plan of last winter, the Badile, had crept back into my head. The Badile! Who named these mountains? We had just had a fortnight in the Dolomites, and the mere sound of their names already filled the soul with longing. And now Promontogno, Sciora, Badile—these were singing through our heads.

This new idea put everything into the melting-pot again. It had all been so simple before. I had already done the Furggen, and it was a fine memory. But at Visp we had to make up our minds, and instead of turning right for Zermatt and the Matterhorn, we continued along the valley of the Rhône, along the great road bordered with poplars, heading eastwards. Beside me I could sense Bernard's eagerness, as on the eve of a great battle.

The Sciora hut was burnt during the war, and we slept between the coarse linen sheets of the *pension* near by. It is like a very well-kept old inn. At half past three next morning the mistress of the house, stout and kindly, brought us our ham sandwiches and sent us on our way with a "Buona fortuna" before shutting the heavy door behind us. Then a workman engaged on building the new hut accompanied us as we walked up. Lantern in hand, he showed us the route that he followed each day; and I thought of Cassin, eleven years before, climbing up to explore this untouched face. . . .

365

By the time we arrived at the foot of the wall it was half past eight. On the right we could identify the line of attack of the two climbers from Como, and for a moment we were tempted to go left, to the foot of the great central couloir. But the sun, warming the higher part of the face, started stones falling; they came tumbling down to smudge the little glacier below. We put on the rope and shared out the loads; whenever possible I would be climbing with a very light sack. Bernard's sack was very much heavier.

The glacier was very low, and the initial slabs were worn smooth. We looked for and found the snow bridge over the gap. Just as I began to cross it, it collapsed, much to the amusement of the workman, who had stayed to watch us start. This made the take-off very delicate, and in the end Bernard gave me a shoulder, following after himself. We then went on together, following a long shelf as far as the first open corner. This brought us up with a start, for up to here it had been easy. We climbed it and found other upward shelves, bringing us leftwards to the foot of a great block detached from the face. This was a real turning-point, for it is here that the north-east face of the Piz Badile begins in earnest.

It is a repulsive place; but higher up a piton in the rock showed me the route. While Bernard passed the gear up to me, I looked up at these open corners rising in diagonals towards the left: one angled like a roof, the other convex, almost vertical, flattening out one hundred and fifty feet below us. I could not help thinking of Cassin arriving at this point, and immediately starting to climb this difficult section as naturally as he had overcome the easy shelves. Undoubtedly these Dolomite climbers are lucky to be constantly "ready for anything"—in a frame of mind which accepts everything that comes: slanting corners and repellent overhangs; traverses followed by drops of hundreds of feet *en rappel*; the lack of stances and stances on pitons; passages where progress is at the rate of thirty feet an hour, or where the only solution is to swing across the void, although you can only see some fifteen feet ahead. Yet one thing was surprising and rather deceptive about this cliff, in contrast with the Dolomites. These slabs, these corners of splendid granite, are less steep and less exposed than the limestone corners; but despite this it is impossible to climb them without pitons, for the rock is too compact, lacking even the smallest hold. There were no airy hundred-foot drops as on the Sass Pordoï or the Spigolo Giallo in the Dolomites, where the rope behind me hung free of the rock. Here the stirrups did not hang, they lay against the slabs. Yet this slanting corner was difficult; you needed to hammer in the pitons with the left hand, and the cracks overlapped downwards. You had to trust a piton driven in upside-down, then a second fixed in the same way. I found this piton work tedious and exhausting, and did not like it at all. It was not so much the fact of leaving those easy shelves behind, or of reckoning that a return would be almost impossible down those slanting corners; but it seemed so futile to be doing nothing but hammer in pegs. Climbing one corner after another, I advanced thirty feet an hour up this wall of three thousand feet—a ridiculous pace. It had been all very well putting in a piton or two in the slabs on the east face of the Crocodile.[6] But what was the point of fastening myself here, in fine weather, to a series of little nails?

And yet, absorbed perhaps by the technical interest, I found myself choosing the right piton from my supply, driving it into the rock, hearing it sing as it went in, and confiding my whole body, with all that it contains of hope and love, to this one iron peg. I gained just three feet, and my interest grew. I redoubled my efforts to pass the angle of the corner, which was no longer sloping but vertical; I lengthened myself and stretched out to gain another few inches. I found another crack for a bent "extra-flat" piton. At last it was firmly fixed, and with the help of the stirrups another six feet were gained. I could no longer see Bernard, but he could judge of my advance from the noise of the pitons and the least movement of the ropes.

There between my feet the slabs swept away, not quite vertical but curved three hundred feet below like a ski-jumping hill. Thanks to a few holds I was able to climb without pitons, and reached the next stance more quickly. I hauled up the big sack on the third rope, and Bernard climbed with the small one. Then it was my turn to feel *him* climb up, from the tremors of the ropes. He recovered the pitons, a tiring, acrobatic feat in itself, and brought them up to me. These iron pegs at least provide the excuse for a smile between second and leader, when the former hands them over. On I went, the richer by all my ironmongery and a smile. The hammering of pitons continued.

There followed more corners and more slabs, till we arrived at last the bivouac site of the Italians; but we did not halt here. The route slants very steeply upwards to the left, over fine slabs with firm, small holds. It was sheer joy to be climbing without artificial aid once more. On we went, stance after stance, rope-length by rope-length, until we reached the little snow-field half-way up the face. Here the Badile seems to lie back, only to soar again in a fresh upward surge. It was now a quarter past 6 P.M., and I left the sack in order to have a look at the way ahead. There is little relief in this immense sweep of smooth slabs; everything is so sloping that we wondered under which of these projecting eaves Cassin could have squeezed himself.

Once again, as at the beginning of the climb, I was tempted by the great central couloir, ninety feet to the left; but the stones, icicles and waterfall which came crashing down it soon scared me off. I skirted under the wall and found Cassin's corner topped by an enormous overhang; there lay the way. But for that evening we were only making a reconnaissance. It was now half past six, and 28th August, on a face long deserted by the sun. It was clearly too late to think of starting on this next step, but I climbed the first, very difficult hundred feet, planted pitons and returned to Bernard. Night was creeping up.

We went down a further seventy feet and prepared our bivouac. It was fine and cold. Despite the gathering darkness we took our time over settling in, so as to shorten the long hours of the night as much as possible. We planted the piton anchoring us to the rock, and put on our eiderdown jackets.[7] We gratefully unfolded the wind-proof smocks which we had hesitated to bring the evening before. We lit the candle and the solid meta-fuel stove. For us two human beings the face of Piz Badile was home for the night.

After this performance we looked at our watches. It was still only eight o'clock, and a long night of sleepless inactivity lay ahead. Tensed with cold, hooked on to the Badile by a piton like pictures hanging on a wall, we endured only for the sunshine to come. The sky was beautiful. But among high mountains the chilly dawn is very slow in arriving. As the wall faces north-east we had hoped that we might receive the early rays to help us start. But when the sun did appear it dallied three hundred feet above our heads, and we decided to climb up towards it. The snow was hard and the frost had made ice of what had melted the day before. At eight o'clock we were at the foot of the open corner. Stiff from cold, I climbed clumsily with the help of the rope left yesterday. But thirty feet higher I was touching rock white and warm with the sun; the vitality which had ebbed from my body sprang out anew, my movements flowed more easily and my pace quickened. Down below Bernard was still shivering, but I reached the stance quickly and brought him up. Then I passed him the ropes and went on.

The morning before we had been surprised by these corners; to-day I marvelled at the audacity of such a route. The ground here is as vertical as a limestone cliff and the climbing airy as you could wish. There is only just the bare minimum to allow you to get up. It was not a succession of slabs that we were climbing, but one immense slab, all but perfect in its regularity and smoothness. Everything about the climbing of it was a joy, and as we climbed I seemed to understand the meaning of our exploit. It was not the increasing nearness of the summit, or the climb in itself, that filled us with a quiet joy, but the feeling that mind and muscles were fulfilling their intended function. Somehow we were "in the right place."

What pleasure Cassin must have had tracing his route up this wall! The certainty of being able to get up must have given him the strength to ignore the awesome aspect of the overhangs above. To reach them we had to climb a thin crack up a sheer sweep of wall leading right up under the overhang. Then we must depend on pitons fixed head downwards, and step in stirrups hanging out over the void, in order to traverse horizontally to the left, under the eaves, and gain the corner that follows. The manoeuver is almost simple, for there is no alternative. Then the corner itself was long and difficult; the ropes did not run easily, for they tended to jam under the eaves. The exit was delicate, on rounded holds, and our hundred-foot length of rope only just allowed me to reach the tiny ledge which served as stance. Then there was the tiresome strain of pulling up the sacks, and Bernard started up, again performing feats of acrobatics as he recovered the pitons. Soon he emerged beside me, handing me triumphantly the precious metal so that I might use it yet again.

The huge scale of the cliff was brought home forcibly to us at this point by the height that we had gained. After a delicate climb up a wall I reached a minute ledge by a tiny crack, the ledge on which the Italians had made their second bivouac. So the great buttress had been overcome! Above us was a large, light-coloured slab, very recognizable from the description; and on our right the start of the crack by which we must climb it. But it was mid-day, and we stopped to eat on this platform of sad memories. Usually pitons simply mark a route, but on bivouac sites they convey a feeling of joy or sadness. Here men sang because they were cold; here they ate, not because they were hungry, but to keep up their failing strength, before they left this terrace for a night their bodies had warmed.

But we could not linger; dark clouds now covered the sky. We started up the crack, which, higher up, widens into a cleft and finishes on the north ridge. The climbing was delicate without being difficult, for crack and cleft were drenched by streams of water from the melting snow-fields above. We climbed with care, but we had to hurry too, for the bad weather that invariably accompanies big climbs seemed to be getting worse around us; the clouds darkened, the light faded, the rock appeared flat and featureless. Horrified at the thought of a storm in this fissure, where the sheet of water would so soon be transformed into a torrent, I climbed fast, very fast, and rather roughly. Behind me the ropes were heavy with moisture. Above, the cleft was barred by vertical walls forming a difficult obstacle, demanding care and attention. Meanwhile the rock grew greasy under its film of water. It began to rain, but we seemed to be making our way through a curtain of vapour, frigid almost tangible and hard to penetrate. There was nothing ethereal about these regions, and yet I felt myself as light as if I had abandoned my human frame; I almost ran up the rocks.

A stream of water flowed from the holds to which I was clinging, trickled down my arm and froze me to the shoulder, which was already soaked by the rope running over it as I secured Bernard. Bernard climbed very fast, and we gained height rapidly. But this couloir which had looked so short from Cassion's bivouac, was in fact over six hundred feet high; that meant seven or eight rope-lengths, and that is a lot of rope to be handling.

Luckily there was a brief clearing of the weather, and we made use of it. But higher up the angle steepened and I had to use pitons, which lost us precious time. My thoughts were very clear, despite the anxiety and my state of exaltation. I was afraid of the storm and used all my strength to hammer the pitons into the cracks. Meanwhile Bernard, who had been carrying the big sack, was now burdened with mine as well. When he hoisted himself up by the soaking rope to gain time, a little fountain bubbled down his sleeves. Once, looking up, he said:

"If only Mother could see me now!"

Alas! The clearing did not last long; the rain began to fall more heavily. Fortunately I had just surmounted the last steep rise and had reached a ledge. While securing Bernard I tried to study the ground ahead, but visibility was limited to a few yards. I sensed that we were at the level of the sloping shelf which must be followed to the left when one leaves the couloir. It was very tempting to continue straight up towards the north ridge, but in bad weather this couloir may become a trap. For a moment we hesitated before launching out along the shelf, which is very narrow. We thought of Cassin, held up by bad conditions and by his large party, but still determined not to abandon the face. At this moment the storm burst, and we were afraid of the waterfall coming down the gully. It was only five o'clock, and if we had gone on we would just have had the time to reach the summit that evening.

I traversed eighty feet along the shelf, which widened but was coated with snow. The storm became violent. Just as Bernard joined me there was a flash of lightning, very close. As there was no rock spike I drove in a piton and we pulled on our smocks. To continue was out of the question; there was nothing for it but to wait to see how it would turn out.

It turned out badly. From an inky sky heavy rain pelted down upon us. Between repeated thunderclaps lightning struck very close, blinding us with its dazzling, dread glare and hurting our eyes. We were drenched to the skin, cold to the marrow. Bernard looked at his watch: it was six o'clock. Another bivouac on the face!

Then began an interminable vigil. A respite of ten minutes would have allowed us to advance a little close to the summit. Yet it was not so much the top that we longed for, as to move a little instead of staying anchored to our piton; to *do* something rather than just wait. Our muscles already felt stiff and cold; the inaction was slowly destroying us. For we were climbers, built for climbing, not to remain stormbound for hours on end. We would gladly climb anything, a chimney, a crack, a slab. We would climb silently, simply climb, stretch out and stand upright. Bernard would feel the wet nylon rope slip between his fingers while I climbed. It need only be one rope-length in our accustomed way. It was not just a whim. It would do us so much good! I would say to Bernard: "I'm at the stance, come on," and he would take the two sacks without complaining of their weight, so thankful would he be to leave this shelf. . . .

But now this dream was no longer possible. It was 7:30 P.M. and there had been no break. Now night was upon us, and we were doomed to the shelf. All around us lightning flashed and a few hailstones fell. Bernard again consulted his watch: the flashes were coming every three minutes, and each time we were afraid. Against the wind which knocks you down and sends you gradually to sleep, against the cold which shrivels you and freezes your blood, against the stinging snow which sows death—against all these the mountaineer can struggle. But the lightning strikes, stiffens and kills at one blow. And each time it whitened the night for a second, we cowered fearful against the rock, mere shadows of life.

How I longed for the snow which falls after a storm, the snow which covers everything in the ensuing calm! I recalled the storm which caught René Mallieux and myself two years before, while we were doing rappels down the Aiguille du Roc.[8] It was six o'clock, at the end of September, and we had had to bivouac at the gap. All night it had snowed; we were soaked and frozen, for the light snow penetrated everywhere. Above all we had to be careful not to fall asleep. From time to time I would pull out my hand to sweep away the snow that was cloaking us. By the early morning a foot and a half of fresh snow covered everything. I withdrew my hand, slightly frost-bitten, into a pocket damp with melting snow, and hesitated to take it out again. But I said to myself: "I am the guide, and the guide *must* be invulnerable." With that thought I felt sure that my fingers would not be frost-bitten. But now, faced with lightning, I was miserable and powerless.

The cold held us more and more in its grip. For something to do we decided to make tea. We brought out the stove, set it up as well as we could between us, put the meta-fuel inside the windshield and the snow in the pan. But it was all quite useless, for no sooner had we struck a match than it was blown out by the wind. And when we were lucky enough to light the meta, it was the meta which immediately went out. After using all the matches we remained crouching stupidly over our useless stove, until, to pass the time, Bernard brought out the cigarettes. But as we had no more matches, our craving for a smoke also remained unsatisfied.

The flashes became less frequent. We had the impression that the storm was moving off towards the Bernina, casting a strange light on the lake of Silvaplana. We unbent our legs, stretched them out and let them hang over space. We had been crouching against this rock, motionless on this narrow shelf, for hours! Below us, in a single sweep, the slabs of the Badile swept away unbroken. . . . Bernard dropped a glove . . . a few more hailstones fell . . . we ate a little. . . . Far off the lightning flickered over St. Moritz.

As the storm moved off we made plans for the morrow. It was still raining and we shivered, but already we were looking ahead. If only the rock was not too wet, if only a ray of sunshine would touch it . . . for we had still to do a very exposed traverse, whose difficulty was stressed by Cassin in his technical note on the climb. There would be certain precautions to take so as to climb at all; we must wriggle our feet in our boots and rub our limbs. But our clothes, right down to our shirts, were saturated with rain, first warmed by contact with the skin but played on by the wind when we started moving and moulded into a sheet of ice.

Now that the thunder and lightning had moved off, we could hear the stone-falls crashing down the face of the Piz Cengalo (11,056 feet) opposite. But the fireworks of the night before were lacking; they had been a fine display against the blackness of the night. Instinctively we lowered our heads between hunched shoulders, curled our legs under us and tried to stop breathing. . . . Then the lightning returned; a flash lit up the rocks around, and I could see the rain dripping like milk on Bernard's rounded back and shining hood. I heard a faint noise, like paper being crumpled; then, immediately after, a deafening crash. The whole cirque of mountains around was shaken, the echo rolling from wall to wall.

We had had no more than a respite in the storm. In my misery I felt frightened. Lightning flashed and sizzled around us, the thunder roared. Bernard told me the time: it was just before midnight. The nightmare had been going on for six hours. No sooner did the restful darkness return, our tense, cramped bodies relax, and our fear for a moment release us, than another ball of fire would strike the rock.

Often before we had been shaken, buffeted, tested by storm; we had even been in danger of being dislodged from our holds, but there had always been an outlet in retreat: leaping from rock to rock, down the snow slopes, speeding downwards and losing height rapidly, moving fast and with precision. All this was stimulating. But this night we were not on the move. We must content ourselves with simply being there, anchored to the spot.

The night dragged endlessly.

In the early morning, when the storm ceased, we made the horizontal traverse of which Cassin writes in his note. Then two rappels landed us in the great central couloir. There a poorly defined arête, sheltered from stone-fall, led to the summit. It was midday when we arrived, to meet two climbers who had come up by the ordinary way on the south flank. After such a struggle we rejoiced in the presence of other humans. Everything tasted new: sun and rock, men, colours, tobacco, and an orange which they offered us. Our gaze ranged over the surrounding peaks. Once more the weather was fine and the mountains inviting. Then together we descended happily by the ordinary way to the Gianetti hut.

I had had the finest reward of all. I had indeed succeeded in doing the Badile as a guide; but above all, and the greatest prize of all in my job, my confidence in my companion was justified. The guide would not be so strong if he did not give something of himself. And Bernard, who had made his début two years before, had now won his spurs on the slabs of the Piz Badile.

—1954

Notes

1. Hidden peak, 26,470 feet, is near K2 in the Karakoram, and at the time of writing has not yet been climbed. Deudon was a member of the French expedition which attempted to climb it under H. de Ségogne in 1936.

2. A row of five small, very sharp rocky pinnacles (the highest 13,481 feet) on the flank of one of the buttresses of Mont Blanc. First traversed throughout by Armand Charlet and party in 1928.

3. A peak on the Brenva side of Mont Blanc, 10,742 feet. One of the lower peaks available from Courmayeur, first climbed in 1898. The hardest route on it is that made up the east face by G. Rébuffat, B. Pierre and J. Deudon, 1948.

4. Mountain of 8,285 feet near Chamonix.

5. Crags near Chamonix, used for practice climbs.

6. One of the Chamonix Aiguilles, 11,942 feet high.

7. The French use the word *duvet* for these jackets.

8. A very sharp pinnacle on the side of the Aiguille de Grépon (11,424 feet) above Chamonix.

Sir Edmund Hillary
from *High Adventure*

The highest point on the surface of the earth finally succumbed to a New Zealander named Edmund Hillary (1919–) and his Sherpa companion Tenzing Norgay on May 29, 1953, after several valiant attempts by British and Swiss teams. When Sandy Irvine and George Leigh Mallory, with oxygen apparatus, failed to return from their 1924 summit attempt, professional climbers wondered whether Everest was a mountain that would forever remain unconquered by humankind. Hillary's account reveals in detail how a mixture of good luck, stamina, and an incredible tolerance for pain propelled them to the top. The rush to the top became a national passion for the British before World War II, with serious attempts by England's best climbers in 1922, 1924, and 1933. In 1951, Eric Shipton led a reconnaissance mission accompanied by Hillary, Michael Ward, Eurle Riddiford, and Tom Bourdillon, and was criticized for turning back at the Western Cwm. Subsequently the British Himalayan Committee turned over the leadership of the next British expedition to a military officer, John Hunt. Hillary and Tenzing were clearly the fittest members of the group, and the quickest to adjust to the mind-numbing altitude. Hillary and Tenzing spent a night at 27,900 feet, loaded their oxygen gear the next morning, and headed for the summit. After scaling a tricky rock face now known as the Hillary Step, and cutting a series of ice steps, the two found themselves at the top of the world. Everest remains one of the most popular mountains for professional climbers. Hillary is regarded as a national hero in his native New Zealand.

SUMMIT

At 6:30 A.M. we crawled slowly out of the tent and stood on our little ledge. Already the upper part of the mountain was bathed in sunlight. It looked warm and inviting, but our ledge was dark and cold. We lifted our oxygen on to our backs and slowly connected up the tubes to our face-masks. My 30-lb. load seemed to crush me downwards and stifled all enthusiasm, but when I turned on the oxygen and breathed it deeply, the burden seemed to lighten and the old urge to get to grips with the mountain came back. We strapped on our crampons and tied on our nylon rope; grasped our ice-axes and were ready to go.

I looked at the way ahead. From our tent very steep slopes covered with deep powder snow led up to a prominent snow shoulder on the South-east ridge about a

Sir Edmund Hillary, *High Adventure* (London: Hodder and Stoughton, 1955), pp. 198–209 of *High Adventure* copyright © 1955 by Sir Edmund Hillary. Originally published by Hodder and Stoughton, London. Included by permission of Sir Edmund Hillary and Celebrity Speakers (NZ) Ltd.

hundred feet above our heads. The slopes were in the shade and breaking trail was going to be cold work. Still a little worried about my boots, I asked Tenzing to lead off. Always willing to do his share, and more than his share if necessary, Tenzing scrambled past me and tackled the slope. With powerful thrusts of his legs he forced his way up in knee-deep snow. I gathered in the rope and followed along behind him.

We were climbing out over the tremendous South face of the mountain, and below us snow chutes and rock ribs plummeted thousands of feet down to the Western Cwm. Starting in the morning straight on to exposed climbing is always trying for the nerves, and this was no exception. In imagination I could feel my heavy load dragging me backwards down the great slopes below; I seemed clumsy and unstable and my breath was hurried and uneven. But Tenzing was pursuing an irresistible course up the slope, and I didn't have time to think too much. My muscles soon warmed up to their work, my nerves relaxed, and I dropped into the old climbing rhythm and followed steadily up his tracks. As we gained a little height we moved into the rays of the sun, and although we could feel no appreciable warmth, we were greatly encouraged by its presence. Taking no rests, Tenzing ploughed his way up through the deep snow and led out on to the snow shoulder. We were now at a height of 28,000 feet. Towering directly above our heads was the South Summit—steep and formidable. And to the right were the enormous cornices of the summit ridge. We still had a long way to go.

Ahead of us the ridge was sharp and narrow, but rose at an easy angle. I felt warm and strong now, so took over the lead. First I investigated the ridge with my ice-axe. On the sharp crest of the ridge and on the right-hand side loose powder snow was lying dangerously over hard ice. Any attempt to climb on this would only produce an unpleasant slide down towards the Kangshung glacier. But the left-hand slope was better—it was still rather steep, but it had a firm surface of wind-blown powder snow into which our crampons would bite readily.

Taking every care, I moved along on to the left-hand side of the ridge. Everything seemed perfectly safe. With increased confidence, I took another step. Next moment I was almost thrown off balance as the wind-crust suddenly gave way and I sank through it up to my knee. It took me a little while to regain my breath. Then I gradually pulled my leg out of the hole. I was almost upright again when the wind-crust under the other foot gave way and I sank back with both legs enveloped in soft, loose snow to the knees. It was the mountaineer's curse—breakable crust. I forced my way along. Sometimes for a few careful steps I was on the surface, but usually the crust would break at the critical moment and I'd be up to my knees again. Though it was tiring and exasperating work, I felt I had plenty of strength in reserve. For half an hour I continued on in this uncomfortable fashion, with the violent balancing movements I was having to make completely destroying rhythm and breath. It was a great relief when the snow conditions improved and I was able to stay on the surface. I still kept down on the steep slopes on the left of the ridge, but plunged ahead and climbed steadily upwards. I came over a small crest and saw in front of me a tiny hollow on the ridge. And in this hollow lay two oxygen bottles almost completely covered with snow. It was Evans' and Bourdillon's dump.

I rushed forward into the hollow and knelt beside them. Wrenching one of the bottles out of its frozen bed I wiped the snow off its dial—it showed a thousand-pounds pressure—it was nearly a third full of oxygen. I checked the other—it was the same. This was great news. It meant that the oxygen we were carrying on our backs only had to get us back to these bottles instead of right down to the South Col. It gave us more than another hour of endurance. I explained this to Tenzing through my oxygen mask. I don't think he understood, but he realised I was pleased about something and nodded enthusiastically.

I led off again. I knew there was plenty of hard work ahead and Tenzing could save his energies for that. The ridge climbed on upwards rather more steeply now, and then broadened out and shot up at a sharp angle to the foot of the enormous slope running up to the South Summit. I crossed over on to the right-hand side of the ridge and found the snow was firm there. I started chipping a long line of steps up to the foot of the great slope. Here we stamped out a platform for ourselves and I checked our oxygen. Everything seemed to be going well. I had a little more oxygen left than Tenzing, which meant I was obtaining a slightly lower flow rate from my set, but it wasn't enough to matter and there was nothing I could do about it, anyway.

Ahead of us was a really formidable problem, and I stood in my steps and looked at it. Rising from our feet was an enormous slope slanting steeply down on to the precipitous East face of Everest and climbing up with appalling steepness to the South Summit of the mountain 400 feet above us. The left-hand side of the slope was a most unsavoury mixture of steep loose rock and snow, which my New Zealand training immediately regarded with grave suspicion, but which in actual fact the rock-climbing Britons, Evans and Bourdillon, had ascended in much trepidation when on the first assault. The only other route was up the snow itself and still faintly discernible here, and there were traces of the track made by the first assault party, who had come down it in preference to their line of ascent up the rocks. The snow route it was for us! There looked to be some tough work ahead, and as Tenzing had been taking it easy for a while I hard-heartedly waved him through. With his first six steps I realised that the work was going to be much harder than I had thought. His first two steps were on top of the snow, the third was up to his ankles and by the sixth he was up to his hips. But almost lying against the steep slope, he drove himself onwards, ploughing a track directly upwards. Even following in his steps was hard work, for the loose snow refused to pack into safe steps. After a long and valiant spell he was plainly in need of a rest, so I took over.

Immediately I realised that we were on dangerous ground. On this very steep slope the snow was soft and deep with little coherence. My ice-axe shaft sank into it without any support and we had no sort of a belay. The only factor that made it at all possible to progress was a thin crust of frozen snow which tied the whole slope together. But this crust was a poor support. I was forcing my way upwards, plunging deep steps

375

through it, when suddenly with a dull breaking noise an area of crust all around me about six feet in diameter broke off into large sections and slid with me back through three or four steps. And then I stopped; but the crust, gathering speed, slithered on out of sight. It was a nasty shock. My whole training told me that the slope was exceedingly dangerous, but at the same time I was saying to myself: "Ed, my boy, this is Everest— you've got to push it a bit harder!" My solar plexus was tight with fear as I ploughed on. Half-way up I stopped, exhausted. I could look down 10,000 feet between my legs, and I have never felt more insecure. Anxiously I waved Tenzing up to me.

"What do you think of it, Tenzing?" And the immediate response, "Very bad, very dangerous!" "Do you think we should go on?" and there came the familiar reply that never helped you much but never let you down: "Just as you wish!" I waved him on to take a turn at leading. Changing the lead much more frequently now, we made our unhappy way upwards, sometimes sliding back and wiping out half a dozen steps, and never feeling confident that at any moment the whole slope might not avalanche. In the hope of some sort of a belay we traversed a little towards the rocks, but found no help in their smooth, holdless surfaces. We plunged on upwards. And then I noticed that, a little above us, the left-hand rock ridge turned into snow and the snow looked firm and safe. Laboriously and carefully we climbed across some steep rock, and I sank my ice-axe shaft into the snow of the ridge. It went in firm and hard. The pleasure of this safe belay after all the uncertainty below was like a reprieve to a condemned man. Strength flowed into my limbs, and I could feel my tense nerves and muscles relaxing. I swung my ice-axe at the slope and started chipping a line of steps upwards—it was very steep, but seemed so gloriously safe. Tenzing, an inexpert but enthusiastic step cutter, took a turn and chopped a haphazard line of steps up another pitch. We were making fast time now and the slope was starting to ease off. Tenzing gallantly waved me through, and with a growing feeling of excitement I cramponed up some firm slopes to the rounded top of the South Summit. It was only 9 A.M.

With intense interest I looked at the vital ridge leading to the summit—the ridge about which Evans and Bourdillon had made such gloomy forecasts. At first glance it was an exceedingly impressive and indeed a frightening sight. In the narrow crest of this ridge, the basic rock of the mountain had a thin capping of snow and ice—ice that reached out over the East face in enormous cornices, overhanging and treacherous, and only waiting for the careless foot of the mountaineer to break off and crash 10,000 feet to the Kangshung glacier. And from the cornices the snow dropped steeply to the left to merge with the enormous rock bluffs which towered 8,000 feet above the Western Cwm. It was impressive all right! But as I looked my fears started to lift a little. Surely I could see a route there? For this snow slope on the left, although very steep and exposed, was practically continuous for the first half of the ridge, although in places the great cornices reached hungrily across. If we could make a route along that snow slope, we could go quite a distance at least.

With a feeling almost of relief, I set to work with my ice-axe and cut a platform for myself just down off the top of the South Summit. Tenzing did the same, and then

376

we removed our oxygen sets and sat down. The day was still remarkably fine, and we felt no discomfort through our thick layers of clothing from either wind or cold. We had a drink out of Tenzing's water-bottle and then I checked our oxygen supplies. Tenzing's bottle was practically exhausted, but mine still had a little in it. As well as this, we each had a full bottle. I decided that the difficulties ahead would demand as light a weight on our backs as possible so determined to use only the full bottles. I removed Tenzing's empty bottle and my nearly empty one and laid them in the snow. With particular care I connected up our last bottles and tested to see that they were working efficiently. The needles on the dials were steady on 3,300 lb. per square inch pressure—they were very full bottles holding just over 800 litres of oxygen each. At three litres a minute we consumed 180 litres an hour, and this meant a total endurance of nearly four and a half hours. This didn't seem much for the problems ahead, but I was determined if necessary to cut down to two litres a minute for the homeward trip.

I was greatly encouraged to find how, even at 28,700 feet and with no oxygen, I could work out slowly but clearly the problems of mental arithmetic that the oxygen supply demanded. A correct answer was imperative—any mistake could well mean a trip with no return. But we had no time to waste. I stood up and took a series of photographs in every direction, then thrust my camera back to its warm home inside my clothing. I heaved my now pleasantly light oxygen load on to my back and connected up my tubes. I did the same for Tenzing, and we were ready to go. I asked Tenzing to belay me and then, with a growing air of excitement, I cut a broad and safe line of steps down to the snow saddle below the South Summit. I wanted an easy route when we came back up here weak and tired. Tenzing came down the steps and joined me, and then belayed once again.

I moved along on to the steep snow slope on the left side of the ridge. With the first blow of my ice-axe my excitement increased. The snow—to my astonishment— was crystalline and hard. A couple of rhythmical blows of the ice-axe produced a step that was big enough even for our oversize high-altitude boots. But best of all the steps were strong and safe. A little conscious of the great drops beneath me, I chipped a line of steps for the full length of the rope—forty feet—and then forced the shaft of my ice-axe firmly into the snow. It made a fine belay and I looped the rope around it. I waved to Tenzing to join me, and as he moved slowly and carefully along the steps I took in the rope. When he reached me, he thrust his ice-axe into the snow and protected me with a good tight rope as I went on cutting steps. It was exhilarating work—the summit ridge of Everest, the crisp snow and the smooth easy blows of the ice-axe all combined to make me feel a greater sense of power than I had ever felt at great altitudes before. I went on cutting for rope length after rope length.

We were now approaching a point where one of the great cornices was encroaching on to our slope. We'd have to go down to the rocks to avoid it. I cut a line of steps steeply down the slope to a small ledge on top of the rocks. There wasn't much room, but it made a reasonably safe stance. I waved to Tenzing to join me. As he came down to me I realised there was something wrong with him. I had been so absorbed in the technical problems of the ridge that I hadn't thought much about Tenzing, except for a vague feeling that he seemed to move along the steps with unnecessary slowness. But now it was quite obvious that he was not only moving extremely slowly, but he was breathing quickly and with difficulty and was in considerable distress. I immediately suspected his oxygen set and helped him down on to the ledge so that I could examine it. The first thing I noticed was that from the outlet of his face-mask there were hanging some long icicles. I looked at it more closely and found that the outlet tube—about two inches in diameter—was almost completely blocked up with ice. This was preventing Tenzing from exhaling freely and must have made it extremely unpleasant for him. Fortunately the outlet tube was made of rubber and by manipulating this with my hand I was able to release all the ice and let it fall out. The valves started operating and Tenzing was given immediate relief. Just as a check I examined my own set and found that it, too, had partly frozen up in the outlet tube, but not sufficiently to have affected me a great deal. I removed the ice out of it without a great deal of trouble. Automatically I looked at our pressure gauges— just over 2,900 lb. (2,900 lb. was just over 700 litres; 180 into 700 was about 4)—we had nearly four hours' endurance left. That meant we weren't going badly.

I looked at the route ahead. This next piece wasn't going to be easy. Our rock ledge was perched right on top of the enormous bluff running down into the Western Cwm. In fact, almost under my feet, I could see the dirty patch on the floor of the Cwm which I knew was Camp IV. In a sudden urge to escape our isolation I waved and shouted, and then as suddenly stopped as I realised my foolishness. Against the vast expanse of Everest, 8,000 feet above them, we'd be quite invisible to the best binoculars. I turned back to the problem ahead. The rock was far too steep to attempt to drop down and go around this pitch. The only thing to do was to try to shuffle along the ledge and cut handholds in the bulging ice that was trying to push me off it. Held on a tight rope by Tenzing, I cut a few handholds and then thrust my ice-axe as hard as I could into the solid snow and ice. Using this to take my weight I moved quickly along the ledge. It proved easier than I had anticipated. A few more handholds, another quick swing across them, and I was able to cut a line of steps up on to a safe slope and chop out a roomy terrace from which to belay Tenzing as he climbed up to me.

We were now fast approaching the most formidable obstacle on the ridge— a great rock step. This step had always been visible in aerial photographs, and in 1951 on the Everest Reconnaissance we had seen it quite clearly with glasses from Thyangboche. We had always thought of it as the obstacle on the ridge which could well spell defeat. I cut a line of steps across the last snow slope, and then commenced traversing over a steep rock slab that led to the foot of the great step. The holds were small and hard to see, and I brushed my snow-glasses away from my eyes. Immediately I was blinded by a bitter wind sweeping across the ridge and laden with particles of ice. I hastily replaced my glasses and blinked away the ice and tears until I could see again. But it made me realise how efficient was our clothing in protecting us from the

378

rigours of even a fine day at 29,000 feet. Still half blinded, I climbed across the slab, and then dropped down into a tiny snow hollow at the foot of the step. And here Tenzing joined me.

I looked anxiously up at the rocks. Planted squarely across the ridge in a vertical bluff, they looked extremely difficult, and I knew that our strength and ability to climb steep rock at this altitude would be severely limited. I examined the route out to the left. By dropping fifty or a hundred feet over steep slabs, we might be able to get around the bottom of the bluff, but there was no indication that we'd be able to climb back on to the ridge again. And to lose any height now might be fatal. Search as I could, I was unable to see an easy route up to the step or, in fact, any route at all. Finally, in desperation I examined the right-hand end of the bluff. Attached to this and overhanging the precipitous East face was a large cornice. This cornice, in preparation for its inevitable crash down the mountainside, had started to lose its grip on the rock and a long narrow vertical crack had been formed between the rock and the ice. The crack was large enough to take the human frame, and though it offered little security, it was at least a route. I quickly made up my mind—Tenzing had an excellent belay and we must be near the top—it was worth a try.

Before attempting the pitch, I produced my camera once again. I had no confidence that I would be able to climb this crack, and with a surge of competitive pride which unfortunately afflicts even mountaineers, I determined to have proof that at least we had reached a good deal higher than the South Summit. I took a few photographs and then made another rapid check of the oxygen—2,550 lb. pressure. (2,550 from 3,300 leaves 750. 750 over 3,300 is about two-ninths. Two-ninths off 800 litres leaves about 600 litres. 600 divided by 180 is nearly 3½). Three and a half hours to go. I examined Tenzing's belay to make sure it was a good one and then slowly crawled inside the crack.

In front of me was the rock wall, vertical but with a few promising holds. Behind me was the ice-wall of the cornice, glittering and hard but cracked here and there. I took a hold on the rock in front and then jammed one of my crampons hard into the ice behind. Leaning back with my oxygen set on the ice, I slowly levered myself upwards. Searching feverishly with my spare boot, I found a tiny ledge on the rock and took some of the weight off my other leg. Leaning back on the cornice, I fought to regain my breath. Constantly at the back of my mind was the fear that the cornice might break off, and my nerves were taut with suspense. But slowly I forced my way up—wriggling and jamming and using every little hold. In one place I managed to force my ice-axe into a crack in the ice, and this gave me the necessary purchase to get over a holdless stretch. And then I found a solid foothold in a hollow in the ice, and next moment I was reaching over the top of the rock and pulling myself to safety. The rope came tight—its forty feet had been barely enough.

I lay on the little rock ledge panting furiously. Gradually it dawned on me that I was up the step, and I felt a glow of pride and determination that completely subdued my temporary feelings of weakness. For the first time on the whole expedition

379

I really knew I was going to get to the top. "It will have to be pretty tough to stop us now" was my thought. But I couldn't entirely ignore the feeling of astonishment and wonder that I'd been able to get up such a difficulty at 29,000 feet even with oxygen.

When I was breathing more evenly I stood up and, leaning over the edge, waved to Tenzing to come up. He moved into the crack and I gathered in the rope and took some of his weight. Then he, in turn, commenced to struggle and jam and force his way up until I was able to pull him to safety—gasping for breath. We rested for a moment. Above us the ridge continued on as before—enormous overhanging cornices on the right and steep snow slopes on the left running down to the rock bluffs. But the angle of the snow slopes was easing off. I went on chipping a line of steps, but thought it safe enough for us to move together in order to save time. The ridge rose up in a great series of snakelike undulations which bore away to the right, each one concealing the next. I had no idea where the top was. I'd cut a line of steps around the side of one undulation and another would come into view. We were getting desperately tired now and Tenzing was going very slowly. I'd been cutting steps for almost two hours, and my back and arms were starting to tire. I tried cramponing along the slope without cutting steps, but my feet slipped uncomfortably down the slope. I went on cutting. We seemed to have been going for a very long time and my confidence was fast evaporating. Bump followed bump with maddening regularity. A patch of shingle barred our way, and I climbed dully up it and started cutting steps around another bump. And then I realised that this was the last bump, for ahead of me the ridge dropped steeply away in a great corniced curve, and out in the distance I could see the pastel shades and fleecy clouds of the highlands of Tibet.

To my right a slender snow ridge climbed up to a snowy dome about forty feet above our heads. But all the way along the ridge the thought had haunted me that the summit might be the crest of a cornice. It was too late to take risks now. I asked Tenzing to belay me strongly, and I started cutting a cautious line of steps up the ridge. Peering from side to side and thrusting with my ice-axe, I tried to discover a possible cornice, but everything seemed solid and firm. I waved Tenzing up to me. A few more whacks of the ice-axe, a few very weary steps, and we were on the summit of Everest.

—1955

Charles Neider
from *Edge of the World*

Besides his Antarctic explorations, Charles Neider (1915–2002) was a noted photographer, well-published writer of novels, essays, anthologies, and scholarly works. He compiled a number of anthologies of firsthand accounts of adventures, exploration, and nature, including Man against Nature, Great Shipwrecks and Castaways, *and* Antarctica. *He was also a recognized Mark Twain scholar, and edited numerous editions and collections of Twain's works. In this selection, he describes the helicopter crash into Mount Erebus at the South Pole, a crash that he and his companions nearly did not survive due to lack of provisions and survival gear. Neider died at his home in Princeton, New Jersey, at age eighty-six while this volume was being prepared.*

At around 11,500 feet we saw Erebus's crest clearly. Light smoke, probably mixed with steam, was issuing from the crater. We were on the volcano's northwest side and close to the top of the clifflike second crater. Erebus has three craters, the third being the topmost. We saw many rock outcrops, for here the mountain was exposed to the warming effects of the summer sun, which, as we know, slowly dips as it rounds the sky counterclockwise, reaching its nadir at midnight, when it is above the Pole.

Palmer said calmly, "I'd like to clear it but we've got too much weight."

At about 12,000 feet he said, "It's as high as she'll go," yet he seemed to be pushing the craft to go still higher.

Erebus's crest felt very close to us. At moments we seemed to be heading directly for it. During my current visit to Antarctica I had several times imagined Erebus to be Ross Island's godhead, and its crest to be the mountain's face, remote from mortals, a legendary place where great prophecies were pronounced. This despite my knowledge of the meaning of the name. In Greek mythology Erebus is a son of Chaos and also the dark nether place through which souls pass on their way to Hades. At times I had thought of the mountain as a symbol of Antarctica, a continent both extraordinarily beautiful and dangerous. I had seen the mountain from many sides, always at normal distances. What I was now experiencing were abnormally intimate views of the northwestern side of that face.

From Charles Neider, *Edge of the World: Ross Island, Antarctica* (Garden City, NY: Doubleday and Co., 1974; Cooper Square Press, 2001). Text from pages 360–399 of *Edge of the World*, copyright © 1974 by Charles Neider. Included by permission of the Estate of Charles Neider.

I made out Beaufort Island on our left and some open sea to our right. It occurred to me I should ask Palmer to abandon this madness and take me immediately to Cape Bird as scheduled. But I was not about to cry chicken.

"If he wants to keep climbing that's his business," I thought.

What an idea: as if my life were not my business.

The craft was straining; it seemed to be trembling. My altimeter registered more than 12,500 feet. The reader will recall that the elevation of Mount Erebus as indicated on current official maps is 12,450 feet and he will no doubt wonder if, since we were higher than this, we could see into the crater itself. I should like to remind him that the figure of 12,450 feet represents elevation based on triangulation at sea level, and that my readings were in barometric terms, that Mount Erebus is in a low-pressure area, and that in such terms its elevation is approximately 13,300 feet. I saw some open sea, a lot of pack ice, and the watery horizon in the north, where there was still a good deal of lovely blue sky. Cape Bird was under thick cover.

We were approaching the crest from the northwest now. It rose to a mildly sloping peak, at the top of which was some dark stuff with the hue and texture of an ash heap. I was shooting through the windshield and through a strange apparition: a distorted reflection of a helmet surrounding a mongoloid face. At the crest, in addition to the ash heaps—the central one was the largest and darkest—were some snow and some precipitous rocky areas; the gullies of the latter were snow-filled. There was a moment when we seemed to be almost on a level with the top of the mountain. I was shooting out of my hatch now. We were spiraling very slowly clockwise. Beyond the heaps was the smoking crater itself.

I was both willing and ready to take advantage of the situation if we cleared Erebus, yet I kept silent, whether because I had something to gain by Palmer's overflying the crater or because I was determined not to cry chicken I shall probably never know. Technically the pilot is solely responsible for his craft, and nothing I said or failed to say could mitigate this fact. But I *might* have succeeded in persuading him to descend if I had tried. Possibly he had gone too far out on a limb and needed me to save his face. Perhaps if I had felt less distance between us in our wardroom meetings I would have been kinder and have given him, presuming he needed and wanted it, the overt excuse to lose altitude voluntarily.

I am not unaware of the fact he may have taken a great risk in a desire to do me a service, as he had already done me one by inviting me to sit in the cockpit with him, and that I was responding meanly. Or, knowing that I was gathering material for a book about Ross Island, he may have tried to impress me in the hope of playing a role in it. On the other hand, inasmuch as I would have been much safer in the cabin than in the cockpit during a crash, and inasmuch as he was inviting a crash by his rashness, he may have done me a disservice by inviting me to share the cockpit. These are subtle and painful matters and have puzzled and troubled me ever since.

Suddenly we seemed to hang still. Then we descended quickly, not flying but falling. Yet it was not a vertical fall but a forward one, as if we were trying to land too rapidly.

Palmer cried in a brittle, bitter tone, "We've got a downdraft! We're going down!"

For an instant I thought he meant we had merely failed to clear Erebus. Then I realized that our single, turbine-powered engine had air-starved in the too-thin air. This was bad enough. In addition we were being shoved down by a powerful downdraft.

And so Palmer had made the mistake of flying around to the opposite side of the updraft. The updraft, on the southeast side of Erebus, was due to the prevailing southeasterly, that bitter, life-endangering wind that swept down from the polar plateau and across the Ross Ice Shelf. The downdraft was on the northwest side. Until this moment, and during the other helo flights I had been fortunate enough to experience in a cockpit, I had enjoyed the feeling of having nothing between me and the outside world but a thin Plexiglas shell. Now I felt I was in a free fall, with not even the shell to protect me, and that on impact the back of the craft would slam against me.

The wild, desolate, rocky landscape rose up to greet us. Strangely, I thought for a moment that Palmer was possibly trying to land somewhere—anywhere—in order to have a look around or to think things through. I hoped he retained enough control of the craft to be autorotating but I could not really believe he had sufficient altitude for an autorotation or that an autorotation was possible in such a downdraft.

A white mass of snow came at us, magnifying with great speed and intensity. There were gray and black boulders and rock aprons and shoulders everywhere. There was insufficient time to experience fear, yet there was time for fascination, for observation and above all for acute experience.

Palmer, shouting "Mayday! Mayday! Mayday! Any station! Any station!" desperately flipped toggle switches.

The snow and ice masses rose up and slammed us. We bumped, buckled, spun around, skidded. I wondered if I was about to be killed. Suddenly we were motionless. There was a terrific silence. I unfastened my harness, removed my helmet, realized I was in one piece and that my cameras, which hung from my neck, hadn't been damaged. The engine had quit. The rotors were still. We weren't on fire.

Palmer, having unharnessed himself, jumped up, his face contorted, and shouted, "Fuck! Fuck!" in disgust and exasperation, flipping some overhead switches.

"Take it easy, Stu," I said.

I went outside for a look around. The crest looked unbelievably close, and bad weather was moving in from the west and north. It was obvious the latter would soon engulf us. We had dropped down onto a colorless world: nothing but blacks, grays and whites. The blue of the sky was so rapidly being transfigured into a milky gray it hardly counted as a color; in any event it would not be a color for long. The only colors were those we had brought with us: for example, the brilliant red of my USARP

383

parka. The helo's tail pointed in the direction of the crest. The cockpit faced rock aprons, huge black and gray boulders and two large ice fumaroles just beyond the boulders. In the crest's direction was a series of parallel-like and horizontal rock ridges, rising one above the other, interspersed with boulders and patches of snow and ice. The smoke issuing from the crater beyond the ash heaps was blowing away from us. On the craft's starboard side were more rock aprons and boulders. On its port side was a long stretch of naked and fairly level rock; but there too were many boulders the helo had miraculously missed. We had come down on the upper portion of the plateau of the second crater, whose great cliff was not too distant in the direction of the ice fumaroles. I wondered how it would have felt if we had gone spilling down that cliffside.

It struck me as being about the worst place for a ditching imaginable: difficult for single-engine helos, the only kind available in Operation Deep Freeze then, to ascend to for a rescue; almost impossible for them to start an engine at if it conked out; death to walk down from past the rock and ice cliffs and ice slopes and ice falls and crevasses I knew about from extensive reading, from studies of high-altitude photographs and from having observed some of them at firsthand from helicopters. Doubting that my companions suspected what a man-killer Erebus could be, I resolved to keep such knowledge to myself as long as possible.

An examination of the craft revealed that the landing gear had been badly damaged. We had hit the deck on the port side. The port tire had blown. The port wheel had been slammed out of position on its axle. The struts connecting the port pontoon with the fuselage had been telescoped and their covering shredded. The pontoon was almost vertical instead of horizontal. The small tail wheel had been partially rammed into the fuselage. The starboard wheel had been bent out of shape. Its tire was almost flat. But the pontoon looked all right. The helo was resting on its hull and tipping strongly to port. One of the rotor blades was almost only head-high.

We were now all outside and greatly relieved to be uninjured. It seemed a miracle that we had found a bit of level, snow-covered ground among all the rocks and boulders. Also miraculous was the fact we hadn't come down in straightforward, tricycle fashion. If we had, we would have had sufficient momentum to pile up on the boulders and burst into flames. Coming down on one side had caused us to swivel around and skid sideways; this had given us sufficient traction to brake us short of disaster. And fortunately the snow had been soft and deep enough to act as a shock absorber. If we had hit down on ice or flat rock we would have pancaked.

Studying the damage, once again Palmer cried "Fuck!" in despair, his face showing anguish. It was inevitable that such behavior, coming from the leader of our group, would be infectious. The crewman's face trembled, he worked to control his emotions, he said "Fuck" in a low voice, bit his nether lip and swung his head from side to side. But Enderby looked stolid although pale. I learned from him later, at McMurdo, that he had thought Palmer had landed deliberately.

Palmer said as if to himself but very clearly, "I'm going to be shipped out."

He remarked several times how lucky we were one of the rotor blades hadn't hit the snow; if it had, we would have been flipped over. He entered the cockpit and tried to start the engine. The crewman stood by outside with a fire extinguisher. We had plenty of battery power but the engine could not grab hold. I had heard a story about a Coast Guard helo going too high somewhere on Erebus, landing, shutting down its engine and being unable to start it without the help of other helos, special batteries and special equipment. And that hadn't been near as high a we now were. Palmer called out to the crewman that he had a red warning light indicating fire.

"Look for a fire!" he shouted.

The crewman replied he didn't see any sign of a fire but that smoke was pouring out of the exhaust. The smell of fire in the cabin was too strong to be ignored. I asked Enderby to remove my survival tent and gear from the craft and to set the tent up as best and as quickly as he could at sufficient distance from the helo to protect it if the helo burned. Whether the craft burned or not, we would need the tent if the temperature kept dropping. I told him not to bother staking the tent down thoroughly.

"Just secure it against a possible gust of wind. Then give me a hand with the food."

I started lugging cartons out of the craft. The effects of the altitude, which became apparent the moment one moved about or worked, were unpleasant now: breathlessness, a pounding of the heart, dizziness, quick fatigue, the possibility of blacking out. But they were mild for me as compared for my companions. I was surprised when, quite early, the crewman complained of a vicious headache. Then Enderby and Palmer said they had very bad headaches too. I explained my lack of a headache to myself as being the result of all the swimming I had done and the oxygen hunger I had deliberately endured.

After a while the smoke stopped and the smell of fire disappeared. We were still warm from the craft's heating system. Things could be worse. They could also be somewhat better: for example if the HF (high frequency) radio was functioning. But the HF radio required a lot of juice, and we had lost the radio with the engine's failure. You lose your single engine and go down, and to help along your morale you also lose your HF radio.

Palmer fetched a line-of-sight hand radio and walked around the craft, saying, "Mayday! Mayday! McMurdo! McMurdo! Any station! Any station! This is copter one four zero four down on the northern slope of Mount Erebus!"

He handed me the radio—it was small, with a flexible, tubelike antenna—and asked me to keep calling. So I walked around outside and pressed the transmission button and said over and over, "McMurdo Station, McMurdo Station! Mayday, Mayday, Mayday! McMurdo Station, this is helo one four zero four down on the northern slope of Mount Erebus!"

But I felt very dubious about the effort, for the gadget was a line-of-sight thing, and Erebus was between us and McMurdo.

Again Palmer tried to start the engine and again he received a fire signal. Coming outside, he told me he believed the engine was all right but that the air was too thin to permit the engine to take hold.

He said, "We'll have to walk to a ridge overlooking McMurdo and use the hand radio from there. Chuck, you know Ross Island best. Can we walk to the top?"

I said it would be foolhardy to try it. Visibility was poor and getting worse. We were going to be socked in very shortly. The temperature was rapidly dropping. We might have to contend with bad ice slopes, even crevasses. And we had no crampons, no rope and only one ice ax. Furthermore, we had the altitude effects to contend with.

Palmer walked around examining the craft, uttered a few more "Fucks," then turned to me and said, "Chuck, I'm sorry to have gotten you into this place."

"Forget it, Stu, it's okay."

"We'll *have* to get to a ridge," he said. "If not up there, then a lower one, maybe lower than here. Van and I will look for a ridge."

I advised him to stay on outcrop whenever possible and to probe with the ice ax when he was on snow.

He said, "Hell, let's walk down the mountain and get away from this altitude."

I said, "You wouldn't get three hundred yards before you'd be dead. There are snowbridged crevasses. You could fall through and go down thirty or forty feet. Even if you survived the fall and we had rope and gear and know-how to rescue you with, there'd be little time. Down there, below the surface, you'd be at mean temperature, probably fifty or sixty below. And there are icefalls and ice slopes. We have no belaying equipment, only one ice ax, and no knowledge of the fastest way down. The best way down I know about is at Royds, but we're too far north of that. And how would we see in that mass of clouds? We wouldn't stand a chance."

He looked startled.

"We're trapped," I said. "We'd better stay close to the craft. It's our best chance of being found."

I wanted to say more. I wanted to ask, "Why don't you drain the helo's fuel and lubricant while they're still warm, so we can use them for heat and for smudge pots?"

For it was standard polar survival procedure to drain fuel and lubricant immediately after a crash.

But I could sense that he still hadn't accepted the fact the craft was here to stay, that he was hoping the engine would somehow fire, catch hold and extricate us from our most unusual predicament; and clearly I was eager to share his hopes even though I wondered vaguely if the engine system had been damaged in the crash, for otherwise I would have said what was on my mind; or wouldn't I?

Much was uncertain. Had McMurdo heard our HF mayday signal? But even if it had, it knew neither our identity nor our location. Was the hand radio working?

And so Palmer and Enderby headed southwestward, Enderby probing the way and Palmer looking unearthly in his huge helmet. If they remained as much as possible on the plateau on which we found ourselves, which contained a substantial amount of outcrop, and if they used the ice ax responsibly they would be reasonably safe. Soon they disappeared below a nearby ridge, leaving me alone with the crewman.

XXV
THE HELICOPTER

I walked to an outcrop to study the crash scene from a distance and to view the helo, this poor kitelike box that through mismanagement had fallen out of the sky; this outpost of civilization in a bleak and savage wilderness; this comfortable "home"; but a home which, because it was a metal fuselage, was a heat sink, beautifully capable of dissipating our body heat into space; therefore a home that could destroy us if we depended overmuch on it; this representative of high technology, costing half a million dollars, but a technology, as for example in the case of the HF radio, that had failed us; or that we had significantly failed.

The cloud cover that had been steadily moving in on us had by now engulfed us like a thick fog. Who would have dreamed it had the audacity to climb so high? At times one had to resist the notion it was malevolent. For weeks Erebus had been clear. Now, in the increasing warmth of the austral summer, more and more seawater was free of its frozen state and creating massive fogs and clouds. The cover made the largest, blackest boulders appear to be faint gray shadows in a vast milky stuff. Visibility was seventy-five to a hundred feet. Beyond that range, in every direction, including overhead, was a potentially murderous white wall. What a thing to happen at a time when we had strayed grossly from our flight plan! We might as well be underground for all the good it would do to set off flares and smoke bombs.

The crewman, wearing a white spherical helmet, a khaki flight suit, light khaki flight gloves and beat-up desert boots, was standing uncertainly in front of the open hatch. He was a gracefully tall man with a pleasant, easy-smiling, longish face. Little brown hairs sprouted from his bony chin in what, hopefully, was the beginning of a beard. I had paid little attention to him. One saw helo crewmen but looked through them. What did we have in common? Usually very little. But this present crewman and I had a good deal, despite the fact that we had been born greatly apart, he in Illinois in 1950, I in Russia in 1915. We might well die together; or, if not together, in tandem. And I believe we also felt the uncommon bond of representing life in a mostly inorganic world. I thought "mostly"; in the faith there must be little outposts, faint stains, of life here, even though none were presently visible.

Realizing that I didn't know his name, I walked over and asked what it was. It felt odd to be making such a request inasmuch as we had crashed and worked together and he had been addressing me as Doc. But I had been uncertain as to whether we would lift off and remain strangers to each other. Now I knew we were not going to take off—not in one four zero four, which had found its last resting place. We were going to get to know each other before we were out of this.

"Jack Eights," he replied.

387

I gave him my name but he called me Doc throughout the episode although Palmer and Enderby called me Chuck. He looked unhappy. I suspected he felt very lonely. I knew I did, yet I had relished the feeling of loneliness, or rather of being alone, in Taylor Valley and at Capes Evans and Royds. Four had been diminished to two; temporarily it was only he and I against raw nature here in the form of Erebus: Erebus the white, the beautiful; an angel capable of vomiting up molten lava, of destroying life with either heat or cold.

I asked him to help me secure the tent. We were lucky the wind was mild, but would it continue to be? Our lives might depend on the tent. He worked at the ropes and poles while I hammered at the rock pegs with a fire extinguisher. We had thin cylindrical metal pegs, meant for Cape Bird, instead of square wooden ones. In snow and ice and in a steady, grinding wind the metal pegs, providing less friction, would work loose more readily. The sound of metal on metal ricocheted around us. The temperature was dropping steadily.

Occasionally Eights looked on the verge of panic. Once he said harshly to himself, "Fuck! What am I doing here?"

He was, as we know, only twenty. When I saw him like this something paternal stirred inside me.

"We'll be all right," I said.

Glancing up, he asked hopefully, "Think so, Doc?"

"Yes. I wouldn't miss this for anything."

He smiled. He seemed more relaxed after that. Possibly I represented for him the responsibility and reliability of middle age. And perhaps he had already begun to doubt Palmer's ability to bring him intact out of the situation and had begun to look to me to do it. Maybe he was impressed by my relative calmness, which resulted, I believe, from my being acquainted with the facts of life in Antarctica. Also, I was fascinated by everything and was trying to observe and remember acutely. What must have seemed a naked disaster to him seemed to me at times, in addition, a remarkable opportunity.

There was more work to be done, but his head was splitting, and I was breathing very heavily and rapidly. We rested awhile, watching the weather. He drew out his sheath knife, saying, "Doc, I've always wanted to stick this into a helo and now I can."

I laughed. But, not wanting to witness the sticking, I turned away and walked to a distant outcrop to take a few shots of the boulders showing in the cover. It occurred to me that if he was temporarily mad enough to tilt with a dead helo he might also be sufficiently unhinged to stick a knife into a man. I went back to him. He said his feet were numb. His boots could be called boots only by extravagant courtesy. I suggested he stand on rock because rock, being dark, had absorbed the sun's heat better than snow and ice, which had reflected it back. We made our way across hard, squeaky snow to an outcrop near the ice fumaroles, going on the path we had probed earlier with the ice ax. His feet felt better on the rock.

If our luck had been bad before, it became rotten now: the cover got so thick it approached the dreaded whiteout condition. In response, the outcrop grew bitterly

388

cold. Soon it made little difference to our feet whether we stood on rock or snow. We glanced skyward longingly, hoping the cover would break up and permit the sun to give us back our body heat. I judged our present temperature to be about five below.

Eights entered the cockpit and said through the open starboard hatch he thought the engine would start if we had some sunlight to warm it and a head wind to blow air into the turbine intake. There was still plenty of battery power. The engine made lots of noise, spewed smoke out of the exhaust and emitted a strong smell of fire. A red warning light flashed on the instrument panel.

Emerging from the craft, Eights murmured, "Christ, Christ, we're fucked," his lean face showing despair.

He asked me to spray a long fire extinguisher's contents into the turbine intake as he again tried to start the engine. The carbon dioxide in the extinguisher was depleted; only air was coming out; hopefully the latter would help the engine to grab hold. I climbed onto the fuselage and did what he requested. The effort was useless. Without a thicker air mixture the engine was dead.

I wandered off in the direction Palmer and Enderby had taken, going farther from the helo than before, intending to shoot the scene so I would be able to convince myself, in the event we were rescued, that the weather had been as bad as it now looked. I saw narrow, long, green crevasses. Although it seemed unlikely, judging by the terrain, that I would encounter wider ones, I could not be sure, so I made my way with some caution. The mostly white craft would not easily be visible from the air. The bottom of the hull was white, as were the cabin and the engine housing. A red stripe ran down the back of the cabin. The front exterior of the cockpit as well as the tail were red. The rotors were black, with orange tips. Up on the turbine housing were the numerals 1404.

I had stopped at a large deep cleft in some rock. Glancing into the cleft, I saw a patch of pink lichen: the non-human life I had hoped was here with us.

"Doc?" Eights called anxiously.

I headed toward him to see what he wanted. He left the helo to meet me.

"We'd better not get separated," he said, handing me a khaki plastic whistle with a braided black cord.

I didn't blame him for not wanting to be left alone in a place where everything was so unfamiliar and threatening. He had recently arrived on the ice for the first time. He had been living on the warm, crowded *Staten Island*. He had visited warm, crowded McMurdo. And now he was near the top of Mount Erebus, with his life's supply of heat steadily diminishing.

He was such a nice-looking boy, and possibly he had been thinking of his parents, or of a girlfriend, or of places in Illinois he especially liked, or of some chore he had meant to do on the icebreaker, or was wondering by what sour luck he had been chosen for this flight, *my* flight, designed solely to deliver me to Cape Bird, and probably he realized I might have decided, had I felt less pressed for time, to scratch it, considering the state of the cover. Was the cover as thick along the coastal route as it was up here? It struck me, from the little I knew of such things, as being capable of lasting many days. If it stayed a long time would we handle ourselves badly or well? I was still ignorant of facts I would soon acquire. I believed then that we possessed the means to fight the cover and the mountain with a sporting chance of coming through, even if we had to hold out for weeks. I wonder now how much of my reaction to Eights was quiet for my having had a share, such as it was, in causing his predicament.

It seemed to me that Palmer and Enderby had been gone too long. We had crashed at approximately 2:30. It was now past a quarter to four. Where were they? Would they find their way back in this white stuff? What if one or both had fallen into a crevasse? What if they were lost—they were without shelter or food. And they were lightly clad. Palmer, as we know, had on only his helmet, his flight suit, his flight gloves, flight boots. And Enderby had on a USARP parka, whose hood he had pulled over his head—I didn't know what kind of shirt he was wearing under it, but I assumed it was the standard heavy woolen one—blue jeans, hiking boots and black gloves. I knew how cold they must feel: I myself was lightly clad for this temperature. I wore thermals, a black cap, a wool shirt, threadbare tan cotton corduroy trousers, a USARP parka, black double gloves and my own hiking boots, and I had begun to experience fits of shivering, as had Eights. The cold that was penetrating our bodies was sending alarm signals to our brains, crying as if in panic, "Beware! Beware! Parts of you are in danger of freezing!" Adrenalin flowed accordingly, whether you wished it to or not. If Palmer and Enderby died it would be a poor beginning to a tragedy that might have the added horror of being long drawn out, with Eights and me following them but more slowly because we had the tent, food and the helo. We ought to have decided how long they would be away. How stupid it had been of us not to have formed a plan. We had had no right to improvise so casually.

Warning Eights I intended to use the whistle, I walked a fair distance in the direction in which I had last seen them and blew a long blast, hoping I would hear a cry in return. I heard nothing human. It was not easy to blow hard at this altitude. You got dizzy; you wondered for a moment if you were going to black out. Between blasts you listened to the eerie Antarctic silence, interrupted now only by the hum of the wind as it caressed jagged volcanic boulders and your ears. I blew half a dozen times at intervals of about five minutes, becoming increasingly alarmed, for I knew that our best chance for survival was to stick together, to remain near the helicopter and to keep up our morale.

I returned to the craft, where Eights had broken out smoke bombs, flares and a Very pistol with shells. I asked him to fire the pistol at the cover overhead. The flare rocketed up, burst, divided into two brilliant red mushrooms and fell, dying. It came nowhere near reaching the cover. Taking inventory of our signaling devices, we resolved not to use them unless the cover lifted and we heard a plane.

Not long afterwards Enderby and Palmer appeared slowly out of the mists southwest of us, looking very tired, Enderby still carrying the ice ax. I was relieved to see them. We were all together again; we hadn't done anything irreversibly stupid. Palmer

390

was shivering; he was obviously unwell for some reason. He said the hand radio was useless; its battery was too cold. Enderby's face was red and drawn. He reported that his feet had gotten wet and were very numb. By questioning Enderby, who gave me the impression of being more stolid than stoical, I learned that they hadn't heard the whistle— what had muffled it? ridges? the cover? the thin air?—and that they had had no trouble following their tracks on their way back. They had not found the ridge they had been seeking, one overlooking McMurdo. They had reached several ridges but each had given way to another. Feeling the cold badly, with the altitude fatiguing them, and having trouble with altitude headaches, they had decided to go no further. What Enderby and Palmer did not reveal then for some reason (I learned it from Enderby back in McMurdo after our rescue) was that Palmer had taken two spills, slamming down on his back so suddenly and hard as to cause Enderby to be seriously alarmed.

Palmer was silent now and his glances tended to be averted. Was it because he suspected he had already said too much by declaring, "I'm going to be shipped out?" Why had he taken Enderby instead of Eights on his search for a ridge? Because he wanted to avoid the sense he had abandoned the passengers. Probably he was still stunned by the falls. I wish now I had known about them. Such knowledge might have lessened my resentment of him. I caught myself thinking, "Going over Erebus is a game in which there can be no sympathy for failure."

Yet there were crucial questions, such as whether he had autorotated—I doubted he had—that I failed to put to him in order to spare him possible embarrassment. His mental state was important to our safety; he was still our leader, who would pull us through. I failed utterly at this time to grasp our true condition, for example to take stock of our survival gear. Much later, on reviewing the episode, I was astonished it had taken me so long to grasp the real situation.

A strong north wind came up and whipped the tent flaps, strings and openings. Enderby pounded at the tent stakes and checked the poles and ropes. I thought, "Prepare yourself for a long stay and prepare the others." We gathered in the tilted helo cabin, which still felt warmer than the outside, and shut the hatch. I told Palmer what I had already explained to Eights about the metal fuselage being a heat sink. He was skeptical. He said the cabin was a good place to remain in; it was more roomy and more comfortable than the tent. I said that the tent, being much smaller than the cabin, was easier to warm with our bodies. He remained dubious even when our feet began to freeze from contact with the floor.

It slowly became clear to me that there was a failure of leadership on his part. He seemed unwilling or unable to take command, and was understandably reluctant to hand it over to me. However, it became increasingly unnecessary for him to relinquish it formally. As he turned more and more inward the two young men looked to me for suggestions and orders and I found myself having with painful embarrassment to take over his role out of necessity.

He asked me—I was closest to the cockpit—to see what the windshield thermometer read. I reported it was at –25°C, or about –15°F. The two scales begin to merge at low temperatures. At forty below there is no difference between them. They diverge again below that figure. The wind had a permanent feel to it.

And now, quite suddenly, certain unpleasant facts came to light. Enderby stood up, looked at me with a pale face full of embarrassment, and said in a small voice, "Chuck, I forgot to bring my survival gear."

It struck me as especially ironic that he, who worked in the Field Center, which was supposed to know something of the hazards of Antarctica, should be guilty of this lapse. Perhaps he had thought, "It's only a turnaround flight. We're in the middle of a heat wave. Why bother to drag my survival bag along?" but probably he hadn't. The history of Antarctica was dotted by people who had taken the continent for granted, sometimes to their sorrow. Now his sorrow was mine also, for I would have to share my survival gear with him. Of course, he had not known the weather was foul on the McMurdo-Bird route. Still, that route was as long a flight as you could make on Ross Island, and he ought to have taken survival gear along on even a short flight: it was the rule, designed to save limbs and possibly lives.

Then Eights told me that the helicopter's four survival packs, each weighing about fifty pounds, were not on board. They had been removed for the shuttle flights between McMurdo and Willy Field and, through some confusion, had not been replaced. Furthermore, he said, he had brought no personal survival gear and nor had Palmer. Palmer, staring at the floor, remained remote and silent.

The harsh facts of our situation were now beginning to take full hold of me. My companions had trilled with Antarctica. They had been lulled by the heat wave at McMurdo; by the comforts provided by the nuclear plant; by the security suggested by all the aircraft and heavy equipment and men. I was by far the oldest of the group, with the least chance of coming through, despite my good physical condition. When I considered that my ability to survive would be greatly lessened by my having to spread my gear thin to help my companions a bitterness rose temporarily to my palate. My careful habits had proved insufficient to my safety. The lesson was simple: it was not enough to provide for yourself unless you were traveling alone.

An intuition caused me to ask Enderby suddenly, "Did you pack matches in my gear?"

Enderby paled, looked stunned.

"No. I forgot."

I turned to Eights.

"Are there matches on board?"

"No, sir."

"Anybody got any matches?" I asked.

There was no reply.

We were losing moisture with some rapidity. When one of us spoke, clouds of steam escaped him. The continent was notoriously dry; its air was like a sponge. But now we had the added complication of the special dryness of high altitude. It seemed obvious to me—a thought that I expressed to my companions—that our lives would first be threatened by severe dehydration, which would cause certain organs to collapse, and that somehow we would have to make a fire and heat snow to make water. The snow outside was already too cold to put in one's mouth safely, and the temperature was steadily falling.

By now the engine's lubricant had no doubt congealed and could not be drained; it should have been drained within a half to three quarters of an hour after the crash. With the lubricant and using wicks we could have made flares as well as smudge pots. But the helo's fuel was still fluid at this temperature. We could drain it, using a section of the canopy or some other articles as the container. We could improvise a stove out of a large can or whatever else was handy and, using bits of gravel or small rocks as a base, pour fuel on them and burn the fuel for heat, for making water, for thawing food and for cooking. The helo's fuel, if carefully conserved, could last us quite awhile. But it was useless without matches. If the sun were out and we had a magnifying glass—perhaps one of my camera lenses could be used as one—we might make a fire, for the sun was strong in this dry air, especially at our altitude, despite the fact that it hung low over the horizon. However, given our cloud cover, I did not think we had a right to be optimistic about its reappearing soon. I wondered if the helo's battery could be used to make sparks and then a fire, and wondered also how long the battery would hold up at this low temperature. Possibly it was already dead.

Eights's feet were the first to go. I pulled my mukluks out of my orange seabag—they were rated to forty below, I had been told in Christchurch—and gave them to him. He had no headgear aside from his helmet, and only his flight suite and flight gloves. I gave him my khaki woolen balaclava and a pair of heavy gray mittens. To Enderby I handed fresh woolen socks to replace his wet ones. Palmer had no headgear other than his helmet. I had no headgear to give him. I handed him a double pair of gloves to be used in addition to his thin flight gloves. Luckily he was wearing sturdy leather boots, as was Enderby. My own boots were inadequate: the soles had been ripped by my climbing around the volcanic terrain of Royds and Evans. My feet felt frozen, especially the left one, which had been run over by a car and which, ever since, had been the weak one. My legs were turning numb. After considering the matter a moment I asked if it was all right if I put on my windpants, explaining that I was losing sensation in my legs.

"Hell yes!" Palmer said loudly out of his silence.

I said, "This gear belongs to all of us."

Then—I hated myself for doing it, for I had only one pair of windpants—I pulled them out of the survival bag, removed my boots, laboriously donned the black pants, then put the boots on again, my head spinning with the effort of bending over, my hands thick, clumsy, my thoughts murky. I felt guilty, nasty for wearing the windpants when no one else had windpants. On the other hand, only Eights had mukluks and he was delighted to have them and to know he was not going to risk the loss of his feet. Then I thought that, after all, the pants were mine and that I was the oldest of the group and presumably the least able to take the thing that might be coming: a tremendous test of our ability to cling to life. A second thought came forcefully: at what price was it worth hanging on? At the cost of one's honor? Then I thought that if we had all brought our survival gear and the helo's four survival packs we wouldn't be in a very bad way unless a long-lasting blizzard blew up. We could set up a couple of tents and be comfortable in our sleeping bags. We could rest and sleep the time away until we were found, even if it took a couple of weeks.

Well, we were in for it and it would take a few miracles to get us out. I was convinced we must soon move into the tent. I could say simply, "I'm moving into the tent" and let whoever wanted to follow me follow. But that would humiliate Palmer and lower his morale still further. If it continued to decline, his will to survive would fall with it; with a weak will his chances of survival would greatly lesson and he might do something to decrease them further: for example, he might take a serious fall. If one of us suffered badly the others would have to minister to him. In the process we would lose our own narrow margin of safety and we might all go down into irreversible damage or death. So I refrained from saying, "I'm moving into the tent" not out of altruism but out of self-interest. For the clear fact was that our lives depended on each other.

XXVI
THE TENT

It was now about 4:45, two and a quarter hours after the crash. Our mayday signals had obviously not gotten through, for if they had we would have heard C-130 engines overhead long since. We should have reached Cape Bird at about 2:30 or 2:40 and notified McMurdo Station of our arrival. By an hour later McMurdo had no doubt become thoroughly alarmed. I expected that the coastal route between McMurdo and Bird was being completely although hazardously searched. Cape Bird had probably already been visited. We wondered if an SAR (search and rescue) Condition was in full operation.

We took stock of our means of survival. We had one Air Force survival tent, designed for single or double occupancy, one Bauer sleeping bag, two cot mattresses, one ice ax, one canteen of water (already frozen), a good deal of food, much of which would need thawing out, and no apparent means of making a fire. We also had the helo's insulation and a lightweight brown blanket that I assumed belonged to the helo but whose ownership I have not been able to establish with certainty. Enderby later told me it may have been part of my camping gear; he wasn't sure. In addition we had the clothes we were now wearing and a pair of bear paws in my seabag that no one, I think out of delicacy, used because it was the only pair among us.

Our situation was not good but it could have been much worse. No one had been injured in the crash. We had a tent and therefore were not obliged to stay in the helo. Without a tent we would have been forced to remain in the craft, for we lacked the tools for digging body trenches in the hard snow. We had the sleeping bag, which, when unzipped, could serve as a blanket. We had the brown blanket. We had the survival gear I had brought along.

The cold began to feel savage. The temperature was steadily falling and the wind was still rising. The metal fuselage was rapidly draining us of body heat even though we tried to avoid metal contact. When I repeated forcefully that we would freeze in the cabin, Palmer said, "maybe we'd better move to the tent."

I asked Eights to strip the cabin of its insulation and told Enderby to crawl inside the tent and prepare a flooring with the stuff we would hand him. Palmer and Eights stripped the helo of everything that looked useful, including the seats, and handed it to me. I carried the stuff to the tent about twenty or twenty-five feet away and gave it piecemeal to Enderby through the complicated, wormlike entrance. All I saw of Enderby during this operation was his hands. I also passed to him the two cot mattresses, the canteen and the sleeping bag.

When I crawled in to examine his handiwork I made my way through a billowing red tube of light material, then through some white, gauzelike stuff that served as a curtain-door, and fouled myself at times as though in a shroud—I felt like a crawling blind man—and even the extra little exertion of getting down on all fours made itself felt by a wild beating of my heart. I was surprised to see how neatly he had arranged things. He had spread the helo insulation on the tent floor, the mattresses side by side on the top of the insulation, and had made a blanket of the sleeping bag. It all looked unexpectedly cozy.

"What a fine boy he is!" I thought.

We gathered together our necessaries and set them down near the tent entrance, that is, the one facing the summit. The opposite one Enderby had tied into a great knot as a protection against the wind. We had a Very pistol and shells, flare, smoke bombs, dye markers, and cartons and crates of food; fruit, vegetables, bread, frozen steaks, frozen rock lobsters, even milk chocolate.

Palmer and I agreed on a plan: to huddle in the tent and to try to ward off permanent damage while we got used to the altitude. Each man's thermal margin was so small, even in the tent, as we were soon to discover, that if one of us had reached an irreversible stage, with the psychological consequences this would have entailed, and required ministering to, the others would probably have gone down in domino fashion. Eights asked me how long it would take to get used to the altitude. I replied that the effects would probably increase before they diminished. My friend Dale Vance, now at Vostok Station, had felt fairly good there the first day but for the next ten had had headaches, insomnia and some nausea. We were approximately as high as Vostok.

You sense that the altitude was like an animal, lurking to assail you, and although you were cautious, being by now aware of its potency, it worked on you suddenly: when you were walking or working or even just standing still and talking. It made you breathless, caused your speech to be fuzzy, disarranged your thoughts. Your words came out too slowly or mixed up. It was easy to do something stupid or dangerous. In addition, the altitude prevented you from warming up by jogging in place. To try jogging was to invite blacking out or vomiting. However, the altitude effects were inconstant and fortunately they were infrequent. But my companions were plagued by intense headaches which I took to be as bad as migraines. In addition to the altitude, always you sensed the power and personality of Erebus. This domineering, remote volcano now had an intimate place in our minds, our lives and perhaps in our death.

Glancing at my companions—we were still outside—I found myself wondering who would outlast whom. I thought of my age. In nine days I would be fifty-six. How long would my heart endure the demands being put on it? It beat very rapidly and pounded even when I did not exert myself. I told myself I must not think about my age; I must put all negative thoughts aside if I meant to survive. I must keep up my morale and the morale of the others. Above all I must behave well. For this, in the end, was what it was about, my having come to Antarctica. It was the subject that had intrigued me so long and intensely: getting at the heart of a magnificent, wild continent. Whenever I remembered my wife and daughter and thought of what my death would mean to them I put them quickly out of mind. I could not afford to let myself be softened by sentiment. Anyhow—and this struck me as very odd—I felt that my truest loyalty was to my present companions, strangers to me. It was with and for them I must behave well; but primarily it was for myself.

And then there was the cold: that thief of one's life's warmth. We kept glancing hopefully at the sky, and when the scud showed patches that seemed thinner than usual our hearts sang, and we grinned, cracked jokes. If the sun were to come out we'd be warm. My left foot was worrying me; it had begun to lose all feeling.

Palmer entered the tent. Enderby was outside somewhere, Eights was in the helo cabin. We needed rocks with which to secure the tent flaps in order to minimize the seepage of wind in the tent. I took the ice ax to some boulders and tried to break chunks off. The volcanic stuff was unbelievably hard. All I managed to achieve was to stimulate my hands with the shock of the blows. One would need a pickax to dent such material. Eights, having emerged from the cabin, suggested inflating the helo's one-man life rafts and placing them against the sides of the tent; this would to some extent hold down the flaps. We inflated the rafts but not to much effect. Later, when we were huddling in the tent, we would feel minutely the variations in the wind's strength. When the wind subsided, the tent grew noticeably warmer. When it rose, we immediately felt threatened, and involuntary alarm signal went off throughout our bodies, various appendages crying out that they were in imminent danger of dying.

I walked to a distant outcrop to take some photographs. Returning to the helo, I found Eights standing in front of the cabin hatch, munching on a chunk of cabbage. In one gloved hand he held a whole head, from which he had cut a hunk with his sheath knife. He had thrown the outer leaves onto the snow. Picking them up and tossing them into the cabin, I said, "Our lives may depend on these. There's no telling how long we may have to hang on. Don't throw *anything* away."

He stopped eating.

I thought, "Stu has made no move to inventory the food and to prepare to ration it. What's he thinking of? Is he positive we'll be rescued? Doesn't he realize this cover can hang on for days, during which fatigue will worsen, causing irritation, illness, accidents? But first will come the dehydration."

As if reading my mind, Eights asked, "Why can't we eat snow, Doc?"

I said the temperature of the snow was now probably twenty or twenty-five below; that the temperature of a freezer compartment in a house refrigerator was about five above; that the snow would injure lips, tongue and palate.

He said, "We've got lots of fruit."

"Which will be like billiard balls soon."

I went to the cockpit to read the thermometer. It registered –35°C, the equivalent of –31°F. The wind was blowing steadily. What was the effective temperature? Fifty, sixty, seventy below?

Eights and Enderby crawled into the tent. I followed them. We lay on our backs under the sleeping-bag blanket at right angles to the entrance and would continue to lie like that, without the luxury of lying on our sides. Any motion on the part of one of us disturbed the others and robbed them of body heat. I was nearest the entrance. Farthest from me was Palmer, lying parallel to me; next to him was Eights, lying opposite him; and next to Eights was Enderby, lying opposite me.

The unzipped sleeping bag wasn't large enough to cover us adequately. We shifted the brown blanket from time to time on an emergency basis. My right side and thigh, only partially covered, grew very cold. I asked Enderby how his feet were. He said he had lost feeling in them. I invited him to place them under my parka, which he did. I felt like crying about him. He had come on a simple turnaround flight and now he might die here. He and Eights aroused painful fatherly feelings in me. Of the four of us they had the most to lose by dying now; it was right that they were in the middle, where it was warmest. I had the least to lose. I lived a long and complex life, containing its share of tragedy, and I did not discover a strong desire to cling to it.

My own feet were a problem, especially the left one. For a while I hoped they would recover under the blanket—we had removed our boots—but I realized slowly it was not responding. I tried wiggling the toes. I rubbed it against my right foot. I curled the right foot over it. Finally I handed Enderby my two left gloves and asked him to put them on my left foot. Slowly the foot came around but then my right foot began to go. At the same time I felt sleepy; I wanted to sleep in order to conserve strength. But if I slept I would fail to stay on guard for my foot's sake. How would it be to return to the world footless? So I determined not to sleep unless my whole body was secured. Meanwhile it became plain that it wasn't just my right foot that was in trouble but my right side from the hip down.

Palmer said, "I'm not going to make it if my left leg doesn't get more cover," and Eights rearranged himself, in the process unavoidably rearranging Enderby and me, and the brown blanket was passed to Palmer temporarily.

We huddled close together, shivering fitfully. It was remarkable how small our margins of body heat were. We would all have to be on a constant alert if we were to succeed in warding off permanent damage.

We were struck by what the red tent did to colors. The green sleeping bag had become a deep navy blue, my red parka a pale yellow-orange. Eights kept commenting on this transmutation of colors. He seemed more relaxed now, although once I overhead him saying to Enderby, "Every once in a while I feel panicky." He cracked jokes and exhibited a comic, mugging side. He could not seem to let go of the subject of colors.

Then we heard C-130 engines in the north for a while; in the south; in the west. So there was no doubt the search was on. One wanted to shout, "Here we are!" and to send up flares. We took turns crawling out of the tent to see if there was a break in the cover. Each exhausting effort dissipated some of our body heat. Each shivering returning man brought in more cold.

Invariably the report was, "It's the same."

I thought, "If only there was a tiny Plexiglas window in the top of the tent, through which we could observe the weather. What a lot of body heat it would save!"

For a while all wanted was for the cover to break up. That would signify *the next step*, without which there could be no help for us. The long hours passed.

Then, to my great astonishment, Palmer asked casually, "Would anybody mind if I smoked?" and broke out a little lighter.

And Eights, asking the same question, withdrew from a pocket an identical lighter.

"Great Christ!" I thought. "I'm dealing with children!"

One charitable explanation I could put on their having failed earlier to reveal the existence of the lighters was that they were positive we were not in a genuine survival situation; we could carry on our lives in normal fashion; we were sure to be rescued. But if that was the case why had they shown signs of panic? Were their minds, then, dissonant with their bodies? Did their minds say, "There's nothing to worry about. I'll be taken care of"? Or did they say, "There's too much to worry about, and I'll just smoke to comfort myself"? Another charitable explanation was that they had misunderstood, or had failed to grasp, or had disagreed with, or had discounted, my warnings of the dangers of dehydration. A less charitable one was that it graveled them to be helped by a middle-aged civilian, a writer at that, somebody who typically spent much time on his behind.

At any rate, we could make a fire after all! I, a non-smoker, did not enjoy the prospect of the small tent's being filled with smoke. Apparently an abstainer could not escape cigarette smoke even near the crater of Mount Erebus. But if smoking was good for Palmer's and Eights' morale, I was for it—for the moment. So I did not raise an objection. Enderby didn't either. Nor did I ask why the lighters hadn't been mentioned previously. Anyhow, I hoped they would not enjoy smoking at this altitude and would quickly give it up. I was wrong. They seemed to find comfort in it.

We were all sitting up now. The tent felt very crowded but not as much as when we were prone on our backs, our heads against the tent walls or helo seats, our chins thrust down, cricks developing in our napes and in our throat muscles. The narrow tent was not meant for use by persons lying at a right angle to the entrances. How long would it take before such crowding made us exceedingly irritable, debasing the quality of our social behavior, lowering our will to survive and causing a proneness to accidents?

The problem arose of where to put the cigarette ashes. Palmer offered his helmet. I suggested to Eights he use some tinfoil from one of the milk chocolate bars we had with us. He did. He was greatly intrigued by the vivid, electric green of the cigarette flame. He had begun to expand. He was very charming now, I thought. Often, happening to glance his way, I discovered him staring intently at me. He and Palmer finished their cigarettes and we lay down again.

The time slipped by. At one point I focused sharply on Joan, my wife. I felt I was communicating with her. I imagined saying intensely to her, "Lift the cloud cover. It's an urgent matter. If you wish for it hard enough it may go away." Then it struck me that if there *was* anything to ESP I might alert her to my situation, which would be terrible, for it would make her aware of her inability to help me. So I quit this game.

I thought I was a bit old for my heart to be beating as hard, as fast and as strangely as it was. It hammered against my chest cavity like a live, wild thing: jumping, twisting, bouncing in a way I had never experienced. When I had swum hard my lungs had worked hard in rhythm with my heart. Now they worked heavily but quietly while my heart, like some wild caged bird, beat so powerfully I experienced it as a unique, alien entity, some small but mad bit of life that had gotten trapped inside me and was frantically trying to escape. I think it was the altitude that caused it to behave like that. If it was fear, it was for me an entirely new kind, without overtones in my mind and in other parts of my body, as far as I knew. I do not recall feeling fear during the episode, not fear in the very personal sense; certainly at times I was alarmed for us as a group. Quietism seemed to have possessed me. I felt ready to die peacefully; I knew that freezing was a peaceful death. It did not seem at all like a big deal to take off. It felt, as a matter of fact, like a pretty good moment for me to go, and I was comforted by the fact I was well and specially insured. It occurred to me more than once that, financially speaking, I was probably worth more dead than alive. I wondered how long this little bird in my chest could keep beating its wings in such a mad way and I thought what a messy situation it would be for all of us if I had a heart attack.

My bare left hand was in a parka pocket with a furlike lining. My double-gloved right hand lay on my chest. Now and then I was aware that the middle finger of my right hand was slowly assuming a hook shape and that the knuckle was extremely sore. Once, when I removed the gloves and glanced at the hand, I saw that the tendon was taut and whitish under the palm flesh. It was very difficult for me to straighten the finger. I wondered what had happened to it.

There were hours of silence, during which I asked myself what my resources for hanging on were. It seemed to me that Erebus could be personified as cunning and that if I was to survive I must be more cunning than it. I must be more cunning than I had ever been in my life. Above all I must not fight the mountain head on. I noticed that if I kept my face beneath the blanket my face became warm from the breath, and that the energy conserved in not having to warm my face as much as when it was exposed, went into warming my right thigh and foot, making their temperature bearable. This was not something I imagined; I tested it. With my face exposed, my right thigh and foot felt achy, numb. With my face covered they began to relax with more heat. It was an example of being cunning, I thought. I reported this minor discovery to my companions, although without using the idea of cunning; they soon confirmed it. I also noticed that whenever I sat up I had strong abdominal cramps and felt on the verge of vomiting. To vomit would mean to leave the tent and lose much body heat. So I took to sitting up very slowly, calming the cramps with an effort of mind and not mentioning them in order to keep the group's morale as high as possible.

Palmer announced that he needed "to take a dump" but would try to hold it in. Defecation meant leaving the tent and exposing yourself to cold and wind. A trifle, perhaps; but by their sum a series of trifles could determine if you survived or not.

I resolved I would try to survive. But for whom? My wife? My daughter? Myself? It seemed redundant, self-serving, meaningless to survive for oneself. Although it was clear to me that I ought to try to survive for my daughter's sake because of her youth (she was thirteen), I felt the need to survive for my wife, who, I told myself, needed me more than she knew. And so when I felt very tired—I hadn't had a good night's sleep in days and last night I had slept for four hours—and on the verge of not caring any longer what happened to me, of drifting off somewhere—to sleep or gangrene or death—I thought of her needing me, and then my eyes opened wide beneath the sleeping-bag blanket, and that popping open roused me with a lunge to full consciousness, or to superconsciousness, as it seemed to me then. Over and over, thinking of her needing me, I came wide awake and determined I would *live*. If I didn't have the will to live for myself there was no doubt I had it for her. Perhaps this exercise in determining to live for someone else was also a part of being cunning.

Occasionally I realized how silent it was when the wind died down. This was the great Antarctic silence; a ringing of blood in one's ears. But mostly I didn't hear it because my breathing was heavy: my chest rose and fell with force to provide me with sufficient oxygen, and if I started to drift off toward sleep I would awake with the feeling I was out of breath.

Cunning: I warned my companions not to eat bread because bread was gas-forming and because the expansion of gases at twelve thousand feet was considerable as compared with that at sea level. Dale Vance had overeaten at one of his first meals at Vostok and had lain on his back for hours, gasping. Sea level? By air miles we were so close to it, and to McMurdo, and to warmth and security.

I wondered at times why Palmer didn't try to use the HF radio on battery power. I knew I was ignorant on the subject and so I didn't mention it to him. I assumed the HF radio required more juice than the battery could provide. About a year later I happened to be talking with Jim Brandau about this matter. Brandau asked me if we had heard planes while we were on Erebus. I said yes, often. He looked surprised. He said it took a lot of power to send HF signals that would bounce off the ionosphere and go beyond the horizon, more power, probably, than could be obtained from a battery, but that Palmer should have tried the HF radio on battery in an effort to contact the plane within sound of us, and that he might have succeeded.

Palmer was perhaps at least partially in a state of shock. He had taken two bad falls, as we know. They had occurred because he had failed to notice that certain patches of snow were a lighter shade than others and had not avoided them. Such patches often indicate a thinner layer of snow over ice and can be treacherous to walk on. Enderby had stayed clear of them. He had either failed to warn Palmer or Palmer had ignored the warning. As Enderby described the falls to me when we were back at McMurdo, Palmer's legs had flown from under him; he had landed heavily on his back; and he had reacted with great surprise and a good deal of bewilderment. Probably the two falls influenced his subsequent abandonment of any serious effort to provide leadership for our group. Such falls were what could come of ignorance. They were also the result to some extent, I suspect, of hubris. A more modest man would have walked in Enderby's tracks, especially inasmuch as Enderby carried the ice ax and occasionally probed the snow with it.

Some months after the crash episode it occurred to me that the state of one's conscience during a crisis can determine whether one behaves badly or well. Thus the fact that I was the only one of the group with survival gear placed me in the position of the giver rather than the receiver and left me with a fairly clear state of mind. Palmer was in the worst position of us all: he had brought us onto Erebus and was now technically responsible for our welfare. Affecting his behavior must have been the realization that his career if not his life had abruptly reached a turning point.

The extraordinary thing is that not once during the long hours when we waited for a rescue did any of us ask him, at least so far as I know, any direct, pertinent questions which might have revealed his motives, his intentions or what precisely had happened; nor did he offer such information. I suppose we had better things to think and talk about than what was now in the past. We were concerned with our future, or rather with the question of whether we had one. I suppose too that a sense of delicacy prevented us from raising questions that might have injured his morale. He turned inward almost from the start and psychologically moved increasingly away from the rest of us. From time to time he coughed, and once he said he believed he had pneumonia.

There were various practical aspects of the question of being cunning. For example, when I lay with my face exposed and opened my eyes now and then, I didn't mind the pink, dappled light of the red tent—how misleading that light was! How it always tricked us into thinking the cloud cover was lifting!—but when my face was under the blanket and I then had to uncover my eyes and look around the tent, the light was atrocious, it assaulted my eyeballs violently, causing nerves to throb madly

401

all the way from my eyes deep into my head, and I knew I could not sustain many such seizures without becoming snow-blind. So I developed a little strategy to minimize the assault. I covered my eyes with my fingers, slowly opened my eyes, then tentatively, carefully, spread my fingers until the light was bearable. It was strange that the light was so intense while the cloud cover was so thick.

Cloud cover: that was mostly what I thought about, wondering when it would lift and asking myself how to be patient, even if I had to wait for days. Patience too was a way of being cunning. Unless you were patient Erebus would surely defeat you. You must be as simple-minded, in some ways, as a penguin. At Cape Evans in the nasty, bone-destroying southeast wind that had come off the polar plateau and the ice shelf, I had observed Adélies lying on their breasts out on the sea ice, seemingly asleep, waiting for the bad weather to pass. This was what I too must do. And it was what we were doing; lying low, waiting for that momentous time when we would be able to use our flares and smoke bombs. The cover was endlessly on my mind and endlessly the subject of tent conversation when there *was* conversation. Mostly there was none; there were vast silences when it was easy to assume my companions were asleep. The silences conserved energy. They allowed us to animalize in this primitive moment, to sink somewhere inside ourselves to a secret place where we could concentrate entirely on clinging to what strength each of us had. But what if the cover hung on day after day? Would there come a time when we would crack?

There were also less pleasant aspects of being cunning. Palmer was snoring, which meant he was asleep and regaining strength; he would be in better shape than I in the morning. In a crisis—as if this in the tent was not enough to justify the name of crisis—he would outlast me. So I began to think what I could do to be more cunning than he.

Hours passed, passed. He and Eights lit up again.

I said half jokingly, "Easy on those lighters. Our lives may depend on them."

Neither Eights nor Palmer responded to the remark. I was profoundly irritated by Palmer's failure to requisition the lighters for the common good. When they lit up a third time, I resolved that at the fourth I would ask them to stop smoking and make the lighters common property. I hoped the confrontation would not be ugly. Fortunately it never came.

Palmer finally couldn't hold it in any longer; he crawled outside to "take a dump," returning with a rueful expression and reporting, "It froze while I was wiping it."

I suggested it wasn't necessary to move our bowels in the open. We could defecate in the cabin's large metal cabinet that contained cans of lubricant. It would be a simple matter to line the cabinet's bottom with a helo seat cover. This would permit us to dispose of the feces from time to time. One could shut the hatch and keep out the wind, and one would have the cabinet's side to sit on. My companions agreed, so I removed my gloves, withdrew a Swiss army knife from a parka pocket and cut away a seat cover. To my surprise, although the cover was very cold the foam rubber inside it was much warmer, and the styrofoam was even warmer. These materials

402

were not as efficient heat conductors as the plastic cover. So this too was an aspect of being cunning; saving body heat by using as pillows foam rubber and styrofoam instead of whole seats.

At times my abdominal cramps rose to a pitch and I too felt I might need to defecate. I held on, hoping I wouldn't vomit. I thought how disastrous violent indigestion could be in our circumstances.

At one point, to make sure I hadn't been mistaken, I made a special trip to the cleft in the outcrop where I had seen the lichen. There the bit of life was, a striking pink suggestion of the warmth of human blood. What a lonely, dreary place the lichen lived in, yet its existence deeply comforted me by suggesting that even here there were fascinating things to occupy one's mind, however little of one's life might be left.

Occasionally we heard planes. They always sounded far away. How long would they keep looking for us? Palmer said they'd never quit; this was no civilian matter; the search would continue until the mystery was solved. It was comforting to hear it but was it a reasonable view? I doubted it. We might have fallen into the open sea without a trace, or into a giant crevasse. The search could not go on indefinitely. If it stopped, *then* what would we do?

Unlikely though it may seem, at times I was glad to be in this spot, for if I survived, what a tale I would have to tell! Over and over a gear slipped in my thinking as I projected myself into the future and found myself a rare bird, one who had crashed on Erebus and lived. It was pleasant and perhaps necessary for me to dream like this; it lessened the burden of waiting; but the dreams always ended abruptly when, with a thud, I recalled I was in the present and that my future might never come.

Several times I donned my boots and left the tent to observe and to take photographs. It was very pleasant to be alone. What beautifully subtle if menacing scene it was! In my mind I threw my life away on each of these solitary excursions. If one died now one would have the satisfaction of knowing one had died fairly well. The glow that one could not be robbed of and that sustained one again and again was the knowledge that one was behaving decently, as far as one knew. This knowledge was the best gift one had, and the best one could hope to bring down off Erebus.

Saying his headache was killing him, Eights went to the helo and fetched a first-aid kit, which contained morphine but no aspirin.

"Shall I take some morphine, Doc?" he asked.

I said if he did he would fall into a deep sleep and wouldn't know if he got badly frostbitten. I told him where in the cabin he could find my toilet kit and got aspirin from it. He swallowed two or three tablets of aspirin without water, but his headache did not respond. Enderby said *his* headache was going away.

A little later Eights sat up, broke out a bar of milk chocolate and ate some of it. Palmer said nothing, so I said, "Stu, I don't think we have a right to eat at will. We should ration everything we've got. There's no telling how long it will be before we're found. We may have to hold out for weeks."

Palmer said, "I thought it was the other way around, that we eat as much as we want while we're still in good shape."

"Stu," I said, "you're still fresh from McMurdo, from the ship. You're well fed. The time may come when we'll desperately need food and water to survive."

He thought a moment, then suggested we all eat a bit of chocolate and an apple to stave off hunger. My companions each placed a small apple in an armpit, meanwhile munching chocolate.

Later, lying with my eyes closed, I found myself thinking, "You son of a bitch. You threw my life away."

But I knew I must stop resenting him, for if I didn't I would soon hate him, and his knowledge of the hatred might lower his morale even lower than it was. Without high morale we could not show the volcano what human beings were capable of. No, in this place Palmer and I were one, bound together like Siamese twins. To hate him, or just to resent him, was to threaten my own morale and survival as well as that of the two young men.

The hours passed: in silence. Always, except for the wind and the sound of engines, there was silence. Then the engines faded out. Did this mean the search had stopped temporarily? If so, when would it be resumed? If we were not found in time when *would* we be found? *We* knew we were all right but those searching for us were no doubt wondering in what condition they would find us, if find us they did. Occasionally I saw myself with their eyes, for I had come so close to not being all right that it was as if I had tasted the experience of being smashed, frozen. *If* we were found, how would it happen? And if we were *not* found?

The ceasing of the engines brought apathy. There was no longer an urgent need to check on the cloud cover, for even if the cover lifted now, what good would it do us if there were no planes in our vicinity? The hours were passing without signposts. On eternity's edge time itself grew apathetic.

XXVII
Found

After a time we heard engines again. They sounded quite low and seemed to be helos. I scrambled out of the tent. And engine approached, dimmed. Another seemed to draw close but faded. The cover was too thick for me to see planes. I returned to the tent.

Lying half-conscious, I thought I heard a helo coming close and *above* us. The sound was very faint but I was sure it belonged to a helo. I alerted Eights, who, after listening a moment, agreed with me. I shouted to Enderby to take a look. He was more agile than I. He rushed out in stockinged feet. The engine sounded louder.

Then we heard his electrifying cry: "I *see* it!"

We had left the loaded Very gun in an open carton beside the entrance shroud.

I shouted, "Fire the Very pistol directly at him!"

404

I heard the gun go off. Eights was tearing outside.

"They *see* us!" Enderby cried.

In that twinkling everything changed for us.

"Wave him off! Don't let him land!" Palmer shouted.

This was sound advice, for we had not selected and marked a landing pad, or indicated by smoke bomb the wind direction.

A moment later Eights cried that the helo was dropping two survival packs. Palmer and I were fumbling with our boots. My hands were not cooperating. I crawled through the shroud, belly cramping, head swimming. Palmer was behind me, coughing heavily.

A Coast Guard helicopter was departing beyond a high ridge just to the right of the crater. On that side of the crest the sky had cleared a bit and the sun was showing milkily. My watch read precisely midnight, which meant it was due south where the sun was. We didn't realize then that the helo would not return until about 2:30.

Eights and Enderby retrieved the survival kits, which contained no headgear and footgear but which did have matches and fat white candles and lots of mosquito netting. We laughed. We felt wonderfully refreshed.

I went to the helo cabin, where my two caseless cameras were white with frost, removed the lens covers and began shooting the damage to the helo, knowing the Navy would want close-up shots for the investigation that was sure to come. It was not easy to keep one's mind clear at that altitude while portions of one's body kept sending signals warning of the danger of irreversible frostbite. One had to caution oneself to do everything in slow motion. It was now as well as earlier that one's practice with cameras in the temperate zone became crucial. While I was photographing the telescoped strut that ran from the fuselage to the port pontoon, Eights stripped metal from it, commenting on how easily it came away. Later he amused himself by lobbing red flares into the mouths of the two ice fumaroles. The red glow was very conspicuous in the fuzzy gray world.

When the cameras ran out of film I carried them into the tent and rewound the cassettes as slowly as I was able. I was still wearing the double gloves. I could feel from the tension of the rewind knob that the film remained intact. Back at McMurdo, trying to reload cameras while wearing the gloves, I had failed in the experiment, as I had failed when wearing only the large, bulky shell. I had no alternative now but to reload the cameras with naked hands. I had not brought along anti-contact gloves but in any case they would have prevented only adhesion of skin to metal, not frostbite. I remembered what had happened to the fingers of my right hand when, earlier in the crash episode, frustrated by a Very pistol shell that was stuck in its casing, I had removed the gloves from that hand and freed the shell. It had been strange to the point of fascination to observe the fingers rapidly turn a dead white almost to the knuckles. Since metal and skin had been extremely dry there had been no adhesion.

The frost on the cameras had by now seemingly ablated. I touched the cameras tentatively and found that my fingers did not stick to them. As I reloaded, my fingers

405

burned, and turned very white, and then I lost feeling in them but they kept responding to my commands. Going outside to continue shooting, I discovered that the lenses were frosted over by condensation of moisture from the tent's interior. I set the cameras on the floor of the open helo cabin, where they cleared by ablation, then shot skid marks, pontoons, wheels, struts.

Before we were found—and it was still by no means certain we would be rescued: the cloud cover was playing tricks over the summit—it had seemed to me that there was really a simple equation inherent in our situation. I had been fairly sure our lives had been forfeited. The only relevant question was, it had struck me, would one die well or badly. If by some miracle we were rescued, I had thought, the sole thing of lasting value one could hope to bring off this mountain was the knowledge one had behaved well. Frankly, I had not relished the prospect of having to deal, for the rest of my life, with the memory that I had behaved otherwise.

Failure to do one's duty, duty being for example work one had committed oneself to, in my case to bring back data gathered during my visit to the continent, was an element in behaving badly. If I failed to take pictures during such an episode what could I tell myself later? That I had been too cold, tired, sleepy, numbed, frightened? But such excuses, if they didn't wash now, and they didn't, would hardly wash later. I would have to deal with the fact I had let myself down, and I wasn't ready to pay so considerable a price. As a result, I had few qualms about risking parts of my body by leaving the tent periodically to take photographs. Besides, it was fruitful to confront oneself alone from time to time; and keeping busy helped one to be mentally resilient. In addition, I had thought, if we died on the mountain, the photographs, when found, would be a partial record of what had happened to us as well as a suggestion that I had died while at work rather than in a state of funk. And if we should be rescued there would be a record of what had occurred.

At about 12:30 a Herc appeared and flew under the high cover in huge circles over us. He never let go of us, and once he made a low pass and I gathered he was shooting us. It was a tremendous morale boost to have him up there.

Still shooting, in a while I realized I had better warm my left foot. And my hands had gone strangely very bad despite the double gloves. So I crawled into the tent to work on the foot.

Palmer, sitting under the brown blanket, was warming a stockinged foot with a lighted candle. The candle's green flame was close to his foot and the blanket.

I thought, "He's showing the same poor judgment he showed when he tried to overfly Erebus. If this tent goes up in flames, and presuming we escape, all our gear will go with it and we may well go under even though we've been found, for there's no telling how long it will be before they come for us, or *can* come for us."

I said, "Take it easy with the candle, Stu," but he didn't respond.

I asked Eights where the hand radio was. He said he had tried to communicate with the rescue helo both by beep and by voice but had failed even to pick up the craft, and had got so disgusted he had thrown the radio into the crashed helo's cabin.

406

"They should have dropped us a radio so they could tell us their plans," he said. "Or at least they could have dropped us a note."

When Palmer tired of the candle Eights asked for it and warmed his naked right hand over it, staring at the flame, and the flame singed the elbow of Enderby's parka and came close to the tent wall. Then, after I warned him, Eight set the candle down on a small piece of styrofoam and studied it, fascinated by the flame's unbelievably pure and intense green.

He and Enderby wondered aloud when the rescue attempt would be made and how. Would Coast Guard helos hazard an attempt? Or would a Herc try to skylift us out one at a time?

Palmer said, "They're not going to skylift me. You get a hell of a jerk when they do that. And you'd freeze to death before they pulled you inside."

The speculation between Enderby and Eights continued awhile.

Palmer said, "They can't take us out all together. We'll probably go out two at a time. We ought to decide who's going out first."

For myself, I didn't care whether I went out first or last. We had been found, and if I were the last to be scheduled to go, and got socked in by weather for days, my position was known, I'd have the sleeping bag to myself, and matches and candles, and I could lie low, and drink enough water to keep from getting seriously dehydrated, and I'd be fine.

I said, "I volunteer to go last."

After an awkward silence he said, "I'll go out with you."

"Take it easy," I told myself. "He did behave well in looking for the ridge. He did wave the helo off. He did invite you to fly in the cockpit with him. And possibly he did autorotate, select the landing spot, save our limbs if not our lives."

But later, when I returned to the tent after shooting some more while my companions were under the sleeping bag, Eights said, "You and I will go out last, Doc."

I said, "I thought Stu and I were going last."

"Stu's not feeling too good," Eights said.

Palmer said nothing.

As I slid beneath the blanket I expected to resent or even to hate him. I was wrong. My resentment seemed to have burned itself out at the time when I had told myself I couldn't afford it. Actually, I felt paternal toward him now, as I did toward the two young men, and discovered, on looking back on the long hours of hoping, that at times I had already felt that way toward him. I discovered also that I had been afraid at times, in little bursts, but that the essential thing was not whether one was afraid but whether one's fear could be controlled.

Then suddenly we heard a helo approaching—with that beautiful familiar chopping sound—and we were lacing our boots and crawling outside, and we spotted not one but two Coast Guard helicopters circling over Erebus, and the scene was unreal, for here we were on this ice and snow and rock shelf, and there was the red tent, well staked down, its rope taut, the cloth brilliant, and the stricken helo leaning to port,

407

heavy on its hull, and Eights setting off violet smoke bombs, and up there was the volcano's summit, obscured by scud and smoke, and beyond the summit was a milky, wan sun, the summer sun that for months never set, the sun that had burned me badly at Royds, and up there in that fairyland the two helos were circling, feeling their way carefully, and I thought, "My god, that's hairy," and I wondered if they too would air-starve, and meanwhile the Herc watched over all of us, and I tried with all my might to observe and remember everything.

We had selected a landing pad—an apron of sloping, almost naked rock not too far from the tent—and Eights and Enderby now marked it with my green rucksack and some food cartons, and Eights signaled the first rescue helo (1377, from the *Staten Island*) to a landing. I naively stood nearby and watched the helo touch down. The blizzard caused by the rotors hit me full in the face, and my eyes were blasted by ice and snow particles. Blinded, I whirled to give the blizzard my back. After a moment, glancing at my frosted cameras sitting on the cabin floor, I saw that the lenses, or rather the UV filters, were white with snow. I wiped them clean with a gloved finger.

The pilot of 1377, Neil Nicholson, whom I knew, dressed lightly but looking confident and warm, left the craft and walked rapidly to 1404, his helmet making him look like a megacephalic Martian out of a science fiction tale. He came up beside me. I was studying my gear on the cabin floor, deciding what I had to take out with me. He touched my arm and asked with a glance of concern, "Are you all right?"

It struck me suddenly as extremely remarkable that the eerie, immense and in some ways marvelous silence of Mount Erebus was being shattered by 1377's barbaric sounds; yet I was grateful for those sounds; they were made by a *live* engine; and I found myself responding with a new and special intimacy to the noises a helo made as against those made by a C-130 like the one circling, circling above us.

I shook my head affirmatively.

Again he asked, "Are you all right?"

Again I shook my head.

"We've got to get out of here fast," he said. "The weather is very bad and may close in again. Leave everything behind except maybe a camera.

"I'm not leaving without my professional gear," I said.

He glanced at my face, shrugged, and walked away.

Enderby fetched the Kiwi mail from the cockpit and handed it to Palmer, who ran to 1377 and boarded it. Meanwhile the second rescue helo had disappeared. I hoped it hadn't crashed. It would be terrible if someone got killed while trying to save us. Taking my cameras, I went to an outcrop near 1377 and observed what Nicholson, his crewman (who was wearing a brilliant red flight suit) and Eights were doing to mark the pad for the second helo. A vivid red line was drawn on the outcrop to indicate the position of the front of the cockpit. Smoke bombs marked the position of the rear wheel. Nicholson had hung my blue towel from a tent pole as a wind sock and was now marking the pad with flares, dye markers and smoke bombs. The preparations were very colorful in the gauzelike, black-and-white terrain: red, orange and purple smoke poured along the base of the pad, was caught by the rotor blasts and sent northward, southward and then directly at me, choking me. Feeling tremendously lucky to be there with cameras that seemed to be functioning well, I believed this was my best moment on the ice. I kept warning myself to remember to check light meters, to advance frames slowly, to double-check focus, to compose carefully, and above all to work in slow motion, being mindful of the effects of high altitude on one's judgment.

Then I realized that my double-gloved hands had been screaming for some time, as if they were being crushed by giant pincers, and I wondered vaguely why they were making such a fuss—my face felt fine—and I wondered if reloading the cameras barehanded had something to do with it. The fact was that the double gloves were not sufficient protection for hand work at that temperature. One needed to wear bear paws to be comfortable. As we know, I had brought a pair in my survival bag but one of my companions was now using them. Anyhow, it was not possible to take photographs while wearing them.

And then Neil Nicholson stripped to the waist and replaced the towel with his undershirt because the towel was too heavy to flutter in the current breeze, and I thought, "It's thirty below and he has a small, very white paunch. He has a great deal of body heat from the warm helo to be able to do that."

I intended to photograph him like that but my hands failed to respond to my orders. All feeling had left them. I was not to regain full sensation in the finger ends for from six to eight months, and at this writing a certain amount of circulatory and neural damage seems to be permanent. I let my cameras hang from my neck while I clapped my gloved hands together. It was like clapping boards, for all the feeling there was in it. Enderby ran over to me and handed me the bear paws he had been wearing, and he ran to the helo and boarded it, and I kept slamming my hands together in the bear paws.

Suddenly, Nicholson, now in the cockpit with is copilot who had never left the helo and who had not shut down the engine, raced the rotors for liftoff, and I stood there idiotically, having already forgotten what had happened when 1377 had hit the deck. My face felt as if it were hit by a metal curtain, and pellets of ice stung my eyeballs. I wheeled, and hung on the outcrop, digging with my toes and bracing to be kept from being blown off. The helo's liftoff caused such a whiteout that for whole minutes nothing could be seen. The whiteout cleared, and, by God, there was the second helo, descending, and Eights ran to the pad and signaled it in.

"Let's *go!*" he shouted to me, and boarded the craft.

With gear hanging from my shoulders and cameras from my neck, I ran to the hatch and fumbled to climb aboard, but my knees were weak, my hands couldn't clutch, and my gear was pulling me backwards toward the pad. It was a high step to the cabin floor. The bearded crewman, warm, fresh, reached out above me, grabbed my armpits and with a tremendous jerk hauled me aboard.

I removed my gloves and fumbled with my seat belt. The crewman, noticing I was having trouble, belted me in. My hands were dead white, especially from the knuckles to the nails. To the left of my seat I felt a current of warm air. I hung my left hand down in it. The crewman bent over to increase the air flow. I warmed my hands in it alternately until they hurt very badly and I knew they would be all right. Eights slouched back in his set, his long legs outstretched, his arms limp. His eyes were closed. The crewman offered us coffee. I had given up drinking coffee about a year ago, so I declined it.

"Gee, Doc, take it," Eights said. "At least it's warm to hold."

I accepted a cup. . . .

—1974

Peter Matthiessen

from *The Snow Leopard*

Peter Matthiessen (1927–) undertook a journey of Buddhist enlightenment in 1973 to Dolpo on the Tibetan Plateau accompanied by George Schaller (referred to as "GS" throughout the book). Schaller is also an internationally acclaimed writer, naturalist, and author of The Serengeti Lion *(1972) and* Mountain Monarchs *(1977). Matthiessen describes the mountains and mountain people of this region as he and Schaller search for the seldom-seen snow leopard. Because of the mountainous terrain, Matthiessen and Schaller were forced to make several hair-raising journeys through ice- and snow-filled ridges and gorges. Their goal was to reach Shey Gompa, the "Crystal Monastery," very rarely visited by Westerners. Interspersed with reflections on Buddhism and the philosophy of enlightenment are memories of Matthiessen's wife Deborah (referred to as "D" in the narrative), who had died of cancer before the trip.*

October 19

With a full pack, I leave at dawn, and make good time up to the sun, at 15,500 feet. The trek is fun, for knowing the way I can enjoy details. On bare places in the ice-fretted snow, rubbery red succulents grow among the stone, and many stones hold fossils from the epochs when these earth summits lay beneath the sea.

In the snow mountains—is it altitude?—I feel open, clear, and child-like once again. I am bathed by feelings, and unexpectedly I find myself near tears, brought on this time by the memory of an early-morning phone call from the hospital, in the last week of D's life. For days, D had been in what the doctors thought was her last coma, yet a nurse's voice said that my wife wished to speak with me: she had to assure me that there was no mistake. Then I heard this very weak clear voice out of D's childhood, calling as if I were far away across a meadow, "Peter? Peter? Come right away! I'm very, very sick!" She must have sensed that she was close to death, and the bewilderment in her voice broke my heart. I ran there through the winter streets, past pinched city faces glaring in suspicion, steam rising from beneath the street in frozen wisps, blowing away.

Now, halfway around the world, as tears freeze at the corners of my eyes, I hear strange sounds, a yelping like a lonely mountain fox, and a moment later burst out laughing, thinking how D herself would laugh at an idea so delicious as wailing with lost love in the snow mountains. The tears and laughter come and go, and afterward

411

I feel soft, strung out, and relieved magically of the altitude headache with which the day had started.

At the snowfields depot there is nothing but snow and silence, wind and blue. I rest in the warm sun, enveloped in the soft shroud of white emptiness; my presence in such emptiness seems *noticed*, although no one is here.

When Phu-Tsering comes, we pitch two tents in the gravel gully between drifts; the loads lie in a mist of wind-blown snow. My missing stave is here, stuck in a snowbank by the B'on-po who made off with it when he passed my tent at the start of yesterday's climb. Now Dawa arrives, it is just past noon, and when we finish these chapatis, we shall carry three loads to the pass, descending again to this camp for the night. Despite his bitter experience in the Dhaulagiris, Dawa wears a rag over his eyes only because I forbade him to leave camp without it. Earlier this year, he worked at the base camp of an American expedition to Annapurna Four: he has had no experience as a mountaineer, and not much, it appears, as a grown man.

It is windless and hot, and the knee-deep snow has softened in the sun, and our boots break through the steps made by GS's party while the snow was hard yesterday morning. I am toting a burlap sack of lentils in a broken basket, and can testify that the porters would have quit within the first one hundred yards in the unlikely event that GS had charmed them into going on. The thin straps bite at my shoulders, the broken wicker stabs holes in my parka, and the basket itself on its crude harness rolls heavily from side to side, throwing me off-balance: I pant so in the thin air that I feel sick. I keep my gaze fixed on the misted footprints that weave back and forth up the steep slope, so as not to be disheartened by the distance still to go; the sun is shimmering in waves off the bright snow.

With no landmarks, only this hallucinating whiteness blurred by the salt sweat in my vision, the way to the pass mounts in crazy spirals to a white crescent on the blue. From somewhere comes the rumble of an avalanche. Here I am at 17,000 feet, in desperate need of air; instead, I am floundering through soft snow beneath sixty pounds of lentils. Every few feet, I come to a gasping halt, lungs bursting. The stress brings an upsurge of yesterday's rage; I curse the thrift that has brought us, so to speak, to this pretty pass. Today we shall have carried loads from Cave Camp to the Kang, four thousand feet up through ice and heavy snow; two more loads apiece must come up from the Snowfields Camp tomorrow. Why aren't GS and Jang-bu back today to help? Why are we setting out willow sticks for Tukten and Gyaltsen, when it is plain that the absent Sherpas will never get this far without a guide? If GS had packed a sack of lentils more than a thousand feet up a steep slope, knee-deep in this blazing slush, he would send no more damned messages about two easy trips a day.

Then I come to my senses, as if hearing a distant bell: all this raging is absurd. I know this man, and if he has stayed in Shey (the alternative explanation for his absence—accident—is unthinkable) he has good reason. My anger is wasting energy I badly need, and realizing this, it is easy to put it aside.

As the slopes steepen, I am almost on all fours, knuckles brushing the snow, and this simian stance shifts the weight forward, saving my lacerated shoulders. Three thoughts carry me ahead: the prospect of the northward view over Dolpo to Tibet; the prospect of a free descent across these brilliant snowfields to hot tea and biscuits; and the perception—at this altitude, extremely moving—that these two hands I see before me in the sun, bracing the basket straps, hands square and brown and wrinkled with the scars of life, are no different from the old hands of my father. Simultaneously, I am myself, the child I was, the old man I will be.

Three hours of brute labor are required to reach the pass, where a very cold wind from the north makes us lie flat out on our bellies. What the Kang turns out to be is the only point on a narrow spine between two crags where a descent might be attempted into the great snow bowl beyond. Even here, the drop in the first hundred feet is too precipitous for creatures without hands; a slip would mean a roll and tumble of a good half-mile.

At 17,800 feet, Kang La is much higher than any peak in the United States outside Alaska, yet in three directions rise mountains of greater altitude, for excepting Tibet, Nepal is the highest country in the world. The horizon north across the mountains, in deep purple shadow, is the Land of B'od. These ravines on the north side of the Kang are deep in twilight; one of them must lead down to Shey Gompa.

Confronted with this emptiness, it is not hard to imagine that somewhere down among those peaks—like that green place under the Jang Pass in the Saure ravine— the center of the world, Shambala, might exist. Tradition says that the venerable Lao-tzu, having propounded the Tao to the Keeper of the Pass, vanished with his ox into such emptiness; so did Bodhidharma, the First Patriarch, who carried the Dharma from India to China. But what I see in this first impression is a chaos of bright spires, utterly lifeless, without smoke or track or hut or passing bird.

To the south, under the Kanjirobas, the point of brown color that is camp lies in full sun. I retreat down the snow slopes, starting to run, as the oppression of that northern prospect lifts away. The glaciers glow in sunset light, as the ice face of Kanjirobas comes in view. In the last of a flying, swift descent I leap and bound.

At sundown, a black eagle crosses between peaks; then bitter cold descends from the swift fierce stars. With no fuel to spare, we turn in quickly, to wait out the night.

October 30

At daybreak, when I peek out at the still universe, ice fills my nostrils; I crouch back in my sleeping bag, cover my head. If GS and Jang-bu do not come today, there are hard decisions to be made. Since our path of retreat is a descent down icy boulders, this is no place to be caught in a storm, and, anyway, we cannot stay, as fuel is almost gone. The spell of silence on this place is warning that no man belongs here.

At dawn, the camp is visited by ravens. Then a cold sun rises to the rim of the white world, bringing light wind.

This morning we shall carry three more loads up to Kang La, and then three more. That will make nine; there are fourteen altogether. To avoid the bitter cold, we wait until the sun touches the slopes, then climb hard to take advantage of the snow crust, reaching the pass in an hour and a half. In the snowbound valleys to the north, still in night shadow, there is no sign of our companions, no sign of any life at all.

The Sherpas start down immediately; they, too, seem oppressed by so much emptiness. Left alone, I am overtaken by that northern void—no wind, no cloud, no track, no bird, only the crystal crescents between peaks, the ringing monuments of rock that, freed from the talons of ice and snow, thrust an implacable *being* into the blue. In the early light, the rock shadows on the snow are sharp; in the tension between light and dark is the power of the universe. This stillness to which all returns, this is reality, and soul and sanity have no more meaning here than a gust of snow; such transience and insignificance are exalting, terrifying, all at once, like the sudden discovery, in meditation, of one's own transparence. Snow mountains, more than sea or sky, serve as a mirror to one's own true being, utterly still, utterly clear, a void, an Emptiness without life or sound that carries in Itself all life, all sound. Yet as long as I remain an "I" who is conscious of the void and stands apart from it, there will remain a snow mist on the mirror.

A silhouette crosses the white wastes below, a black coil dangling from its hand. It is Dawa Sherpa carrying tumpline and headband, yet in this light, something moves that is much more than Dawa. The sun is roaring, it fills to bursting each crystal of snow. I flush with feeling, moved beyond my comprehension, and once again, the warm tears freeze upon my face. These rocks and mountains, all this matter, the snow itself, the air—the earth is ringing. All is moving, full of power, full of light.

––––––

Eager to make my second climb while the snow is firm, I travel quickly. This time I have a sack of onions in my basket—how *onion* is this onion reek in the stiff snowbound air! —and the onions seem much heavier than, in their onion nature, they have any right to be. Later I find that the sly Phu-Tsering has cached two gallons of cooking oil beneath the onions; he giggles gleefully behind me.

Already the snow has lost its edge, and I break through here and there on the ascent: this trip takes a good half hour longer than the first, although an hour less than yesterday. The pass is reached a short time after noon, and Phu-Tsering, first to gaze down into the snow bowl, turns back toward me, his grin of pleasure turning to a frown. "There is Chorch." He sighs. "No porters." Wearily, Dawa and I sit back against bare scree to shed our harness. Far below, Chorch in his bright-blue parka is plodding upward; lower till, Jang-bu rests on a white rock. In full sun, the mountains to the north look less forbidding, but it is clear from the way GS is moving that the route to Shey lies under heavy snow. We gaze down, stupefied, as the hot sweat on our backs turns cold.

Today the thin air and heavy load bother me less than the shining snow, which after two days has cooked my head, eyes, brains, and all—in my addlement, I reel

414

around on the high rim of the world. Phu-Tsering and Dawa are also burned and dizzy—Dawa, despite repeated warnings, is still careless about his eye rag—and as we are hungry after our two climbs, we descend to Snowfields Camp again without waiting for GS and Jang-bu. Though none of us say so, we are all disheartened; this job of moving fourteen loads from Snowfields Camp up over Kang La and down to Shey will have to be finished by just five of us.

In early afternoon, our friends reach camp with their bad tidings: at Shey, there are no porters and no food. The early October storms that held us up in Dhorpatan have been blizzards in these peaks, just as we feared, and the unseasonal snow had caused the people to lock up the Crystal Monastery, abandon Shey, and cross the eastern mountains to Saldang, leaving two women to guard the remnant stores.

GS brings up of his own accord what he refers to as his "curt note" of two days before, explaining that it was so cold and windy at the Kang Pass that he could not write more than bare essentials; he had ordered me to pay off the two Ring-mos because his frozen fingers could not count out money, which might have blown away into Tibet. I admit to him that I didn't care much for the note and offer to say why, but he anticipates my objections, saying that the note meant no criticism of my actions but only recognition that my instincts about the route had been correct, whereas he had held us up by "waiting too long on the wrong mountain." That he wrote it as he did, and that I took it so amiss, he ascribes to the pressure of the days preceding and also to the high-altitude irritability that has ruined so many mountain expeditions. Everything he says rings true to me, and I feel foolish: I recall my first visit to high altitudes, in the Andes, when I was so volatile that any sudden noise inspired fury. Quickly and happily we drop the entire business. We are glad to see each other—and a good thing, too, since in this camp we shall have to share this one small tent—and full of excitement about Shey, for there is good news, too: the blue sheep there are plentiful and tame, and the rut we have come so far to see has scarcely started.

Early tomorrow, if fair weather holds, we shall pack the last five loads up to Kang La, then slide all fourteen down the northern face to a strange black tarn in the bottom of the snow bowl. From there the loads will be moved in relays, three hours downriver to Shey. At Snowfields Camp we shall leave a cairn with food for Tukten and Gyaltsen, and instructions to ignore advice from the denizens of Ring-mo and to push on to Shey; being lightly loaded, they might reach Shey from Snowfields Camp in a half day. If the pass is closed by blizzard, they should try to reach us by a long alternate route, from Murwa by way of Saldang; there are three high passes on that route, say the Shey women, but none of them is so formidable as this one. All else failing, they are to await us at Dunahi.

———

In a dream I am walking joyfully up the mountain. Something breaks and falls away, and all is light. Nothing has changed, yet all is amazing, luminescent, free. Released at last, I rise into the sky. . . . This dream comes often. Sometimes I run, then lift up like a kite, high above earth, and always I sail transcendent for a time before awaking. I *choose* to awake, for fear of falling, yet such dreams tell me that I am a part of things, if only I would let go, and keep on going. "Do not be heavy," Soen Roshi says. "Be light, light, light—full of light!"

In recent dreams, I have twice seen light so brilliant, so intense, that it "woke me up," but the light did not continue into wakefulness. Which was more real, the waking or the dream? The last Japanese character written in this life by Soen Roshi's venerable teacher, and the last word spoken, was the word for "dream."

October 31

Today is the last day of October.

I am tired, and the early climb takes a half hour longer than the climb at the same hour yesterday. At the rim we rest briefly before starting the descent into the blue shadows of the bowl. I plant my stave, then kick a foothold into the snow wall, then move the stick down, kick another step—"Never move more than one thing at a time!" GS calls—until, reaching a point just above a chute of sharp jutting shale, I level a platform for both feet and prepare to receive the loads. Out of the sun, the air is very cold. GS lowers my backpack, then a sack of lentils, then our supply of flour in a big neoprene bag. I work the lentils and the flour over to my right, to a point where they will clear the stretch of shale, then let them fall. The lentils in their squashy sack soon come to rest where the wall becomes steep slope, a hundred yards below, but the slick neoprene bag sails so far down into the bowl, and at such speed, that the Sherpas, whose heads have now appeared over the rim, give it a cheer.

With my backpack, punching with my stick, I descend carefully to the lentils, then keep on going, sliding the rough sack alongside. Even here, the bowl side is so steep that facing the slope on all fours, I am almost upright, and I must kick steps into the hard crust as I go down, to avoid a long and lacerating fall.

The figures above, bringing more loads to the rim, look very small; I see Phu-Tsering make his way down to the platform. Then, from the sky, as the imminent sun shoots cold rays over the ice rim of the Kang, comes a cry of warning.

A load is falling.

Black figures on the sky, a doomsday sun, the blaring ice, and this dark bounding thing, quite small at first, looming larger with each carom as it comes: a load is falling. Clumsy with my pack, I clutch the crust, afraid that any move may be the wrong one, since trajectories of the dark thing are so erratic; I kick desperately at the ice, making a purchase for a leap aside at the last second. Someone yells as the lunging shape strikes the slope above me and takes off again, filling the sky: that it will strike precisely where I lie seems astonishing even in this last hallucinatory second. I leap leftward, and GS's big case—books, spare boots, camera equipment—splits the glazed snow where I had been and whistles downward. I have lost my hold on the slope, and start to fall, but my stave, punched through the crust, comes to my rescue, and I lie spread-eagled, forehead to the snow, gasping for breath. Far above, GS's voice is high, berating Phu-Tsering for his carelessness. Later, when I tease Phu-Tsering ("I thought you were my friend!"), he laughs wildly out of nervousness, saying, "I sorry!"

We hoped to have the loads down to the snow lake by midday, but the warmth and windlessness now work against us. In the steep stretch, the loads slide well upon the crust, even with one man for three loads, but later, when the sun is overhead, they bog down and must be dragged through softening snow. Frequently we sink up to the crotch, and it is midafternoon before the first loads reach the snow lake; the rest lie scattered on the slopes above. GS, on snowshoes, had fared better than the rest of us, but we are all soaked and exhausted.

The sunset behind the steep walls of the bowl will bring instant cold. The Sherpas, unladen, set off rapidly for Shey, although they cannot reach there before dark. Much as I wish to go to Shey this evening, it is folly to set out wet and tired down a tortuous three-hour course of drifts and ice-stream boulders and floes: I say I shall camp here. GS agrees. Although we did not eat at noon, we are too tired to be hungry. And so we bivouac by the strange pond—a depression of black clay where, at this season, snow and ice melt at midday—and share the last tin of sardines, and are huddled in our sleeping bags when darkness comes in the late afternoon.

A sundown wind has died away to utter stillness, and a good thing, too, since the snowbanks all around are deep and dry, all set to drift. GS is a remorseless sleeper, but for me the night will be a long one. I think about the great black eagle that crossed the sky at twilight: this can only be the golden eagle, which I last saw in western mountain lands of North America. Perhaps this eagle is the one that passed over Snowfields Camp at just this time of day. What can it be hunting, this heroic bird, in bitter white waste, at the edge of darkness?

—1978

Galen Rowell

from *In the Throne Room*
of the Mountain Gods

Galen Rowell's (1940–2002) account of the 1975 American expedition to K2 was one of the first brutally honest tell-all climbing exposés. Using excerpts from expedition members' diaries and letters, Rowell provides a multiperspective view on this near disastrous trip, marred as it was by violent arguments, paranoia, irrational behavior, and legal threats. Fred Stanley and Fred Dunham (dubbed the "Freds") threatened to quit the expedition, claiming that leader Jim Whittaker, his twin brother, Lou Whittaker, and Jim Wickwire ("Wick") had formed a secret pact in Seattle to use the other members of the group as packhorses to help the other three make it to the summit. Rob Schaller, Steve Marts, and Leif Patterson were also drawn into the controversy. The expedition was further plagued by continual labor disputes with the Balti porters hired to carry the loads. Lou and Jim Whittaker founded Rainier Mountaineering, Inc., which has guided thousands of people to the summit of Mt. Rainier, and both brothers have been active in environmental causes in the Pacific Northwest. Rowell's account is illustrated throughout with his striking photographs of K2 and little-visited areas of Pakistan. Rowell died in a plane crash while this volume was in preparation.

THE REVOLT

On June 16, I climbed to Camp II with Lou, Wick, Rob, and Steve. Jim and Dianne stayed below to help with the lower end of the winching system up to Savoia Pass. The two Freds were in base camp with Leif, both very subdued after a wild confrontation with the rest of the team. I sympathized fully with their emotions about the expedition, but not with their threats to go home. During the approach, both Freds had been more upset than anyone about the porters' failure to honor their contract when the going got rough. Now, to my way of thinking, they were doing exactly the same thing. We owed it to each other, even if we were no longer friends, to stick together long enough to make a serious attempt on the mountain. Otherwise, many man-years of effort and hope would have been spent in vain.

The Freds believed that the Whittakers and Wickwire formed a conspiracy in Seattle to place themselves on the summit to the exclusion of others. I didn't believe it. The kinds of partnerships that are often called conspiracies are usually nothing more than

Galen Rowell, *In the Throne Room of the Mountain Gods* (San Francisco: Sierra Club Books, 1986). © 1986 by Sierra Club Books. Originally published in San Francisco by Sierra Club Books. Text from pages 234–242 of *In the Throne Room of the Mountain Gods* included by permission of the publishers, Sierra Club Books.

expressions of mutual self-interest. Wick and Lou *seemed* as if they were involved in a conspiracy because each was individually motivated toward the same goal: being first on the summit. Jim recognized them as the winners of a self-styled competition. But if an agreement on the summit team existed beforehand, why had Wick and Lou pushed so hard to prove themselves? If a conspiracy had really existed, why didn't they just take it easy, waiting for Jim to pull them out of a hat after we prepared the lower camps?

Each of us had a slightly different interpretation of the Freds' revolt. Unfortunately, Fred Dunham did not keep a diary, but what follows are the descriptions that the other team members recorded at the time.

Lou Whittaker:

Big crisis today! Last night the Freds talked til midnight and today Stanley says he has *quit* the expedition. Feels he has no say in anything and that Jim and Wick and myself are running the expedition without letting anyone else have a vote. They were both very quiet yesterday after a ribbing that they got when they laughed because Wick and I were turned back from Camp II because of snow. Jim said usually when someone tries to do what we all want, like try to climb the mountain, failure would not be something to delight in. . . . The Freds have been so negative on everything— the country, the coolies, the HAPs, Manzoor, and now the rest of the team. I think a fear of the mountain may have them both stymied.

Dunham said he would carry tomorrow but Stanley may not. . . . He is really in a pout right now like a five-year-old—hard to sympathize with. . . . I didn't think I was being too strong with the Freds, but Wick said we (Jim and I) can tend to bulldoze through problems and can come on very strong.

Rob Schaller:

Two days ago we had a real crisis with the two Freds, both suddenly admitting to being alienated by the Big Three and not feeling a part of the expedition. Stanley believes there is a conspiracy to get the Big Three on the top and we are only coolies to accomplish that purpose. He seems to have transferred his hostilities toward the Baltis to the rest of us. . . . Stanley talks seriously of leaving and I talk with him for hours but to little avail.

Dianne Roberts:

I haven't been able to sort out the thing with the Freds in my own mind. A few days ago they began being deliberately uncommunicative after going to Camp II with Lou and Wick. Then in an odd series of conversations they revealed, first to Galen and Steve, then to Wick and Jim, that they were totally pissed off with the way things were going, that they felt cut off and ignored by the others, that their opinions were being laughed at and a lot of other paranoid bullshit including the accusation that Jim, Wick, and Lou were involved in a conspiracy (hatched in Seattle) to get the three

419

of them to the summit of K2 by employing the forced labor of the rest of the team. Whew. It came as a shock to everyone—both in its content and in its intensity, but it did serve as a catalyst to bring out feelings that have been brewing for weeks. The rest of us (except Leif) sat at Camp I talking about it for most of one afternoon and the next morning. Galen got into it a lot, trying to justify, or at least explain the Freds' outburst in terms of the "autocratic/dictatorial" running of the expedition all along the way. Hell—all kinds of accusations were flung about with rare abandon. But not too much of it made any sense—except the clear revelation that our group has been divided in half all along, with neither half understanding the other since the beginning.

Jim Whittaker:

Stanley is really running off at the mouth. Claims he is going to quit the expedition— that Lou, Wick, and I have a pact, made in Seattle, that the three of us are going to reach the summit of K2 and he is just going to carry for us. Claims no one else will get a chance. He says that I am a dictator, Wick is ignoring everyone else but Lou and I and to hell with everyone.

Manzoor Hussain [in a letter written after the expedition]:

Fighting and quarrels had started between Freds and Lou and Wick. . . . In fact the team had started breaking itself into four sections right from the beginning. Fred Dunham and Fred Stanley formed one section (the extremist left). Lou Whittaker and Jim Wickwire, another (whom everybody called the most ambitious for the peak). Steve Marts, Rob Schaller, Galen Rowell and Leif Patterson formed the third section (the moderate ones). . . . Jim Whittaker and Dianne Roberts formed the fourth section, isolated from whatever was happening in the expedition. Fred Stanley had a bitter quarrel with Jim Whittaker and thought he was amongst foes rather than friends.

Leif Patterson:

The fifteenth opens with a tremendous crisis. Dunham is disgusted with the way things have been going. Stanley wants to quit. They have some poignant reasons. Feel pretty bad, as if expedition is falling apart. . . . Last night Galen had a long talk with the Freds. Very late in the morning some of the party sets off without resolution of the dispute. . . . My line with all I talk to in the team is that we need each other, that we must be honest toward each other. Imagine then, that same evening, just before Rob arrives in Camp I, a radio conversation with Wick in the same camp. Wick instructs Manzoor to send a telegram to Wick's wife, censuring Joanne [Rob's fiancée] for giving personal information about Rob to newspapers—and threatening Joanne with later court action. Why isn't Rob notified? Why isn't telegram sent directly to Joanne?

Where does this information about releases come from up here? This is intrigue behind each others' backs, a real shock to me.

On morning of June 16th, Fred Stanley cuts in on the radio to have it out with Jim Whittaker. He inquires about the telegram, which cannot now be hidden from Rob. Whittaker refuses any discussion. Fred is bitter. But the net result is that the telegram is called off—a good thing.

[After a carry to Camp I] Fred Stanley and I . . . had a talk . . . got along fine. Fred is very strong and very conscientious. Why won't the upper echelons in our team recognize his fine qualities? Fred is deeply disappointed. He came to climb with Wick and Dunham as much as to scale K2—and what has he got from Wick?

Fred loves to needle Whittaker. It is not the right approach. I have a plan: if Camp III gets established, I want the two Freds and myself to take the lead in putting in Camp IV, provided only our health will hold.

My lungs are not clear. . . . This is such a messed-up trip: my own sickness would mean little in a good team of first-rate friends. But the team is an unhappy one. It is nearly split apart from inner tensions. It is my lot to help pull together, unify, and without sufficient health I cannot succeed in that. I believe that you do not remedy a disastrous confidence crisis merely by talking it over. That is a first step. But the crisis was precipitated by cumulative *actions* in the first place, and actions cannot be eradicated by words, only by other actions. I believe we can still overcome difficulties and unify our team by actions which will allow each individual recognition for his efforts, and by honesty. The Wick-Lou summit consideration should be dissolved. Wick should do his job as deputy leader, which would first and foremost be to mend his relations with this close friends: the two Freds and Rob. The summit must be there to tempt all of us, not only a couple of gung-hos. The illness afflicting us as a team is already dangerously far advanced.

Jim Wickwire:

A major new crisis has hit the expedition: the possible defection of the two Freds. The problem has been brooding for some time. Both have felt they have had little involvement in expedition decision-making, that any ideas or comments they have about what should be done are not listened to or are rejected out of hand. Fred Dunham has been in deep gloom since the Manzoor radio incident of the tenth. Last night after dinner Fred D. unloaded to Galen and Steve how unhappy he was that "his friend Jim Wickwire had been distant," and that he was fed up with constantly being put down by Jim. Last night, I could hear both of them talking in subdued voices far into the night. Something serious was up and was confirmed by Galen's relation of his discussion the previous evening with Dunham. Apparently, Stanley felt the same way and there was talk of their leaving the expedition.

I could not accept the assertion that the entire problem was one of a clash of personalities. Granted, Jim has come on a trifle strong at times; Lou, too, but I believe . . . that both of them are intimidated by the mountain and by the time and distance from persons they care a great deal for.

After breakfast, Jim and I went to their tent to talk with them. Jim led off, saying that his principal objective was to get up the mountain and that everything he had done had been directed toward that end. That to reach the summit every person on the team was important and if he stepped on their toes he was sorry. Fred S. remarkably responded: "Nice pep talk, but I don't believe a word you said." I angrily interjected, "That's completely unfair." And so it went, in a very unsatisfactory way, for a few minutes with Jim there and then for another half hour with them alone. . . . Finally I walked away. Just before leaving for Camp I, talked briefly to Fred Dunham, who said he would continue to work for the expedition because of what he felt was an obligation to those persons who had made contributions at his behest. During the discussion with both Freds, I conceded I wanted to get to the top of K2, that was why I was here, and if I didn't make it to the top, I wanted to leave here with no regrets and knowing that I had given everything to the effort of getting there. Curiously, Fred Stanley said that the reason he came on the expedition was because of Fred's and my presence. That's nice, but not a sufficient reason for coming all the way to Pakistan and K2. . . .

Spent the entire afternoon in our tent discussing pros and cons of what to do. Galen, Jim, Dianne, Lou, and Steve. Nothing conclusive, except maybe to offer them the route-finding to Camp III. To me this is an admission we have been wrong. I don't think we have. At least to the extent they think. . . .

Rob . . . spent nearly four hours with the Freds in their tent that afternoon. No startling new allegations. They feel the expedition is divided into two camps: Jim, Lou, and I in one; everyone else in the other. They thought it would be poetic justice if Steve Marts and a Balti got to the summit and none of us did. Or, better yet, and here is a real twist, both Whittakers get to the summit and I don't. These are my friends? . . .

Motivation on any Himalayan expedition is the name of the game. If you don't have a lot of it, you won't put up with what you have to go through to reach the high summit you are striving for. I admit to having very strong motivation for climbing K2. I make no apologies for it. The Whittakers have it. They should not have to make apology for it. Rob and Leif—and I think Galen—also have it. But the Freds don't. That's why I resent and refute the notion this is all some giant put-down of them by us. Of course there have been and will continue to be personality clashes, but to hang it all on that is utter bullshit.

But in the last analysis, I am spending four months in Pakistan because I want to reach the summit of my dream mountain. For various reasons the Freds (particularly Stanley) are opting out. Lou has the same dream I do, and—if the route goes, and if we stay strong—we will go to the summit together. And if we don't, it will not be because we haven't given the effort of our lives.

(Next morning) Things have really gone to hell vis-à-vis Stanley. At 8:00 A.M. he came on the radio and wanted to know the basis for the telegram to Mary Lou. Rob and Steve were in the tent for breakfast, and I hadn't yet told Rob about the telegram, mainly because I was reluctant to compromise Steve as the source. Stanley was insistent, so in Rob's presence, I explained the genesis of the telegram. Rob nodded in understanding. Stanley charged that I had stabbed Rob in the back. There followed one of the most irrational, hate-filled diatribes I have ever heard, directed at Jim and me. He yelled that there was a conspiracy among Jim, Lou, and me to put the three of us on the summit to the exclusion of all the others. . . . There had been discussions about who was strongest in the team . . .—Lou, Jim, and me—but absolutely no pact to put all three of us on the summit. We had simply looked around and concluded that we had greater motivation than the others, except perhaps for Leif and Rob. . . .

A few minutes ago Galen said that on the approach march the other five felt alienated from Jim, Lou, and me, as though we had formed a group with its own ambitions for the summit—that we had not been warm and compatible on the approach. Compatibility is a two-way street, and he would place the entire burden on us to walk the full length of the street. To me, the whole thing is a commentary on the insecurity of the others, an indication of their need to be wet-nursed. I was happy on the approach just to be here in this great country. Why should I have sought out those who did not share my feelings as opposed to one who did—Lou? Friendship is mutuality, not sitting back waiting for your "friend" to come minister to you.

Fred Stanley:

Last evening when I got to camp with Steve, the porters and Manzoor welcomed us, untying our rope and carrying our packs to our tents. A kind of warm glow came over me. I got into my sweater and down vest and wind shirt, got my cup out, and headed for the cook tent. . . .Dinner was ready. I was feeling pretty good and somewhere into the conversation I mentioned that Fred and I could hardy contain ourselves at the irony of Wick and Lou starting out for Camp II the previous *afternoon* and then returning fifteen minutes later (in a snowstorm) after all their noise and valorous talk. That is, I started to mention it and Jim jumped on me, shouting me out, saying how the two Freds were happy about their failures . . . how we're always happy when something goes wrong, how we were happy when he didn't make Camp I from base camp in forty-five minutes as he had bragged he would (this I knew nothing of), etc. I just shut up and slowly finished my dinner. . . .

I am really at a low ebb. I have lost all enthusiasm for the expedition, wishing there was some way out without leaving the rest in the lurch. Each person in this small group counts a lot. The talk this morning is to have Wick and Lou return to the lead with Rob and Galen going to II to set up the winch system. I left earlier when the talk turned to the virtues of the first two fixing the route or not, to finish my cocoa and pancakes in peace away from the sound of the Whittakers' voices drowning out Galen's and even Fred's, I think. . . . Lou and Jim can always shout a little more than the other guy is willing to, knowing it's no use to argue with them, or they can attack

423

him personally, saying his knowledge of fixed lines in Yosemite is of no use here, etc. Jim asked Fred—it sounded like a challenge to me—if he had any objections to Wick and Lou going into the lead again. I really don't give a shit. I was even hoping I would wake up good and sick this morning so I could just have an excuse to lie about—maybe even go down. If I had Alex Bertulis's address I would send him a letter telling him how lucky he was to get off this thing when he did even as he did. A blackballing by Whittaker raises him a notch in my eyes. And I know damn well no one besides Wick, Lou, and perhaps Jim have a chance for the summit. . . .

Wick is sitting on the fence, I think, wanting to stay in good with Jim and Lou, certain that Lou as the leader's brother and he as deputy leader will be the ones for the summit. . . . I hope it's a picket fence and he gets one up the ass. . . .

Jim sent a couple of telegrams . . . saying how we were gouged on the approach but how nice things are going now. . . .

Fred just came in from what he called a psychotherapy session with Galen and Steve. He said they talked over some of the same feelings we've all had. Galen says he's just going to enjoy the company of others and work toward the success of the expedition. I tell Fred that's what I find depressing. The success of the expedition means putting a Whittaker on the summit. . . .

I've never had any great Nazi fervor about climbing K2 as perhaps Wick has. I came on the expedition for enjoyment and have had little. I can still remember Jim saying things will get better when we reach the mountain, the morning Lou threatened Fred at Concordia. They've gotten worse. Galen has struck up a psychoanalysis session with the rest of the group this morning, discussing Fred and me and himself, also. I believe he's found it an opportunity to bring out his problems with the Whittakers and air them— a good catharsis for him. Lou, Wick, and everyone are getting into the act now, psychoanalyzing us. I can't hear it all, actually only a phrase or two, but I sure have to chuckle. It sounds to me like Galen's good intentions of trying to get us treated better, listened to, respected for our positions, not put down every time we open our mouths, are being shouted down.

Wick is talking vehemently. I hear noises about fragile egos, losing a few on Himalayan expeditions, crying in the tent. . . . Fred came back saying the Jims wanted to talk to us. I finally got them to understand I didn't really care to talk about it other than to say I was unhappy with personal relationships and was ready to bail out. Fred said he was ready to stay and do as he was told. . . . Jim made a pep talk and plea that he was doing things as he thought they ought to be done and was only interested in getting the expedition to the summit, and unless I was willing to talk about it there wasn't much he could do. What it boiled down to was he was begging for bodies to stay on; otherwise the expedition had had it. He finally left and Fred talked a little more with Wick, who tried to explain his position and actions, talking about safety, our supposed preoccupation with safety, technique, technical competence. . . . All I could think of was what does this have to do with the Whittakers treating people like shit?

424

I remembered just a minute ago that when I was a kid we used to talk about digging a hole deep enough to come out in China. What reminded me was that I just pissed a hole in the snow. . . . I'd like to jump down it and come out in Washington.

Rob came by earlier and said he tried to keep out of the morning's psychoanalysis and we talked about the situation. He said he's felt out of it—left out by the Big Three ever since Rawalpindi. . . . He seems to think as Galen, that things will get better if we five stick together, that there are or will be changes in the Whittakers. . . . Wick's aloofness to him since getting to Pakistan has hurt him. . . .

I think Wick was pretty shook this morning and I don't blame him, but I haven't laid awake the past two nights for no reason, either. When I replied "you and Fred" to his question of why did I come along on the expedition, he said that was a pretty poor reason. It was enough for me and half that reason is gone now. I don't think I've anything to prove or find out on K2. I was along for an adventure with friends.

A radio call (from Camp I) at 6:00 P.M. while we (Fred, Leif, Manzoor, and I) were finishing dinner: Wick wanted to send out a telegram to Mary Lou (his wife).

WE HAVE REPORTS JOANNE [Rob's fiancée] IS ACTING AS OFFICIAL OR UNOFFICIAL LIAISON WITH NEWS MEDIA REGARDING EXPEDITION MATTERS. SHE IS NOT AUTHORIZED TO DO SO. OUR CONTRACTUAL OBLIGATIONS TO NATIONAL GEOGRAPHIC SOCIETY AND SIERRA CLUB REQUIRE CAREFUL REVIEW BY US OF ALL INFORMATION RELEASED TO NEWS MEDIA. ALTHOUGH WE CANNOT PREVENT JOANNE FROM TALKING TO MEDIA, PLEASE ADVISE SHE FACES LEGAL ACTION IF SHE CONTINUES TO RELEASE FIRST-PERSON DIARY ACCOUNTS OR PHOTOGRAPHS TO MEDIA. OTHERWISE, EVERYTHING FINE. LOVE YOU AND MISS YOU SO.

The threat of legal action caught us by surprise and really floored us. Jim came on to Manzoor and said, "Yes, I think that's something that should be sent." I had looked out the tent door just a few minutes before to see Rob moving (in the distance) up the last slope to Camp I. Fred got on the radio and asked to speak to Jim. Jim Whittaker came on and asked, "Which Jim?" (Wick or Whittaker) and Fred said it didn't matter, he just wanted to find out the source of the rumor. Jim said he thought he'd let Fred talk to Wick, Rob was coming into camp. Wick came on, and without answering the question, said a few words and said the next radio contact would be at eight in the morning and signed off. We sat back shocked. What a stab in the back to Rob. . . . Leif said he just couldn't believe the deceit, the behind-the-back things going on in this expedition. We agreed to make sure in the morning that Rob knew of the telegram. We thought of sending another saying to Joanne this was not an expression of the whole expedition.

We talked on; Fred finally left. . . . Leif kept remarking that the five of us had the power to get the expedition running the way we wanted it. I realized that we could, on our own, stock the camps as high as we wished for as many as we wished. It's his opinion that the summit team will be chosen by expedition vote. . . . During the conversation he managed to impart to me some of his fantastic strength. Enough that I

425

decided to stick around for a while and start being the person I'd like to be in situations like this. . . .

After talking with all the climbers other than the Big Three, I realize they all have many of the same feelings I do, that if there come any corporate votes, it'll be 5 to 4 (corporate votes affecting me brought up by our legal eagle, Wick). . . .

I woke at seven this morning, my mind immediately in high gear—one of those situations when everything is spread before one with perfect clarity. . . . Everything I would have liked to have said to Wick and Jim the previous morning is completely sorted out in my mind now. I am looking forward to the radio contact and tell the others I would like to make it. I also prepared to do a thing I was less than proud of—recording a conversation with others when they didn't know it. Something I wanted as a personal reference . . . something I can present to Wick or Whittakers if things are said which there is going to be a question about. At eight Jim is on. I ask for Wick. He is on. I ask him if he is ready to supply the source of his rumor. In his careful lawyer's voice and words, he replies that it has only just now come to his attention that possibly first-person diary accounts of the expedition have been printed in the Seattle papers. I think he hemmed and hawed before this, saying he wanted to speak to Rob first. At some point he said that before he went further he wanted to know if I was still a member of the expedition in light of the previous day's happenings. I replied that I was still a member of the expedition until I was run out by them the way Alex was. Jim burst in on the conversation somewhere and I told him that he, Wick, and Lou were going to have to quit treating the rest of us as piles of shit into which they could kick their crampons to get a little higher on K2. I also said they should forget about any plans made in Seattle to put them on the summit first; Jim said I was bordering on insanity. Wick finally came back on the radio to speak to Manzoor and told him to cancel the telegram. Fred, Leif, and I spent a while discussing things afterwards, at least relieved by Wick's cancellation of the telegram, but not otherwise very happy.

—1986

Reinhold Messner

from *The Crystal Horizon*

*Climbing solo has become the latest challenge of professional mountaineering. Reinhold Mess-
ner (1944–) is widely recognized as the world's greatest living climber, and he pioneered
alpine techniques on Himalayan mountains involving short, lightweight bursts to the summit
after sufficient acclimatization, rather than months of siege-camping with successive camps. In
1980, Messner became the first mountaineer to climb Everest alone (and without supplemental oxygen), a doubly stunning feat that was not believed possible even by Everest veterans.
Earlier in 1978, he and Peter Habeler were the first to reach the summit of Everest without oxygen, despite warnings from physiologists that they would be unable to sustain themselves at
that altitude without the bottled gas. Messner's controversial solo ascent almost ended prematurely and tragically when, climbing alone and obviously without a rope or companions to rescue him, he fell into a crevasse from which he slowly extricated himself. The journey to the top
was painful for Messner, but it was even more excruciating on the way down.*

The night is tolerable. The storm has abated. In the sleepless intervals endless thoughts
go round and round in my mind. I feel this thinking as something tangible. From the
back of my mind springs one fragment of thought after another, to and fro, like points
of condensed energy, finding no way out, with a life of their own. As if there were an
energy in my field of force which is independent of me. Indeed it belongs to me, but exists without my so much as lifting a finger, without impulse. Even in sleep.

It comes and goes against my will. So it is also with this almost tangible power
around me. A spirit breathes regularly in and out, which originates from nothingness
and which condenses to nothingness. Only somewhere between these extreme forms
do I perceive it, even with my senses.

There is also my plan for tomorrow. Is it possible in "x" hours to climb "y" metres? Over and over again, this question. I answer it irrationally, I answer it emotion-
ally—a game, like the counting of petals—she loves me, she loves me not. Six hundred metres of ascent perhaps? Seven hundred? As far as the "second step"? Then the
weather penetrates my half-wakeful consciousness. The wind has not entirely calmed
down; nevertheless I feel its decrease as something like peace. The quiet before the
storm? The moon shines but still the night is warm. I am no longer freezing. Is the

monsoon break over? Is it still ice crystals the wind hurls against the tent or is it snowing already? If it snows suddenly, and a lot, I shall be able to go neither up nor down. Then I shall be trapped. In my inertia I don't know which I prefer, good weather or snow. What should I do in the case of avalanche danger? How long could I survive here? These questions, to which my imagination knows no answer, and also wants to give no answer, pursue me into my dreams. Again chains of thought without conclusion, independent streams of energy in my mind. Certainly the avalanche danger is a slight higher up but this grainy new snow is like a morass, it not only holds one back, it also saps one. Once exhausted I am lost forever.

As the morning dawns sluggishly I notice that the wind is dropping again. That lends me wings. I manoeuver the gas burner into the sleeping-bag to warm it up. An hour later I am drinking luke-warm coffee. With that I chew the hard, coarse brown bread from South Tyrol again. All the small chores in the constriction and cold of the tent add up to a bodily ordeal. I work with numb fingers; uninterruptedly, hoar-frost trickles from the canvas. To be able to stretch out fully, or to stand up to adjust my clothes is a luxury which I cannot perform in here. Such a tent would weigh at least three times as much as my special construction. Once more I force myself to cook. The dry lumps of snow produce an unpleasant noise between my fingers. It is an eternity before my fist-sized pot is full of water.

For an hour I lie still with my clothes on in the sleeping-bag, drink and doze off. I don't want to look at the time. When I open my eyes I often don't know whether it is morning or evening.

I feel a driving unrest in my innermost being. It is not fear which suddenly seizes me like a big all-embracing hand. It is all the experiences of my mountaineering life which spread out in me and press for activity. The exertion of thirty years of climbing; avalanches, which I have been through, states of exhaustion which have condensed over the decades to a feeling of deep helplessness. You must go on! Time won is energy saved. I know what can happen to me during the next few days, and I know how great the grind will become below the summit. This knowledge is now only endurable in activity.

I must go, and yet each smallest chore is an effort. Up here life is brutally racked between exhaustion and will-power; self-conquest becomes a compulsion. Why don't I go down? There is no occasion to. I cannot simply give up without reason. I wanted to make the climb, I still want to. Curiosity (where is Mallory?), the game (man versus Mount Everest), ambition (I want to be the first)—all these superficial incentives have vanished, gone. Whatever it is that drives me is planted much deeper than I or the magnifying glass of the psychologists can detect. Day by day, hour by hour, minute by minute, step by step I force myself to do something against which my body rebels. At the same time this condition is only bearable in activity. Only a bad omen or the slightest illness would be a strong enough excuse for me to descend.

As the sun strikes my tent and slowly absorbs the hoar-frost from the inner wall I pack up everything again. Bit by bit, in the reverse order to which I must unpack again in the evening. Only two tins of sardines, a gas cartridge as well as half the soup and tea, do I leave behind in a tiny depot, to make my rucksack lighter. I must make do with the remainder of the provisions. It is almost 9 o'clock.

The weather is fine. Tomorrow I shall be on the summit! The moment I crawl out of the tent my confidence is back once more. As if I am breathing cosmic energy. Or is it only the summit with which I identify? The air above me seems to be thin, of that soft blue that looks transparent. The mountains below me I see only as wavy surfaces, a relief in black and white. Take down the tent, fold it up! I command myself. But now these impulses no longer come from the mind, they come again from the gut.

Each drawing of breath fills my lungs with air, fills my being with self-realization. There can be no doubt. I set out on my way. The first 50 metres I go very slowly, then I find my rhythm again. I make good progress. At an avalanche fracture I hesitate. I climb somewhat to the right of the North Ridge; the ground becomes steeper. There is more snow here than down below.

Suddenly the weather worsens. Like massive wedges, grey white cloud formations force themselves over the passes from the south into Tibet. Already the valley bottoms are filled with monsoon mist. Instinctively I keep further to the right. The weather on Everest is often not what it seems. Is it the monsoon or a sudden fall in temperature? Is a storm coming on?

You must have experienced the wind in the region of the summit to know that it can easily sweep people away. Now streaks swim in the sky; this battle with the mountain air makes me nervous. The halts for rest between climbing become longer. Hesitation. Uncertainty. The slopes are not steep, an average 40° perhaps. But above 7,900 metres all terrain is strenuous. Around me the morning air is still clear. Over the Rongbuk Valley, strands of cloud form constantly, shunt as far as the eastern horizon and evaporate.

SISYPHUS ON EVEREST

As always at great height I need a long time today to get the life-giving energy circulating again. It is as if the harmony had been disturbed. Through movement—right foot placed, weighted, released, dragged, left foot . . .—a field of energy develops in my body. After the initial kick-off the sluices open, guy-ropes slacken. With the reduction of anxiety, currents concentrate throughout my body—immeasurable, intangible forms of energy.

On this morning of 19 August I climb for a long time—much longer than normal—with this power dammed up. It is as if something were blocked, not so much to do with the height but with me, so that I scarcely make headway.

Yesterday it was so easy. Now each step is an ordeal. Why am I so slow? The rucksack weighs more heavily, although it has become lighter. I feel myself lost, vulnerable. However, I cannot make myself believe that there is a God who governs this world, who concerns himself with each single one of us. There is no creator outside of me, outside of the cosmos. I don't know when this faith was lost to me, I only know that since then it is more difficult not to feel myself alone and forsaken in this world. The snow lies deeper here. When my boots sink in, an odd noise results: it is as if someone were behind me.

At last I must accept being alone, inevitably alone. In the long stops for breathing something like homesickness comes over me. My need for security overcomes me, and with that I know that all hopes that someone waits for me down below are, like the anxiety before my solo climb, impeding, paralyzing. Only when moving, seeking and seeing does it become possible for me to accept this loneliness.

When I think, the energy at my disposal is quickly used up. With willpower alone I can get no further now but when I disengage my brain I am open to a power from without. I am like a hollow hand and experience a regeneration. The balled fist or outstretched fingers contribute with exhaustion to helplessness. Only when I am like a hollow hand does an invisible part of my being regenerate, not only in sleep, but also in climbing.

The rhythm of climbing—rest is determined by energy, and this energy determines my rhythm. The stops between climbing are already longer than the fifteen paces I make now each time. This is my measure of time, step by step. Time and space are one.

It is so difficult to cope, to take upon oneself all responsibility, not only for one's actions, but also for being here at all, especially if the whole body is desperate through exertion. In spite of the risk freely entered into I cannot, like Wilson, entrust myself wholly to a God. To what, then? During the ascent I am like a walking corpse. What holds me upright is the world around me: air, sky, earth, the clouds which press in from the West. The experience of proceeding one step at a time. The sense of one's will as something tangible prior to the last two paces before resting. The terrain is easy. Nevertheless it demands my whole attention. That I can stand, that I can proceed, gives me energy to think ahead, to want to get ahead. At least as important as success is joy at one's own skill. It is astonishing how often I have overlooked this part of the pleasure of climbing and have talked solely of loads carried to the summit. High altitude climbing requires a whole range of proficiencies, knowledge and inventiveness. The higher you go, the more man himself becomes the problem. Ability also to solve problems of this sort is what makes a good climber. I see the usefulness of climbing not in the further development of technique, rather in the development of the instinct and proficiency of man to extend himself. Learning about his limitations is just as important as his claim to be able to do anything.

With my snail-like advance I have lost the ability to estimate distance. Also sense of time. Am I about to break down? As I once said, the development of the self is part of my motive, yet what constitutes development when comparisons cannot be made? If I am frequently said to have a compulsion to succeed, this is characteristic of the people of today, for whom experience of an effort, and not the learning process itself, is what counts. He who only perceives his body as a vehicle for success cannot understand me, can not follow my thoughts. I carry on—without calculating or anticipating how far I have got. This climbing, resting, breathing has become a condition which completely absorbs me. It is merely movement along a fixed line. The forward-thrusting impulse in climbing is often referred to as aggression; I prefer to call it curiosity or passion. Now all that has gone. My advance has its own dynamic force, fifteen paces, breathe, propped on the ski sticks which are inwardly and upwardly adjusted. With the knowledge that God is the solution. I confess that in moments of real danger something acts as a defense mechanism; it aids survival, but evaporate as soon as the threat is past. I am not at this moment under threat. It is all so peaceful here around me. I am not in any hurry. I cannot go any faster. I submit to this realization as to a law of Nature.

My altimeter shows 7,900 metres. But altimeters have the capacity to become inaccurate up high. Generally they show less than the actual height. It is also possible that the air pressure has altered during the night. I no longer take the altimeter seriously.

The weather is still fine, and I want to go on. Retreat no longer comes to mind. About 100 metres above the campsite I decide that climbing up the ridge is becoming too dangerous. Also too strenuous, for there the snow lies partially knee-deep. All the hollows are filled in. And above me a single giant-sized trough. Not only the avalanche danger, but the exertion above deters me. A feeling of hopelessness grips me as I poke the right ski stick into the floury mess. Snow slab danger! The topmost layer is firm but gives way with a crack when I step on it. Underneath the snow is grainy. On my own, under these conditions, I would quickly tire myself out.

Then I see that on the North Face the snow slabs have gone. What luck! There the foundation is hard. Yes, that's the way! Without thinking much I begin to cross the North Face. Instinctively, as if pre-programmed, I want to get to the Norton couloir and to climb it tomorrow to the summit. The traverse of the North Face extends a long way, and gains little height, but is good going in the firm monsoon snow. I don't need the ice axe; leaning on the ski sticks I cross the slope. The rucksack with the tent, which I have tied on outside so that it can dry, is still heavy. At almost 8,000 metres even standing with this rucksack on my back is an exertion. Without the ski sticks I would stagger, collapse. I rest like a four-legged creature; in this way the weight of the rucksack does not constrict my breathing.

When I continue again, I do it likewise, largely bending forward, having also shortened the ski stick in my left hand which is on the uphill side. I have completely given up counting my steps; I have not the inclination or strength to take any pictures. Rhythmically—go—rest—I progress like a snail. And out of this progress energy flows to me; it suffices exactly to maintain this rhythm.

The terrain is inclined and rolling. The stretch as far as the great snow couloir seems short. Without asking myself how many dips must lie between me and my planned bivouac spot I climb unhesitatingly upwards. My confidence grows. I no longer feel the loneliness as isolation, much more as detachment. The bridge of wife and friends, the embodiment in a community—supports which I need—I experience now for what they are: aids to endure the awareness of loneliness.

I am now directly under the "first step." Above me projects a blunt flat-topped buttress shaped like a sickle. It is snowed up, and to the right of it stands an unfriendly steep wall, dark; snow lies only on some of its ledges. The rock outcrops in the monsoon snow increase. With that my perception grows of already having been here before—do I know this route?

What disquiets me is the weather. No wind. The sun burns. Clouds press in from the south. Like wedges they push their grey white masses northwards. Yes, there is no doubt; the monsoon storms are sending out their scouts.

Nevertheless I climb on determinedly. Always upwards to the right. I stop in exact line with the summit; or what I take to be the summit—the final point up there is presumably invisible—makes no overpowering impression on me. I stand close under the North-East Ridge and the route appears flattened.

The view too is restricted: on one side by the mass of the mountain, on the other by the rising cloud ceiling. The North peak appears now flat and small; it separates the mist welling up from the valley. Only after longer rest stops am I capable of such observations. Between the North Ridge and the Norton Couloir I am standing on a mountain side which has no equal in the Alps. A slanting trapezium, two and a half kilometres high and almost a kilometre wide.

I progress so slowly! How long my pauses to breathe are each time I don't know. With the ski sticks I succeed in going fifteen paces, then I must rest for several minutes. All strength seems to depend on the lungs. If my lungs are pumped out I must stop. I breathe in through my mouth and expel the air through mouth and nose. And while standing I must use all my will-power to force my lungs to work. Only when they pump regularly does the pain disappear, and I experience something like energy. Now my legs have strength again.

I took the spontaneous decision to follow the North flank of Mount Everest even though I wanted to be on the look-out for signs of Mallory and Irvine. But I do not resent my change of plan, not only because there is so much snow, but also because I know of their failure. I am on the best route to the summit. The going is at times tiring, at times agony, it all depends on the snow conditions. The downward-sloping slabs luckily lie buried beneath a layer of névé and up to now I have been able to go round all the rock outcrops. I can see the North-East Ridge above me, but know that at the moment nothing of the pioneers can be found there. Mallory and Irvine climbed along this ridge, exactly on its edge. That is no guess. I am convinced that Odell saw them on the "first step," on that knob which rises out of the line of the ridge. I know now that they failed on the "second step." In the deep trough above me Mallory and Irvine lie buried in the monsoon snow. This hunch absorbs me like an old fairy tale and I can think about it without dread.

It is as if I saw now the origin of a legend, as if I have perceived the truth. The observations of the Chinese climber Wang in 1974, who told the Japanese Hasegawa of his discovery five years later before an avalanche killed him below the North Col, appear now just as struck from my memory as the contradictory descriptions of the two steps. "First" and "second step" now lie above me. There Mallory and Irvine live on. The fate of the pair is now free from all speculation and hopes. It is alive in me. I cannot tell whether I see it as on a stage or in my mind's eye. At all events it is happening in my life—as if it belongs to it.

Close up, the "second step" appears to overhang. Only a little snow adheres to it. No, without pitons and ladders like the Chinese installed it is literally impossible to climb over it. Likewise today. A few months back the Japanese climber Kato also used the climbing aids left behind by the Chinese.

Between the two steps, therefore, Mallory and Irvine are presumed dead, without previously having reached the summit. I don't ask myself how they died, I only see them turn back. Mallory and Irvine, decades-long legends, live for me forever up there, and not just in Odell's words.

Disappointed and exhausted they turn round below the "second step." In the failing daylight the difficulties increase. The two force themselves to make the laborious descent. They get slower and slower. Night falls. Only energy from success could have saved them. The vision fades. How the pair died can not be answered until someone finds Mallory's body or the camera which Somervell had lent him. Perhaps it can never be answered conclusively. That the two of them did not reach the summit is for me, however, beyond doubt.

After a longer rest my breathing is quiet and regular. Is that someone talking nearby? Is somebody there? Again I hear only my heart and my breathing. And yet there they are again. In this silence each sound, each atmosphere-drowning noise sounds like a spoken word. I jump frequently because I believe I hear voices. Perhaps it is Mallory and Irvine? With my knowledge of the circumstances surrounding their disappearance, which has occupied me many years, now each noise brings a vision alive in me. At any rate I believe sometimes that it is their calls which a breath of wind carries to me or takes away. But I do not recognize their voices for I have never tried to imagine them. So, do Mallory and Irvine really live on? Yes, their spirit is still there—I sense it distinctly.

I gaze at the "second step" and already two beings fill my imagination, release phantoms; in the driving mist everything seems so near, ghostly. In spite of my tiredness I stare up again and again at the knife-edge above me. The "second step" rears closer. A relatively easy snow gully leads to a steep groove. Quite distinctly I perceive a barrier at the top. At this moment I do not know that in May 1980 Yasuo Kato and Susumi Makamura took forty minutes over the "second step." I see the real proof that Mallory and Irvine, with their comparatively primitive equipment, failed there in 1924.

Because the swelling mist envelops everything and because I am exhausted by the climbing, everything around me disappears. With my eyes hurrying on ahead a few metres, I look for the way to go. Brightness pierces me when the sun breaks through the clouds: flashing snow crystals move past me like water from a spring.

In spite of the gloomy snowy waste around me which ebbs and flows with the pulsating clouds, I feel no panic. I know the route. And the track behind me is still there. True, it is snowing lightly, but it is warm. I approach the Norton Couloir over enormous, gentle waves—I have two behind me already. I can't see it, I only sense it.

433

Nevertheless I am not for a moment afraid of being too high. Is it the tiredness which makes me indifferent, or is it this feeling of knowing the way that gives me the assurance of a sleepwalker?—I am convinced that all is well.

Every time I cross a rib there are more lumps of rock. In a row above and below me they make a sort of border. Far above and far below they disappear into the mist. These are the rock islands which show me the way. Like cairns they all have a definite form and each dark speck has a meaning, each gives support to my eyes and to me. Meanwhile the mists around me have become so dense that the sun only now and then breaks through. Direction-finding becomes more difficult. Sometimes the breathless silence after resting fills me for a few moments with terror. Have I already gone too far? When the silence becomes unbearable I have to continue climbing. Always obliquely upwards. The pounding in my body and the gasping for breath after each ten paces lets me forget the emptiness about me. For a pain-filled eternity there is nothing at all. I exist only as a mind above a body. While resting I literally let myself fall: with my upper body leaning on the ski sticks, the rucksack tipped on to the nape of my neck, I go through a period of only breathing out and breathing in. Then I perk up again, and with the first step experience the exertion of the next section. Onward!

Sometimes I feel as if I am stuck in the snow. Nevertheless, I don't let myself get discouraged. I move continually to the right up the North Face. The whole face is like a single avalanche zone. New snow trickles down from above and it is sleeting. I tell myself that it is only a temporary disturbance; the snow will consolidate itself. "It will hold for two days yet," I say to myself.

The ascending traverse continues endlessly with many but regular pauses. Because of the exertion and concentration I have not noticed that the weather has become so bad that I ought to turn back. All around everything is covered in mist. I squat and rest. Perhaps I should put up the tent. The spot seems too insecure to me. I must bivouac on a ridge. If it snows any more that means avalanche danger. These are not rational thoughts, but come from the instincts which lie deep within me. For at least another hour I force myself on still further. On a blunt elevation which runs across the face like a giant rib I squat down again. For awhile I feel only heaviness, indifference, numbness. Then the clouds tear themselves apart. The valley appears: grey, lightly covered in snow, soon masked again by mists. Not only do the mountains seem flattened, also the slopes beneath me and the snow shield in the big couloir. I see all that with the feeling of no longer belonging to the world below. When I notice it is 3 o'clock in the afternoon, it sinks in: I am still about 200 metres to the east of the Norton couloir. When I then peer at the altimeter it shows 8,220 metres. I am disappointed. It's more than that surely! It's not only that I would be delighted to have got as far as 8,400 metres, but that I have exerted myself much more than yesterday. It is misty and snows lightly, I can't go any further today. And yet that is an evasion; I do not know whether there is a bivouac place higher up.

I am dead tired. Conscious of this I scarcely make it to the next rocks. Earlier than planned I erect my tent. On a rock bollard, safe from avalanches—snow slides would branch off to the left and right of it—I find a 2 by 2 metre big, almost flat surface. While I make the snow firm I remain standing up. I ask myself how I shall find my way back if the weather stays like this. This doubt and the knowledge of all that can happen condenses into fear. Only when I work am I inwardly at peace. The quiet light snowfall, the stationary clouds, the warmth, all that is sinister to me. Is it the monsoon or only anxiety? A fall in temperature is on the way, it seems to me. If I cannot get back for days my reserves will be soon used up. The avalanche danger on the North Face and below the North Col grows with every hour.

An hour later my tent is standing on the rock outcrop. Once again I anchor it with ice axe and ski sticks. I can camp here protected from the wind. Also, if there is a storm there is scarcely any danger. I place the open rucksack in front of the tent flap, and push the mat in. Lumps of snow for cooking lie ready to hand. All is prepared for the long night. A feeling of relief comes over me.

I take only two pictures then abandon photography again. It takes too much energy to take the camera out of the rucksack, walk away ten paces, rest, press the self-release. Then I must go back. And for what? Documentary proof, reports, all that has become meaningless. It seems to me much more important that I make myself something to drink.

Tonight I keep my clumsy, double-layered plastic boots near all my clothing; they must not be allowed to become cold. I sense my clothes as something alien. The layers between skin and outer covering feel like unpleasant stuffy air; hence the feeling of being in a strait-jacket. While I lie in the tent—too tired to sleep, too weak to cook—I try to imagine advanced base camp. Nena will now be making tea. Or is she looking straight up here? Has it cleared up meanwhile? Perhaps the weather is improving. Time passes too fast and too slowly. Only when I mange to switch off completely does it cease to exist.

On the evening of this 19 August Nena writes in her diary:

It is 8 P.M. and twilight invades the narrow glacier valley. The snow began suddenly and still continues to fall. I could not see Reinhold the whole day. But I know that he is up there, perhaps somewhere in the vicinity of the "second step." Tomorrow, he will go to the summit. Hopefully the weather will improve again. The heavy black clouds came from nowhere, towering up, splitting snow and sleet. What does it mean? I can do nothing but think of him constantly. If this flurrying doesn't stop, he is lost. How much snow has fallen? How dangerous are the avalanches up there? How difficult is the descent in new snow? How long will it take him back to the North Col? Somehow I am sure that Reinhold will do only what is right.

But there is something incalculable in this man. His whole being is possessed, is energy, action. I am anxious, but I don't mind. Above all I am vexed because the weather is playing him such a dirty trick. That's unfair. I sit in the empty tent and force myself to eat and drink. I try to read about medicine and inflammation of the lungs. But my thoughts are up there in the whirling snow. I am madly excited and

435

sad, both at once. I keep repeating the traditional Tibetan prayer "Om mani padme hum," over and over again.

When it gets dark I put on something warm and venture outside. Didn't I just know it? The 7,000 metre peaks are clearing, the clouds melting away. The wind is coming up. It drives the new snow off the ridges. I shout and scream. He does not hear me, cannot hear me. Nevertheless I speak to him: "I am with you!"

———

How does one live at this height? I am no longer living, I am only vegetating. When one must do everything alone each manipulation takes a lot of willpower. With each job I notice the effect of the thin air. Speed of thought is greatly diminished and I can make clear decisions only very slowly. They are influenced by my tiredness and breathing difficulties. My windpipe feels as if it were made of wood, and I am aware of a slight irritation of my bronchial tubes.

Although I have not been able to prepare any really hot drinks, because water boils at a lower temperature on account of the height, I still keep on melting snow. Pot after pot. I drink soup and salt tea. It is still too little. I am not very hungry. I must force myself to eat. Also I don't know what to eat without making myself sick. Should I open this tin of sardines now or something else? The slightest efforts require time, energy and attention. All movements are slow and cumbersome. I decide on cheese and bread, chicken in curry sauce, a freeze-dried ready to serve meal which I mix with lukewarm water. I stick the empty packet under the top of my sleeping bag. I shall need it during the night to pee in. It takes me more than half an hour to choke down the insipid pap. Outside it gets darker. The many small tasks in the bivouac take as much energy as hours of regular climbing. The difference between arriving at a prepared camp, to be cared for by Sherpas or comrades, and evening after evening having to make camp and cook for oneself is tremendous. Perhaps it is the essential distinction between the classic big expedition and the modern small expedition. Going to sleep is by itself a big exertion. Up here I cannot simply get into bed, stick my head under the covers and fall asleep.

Once more I sit up in my sleeping-bag. First I loosen my boots. Tomorrow morning I want to have warm feet and boots not frozen stiff. So I first change my socks, then pull my boots on again. Once more I push feet and boots right back into the sleeping bag. I throw away the damp socks. Then, outstretched, propped up on my arms, I stick the rucksack under the mat as a pillow. I arrange the cooking equipment so that I can get at it next morning from the sleeping-bag. Constantly I have to shift my body a little and keep my head up, not in order to sleep well, but only to be able to endure the night.

These movements in the narrow tent make me breathless. I am forced to breathe deeply. In between, I pant again. I have had numb fingers for hours. In spite of the occasional slumber of exhaustion—an inadvertent dozing—I cannot fall asleep properly during the night. I am endless like the night.

436

In the morning I am just as tired as the evening before, and stiff as well. I ask myself whether I really want to go on. I must! Then I use the little strength I have to move my body. I know well enough from experience that I can still carry on for a time, but I try to push everything aside—to think of nothing, to prolong a deliberate state which allowed me to endure the whole night.

I have only to get going and keep moving in order to have some energy again. The will to make the first decisive move still fails me. When I open the tent flap this morning, it is already day outside. A golden red glow bathes the summit pyramid; to the east, fields of clouds stretch away into the distance. Automatically I remember the monsoon. It is an eternity before I hold the first pot of warm water between my hands. There is ice lying in the tent. I can't eat anything.

While I fish lumps of snow into the tent I peer up into the Norton Couloir. Fairly steep. Smoky grey clouds cling to the mountain sides. The air is glassy, as if it were full of moisture. I feel a bit chilly in spite of the favourable temperature. Ice by the rocks and tent! However, cold is no problem on Mount Everest during the monsoon period. I am sure that it thaws in high summer when it is windless and misty, even on the summit. My three layers of clothing—silk, pile suit, thin down suit—are sufficient when almost undone.

Two years ago in May 1978 I endured up to minus 40°C. at night. Now it is minus 15°C. maximum, perhaps only minus 10°C. Nevertheless I must not be careless. As long as the sun is not shining I wear gloves, fasten my boots loosely. At this height a few degrees below zero can cause frostbite. I think only of going on. As if retreat, failure, had never crossed my mind. But what if the mist becomes thicker? Ought I to wait a bit? No, that is senseless. In any case I am already very late. I must get outside. At this height there is no recovering. By tomorrow I could be so weak that there would not be enough left for a summit bid. It's now or never. Either—or. I must either go up or go down. There is no other choice.

Twice whilst melting snow I take my pulse. Way above 100 beats per minute. I feel all in. No more trains of thought. Only commands in the mind. The night was one long ordeal. Painful joints, mucous in my throat. Morning is depressing. On this 20 August I leave everything behind: tent, ski sticks, mat, sleeping-bag. The rucksack too stays in the tent. I take only the camera with me. So just as I am I crawl out of the tent, draw my hood over my head and with bare fingers buckle crampons on to my boots. I retrieve only the titanium axe from the snow. Have I got everything? It must be after 8 o'clock already. Without the load on my back things are easier. But I miss the ski sticks as balancing poles. With the short ice axe in my right hand I feel secure, certainly, but for traversing it is a poor substitute.

Only when I climb directly upwards do my gloved left hand and the ice axe fumble about in the snow beneath my head. I proceed on all fours. While resting I distribute my whole weight so that the upper part of my body remains free. I kneel in the snow, lay my arms on the rammed-in ice axe and put my head on this cushion. I can still survey the steep rise above me, orientate myself, weigh up difficulties.

437

Fortunately an uninterrupted snow gully runs up the Norton Couloir. So long as I can see and plod I am confident.

Once, before I reach the bottom of the broad trough, I look out for a longer rest possibility. The tent, a yellow speck, appears as through a weak magnifying glass. Is that only the light mist or are all my senses fooled? I remember the place and then climb up the rise above me to the right. Pace by pace. Step by step. Already after a short while I miss the rucksack like a true friend. It has let me down. For two days it has been my partner in conversation, has encouraged me to go on when I have been completely exhausted. Now I talk to the ice axe. But a friend is little enough in this state of exposure. Nevertheless, the voices in the air are there again. I don't ask myself where they come from. I accept them as real. Lack of oxygen and insufficient supply of blood to the brain are bound up with it, are certainly the cause of these irrational experiences which I got to know two years ago during my solo ascent of Nanga Parbat. Up here in 1933 Frank Smythe shared his biscuits with an imaginary partner.

The rucksack has indeed been my companion. But without it things go easier, much easier even. If I had to carry something now I would not make any progress. I decided to make the ascent because I knew that on this last day I could leave everything behind. In the driving clouds, following my instinct more than my eyes I look for the route step-by-step. Again the distant memory of this couloir. I live in a sort of half-darkness of mist, clouds, snow drifts and recognition of individual sections. I was here once before! A feeling that even lengthy reflection cannot dispel.

An hour above camp I come up against a steep step about 100 metres high. Or is it 200 metres towering up in front of me?

The climbing is made easy by the snow. My whole foot always finds a hold without the crampons hitting the rocks. For hours repeatedly expending oneself, dying, bracing oneself, exerting one's will, letting oneself fall, collecting oneself. The rock islands to left and right of the great gully are yellowish with brighter streaks here and there. Often I see everything double and am uncertain where I should go. I keep more to the right. The slope is now so steep that I rest in the climbing position.

I literally creep along now. Only seldom do I manage to do ten paces without stopping to gasp for air. The view disappoints me. Yesterday morning it was still impressive. Now when I look down on the long glacier with the moraine ridges everything appears flat. The landscape is blunted, deadened by the new snow. Despite the swelling mist I lose all feeling of distance.

Light powder snow on a semi-firm base here. The rock slabs underneath, lying one on another like roof tiles, are approximately as steep as a church roof, and are almost completely snow covered. I leave the gully where it becomes wider and forms a pear-shaped bay. I take bearings on a blunt ridge up to the right. The going must be easier there.

It is getting steeper. When I move I no longer pound like a locomotive, I feel my way ahead hesitatingly. Jerkily I gain height. This climbing is not difficult but downright unpleasant. Often I can find no hold in the snow and must make out the steps by touch. I cannot afford to slip here. For the first time during this solo ascent I feel in danger of falling, like increased gravity. This climbing carefully with great concentration increases my exhaustion. Besides, the mist interferes more and more. All I see is a piece of snow in front of me, now and then a prospect of blue sky above the ridge. Everything goes very slowly. In spite of the enormous strain which each step upwards requires, I am still convinced that I shall get to the top, which I experience now in a sort of anticipation, like a deliverance.

The knowledge of being half-way there in itself soothes me, gives me strength, drives me on. Often I am near the end of my tether. After a dozen paces everything in me screams to stop, sit, breathe. But after a short rest I can go on. Worrying about the bad weather has cost me additional energy. And the ever-recurring question of the descent. But simultaneously in the thickening mist I experience an inspiring hope, something like curiosity outside of time and space. Not the demoralizing despair which a visible and unendingly distant summit often triggers. It is now all about the struggle against my own limitations. This becomes obvious with each step; with each breath it resolves itself. The decision to climb up or down no longer bothers me. It is the irregular rhythm, the weakness in the knees. I go on like a robot. Against all bodily remonstrances I force myself upwards. It must be! I don't think much, I converse with myself, cheer myself up. Where is my rucksack? My second friend the ice axe is still here. We call a halt.

The way up the Norton Couloir is logical and not so difficult as I expected. I shall find my way back. When I reach the blunt rib above I should be able to see the summit. If the cloud breaks. Up there it seems to be flatter.

The fancy to have climbed here once already constantly helps me to find the right route. The steep step shot through with brightly coloured rock lies beneath me. I still keep to my right—not so long ago an avalanche went down here. The snow bears. Under the blunt ridge it becomes deeper, my speed accordingly slower. On hands and knees I climb up, completely apathetic. My boots armed with crampons are like anchors in the snow. They hold me.

As I stand on the rib I hear the wind amongst the stones. Far below this rock rib continues as a buttress. For a short while the mist is so thick that I can no longer orientate myself visually. I continue somewhat further along the rib, where the least of the snow lies. For an hour. Until a dark vertical rock wall bars the way above me. Something in me draws me to the left, I pass the obstacle, and continue still keeping to the right. How long? My only adversary is the slope, time no longer exists. I consist of tiredness and exertion.

I guess myself to be near the top but the knife edge goes on for ever. During the next three hours I am aware of myself no more. I am one with space and time. Nevertheless I keep moving. Every time the blue sky shows through the thick clouds I believe I see the summit, am there. But still there are snow and stones above me. The few rocks which rise out of the snow are greeny-grey, shot through here and there with brighter streaks. Ghostlike they stir in the wispy clouds. For a long time I traverse

439

upwards, keeping to the right. A steep rock barrier bars the way to the ridge. Only if I can pass the wall to the right shall I get any higher.

Arriving on the crest of the North-East Ridge I sense the cornices, stand still. Then I lie down on the snow. Now I am there. The ridge is flat. Where is the summit? Groaning I stand up again, stamp the snow down. With ice axe, arms and upper body burrowing in the snow, I creep on, keeping to the right. Ever upwards.

When I rest I feel utterly lifeless except that my throat burns when I draw breath. Suddenly it becomes brighter. I turn round and can see down into the valley. Right to the bottom where the glacier flows. Breathtaking! Automatically I take a few photographs. Then everything is all grey again. Completely windless.

Once more I must pull myself together. I can scarcely go on. No despair, no happiness, no anxiety. I have not lost the mastery of my feelings, there are actually no more feelings. I consist only of will. After each few metres this too fizzles out in an unending tiredness. Then I think nothing, feel nothing. I let myself fall, just lie there. For an indefinite time I remain completely irresolute. Then I make a few steps again.

At most it can only be another ten metres up to the top! To the left below me project enormous cornices. For a few moments I spy through a hole in the clouds the North Peak far below me. Then the sky opens out above me too. Oncoming shreds of cloud float past nearby in the light wind. I see the grey of the clouds, the black of the sky and the shining white of the snow surface as one. They belong together like the stripes of a flag. I must be there!

Above me nothing but sky. I sense it, although in the mist I see as little of it as the world beneath me. To the right the ridge still goes on up. But perhaps that only seems so, perhaps I deceive myself. No sign of my predecessors.

It is odd that I cannot see the Chinese aluminum survey tripod that has stood on the summit since 1975. Suddenly I am standing in front of it. I take hold of it, grasp it like a friend. It is as if I embrace my opposing force, something that absolves and electrifies at the same time. At this moment I breathe deeply.

In the mist, in the driving of the clouds I cannot see at first whether I am really standing on the highest point. It seems almost as if the mountain continues on up to the right. This tripod, which rises now scarcely knee-high out of the snow, triggers off no sort of euphoria in me. It is just there. Because of the great amount of snow on the summit it is much smaller than when I saw it in 1978; pasted over with snow and unreal.

In 1975 the Chinese anchored it on the highest point, ostensibly to carry out exact measurements. Since then they state the height of their Chomolungma is 8,848.12 metres. I don't think of all that up here. This artificial summit erection doesn't seem at all odd. I have arrived, that's all that matters! It's gone 3 o'clock.

Like a zombie, obeying an inner command, I take some photographs. A piece of blue sky flies past in the background. Away to the south snow cornices pile up, which seem to me to be higher than my position. I squat down, feeling hard as stone. I want only to rest a while, forget everything. At first there is no relief. I am leached, completely empty. In this emptiness nevertheless something like energy accumulates. I am charging myself up. For many hours I have only used up energy. I have climbed myself to a standstill, now I am experiencing regeneration, a return flow of energy.

A bleached shred of material wrapped round the top of the tripod by the wind is scarcely frozen. Absentmindedly I run my fingers over it. I undo it from the metal. Ice and snow remain sticking to it. I should take some more pictures but I cannot brace myself to it. Also I must get back down. Half an hour too late means the end of me. At the moment I am not at all disappointed that once again I have no view. I am standing on the highest point on earth for the second time and again can see nothing. That is because it is now completely windless. The light snowflakes dance and all around me the clouds swell as if the earth were pulsating underneath. I still don't know how I have made it but I know that I can't do any more. In my tiredness I am not only as heavy as a corpse, I am incapable of taking anything in. I cannot distinguish above and below.

Again a shred of blue sky goes by with individual ice crystals shining in the sun. The mountains appear far below and quite flat, between the black-white of the valleys. This time I am too late with the camera. Then clouds, mist again; now their primary colour is violet.

Is night coming on already? No, it is 4 P.M. I must be away. No feeling of sublimity. I am too tired for that. And although I don't at this moment feel particularly special or happy, I have a hunch that in retrospect it will be comforting, a sort of conclusion. Perhaps a recognition that I too shall have to roll that mythical stone all my life without ever reaching the summit; perhaps I myself am this summit. I am Sisyphus. . . .

—1989

Deb Piranian

"Reflections on My First Expedition"

Deb Piranian's (1951–) interest in climbing began when she received a copy of Maurice Herzog's book Annapurna *for her tenth birthday. She moved to Washington State for graduate school and to finally begin mountaineering. Washington, California, and Canada became her playgrounds for kayaking, mountaineering, and rock climbing. After receiving her Ph.D. in Slavic Linguistics, she started working for Outward Bound, concentrating on women's courses, wilderness therapy, and international courses in the former Soviet Union. After many years of working as a psychotherapist, Deb shifted to working within organizations doing leadership and team development training along with training on the "human side" of business. Some of Deb's more memorable climbs include the attempt on Mt. Kongur and Denali, as well as a successful ascent (under adverse conditions) of The Nose on El Capitan with another woman. She currently spends most of her climbing time on rocks throughout the Southwest.*

One night in January 1986, I was aroused from a deep sleep in my Leadville, Colorado, home by the phone's ringing.

"Hello, Deb? This is Nancey Goforth in Alaska. Do you remember me? Did I wake you up?"

"Ya," I answered, still mostly asleep. "I have to get up really early tomorrow for work." I had two part-time jobs, one as an instructor for Colorado Outward Bound, the other as a lift operator at a ski area. I had to be up by 5 A.M.

"Well, I won't keep you. Let's set another time to talk."

"How about Friday morning; I'll be home."

"OK. But just so you know what I'm calling about, I was wondering whether you'd be interested in an all-women expedition to China this summer. Anyway, we can talk on Friday. Bye."

By the time I had crawled back into bed, I was wide awake. China! A women's expedition! It was only Tuesday.

For the next few days, thoughts of China and the expedition permeated all my waking hours. I was on a continual adrenaline rush. Sitting still was impossible. My mind raced: "What gear would I need? What kind of training program should I start?" I was motivated to go to the gym, even after long days of work outside. I stayed up later than usual and did not mind early mornings.

I wanted to go, but had fears and hesitations. My partner, Jeff, and I had made major climbing plans for the summer. I did not like backing out on those. He pointed out that our plans could happen any time, but the expedition was a rare opportunity. Then came the internal doubts. I had been climbing for years, but the last three had been devoted mostly to rock. Although I had spent extended periods of time in the mountains, I had never been on a major expedition. Did I have sufficient skills? I needed to share these doubts with Nancey to see whether she still thought me a worthwhile member. She did.

That short, late-night conversation led to my involvement in the 1986 Women's Expedition to Mt. Kongur (25,325 feet) in China. The highest peak in the Pamir Mountains, a northwest range of the Himalayas, Mt. Kongur had only been climbed once, in 1981 by four British climbers.

In March, the whole team gathered for the first time in Colorado. The goals of the meeting included teambuilding, logistics and having fun outdoors together. I was nervous and excited as I drove to the gathering. I had met only two of the women in person. One was Nancey Goforth. We had met in Seattle several years before to talk about Outward Bound and we had numerous acquaintances in common. Because of her non-sporty dress, people seldom guessed that she had been on many expeditions, including a first ascent. At our gathering she told us that colleagues in her nursing program in Anchorage found out about her mountaineering life only after she started selling T-shirts for our expedition. The other woman I had met was Pat Dillingham. I felt comfortable with her. She worked in corporate training and was focused and organized. She turned out to be the primary one to keep us on task in the many meetings throughout the expedition.

I had talked with Kath Giel, the expedition leader, on the phone, but had never met her. At the meeting she struck me as friendly, enthusiastic and organized. At the time she worked for a utility company in California.

By the end of the gathering, I had some sense of the other women. Joan Provencher, a house painter from California, was quiet and looked strong. Nancy Fitzsimmons, from Idaho and an instructor for both the National Outdoor Leadership School and Outward Bound, was practical and down to earth. Our base camp manager, Suzanne Hopkins from Massachusetts, was a political activist. It was she who questioned seeking donations from companies that had political dark sides.

The other two women were from Colorado. Carole Petiet, a psychologist, was in charge of the psychological research we planned to undertake. Her tall, slender build belied the strength she would show on the mountain. The March gathering was at her home. Kathy Nilsen was a nurse in Aspen. She was an infinite source of humor, something I came to value dearly. When events seemed bleak in China, she could make us laugh, putting everything back in perspective.

The first night together, we each filled out a questionnaire as part of the psychological study. To become more cohesive as a team, we shared parts of the questionnaire: "What are your strengths and weaknesses? What is something that even a close

443

friend may not know about you? We worked through some logistical questions and put on a fundraising show at a Women's Week at the University of Colorado, Boulder. We even went backcountry skiing for a day. Driving home from the gathering, I was excited. It felt like a good group of women, and I was pleased with the process and sense of team so far. I dreamed of our becoming nine inseparable friends.

The next time we were all together was at Kath's home in Albany, California, the week before leaving. We could have used two weeks. There were endless lists of last-minute details, plus food and gear to pack. Numerous relatives and friends dropped what they were doing to help us for that week. We did more psychological and neurological testing for the studies. We sampled donated food and checked donated gear. At one point, Kath's small front yard had five tents set up; in between sat Suzanne and Pat, reading the instructions for the video camera with which we were going to film the expedition.

All that would have been more than enough, but there was still fundraising. We had a budget of $65,000. Being the first all-women expedition in China, we had a unique slant to offer the media. At first the media coverage was exciting. "Look! Our picture is in the paper! We're on the ten o'clock news!" But pressure came with the media coverage; we were presented as experts, as wonder women. I came to understand, especially after the expedition, the media's love of extremes. One article, based on their selective excerpts from our group journal, created the impression that we had been constantly fighting for our lives. It hardly seemed like the same expedition I had been on.

Finally we left. We flew into Beijing and had a day of sightseeing. I was struck by the similarity to the Soviet Union—the gray atmosphere and dilapidated buildings, roads and vehicles. We were whisked to the Ming Tombs and the Great Wall by our interpreter, a young woman with minimal English. The Wall, truly one of the great wonders of the world, stretched for thousands of miles along ridgetops, with subsidiary walls going off on adjoining ridges.

We also had our first face-to-face encounter with the Chinese Mountaineering Association (CMA). The Chinese had never dealt with an all-women expedition. Previous "women's" groups always included men, usually in leadership roles. Our first obstacle was a CMA official named Mr. Ying, whom we quickly renamed Mr. Ying-Yang because of his obvious efforts to create obstacles for us. He told us it was "surely impossible" to take all our baggage and specially crated oxygen on the plane with us to Urumchi (Urümqi), our next destination, and it would have to be shipped separately, which would take several weeks. "You have many problems. Why don't you just go trekking," he advised us. We decided to ignore his negativity and to counteract with the assumption that everything would fly with us. The next morning at the airport, we piled our seventy-five pieces of baggage in front of the check-in counter, blocking the area. All our baggage, including the oxygen, came with us on the plane.

In Urumchi, we met our two liaison officers, Su and Muhameti. Su spoke reasonable English, liked to be the center of attention and was an avid and talented photographer. Muhameti was Uighur, the predominant "minority" in northwestern China. Because of his Uighur language, he was invaluable in dealing with the local people, especially our camel drivers. Several years before, he had worked as a liaison officer for the Japanese expedition attempting the north side of Mt. Kongur, on which several climbers had been killed in an avalanche. A gracious and humble man, Muhameti consistently tried to make our experience both positive and meaningful.

After numerous delays due to dust storms, we flew on to Kashgar (Kashi), an ancient oasis town on the Silk Road. The people in and around Kashgar are mostly Uighur, Kazakh and Tadzhik, thus they are Turkic and Iranian, not Asian. They are also Muslim. For me, this was the most fascinating part of China. It was like stepping into a different world, even a different era. There were few multistory buildings in Kashgar; most buildings were hundreds of years old. People got around mostly on foot, by bicycle, on donkeys or on horse-drawn carts, and we soon learned that the carts with a blue or red canopy were taxis.

While in Kashgar, we had our second run-in with Mr. Ying-Yang's efforts to thwart our mountaineering attempts. We had shipped Gaz cartridges for our Bleuet stoves, which were to be our only source of fuel high on the mountain, well ahead of time from the United States. In Beijing, Mr. Ying had told us they had not yet arrived but that it was "surely possible" to buy some from the CMA in Kashgar. Although we were able, with the help of Su and Muhameti, to buy high-altitude cartridges from the CMA that were left over from a Japanese expedition, Su told us that Mr. Ying had called from Beijing with instructions not to sell us any.

Leaving Kashgar, we drove by jeep and truck along the Karakoram highway. Right outside of Kashgar and the green of its oasis, we found ourselves in the bleakest countryside I have ever encountered. The whole area was a flat field of large gravel. Only the tire ruts distinguished the road from the surrounding area. Gradually, barren hills showed on the horizon. At one point we passed a "highway crew": people removing rock cut from the cliff road with crowbars and moving it to the river side in wheelbarrows. The road grader was a camel dragging a heavy piece of metal along the road. The rocky hills gave way to snow- and glacier-covered peaks. What were named nominal peaks there would have been major mountaineering attractions anywhere in the United States. At last we reached our destination, Karakol Lakes at 12,000 feet, situated in a high desert plain surrounded by towering mountains.

We spent two nights there acclimatizing, visiting a local settlement and trying to figure out which of the distant peaks showing themselves among the clouds was our destination, since no topographical maps of the area were available.

Ever since we had met Su and Muhameti, they had made comments implying that they wanted to go above our base camp and be involved in the climb. We were definitely against it; this was to be a women's expedition. We decided we needed to impress upon them our experience. The night before leaving Karakol Lakes, we had a meeting with all eleven of us. "In the interest of getting to know each other," we each shared our background and achievements. It felt strange to brag about ourselves, but by the end of the meeting Su and Muhameti said that they were impressed and that we obviously knew what we were doing. They dropped all talk of going above base camp. In some sense, I think, they were relieved. Neither of them had much mountaineering experience. I suspect they had felt responsible to "protect" us on the mountain.

The walk to our base camp at 14,800 feet (elevations are approximate, based on altimeters) could have been done in one day had the camel drivers with our gear not tried to undermine us. Muhameti told them that they would not get paid if they did not take us all the way. By then, the drivers had procrastinated and dramatized long enough that we had to spend a night on the way. In the morning, everything was covered with snow, but it melted as we hiked the last eight hundred feet to base camp.

We spent the first day setting up tents and organizing gear. We had agreed to take a rest day the next day for people to acclimatize; we had come up almost 10,000 feet in three days. On the "rest day" I felt tired, but could not resist hiking up higher. Under a gray overcast sky I hiked above the camp to where I could see the Koksal Glacier where it squeezes between two ridges. There were more crevasses than glacier surface. Awed by the sight, I couldn't help being glad that our route was elsewhere.

The next day, Nancey and Kathy came down with respiratory infections. Kathy said she had felt the beginnings of it in Urumchi and, perhaps, should not have gone running there. Nancey was pretty sure she had picked up hers in a small settlement near the Lakes where she had drunk tea from a local's cup. Within a day, everyone except Nancy, Pat, Suzanne and myself were sick and on antibiotics. Suzanne was base camp manager, and a back injury prevented her from carrying loads, but Nancy, Pat and I were anxious to get on the route and start carrying loads. So, with great excitement, the three of us set off up the Corridor Glacier.

Each new view around a corner was exploration: What will we see? What is the best way to go? How long will it take to get to that col? What looked like a forty-five-minute distance turned out to take three hours, so unaccustomed were we to the scale of these mountains. Being neophytes to big expeditions, we were not clear about the best way to organize movement up the mountain, where to put caches or establish camps. Nancey and Kathy had the most expedition experience but were extremely sick. It was all they could do to wake up and crawl out of their tents to pee; they were certainly in no state to help plan an efficient system. So for the first three or four days, until the others began to recover and help carry loads, the four of us who were not sick made many of the organizational decisions.

The system we established remained more out of inertia than pure merit. We had two caches between our base camp and the advanced base camp—one at 16,200 feet and the other at a col at 17,300 feet. The lower one proved of some value as people recovering from sickness started to carry loads. It gave them a short, "conditioning" goal. However, as it turned out, having two caches was inefficient. As we adjusted to altitude, we could make longer carries. We still needed an intermediate stop between the two base camps; it was too far to make the round-trip in a day without a rest day. However, with two caches, we tended to set our sights on shorter distances.

Gradually, the other women got better. Everyone was eager to be involved in moving up the mountain and started carrying loads as soon as they felt better. Unfortunately, I think for some it was too soon. Nancey, Kathy and Joan never fully recovered. After a few days of carrying, they would be back in their bags sick. I cannot help but think that if they had been able to resist the strong drive to be out and involved, had taken a few extra days to more fully recover, they might not have continually relapsed. Of course, hindsight is twenty-twenty. As it was, they all got to the advanced base camp, and Kathy and Nancey made a trip to Camp I.

We spent two weeks traveling back and forth between the base camp and advanced camps, carrying gear and food. It was exciting to finally move up to the advanced camp, at 17,000 feet in the middle of the upper basin of the Koksal Glacier before it squeezed down toward base camp. With hindsight, I can now see that we carried too much food and gear above base camp. Our plan was for everyone to be at least as high as the advanced camp, if not higher, so we carried up food and fuel for eight people. We did not take into account the likelihood that at least some of us would be sick. We realized later that we should have carried up enough for five or six people; if we had been lucky enough to get all of us that high on the mountain, we could have carried up more supplies as needed.

For the advanced camp we had VE-25 tents, the largest of The North Face dome tents, and MSR stoves (both donated). For higher camps we had brought modified Bleuet stoves and smaller tents. Essentially, we had carried double the gear we needed to Advanced.

As people adjusted to the altitude, they worked on setting up Camp I at 19,300 feet on the southwest rib. On the morning that Pat and Nancy planned to move to Camp I, Nancy said she was too tired to go. Kath asked whether I would go; Pat was anxious to move up. Ignoring my own tiredness, I agreed. It was special to be the first to sleep there. We melted water, forced ourselves to eat and drink, and marveled at the view. Off in the distance, 7,000 feet below, we could see Karakol Lakes and the brown of the surrounding high desert. We could see into Pakistan and the Soviet Union. The next day we were tired and had headaches. Between resting and melting water for drinks, we worked on a snow cave for Carole, Nancy and Kath, who joined us that day.

The next night was one of the worst in my life. My head felt like it was splitting into pieces. Ordinary medication did nothing. I cried from pain and constantly shifted positions, hoping to find a more tolerable one. In the morning, at the seven o'clock radio contact, I asked the nurses (Nancey, Kathy and Carole) what stronger medication we had that I could take for headaches. After a few questions, they said I needed to descend; it sounded like edema. I felt like crying from disappointment as Nancy and Pat accompanied me down. Within 1,500 feet I felt tolerable. By the time we reached the advanced camp, I felt okay. It was hard to watch Nancy and Pat turn around to go back up.

Nancey was glad for the company. The previous day, she had been knocked off her feet by a sudden shift of the glacier. We had probed the area carefully when we had originally set up the advanced camp, but things were changing. We spent the next week together reading, eating popcorn and freeze-dried cinnamon apples, organizing gear, sleeping and talking. We went up to Camp I once, but I started getting a headache again. As our time on the mountain drew to a close, we cleared out everything extra from the advanced camp and moved down the mountain. Back at the base camp, overwhelmingly disappointed, I swore I would never go on another expedition. I wanted to get away from the mountains, go sightseeing in Kashgar and Beijing, and go home. I missed Jeff more than I had anticipated.

Meanwhile, Nancy, Kath, Pat and Carole at Camp I pushed higher. Camp II was set at approximately 21,000 feet. But when the weather deteriorated and avalanche conditions developed, they decided the summit was not worth the risk. In addition, our time was running out; the date for the camels to pick us up at base camp was set and could not be changed. That was unfortunate because there was still plenty of food and fuel at the advanced camp to wait for conditions to improve. Our only shortage was time.

Extra time would have also given people a chance to rest. Carrying loads had taken a toll. Carrying too much gear to the advanced camp, not having had a terribly efficient system, and sickness had eaten up time. Above 19,000 feet there is so little oxygen that your body deteriorates even on "rest" days. To really recover and regain strength, you need to return to lower elevations. If we had had more time, people could have returned to base camp for a number of rest days after stocking Camp I and then gone back up for a summit push. If . . .

It was a great relief when we were all safely back at base camp. We had a meeting to discuss our successes and what we could have done better. Watching the video of this meeting back in the States was painful. We had been so down about not making the summit, yet we were not talking about that. As we each talked about "successes," our faces shouted out sadness. At that meeting we were unable to share our pain with each other. It is true that reaching the summit was only the goal and that the process of the whole expedition was significant, but at that moment all we seemed to see was the goal not reached.

As if in accordance with our mood, a heavy snow fell the last night in base camp. The next day we walked out of the camp, each in our own world under a gray sky that matched the gray snow, eliminating any distinct horizon.

After seven weeks in the mountains, we retraced our steps through China. With the stresses of the mountain behind us, we felt more patience to go sightseeing and enjoy the culture. We began to talk some in smaller groups about the disappointments, but we were no longer a cohesive group with a common goal. We each had separate plans ahead of us.

I came away from the expedition full of new experiences and understanding, although at the time I did not appreciate them all. What I had known intellectually about expeditions, I came to understand on a personal, experiential level. The familiarity with expeditions gained on Mt. Kongur proved invaluable when, several years later, I ventured onto Denali with two friends who had no previous expedition experience.

There was also the time shared with the eight other women. We did not all become the inseparable friends I had hoped. Some of the time together was joyful, some of the interactions were rough and painful, but I feel a bond with most of the women because of our time together.

As I originally went through my journal to write this article, I was struck by two things. One was my own concern with doing everything correctly. I wanted a perfect expedition with no mistakes (whatever that means). The second was the marvel of the process. Yes, it was extremely disappointing not to reach the summit, or even the technical parts of the climb. However, I now appreciate that those would have been only final steps in a long journey. Not making those steps cannot negate all the steps we did take. With each of those steps came new experiences and understanding, and I feel incredibly fortunate to have been part of the journey.

—1992

Pete Sinclair

from *We Aspired*

Pete Sinclair (1935–) served as a climbing ranger in the Grand Teton National Park during the 1960s, a time he recalled in his autobiographical We Aspired. *He supervised a number of rescues in the park and founded the Jackson Hole Mountain Guides. He also taught English at Evergreen State College.*

NORTH

Mt. Sanford, though not a big Alaskan mountain, was the biggest mountain I had ever seen. We had changed drivers in the pink and gray dusk of the approaching solstice about an hour before, at Tok Junction, so I hesitated to wake up Barry. There were four of us in two cars: "Millicent," Barry Corbet's '40 Chevy, and "Bulldog," Jake Breitenbach's '50 English Austin. (Jake wore Italian racing gloves when he drove.) Bill Buckingham and I rode shotgun. June 5, 1959, the last year a person could light out overland from the States to a U.S. territory; we were headed south, which was strange after three days of going north over two thousand spine-shrinking, tongue-dusting, mosquito-slapping, windshield-nicking, tire-popping miles. Bulldog and Millicent were as festooned with used tires as tugboats are. At Jake's suggestion, we stopped counting flats and timed tire changes instead. Four and a half minutes was the best we could do on Millicent, but we got a doorhandle-to-doorhandle time of three minutes fifty-eight seconds on Bulldog's left rear tire.

Much of the gravel highway between the northern mountains was long, level, and straight, logical if you thought about it, but I hadn't. Down these interminable stretches, holding the jiggling wheel at top dead center, we felt the road at work dismantling the cars. The trees were recent second growth. There was a limit to how long we could hold our breath at the vastness and the dust. When we exhaled, we found that we were tired, dirty, stiff, bored, and unenvious of the pioneers. The Alcan equivalents of old Fort Bridger combined filling station, garage, wrecking yard, general store, diner, bar, post office, and community center. Their construction was log or rough-sawn board and batten, your basic abandoned early logging camp. They all looked rustic and homey to us. We stopped at one about every four hours for gas. Twice a day we'd stay for an hour to get our tires patched and to eat ham and eggs.

Due to some mysterious economic principle, the further up the highway we went the cheaper the ham and eggs got. The price bottomed out at eighty-five cents between Watson Lake and Whitehorse, then rose gradually until we crossed into Alaska, where it jumped a dollar. In Alaska, you have to be a high roller just to eat breakfast.

Beside the summit of the mountain a rainbow formed, a double rainbow, a truncated double rainbow: not an arch but a square as big as the upper part of the mountain. There was the square rainbow to the left, the white Mt. Sanford triangle in the center, and to the right were dark foothills shaped to a rectangle by clouds above and ground fog below. Sorry Barry, you've got to see this.

He looked, didn't get it, was polite, tried to work up some enthusiasm, fell asleep again. I understood. The membranes in my eyes, too, felt like rice paper dusted with talcum powder. I was embarrassed by my aesthetic gush. Still, a square rainbow, a mountain for a triangle, a forest for a rectangle, a night without dark. I'd expected big things of Alaska and here was God doodling in color.

Even allowing for the year since having scoured off the memory of the spines and sharp edges of youth, 1959 was a special year. Jake was still alive and Barry had his legs. Life was sweet and we could taste it. We were twenty-three to twenty-five, too young for World War II, too privileged for Korea, and too old for wars to come. We had been children before Hiroshima. Like Robert Frost's bird singing in its sleep, we had come through the interstices of things ajar. We were the high school and college generation of the 1950s, as it seems to me now, the last innocent Americans.

We were in Alaska to climb Mt. McKinley. The bulk of our gear had come up by barge from Seattle. A friend of Jake's in Anchorage (Rick Smith) gave us the use of his basement for sorting and repacking, as friends of Jake's in Seattle (the Kamerers) had given us the use of their lawn, kitchen, and sewing room. There weren't many climbers in the country then. We all pretty much knew or knew of each other. We also knew or knew of folks like Rick Smith and Kent and Sonja Kammerer, who offered floor, shower, and spaghetti feed—people who made for us a sanctuary of ordinary life. That the country could have been that small only thirty-four years ago!

The next day the barge with our baggage came and we went from Anchorage to Talkeetna on the Department of Interior train, stopping to let passengers on or off at what appeared to be trail crossings in the bush. The Matanuska and Susitna valleys were surprisingly lush, cool jungles giving off soft, green light. We drank beer in the dining car in the morning, feeling just slightly sinful; nearly everyone else in the car was joyously drunk. Also, we'd read Hemingway and Homer. Drinking is part of adventuring: one last round, boys, a libation to the gods, boys, before we go off in search of the Great Death.

We chose to use the Athabaskan name, Denali, for Mt. McKinley. Of the four of us, only Jake had been on Denali before. From the airstrip in Talkeetna, we got glimpses of it among the clouds over the Alaska Range. Unable to distinguish mountain from cloud, I took the short view, concentrating on sorting our gear into drop loads and plane loads. The mountain would wait.

After we sorted our gear, we cut fir boughs to drop on the glacier to give the pilot, Don Sheldon, something to judge depth by. Sheldon flew Jake in first. He found a slope on the glacier that was a hair steeper than he could taxi up at almost full throttle. He landed by cutting back until he touched down and then giving it almost full throttle. The Super Cub roared up the landing site, gradually losing way. Just as the plane was about to stop and start sliding backwards, Sheldon turned so that his skis were across the fall line. He kept a little power back in case he fell into a soft spot, as in fact he did while landing Jake. The glacier was almost too soft to land on, so Sheldon put Jake to work packing a landing strip while he returned for me. This was my second plane ride, the first had been in an Air Force jet fighter. Packed in gear up to my neck, I peered left and right at unnamed, unclimbed, Rocky Mountain-size peaks lining the Kahiltna Glacier. Denali was out of view beyond the clouds above these peaks. It was as if we were tunneling our way up to the mountain. Sheldon said that the clouds had been higher on the first flight and they'd been able to take a look at the lower part of the route and pick a drop site. Good news which I would have received with more enthusiasm if Sheldon had been able to give it without turning around and looking at me. I wanted him to look the way the plane was pointed, toward the rising glacier and hemming walls.

It looked like we were going to run out of clearance between glacier and cloud, with no room to turn around. It looked like we were flying into the toe of a giant white sock. Then we came to a wide place where the glacier had arms branching off both sides. We circled right and there was Jake, the evergreen cuttings, and the track he packed.

We drop down and drift over a large crevasse, and another, and then we are on the track, and then we run off the end of it because we went faster on the packed snow, leaving Jake behind. And now the turn, and then the snow gives way under the right ski, and we sink down until we are held up by the wing resting on the snow. With the engine off, it is very still. I can hear Jake's snowshoes as he approaches. Sheldon is grinning, which I understand to mean that we are in a hole and not in a crevasse. Jake laughs as he begins to dig out the door for us. I think that it takes a lot to get someone nervous around here; then I too laugh and decide that I'm going to like it here.

By careful tilting and tugging and by placing a pack frame under the ski, we got the Super Cub back onto the surface of the glacier. Sheldon decided he had to have one of those pack frames, an invention of Jake's.

After taking off, Sheldon circled and waved his wings. We guessed that that was it for the day, but waited up until midnight anyway. Jake talked about logistic possibilities: how many loads from Landing Camp to Base, how heavy, in what order, how long. I tried to pay attention. Soon it became apparent that Jake wasn't paying attention either. He was just saying the words that he, as leader, was supposed to say. We had been in a state of anticipation for almost a year; it had become a habit. It took a while for what was there to assert itself.

Our chatter about what we were going to do stopped. We got in our sleeping bags, put on our wool caps, stuck our heads out of the door of our orange tent, and took a look around. We picked out climbing routes on the rock above us. Our route started from the next arm up on the glacier. We were picking out routes on a ridge that divides that arm from the one we were on. We didn't have to climb the ridge; we'd just walk around the end of it. Picking out routes was just a way to make ourselves feel at home. After a bit is dawned on me that this ridge, on which I had been selecting rock-climbing routes as if it was a practice cliff, was the Kahiltna Peaks, as high off the glacier as the Tetons are above Jenny Lake!

By midnight next (June 8, 1959), Bill and Barry had landed and we had moved most of our gear five miles up the glacier. In another twenty-four hours we had established Base Camp at the foot of the ridge we wanted to climb. It was a miserable two days. The heat on the glacier was intolerable. I was treated for heat stroke during a lunch break. Our loads were enormous. My intestines lost their grip. But the tedious work ended and soon slipped from memory; the climb proper was about to begin.

The ridge we wanted to climb was the southwest spur of the South Face, now called the Southwest Rib. We were on the west side of the spur and had to climb through the icefall formed by the glacier squeezing around the protruding spur. Our camp lay below the line where most of the ice and snow cascading off the icefall came to rest. Nevertheless, our tents were surrounded by debris that came from a hanging glacier on the north wall of the Kahiltna Peaks.

Because of fine route finding by Bill and Barry, the icefall turned out to be a minor problem. From high up on it, on our last carry out of Base Camp, we watched impassively as an avalanche washed over our abandoned camp. It was as difficult to attend to such past dangers as it was to attend to the magnificence of the terrain. The long view was the length of a rope, the short view was just in front of our feet. My foot went through a snow bridge over a crevasse, and I felt a surge of adrenaline (panic). I shifted my weight to the other foot, planted my axe, and that was it. Within two steps I forgot the incident. I was forgetting how to worry.

From Base Camp, we could see the upper mile of the rib, but it was like looking through binoculars at mountains on the moon. The route through the icefall took us eastward, past the base of the rib, then made a left turn around the bottom tip of the rib, and headed us north toward the face. From the top of the icefall, twelve hundred feet above Base Camp, we took our first clear look at what we had come to climb.

The South Face, two and a quarter miles across at the fifteen-thousand-foot contour, has two facets divided by a central rib.[1] We could see only the left (west) facet, that portion of the face bounded by the Southwest Rib and the Cassin Ridge. We made our camp, Icefall Camp, over against the rock of the Southwest Rib and looked up.

———

The ice sloped down to form a swale and then ascended to the base of the face, three-quarters of a mile away. We were at the left edge of a semi-circular amphitheater, a mile and a half in circumference from our rib around the top of the glacier to the base of the Cassin Ridge. The wall of the amphitheater, from its base at the top of the glacier to the summit of Denali, was just under nine thousand feet high. We had before us an honest-to-God awesome prospect.

We were there because no one had done anything on the South Face before. Our reason for thinking that we could do something was that any route up the face appeared to require rock climbing, and, though we had little experience on mountains like Denali, we were Teton rock climbers. Bill, Barry, and Jake were Teton guides. Jake and Barry had a fantastic season in 1957. Bill had grown up in Jackson's Hole and had climbed every major peak in the range solo at the age of thirteen. I had started climbing with Jake and Barry at Dartmouth in 1954 but, because of various dealings with the military, had never been in real mountains until I went to Jackson's Hole in August, 1958. There, Sterling Neale, another Dartmouth climber, gave me a crash course in Teton climbing. He got me in good enough condition so that I was able to join Barry, Jake, and Bill on the second complete ascent of the South Buttress of Mt. Moran. Southern exposures are so much pleasanter to climb than northern faces that, after five beers in Jackson after that climb, someone suggested that we have a go at the south side of Denali. As is usual with projects like this, it grew rapidly in the early stages, until it included a fair portion of the climbers and skiers wintering over in Jackson's Hole, and then began to shrink. Ultimately, there were only the four of us who had made our boast in the Jackson mead hall. We weren't really an expedition any more, just an alpine climbing team. Well that was all right we decided. Hermann Buhl thought it was good to go to the big mountains in small teams; we'd give it a try.

All of these plans, and our implied boasts, had been made in the valley. Now we were face to face, so to speak, with the consequences. From our point of view, near Icefall Camp, the face itself was unclimbable. Up across the middle of our facet of the wall was a rock band with blank sections in it. It was hard to judge how big these blank sections were. The map showed the rock band to be twenty-nine hundred feet, almost the height of El Capitan. The blank sections in the rock band could easily be as much as five hundred feet. But that alone only made the face almost impossible. Someone who could climb the Eigerwand could somehow find a route up this band. We judged the route impossible because of the two great glaciers which framed the El Capitan-sized band above and below. The two-thousand-foot glacier plastered to the face above the rock band sent down chunks of ice that did not seem big, in the scale of the face, but were actually the size of log cabins.

The view to the right of the face ended at the Cassin Ridge, obscuring the facet to the east. This central rib did not look unclimbable, but it looked unclimbable by us then and by any standard of competence we could then imagine aspiring to—even after five beers in the Log Cabin Bar.[2] There was something about looking at the face that I must have experienced when, prior to memory proper, I looked about me and realized that the world had not been constructed for a person my size, that a person was going to have to get bigger if he wanted to get along around here.

454

When we finished contemplating the "brutal immensities," as Buckingham called the features of Denali, we turned to our own project, the Southwest Rib. We spent a day and a half searching for a way to get to its crest. To us, the rib appeared to be a ladder placed against the wall to carry us past the two glaciers and the rock band. Jake and I searched the rock immediately above the camp. We hoped to make an ascending traverse back southward across the flank of the rib to the crest. After days of snow-slogging, the rock climbing was fun and relatively easy, but the flank of the rib was, in effect, a face. It only took us thirty minutes to climb it to the crest, but it wasn't a way to go because the technical work needed to ferry loads across and up it would be slow. Also, we'd run into a small blank section. We'd have to hit the crest further up.

The next day, Bill and Barry did that, climbed to the crest by a route closer to the South Face, and discovered, yet closer to the face, a giant couloir that appeared to lead all the way back down to our glacier. Above, there seemed to be only two large snow hummocks to climb to bring us to the place where the rib leveled out and abutted into the face, five hundred yards to the left of the El Capitan-sized rock band.

We did not welcome this opening up of the route as joyfully as we ought to have. We had been expecting to gain the face by the rib ever since we saw the first photographs of the face. It was unnerving that our first move was a wrong move. And, in abandoning the rock of the rib for the snow of the couloir, we gave up our special qualification for attempting the route. But there was no way to avoid it, it was too obviously the way to go. By the evening of June 12, Bill and Barry had placed eight hundred feet of fixed-rope in the bottom of the gully, which turned out to be not a snow but an ice gully. We would attempt the mountain not as a team of specialists but as one of fairly young climbers with just over the minimum qualifications.

I had not participated in the discussion that led to the decision to use the gully. The first time I looked up it, it seemed to sway, making me the first climber to get vertigo by looking up an exposure. The bottom of the gully was steeper than the top. When Bill and Barry went out to fix rope up it, having seen only its upper section, they passed it by as being too steep to be a part of the gully they had seen. This gully they'd lost track of, much wider, longer, and steeper than the Teton Glacier, was but a minor feature beneath the great South Face. Jake, Barry, and Bill called the angle of the ice sixty degrees because it was steeper than the ice wall on the West Buttress that was called fifty degrees. The exact angle of the ice was a matter about which I could feel complete indifference since this was to be my first ice climb.

With a minimum of internal hysteria, I made my first carry up the eight hundred feet of three-eighths-inch manila rope that Bill and Barry had put in. I climbed the gully as if the fixed rope were not there—which, as far as I was concerned, having never trusted my precious body to anything smaller than seven-sixteenths-inch nylon, it wasn't. After surviving the first 120 feet of descent for the second load, I stopped imagining myself hurtling down the gully and trusted my weight to that puny thread.

So this is how it is in the big mountains, I thought to myself as I waited at the top of the lowest section of rope until Jake cleared from the rappel. What else do you have to do to be ready for Annapurna? Bill and Barry were fixing the upper section of the gully. They were hundreds of feet above, but I had a comforting image of being connected to them by the ice chips streaming down from where they were cutting steps. Little shards of ice danced and tumbled down the surface, glittering like bubbles on a brook. I followed them with my eye to their source, reading the surface of the ice by their path. Bill's axe rose and fell like a fly rod casting into the depths of the ice. Barry looked around from his relaxed belay. Above them a black dot was bounding gaily on the surface of the glacier like a water bug.

"Rock! Rock! Rock!" I yelled. I hugged the ice, trying to melt my way into it. At last glance the rock had almost reached Bill and Barry. By the time it got to me, it had reached terminal velocity. The corners and edges of the rock ripping through the air hummed a terrifying tune. Missed. I lifted my face from the ice to glance at Bill and Barry. Jake! No, the rock had exploded a small crater in the snow a few feet in front of him. The rock had passed within twenty feet of each of us.

The gully, the fixed rope, the falling rock, were to me an examination. I wasn't sure that I had passed. I wondered if the others had also worried about themselves first. But I hadn't quite done that; I did yell a warning before taking cover. Did I think, "Him, not me?" No, I did not have that thought. Did I have that wish unspoken? I might have. If Jake had been killed, I would have been certain that I had permitted it.

We went on to the top of the gully. And there we stopped. The top of the gully was not a col or saddle or cornice, it was a large double mound of ice of uncertain origin. We spent most of the next three days of perfect weather at these "snow bumps," as we had named them from below, stuck as effectively as if five feet of snow had fallen. Perhaps it was the rattlesnake whir of the rock. Perhaps it was the steepness of the ice or the fact that in deciding to abandon our snowshoes we might have cut off our retreat. Maybe things had gone too well. Some wyrm of unconfidence found its way to our courage-hoard. We named this camp Concentration Camp.

The next day, the eighth straight of good weather, Bill and I climbed the first bump, to be stopped by a level area on top. Although it was level, the snow was crisscrossed by a confusion of snow and ice structures whose logic and origin escaped us. To the east was the ice gully; to the east was a three-thousand-foot drop. There was only forward or back. Bill had barely started to cross when he sank to his waist.

"What is it?" I asked.

"I don't know, but I'm getting out of here," came Bill's ominous reply.

But, before he could reach the camp, Bill had one more problem to deal with: my very first experience descending ice had happened within the past twenty-four hours and that was with a fixed rope. In those days there was no such thing as adequate protection on ice. Our axes were of no use, so I had to go down on crampons only, facing out from the mountain. And there would be no practice tries. When my body was properly in balance over my crampons, my mind was of the opinion that I was leaning forward, about to go down, down, down two thousand feet of hard, blue-white ice. It did not look right, this descending ice; it didn't look like something a person ought to do. Like Christ leading a disciple across the water, Bill showed me that it could be done. He said it was like friction climbing, which is exactly what I feared it was like, but I did what he told me to do. I made the first step correctly and the subsequent steps also, so that when we got back to the tent I was feeling a little bit chipper.

It didn't last. That evening a gloom heavy as remorse after sin weighed us down to thoughts like "If we leave now, tomorrow morning, maybe we can still get out alive."

Our climb was a deliberate experiment in climbing on an expedition-sized mountain with an alpine climbing team. We had to talk the Park Service into letting us try it. Nearly everything had gone as we expected. Any size expedition, the bigger the better, could have gotten to the base of the gully. To get to where we were and to where it seemed we had to go, we were just the right number. We had abandoned materials all along the route until we were down to what we could carry in four enormous loads. Of the 1,725 feet of fixed rope that we had brought, 1,600 feet were gone, fixed in the gully below us. Our snowshoes were stuck heel first into the snow at the base of the fixed rope. Not one snow bridge that we had used in the icefall was still intact. Retreat would not be easy.

When Bill turned back that morning, I feared that it might be because he couldn't trust me to do my part. But that was not what was going on, at least not that any more than the dozen other things we randomly chose to worry about. What had happened is that we had encountered precisely the difficulties we had told each other we would encounter, while we had secretly hoped that things would turn out to be easier.

Just as the maps and photographs indicated, the south side of Denali was steep. Rocks fell off the mountain when there were people in the fall line as they did when there were not people in the fall line. There might be good campsite where we wished one to be and there might not. Manila rope three-eighths inch in diameter is exactly as it appears, not nearly as strong as seven-sixteenths-inch nylon rope. The fact that we had surmounted with ease the difficulties we had made extraordinary efforts to find did not increase our confidence. That just made us wonder when it was going to happen. "It" was . . . what? A storm.

We first decided that we couldn't go up because there would certainly be a need for fixed ropes ahead. All the fixed rope we brought was already fixed and had to stay fixed so we could retreat in case of a storm. Later we argued that there were probably four thousand more feet of ice ahead, which would be easier if there were snow on it, so we could kick instead of cut steps and could do without fixed ropes. Therefore, further progress could not be contemplated until a storm brought snow. When Buckingham had enough of this creative speculation, he stopped it by observing, "We

457

came here to climb. It would be ridiculous to retreat with the report that we couldn't do the route because the weather was too good."

That stopped the silly talk, but it didn't get us going. On the next day, when it was Jake and Barry's turn to lead, Jake insisted on turning back before they even got to the high point Bill and I reached.

All the gloomy talk scared me, and I would have been happy to turn back. So far I had had a wonderful time. I was willing to take that back to the valley. I had the least idea about how to read the terrain for foreseeable dangers, but when Jake and Barry turned back from terrain that *I* found easy, I knew that it was the geography of the soul that was holding us up.

Jake had had me as his partner since we landed. I suspected that sending me up with Bill was a subtle move by Bill and Barry to release Jake from the grip of his depression, that they felt that it didn't help Jake to have a look after me. I had done my share. Any worries I had I kept to myself. I cleaned the dishes without complaining. But if they knew only half of what I knew about what I didn't know, they had something to worry about. I didn't mind not having major responsibilities until Jake turned gloomy. I ought to be helping, but I knew not how.

The only worry Jake spoke about was that we might "extend ourselves" beyond a point from which we could retreat. He had climbed Denali before and felt, justly, that we didn't know what it could be like there in bad weather.[3]

———

It might have been our unorthodox expedition that bothered Jake. It was as much his plan as anybody's but it might have appealed to his logic and not his heart. We were unorthodox in that we did not really have camps; we bivouacked in tents. We weren't living right. The British had invented mountaineering in the first place. The philosophy of expedition climbing was a product of their military and colonial genius. We were a guerrilla band. The distinction isn't one of safety versus risk; no one matches the British for sheer daring. The issue is more one of style. The classic mountaineering expedition is large not because it's safe that way, it isn't, but because it takes a large expedition to carry the necessities. Going into the jungle is no trick. Having an afternoon tea in the jungle is. The touch that the British carried into the darkness was gracious living. It was not enough to drink tea from china cups, to present a good show; the tea actually had to taste good. Jake was American and therefore informal. He wore suntans and rolled shirt sleeves for all occasions, a jacket over the rolled sleeves for formal occasions. But his trousers were always unwrinkled, and his shirts always white and fresh. There was a crispness to his informality.

Jake had been talking about us overextending ourselves since Bill and Barry found the gully. Now, at the top of the gully with all our fixed rope below us, we were certainly at least extended. We all talked superstitiously about the phenomenal weather. We all had seen the avalanche cover our base camp. We all had been near

458

the falling rock. We all wondered if we could do what we'd been doing if the weather went bad. Doubt drained our energy like a low-grade infection.

When Barry and Jake returned to camp on June 15, it seemed to mean we were defeated. Then Barry asked me if I'd like to go up with him. He just couldn't give up without taking a look himself. I worried that his asking me might be a little hard on Jake, but by the code of the mountains, Barry not only had the right to make the request, he had a right to expect support. If he regarded me as adequate support, that was his affair.

The first bump went easily. This was my third day of ice climbing, and I was beginning to get the hang of it. I was in a perfect environment for quick learning.

Barry diagnosed the weird area between the two bumps, where Bill had sunk to his waist, as "an area of fossilized cornice." Giving it a name helped. No one but me appeared to think that if the name was a correct description, it was possible that we would sink up to our armpits and find our feet hanging free in the air.

We crossed over to the second bump. It was steeper than the first bump, and getting on it required traversing a small, yet steeper section of ice. I realized then that we might not be defeated after all if I could fill in for Jake. We could go on if I could lead the pitch. Barry could establish a bombproof belay on the level section. If I couldn't climb the pitch with that degree of protection, then we probably ought to turn back. None of this was stated of course, but for the first time since we left Seattle, I understood that I had a contribution to make.

A person can sometimes climb pretty well when he knows he can't get hurt. It's like playing poker with a pat hand. It's not really poker, but it sure is fun. I did the pitch in good style for a first lead on ice. Then Barry led a pitch and it was my turn again. The protection for my second lead was practically worthless, but I'd learned what crampons would do. I was half a rope length out on the lead when it began to snow. We turned back because we already had what we needed, a way over the bumps. The sky had cleared again when we reached the tent.

We began the discussion again, this time knowing we were going to decide to go up. The retreat might be impossible, "So," said Buckingham, "the only way back might be over the top." That did it. Retreating up the mountain was exactly the right idea. This gave Jake the opening he needed to recoup his leadership. We didn't literally have to go over the top with our camp. There might be a route from our rib over to the West Buttress Route. Jake thought he had spotted a traverse when he climbed the mountain by the West Buttress Route. The photographs also indicated that there might be one. Jake had thought of the traverse as a possible way to the summit if the upper part of the rib stopped us. Since the traverse was below the level of the ice wall on the West Buttress, it might even be an easier route down than the standard West Buttress Route, allowing us to avoid the danger of descending that ice wall without having fixed it with rope. It really was all a matter of how one looked at things. The whole climb had a new gestalt. Someone casually mentioned that we still hadn't figured out how we would get down the Kahiltna Glacier without the

459

snowshoes we left at the base of the gully. After thinking about that a bit, we pretended it was never said.

Barry was so delighted with the decision to go up that he volunteered to go down into the gully to retrieve eight hundred feet of our fixed rope. Buckingham asked to join Barry because he hadn't been out of the tent all day. I didn't object; neither did Jake.[4]

———

The weather was perfect, the route was perfect, we were not perfect. Jake probably experienced both joy and fear in the mountains more purely than the rest of us. We all felt some fear. Bill's weapon against it was calculation and wit. If he couldn't think his way through it, he'd disarm it with a phrase. Barry's weapon was action. If Barry was on a climb that scared him, he got up earlier in the morning. My trick was to leave a piece of equipment behind, nothing serious enough to stop the climb, but a plausible excuse if I couldn't do it. Jake didn't have a trick. He had to wait it out.

The two bumps took nearly a thousand feet of fixed rope, requiring the use of a climbing rope in addition to the three-eighths-inch manilla. We emerged from the top of the second bump onto a sun-lit snow meadow several hundred feet across. We were high enough now so that we could look across the shoulders of Mt. Foraker to the Susitna River Valley ten thousand feet below us. Nobody but us had ever looked out on the world from here. That had been true all the way up the route, but this was the first place that made us think it. We named the camp Paradise. We had cut a Jacob's ladder of about five thousand steps to get there.

Then there was Camp Fatigue. The day was hot. The altitude was getting to us. Our loads were over eighty pounds. Another day like that and we would have started thinking about going home again.

The climbing the following day, from Fatigue to Balcony, was on rock, and it was great fun because we lightened our loads. At the point where the traverse over to the West Buttress could be made, we cached all supplies not needed for the three days we gave ourselves to get to the summit and back and climbed on. We were high enough to see approaching weather and it was certain that a storm was coming, but there was no talk of retreat. It was a great relief to have made the commitment. For the first time since childhood, I was where I wanted to be, doing exactly what I wanted to do, with the people with whom I wanted to do it.

—1993

Notes

1. This central rib of the South Face is now called the Cassin Ridge after Riccardo Cassin, who, leading a party of five other climbers from the Lecco Section of the Italian Alpine Club, climbed the rib two years later, July 19, 1961.

2. The life history of a difficult mountain route has seven stages: (1) invisible or un-image-able, (2) unclimbable, (3) possibly climbable but suicidal, (4) first ascent, (5) difficult route, (6) a classic route, and (7) once considered a classic route.

3. Some years later, Barry, back on McKinley for a rescue, returned with a tale of their six-foot-high Logan tent being buried in one day's snow.

4. A year or two later, Yvon Chouinard told me that this moment, the moment we decided to go on, was a historic moment in the history of American mountaineering. The climb was not terribly difficult even by the standards of that time, but, said Yvon, "it was the first time an American team committed itself totally to a mountain route." Yvon might be right. It might be that what struck us at Concentration Camp through three days of gorgeous climbing weather was the thought that we were at a threshold that hadn't been crossed by anyone we knew.

Greg Child

from *Postcards from the Ledge*

The Australian climber Greg Child (1957–) began his mountaineering career as a rock climber.
He has distinguished himself on difficult routes on El Capitan. He has also participated in over
a dozen Himalayan climbing expeditions. His photography and articles on mountaineering
have appeared in numerous magazines, and he is the author of several books of adventures.
Child also authored the climbing textbook Climbing: The Complete Reference.

WHATEVER HAPPENED TO LUKE SKYWALKER?

The dirtbag climbers from my past sometimes visit my dreams, like ghosts in the night, their faces, nicknames, and scurrility hovering against the granite backdrop of Yosemite Valley. They are the ones who stood in the shadows, never admitted into the scene because we real climbers could sniff the air and sense they were climber-impersonators and not the genuine article, and because they were weird and scary, characters beamed in from a Hunter S. Thompson story. Rascals and blatherskites, petty criminals and acid casualties, kooks and misfits, natural-born losers and so-ciopaths, they had enough experience on the rocks to masquerade as climbers, and they flocked to Yosemite's Camp 4, a.k.a. Sunnyside Campground.

I'm talking about the climbers' Yosemite of 1970-something, maybe the early 1980s, and I'm talking about an environment where being weird was fairly normal, where renegade behavior was fashionable among real climbers. Dirtbag climbers, however, were a cut below those of us who shared tent space with bubonic ground squirrels and scavenged the cafeteria leftovers of Japanese tourists. Dirtbags were predators, thieves, and con artists who disguised themselves as climbers and preyed on those of us who came to Yosemite with nothing but climbing in our hearts.

Luke Skywalker, where are you now? Stepping out of the shadows one week in 1980, he made a plausible facsimile of a climber at first, even trying an El Cap route or two, but his icy stare and his disjointed mutterings and crazed cackling while on belay freaked out his partners so badly that they signaled retreat after a few pitches. No, Luke was to climbing what decaffeinated is to Starbucks. He was ersatz. His real identity was forgotten when some wit nicknamed him after the intergalactic traveler from the then-popular movie *Star Wars*.

I met Luke on Half Dome. I had just humped a massive haulbag up slab and through forest to the foot of a route called Zenith when I heard a deranged-sounding scream from the cliffs above, followed by the ping of a dropped piton bouncing down the wall. My partners, a New Zealander whose nickname was The Dog and a Brit whose nickname was Egg, scattered for the shelter of rocks while the steel missile ricocheted into the woods.

"That must be Luke Skywalker up there," suggested Egg while balancing another cigarette on his lower lip and torching it with a Zippo lighter.

Luke, it was known, had taken to soloing big walls, or at least trying to, because no one would climb with him anymore. It was also suspected that Luke was in the habit of divesting climbers of their climbing gear, since his climbing rack seemed to expand with every wall he attempted, a peculiar anomaly for someone who left retreat anchors everywhere.

We'd been warned he'd been seen heading for Half Dome to solo the old Royal Robbins route, Tis-sa-sack, and there he was, swinging about in his aiders, in the 500-foot leaning corner above us called the Zebra, so named for the black stripe weeping over the white rock.

Luke swung his hammer around his head and flailed with his hands and screamed. See us, 500 feet below, he yelled down something about a swarm of bees. Indeed, an eerie buzz did emanate from the wall. Farther down the valley, to the west, the afternoon sky was turning a strange shade of magenta and orange as smoke from a massive controlled-burn choked the sunset. Luke continued raving a few minutes more, then slid down the line of ropes he'd installed up to his high point. Near the ground he tossed his rack down with a loud clang and angrily damned it to hell.

"Out there," said The Dog. His real name was Nic Craddock, but we called him The Dog because of his studied scruffiness. Whenever he said, "Out there," it meant things were about to get weird. He was never wrong about this.

Luke marched toward us and greeted us like we were all old friends, though this was the first time we'd laid eyes on him. Only his reputation preceded him.

"Hey, man, I see a cigarette, got a spare? Thanks. Got any 'biners I can borrow? I'm kinda short. How are you guys set for food? I could really use a good meal before I set off tomorrow. Maybe I should hike down to the supermarket and bring up more munchies, I dunno, hey, you got five bucks you can lend me? Oh, man, you wouldn't believe the bees up there, I got swarmed, thought they were gonna sting me to death. Complete freak-out, had to rap off. Goddamn bugs. It was intense."

Luke spat all this and more out of his mouth in a machine-gun staccato. His eyes had a penetrating yet translucent quality; there was a jittery twitch to his facial expressions, the calling card of way too many acid trips. I felt uncomfortable in his presence, and a shiver went up my spine, as if someone were doing a jig on my grave. We slipped away from Luke and found a flat place to bivy, but he followed us, laying his sleeping bag beside ours, curling up like a stray pup at our feet.

"Out there," repeated The Dog with a whisper and a nod.

Around midnight a rustling sound from our haulbag woke me and Egg, so called because of his yolk-colored hair; his real name was Graham Everett. I expected to see a raccoon nosing into the bag, and I grabbed a stone to fling at it; but the moonlight revealed Luke digging through our possessions. Seeing us sit up in our sleeping bags, he froze. We stared at each other. Nothing was said. A long minute passed, and then Luke slowly replaced the things he'd removed from our haulbag and went back to his sleeping bag. Heightened by moonglow, Luke's Neanderthal gaze had a dangerous depth, full of awful possibility and stunted morality. He'd used it as a weapon, staring us down with his opaque glassy orbs, and he successfully put the frighteners on us. Egg lit a nervous cigarette and whispered something about getting our heads bashed in with a piton hammer while we slept. So we didn't sleep, but kept watch on Luke all night, at least till sunrise, when we dozed off and Luke disappeared up his ropes to do battle with Tis-sa-sack and the bees.

When we entered the bug zone that day, we found that the humming wasn't made by bees but some harmless, lethargic, dronelike flies that had hatched in the millions, all of which were now looking for a home and a purpose, at an altitude a thousand feet above the base of Half Dome. We watched swallows and yellow jackets intercept the flies like fighter planes swooping through a squadron of bombers. But to Luke they were killer bees, and in a final fit of screaming he retreated, yelling the whole way down.

Zenith had been climbed the first time the previous summer by the bigwall maestros Jim Bridwell, Dale Bard, and Kim Schmitz. The rock on this climb is layered like onion skins: a mass of flakes stacked one over another, expanding, elastic, hollow. Most of the climbing is on aid placed behind these shaky flakes. It made for a creaky insecurity as you felt the piton or nut you hung from slip downward as the flake it was lodged behind flexed open a millimeter. The ultimate expanding formation on the route was dubbed the Space Flake—eighty feet long, thin as a cookie, guillotine sharp, and booming like a drum. We climbed this wild, diagonaling feature with nuts and cams and stacked pitons poked into its underside. It seemed that a mere fart would be enough to dislodge this scimitar of rock, the result of which would be the surgical removal of all traces of climbers from the wall. In recent years a large chunk of it has fallen off.

On the sixth day we climbed into the middle of the wall, where the rock was white and bleached like bone. Rain had never touched this overhung face, and not even lichen clung to the wall. Climbing a corner system, Egg was knocked backward onto the rope by the rush of thousands of flies exiting the crack he had shoved his hands into. They sheltered in there to escape the heat of the day, and the rush of musty air from their foul nest had the whiff of Beelzebub.

By the seventh day we were growing nerve-wracked and argumentative from the constant insecurity of pitch after pitch of expanding flakes. Even our bivouac that night was off a huge orange biscuit stuck to the wall. As we hung our port-ledges from nuts, cams, and pitons all wedged behind the flake, The Dog lectured us about

464

earthquakes, which, in California, have no manners and come when least expected. His information was not appreciated, causing us to conjure up a shared vision of our flake flapping in a quake, spitting out the anchor, and sending us to ground zero. Flying in formation down the wall on our porta-ledges, we would surely be bickering, each of us blaming the other for not adding a bolt to the belay.

We reached the top on the eighth day after nailing a toast-thick flake, then joining the final pitches of Tis-sa-sack. The next day we were back on the valley floor, drinking beers and inhaling sandwiches outside Degnan's Deli. Around us moved a procession of dirtbags, misfits, and oddballs. After our cozy solitude on Half Dome, contact with the human race was unappealing and we wanted out. We talked about going right back onto another wall and debated whether or not we seemed like dirtbags to the people around us. We agreed that we were dirty but not dirtbags, that we didn't fit into society at that point in our lives but we weren't misfits, that though we were oddities we weren't oddballs. And anyone could see just by looking that we weren't tourists. Climbers, we agreed after another six-pack, were as indigenous to Yosemite as bears, and we belonged there just as much as any Winnebago.

Budweiser-driven elitist climber drivel lolled off our tongues. Soon we had a crowd around us. They lapped up our wisdom and our tales of Zenith so long as we fed them beers. As the session wore on, I saw that several dirtbags and misfits had infiltrated the audience. There was the Bearded Lady, a poor girl who started off as a normal-enough climber but who suffered some hormonal tragedy that left her bereft of mind and gave her a swarthy five-o'clock shadow. She supported herself by stealing tips from tables in the restaurants. And there was the dude who pedaled his bike around the loop road morning, noon, and night, and had the habit of riding up to you, hitting his brakes, and then hopping off the bike and spinning his front wheel in front of your face. "Spinning," he'd say with a screw-loose smile, then scoot off. I saw that those around us were nodding in agreement with our diatribe against the dirtbags and unsavory elements who were spoiling Yosemite. They had no idea we were talking about them. I realized then that "dirtbag" is a relative term and that they didn't see themselves as lost souls at all.

"Did ya hear about Luke?" a passing climber asked us. Eagerly, we listened.

But some background first. All summer long, thieves had been stealing from climbers, out of tents, from cars, from packs left at the base of climbs. Even the walls were not safe (as we discovered when Luke raided our haulbag); someone was nocturnally jumaring the rope of climbers fixing on El Cap and stealing the equipment from their high points. One fellow whom Luke hung out with had been fingered by a climber who stumbled across a dirtbag nest in the boulders behind Camp 4 and found said dirtbag sleeping on a piece of ornamental carpet that had been boosted from his van, along with everything else he owned. But the rangers let the dirtbag off, saying they had to have more than a ragged shred of carpet to justify an arrest; they had to have the loot. The dirtbags might have been dirtbags, but they had an efficient system for getting the gear out of Yosemite to the fence who sold it for them.

465

Now here's the punch line: some climbers decided to lure the thief with a sting, by leaving a fat rack at the end of a rope on El Cap and then waiting in the woods. It didn't take long till Luke turned up, jumared the rope, took the rack, and rappelled down. The vigilante climbers met him at the bottom of the wall with piton hammers in hand.

"I thought you guys left already," Luke said with a whimper.

Being locked up slowed Luke down for a few days, but he was soon out. Through some legal technicality, the charge didn't stick. A climber's word against a dirtbag apparently wasn't enough. People joked that Luke would have to murder someone to get thrown out of Yosemite, that the corpse would have to testify, and that no one would believe the corpse.

He did leave, though. On a rainy and frigid fall night, a Canadian hellion named Darryl Hatten (who would later be ousted from Yosemite for riding a bicycle through a restaurant and causing indigestion to many tourists) visited Luke's abode—a plastic tarp draped over a picnic table. Darryl carried a knife and a bucket of cold water. He slit the tarp, doused Luke with the icy water, and threatened Luke with unspeakable atrocities. Darryl's threats had a convincing quality, even though he was really a gentle giant, and Luke fled Yosemite, shivering and wet.

Luke was gone, but other dirtbags replaced him. The climbers continued to climb; the dirtbags continued to steal. I seldom visited Yosemite after the mid-1980s. It seemed that the mood of the Valley had changed: too many people, too many rip-offs, rules, and rangers. Maybe it was I who had changed. But, on a rare visit to Yosemite a few years ago, while sitting around a campfire with an old wall partner and dredging up the past, I did hear an update on Luke. The source, said my friend, was an L.A. newspaper that contained the grisly tale of a young man who beat his grandmother to death with a hammer when she refused to loan him money. He beheaded her and was apprehended while driving around with the corpse in his trunk. The photo of the murderer, my friend insisted, was Luke.

I thought of Luke's piercing eyes transfixing me that night below Zenith, and the suggestion of evil in that glare. A campfire chill rattled my bones. It had been a close call, but climbing is always full of close calls.

—1998

466

Alan Weber

"Disaster Deferred"

Many rock climbers have experienced a day like the one described below by the editor, punctuated by small, but dramatic events that force one to ponder the ars ascendi. The unscathed and closely-shaved will afterwards approach the experience of climbing with a more mature perspective. Weber (1963–) is a research fellow at Cornell University. His interest in the outdoors was spurred by his father Jon Weber, a speleologist, geologist, and adventurer. He has rock and ice climbed throughout the Northeast and Northwest United States, and adventured throughout the South Pacific and Australia.

When I was an undergraduate at Cornell University I climbed and scrambled on anything vaguely rock-like, including buildings, dams, erratic boulders and quarries. The region surrounding Ithaca, New York, is not especially suited for climbing, because although the area contains several deep gorges (you may have seen the bumper sticker, "Ithaca is Gorges") carved by streams making their way into Lake Cayuga, the rock surrounding the lake is mostly composed of loose shale which sloughs off in crumbly clumps in your hands. I remember when I learned the word *friabilis*—crumbly—in Latin class, and the first thing that came to mind was gorge shale. While bouldering around in the gorges, my companions and I would turn smugly to each other and fire off mock Latin barbs:

Hodie friabilis, stultus (It's crumbly today, O doltish one).
Nego, inurbanus, ascendo (I deny your proposition, O rustical fool; I shall ascend).

Since the statute of limitations may not have expired on some of our exploits in the state and county parks, I unfortunately cannot elaborate further on some of our local climbing adventures. As luck would have it, the only accidents we ever suffered were ripped breeches, mouthfuls of mud, and some sliced fingers; and let me say that shale makes a beautifully clean incision that can be quickly stitched, and, more importantly, can easily be passed off to university officials and local authorities as having been inflicted by carelessly slicing a tomato.

I had learned to climb in Pennsylvania from Tom Smythe, a friend of my father's from the old school of climbing. He had climbed in the Himalayas and still travels to South America for expeditions. He taught me to climb from the ground

---

up, so to speak, with the absolute minimum of gear. Before the advent of the new high tech gear, climbing was a simpler sport—a mountain could be scaled using boots, several coils of rope, carabiners, and a hammer and pitons—wedge shaped spikes of iron jammed into the rock. The rope we used was goldline, which has thankfully disappeared from the climbing scene. Goldline was a stretchy nylon rope with a unique dirty yellow-green color that is still fixed firmly in my mind. Prefab harnesses were scorned, and often you rigged one up yourself with carabiners and webbing.

The problem with goldline was that it was extremely stretchy, which meant when you took a screamer, you could be assured of bouncing around a few times, banging into outcrops and boulders on your way up and down. On the other hand, this stretch would also absorb a great deal of the shock of a fall instead of jerking the climber abruptly to a halt like the newer, stiffer kern-mantle ropes. This extra stretch was important, since one older conventional tie-in for rock climbing involved directly tieing into the rope with a bowline knot around the waist. This versatile, strong, and adjustable knot, still used in boating, has the advantage that it can be easily tied with one hand in a matter of two or three seconds. Anyone who has fallen on a bowline around the waist knows that it is not one of life's more pleasurable experiences, since the rope cinches up around the rib cage and can cut off your breathing. An unconscious climber hanging from a rope high in the mountains is as much a liability to themselves as to those who must rescue him.

Do I want to go back to the old days of climbing and the old, primitive techniques— simpler, but perhaps more dangerous and less forgiving? Certainly, some older climbers have turned away from certain trends in modern sport climbing—any kind of artificial aid is "cheating" for them. They feel that anyone with an electric rock drill and some metal bolts can walk up the flattest, smoothest face ever thrown up by nature. In the 1920s, George Leigh Mallory and Sandy Irvine strapped on the first primitive breathing apparatus to their backs and headed into the Everest mists, never to be seen alive again. The naysayers who protested that supplemental oxygen was unsporting, and furthermore, simply wouldn't work, were vindicated. Although the generation of die-hards who viewed supplemental oxygen as cheating are now all gone, many climbers wonder how far technology should intrude into the sport. Jon Krakauer's book on the 1996 Everest disaster demonstrated that with enough logistical support, expensive equipment and willing Sherpas, any untrained outdoor enthusiast (with enough money) could defeat the world's tallest mountain. On the other extreme, Reinhold Messner has climbed Everest solo and without supplemental oxygen. Where does one draw the line for the race of Messner's, and what is the minimum amount of gear required for safety? Thus far no minimalist has done a naked ascent of Everest without supplemental clothing, but I should perhaps not joke about such things in print, since climbers are above all a breed who love challenges.

———

Do I want to go back? I can't easily answer that question. With the mass of improved and safer gear on the market, the question of going back to a simpler time, is not as straightforward as, say, the folk music revival of the 1960s that abandoned the electric guitar and picked up the unplugged variety. I have out of necessity done crotch burning body rappels with only the rope and my fear guiding my tired body down the rock (warning kids: don't do this without heavy clothing and lots of practice). I am glad I knew how to escape a dangerous situation with minimal help from climbing technology. Let a thousand varieties of climbers bloom.

An adventure in the Schwangunk Mountains of central New York a number of years ago brought to a head the questions about climbing gear and the psychology of climbing that had been brewing in my mind for a number of years. I hooked up with a group of seven climbers one July weekend and we drove out from Ithaca on Highway 17 in a crumbly Buick to the Gunks, as they are affectionately known. This tale also has a love interest, which would be better told in another story. Alexandra, while not a climber, enjoyed the company of climbers, and decided to travel with us. I often wonder if some of our follies on this trip were not related to our macho desire to impress her.

———

After we arrived at the Gunks and unloaded the ropes and gear, we decided to split into smaller climbing groups. I was paired with a German chap who exuded confidence and experience. Although in the back of my mind, I thought that the huge rack of gear hanging from his shoulder was more suitable for El Capitan than our humble Gunks pitches, I assumed that he had just arrived from an expedition in the Alps and didn't have time to sort his gear. We surveyed the rock and briefly discussed possible routes up the face, although in retrospect I wish we had talked more. I took his silence and firmly pursed lips to mean that he had already mentally mapped out our ascent, and that reaching the top was a simple formality! We agreed that first Gunther would lead and then I would follow next, retrieving the protection or "pro," the nuts and hexes wedged into the rocks. For those who have not climbed before, the setup goes something like this: a belayer stands or sits on the ground or ledge, tied to some immovable object while the lead climber climbs up the rock face with the rope tied to his harness. Every few feet, the lead climber jams a metal device into the rock and threads the rope through a carabiner attached to the device. Thus if the lead climber falls, the belayer stops the rope from playing out with the devices in the rock acting as an anchor point, breaking the climber's fall. When the lead climber runs out of rope, he secures himself to the rock with a piece of protection and becomes the belayer for the follower. The second climber then follows the leader's route, pulling out the protection as he goes.

I tied myself to a tree and prepared to belay Gunther. After the customary signals, Gunther began to climb. What I considered to be the first pitch of the climb actually began about fifteen feet up on a ledge preceded by some boulders and ledges, which were wide enough to walk up like stairs. Strangely, Gunther paused and hesitated. I had assumed that he would just walk up to the ledge and then begin climbing. Instead, he pulled out some protection and began placing it in the rock. I thought this was odd, but reasoned that he was simply being careful. Falling fifteen feet can be painful, perhaps fatal if you landed on your head. I secretly applauded his approach, because I for one have always erred on the side of safety in climbing. The Tom Smythe school had taught me that falling was bad form, dangerous, and an indication that you were taking too many risks. At altitude, just as everything is steeper, slipperier, and less attainable due to anoxia, falling takes on a magnified seriousness. Climbing can be an extremely safe sport—only very rarely does climbing gear fail, and most of it is designed to bear the shock of many thousands of pounds of force. Occasionally rock will shear off—a trusty looking hand hold will rip right out of a solid face—or a sharp rock edge will slice a rope in two, but even then, this is what properly placed gear anticipates. The danger is often greater for the belayer below who gets showered with debris, especially in ice-climbing, when monstrous icicles and ice walls crash to the ground.

I watched with satisfaction as Gunther placed protection, even if it seemed like overkill and overcautiousness, up to the ledge. Our climbing safety philosophies were in harmony. Of course, I was eager to feel the gritty quartzite on my fingertips, and I felt that he was moving much too slowly. When he reached the ledge, I knew that the real climbing would begin. Gunther moved up the rock again, slowly, and I grew impatient, since from my perspective the first part of this climb seemed geared for beginners, something the guidebook might rate as a 5.2. Why was he moving so slowly?

About sixty feet up, Gunther paused unexpectedly. Even from that distance, I could see the sweat pouring from every pore of his body and his skin glistening in the sun. Then his knee began twitching. Within minutes his whole leg was trembling violently. I knew he was in trouble and made sure I was fully extended from my anchor to catch a fall. If his pro was properly set, he would only fall about six feet before his last anchor would arrest his descent. It became clear to me that he was caught in an awkward position, with too much weight on his arms and unable to move up—I wondered, however, why he didn't downclimb to a safer spot. After a few more seconds of intense shaking, he fell.

Gunther let out a tremendous yell as he peeled off the rock and headed downward to his last anchor. To my astonishment, when he flew by his anchor, the hexentric nut popped out of the rock. He continued falling to his next anchor. My mouth opened in horror as that too ripped out of the crack. Number three, pop! Gunther continued screaming. I was too shocked to do anything, even yell. There was nothing

470

I could do, but dumbly hold a rope that was useless to stop the falling climber. He was losing his anchors one by one: was popping the protection out of the rock like a zipper opening. For ten seconds, I felt like I was watching a man die, while I stood by unable to do anything.

I turned my head away when he struck the ground. I knew I had to look eventually, although my mind revolted at the prospect of seeing the broken and mutilated body which I knew I would see. Miracle upon miracle! Gunther was lying moaning in a crumpled heap on the ground several hundred yards into the woods. He had landed on both feet and had rolled over and over again head over heels through the woods. Although none of this was conscious on his part, the rolling had absorbed the shock of the fall. I unclipped and rushed to him. He was badly shaken, but he attempted to stand up. He seemed to be intact, but when I tried to help him up he collapsed on his right foot and winced. All during this time he insisted that he was all right—just a flesh wound—that he didn't need any assistance.

Gunther was very embarrassed about the fall; he had not set the protection properly, and his mistakes had almost cost him his life. If I had been more perceptive, I would have noticed the shiny newness of his equipment. If I had talked with him more, I would have known that his knowledge of climbing came mostly from books, not practical experience. At the time, I was only interested in getting him some help, but later I became angry both at myself and Gunther. What if he were belaying me on the second pitch, and I fell? What if he had not set his belay anchor properly? I would have pulled him off the rock and we might have both met our Maker.

———

It took two other climbers to convince Gunther that he really was injured, that his ankle was probably sprained and that climbing was over for him for the day. The same pride and overconfidence that led to his accident also prevented him from admitting his mistakes that day and more importantly prevented him from accepting help. I thought of Oedipus. It was clear that he couldn't hobble out of the woods alone, so I helped him to the road. He continued to insist that he did not need to go to the hospital.

Fortunately, we ran into some climbers who were driving through western New York that day and who agreed to drop him off in Ithaca. I said goodbye to Gunther and returned to join the other group of climbers. I later learned that despite the entreaties of the climbers who were driving him home, Gunther still refused to go to the hospital for x-rays. I also found out later that when he finally took off his high-topped climbing shoe at home, his ankle collapsed into a formless mass, the bones inside were splintered and crushed. His shoe was the only thing holding his foot and ankle together. He had to be rushed to the hospital for emergency surgery and reconstruction. The only thing I could admire in Gunther at this point was his incredible tolerance for what must have been excruciating pain.

I decided to continue climbing that day, despite the accident, and I agreed to belay for Fred, someone who, although only an acquaintance of mine, I knew to be an excellent and prudent climber. I was with a more experienced group now and I convinced myself that the accident with Gunther was just a fluke. I had drawn the short straw and had ended up with the least experienced climber.

Fred began leading and I watched him as he moved further and further to the right, placing protection. This time I watched the placements with a more critical eye, and they seemed sound. He moved to a corner on the wall and swinging his right leg around, he disappeared around the corner. The continual tension on the rope told me to keep playing out rope for him. For obvious reasons, it is generally not a good idea to move out of the line of sight of your belayer. Although a good belayer can tell the whereabouts of his climber even in total darkness by feeling the tension on the rope, it is better to be able to see directly what is going on.

———

It was not long before a sharp tug on the rope indicated that Fred had fallen. I caught him easily. I called to Fred to see if he was all right. No answer. I called again, raising my voice. Still no answer. Most of the rope was played out, and he must have been a considerable distance away. I yelled again. Obviously the rock wall was bouncing my voice directly back to me. After several minutes of yelling, the rope went slack. Another climber appeared around the corner and told me to take Fred off belay, since he was now in a safe spot. After I climbed up to Fred who was able to belay me, I learned that he had taken a long leader fall which had bruised and cut up his face and broken his glasses. He was not seriously hurt and he was able to rappel down to the base of the cliff. I rapped off after him. When I reached the ground, I reflected again on what had gone wrong. He should not have gone so far, and moved out of sight and calling distance of his belayer. This time, however, the gear had saved him.

I concluded that the climbing gods were in a foul mood and that to continue to climb that day would be tempting fate. In fact, after that day, I gave up climbing for about four years. Driving home, I had time to run through the sequence of events. After years of safe climbing, one accident and one near accident. Fred thoroughly knew the fundamentals of climbing, had set his protection properly, and was able to bounce back from a momentary miscalculation. But Gunther had relied too much on his expensive gear. He believed it would protect him like a magic talisman. But his experience had let him down—almost killed him.

—2003

Glossary

ABSEIL—same as rappel

AIGUILLE—literally, a needle of rock

ARÊTE—narrow rock or snow ridge

BELAY—(n.) rope system held by a belayer used to catch a falling climber and (v.) the act of protecting a climber from falling with such a rope system

BERGSCHRUND (RIMAYE)—the crevasse which forms by a glacier breaking away from the walls of the mountain

BIVOUAC—a hasty camp or resting place, as opposed to a fully equipped camp

CARABINER (or KARABINER)—ring-shaped metal climbing device for attaching ropes, harnesses, etc. and numerous other climbing uses

CHIMNEY—(n.) a large crack in the rock large enough for a climber to ascend or descend and (v.) the act of climbing in this crack by pressing parts of the body against the walls

COL—a slight dip between two peaks

CORNICE—a lip of snow or ice projecting over a ridge, sometimes the source of avalanches

COULOIR—literally, corridor, a narrow passage in a mountain

CRAMPONS—metal spikes worn over heavy boots for traction on ice or snow

CREVASSE—a gulley or fissure formed by the cracking of glacier ice

CWM—(pronounced "Koom") a Welsh word for a valley

FIGURE EIGHT—metal device shaped like an eight for belaying and rappelling

GLISSADE—a slide down a snow or ice slope, either accidentally or controlled with an ice axe

HARNESS—(waist or chest) device made of webbing and attached to a belay rope to hold a falling climber

ICE AXE—multipurpose staff with a pickax-type head and pointed end for securing belays, cutting ice steps, and climbing ice walls with crampons

LEAD CLIMBER—preferably the most experienced member of a climbing party who climbs first and sets protection in the ice or rock

PITCH—a section of rock or ice wall between secure belay points

PITON—metal spike with a ring hammered into the rock to hold ropes, gear, and climbers (to protect them from falling) or for artificial aid in climbing difficult walls; now generally replaced by removable metal wedges called chocks

PRUSSIC KNOT or LOOP—knot used to attach to a larger rope or for ascending a rope, although mechanical ascenders (such as Jumars) are now more widely used

GLOSSARY

RAPPEL—to descend a doubled rope either by wrapping it around the body or through a variety of metal devices
SÉRAC—a large block or tower of ice
TRAVERSE—(n. and v.) to travel horizontally across a rock or ice face
VERGLAS—thin, transparent coating of ice

OTHER TITLES OF INTEREST

AFRICAN GAME TRAILS
An Account of the African Wanderings
of an American Hunter-Naturalist
Theodore Roosevelt
New introduction by H. W. Brands
616 pp., 210 b/w photos
0-8154-1132-4
$22.95

AFRICA EXPLORED
Europeans on the Dark Continent,
1769–1889
Christopher Hibbert
344 pp., 54 b/w illustrations, 16 maps
0-8154-1193-6
$18.95

ANTARCTICA
Firsthand Accounts of Exploration
and Endurance
Edited by Charles Neider
468 pp.
0-8154-1023-9
$18.95

ARCTIC EXPERIENCES
Aboard the Doomed *Polaris* Expedition
and Six Months Adrift on an Ice-Floe
Captain George E. Tyson
New introduction by Edward E. Leslie
504 pp., 78 b/w illustrations
0-8154-1189-8
$24.95 cloth

BEYOND CAPE HORN
Travels in the Antarctic
Charles Neider
414 pp., 14 maps
0-8154-1235-5
$17.95

CARRYING THE FIRE
An Astronaut's Journeys
Michael Collins
Foreword by Charles Lindbergh
512 pp., 32 pp. of b/w photos
0-8154-1028-6
$19.95

THE DESERT AND THE SOWN
The Syrian Adventures of the Female
Lawrence of Arabia
Gertrude Bell
New introduction by Rosemary O'Brien
368 pp., 162 b/w photos
0-8154-1135-9
$19.95

EARLY AMERICAN NATURALISTS
Exploring the American West 1804–1900
John Moring
320 pp., 10 b/w photos
0-8154-1236-3
$27.50 cloth

EDGE OF THE JUNGLE
William Beebe
New introduction by Robert Finch
320 pp., 1 b/w photo
0-8154-1160-X
$17.95

**EDGE OF THE WORLD:
ROSS ISLAND, ANTARCTICA**
A Personal and Historical Narrative
of Exploration, Adventure, Tragedy,
and Survival
Charles Neider
with a new introduction
536 pp., 45 b/w photos, 15 maps
0-8154-1154-5
$19.95

THE FABULOUS INSECTS
Essays by the Foremost Nature Writers
Edited by Charles Neider
288 pp.
0-8154-1100-6
$17.95

GREAT SHIPWRECKS AND CASTAWAYS
Firsthand Accounts of Disasters at Sea
Edited by Charles Neider
256 pp.
0-8154-1094-8
$16.95

THE GREAT WHITE SOUTH
Traveling with Robert F. Scott's Doomed
South Pole Expedition
Herbert G. Ponting
New introduction by Roland Huntford
440 pp., 175 b/w illustrations,
3 b/w maps & diagrams
0-8154-1161-8
$18.95

IN SEARCH OF ROBINSON CRUSOE
Daisuke Takahashi
256 pp., 23 b/w photos
0-8154-1200-2
$25.95 cloth

THE *KARLUK*'S LAST VOYAGE
An Epic of Death and Survival in
the Arctic, 1913–1916
Captain Robert A. Bartlett
New introduction by Edward E. Leslie
378 pp., 23 b/w photos, 3 maps
0-8154-1124-3
$18.95

KILLER 'CANE
The Deadly Hurricane of 1928
Robert Mykle
320 pp., 24 b/w illustrations
0-8154-1207-X
$27.95 cloth

LA SALLE
A Perilous Odyssey from Canada to
the Gulf of Mexico
Donald Johnson
296 pp., 25 b/w illustrations
0-8154-1240-1
$26.95 cloth

**THE LIFE AND AFRICAN
EXPLORATIONS OF LIVINGSTONE**
Dr. David Livingstone
656 pp., 52 b/w line drawings and maps
0-8154-1208-8
$22.95

MAN AGAINST NATURE
Firsthand Accounts of Adventure and
Exploration
Edited by Charles Neider
512 pp.
0-8154-1040-9
$18.95

MEMOIRS OF MY LIFE
Explorer of the American West
John Charles Frémont
New introduction by Charles M. Robinson III
696 pp., 89 b/w illustrations
0-8154-1164-2
$24.95

MY ARCTIC JOURNAL
A Year among Ice-Fields and Eskimos
Josephine Peary
Foreword by Robert E. Peary
New introduction by Robert M. Bryce
280 pp., 67 b/w illustrations, maps,
& diagrams
0-8154-1198-7
$18.95

MY ATTAINMENT OF THE POLE
Frederick A. Cook
New introduction by Robert M. Bryce
680 pp., 45 b/w illustrations
0-8154-1137-5
$22.95